CENSUS OF INDIA 1941

Census of India 1871-1951, 9 Sets In 384 Bindings (9788121258876) Rs. 700000

Census of India 1941, 25 Vols. In 19 Bindings (9788121271219) Rs. 29000

1. India - Tables and Administrative Report (9788121274159) Rs. 1275 (Vol. 1, Pt. 1 & 2)
2. Madras and Bombay - Tables (9788121274135) Rs. 1220 (Vol. Vol. III)
3. Bengal - Tables and Caste Tables (9788121274098) Rs. 820 (Vol. IV, Pt. 1 & 2)
4. United Provinces, Punjab, Bihar, Central Provinces & Berar - Tables (9788121274050) Rs. 1900 (Vol. V to VIII)
5. Assam, North - West Frontier Province, Orissa - Tables (9788121273978) Rs. 920 (Vol. IX to XI)
6. Sind, Andaman And Nicobar Islands, Baluchistan - Imperial Provincial And Sample - Tables (9788121273916) Rs. 1450 (Vol. Vol. XIV)
7. Coorg, Delhi, Baroda, Central India - Tables (9788121273855) Rs. 2100 (Vol. Vol. XVIII)
8. Cochin - Report & Tables (9788121273770) Rs. 1075 (Vol. XIX, Pt. 1 & 2)
9. Gwalior - Tables (9788121273756) Rs. 1850 (Vol. XX)
10. H. E. H. The Nizam's Dominions Hyderabad State - Report (9788121273732) Rs. 1175 (Vol. XXI, Pt. 1)
11. H. E. H. The Nizam's Dominions Hyderabad State - Tables (9788121274111) Rs. 3950 (Vol. XXI, Pt. 2)
12. Jammu And Kashmir - Essay And Tables (9788121273718) Rs. 2000 (Vol. XXII, Pt. 1 & 2)
13. Mysore - Report (9788121273695) Rs. 1525 (Vol. XXIII, Pt. 1)
14. Mysore - Tables (9788121273671) Rs. 2100 (Vol. XXIII, Pt. 2)
15. Rajputana And Ajmer-Merwara- These Ten Years (9788121273657) Rs. 925 (Vol. XXIV, Pt. 1)
16. Rajputana And Ajmer-merwara - Tables (9788121274074) Rs. 1260 (Vol. XXIV, Pt. 2)
17. Travancore - Report (9788121273633) Rs. 1325 (Vol. XXV, Pt. 1)
18. Travancore - Tables (9788121273619) Rs. 1300 (Vol. XXV, Pt. 2)
19. Travancore - State Tables and Administration Report (9788121273596) Rs. 1620 (Vol. XXV, Pt. 3 & 4)

CENSUS OF INDIA, 1941

BOOK - 12, VOLUME - XXII

JAMMU AND KASHMIR

PART 1&2 - ESSAY AND TABLES

CAPT. R. G. WREFORD

GYAN

Published by

Gyan Publishing House
5, Ansari Road
Daryaganj, New Delhi-110002
Phone: 011-47034999, 9811692060
E-mail: books@gyanbooks.com

Distribution Network
gyanbooks.com
India, USA, Canada, UK, Australia

ISBN: 978-81-212-7121-9 (Set) 25 Vols. In 19 Bindings

ISBN: 978-81-212-7371-8 (PB) Vol. XXII, Pt. 1 & 2

First Published, 1943

2nd Impression 2024

Printed at: Gyan Press, Delhi.

CENSUS OF INDIA 1941

Census of India, 1941

VOLUME XXII

JAMMU AND KASHMIR

PARTS I & II

ESSAY AND TABLES

BY

CAPT. R. G. WREFORD

CENSUS COMMISSIONER, JAMMU AND KASHMIR STATE

JAMMU:

Printed under the supervision of
J. Sharma, C. P. C. Tech., M. P. G. (Manchester), Superintendent, The Ranbir Govt. Press.

1943

TABLE OF CONTENTS

Part I

ESSAY

THE CENSUS 1941

Part II

TABLES

ERRATA.

Page 3, column I, line II *read* " known as Khuls".

,, 8, ,, 2, ,, 24 ,, " stokers in the".

,, 9, ,, I, last line ,, " Sunni sect, *viz*, Wahabis".

,, 15, ,, I, line 30 ,, " village proprietors with".

,, 17, ,, 2, ,, 5 ,, " manure available is".

,, 23, ,, 2, 8 lines from end *read* " Doyan Khul (canal)".

,, 28, ,, I, line 44 *read* " 26¼ lacs".

,, 30, ,, 2, ,, 45 ,, " has ever been".

,, 33, ,, I, ,, 46 ,, " 35 per cent for the".

,, 37, ,, 2, ,, 24 ,, " into the subject".

,, 38, ,, I, ,, 21 ,, " Harijans, Sikhs and".

,, 39, ,, I, ,, 7 ,, " in 1924 ; for figures".

,, 39, ,, 2, lines 23, 24 *read* " future students in schools will".

,, 39, ,, 2, line 25 ,, " at their option".

,, 39, ,, 2, ,, 26 ,, " one script, *i. e.* Persian".

,, 40, ,, 2, ,, 2 ,, " easily realised".

,, 43, ,, I, ,, I ,, " cured more frequently".

,, 253, Para 5, line 2 *for* the word "numbers" *read* "number".

,, 254, ,, 9(v), last line *for* the word "Wih" ,, "with".

,, 302, ,, 9(b), *for* the word "includes" *read* "include".

,, 302, ,, 10(b), *for* ,, ,, "besed" ,, "based".

Page 333, under Inner Sub-branch against Central Group *for* the word "Rajastnani" *read* the word "Rajasthani".

Page 342, 3rd line, *for* the words "ndian christians" *read* the words "Indian Christians".

Page 350, in column 8 against " Jammu and Kashmir State " *for* the figures " 12875 " *read* the figures " 13875 ".

Page 354, in the third line of paragraph II *for* the word " is " *read* the word " are ".

Page 356, in the last but one line under column I, *for* the brackets and words " (Leased Areo)" *read* the brackets and words " (Leased Area) ".

Page 357, in column 10 under Chuhra against Jammu *for* the sign and figure " -8 " *real* the sign and figures " -89 ".

Page 369, under column 35 against Srinagar city *insert* the figure " 4 ",

Page 376, in the heading of column 12 *for* the figures "1941 i" *read* the figures "1941".

FOREWORD

In past years the Census Report was so to speak tied on to the tables of which to a large extent it was a translation in words. With the developments in departmental administration and specialist provision which are a feature of all governments, it is no longer necessary for Census Superintendents to attempt a separate dissertation on every table. Nor is it desirable.

The principle should rather be that the tables are produced for the use of departments concerned and of the public as a whole. The departmental specialists will deal with this specific aspect and what the Census Superintendent should aim at is a synoptic survey which will take and keep the whole province or state in view throughout and try to represent it as an organic and developing whole.

The essay form has been adopted as far as possible in order to produce the utmost degree of continuity and interest. Tables have been reduced to a minimum in order to enhance its readability and the theory is that the essay should be capable of being read quite separately by a stranger who from it alone without other assistance would gain a definite idea of what the province or state stands for, what its main conditions and problems are and in what direction it is developing.

The essay is not a gazetteer and deliberately omits ordinary standard detail which can be obtained in departmental publications. Readers are therefore referred to these publications for such matter.

NEW DELHI : M. W. W. M. YEATTS,

February 27th 1942. CENSUS COMMISSIONER FOR INDIA.

INTRODUCTION

The Report.—The 1941 Census Report is in four parts. Part I takes the form of an essay. It describes the boundaries of the Jammu and Kashmir State, its physical features, the system of administration, the constitutional changes made during the decade, the distribution and composition of the population, departmental activities and the bearing they have on the well-being of the people, the more important aspects of the facts recorded by the Census and the ability of the country to support an increasing population.

Part II gives the results of the Census in tabular form; it contains Imperial Tables, State tables and Subsidiary tables. Each Imperial table is preceded by brief explanatory notes and followed by subsidiary tables. At previous Censuses the subsidiary tables were published in Part I at the end of the chapter discussing the table to which they pertained.

Part III consists of Village Tables and Housing Statistics. The former show the population, chief communities, literate persons by sexes in each village, number of occupied houses and the population at the previous Census. The villages are grouped by districts, tehsils, charges and circles; figures are given separately for the two cities of Jammu and Srinagar. Notes precede the tables of each district. The Housing Statistics represent an attempt to tabulate the information regarding housing conditions recorded in the House Lists; they leave much to be desired but constitute a new feature. At the next Census it may be possible to obtain more accurate data in this respect. Part III is of purely local interest and the distribution of copies has been restricted to officials, representatives of the press and others in the State.

Part IV discusses the Census operations and administrative matters. It is primarily intended for the information of His Highness' Government and those conducting operations in the State at the next Census. It is being printed for local issue only.

Parts I and II are produced together in one volume. In previous reports each Imperial Table was discussed at great length chapter by chapter; on this occasion there is no such detailed discussion. There are no graphs or diagrams. An endeavour has been made to give the general reader an accurate picture of conditions in the State relating to those questions with which the Census is concerned without the necessity of having to wade through a mass of technical detail. The essential facts are available in the tables; where it is thought that they are defective in any respect this has been plainly stated in the notes.

II. Census Operations.—The first attempt to take a Census in the Jammu and Kashmir State was made in 1873; it was little better than an estimate. In 1891 regular Census operations were carried out synchronously with the rest of India but they did not cover the Gilgit Agency. In 1901 the second regular Census was taken. The results of both the 1891 and the 1901 Censuses left much to be desired. The Census taken in 1911 was the first complete Census conducted in strict conformity with the principles and instructions emanating from the Census Commissioner for India. The Censuses conducted in 1921 and 1931 followed closely the methods of 1911.

The 1941 Census staff has benefitted by the experience gained during the last three decades and I acknowledge the debt owed to our predecessors. The operations have been carried out in accordance with the instructions issued by the Census Commissioner for India with such minor modifications as were necessary to meet local conditions. Zero hour was sunrise on March 1st 1941, to which date and time all births and deaths were related. There was no communal discord. The weather was satisfactory throughout the period of enumeration. A few complaints were received which were investigated immediately and disposed of without difficulty. All communities appear to have been satisfied with the results. The only question which gave rise to any irregularities, as far as is known, was that relating to 'Mothertongue'. The Persian-Devanagri script controversy had its effect on the answers recorded in this connection. Clear instructions were issued to enumerators that 'Hindi' and 'Urdu' should both be recorded as 'Hindustani'. Even so it is feared the record for Mothertongue has been vitiated in certain areas because those active in the script controversy carried on propaganda to influence those of their persuasion to show Urdu or Hindi as their mother-tongue, irrespective of the facts.

The normal Census divisions, consisting of districts, tehsils, charges, circles and blocks were created. District Officers (Wazirs Wazarat) automatically became District Census Officers in addition to their usual duties. Similarly, Tehsildars became Tehsil Census Officers. Charges, circles and blocks varied in size according to local conditions. The average charge in non-city areas consisted of 6·5 circles with 2,888 occupied houses and a population of 14,934. The average circle in non-city areas consisted of 12 blocks with 445 occupied houses and a population of 2,304. In city areas the average block consisted of 46 houses with a population of 326. A 'house', as at previous Censuses, was deemed to consist of a single commensal unit. The Revenue Department furnished the bulk of the personnel but most departments supplied their quota for the smaller Census divisions. Many of the enumerators were non-officials. In all there were 258 Charge Superintendents, 1,706 Supervisors and 19,997 Enumerators.

In 1931 the actual Census was preceded by a preliminary enumeration. This record was subjected to a final check carried out between the hours of 7/00 P. M., and midnight on Census Day. The aim was to obtain the equivalent of an instantaneous photograph of the population. To subject the record of some weeks' laborious effort to a hectic five hour check did not necessarily produce a better record. On this occasion there was only one enumeration which was continuous over a period of one month. Our aim was to complete the record three days previous to Census Day so that supervisors might have time to check enumerators' work and get obvious errors corrected. The record thus obtained was subjected to a necessary minor revision on Census Day when births and deaths which had occurred during the period of enumeration were adjusted with relation to sunrise on March 1st. In the case of deaths up to zero hour the slips already written were cancelled under supervisors' initials; in the case of births a slip was filled in. The enumeration was based on normal place of residence. Temporary absences were ignored. The criterion in all doubtful cases was whether a person would be at his normal place of residence on March 1st.

It will be obvious to those having the slightest knowledge of the geography of the State why some modifications had to be made in the enumeration time-table to meet local conditions. For example, many villages situated in the high mountainous areas of Ladakh, Astore, Gilgit and Karnah are usually cut off by snow in February of any year making movement very difficult and good enumeration practically impossible. The whole of these areas was enumerated non-synchronously, work commencing on December 1st and being completed by the end of that month. There are many villages in other districts where similar conditions obtain. These too were enumerated non-synchronously during the period mentioned. There is little movement in such areas during the winter. Special arrangements were also made to enumerate the population living in boats and those to be found in forest and road construction camps, hotels, wayside halting-places, jails, and hospitals. All these were enumerated where found on Census Day. At previous Censuses passengers on running-trains and other transport services were stopped and enumerated. Since the population was enumerated on this occasion on the basis of usual place of residence special measures for enumerating such short period travellers were dispensed with.

Arrangements were made in advance for the preparation of enumerators' abstracts, circle, charge and tehsil summaries, and for the collection and despatch of the record to headquarters. District officers were required to calculate provisional totals for their respective districts and to communicate these to the Direction Office as soon as possible by hand or telegram according to circumstances. Prompt communication of the totals was asked for but not undue haste. The work was carried out satisfactorily. The provisional totals for the whole State were communicated to the Census Commissioner for India well within the period fixed. These gave the population for the whole State as 4,021,658. Compilation of the record showed the correct figures to be 4,021,616—a difference of 42 persons or an error of just over one per hundred thousand.

III. Tabulation and Compilation.—It is not proposed to discuss the work of abstraction and compilation in detail here; this finds its place in Part IV of the report. In the past it has always been the practice to have two offices for tabulation—one located at Jammu and the other at Srinagar. At this Census the whole of the work was concentrated in one office at Srinagar. There are no linguistic difficulties to make it necessary to open offices in different localities. The record is not too large to handle in one office. The advantages gained by having one central office are obvious ; the most important are closer supervision, quicker issue of instructions and disposal of references and uniformity of treatment. The Tabulation Office was accommodated in a building within 300 yards of the Direction Office. As answers to questions at this Census were recorded direct on to the slips to be sorted for tabulation there was no necessity for slip-copying except in the case of a few special household schedules ; the use of these was strictly limited and the number involved very small. The use of the original record for tabulation necessitated the close scrutiny of the slips forming the record, the correction of obvious errors and the removal of blank and cancelled slips. This proved a troublesome and laborious process but that is an administrative matter which is discussed in Part IV. Tabulation commences with the checking of the record received against district, tehsil, charge and circle summaries and the enumerators' abstracts ; it was commenced on 26th March 1941 and completed on November 15th 1941 ; half the staff was dispensed with and the rest retained for compilation work for which we allowed a period of 3 months. The Compilation Office was closed on February 11th 1942. The checking of tables and the preparation of the remaining subsidiaries was carried on and completed in the Direction Office.

IV. Accuracy of the Record.—The ability and readiness of an unpaid Census agency, many of whom are unavoidably of a low standard of education, to record complete and correct answers to a long and, in some respects, difficult questionnaire is obviously subject to limitations. It may, however, be accepted as a fact that the great majority of the enumerators made an honest attempt to grapple with the onerous duties entrusted to them. It must be stated in clear terms that the answers to some questions were not accurate or complete. Consequently some tables do not represent a correct record of the real position. The tables relating to the actual population, its distribution, variations and communal composition may be accepted as correct subject to a very small margin of error ; the same may be said of the tables relating to birthplace. Table VII, Age and Civil Condition, is subject to the defects inherent in all age tables prepared by the Census agency. Some people have a deep-rooted objection to giving their correct age on any document in any country. In India large numbers of the population do not know their real age and can only make a guess. Such guesses are frequently inaccurate. There is, and always has been, a definite tendency to give a round figure such as 20, 30, 35 and 40. For any age over 50 the figures for the most part must be treated as approximate only. These defects are not peculiar to this State ; they are common to the whole of India. But as they have always existed the age table at this Census is reliable for the purpose of comparison with the figures given at previous Censuses.

The answers to the questions on which Tables VIII and IX are based were incomplete and very unsatisfactory. These tables must therefore be considered defective and practically useless for statistical purposes. They indicate a general condition only. Table X gives a more accurate record of the real position than the same table for 1931 but unemployment under all heads may be assumed to be in excess of the figures given. This is due to the fact that some are diffident in admitting that they are unemployed. Table XI may be accepted as reasonably accurate and Table XII too, except to the extent that Hindustani has been shown as Mothertongue. The number of persons living in the State whose true Mothertongue is either Urdu or Hindi, both shown as Hindustani in the table, is very small. The remaining tables may be accepted as reasonably accurate.

V. Cost of the Census.—The total expenditure on Census operations, excluding some minor charges which at the time of writing have not been adjusted, comes to Rs. 1,48,000. It is anticipated that the minor charges referred to will be more than covered by receipts on account of the sale of furniture etc., when the department is closed. The exact figures will be given in the Administration section of the report—Part IV. On the basis of the figure given above the cost works out at Rs. 36·8 per thousand of the population. The cost in 1921 and 1931 was Rs. 1,46,332 and Rs. 1,49,508 and the rate per thousand of the population Rs. 44 and Rs. 41 respectively.

VI. Public Attitude.—The political atmosphere throughout the country was calm during the whole period of the Census operations. The public showed no hostility to the Census in any form; their attitude was either apathetic or they co-operated to the best of their ability. It is not easy to convince the public that the Census is their census and that full co-operation is likely to be advantageous to them as well as to the administration. There was no occasion to take proceedings under the penal clauses of the Census Act. The press gave us their co-operation and were helpful in giving publicity to notices and communiques. The only Census questions which gave rise to hesitancy and reluctance were 7 and 8, relating to the number of children born to a married woman and her age at the birth of her first child. These questions were not correctly answered in many cases; in a large number they were not answered at all. The fertility tables prepared from them should not be regarded as accurate.

VII. Acknowledgements.—The All-India Census becomes more exacting and a greater strain on those responsible for its conduct every decade. The Government of India decided to restrict tabulation and to confine compilation to a few of the more important tables and to file the Census record for future reference. His Highness' Government decided to complete the work in every respect.

Before concluding these introductory notes I should like to acknowledge the assistance received from all quarters. To the thousands of unpaid Census workers, both official and unofficial, I can only offer our very sincere thanks. We are grateful to Mr. M. W. W. M. Yeatts, C. I. E., I. C. S., Census Commissioner for India, for his guidance and advice. I am indebted to the Hon'ble Dewan Bahadur Sir N. Gopalaswami Ayyangar Kt., C. S. I., C. I. E., Prime Minister, His Highness' Government, Jammu and Kashmir for his sympathetic understanding of our difficulties and problems and his prompt assistance to us in our efforts to overcome them. I acknowledge with pleasure the co-operation of all those officials and representatives of the public who kindly responded to our requests for notes on departmental activities and conditions of living. Finally, I must express my great appreciation of the loyal co-operation I have received throughout from my staff.

SRINAGAR:

June 30th 1942.

R. G. WREFORD,

CENSUS COMMISSIONER,

Jammu and Kashmir State.

CENSUS OF INDIA 1941

VOLUME XXII

JAMMU & KASHMIR STATE

PART I.

Boundaries and Area.—The Jammu and Kashmir State lies between 32.17′ and 36.58′ North Latitude and 73.26′ and 80.30′ East Longitude. To appreciate fully the political importance of its geographical position one must look at a map of Asia. On its northern borders three empires meet—the British, the Russian and the Chinese. The independent kingdom of Afghanistan lies to the north-west, the Punjab to the south and the North West Frontier Province to the west. On the east it is bounded by Chinese Tibet and on the north and north-east by Russian and Chinese Turkistan. It has an area of 84,471 sq. miles and is the largest State in India. The chief rivers are the Indus, the Jhelum and the Chenab all of which thread their way through the territories of the State later to form the main part of the mighty waterways which irrigate and fertilise the Punjab and Sind provinces of British India.

2. Natural Divisions.—The natural or geographical divisions of the State, first adopted for Census purposes in 1911, are The Submontane and Semi-mountainous tract, The Outer Hills, The Jhelum Valley and the Indus Valley. The first consists of the plains bordering the Punjab and the broken mass of foothills lying at the base of the great mountain ranges of the Himalayan series. This division contains the following administrative units:—

> the tehsils Kathua and Jasmergarh of the Kathua District, the whole of the Jammu District and the tehsils Bhimber and Mirpur of the Mirpur District.

The Chenab and the Jhelum both flow through this division. The northern parts of this division consist chiefly of foothills, known locally as 'Kandi', which rise to a height of about 2,000 ft.; for the most part they are stony and arid. They thirst for the water which cannot reach them. In the 'Kandi' areas cultivation is meagre and scattered; the crops depend very largely on timely rains. The area of this division is 2,609 sq. miles. The population at the time of the recent Census was 814,028.

'The Outer Hills' division consists of the lower hills lying roughly to the south of the Pir Panjal. The latter separates the two main provinces of the State, Jammu and Kashmir, from each other. A large part of this area lies at an altitude of between 2,000 and 4,000 ft. but in the Udhampur District, and in other areas too, the hills become mountains and reach a height of over 15,000 ft. Bhadrawah (5,540 ft.) and Kishtwar (5,360 ft.), the headquarters respectively of the two tehsils bearing the same names, are both in close proximity to high mountains. The following administrative units are situated in this natural division:—

> the Basohli Tehsil of the Kathua District, the Kotli Tehsil of the Mirpur District, the entire districts of Reasi and Udhampur and the Poonch and Chenani Jagirs.

The chief river is the Chenab which enters the Udhampur District from the Chamba State and the Great Himalayan range to the east and continues through the Reasi District and the Akhnur Tehsil of the Jammu District finally to reach the Punjab near Sialkot. In the lower areas of this division rice and wheat are mostly grown; higher up maize is the chief crop and staple food. From elevations of about 5,000 to 8,000 ft. the mountain sides, where not exposed to the scorching winds of the plains, are clothed with magnificent pine and deodar forests, particularly in the tehsils Ramban, Kishtwar and Bhadrawah of the Udhampur District. Bhadrawah has often been called a miniature Kashmir. The Reasi District is known to be rich in minerals which, as yet, are almost untouched. Except in the fertile valleys, cultivable land is scarce and scattered consisting of comparatively small plateaux and patches of cultivation. Rainfall is plentiful—the highest in the State—thanks to the warm moisture laden winds which strike against the high Pir Panjal range and deposit their waters on the surrounding country. The area of this division is 9,769 sq. miles ; the population was returned at 1,167,405. These two natural divisions—The Sub-montane tract and The Outer Hills—together constitute the entire Jammu Province, including the Poonch and Chenani Jagirs.

The Jhelum Valley division corresponds to the administrative districts of Anantnag, Baramulla and Muzaffarabad that is to say, the Kashmir Province. Seven of the tehsils of the two first named districts— Srinagar, Anantnag, Kulgam, Pulwama, Baramulla, Sri Pratapsinghpura and Uttarmachhipura—form what is usually known as the Kashmir Valley. The Jhelum rises at Verinag at the southern end of the Kashmir Province and flows through the middle of the Kashmir Valley. It receives the waters of numerous tributaries on both its banks before it enters the Woolar Lake out of which it flows on through the gorge at Baramulla ; its chief tributaries are the Liddar and the Sind, both on its right bank. They have their source in the everlasting snows and in their course pass through magnificent mountain scenery which has to be seen to be believed. No words are adequate to describe the beauty and grandeur of the Liddar and Sind Valleys. The Kishanganga river, having its source on the southern slopes of the mountains in the neighbourhood of the Burzil and Kamri Passes, joins the Jhelum on its right bank at Domel in the Muzaffarabad District ; thus the valley of the Kishanganga forms part of the natural division known as the Jhelum Valley. On the left bank of the Jhelum, roughly west, is the Pir Panjal Range from the slopes of which numerous small streams flow into it. For the most part they are little more than mountain torrents. The country to the south and west of the Pir Panjal gets more rain than the Kashmir side of the watershed. The mountains surrounding the Jhelum Valley average about 12,000 ft.; many of the peaks exceed 14,000 ft. At the southern end of the valley they dip to about 9,000 ft. where the Banihal pass gives an exit to the Jammu Province. The main Kashmir Valley averages about 5,500 ft. with Srinagar (5,200 ft.) at its centre. The higher areas under cultivation in the Liddar and Sind Valleys exceed 7,000 ft. The major part of the Muzaffarabad District and the higher elevations of the Anantnag and Baramulla Districts are too high and mountainous for cultivation. The lower and flatter areas produce rich harvests of rice and maize ; wheat and barley and many other crops are grown too but rice and maize are by far the most important. All kinds of fruit trees grow in abundance. Most of the food grain supplies of this division are grown in what is commonly known as the Kashmir Valley ; this consists of the valley of the Jhelum from its source to Baramulla and the subsidiary valleys on both banks. The area of this division is 8,539 sq. miles and the population 1,728,705.

The Indus Valley or 'Tibetan and Semi-Tibetan Tract' consists mainly of the middle reaches of the Indus, which, taking its source from the Mansarowar Lake in Tibet, traverses the frontier districts of the State from south-east to north-west as far as a point near the peak Haramosh (24,270 ft.). It then takes a south-westerly course passing the Nanga Parbat massif to its north, on through the Chilas illaqa of the Gilgit Agency to independent tribal territory and later to the North West Frontier Province and the Punjab. With the Karakoram to the north-east, the Hindu Kush to the north-west, the central range of the Himalaya to the south and the subsidiary ranges of all three of these great mountain systems running through it at all angles and all heights, this division consists practically entirely of snow capped mountains, high plateaux, ravines and wastes. The area contains the giants Mt. Godwin Austin (28,250 ft.) and Nanga Parbat (26,660 ft.). There are literally hundreds of peaks exceeding 20,000 ft. in height many of them not even bearing a name. This division corresponds to the administrative units Ladakh District, Astore Tehsil, Gilgit (Leased Area) and Gilgit Agency. As its name indicates the Indus is the chief river. At the northern end of the small Bunji plain, as it leaves the Haramosh range, it is joined by the Gilgit river. The latter rises near the Durkot Pass in the Yasin illaqa of the Gilgit Agency and is itself fed by the Hunza river which rises near the Pamirs and makes its junction a few miles from Gilgit. The Astore river, which has its source on the northern slopes of the Burzil, joins the Indus at the southern end of the small Bunji plain as it turns into the great gorge below Gor leading to Chilas.

The Ladakh District is very dry and almost rainless. The Astore District is much better off in this respect; Gilgit (Leased Area) and Gilgit Agency are better off too but not below altitudes of 7,000 ft. The cultivable area in all districts is a very small proportion of the total area. Such cultivation as there is depends entirely on irrigation by small canals, known as Kuhls, fed by the melting snows, except in the Astore District where the rainfall is sufficient for maize and other crops grown in hilly tracts at elevations between 7,000 ft. and 9,000 ft. In Ladakh grim, a kind of barley, is grown at altitudes as high as 15,000 ft.; it is the most important crop. In the Astore District maize is the chief crop. Gilgit (Leased Area) and Gilgit Agency are more fortunate in the matter of elevation, climate and irrigation. Wheat, barley, maize and dhals are produced and some rice of poor quality. The area of this division is 63,554 sq. miles and the population 311,478.

The 'Natural Divisions' discussed did not exist as such until the Census of 1911. Previously the population had been shown by administrative units. The natural divisions made in 1911 have been adopted at all subsequent Censuses. They are based on a somewhat arbitrary division. This was unavoidable since they had to correspond with some definite grouping of administrative units to facilitate comparison of figures. The fact is the whole country is mountainous except for a comparatively small area bordering the Punjab; one can only say a certain area is less mountainous than another or that the mountains are bigger in one division than another. Within the limits of each conditions vary considerably. In the Indus Valley division altitudes vary from about 3,000 ft. to Mt. Godwin Austin's 28,250 ft.; rainfall varies from practically nil to a reasonable figure. Temperatures range from over 120 in the shade in the rocky gorges of the Indus in summer to below zero in many of the populated villages of the higher altitudes in winter. Similar variations in conditions are found in all the other divisions to a smaller degree. The rich soil and the abundant crops of the central parts of the Kashmir Valley provide living conditions which are beyond comparison with those obtaining in the mountainous wastes of a large part of the same division. Even in populated areas conditions vary with every rise of a few hundred feet in altitude. In the comparatively short distance of 30 miles from the centre of the Kashmir Valley in an easterly or westerly direction we rise in altitude from 5,200 ft. at Srinagar to 10,000 ft. on the slopes of the surrounding mountains. The Outer Hills division contains some areas with rich soil and abundant crops and others which are sandy, stony or mountainous wastes; some areas with a temperature which is tropical and others where it is almost arctic. In the Sub-montane division living conditions show less variation than in the others, but even here they vary considerably. It is, therefore, reasonable to say that the natural divisions have been created on an arbitrary basis and one must not assume that the living conditions are even approximately the same throughout any of them. The fact is the nature of the country is such that no practical scheme of natural divisions is possible which would bring into the various divisions so made all parts of the population living under the same conditions. The best division for practical purposes would be a provincial one consisting of the Jammu Province including the Poonch and Chenani Jagirs, the Kashmir Province and the Frontier Districts.

3. **Administrative Units.**—For the purposes of administration the State is divided as follows:—

(i) the Jammu Province,
(ii) the Kashmir Province (including Astore),
(iii) the Ladakh District,
(iv) Gilgit (Leased Area) and the Gilgit Agency.

Units (iii) and (iv) together with the Astore District of the Kashmir Province, correspond to the group designated 'Frontier Districts' in the tables given in Part II of the report. At the 1931 Census the present districts of Astore and Gilgit (Leased Area) together formed the Gilgit District. The present Astore District is the Cis-Indus part of the old Gilgit District; Gilgit (Leased Area) is the Trans-Indus part. The Gilgit Agency, shown in the Census Report for 1931 and previously as 'Frontier Illaqas', consists of areas which, whilst owing allegiance and paying tribute to His Highness the Maharaja Bahadur of Jammu and Kashmir, are administered on behalf of His Highness' Government by the Government of India's Political Agent at Gilgit. The designation 'Gilgit Agency' has been shown on this occasion instead of 'Frontier Illaqas' as it is deemed to be a more precise and at the same time more comprehensive term than the somewhat vague designation 'Frontier Illaqas'; it refers to the same areas, neither more nor less. The Poonch and Chenani Jagirs, situated in the Jammu Province, are administered by their respective Jagirdars subject to the overlordship of His Highness the Maharaja Bahadur of Jammu and Kashmir.

4. **District Changes.**—There was no change in external boundaries during the decade ending 31st December 1940 but there was one important change of administrative boundaries. Reference has already been made to the partition of the old Gilgit District into two separate units—Astore and Gilgit (Leased Area). In the middle of the decade (1934) negotiations were concluded between His Highness the Maharaja Bahadur of Jammu and Kashmir and the Government of India by which the Trans-Indus part of the old Gilgit District was leased to the Government of India for administrative purposes. This area, designated Gilgit (Leased Area), has since been administered on behalf of His Highness' Government by the Government of India's Political Agent at Gilgit. In the present tables the areas of Astore and Gilgit (Leased Area) have been shown as 1,632 sq. miles and 1,480 sq. miles respectively. Together they make the total of the area of the old Gilgit District as shown in the 1931 tables *viz.* 3,112 sq. miles. For a short time after the lease of the area referred to, the Cis-Indus part of the old Gilgit Wazarat, now designated Astore, was included with the Ladakh District for administrative purposes. Subsequently it was transferred to the Kashmir Province and placed under a revenue official directly responsible to the Governor of the Kashmir Province but its geographical position makes it a part of the Frontier Districts. Subject to the changes discussed administrative units remain the same as those shown in the 1931 tables. There is no occasion to detail them here; the districts of the two provinces are shown in the Imperial Tables; the tehsil sub-divisions of the districts are given in the State Tables.

5. **The Government of the State.**—The main purpose of a Census is to ascertain the increase or decrease of population in the whole area and in particular areas during the previous decade. The most important questions arising from the results shown are whether the country can support an increasing population without deterioration in the standard of living, assuming there is an increase, and what are the causes of any actual decrease or abnormally low rate of increase. All other questions are subsidiary. The nature of the administration of any country has an important bearing on living conditions and before we examine the tabulated results of the Census it will be well to discuss the existing administration and the constitutional changes which have occurred in the past ten years. The country is governed by His Highness the Maharaja Bahadur of Jammu and Kashmir with the assistance of a council of ministers presided over by the Prime Minister, the Hon'ble Dewan Bahadur Sir N. Gopalaswami Ayyangar, C. S. I., C. I. E., and a Legislative Assembly, known as the Praja Sabha, consisting of elected representatives, nominated members and official members. For the proper administration of law and justice there is a High Court of Judicature. The full bench consists of the Chief Justice and two other judges. There is a Board of Judicial Advisers to assist His Highness with advice in appeal cases. Whilst legislation may be initiated by the Assembly subject to the rules of procedure, or by the Prime Minister and the ministers associated with him to form the Council, all legislation must receive the assent of His Highness before it becomes law. All activities of the State are directed by Heads of Department responsible to the ministers who hold the portfolios for their respective departments. Except in the case of reserved subjects, members of the Praja Sabha are entitled to discuss the activities of any department. At the time of the 1931 Census the representatives of His Highness' subjects were not associated with the government of the State. Since then there have been important constitutional changes. It will be suitable to discuss here what they are and the immediate causes which gave rise to them.

6. **Grievances Commission.**—Riots occurred towards the end of the summer of 1931. For some years previously there had been political unrest throughout India and dissatisfied elements in this State were not slow to adopt the movement started there. Communal claims led to the excitement of communal feelings. Small incidents which would have been considered of little or no importance in normal times were seized upon and magnified; dis-affected elements were alert to find fuel to add to the fire of discontent they had kindled. There were some who felt they had a legitimate grievance. In the excited atmosphere which had been engendered minor indiscretions, having no malicious purpose, were exaggerated and represented by interested parties as deliberate attacks on this religion or that community. His Highness ordered immediate enquiries; some officials were found to have failed in the discharge of their duties in one respect or another and remedial measures were taken.

In November 1931 His Highness appointed

a Commission to enquire into the grievances and complaints of all sections of his subjects. The Commission was presided over by Mr. B. J. Glancy, I. C. S., now His Excellency Sir Bertrand Glancy, Governor of the Punjab, whose services were lent by the Government of India at His Highness' request. The inquiry was conducted in a very prompt and thorough manner. The Commission's recommendations were submitted in March 1932 and received immediate attention. Orders were issued in April 1932 that steps should be taken to implement the recommendations as early as possible. At the same time as he appointed the Commission to inquire into grievances and complaints His Highness was pleased to declare that, as had already been announced, it was his intention that measures should be devised for associating his subjects with the Government of the State. It was ordered that, as soon as the Commission appointed to inquire into complaints and disabilities had finished its work, a conference, at which the various interests concerned would be represented would meet to discuss the introduction of constitutional reforms in accordance with His Hidghness' intention.

7. **Constitutional Reforms.**—The Kashmir Constitutional Reforms Conference commenced its work about the middle of March 1932; its report was submitted in April. The Conference recommended that a Legislative Assembly should be established as soon as possible and made suggestions regarding its composition, powers and functions. At the same time the Conference suggested the appointment of a Committee to collect the necessary data on which further action could be based. His Highness in Council was pleased to accept the recommendations of the Conference.

In May a Franchise Committee was appointed under the presidency of Sir Barjor Dalal. In March 1933 Sir Ivo Elliot, Bart., I. C. S. (retired), was appointed Franchise Officer. The proceedings of the Committee were given the fullest publicity. Their report was submitted in January 1934 and by an order dated February 24th 1934, published in the Government Gazette, His Highness the Maharaja Bahadur was pleased to accept the recommendations of the Committee and directed that regulations be prepared to give effect to them. It was decided the Assembly should consist of 75 members; of these 33 were to be elected and 42 nominated. The elected members were to consist of 21 Muslims, 10 Hindus and 2 Sikhs and the nominated element comprised 12 officials, 14 non-officials and 16 State Councillors. The latter were selected from those who, as ministers and in other capacities, had had long experience in the administration of the State. In the selection of nominated non-officials and State Councillors care was taken to ensure the representation of all communities, interests and localities. The majority of those competent to represent the views of the people giving evidence before the Franchise Committee had favoured separate electorates and this system was adopted. For various and sufficient reasons adult suffrage was not adopted; the chief of these were the low standard of education amongst the masses, the vastness of the area and the paucity of officers competent to conduct elections. The franchise was given on a liberal basis. In the case of women it was limited to those who had passed an examination equal to or higher than the Middle School Certificate. Candidates for membership of the Assembly were required to have attained the age of 25 and to be literate either in the Persian or Devanagri script. A candidate for election was also required to be a registered elector of the constituency in which he stood and to have resided in the area for twelve months preceding the first day of the month on which the roll was published. It is unnecessary to discuss further the various stages preparatory to the inauguration of the Legislative Assembly. It is sufficient to say that the Praja Sabha (State Assembly) was formally inaugurated by His Highness the Maharaja Bahadur on October 17th 1934 in a special Durbar in the Rajgarh Palace. By Regulation No. I of 1991, which is the foundation of the existing constitution of the Jammu and Kashmir State, all ultimate powers are reserved to His Highness the Maharaja Bahadur. Under the same regulation certain subjects are reserved which it is unnecessary to give in detail here. The administration and government of the State is vested in a council of ministers presided over by the Prime Minister. The Praja Sabha has the power of interpellation, of passing resolutions, of discussing the budget and of introducing and passing legislation. Its authority is adequate in that, subject to certain provisions, it has the power to legislate for the whole State or any part thereof and for all subjects of the State wherever they may be. In cases of emergency, His Highness may give assent to an ordinance submitted by the Council but such ordinance shall become law for a period not exceeding six months. Copies of money bills involving the imposition of a new tax or duty or increasing an existing tax or duty must be supplied to every member of the Praja Sabha and a day or days allotted for discussion to enable members to ask questions and move resolutions. If a resolution be passed the bill in question cannot be passed until the resolution concerning it has been taken into consideration. The annual budget is placed before the Praja Sabha which has the power to ask questions and to move resolutions concerning it. If a resolution on the budget is supported by a majority of votes the President of the Praja Sabha is required under the rules of procedure to declare what action, if any, the Council will take on the resolution. Legislation relating to or affecting the religious rights, ceremonies, endowments or personal law of any community cannot be introduced without the previous sanction of His Highness the Maharaja Bahadur and the consent in writing of not less than two-thirds of the members of the Praja Sabha belonging to the community affected. Every bill passed by the Praja Sabha requires the assent of His Highness who may assent to the bill or return it for reconsideration. The constitution sanctioned under Regulation No. I of 1991 remained in force upto 27th Bhadon 1996, corresponding to 7th September 1939, when His Highness the Maharaja Bahadur was pleased to repeal the Regulation and promulgate the Jammu and Kashmir Constitution Act No. XIV of 1996 in its place. The new Act effected certain improvements in the text of the Regulation No. I of 1991 which were considered necessary. It defined the constitution and powers of the High Court of Judicature and provided for the establishment of a Board of Judicial Advisers to assist His Highness the Maharaja Bahadur in the disposal of appeals against the decisions of the High Court and such other matters as His Highness might choose to refer to the Board for advice.

On the 11th February 1939 His Highness the Maharaja Bahadur had been pleased to announce another instalment of constitutional reforms which extended the powers of the Praja Sabha and gave the representatives of the people greater opportunities of associating themselves in the administration of the State. Briefly, this further instalment of reforms reduced the number of nominated members of the Praja Sabha and increased the number of elected representatives to 40 in a House of 75, provided for the creation of four posts of paid Under-Secretaries to be filled by non-official members and created the post of Deputy President of the Praja Sabha to be filled by the election of a member of the Praja Sabha. It laid down that the annual financial statement, so far as it relates to items not charged to the revenue of the State, should be submitted to the vote of the Praja Sabha in the form of demands for grants. By the new provisions legislation relating to taxes, as distinct from fees and penalties, which was previously initiated by the Council of Ministers, was brought within the authority of the Praja Sabha subject to certain restrictions. Whilst these constitutional reforms give the representatives of the people ample opportunity to associate themselves with the administration and government of the State they in no way impair the inherent powers of His Highness the Maharaja Bahadur. Members of the Praja Sabha enjoy freedom of speech and no member is liable to proceedings in any court in respect of anything said or vote given by him in the Praja Sabha or any committee thereof or in respect of the publication by or under the authority of the Praja Sabha of any report, paper, vote or proceedings.

8. **The Legislature.**—Since it was inaugurated in 1934 the Praja Sabha has passed much useful legislation; it has solid achievements to its credit. Up to the end of 1940 nearly a hundred of its bills had received the assent of His Highness the Maharaja Bahadur and had become Acts. These cover a wide field and relate to the suppression of traffic in women, prevention of infant marriage, excise, State aid to industries, panchayats, criminal law, civil procedure code, land alienation and right of prior purchase, co-operative socieites, aid to agriculturists and land improvement loans, grain control, stamps, income-tax, land revenue, press and publications, court fees, grazing, tenancy, wireless telegraphy, water-mills, tolls, preservation of ancient monuments, town planning and improvement, partnerships, transfer of property, insurance etc. Many of these are amendment Acts; some represent original legislation. The list is sufficient to indicate that the Praja Sabha has a very real say in legislation affecting the living conditions of the people. This is a factor of importance when we are considering the ability of the country to support an increasing population. The provision of adequate means of subsistence for all sections of the people is the most important of all problems when we have to consider the needs of a rapidly increasing population. Unless timely measures are taken misery must result and the problems of government increase in every direction. It is from this angle that the question of a rapidly increasing population must be considered in India. The existing standard of living of the masses is not such as to permit of any deterioration without results which may have grave repercussions. It was considered necessary to give some idea of the geographical, administrative and constitutional features in the State as a background before proceeding to discuss the results of the Census and their

bearing on the conditions now existing and likely to obtain in the future.

9. **Population.**—The facts regarding the composition and distribution of the population are given in Imperial Tables I and V and their subsidiaries and in State Table I.

Imperial Table I and State Table I together give detailed information concerning the area, houses and population of the State as a whole and of its districts and tehsils separately. The subsidiaries to Imperial Table I give figures showing the density of population for the whole State and various parts of it, details regarding cultivable and cultivated areas and the proportion of females to males for all districts.

Imperial Table II shows the variations in the actual population for the whole State and in each district for the past fifty years. Its subsidiaries show the percentage variations and changes in density for each decade and a comparison between the variations according to the Census returns and those shown by the vital statistics.

Imperial Table III and its subsidiary show the distribution of the urban and rural population in density groups and the proportions of the population living in each.

Imperial Table IV classifies towns according to population and shows the variations in the population of each since 1891. Its subsidiaries give the percentage variations and the number of females per thousand males in urban and rural areas respectively with separate figures for the two cities—Jammu and Srinagar.

Imperial Table V gives details of the urban population by communities separately for all towns in the State, by districts and for the State as a whole. Its subsidiaries show the number per thousand of the total population, and of each community, who live in towns for each Natural Division and the communal composition per ten thousand of the urban and rural populations separately.

It is not easy to visualise the size of a country by its area in square miles; comparisons usually give a more accurate idea. Jammu and Kashmir State (84,471 sq. miles) is slightly smaller than England, Wales and Scotland put together (88,749 sq. miles) ; in India it may be compared with Bihar and Orissa taken together (83,054 sq. miles), Hyderabad State (82,698 sq. miles) or with Bengal (77,521 sq. miles). But area alone is of little importance ; we are concerned with the people occupying any given area and more particularly with their numbers—the density of the population. The density figures for the whole State and by districts are given in Subsidiary (i) to Table I. There is no necessity to discuss them in detail here. It may however be observed that the figure for the whole State has risen to 48 against 43 in 1931. The 1931 density figures for Great Britain, which comprises England, Wales and Scotland, and for Bihar and Orissa, Hyderabad State and Bengal, which are comparable with the State in area, were 480, 454, 175 and 646 respectively. It must be remembered however that the State is one of the most mountainous countries in the world and that the figure for the State includes the mountainous wastes of the sparsely populated Frontier Districts; the figures for all other districts of the State compare well with those for Hyderabad's 175, the figure for Jammu Province being 160 and for Kashmir 202. The factors affecting density in any area are numerous but the greatest is probably industrialisation. In this respect the Jammu and Kashmir State cannot compare with Great Britain, Bengal and Bihar ; it has a few industries but the more important of these—forest exploitation, sericulture and fruit growing—are closely allied with agriculture and the State must be described as almost entirely agricultural. If we consider the proportion of cultivable area to the total area (5·6 per cent.) it will be realised that the density is actually very high for the inhabited tracts and when we remember that the bulk of the population is dependent on agriculture it becomes obvious that a continuing increase of population at the rate of 10 per cent. per decade for a period of two generations is going to give rise to very serious problems in the absence of industrial development or more intensive cultivation. The pressure of population on the land is already a problem and fragmentation of holdings is probably proceeding faster than consolidation ; the holding on which the average peasant family relies for its subsistence is gradually becoming smaller. The Frontier Districts have been cited above as sparsely populated mountainous wastes ; the description is justified. Scrutiny of Subsidiary (i) to Table I will show that other areas are very mountainous too and that only 6·3 per cent. of Udhampur District is cultivable and 8·4 per cent. of Muzaffarabad. The most favourable conditions are found in the Jammu District but even here the percentage is only 38·5. The actual area cultivated in any district is even less. On this basis the density figures indicate rather serious overcrowding of the land ; they exceed 1,000 in most districts in the State and approach 2,000 in some areas of the Frontier Districts and in the Anantnag District. It is a simple matter for those who wish to go into details to calculate the actual figures for any particular district.

Since the State is so largely agricultural irrigational facilities and adequate rainfall are matters of prime importance; the figures for both are given in Subsidiary (i) to Table I. A steadily increasing population in an agricultural country requires an expanding area for cultivation or, in the absence of more land to put under crops, more intensive cultivation of existing areas; the latter is not usually possible without the use of fertilisers and an assured water supply and this points to the construction of more canals to ensure regular and ample irrigation. A considerable gap is shown in Subsidiary (ii) to Table II between the variation since 1931 according to the Census and the increase revealed by the Vital Statistics. The method of collecting and recording the Vital Statistics leaves much to be desired and too much reliance should not be placed on them. However, Col. Sir Ram Nath Chopra, I. M. S. (retd.), Director of Medical Services in the State has kindly written a note discussing vital statistics, diseases, epidemics and health matters generally which is printed as an appendix to this essay, and further discussion of the subject here is unnecessary.

10. **Migration.**—Another important matter affecting the population is migration. Imperial Table VI and its subsidiaries give the figures available; for reasons given in the notes to the table they are incomplete. However, it may be said at once that at the time the Census is taken, in the early spring of any year, the population of the State is at its lowest. In the past there has been little movement into the State or out of it from one year to another or from one decade to another which has any permanent effect on the population. As time goes on, if the population increases at its present speed, either the local means of subsistence must be increased by industrial development or the land must be made more fruitful. It is more than probable there will be both industrial and agricultural development as well as an increase in emigration. To return to the point. Both emigration and immigration are at present mostly seasonal. Since the great majority of emigrants leave the State chiefly for the Punjab and North West Frontier Province in search of employment, in the late autumn when their crops have been harvested and return in the spring as soon as the snow is off the land and they can attend to field works, they are absent when the Census is taken at the end of February or early in March. The bulk of the immigrants to the State are either tourists who want to see the beauties of Kashmir or men and women from India, of every station in life, anxious to escape for a while from the heat and dust of the Indian plains to the coolth and restfulness of Kashmir and its many beautiful valleys. These visitors commence to arrive in March and have gone by the end of November; a few stay to become temporary residents; most of them are not here when the Census is taken. Besides these seasonal migrations there are movements which may be described as semi-permanent. From most districts of the Jammu Province, but more particularly from Poonch Jagir and the Mirpur District, men in considerable numbers leave their homes for fairly long periods at a time. Some are taken as recruits in the British Indian Army; others get employment as domestic servants, as seamen and stokers n the mercantile marine operating from Indian ports, as labourers on the railways or as traders both in and beyond India. These represent a loss to the population but from one decade to another, in the past, the numbers involved are believed to have been fairly constant. At the recent Census the numbers were probably higher than usual owing to the war and the impetus given to recruitment for the services and to all trades and industries meeting war requirements both directly and indirectly. Movements other than those mentioned are mostly purely local.

One more point demands mention owing to its bearing on the future population; this is the proportion of the sexes. Various aspects of the question are presented in different subsidiary tables but the position for the whole State and for each district for the last forty years is clearly shown in Subsidiary (iv) to Table I. Before discussing the activities of the various departments in the State and their bearing on our subject it will be convenient to refer to the communities which together constitute the population.

11. **The Muslims.**—The communities of the State are classified by religion. The details are given in Table XIII. Muslims are the most numerous. They number over thirty-one lacs and constitute 77·11 of the total population. During the decade they increased by 10·07 per cent. Over sixteen lacs live in the Kashmir Province and over twelve lacs in the Jammu Province (including Jagirs); the sparsely popu-

lated Frontier Districts hold just over 270,000 out of a total population of 311,478. Racially, most of the Muslims of the Jammu Province and its Jagirs are closely connected with the tribes of the Punjab and are of the same original stock as the Hindu elements of the population but the Gujjars are an important element. The Muslims living in the southern part of the Kashmir Province are of the same stock as the Kashmiri Pandit community and are usually designated Kashmiri Muslims; those of the Muzaffarabad District are partly Kashmiri Muslims, partly Gujjar and the rest are of the same stock as the tribes of the neighbouring Punjab and North West Frontier Province districts. The Muslims of the Ladakh District are mostly Mongolian (Baltis) by race but in the Skardu Tehsil many are of Dardic origin. In Astore and the various illaqas of the Gilgit Agency they are mostly Dards. There has naturally been a certain amount of inter-marriage between the Muslim elements of the different racial stocks since the large scale conversions to Islam from the fourteenth century onwards.

There were few, if any, Muslims in the territories now comprising the Jammu and Kashmir State previous to the beginning of the fourteenth century. These few infiltrated from the neighbouring areas of the Punjab into the Jammu Province. In the Kashmir Province the whole population for all practical purposes was Hindu up to about 1325 A. D. and in the Frontier Districts they were either Buddhists or belonged to primitive tribes. About this time Syed Abdur Rahman, better known as Bulbul Shah, obtained many converts to Islam. He was followed by Hazrat Mir Syed Ali Hamdani whose piety and learning made such a great impression on the people that large numbers are said to have embraced Islam. Islam continued to spread without any differences in its ranks up to the period of Sultan Hassan Shah. A little later Mir Shamas-ud-Din Iraqi arrived in Kashmir from Khurasan and commenced to preach the tenets of the Shia sect. He experienced many vicissitudes but eventually some of his followers gained influence at court and by 1554 A. D. Ghazi Chak, a Shia, became King of Kashmir. The dynasty lasted 32 years. There are said to have been acute differences between the two main sects of Islam—Sunni and Shia—during the period of the Chak dynasty which led Sunni elements to beseech Akbar the Great to conquer Kashmir. The two sects were on good terms during the Moghal period but at intervals since their relations have been strained. There are two minor Muslim sects which are offshoots of the Sunni sect, *viz*. Wahabis and Ahmadis. The latter are also known as Qadianis. Both are of comparatively recent growth and numerically unimportant in the State. The majority of the Muslims in the State belong to the Sunni sect. At the recent Census Shias were recorded as such and numbered 205,999. In addition there are approximately 74,000 in the Gilgit Agency. At this Census Shias were not recorded as such in the Gilgit Agency but merely shown as Muslims. The total Shias in the Jammu and Kashmir State territories at the 1941 Census may therefore be taken as 280,000; the remainder, nearly all Sunnis, total 2,821,247.

Of the various castes and tribes making the Muslim element of the population those describing themselves as Kashmiri Muslims and Gujjars are by far the most numerous; the former numbered 1,270,261 at the recent Census and the latter 381,457. The next important in numerical order are Rajputs, Jats, Sheikhs, Baltis, Sudhans, Syeds and Moghals. The Rajputs, numbering over 226,000 are spread all over the Jammu Province with a few in Poonch Jagir. In the Kashmir Province they are mostly found in the Muzaffarabad District. Jats, over 121,000, are almost entirely located in the Jammu Province, the great majority living in the Mirpur District. The Sheikhs, nearly 110,000, are found in all districts of the State; the largest numbers are located in the Anantnag and Baramulla Districts of the Kashmir Province. Of the 99,348 Baltis all but a few hundreds live in the Skardu and Kargil Tehsils of the Ladakh District. Sudhans, 78 000, are almost entirely found in the Poonch Jagir and the Mirpur District. Syeds, 52,000, and Moghuls, 42,000, are found in every district of the State; the largest numbers are in Poonch, Mirpur and Muzaffarabad. There are a fair number of Syeds in the Anantnag District. The full details of all the important elements of the population are given in Table XIV.

There is no occasion to say much about the Kashmiri Muslims in spite of their numerical importance. They have lived in Kashmir since ancient times and previous to their conversion to Islam from the early fourteenth century onwards were a part of the resident Hindu population of Kashmir.

12. **The Gujjars.**—The Gujjars are in a different category; their origin and first appearance in the State are not definitely known. At the recent Census they numbered 381,457 which is 21,324 less than in 1931. This decrease cannot be accounted for unless it is due to the fact that in many cases they did not describe themselves correctly. Muslims as a whole show

an increase in numbers which compares favourably with the increase of population for the whole State. There is no reason to believe that the Gujjar element of the community was an exception to this tendency. Gujjars show a decrease in the districts Reasi, Poonch and Chenani in the Jammu Province and for all districts in the Kashmir Province. The tabulation of figures for the Gilgit Agency did not separate the various elements of the population. In 1931, 2,454 Gujjars were recorded as living in the Gilgit Agency. However, it is not necessary to attempt to account for the variations ; to do so would be pure guess work when we have no reliable evidence to explain the decrease.

The early history of the Gujjar tribe is obscure ; there are several theories as to their origin. It is suggested, with diffidence, that the theory that they came to India from Central Asia, from a region in the neighbourhood of the Caspian Sea, is as good as any. That they came to the territories now known as the Jammu and Kashmir State by way of the Punjab and the North West Frontier Province does not appear to be disputed. Historians seem to be satisfied that tribes called "Gurjaras" were established in the areas now known as Gujerat and Kathiawar from about 600 A. D. onwards. It is believed that these and other sections of the tribe were the ancestors of those now known as Gujjars in this State. The "Gurjaras" were Hindus at the time they are first noticed in India whatever faith they may have professed previous to their migration to India. They had apparently established a kingdom of their own at the time of Harsha about 640 A. D. but were probably under his suzerainty. Their country was to the south of Sind and extended roughly to the Gulf of Cambay. It seems that they successfully resisted the Arab invasion from the north early in the 8th century A. D. It is alleged that about 750 A. D. the Chapa dynasty of the Gurjaras, which had been in power for about 200 years, was displaced by the Pratiharas who seem to have carried on till about 1000 A. D. when their power was broken by the coming of Mahmud of Ghazni. Nothing much appears to be known of the Gurjaras in the Punjab until 890 A. D. when Raja Shankervarman of Kashmir is said to have invaded Gujerat, the Gurjara kingdom ruled over by one Lakhandev. A region known as Tekka, situated in the area now known as the Punjab, was ceded to Shankervarman. The Gurjara kingdom of Gujerat mentioned does not correspond to the present Gujrat District of the Punjab but the present district of Gujrat is believed at one time to have been a part of it. It is reasonable to presume that Gurjara tribes had extended to the Punjab and it is probable that such places as Gujrat, Gujranwala, Gujarkhan and Gurdaspur, where Gujjar families are still found, derived their names from this fact. The Gurjara kingdom ceased to exist in the time of Akbar the Great when their country was annexed. By this time a number of Gujjars, as we will now call them, had embraced Islam and from now onwards the connection of the northern section with their Hindu ancestors becomes less and less. No claim is made for the historical accuracy of the brief summary given above of the probable early history of the Gujjar tribes. It is nothing more than a summary of the views given in various works in an attempt to link the Gujjars now living in the Jammu and Kashmir State with those believed to have been their ancestors. The migration of a part of the tribe to the territories now known as the Jammu and Kashmir State is attributed to the outbreak of a serious famine in the regions inhabited by the tribe, now known as Rajputana, Gujerat and Kathiawar. The exact period has not been fixed but it is known as the "Satahsiya Famine". It is stated that some parts of the migrating tribes moved to the Punjab whilst others moved further north to the areas now known as Kaghan, Swat, Hazara, Kashmir and Gilgit. The same source states that the Gujjars now living in the Jammu and Kashmir State are parts of two separate migrations, one direct from the Gurjara tribes of Rajputana, Gujerat and Kathiawar, the other, and later migration, from the Gujjar tribes settled in the Punjab. It is stressed that there are still Gujjar families living in the Sialkot, Gujranwala, Gujrat, Jhelum and Rawalpindi Districts of the Punjab. Some Gujjars now living in the Bhimber and Rajouri Tehsils of the Mirpur and Reasi Districts of the Jammu Province claim that their ancestors came from the Gujrat District of the Punjab. It is probable that many of them followed in the wake of the Moghal rulers who used to visit Kashmir. The route of the Moghals from Delhi is known to have been through Gujrat, Bhimber, Rajouri, Behramgala and Shopian to Srinagar. Gujjars have been settled for many generations all along this route. It is on record that the older inhabitants of Bhimber complained to Akbar the Great when he was on his way back to Delhi from Kashmir that the Gujjars were a source of annoyance and suffering to them. The inhabitants of Sialkot made similar complaints. In the 17th century there were Gujjars of high official status in Poonch. They lived at Lohar-Kot or

Loherene, now known as Loran, in the Haveli Tehsil of the Poonch Jagir. They provided ministers to assist the rulers of the area. At the end of the 18th century one of their leaders named Ruh-ullah Khan obtained full control of the country and assumed the title of Raja. He was the most important Gujjar personality of the time. He was Wazir to Raja Khan Bahadur of Poonch. On the murder of the latter, Ruh-ullah Khan ruled as the deceased Raja's representative until he got his own son, Amir Khan, declared Raja of Poonch in 1797 A. D. Ruh-ullah Khan died in 1819 and Amir Khan about 1825. The latter was succeeded by his son, Mir Baz Khan, who was conquered by Maharaja Ranjit Singh of the Punjab. Mir Baz was removed to Lahore where he was murdered by one Pir Bakhsh Khan Chib in 1837 A. D. The dynasty started by Ruh-ullah Khan was known as the Sango line of Gujjars. With the disappearance of Mir Baz Khan their short period of power came to an end and the status and influence of the Gujjars gradually deteriorated. No outstanding Gujjar has since appeared in the State comparable with Ruh-ullah Khan. As the generations have passed since his time, the Gujjar tribe throughout the State has become less important in all respects except in numbers. With the advent of the Sikhs it would seem that the Gujjars split up. Probably small groups of them migrated to different areas in the State away from close contact with Sikh rule. Some probably moved along the old Moghal route through Bhimber and Rajouri to Kashmir *via* Shopian and others over the hills from Poonch to the districts of Baramulla and Muzaffarabad. From these areas they have spread to all districts of the State. The wealthier of the Gujjars keep herds of buffaloes, cattle, sheep and goats; nearly all follow agricultural pursuits. They are no longer nomadic by inclination but settle wherever they can. In almost every nullah in the country a family of Gujjar squatters will be found high up above the ordinary levels of cultivation. They cultivate land at an altitude well beyond the limits of ordinary village lands and do a great deal of damage to forests in the process. The Bakarwals are a nomadic element of the Gujjar tribe; they keep large herds of sheep and goats and a certain number of buffaloes and cattle. Their goats do great damage to forest areas. Whether the assumptions with regard to the early history of the Gujjars and their arrival in this State set forth above are well founded or not, the fact remains that they are in the greatest numbers in the Jammu, Reasi and Poonch Jagir Districts of the Jammu Province and the Muzaffarabad, Baramulla and Anantnag Districts of Kashmir. With the exception of the Gujjars of the Jammu District the community shows little interest in education and in this respect is very backward. The Gujjars of Jammu District are advanced compared with Gujjars in the rest of the State. This is probably due to the fact that they live close to, and have come more in contact with, civilizing influences than other sections of the tribe. The percentage of literacy amongst the rest of the Gujjars is very low. They are a valuable element of the State population but unless they make some effort to acquire at least the rudiments of education the community as a whole is doomed to recede lower in the social scale.

13. **The Hindus.**—The Hindus in the State, including the Scheduled Castes but excluding Sikhs and Jains, total 809,165 or 20·12 per cent. During the decade they increased by 9·90 per cent. The most important numerically are the Brahmans, the Rajputs and the Kashmiri Pandits. Their numbers at the recent Census were 198,004, 168,582 and 76,868 respectively. The number of Brahmans living in the Jammu District is over 63,000. In Kathua and Udhampur Districts there are over 35,000 in each case. Reasi comes next with nearly 30,000 followed by Poonch Jagir with over 19,000 and Mirpur District with over 14,000. There are some 1,335 in the Chenani Jagir. In other districts of the State their numbers are negligible. The Hindu Rajputs are found in large numbers in the Udhampur District with over 61,000, followed by Kathua and Jammu with over 36,000 and 35,700 respectively. Reasi comes next with nearly 21,000 and Mirpur with over 8,000. Their numbers in other districts are very small. Most of the Kashmiri Pandits are residents of Srinagar; over 62,000 live in the Anantnag District in which Srinagar City is situated. Another 11,000 were recorded in Baramulla District. The figures do not exceed a thousand in any other district except Jammu which has 1,367. The Kashmiri Pandits community has a higher standard of literacy than any other. This fact gives it an importance out of all proportion to its comparatively small numbers. The Scheduled Castes together number 152,536. The numbers for each caste and their distribution throughout the State are given in Part II of Table XIV. Adherents of the Arya Smaj movement numbered 87,356. In Table XIII they are included with "Other Hindus". In 1901 they numbered only 79. Reference need only be made to three other elements of the Hindu population *viz.* Khatris, Jats and Mahajans; the two former exceed 25,000

and the latter 23,000. The Khatris are mostly found in Jammu Province, particularly in the Jammu and Mirpur Districts. Each of the other districts has a small number. There are few outside Jammu Province although some 2,000 were recorded in the Muzaffarabad District. Of the 25,000 Jats over 16,000 live in the Mirpur District and over 7,000 in Jammu District. There are 1,430 in Kathua. Elsewhere the numbers are small. Over 10,000 Mahajans live in Jammu District and over 4,000 in Udhampur. Each district of the Jammu Province has its quota. There are very few in other parts of the State. There is little new to be said about the origin of the Hindu elements of the population. Most of them are descended from the indigenous population of the area. Their history goes back to very early times and is rather a subject for the historian. Numbers of them have migrated to British India during past centuries and the community here has received accessions to its numbers by immigration from British India, chiefly from the neighbouring areas of the Punjab. A note on the Dogra Hindu-Rajput community, of which His Highness the Maharaja Bahadur of Jammu and Kashmir is the head, has recently been produced and published by Thakur Lakshmansingh Charak of Jammu and can be obtained easily, by those desirous of details. An interesting genealogical table of His Highness' family is given with the note which traces the Ruling Family's descent back to Maharaja Sudarshan of Ajodhya.

14. **The Sikhs.**—The Sikhs number 65,903. They form only 1·64 per cent. of the population but are increasing at a higher rate than any other community. They increased by 30·08 per cent. during the decade. They are found in varying numbers in every district of the State. The largest aggregations are in Poonch Jagir (14,887), Muzaffarabad (12,922), Mirpur (12,111), Jammu (9,151), Baramulla (8,458) and Anantnag (5,654). Whilst the main influx of Sikhs to the country followed its conquest by Maharaja Ranjit Singh of the Punjab there is evidence to show that there were Sikhs in small numbers in the country as early as the sixteenth century. Guru Nanak visited Kashmir and is said to have made converts. The Gurdwara at Martand commemorates his visit. Guru Hargobind also visited Kashmir by way of Sialkot and probably followed the Moghal route. Gurdwaras at Srinagar, Baramulla and Muzaffarabad commemorate his visit. His teaching probably resulted in a number of the inhabitants of Srinagar and the neighbouring villages embracing Sikhism. Possibly he left behind some of his disciples to carry on his work. Sikhism cannot be said to be indigenous; a few local converts don't make it so. However, it is clear that its existence in the State goes back to a date before the advent of Sikh rule. As already remarked, its beginnings in the Kashmir Province at any rate, would appear to date from the visits of Gurus Nanak and Hargobind. A story appears in previous Census Reports from 1911 onwards to the effect that during the period 1751-1762 A.D. certain mercenary troops were engaged by Raja Sukhijiwan, Governor of Kashmir at that time, to assist him to assert his independence against his master, Emperor Ahmad Shah Durrani of Kabul. According to the story these mercenaries embraced Sikhism in the time of Maharaja Ranjit Singh and were called "Jinsi Sikhs" from the fact that they were in receipt of jins (grain) as military rations. Later, they are said to have settled in various parts of the country and to have started the Sikh settlements now found at such places as Tral, Hummal, Baramulla etc. The story is a bit confused; it states that Raja Sukhijiwan "brought Jinsi Sikhs from Pothwar and the adjoining hills" and goes on to say that "they embraced Sikhism in the time of Maharaja Ranjit Singh". These statements are contradictory. Ranjit Singh did not come on to the scene until long after 1762. If any mercenaries embraced Sikhism in the time of Ranjit Singh they could not have been those brought in by Sukhijiwan. It is possible the mercenaries brought in by Sukhijiwan were Sikhs and not Punjabi Brahmans as has been stated in earlier reports. It is also possible that the descendants of these mercenaries, who may have been Punjabi Brahmans, were here when Ranjit Singh conquered the country and that either they entered his service as Sikhs or embraced Sikhism then. In those days land revenue was collected in kind with the assistance of the military. The unit employed was known as the Nizamat Paltan which consisted of Sikhs. It is probable that these men became known as "Jinsi Sikhs" to distinguish them from the members of other Sikh units because of their association with the collection of grain (jins). This, of course, is pure conjecture but then the story of Raja Sukhijiwan and his "Jinsi Sikhs", although going back to the Census Report of 1911, is only based on a story related by a certain official at the time of the 1911 Census. Whether there was any influx of Sikhs in the period 1751-1762 or not, it is clear that, although there were Sikhs in the country previously, most of them now living in the State are the descendants of those who came to the country with Ranjit Singh's invading army and during the period of Sikh rule (1819-1846). This is supported by the fact that the largest aggregations of Sikhs

are found in those areas of the State closest to the Punjab which had close associations with the Sikh court at Lahore. Ranjit Singh first attacked Jammu in 1808. The Sikhs were not successful at their first attempt to conquer Jammu. But by 1809 Gulab Singh, later the first Maharaja of Jammu and Kashmir, had joined the Sikh army at Daska, near Sialkot at Ranjit Singh's request. It is reasonable to presume that Sikhs commenced to enter the Jammu Province in considerable numbers from this date onwards up to the time of the fall of the Sikh kingdom in 1846.

15. **The Buddhists.** The next in order of numerical importance are the Buddhists. Their home is Ladakh. There are 40,696 of them. They have increased by 5 per cent. since 1931. Very few leave their own country for long. At the Census all but 532 were enumerated in Ladakh. They live in the Ladakh Tehsil and in that part of the Kargil Tehsil adjacent to it. There are none in those portions of the Kargil Tehsil adjoining Kashmir or the Skardu Tehsil. A few live near Padar in the Kishtwar Tehsil of the Udhampur District which lies on the western borders of Zanskar in the southern part of the Kargil Tehsil. The Buddhist community shows a far smaller increase in numbers than any other. This has been the case since the beginning of Census taking. In 1911 it was attributed partly to the practice of polyandry and partly to conversions to Islam. These conversions are not so numerous as to be noticeable and most occur as a result of intermarriage. The scarcity of cultivable land, the absence of forests and the lack of water for irrigation are not conditions favourable to an increase of population. If we add the practice of dedicating both boys and girls to their monasteries in considerable numbers to lead a life of celibacy it is not surprising that the community shows a small rate of increase. In fact, it is the nature of the country itself which has probably given rise to the practice of polyandry and to the dedication of boys and girls to the monasteries. The country cannot support an increasing population in existing conditions and the numbers of the Buddhist community are unlikely to expand much until the conditions in their country alter very considerably. As it is, most of them eke out a bare existence.

16. **Other Communities.**—The members of the other communities living in the State are so few in number as to call for little comment. They are Indian Christians (3,079), European and Anglo-Indian Christians (430), Jains (910), Parsis (29), Jews (11), Primitive Tribes and Others (146).

Of these Indian Christians have shown a considerable increase as compared with 1931 when they numbered 1,942. European and Anglo-Indian Christians have increased from 321 to 430. The Jains have increased from 597 in 1931 to 910; of these 895 were recorded in Jammu City.

17. **Social Customs.**—Social customs are bound to have some effect on the rate of increase of the population, certainly those relating to marriage, divorce and re-marriage. It is probable that the customs of the various elements of the population, as much as any other factors, account for the variations in the increase of the four main communities of the State—Muslims, Hindus, Sikhs and Buddhists.

As already remarked, the Sikh community shows a very big increase. It is so large that it is permissible to adduce reasons other than a natural increase of population. The most likely other cause for this phenomenal percentage (30·08) is defective tabulation in the past due to wrong answers given in the Census record. For instance, at the recent Census a reference was received asking if Sikhs could describe themselves as Brahmans under race, tribe or caste. The answer was in the negative. However, if we examine their social customs we find they provide favourable conditions for an increasing population. The expenses connected with the marriage ceremony are not unduly high, there is little caste restriction, the parties to a marriage have considerable freedom of selection, widow remarriage is recognised, purdah is not practised and migration is negligible. Even before the 'Infant Marriage Act' was passed by the legislature in 1985 (1929 A. D.) the marriage of immature boys and girls was unusual. The Sikhs are monogamous; this is an important point in a country where there is a deficiency of females. All the customs mentioned are favourable to an increase. Further, the community welcomes converts but one seldom hears of a Sikh apostate although the possibility of their existence is not contested.

The Muslims show the next highest rate of increase. As in the case of the Sikhs there are no caste restrictions and the parties to a marriage enjoy a considerable measure of freedom of selection if they be of mature age. Divorce is recognised and the remarriage of widows approved. Converts are readily accepted. The factors cited are all favourable to a natural increase of population. The marriage of immature boys and girls is an adverse factor; so also is the practice of polygamy. Infant marriages were common before the passage of the Infant Marriage Act and it is believed the custom still persists. Although Islam permits a man to have more than one wife at a time, it is the exception rather than the rule for Muslims in the State to practise polygamy. Purdah is strictly observed by a considerable portion of those living in urban areas and where accommodation is restricted the lack of fresh air and exercise must re-act adversely on the birth of healthy children. The fact that in some areas large numbers of Muslim men migrate temporarily may be reckoned as a minor adverse factor.

The customs prevalent amongst Hindus are not so conducive to an increase of population as those followed by Sikhs and Muslims. The expenses connected with the marriage ceremony are usually heavy, caste restrictions are considerable, freedom of selection between the parties to a marriage is unusual, the marriage of immature boys and girls was the rule rather than the exception before the passing of the Infant Marriage Act, divorce is not recognised and widow re-marriage is not permitted except by a small section of the community, purdah is observed to a considerable extent in urban areas. These may all be termed adverse factors. Hindus are usually monogamous but more than one wife is recognised in certain circumstances, more particularly in the absence of a son. Converts are very few as it is not a proselytising religion except amongst a small section. The Arya Samajists advocate the abolition of caste restrictions in the matter of marriage, encourage widow re-marriage and are ready to accept converts; indeed they make proselytism a part of their activities. But these innovations are obnoxious to the conservative castes.

We have not far to go to seek the reasons for the small increase in the Buddhist community. The practice of polyandry is sufficient in itself. If we add to this the fact that it is customary for every family to dedicate at least one of its younger sons to a monastery to become a monk and at least one girl to become a chomo or nun and live a life of celibacy, it is a matter for surprise not that the percentage increase is small but that it should be as much as 5 per cent. Recently legislation has been passed by His Highness' Government, at the instance of what may be termed the young Buddhist Party, prohibiting the practice of polyandry and rendering those who infringe this legislation liable to severe penalties. It remains to be seen whether this legislation has the support of the majority of the community. If it has, the next Census should show a greater percentage increase in the population of the Buddhist community unless other equally effective measures are adopted to check such an increase.

The passing of the Infant Marriage Act is bound to have an effect on the Muslim and Hindu communities in particular over a period of years. Medical authorities have satisfied themselves that there is a greater measure of fertility in marriages between those of mature age than in the case of infant marriages. There is also less infantile and maternal mortality. This legislation is therefore likely to operate in favour of a larger percentage increase in the future in the case of those communities previously practising child marriage. In the past, female infanticide is believed to have been prevalent, particularly amongst the Rajputs. His Highness the Maharaja Bahadur of Jammu and Kashmir initiated several measures to encourage those who used to practise this custom to desist. If the various social reforms initiated, which may be said to have been in an embryonic stage during the decade just completed, have the approval of the majority and receive their active support the returns at the next Census should reflect a more even percentage increase in the population of the three chief communities. The Buddhist community must always show a smaller increase until conditions in the country they occupy and their social customs change very considerably.

18. **The Revenue Department.**—Agriculture plays such an important part in the life and economy of the country that it would be well to study the conditions rather closely. Except for those areas under the administration of the Government of India, on behalf of the State, the country is divided into districts and tehsils under the executive control of the Revenue Department at the head of which is the Revenue Minister who is assisted by a Revenue Commissioner and a Director of Land Records. The senior revenue officer in each of the two provinces of Jammu and Kashmir is called the Governor of the Province. District officers are called Wazirs, tehsil officers, Tehsildars and the latter's assistants, Naib-Tehsildars. There is no need to go into the details of the army of overseers, surveyors, clerks, girdawars, qanungoes, patwaris, chaprassis, zaildars, lamberdars and chowkidars, who together make up the staff of the Revenue Department; their numbers are legion and so are their duties. As the name of the department indicates its primary function is the collection of land revenue.

19. **The System of Land Tenure.**—Before discussing the activities of other departments whose work affects agricultural conditions let us examine the system of land tenure. During the Moghal, Pathan and Sikh periods the lot of the peasant was very hard. In the Kashmir Province he possessed neither proprietary nor occupancy rights. All land was owned by the State. The cultivator was permitted to occupy the land only so long as he paid the rent when it became due; he could neither sell nor mortgage the land he occupied. The system of assessment in those days must be described as harsh. The State's share was not less than 3/5 of the gross produce and, allowing for unauthorised exactions, the cultivator's share probably did not exceed 1/3. Conditions in the Frontier Districts were the same; in the Jammu Province they were better. The descendants of the original occupants of the land in Jammu held proprietary rights; many of the proprietors were land-holders of long standing and cultivated their own land; other cultivators were tenants-at-will. It was the custom to collect the revenue in kind on an estimate of the crops. The State share varied; it was ½ from owners, 2/5 from cultivators resident in the village cultivating State land and 1/3 from cultivators belonging to another village. Usually the land was held by hereditary village proprietor with hereditary tenants under them cultivating the land. The revenue demand was heavy with the result that payments frequently fell into arrears and the State took possession of the land. The rights of some proprietors were confiscated as a punishment for acts of rebellion and disloyalty. In this way many villages and parts of villages became the sole property of the State. From time to time re-measurements and re-assessments were carried out but the methods were not such as could be termed accurate. With the advent of the Dogra dynasty under Maharaja Gulab Singhji Bahadur (1846-58), the conditions both for the proprietor and the tenant were eased a bit for new lands brought under cultivation. In the time of Maharaja Ranbir Singhji Bahadur (1858-85) the State share of the crops was reduced and revenue was made payable in cash or kind at the wish of the cultivator but it was not until the reign of Maharaja Sir Pratap Singhji Bahadur (1885-1925) that a Regular Settlement was carried out to determine the rights of the cultivator and to put revenue assessment on a proper basis; this was commenced in 1887 and completed in 1914. The Settlement operations gave to the cultivator something he had never enjoyed before— security of tenure and a fixed cash assessment. The State still retained ownership of large areas. With the proper measurement of land and assessment of revenue the State share was reduced to about 30 per cent. of the gross produce. In addition, Patwari and Lambardari cesses were levied which amounted to 2 per cent. and 5 per cent. respectively, on the amount of each individual's assessment. Since the first Regular Settlement, revision has been carried out in all tehsils and in some of them twice. The incidence of land revenue has been further reduced and now amounts to about 25 per cent. of the gross produce plus the Patwari, Zaildari, Lambardari, Sanitation, Education and Road Cesses. These together amount to about 12½ per cent. on the actual revenue payable which brings the total up to about 28 per cent. of the gross produce. At the time of the first Regular Settlement in Jammu Province the rights of those possessing lands were recognised and they were recorded as owners; other areas which for various reasons had passed into State possession were recorded as owned by the State. The tenants of State owned land were recorded as tenants-at-will or occupancy tenants according to the period they had been in possession. They were required to pay 'Malikana', over and above the ordinary revenue assessment; the rate of Malikana varied according to length of possession. The tenants of proprietors, other than the State, were usually required by their landlords to pay the revenue assessment due plus 'Malikana' or rent in kind as might have been previously agreed upon. In 1912 to commemorate the coronation of His Majesty King George V all tenants-at-will of land owned by the State were granted full occupancy rights. At the time of the first Regular Settlement in Kashmir Province established cultivators were given 'assami' or tenancy rights. The concession permitted an 'assami' and his heirs to hold the land occupied in perpetuity so long as the revenue assessment was paid but gave no right of transfer either by sale or mortgage; ownership remained with the State. The same concessions were given to the land-holders and cultivating tenants of the Frontier Districts in similar circumstances.

Thus, throughout the State, the reign of His late Highness Maharaja Sir Pratap Singhji Bahadur brought relief; for the first time the cultivator was given a fair assessment and security of tenure. Since the present Ruler, His Highness Maharaja Sir Hari Singhji Bahadur, came to the throne in 1925 the conditions of life for the cultivator have been improved enormously. At the time of His Highness' coronation or Raj Tilak in 1926 important concessions were announced which took the form of grants of State-owned land to village communities. In

1933 His Highness was pleased to confer proprietary rights on occupancy tenants of State land and those with assami rights and remitted the payment of 'Nazrana' usually levied on such occasions ; the Malikana payable by occupancy tenants over and above the amount assessed for revenue was also remitted. These concessions, following those already made, greatly improved the status of the cultivator and in thousands of cases changed his position from a serf to a land-holder.

To protect the thousands of newly created land-holders in the Kashmir Province and the Frontier Districts from the consequences of their own improvidence a Land Alienation Act was passed to control the transfer of land by sale or mortgage. The Act disallowed the transfer of the newly acquired rights to any but a member of the agricultural classes and prohibited the alienation of more than 25 per cent. of any holding for a period of ten years. After the lapse of the period mentioned the provisions will be reviewed. A Pre-emption Act was also passed in order to protect family and village interests and to keep the land as much as possible in the possession of real cultivators. Whilst the status of the peasant cultivator has improved throughout the State in the past fifty years beyond the dreams of his ancestors, the position is not free from difficulties and dangers. The 'assami' now owns his land and has security of tenure but he must be taught to value these rights to the full and to pass on his inheritance to his sons intact. It is all too easy to dissipate the problems of the present by mortgaging the future ; the right to alienate up to 25 per cent. of land holdings has been exercised in the full in hundreds of cases in liquidation of debt. These sales have increased the fragmentation of holdings, which is already a difficult problem, and have resulted in the transfer of much land to members of the agricultural classes who are not cultivators. The tenant or paid agricultural labourer seldom works as conscientiously as the owner cultivator. Alienation of land on a large scale to non-cultivating owners is bound to lead to a reduction in the aggregate food grain supplies produced in the country. This in turn must lead to greater difficulty in the feeding of a rapidly increasing population. Figures showing the average size of holdings in the two provinces Kashmir and Jammu have been supplied by the Land Record Department; they vary from 16 acres in the Jammu District to 2½ kanals in the Anantnag District; there are 8 kanals to an acre. The average holding is 6 kanals in Baramulla and just under 6 in Mirpur. These figures indicate the extent of fragmentation of holdings which already exists. Efforts have been made to bring about the consolidation of holdings but the results to date are not encouraging. The Land Records Department reports that since the cultivator was given proprietary rights and the right to alienate up to 25 per cent. of his holding, that is to say during the past decade, large numbers of land transfers have taken place. The most common cause is debt, either inherited or accumulated, usually as a consequence of improvident habits. In Kashmir, the desire to own land on the part of the richer classes of people living in Srinagar is strong. Prices have soared; land previously valued at Rs. 20 per kanal is alleged to have been sold recently at Rs. 300 per kanal. When His Highness gave the cultivator ownership of the State land he occupied previously as a tenant and the right to alienate a part of it he gave him not only independence but the means to liquidate his debts and to make a handsome profit at the same time. It should be repeatedly impressed upon the cultivator that unless he acts wisely the great concessions he has received may well become a curse. If due to extravagance and improvidence on the part of the present peasant-owners a large proportion of the cultivable area passes from the ownership of the actual cultivator into the possession of non-cultivating classes and absentee landlords the children of the present peasant-owners will be dispossessed and revert to the position of serfs and labourers. The present position as regards the supply of food grains, which is by no means easy, may well be greatly aggravated. The wisdom of restricting the peasant's powers to alienate his land heritage is obvious.

With the object of helping agriculturists to avoid debt and to encourage the development and improvement of cultivable areas His Highness' Government passed the 'Aid to Agriculturists and Land Improvement Act' in 1936. Under this act loans are made available on easy terms to any proprietor or occupancy tenant of agricultural lands for any purpose directly connected with agriculture. In 1937 a 'Kahcharai Act' was passed by which every landholder or tenant is permitted to keep one buffalo for domestic purposes free of Kahcharai or grazing tax.

It is correct to say that conditions of life for the peasant have been transformed in the State since the Dogra dynasty was established by Maharaja Gulab Singhji in 1846. The improvements were slow to begin with; the speed was accelerated from 1890 to 1920. During the last two decades the progress has been rapid.

20. **Agriculture.**—Measures to improve conditions of living for the cultivator have not been confined to the grant of proprietary rights and security of tenure. The activities of the Agriculture, Veterinary, Co-operative and Rural Development and Panchayat Departments are all directed towards the improvement of the conditions under which the agricultural classes live and work and the introduction of more efficient methods. During the past decade the staff of the Agriculture Department has been strengthened in all directions; demonstrations and propaganda have been increased. The chief food crops grown are rice, maize, wheat and barley in the Kashmir Province, maize, bajra, wheat, rice and barley in the Jammu Province and maize, wheat, barley and grim— a kind of barley grown at high altitudes—in the Frontier Districts; the latter is an important crop in the Ladakh District. During the decade the Director of Agriculture has succeeded for the first time in developing successful types of local rice and wheat by pure line selection; improvement has also been effected by the introduction of selected foreign seed for such crops as sugarcane, wheat, maize and vegetables. The distribution of selected seed and improved implements has been increased; this is important if the same area of cultivated land is to support a rapidly increasing population. His Highness' Government has become a constituent member of the Imperial Council of Agricultural Research and funds have been sanctioned for two research schemes; one is connected with fruit tree pests and the other with rice. The peasant is very conservative and is loath to change his methods; he has every reason to be reluctant to give up methods which have given him and his ancestors fairly good results until he has been convinced that the new methods advocated are better than his own. He knows from practical experience what his land can produce best and he knows its limitations. The cultivator's inherent dislike of change makes it absolutely essential that new methods be tested and demonstrated in as many places as possible and as often as possible and that propaganda be well conceived and continuous. This policy the Agriculture Department is endeavouring to implement by means of demonstration, tours, the holding of agricultural shows, the opening of demonstration plots and the issue of booklets and hand bills free of charge. Some advance has been made but conversion from old ways to new is a long term undertaking requiring persistence and patience. Little progress has been made in the use of manures; cattle dung, which is the obvious agent for increasing the fertility of the soil, is very largely burnt as fuel in the Jammu Province; a little is used to manure maize or wheat; rice is seldom manured; the use of green manure is practically unknown and artificial fertilisers are too expensive. In the Kashmir Province wood fuel is plentiful in most areas and the manure available is practically all used in the rice fields. At the higher elevations the Gujjar uses it for maize crops. The owner-cultivator manures his rice fields liberally, about 120 maunds to an acre in some cases, but the fields of the absentee landlord get little manure and the crops of the latter are usually inferior to those of the former. In the Frontier Districts also all available manure is utilised in the fields. The Agriculture Department, supported by the various departments having contact with the cultivator, has tried its utmost to persuade him to use all available manure in the fields but to date its efforts have had no more effect in Jammu than in other parts of India where dung is used as fuel. The reason is clear; the cultivator must have fuel and in many areas wood fuel is non-existent or inadequate. The forests which existed a hundred years ago have been ruthlessly destroyed in many areas by man and goat; the remedy is to prevent the destruction of the sources of wood fuel supplies in every way and to open up new plantations under quick growing trees in selected areas for the specific purpose of supplying more wood fuel for domestic and other purposes. The working of the coal deposits in the Reasi District may well do much to solve the problem.

Fruit growing is an important agricultural industry in Kashmir; it is of little importance in Jammu at present. The value of fruit is appreciated in the Frontier Districts but cultivable land there is so scarce that fruit is mostly grown only where grain crops cannot thrive. In Kashmir there has been a good deal of development in the past 40 years but unfortunately two pests found their way to the country about 1920; these are known as the San Jose Scale and Woolly Aphis. The former in particular has done tremendous damage and still persists in spite of all efforts to eradicate it. The pests mentioned have caused heavy casualties amongst apple, pear, peach and cherry trees. They do not confine their attacks to fruit trees and this makes it all the more difficult to eradicate them. Large sums have been spent in an effort to bring them under control. To facilitate the work of the Agriculture Department in attacking and overcoming these pests the 'Crop and Plant Protection Act' was passed in 1933 by which the treatment of trees harbouring these two pests was made obligatory. Efforts during the decade have been continuous but the pests remain. In spite of these pests fruit growing is providing the means of subsistence for an increasing number of persons in the Kashmir Province. There would appear to be no reason why the growing of quality mangoes and citrus fruits should not be organised and developed in the lower altitudes of the Jammu Province and the growing of apples, pears, peaches and cherries expanded in the Bhadrawah, Kishtwar and Ramban Tehsils at altitudes of 5,000/6,000 ft.

The size of the average agricultural holding has already been mentioned. The Director of Agriculture has expressed the opinion that the fragmentation of holdings is one of the most important factors obstructing the introduction of improved methods. He estimates that if all mutations be registered the average size of holdings will be found to have decreased by 10 to 15 per cent. Increased cropping of the cultivated area is handicapped in the Kashmir Province and the Frontier Districts by the rigours of the winter and in the Jammu Province by the lack of facilities for increased irrigation ; everywhere, except in limited areas near densely populated localities, the lack of manure operates against intensive cultivation. The only immediate practical means of increasing the volume of food crops for an increasing population is by the use of manures, selected seeds and improved methods.

21. **Animal Husbandry.**—An ample supply of good draught oxen as well as milch cows is essential for a well-balanced system of agriculture. The difficulty in the Jammu and Kashmir State is not a shortage of cattle but an excess so large as to constitute a serious problem which is very much aggravated by the fact that most of the cattle are of very poor quality. Figures taken from the Cattle Census conducted in 1940, and quoted by the Superintendent Civil Veterinary Department, show that there are 130 cattle to every 100 acres of cultivated land ; it is believed this is nearly twice the proportion obtaining in British India. It is not surprising that the quality is so poor, both for ploughing and for milking, when the numbers are so large. The problems involved are now receiving continuous attention. In 1926 expert veterinary opinion was obtained but owing to financial stringency little could be done at the time to implement the advice given although some action was taken. In 1933 the Veterinary Department was reorganised and strengthened in every way and active steps were commenced to remedy the results of neglect over a long period. The treatment of ordinary diseases and the prompt control of epidemics, unless they assume serious proportions, is routine work. Epedemics naturally receive special attention. The main problems to be solved are the reduction in the total head of cattle, many of which are useless for any purpose, the production of a good type of plough ox at a reasonable price and in adequate numbers and the provision of a good strain of milch cattle. The problems are more difficult to solve than might be supposed because on the one hand the killing of cattle in the State is strictly forbidden whilst on the other hand export is prohibited Excessive numbers due to uncontrolled breeding must lead to underfeeding and ill-nourished animals susceptible to any and every outbreak of disease. In 1940 there were 30 veterinary dispensaries in the State against 18 in 1930. At the end of the decade the construction of a well-equipped modern veterinary hospital was commenced at Srinagar and at the time of writing is nearing completion. A similar hospital for Jammu is under consideration. The use of goat tissue vaccine and virus has been introduced for giving immunity to cattle against Rinderpest. This vaccine is being produced at the State Veterinary Laboratory. Legislation has been passed to license approved bulls for breeding purposes. Steps to implement this measure are being taken. Funds to implement a scheme for the improvement of the cattle of the country have been annually provided on a more generous scale since 1937. Two small Cattle Breeding Farms have since been established. The aim is the progressive reduction of scrub animals by castration and the importation of selected bulls of approved breeds. For some time to come all efforts are to be concentrated on the production of a better quality general utility animal and the improvement of indigenous stock. When cattle owners begin to appreciate the importance and advantage of having fewer cattle of better quality it may be possible to be more selective and produce two different types, one for draught purposes and the other for milk. In 1930 there were no cattle breeding centres; in 1940 there were 87—all supplied with selected bulls. Legislation was passed during the decade providing for the compulsory castration of undesirable bulls under the orders of an officer of the Veterinary Department and it is proposed to carry out castration on a large scale in those areas first where approved bulls are stationed. In course of time this policy should reduce the number of useless cattle and increase the number of good quality animals. Various measures, including the holding of cattle fairs, have been introduced to popularise the scheme for cattle improvement and in the course of another decade the results of the efforts now being made should become apparent. There

can be no question that an improvement in the quality of draught oxen means better ploughing and better crops, and better milch cows more milk, a better diet and a healthier population. In spite of the enormous number of cattle in the country the supply of milk and milk products is inadequate. The rural population consumes a comparatively small percentage of the milk produced. Most of the daily supply is made into ghee and either handed over to a money-lender in liquidation of debt or sent to the nearest town for sale. At present the cry 'drink more milk' cannot be indulged; all possible steps must first be taken to increase the production of milk. A reduction in the numbers of useless cattle and the improvement of the breed is the obvious remedy. The average daily yield of a cow is about 1¾ lbs. A poor quality animal requires at least half as much feed a day as a good milk producer but an ordinary specimen of a good milking strain will produce at least four times the yield of the existing average cow thus producing twice the amount of milk for approximately the same feed. The total daily milk production in the country from cows, buffaloes and goats has been estimated by the Superintendent, Veterinary Department to be a little under 12 lacs lbs. and the average daily consumption per head of the population of milk and milk products about 4 oz. These figures speak for themselves and compare unfavourably with the daily consumption figures for the rest of India which, at 7 oz. per head, are not high. As in the case of milk products so in the case of eggs and poultry. It has been calculated that the consumption of eggs per head of the population does not exceed five per year. It seems that the villager, other than those living near towns, has not yet realised the full scope of poultry keeping as a cottage industry and the value of eggs as an article of diet but steps are being taken to educate him in this respect and to distribute eggs of improved types.

Sheep-breeding and wool-growing in this country is essentially a cottage industry. In the decade 1921-30, His Highness' Government obtained the services of an expert to advise on the woollen industry ; his report, amongst other things, outlined a breeding scheme designed to improve the type of sheep. Some of the recommendations were implemented during the past decade and a Sheep-breeding farm was started for research work. Merino, Wensley Dale, Cheviot and Border Leicester rams have been imported and cross breeding with selected local ewes commenced. Experiments in stall-feeding in winter, machine-shearing, are being carried out and sheep diseases studied. Since sheep-breeding and wool-growing are questions of All-India importance the Imperial Council of Agricultural Research has contributed to the cost of the scheme. Any improvement in the type of sheep maintained in the country and any increase in the wool crop is of vast importance to the great mass of the population. According to the livestock Census taken in 1940 the number of sheep in the State is just over 20 lacs and the number of goats nearly 15 lacs. These figures indicate the value of even a small increase in the annual wool crop per sheep.

22. **Co-operative Societies.**—The Co-operative Societies Department has been established in the State for many years but its operations have not met with complete success. This in no way reflects on the efforts of those at present in control of the work. In 1940 there were 15 Central Financing Institutions and some 3,788 Primary Societies ; of the latter 2,839 were agricultural and 949 non-agricultural. The total membership rose from 63,364 in 1931 to 94,371 in 1940 and the working capital from just under Rs. 89½ lacs to over Rs. 95½ lacs. The latter figure is made up of Paid-up Share Capital Rs. 2,218,774, Loans and Deposits Rs. 4,653,375 and Reserves and other funds Rs. 2,701,014. The capital owned by the Societies has increased in the same period from Rs. 3,576,180 to Rs. 4,919,788. The objects of the many societies vary but the majority are credit socieites ; others aim at better-farming, consolidation of holdings, purchase and sale, organisation of labour, removal of adult illiteracy, arbitration, better-living and education. The aim of the 'better-living' societies is to improve village sanitation, reduce expenses on ceremonial occasions and check harmful customs. A good deal of propaganda requires to be done to educate the masses as to the real meaning and purpose of the Co-operative movement. Many membe s do not appear to realise that the true aims are thrift, removal of debt and the co-operation of all the members to obtain advantages in many directions unattainable by them as individuals. It is suspected that many join the movement in order to get something for nothing and unlimited credit without payment of interest let alone re-payment of capital. This misconception has to be removed before the movement can become strong, healthy and self-supporting. The liquidation of a number of insolvent societies has taken place during the decade ; this is all to the good. It is a form of pruning necessary for the health and strength

of the main plant. The department is doing good work for the masses. One of its most important aims at present is the consolidation of holdings. During the decade 83 societies were organised for this purpose and scattered holdings totalling 198,104 kanals, equivalent to 24,763 acres, consisting of 51,856 fields of an average size of 4.57 kanals, were consolidated into 6,211 blocks of an average size of 31.92 kanals. The benefits of such work to the cultivator are too obvious to require description.

23. **Rural Development.**- A Panchayat Act was passed in 1935 providing machinery for the creation of Panchayats in rural areas with limited judicial powers; the first were established in 1936. In 1937 the Panchayat Department was overhauled and reorganised; it is now known as The Rural Development and Panchayat Department. In the first year of its existence a grant of Rs. 40,000 was sanctioned for rural development; the next year the grant was increased to Rs. 1 lac and in 1940 the grant was Rs. 1,40,000. As the name of the department indicates it is concerned with the working of the newly created panchayats or village committees and the amelioration of conditions in rural areas; the two are very closely related. It does not at present operate in the Frontier Districts. In their short existence the panchayats have done useful work; the number functioning at the end of the decade was 255. One of the causes of trouble and debt in rural areas is litigation over petty cases. To take such cases to the regular courts involves the waste of time and money of all concerned. The panchayats can probably settle most of these cases with a greater measure of equity than the ordinary courts; intricate legal points seldom arise and disposal is quicker and the costs are negligible. The number of cases brought before the Panchayat Courts up to the time of the recent Census exceeds 25,000; the number for 1939-40 was 8,830. This may be taken to indicate that the decisions given find general acceptance. The amount of money saved in costs on those cases is estimated to have been about Rs. 1,50,000. In addition to their court case work the panchayats are actively engaged in improving the amenities of life and in working for the general communal welfare in their respective villages. In the process all concerned in the movement must develop a sense of responsibility and unity. It is the function of the department to encourage self help, to supplement with government funds the contributions of the village for this or that communal purpose and generally to advise and guide the village communities in connection with improvements to drinking water supplies, sanitation, communications, control measures during epidemics, consolidation of holdings, etc., and to assist them to enjoy healthy and harmless recreation. Since the department was re-organised in 1937 government financial aid to an extent exceeding Rs. 2½ lacs has been given for a variety of purposes such as the provision or improvement of culverts, drains, pavement of village lanes and approaches, water supplies, bathing places, latrines, ghats, bunds etc. In addition, some 200 miles of fair weather roads have been constructed or improved. The principle adopted, and rightly so, is that the village must make an effort itself and collect what it can towards the cost of village improvement works. The department has carried out investigations through a staff of surveyors into economic, social and cultural conditions in over 1,300 villages. Besides providing data for study on many subjects these surveys enable the department to gauge with some degree of accuracy the comparative merits of the many requests for financial aid. An adult-education drive to reduce illiteracy, organised by the Education Department, had much practical help from the Rural Development Department and the co-operation of the panchayats. A number of village libraries has been established and radio sets have been installed in 24 villages. There is indebtedness in most villages throughout the State. The economic surveys carried out are very comprehensive and include investigations into the annual income and expenditure of the individual families constituting a village. The figures produced show that in over 50 per cent. of the cases investigated expenditure exceeds income and in the remaining cases that the margin of income over expenditure is very small. To say that the figures compiled in this respect cannot be accepted as accurate without being subjected to a searching test does not reflect on the department's work. A good beginning has been made and the development of these activities should produce valuable results. But a time comes in all such work when the information collected must be sifted, tested and evaluated. Meanwhile, it would seem advisable that further investigations should be held in abeyance until the information already collected has been digested so that future efforts may be well-directed and the maximum benefit obtained from the work and expenditure incurred. For these reasons it is not to be expected that the progress made in the next few years will be as apparent as that in the early stages of the work but by 1950 the activities of the department should have produced definite and

obvious results over a wide area. Unless information already collected and classified is studied and digested there is a likelihood that a stage will be reached when 'the wood cannot be seen for the trees' and the department will be buried under a mass of undigested statistics.

24. **Marketing.**—In 1934 a Marketing Board came into existence to collaborate with the Agricultural Marketing Adviser to the Government of India, an officer appointed to implement the recommendations of the Royal Commission on Agriculture in connection with the organised marketing of agricultural produce. Its work in the early stages consisted entirely of commodity surveys; the commodities subjected to such surveys were selected by the Agricultural Marketing Adviser to the Government of India and have reference to the production, consumption, import and export of the commodities selected for survey, and their derivatives, throughout India. The detailed information collected is to form the basis of development work to follow. By 1940 a number of commodities had been surveyed and preliminary steps had been taken to formulate measures to improve methods of marketing. The absence of central regulated markets is a serious disability to the best marketing of any commodity. Several schemes for the opening of such markets were under consideration at the end of the decade. The grading of produce according to accepted standards is aimed at; the necessity for this is obvious in any well-organised trade and is for the benefit of both the buyer and the seller in the long run. Little real progress has been made to date and the world war now raging has interrupted the work and put back the clock in this respect for some time to come. With everyone scrambling for commodities, irrespective of quality and price, a policy of careful grading has little chance of success. Grading comes into its own in normal times when trade is following recognised channels and quality and reliability count most. Weights and measures throughout India are confused and conditions in the State are no exception. The exact amount represented by any particular weight or measure seems to vary very considerably in places comparatively close to each other. The question of standardising weights and measures is receiving consideration. The various improvements in marketing facilities which have been mooted cannot be said to have received much local encouragement; there has been a certain amount of uninformed and misguided opposition to grading and it is unlikely that much real progress will be made in the absence of, at least, some local trade support.

25. **Roads and Communications.**—In these days of motor transport one of the most important problems in any country is the provision of good roads and communications. The expansion of the road system and the means of communication is obviously a much harder problem to tackle in a mountainous country like the Jammu and Kashmir State than it is in the plains; a hundred miles of good road may be built in the plains at a cost insufficient to cover a tenth of the distance in mountainous country. The fact must be stated that many districts in the State suffer serious disabilities owing to the absence of roads—not good roads but roads of any kind better than a rough pony track. It would not be fair to blame the administration for the existing defects in the road system. There is no railway in the State except a small branch line from Sialkot which crosses the State boundary at Suchetgarh and runs as far as Jammu City. The extension of the railway further into His Highness' territories would be a major engineering project. It is not a question His Highness' Government can alone decide; it requires the collaboration of government and railway authorities in British India. No scheme worth the name can be carried out in connection with the exploitation of the mineral deposits known to exist in the Jammu Province without an extension of the railway to the heart of the area. The State possesses two excellent motor roads, running through mountainous country, connecting Srinagar with the rest of India *via* Rawalpindi and Abbottabad to the east and Jammu and Sialkot to the south. These two roads known respectively as the Jhelum Valley Road and the Banihal Road join at Srinagar to make one continuous road which is the main artery of communications throughout the Jammu and Kashmir Provinces. The whole import and export trade of the State with India and beyond, as well as such trade as there may be between India and beyond with the Frontier Districts and Central Asia, passes through Jammu or Srinagar over one or the other of these two roads. Since this question of roads and communications is of such great importance to the whole economy of the country it will be worthwhile to see what has happened in the past decade and to discuss the possible developments in the near future. It may be said at once that the main artery Sialkot-Jammu-Srinagar-Rawalpindi-Abbottabad has not only been maintained but vastly improved. Many dangerous corners have been reduced and many miles of road surfaced with tar or bitumen preparations. Other roads existing in 1930 have been maintained in a fair state of repair. But it is with new roads we are chiefly concerned, roads to open up the large

areas previously denied the facilities and advantages of motor transport. Taking the Jammu Province first we find that a fair-weather road has been constructed from Mirpur through Kotli to Rambari giving direct communication by motor in fair weather between the Mirpur District and the Poonch Jagir. The length of this road is 79 miles. It was previously unfit for motor traffic at all. Three new roads in the Mirpur and Jammu Districts are designed to connect Dharamsal Jhangar with Nowshera, Nowshera with Sadhoti and the latter place with Akhnur. This scheme had been completed at the end of the decade with the exception of a bridge over the Nowshera Tawi river at Beri Pattan to link up the Akhnur-Sadhoti and Sadhoti-Nowshera roads. With the completion of this bridge, through wheeled traffic will become possible between Jammu City and Poonch *via* Dharamsal-Jhangar. Another road has been constructed between Udhampur and Ramnagar but this still lacked a bridge over the Jammu Tawi at the end of the decade and traffic had to be ferried across; the construction of a bridge is under consideration. A fair weather motor road from Batote on the main Banihal Road to Bhadrawah was commenced in 1935. It will be 55 miles long and was estimated to cost over Rs. 7 lacs. Unexpected difficulties and set-backs were experienced and the road was not completed in 1940. When ready this road will open up a large area and should give a distinct impetus to trade between the Bhadrawah and Kishtwar Tehsils and the Udhampur and Jammu Districts. The road connecting the Reasi and Jammu Districts has been metalled from the take-off on the Banihal Road as far as Katra and greatly improved but beyond Katra it is a very poor fair-weather road and is scarcely motorable at any time except after a good spell of fine weather. The Jammu-Kathua road has been metalled as far as Samba; beyond that town it is only fit for use in fair weather. It is cut at right angles by the Ujh river and other smaller streams and is impassable in the rains. His Highness the Maharaja Bahadur has recently ordered the Ujh to be bridged. This is a most important road connecting the Kathua and Jammu Districts. In the past a traveller from Jammu to Kathua had to go by train to Pathankote and then back to Kathua by tonga or foot. The same difficulty exists at present in the rains. An all-weather motor road from Jammu to Kathua will be a tremendous gain to the whole area served by the road. A number of bridle paths have been widened and improved and the road construction programme in the Jammu Province may be said to have shown steady progress during the decade though an alarming amount of work has to be done before all districts will get an all-weather motor service to the chief centres. In the Kashmir Province also a number of roads have been improved; some fair weather roads have been metalled and become all-weather motor roads whilst others have advanced from being unmotorable to the fair-weather class. The more important may be mentioned. The road from Srinagar to Charar-i-Sharif has been converted into an all-weather road up to Nagam and a fair weather road up to the Muslim shrine at Charar-i-Sharif. The Anantnag-Pahalgam road leading to Sri Amar Nath Ji has been widened and the surface improved. It is now a good road in all weathers unless damaged by heavy rain. The Pampur-Shopian road has been metalled as far as Pulwama and this section is now a good all-weather motor road; the metalling is to be continued. The Shalamar-Naseem-Gandarbal road and the Gandarbal-Safapur road have been widened and converted into good fair weather motor roads. Other roads throughout the province have been improved and it may be said that the importance of good roads and communications has at last been recognised. Several projects are under execution or receiving consideration and if the present policy is continued great improvements will have been effected before the next Census arrives. The roads to the Frontier Districts must remain pack-transport roads for the most part but the Treaty Road to Leh has received attention and is now motorable as far as Gagangir in fair weather. In a year or so it is hoped to make the road motorable as far as Sonamarg. This should convert Sonamarg into a centre not only for tourists but for the Central Asian trade, if the latter is ever revived. Another important work which has been commenced is the construction of a motor road over the Haji Pir Pass linking up the Poonch Jagir with the Kashmir Province.

26. **Irrigation.**—Next to roads, irrigation is a matter of prime importance if the means of feeding a rapidly increasing population are to be maintained. In the absence of a railway with fixed rates for freight an assured food supply for the Kashmir Province is a vital matter. Motor transport cannot be relied upon because in times of short supply it usually happens that freight rates for motor lorries begin to soar and the expense of importing supplies to give relief becomes almost prohibitive. Ample water for irrigation is available almost everywhere in the Kashmir Province but in many areas use cannot be made of it owing to the difference in levels. During the decade 1931-40 the Zainagir Canal was completed, the Lal Khul and Martand Canals were extended and

two new canals, known as the Nandi and Dadi Canals respectively, were constructed. In 1940 the Martand Canal irrigated 7,578 acres against 6,454 in 1930; it also supplies good drinking water to the area it irrigates. The area irrigated by the Lal Khul increased from 3,879 acres in 1930 to 4,621 in 1940. The Zainagir Canal was commenced in 1923 and completed in 1931. It cost just over Rs. 10 lacs and irrigated 7,538 acres in 1940. The Nandi Canal irrigates land between the Jhelum and its tributary the Vishav. Actually it is an extension and reconstruction of a canal built by the local cultivators the take-off of which was defective and the distribution inadequate and irregular. It was commenced in 1936 and completed at a cost of Rs. 77,640. It irrigated 4,388 acres in 1940 against 700 previously. The Dadi Canal replaces a small water channel constructed by cultivators; it takes off from the Liddar River. The revised estimates for reconstruction and extension amount to Rs. 425,000. Work was commenced in 1937 and nearly completed at the end of the decade. In 1940 it irrigated 1,620 acres. Canal construction has received reasonable attention in the past decade but there are still many areas in which crops could be increased considerably with better facilities for irrigation. It is necessary that the ample water available be used to the greatest extent possible and the existing canal systems improved and extended in all directions. This is the only certain means of increasing food production; the nature of the country is such that the bugbear of most canalised areas—waterlogging—need not be given any thought. The low lying marshy areas have always been more or less waterlogged; most of the rest of the land is on a slope and surplus water drains off quickly.

The need for good canals is greater in the Jammu Province than in Kashmir. The Ranbir Canal was started in 1903 on an estimate of Rs. 17 lacs and was opened in 1905. In 1940 its length, including distributaries, was 236 miles and it irrigated 122,032 acres against 70,738 in 1930. During the decade just over Rs. 1 lac was spent on improvements. It takes off from the left bank of the Chenab near Akhnur.

The Pratap Canal takes off from the right bank of the Chenab about six miles below Akhnur. It is an old canal first constructed in 1873; it was breached and fell into disuse until 1901 when it was remodelled and extended. In 1940 it irrigated 2,798 acres against 1,986 in 1930. The canal also supplies drinking water to the inhabitants of the Kandi tract through which it passes. The Basantpur Canal takes off from the right bank of the Ravi about three miles above the Madhopur Head works. It was opened in 1918 and was expected to irrigate 7,427 acres. These hopes have not been realised; it irrigated 2,206 acres in 1930 and 2,245 in 1940.

The Ujh Canal was originally designed to mitigate the hardships of the people living in a tract of about 2,000 acres in the Jasmergarh Tehsil which was entirely dependent on rainfall both for irrigation and domestic use. It was first constructed in 1923; extensions were started in 1924 and completed in 1933. In 1940 it irrigated 3,268 acres against 2,167 in 1930. It supplies drinking water to the area as well as irrigating it. The Upper Jhelum Canal which irrigates large areas in the Punjab is of little use to land in the State but distributaries from it irrigate the small State areas through which it passes. The area irrigated in 1940 was 1,149 acres against 856 in 1930. The difficulties in the way of irrigation engineers in the Jammu Province are great on account of the broken character of the country. But in view of the fact that the supply of adequate drinking water is an acute problem in many areas, additional efforts should be made to extend the existing canal systems and to open new canals, even if only small ones, wherever it is possible to do so. Several projects for new canals are known to have been under consideration at the end of the decade for both provinces; the sooner construction is started the better. More food grains are wanted in Kashmir and more drinking water in Jammu.

The Frontier Districts are so mountainous that irrigation is very difficult except in the case of small khuls or water channels taken along the contour of the hillside. But in most areas rainfall is very small and cultivation depends 100 per cent. on irrigation. The construction of canals at Kharthong and Saliskote in the Kargil Tehsil is under consideration. They are estimated to irrigate 2,900 and 1,600 acres respectively and would add considerably to the present very limited means of subsistence. A new canal to irrigate land in the vicinity of Leh is believed to be a practical scheme. It is reported that the Doyan Kuhl (canal) in the Astore District was being improved at the end of the decade. Since 1931 the total mileage of canals including distributaries has increased from 393 to 488 and the area irrigated from 89,372 acres to 156,495. The increase in the area irrigated is greater in proportion than the increase in the mileage of the canals; this must be attributed to improved distribution. The canals discussed are those only which have been constructed by the Government. There are hundreds of small canals and distributaries which have been constructed by the villagers themselves wherever local conditions make it possible for them to use the water of the many rivers and small streams: these they repair each year and, if possible, extend.

27. **Public Health.**—It is only necessary to refer to vital statistics and public health conditions briefly. Colonel Sir Ram Nath Chopra, I. M. S., (retired) has kindly written a note and supplied figures to show the general conditions obtaining during the past decade which appears as an appendix at the end of this essay. He has expressed the opinion that the vital statistics are not as unreliable as might be thought. It is unfortunately a fact that the procedure for the notification and recording of births and deaths is defective. The position in the Jammu and Kashmir State is not exceptional; the difficulties and defects obtain throughout India except in well-organised cities and municipalities. The present procedure requires overhauling if the figures recorded are to be deemed reliable for statistical purposes. With the expansion and development of village Panchayats and revision of existing methods it might be possible to obtain a more accurate record; at least in those areas where a panchayat is functioning. As it is we must not place too much reliance on the figures given.

28. **Industries.**—Agriculture is by far the most important industry in the State. Usually the word 'Industries' implies non-agricultural occupations and it is used in that sense here. If good roads, communications and water supplies are prerequisites for successful agriculture, they are essential for the success of industrial enterprises. Imperial Table VIII was designed to show the distribution of the population by occupations and Table IX the distribution of the population in the various categories of industrial workers from managers down to operatives. But, as the notes to these two tables indicate, the defects of enumeration, sorting and compilation together produced such poor results that these tables are worthless for statistical purposes. Excluding Agriculture, our most important industries are forest exploitation, sericulture, weaving of textiles of all kinds, wood-working trades, flour-milling, oil-milling, bee-keeping, working in non-precious metals, rope-making, basket-ware, dairy-farming, tanning, the manufacture of hosiery, papier-mache, perfumes, silverware, carpets, gubbas, soap, rush-mats and chicks, matches, pharmaceutical preparations, ceramics, embroidery, printing, tailoring, building and the exploitation of mineral deposits. Of the minor products taken from the forests and hillsides perhaps kuth, artemisia and resin are the most important at present. The first named is an insecticide; it is also used largely in the preparation of incense, particularly in China; for some years past the market price for this product has been depressed owing to the Sino-Japanese 'Incident'. Artemisia is a species of wormwood from which santonin is extracted whilst resin is tapped from the chir pine and converted into turpentine and certain by-products. To the industries mentioned must be added the manufacture of Indianite, a building material made by a special process from wood. Most of our industries are located in and around the two cities of Jammu and Srinagar and the two towns Anantnag and Baramulla.

The large numbers of visitors to the State each year, a few under 30,000 in 1941, most of whom come to the Kashmir Province, constitute what may be termed the Tourist Trade which provides the means of subsistence for many thousands of the population. These tourists support many of the smaller industries, particularly those which may be called luxury trades, such as wood-carving and cabinet-making, papier-mache, silverware, embroidery, carpets, gubbas, catering, repairs to motors and the provision of accommodation in houseboats, hotels and camps. A Drug Research Laboratory has been opened recently in Jammu and in the course of time the manufacture of drugs from herbs and plants now growing wild in the forests or to be cultivated should become an important local industry.

Some of the cottage industries are being subjected to special investigations by staff working under the control of the Industries Department; these include handloom-weaving, furniture-making, wood-turning, bee-keeping, rope-making, basket-making, poultry-farming, dairy-farming, tanning, flour-milling, oil-milling, and calico-printing. Reports on gubba-making, carpet-making, silverware and wood carving have already been published. There are few large industrial establishments; there are no large mills such as the jute mills of Bengal and the cotton mills of Bombay.

29. **Industrial Organisation.**—Of all the industries referred to only forest exploitation, sericulture, the manufacture of matches, the extraction of santonin, the manufacture of

Indianite and one or two of the carpet factories are independently financed. There may be, and probably are, others but they are few and do not come readily to mind. Of those mentioned forest industries, and sericulture are owned, controlled and financed by the State; the match and santonin industries are privately financed and controlled. The carpet factories, the larger of which are privately owned and financed, obtain subsidies from the State during years of trade depression. The great bulk of the small industries, not all, but especially the luxury trades, are worked on a system somewhat similar to that prevailing in England before the Industrial Revolution, say 150 years ago. The artizans work together in groups under a master craftsman who usually gets his supply of raw materials from a dealer; the latter finances the work, determines the quality of workmanship required, and decides the design of the goods to be made in consultation with the master craftsman. The dealer-financier controls the sale of the finished article and usually has his own selling agency. He is to these small industries what the money-lender is in the rural economy of India. He makes provision for a good return on his capital for any advances he may make to the workers. Some of the small privately owned industrial concerns are financed by the local banks but these must be a small percentage of the total number. In the absence of better organisation and credit facilities the part played by the dealer-financier is essential to most of the small scale industries. Co-operative sale and purchase are not yet developed and it is impossible to dispense with him. It is feared there is a good deal of sweated labour employed in most of the smaller industries.

30. **Forests.**—Next to Agriculture the exploitation of the extensive and valuable forests of the State constitutes the largest industry. The extraction of timber, collection of minor forest products and other activities play a very important part in the life of the rural population; they not only give employment directly or indirectly to many thousands of the inhabitants but are a source of supply, free or at concession rates, of timber for building or repairing houses, fuel, fodder and minor edible forest products. All the forests have been brought under regular working plans and during the decade 1931-40 most of these plans were revised and brought up-to-date. On an average 212 lacs cubic feet of timber and 225 lacs cubic feet of fuel are removed from the forests annually; the actual amount in any year naturally varies according to trade demand and market conditions. In recent years exploitation of the forests has been developed for the greater benefit of the local inhabitants. Formerly, most of the forests were worked under long leases by a few big firms with head offices outside the State. They were powerful enough to enforce their own wage rates for labour and reaped most of the profits. This system has been gradually replaced by short term lump sum leases for comparatively small compartments or groups of compartments. These smaller leases have encouraged local enterprise; many local firms have come into existence and are working successfully. As a result of the existence of a number of small firms labour rates are on a more competitive basis.

The Resin-Tapping industry in the Udhampur District has been reorganised and developed. During the past decade the amount of resin extracted annually averaged 38,000 maunds. Tapping was commenced in the Kathua and Mirpur Districts in 1938; the average annual crop from these two forest divisions is 22,000 maunds. This industry is essentially a subsidiary occupation for the local rural population and the increased means of subsistence in the form of wages is of considerable importance to them.

In the past fir has been worked to a limited degree only. With the advances made in the industrialisation of India this timber has come more and more into prominence. Consequently, in anticipation of the increased demand a new Fir Working Plan Division was started to bring these forests under regular working plans.

Previously, half-wroughts for service rifle butts were manufactured entirely from walnut. In recent years various broad-leaved species such as birdcherry and maple have been used. The factory is located at Baramulla in the Kashmir Province. The following industries in active operation during the past decade depend on the forests of the State for their raw materials:—

(i) The Rosin and Turpentine factory at Miran Sahib on the Jammu-Sialkot branch line of the North Western Railway.

(ii) The Indianite factory at Miran Sahib.

(iii) The Kashmir Willows Factory at Miran Sahib for the manufacture of sports goods with a branch at Srinagar.

(iv) The Half-wrought factory at Baramulla.

(v) The Santonin factory at Baramulla.

(vi) The Match factory at Baramulla.

The possibilities of further development of forest resources are believed to be good. Timber such as fir and broad-leaved species previously in little use are coming into prominence. The prices of some minor forest products were rising at the end of the decade and owing to the war the demand may be expected to expand. Increased demand must result in greater activity and the employment of more labour. Projects under contemplation which should provide employment for considerable numbers, both educated and uneducated, are:—

(i) A factory for the manufacture of drugs based on the results of the work of the Drug Research Laboratory opened at Jammu in 1941.

(ii) The cultivation of Pyrethrum has passed the experimental stage in the Kashmir Province and is now being grown on a field scale. A considerable industry should develop for the exploitation of this plant and provide new employment on a large scale.

(iii) Negotiations have been commenced with big Indian industrialists with a view to starting the manufacture of newsprint. Such a factory will involve a larger capital than can be provided from State resources if the development of beneficent activities is to continue.

The trout streams continue to attract a large number of visitors to the State and their development and maintenance is receiving continuous attention. It is estimated that over 20,000 persons depend directly or indirectly on incomes derived from this source and from other fisheries. The tourist traffic has increased considerably during the past decade. Many camping centres are in or on the borders of demarcated forest areas. The construction of roads, camping grounds and tourists' huts is continuous.

It is estimated that at the end of the decade some 50,000 persons were directly employed in connection with forest exploitation; to these must be added the numbers indirectly affected. The Kashmir Muslim element of the population provides the bulk of the labour working in the forests; they are hard working and have benefited considerably from the expansion and development which have taken place. The Gujjars for the most part continue to follow their hereditary occupation of cattle breeding. The Hindu elements of the population do not readily take to manual labour. It is, of course, their loss; efforts are being made by the Forest Department to induce this important section of the population to look upon manual labour in the forests with less aversion. The chief areas affected by a disinclination of the local people to work in the forests for various reasons are the Muzaffarabad and Pir Panjal Divisions in the Kashmir Circle and the Batote, Lander, Udhampur and Ramnagar Ranges in the Jammu Circle. It should perhaps be stressed that, apart from the large permanent establishment employed by the Forest Department in many administrative and executive capacities, for the great majority working in the forests is a subsidiary means of livelihood. Some few skilled workers, such as fellers and sawyers, move from one district to another according to the seasons but the majority of the labour is recruited from the villages in the vicinity of the work in progress; these men return to their principal means of livelihood—agriculture—at the more important seasons of ploughing, sowing and harvesting.

31. **Sericulture.**—The next important industry is sericulture; the chief stages are rearing the silk-worm, collecting and delivering the cocoons, reeling off the silk from the cocoons and weaving the silk yarn; we must not forget the provision of food for the silk-worm—the leaf of the mulberry tree. As already stated the silk industry is controlled and financed by the State. It provides permanent employment for hundreds and subsidiary occupation for many thousands of agriculturists throughout the State. There are two factories for receiving the cocoons and putting them through the various processes, one at Srinagar and the other at Jammu. The former is easily the larger; in addition to a permanent establishment of nearly 400 persons the average number of daily workers employed in the year 1940 was 2,231. The average for 1931 was 1,707 and it remained just above that figure until 1938 when it jumped to 1,995; the figure for 1939 was 2,040. These daily silk-factory workers may be considered permanently employed; the majority live in Srinagar. The number of rearers of silk-worms employed by the Srinagar factory in 1940 was 51,000; these are all agriculturists and they are spread through-

all tehsils of the Kashmir Province; the average earnings per rearer's household in 1940 was Rs. 8. This is a purely subsidiary means of livelihood and from the figures it will be seen that these rearers between them receive over Rs. 4 lacs in wages annually. To ensure an adequate food supply for the silk-worms the mulberry is a protected tree; its destruction is prohibited except under proper authority. The maintenance of mulberry tree nurseries and continual transplanting and development of new areas is essential for expansion and to replace old and damaged trees. In the year 1921 the number of plants raised and transplanted was just over 20,000, in 1930 just over 41,000, in 1935 70,000 and in 1940 well over 84,000. It will thus be seen that food supplies have been continuously and considerably expanded to meet an ever increasing demand.

The Jammu factory employed on an average 244 daily workers in the year 1940. The number of rearers employed was just over 7,000 at the beginning of the decade 1931-40 and just over 10,000 in the year 1940; these figures indicate steady progress. The annual amount earned per rearer's household worked out at about Rs. 12 representing a total cash distribution in wages for the year of Rs. 120,000, making a total of Rs. 520,000 for both provinces.

A government silk weaving factory has been established at Srinagar recently with up-to-date machinery capable of handling 30,000 lbs. of raw silk annually. At present this factory gives employment to about 100 persons daily. Action has been taken to provide for the continued expansion and development of the silk industry at all stages of production and in the decade 1941-50 the means of subsistence provided by it should be increased.

32. **Tourism.**—Kashmir has been famous for its salubrious climate, beautiful valleys and magnificent scenery not for generations but for centuries. A hundred years ago a few undertook an arduous journey to visit the country; the numbers gradually increased until in the decade 1890-1900, with the completion of the Jhelum Valley Road, they became considerable. The visitor then usually came by tonga; some rode and a few walked. It was not until the motor car reached Northern India that the influx assumed important proportions. Where visitors to the country were previously to be numbered in tens they began to come in hundreds; they are now to be counted in thousands. The tremendous development that has occurred is due entirely to the provision of good motor roads and the reduced costs of travelling. The number of visitors in 1941 as already remarked, was nearly 30,000. The amount of wealth these thousands bring to the country cannot be assessed with any accuracy without the collection of a mass of detailed information but it has been calculated roughly as in the region of Rs. 80 lacs. The money put into circulation by the visitor is now of enormous importance to the economy of the whole country. Many small industries are supported by the visitor and thousands of local inhabitants are entirely dependent for a livelihood and the means of subsistence on a good visitors' season. During the decade 1931-40 the annual number of visitors recorded at the customs barriers into the State has risen from 8,404 in 1931 to 29,292 in 1940. During the same period customs receipts have risen from Rs. 69 lacs to Rs. 78 lacs. It is not suggested that there is any exact relation between the number of visitors in any year and Customs receipts but the former indubitably has a bearing on the latter, both direct and indirect. As long as good roads and cheap transport are available the traffic may be expected to develop further provided the present policy of improving and expanding internal communications continues. It is essential to make more beauty spots and camping sites accessible at a reasonable cost as those more easily reached become overcrowded. His Highness' Government are alive to the value of the Tourist industry and thanks to the facilities provided it is possible for the visitor to enjoy a healthy holiday in beautiful surroundings at a cost proportionate to his mode of life. Every extra visitor means an increase in the means of subsistence. Any heavy falling off in numbers, whatever the reasons, must re-act adversely on the population of the State as a whole and of the Kashmir Province in particular. The complete failure of the tourist traffic for any reason in any year would mean ruin to many small industries, shopkeepers and house boat owners and semi-starvation to many thousands who are dependent on the visitor.

33. **Customs and Trade.**—The progress made in the development of industries, commerce and trade of any country is reflected in the fluctuations of the figures contained in the Customs reports. Fluctuations from month to month or even from year to year may be deceptive but if we examine the figures from one decade to another we can ignore minor and short term fluctuations. By its treaties the Jammu and Kashmir State is entitled to levy import and export duties and to receive goods from foreign countries through British Indian customs posts in Kashmir bond. There is an exception. Goods passing

along the Treaty Road between India and Central Asia *via* Srinagar and Leh in both directions are exempt from State customs duty if the seals are not broken in transit or the goods taken beyond the defined limits of the Treaty Road into the State customs area. During the last two decades the trade of the State has increased considerably in volume but to a less degree in value. For the year 1977 corresponding to 1920-21, the volume of trade, import and export, amounted to 42½ lacs maunds with a value of Rs. 520 lacs. The figures for volume in 1996-97, corresponding to 1939-40, were 57¼ lacs maunds and for value Rs. 575½ lacs. The figures for value do not always vary in direct proportion to the figures for volume. Prices for the same commodity vary considerably from month to month and year to year; in some years the figures for heavy but cheap goods such as grain increase. The decade 1931-40 started with the whole world in the throes of a trade depression unprecedented in its character and intensity. The value of trade in the State as reflected in the Customs returns in round figures fell from Rs. 520 lacs in 1920-21 to Rs. 455 lacs in 1930-31 and still further to Rs. 367 lacs in 1931-32. From the latter year onwards the recovery was slow and it was not until the year 1936-37 that a definite improvement was noticeable. For the next two years there was a small increase but with the outbreak of war the price of food grains in Kashmir rose swiftly and the export of grain was stopped. This had more effect on volume than on value but in other ways too trade has been upset and diverted from normal channels; imports and exports of some commodities have almost ceased whilst in the case of others there has been a large increase. It is too early to discuss in detail the effects of the war on the State. In some respects the country has benefited; in others it has suffered. The volume of import trade in 1920-21, 1930-31 and 1939-40 in round figures was 16½ lacs, 24½ lacs and 26¼ lacs maunds respectively and in round figures the value for the same years was Rs. 273 lacs, Rs. 257 lacs and Rs. 288 lacs respectively. The volume and value of the export trade for the same years in round figures was:—

Volume—26 lacs, 37 lacs and 31 lacs maunds.

Value—Rs. 178 lacs, Rs. 133 lacs and Rs. 207 lacs.

These figures show how widely the relation between volume and value varies. This is not the occasion for a detailed examination of import and export trade figures but some reference seemed necessary because, taken as a whole, they have some bearing on the question whether the increase in the means of subsistence is as great as the increase in the population and likely to continue to be so. Those in the State whose duty it is to study the trend of trade are of the opinion that during the past decade trade in general showed improvement up to the eve of the war. It would serve no useful purpose to attempt to prophesy the trend of trade for the rest of the present decade. Timber and silk are in heavy demand for war purposes and export of these two commodities should continue at a high figure for the duration of the war and for some time afterwards at good prices. In view of the geographical position of Kashmir there should be little, if any, falling off in the tourist traffic. It may be that purchasing power, especially for luxury goods, will be less owing to higher taxation but it is reasonable to assume that the State's main industries will continue to support those dependent on them. What the post-war position will be it would be folly to predict.

34. **Central Asian Trade.**—At the end of the decade 1911-20 the trade between India and Central Asia was flourishing. For the year 1919-20 the trade to Central Asia was valued at over Rs. 48 lacs and from Central Asia at nearly Rs. 42 lacs, giving a total value of Rs. 8,985,510. Next year, 1920-21, the figures rose to over Rs. 47 lacs for exports and nearly Rs. 46 lacs for imports giving a total of over Rs. 93 lacs. This was the peak year of the trade. From that time onwards, that is to say for the last twenty years, the trade has been dwindling steadily in both directions. In some years there was a recovery in trade but such bursts were always short-lived. For the year 1939-40 the figures for exports to Central Asia were Rs. 151,024 and for imports Rs. 230,198, giving a total of Rs. 381,222. Trade between Central Asia and the State has suffered a similar decline. Imports to Kashmir from Central Asia in 1920-21 were valued at Rs. 425,410. The trade declined until 1927-28 when there was a recovery to Rs. 414,910; the figures for 1928-29 were Rs. 442,156—the highest since 1913-14. Political refugees were probably responsible for this short lived revival. From 1928-29 onwards the value of the trade steadily declined; in 1939-40 it was worth only Rs. 78,246—mostly namdas. Since then it has dwindled to practically nothing. Whether the trade will be revived or not remains to be seen. Its decay may be attributed to the lack of stable government and to the hostile attitude to the trade on the part of certain elements in the Sin-Kiang Province and other areas of Central Asia from and to which the trade used

to flow through Yarkand and Leh. The present world war has brought Russia, China and the British Empire into close friendship as a result of mutual interests. It is not, perhaps, too much to hope that at the end of the war the governments of these three empires will be able to take such measures as will not only revive but stimulate the trade on this route. The chief articles imported from Central Asia were cotton manufactures; horses, hides, skins, furs, silks, woollens, namdas (pieces of felt), carpets, gold and charas—an intoxicating preparation made from a species of hemp. The chief articles of export from India were cotton manufactures, hides and skins, silks, tea, leather, paints and colours, drugs, medicines and spices. The imports to Kashmir consisted almost entirely of namdas. The cessation of this trade must have had a very serious effect on the ability of all those living on or near the trade route to earn a livelihood especially the people of the Ladakh and Kargil Tehsils. The market at Leh, through which all the trade used to pass, is now but a pitiful reminder of happier and more prosperous times.

35. **Unemployment.**—The extent of unemployment as recorded at the Census is shown in Imperial Table X but as the notes to the table indicate, the figures given are believed not to tell the whole story. Many educated persons, particularly members of joint families, are believed not to have declared themselves to be unemployed although not occupying a paid post. Most of the uneducated masses don't know what is meant by the term; they have never enjoyed continuous employment from one year to another and to be out of employment temporarily does not in their estimation constitute what is usually understood by unemployment. The figures produced by the Census record are 5,640 for all classes and 3,837 for those educated. It would probably be more in accordance with the facts of the case if we put educated unemployment at 5,000 and the figures for all classes at 10,000. Many youths continue to study at schools and colleges not with any definite aim or to acquire a higher standard of education and learning but because they cannot get a post in government service. It is better that they should do so than sit at home or walk about the streets with nothing to do. On the other hand, this factor results in the over-crowding of college classes at a time in a student's life when small classes and more individual attention are essential to those prosecuting their studies beyond the matriculation standard. Many men of the artizan classes and those working as domestic servants in one capacity or another are not employed for the whole year and it is thought that such persons do not consider themselves as unemployed. Thousands of casual labourers are not fully employed; few of them have regular work throughout the year. The whole problem of Unemployment received the close and continuous attention of His Highness' Government throughout the past decade. In 1936 a Commission was appointed to inquire into the causes of unemployment amongst the educated classes in particular and amongst all classes in general and to make suggestions for a solution of the problem. The Commission's Report was published in 1937. The history of the problem, here and elsewhere in India, was studied, a mass of information collected, evidence taken and the possibilities of effecting improvements thoroughly surveyed. The Commission pointed out that there were no statistics of any kind available to show how much unemployment there was amongst the masses but expressed the opinion that, if the term 'Unemployment' was applicable to a condition of 'Under-employment', there was unemployment to a considerable degree. Some of those answering the Commission's questionnaire were of opinion that there was practically no unemployment amongst the so-called 'Depressed Classes' designated in the Census Report 'Scheduled Castes'. The Commission hesitated to accept this sweeping statement and pointed out that the classes referred to would not always remain uneducated nor continue to follow their hereditary occupations only and that the extent of unemployment in those occuaptions in which they succeeded in getting a place would be aggravated according to the extent of their success. The Commission recognised the existence of a good deal of 'Under-employment' amongst artizans and craft workers, more especially amongst those normally employed in what are usually known as luxury trades, and stated that this condition was more apparent in Kashmir than in the Jammu Province. Unskilled labour and agriculturists were held to be under-employed rather than unemployed. The causes of unemployment were deemed to be trade depression during the first half of the decade 1931-40, faults in the educational system, mechanisation and mass production of goods in other countries reacting on small scale industries in the State, aversion of some classes to manual labour, steady increase in population, lack of industrial development, inadequacy of financial facilities, failure of social customs to adjust themselves to rapidly changing conditions and pressure on the land resulting from fragmentation of holdings.

Having discussed in detail the different spheres of work and activity throughout the State the Commission formulated its suggestions and since these have a direct bearing on the problem today they may be recounted briefly. Under the head 'Services' they advocated, amongst others, the steady expansion of free primary education, strengthening the staff of the Industries, Agriculture, Veterinary and Co-operative Societies Departments and the provision of extra staff in the Forest Department to facilitate the splitting up of large forest contracts into smaller ones. Under the head 'Professions' the Commission recommended the registration of medical practitioners, the subsidising of qualified medical men, vaids and unani hakims working in rural areas, and enforcing the employment of qualified engineers, overseers and sub-overseers as employees or partners in certain classes of contracts under the Public Works Department. Under Agriculture the extension of cultivation in demarcated forest areas was advised where this was possible without harmful results, the setting up of Co-operative Sale Societies, the development of Co-operative Marketing, the extended planting of mulberry trees and the expansion of sericulture, the improvement of cattle breeding, the expansion and better organisation of the fruit-growing industry, the accelerated development of good roads and irrigation schemes, the improvement of communications between villages and the consolidation of holdings. Constructive suggestions were also made with regard to the provision of increased facilities for tourists and the development of industries. In recording its view with regard to the requirements of Education, the Commission recognised the technical nature of the question and advocated the appointment of a committee of educationists to consider its proposals and to report what modifications and changes were necessary. In conclusion the opinion was expressed that there was no facile remedy for educated unemployment and no panacea for all the ills from which the existing educational system suffered nor for the difficulties under which industrial development was struggling. Remedial measures, it was added, involved hard work, courage and expenditure.

There seems to be no reason to find fault with the causes of unemployment listed in the report of the Unemployment Commission. Except the trade depression, which caused such distress in the first half of the decade, all of them are operating today with more or less force but anyone with local knowledge must know that since the report was submitted His Highness' Government have made great efforts to implement the Commission's more important recommendations. Primary education has been expanded. An Educational Re-organisation Committee was appointed in June 1938 and submitted its report and recommendations in March 1939. The staffs of the Industries, Agriculture, Veterinary, Co-operative and Forest Departments have all been strengthened and action taken in many directions to which the Commission called attention. Qualified medical practitioners have been registered and medical men, vaids and unani hakims practising in rural areas subsidised; the whole Medical Department has been re-organised recently and provision made to meet the more urgent requirements of rural areas. The Sericulture Department has been expanded, road construction work accelerated, communications greatly improved, increased facilities provided for tourists and the development of industries given special attention. New industries have been started with capital provided by the State and increased credit and financial facilities provided for private enterprise. The strenuous efforts made during the comparatively short life of the present administration to reduce unemployment and to stimulate trade and industry in every way must be recognised but Unemployment remains a serious problem. With the numbers of educated young men leaving the schools and colleges increasing every year there is no sign of reduction in the numbers of educated unemployed in spite of all the efforts of His Highness' Government in this behalf. No improvement is likely unless and until educated young men turn to trade and industry for occupation rather than continue to seek to obtain some post in government service. The dictum of the Unemployment Commission that there is no facile remedy for educated unemployment and that remedial measures involve hard work, courage and expenditure stands. Since 1937 His Highness' Government have worked hard, shown courage and incurred heavy expenditure. The problem remains unsolved but much has been done to lay the foundations for improvement in the future and it is but fair to say that real industrial development in the State is nearer now than it has even been before. Much depends on post-war conditions throughout the world. India is but a wheel in the world trade machine and the Jammu and Kashmir State but a cog in that wheel.

36. **Possibilities of Development.** – In spite of the somewhat gloomy view taken of the unemployment problem there are grounds for hoping that the work done since 1937 will soon commence to show results. Good roads are under construction in many districts and irrigation schemes are receiving consideration. Apart from the money put into circulation in the form of wages, agriculture and trade must benefit from

the improved facilities for transport and distribution of commodities. To give one instance, the new road from Batote to Bhadrawah should open up the whole of that country and stimulate the fruit growing industry there. An extension from Doda on the road mentioned to Kishtwar will open up a large land-locked area, facilitate the relief of food shortage in years of poor harvests and encourage the increased growing of fruit and walnut trees.

Improvements in the road connections between Mirpur District and the Punjab are urgently required. Easy access to Mangla on the Jhelum would hasten realisation of the project to erect a paper-mill there. There is no motor bridge over the Jhelum river between Kohala and Jhelum, a distance of over eighty miles; such a bridge and connecting motor roads are urgently required to improve communications and facilitate trade.

At the end of the last decade a survey was completed for the extension of a broad guage railway line from Jammu (Tawi) to Akhnur on the Chenab River. Construction in the near future is probably out of the question but with the end of the world war and a fall in the price of materials to normal levels the project should be taken up. But to exploit the possibilities to the utmost the line should go beyond Akhnur and be extended further up the Chenab Valley. The Reasi District is rich in minerals and the working of these deposits depends on rail-head facilities. The position is that the extension of the railway from Jammu to Reasi, or even to Akhnur, will not be justified unless some definite and practical scheme is evolved to work the mineral deposits of Reasi on a large scale ; these cannot be profitably exploited without the facilities provided by rail connection. It seems obvious that the two schemes should be worked out together for the benefit not only of the State and its people but for the railway system in Northern India too. If coal and iron can be worked successfully, and large deposits of both are said to be accessible for comparatively easy working, the advantage to all concerned, and not least to the railways, of an asssured supply of coal does not need to be emphasised.

The State possesses immense possibilities for the development of hydro-electric power schemes. No new schemes have been undertaken in recent years but a large and important Indian engineering company has recently studied the existing undertakings in Jammu and Kashmir and made suggestions regarding improvements and new schemes. The war and the present high prices for all materials preclude the commencement of such enterprises now but as soon as better conditions prevail the development of comprehensive schemes should come under consideration. The possibilities include increased supply of power to Srinagar, provision of electric power to run the proposed paper-mill at Mangla, increase the supply to Jammu and meet the increasing requirements at Miran Sahib and Ranbirsinghpura. In order to take full advantage of the period which must intervene before any large scale project can be taken up, it is understood it is intended to survey thoroughly the transmission lines to Mangla and Jammu and to estimate accurately the material required so that when the opportunity presents itself prompt action can be taken to place definite orders. Meanwhile, it is proposed to instal a small thermal plant at Miran Sahib for industrial requirements there and to give an additional supply to Jammu and for the proposed sugar mill at Ranbirsinghpura. Communications, water and adequate power are the essentials for the development of our industries. Assuming these prerequisites the possibilities may be summarised:—

(i) The expansion of fruit and vegetable growing and the development of a drying, preserving and canning industry.

(ii) The installation of mills for the production of paper pulp and newsprint.

(iii) An up-to-date Research Laboratory has been opened at Jammu to carry out a survey of all the drug producing plants in the State. When preliminary investigations have been completed and the strength of the drugs that can be produced has been standardised, the way will be clear for the manufacture of pharmaceutical preparations on a semi-commercial scale to prove which products can be manufactured satisfactorily on a large scale.

(iv) The production of essential oils is contemplated as a part of the scheme covering the preparation of drugs.

(v) A glass making plant and a tin-making plant are possibilities in conjunction with drug making and other projects.

(vi) Anti-erosion operations on a large scale are contemplated under the direction of the Revenue and Forest Departments and should provide scope for employment on a large scale.

(vii) In the past Japan supplied a large proportion of the world's real silk demand and sold at a price which other countries found unprofitable. The supply from this source is now cut off giving an excellent opportunity to other producing countries to expand and improve the industry. Silk-weaving has recently received a stimulus owing to the demand for parachute cloth; a second weaving plant has recently been opened in Srinagar.

(viii) Surface working of the Reasi coal deposits has been commenced recently; the possibilities of the future are considerable. Other minerals that may in the future be worked are sulphur, borax, graphite, gypsum and iron. The production of sulphuric acid is contemplated as well as a thorough search for petroleum.

(ix) The woollen industry has distinct possibilities but the goods produced must be standardised. The Sheep Breeding and Research Farm at Banihal is in its infancy. In the course of time it might well produce valuable results by improving the quality of the wool grown in the country.

(x) A cotton-weaving industry has been started at Mirpur recently; it is too early to say if it can be maintained on a competitive basis when the abnormal demand created by the war disappears.

(xi) A sugar mill is to be constructed at Ranbirsinghpura and is expected to be working by 1943. An Alcohol distillery is to be installed to work in conjunction with the sugar mill.

(xii) A small industry was started recently for the preparation of oat-meal and pearl barley. The establishment of a factory for large scale production is contemplated. The products have met with immediate success and it is possible they will be able to stand competition from imported preparations even after the end of the world war.

37. **Wages and Indebtedness.**—So far as wages are concerned industrial development should not operate at a disadvantage. The average agricultural labourer's wage is between five and six annas a day; in urban areas the daily wage for a casual labourer is from six to eight annas. Skilled workers and artizans earn from about ten annas to Rs. 2 per day according to their skill and the demand for their services; very few earn as much as Rs. 2 and the average is probably about Rs. 1-4-0. Clerical workers are available in almost unlimited numbers at a monthly wage of Rs. 20; there are many graduates willing to accept any post with prospects at Rs. 30 p. m. to start with. Labour, either manual or clerical, is not organised; there are no labour bureaux for the registration of workers requiring employment. If there were, perhaps rates for all categories would be more even.

No thorough economic survey has ever been carried out in the State and it is quite impossible to state the position with regard to indebtedness with any claim to accuracy. It is, however, safe to say that there is a great deal of indebtedness. The actual amount per head of the population may be small but nevertheless it is sufficient to act as a millstone round the necks of the majority. The peasant's crop of rice, maize, wheat or any other crop is usually mortgaged before it is ready to cut and he is fortunate if sufficient is left to him and his family until the next harvest is due. The ghee (clarified butter) made from the milk produced by the Gujjar's cows and buffaloes is not his to dispose of as he likes; it is due to the village bania or money-lender in liquidation of debt. The embroiderer, wood-carver, carpet-weaver, papier-mache maker, worker in silver and other metals, and others all have to work for wages lower than they could otherwise obtain because having received advances they must carry on with their employer or become involved in more serious difficulties. Many of the house-boats rented to visitors to Kashmir are not the property of the nominal owner but are mortgaged to the hilt to the agencies and others who control the letting of the boat. These instances are not given in an attempt to ridicule the peculiar system of 'credit' which oils the wheels of agriculture, trade and industry in the State but to emphasise that borrowers and those in debt constitute an important proportion of the population and that incentive is weakened by the hopeless condition of indebtedness in which many are placed. The results of hard work so sweet to the free worker are not enjoyed by the man in debt ; he has to pay any extra earnings with most of the rest to his creditor. In many cases heavy debts are inherited and are passed on from father to son. The most usual causes of debt are ceremonies and litigation ; the cost of marriage ceremonies is out of all proportion to earning capacity. The father of a large family of girls is condemned to a life of indebtedness, particularly if he belongs to the Hindu community and lacks ample means.

38. **Transport.**—The absence of railways, except for the short branch line of the North Western Railway which runs from Sialkot to Jammu City and serves a very small area of the State, makes other methods of transport all the more important, particularly motor transport. Previous to the development of motor transport in Northern India, which commenced about 1910, tongas, ekkas and bullock carts carried all imports and exports from and to railhead. The motor lorry revolutionised transport to and from the State. Up to 1939 motor traffic was increasing annually but the requirements of the war have naturally checked this for the present. In 1931 there were 545 cars and 767 lorries registered in the State. In the decade 1931-40 431 cars and 808 lorries were registered. In the spring of 1941 the number of locally registered vehicles operating in the State was 254 cars and 636 lorries. What happens to old and broken cars and lorries ? This is almost as much a mystery as what happens to dead donkeys. To continue, there were 850 lorries, registered within and without the country, in service in the spring of 1941 on State roads. During the decade lorry traffic has increased by about 40 per cent. on the Jhelum Valley route and by about 20 per cent. on the Banihal route ; the increase in car traffic, as distinct from lorries, was about 35 per cent. for the former and 20 per cent. for the latter. On those roads unfit for motor transport commodities are carried by tonga or pack-transport and on the bridle paths and foot paths in the hills by pack-transport and coolies. On the mountain roads to Gilgit and Ladakh wheeled vehicles cannot go ; transport consists of pack animals and coolies, mostly the former.

39. **Telegraph and Telephone.**—Considerable expansion and development has taken place during the decade in the telegraph and telephone services. Telegraph offices have been opened at many distant places not previously connected. Wireless stations have been opened at Jammu and Nowshera cantonments in the Jammu Province. The telephone service has been greatly improved by the construction of a trunk line between Srinagar and Jammu which is linked up with the British Indian system. The capacity of the exchanges at Srinagar and Jammu has been increased and the old magneto system replaced in part by a modern Automatic Exchange. The service has been extended to a number of important centres thus increasing the facilities for visitors to get into telephonic communication with places throughout India.

40. **Municipalities and Town Areas.**—There are two important municipalities—Jammu and Srinagar ; both have advanced during the decade but much still has to be done in both before those responsible for municipal affairs can feel that the more urgent requirements have been satisfied. In Jammu anti-plague measures have been effective during the decade and conservancy arrangements improved. The watering of the streets is now done by water carts instead of by mashkies. A market with well constructed stalls has been opened for the sale of fruit and vegetables. Four public gardens have been provided and the roads have been tarred. Street lighting and the drinking water supply have been extended and improved. Built on the side of a hill, Jammu City enjoys a good natural drainage system and the filling up of unwholesome pits and tanks has added considerably to its health. The scheme of training selected women for midwifery work carried on by the Womens' Welfare Association is claimed to have done much to reduce infantile and maternal mortality. The birth rate shows a good increase during the decade and the death rate an appreciable fall. In Srinagar, similar progress has been made with regard to the watering of the streets and improved conservancy arrangements. A generous contribution was made to assist the work of the Womens' Welfare Association and good results are claimed. Roads have been improved and new landing places constructed on the river banks but much still remains to be done in both respects. Street lighting and the drinking water supply have been extended and improved ; lorry and tonga stands have been provided in various parts of the city in the interests of better traffic control. An effort has been made to relieve congestion by opening up new areas for residential purposes. Srinagar is not so fortunate as Jammu in the matter of drainage. For

several decades the bed of the Jhelum, which passes through the heart of the city, has been rising. After every threat of floods the bunds are raised and now much of the municipal area is below the level of the river for several months of the year. Drainage and sanitation are big questions which will have to be tackled in a big way very soon if health conditions in Srinagar are to be maintained, let alone improved.

Up to 1933 there was little in the nature of local administration in the towns. Baramulla and Sopore in the Kashmir Province and Udhampur and Mirpur in the Jammu Province were Notified Areas under the control of local committees but they did not function well for lack of funds. In 1933 Town Area Act No. IV was enacted and those places declared Town Areas by government were required to conduct their local affairs in conformity with its provisions. The Act was found to be defective in certain respects and was replaced by a new Act in 1940 which enlarged the powers and functions of the Town Area Committees and gave scope for the development of local administration by elected representatives of the public. At the end of 1940 there were 25 Town Areas—10 in the Kashmir Province and 15 in the Jammu Province. Powers were given to Town Area Committees to raise funds by levying octroi, ground-rent, registration fees on the sale of cattle and a number of other minor sources of revenue. Whilst the resources of all are strictly limited most of them are self-supporting with the grants given to them from time to time from the general revenues of the State. The Town Area Committees consist of nominated and elected members; the chairman is usually an official but not always. For some time to come the nomination of officials as members of these committees is likely to continue to assist and guide the elected representatives of the public. The creation of these committees has had a good effect in introducing a sense of civic responsibility. Town roads and lanes have been paved and drained, latrines provided, lorry and tonga stands established, slaughter-houses built, lighting plants installed and arrangements made to combat outbreaks of fire. The funds of Town Areas are supplemented by subventions out of the Sanitation Cess collected at the rate of one pice in the rupee on Land Revenue assessments. In several towns drinking water supplies have been greatly improved and there has been marked improvement in other respects too. These local institutions are in their infancy; with proper guidance by official members and a desire to effect improvements on the part of the elected representatives real progress should have been achieved before the next Census in 1951.

41. **Judicial and Police.**—Any picture of the social and economic conditions obtaining would be incomplete without a brief outline of the machinery for the administration of justice and the work of the police. 1928 is an important date in the judicial history of the State. In that year a High Court was created, comprising a Chief Justice and two Puisne Judges, independent of the Executive. From 1931 to 1933 there was a considerable degree of lawlessness connected with the disturbances already referred to; the magistracy performed their difficult duties with credit. In 1936 a committee was appointed, under the presidency of a judge of the High Court, to inquire into the prevalence of corrupt practices in the public services and to formulate proposals to eradicate them. Order No. 1 of 1928 which governed the constitution of the High Court was repealed by Act XIV of 1996, corresponding to 1939. The new Act provided for the creation of a Board of Judicial Advisers to assist His Highness the Maharaja Bahadur in the disposal of appeals from the High Court. An Appeal Act specified the class of cases in which appeals from the orders of the High Court might be taken to His Highness. The Act of 1939 also provided for the appointment of an Advocate General. The Board of Judicial Advisers performs in the State functions similar to those of the Privy Council in the case of British India.

During the decade the jurisdiction of the High Court was extended to the Poonch and Chenani Jagirs thus giving the inhabitants of the two Jagirs the benefits of an organised judiciary. The number of courts exercising jurisdiction has increased for all classes of cases; the number of practising advocates on the rolls of the High Court has increased from 184 to 287.

The disturbances which occurred in the first three years of the decade imposed a great strain on the police force; large numbers of additional police were enlisted to supplement the permanent force, the strength of which was inadequate to cope with the conditions that arose. Many of these additional police were retained but they lacked the training of the regular force. As soon as circumstances permitted the organisation of the force was overhauled and instructional courses were opened for drill and to impart knowledge of the law and police rules. The practice of sending sub-inspectors for training to the Police Training School at Phillaur was resumed and a new Police Training School was opened in the State in 1938, with a curriculum based on the Phillaur Training School, for the training of head-constables and constables. These measures have indubitably raised the standard of efficiency of the whole police force. The degree of literacy in the lower ranks of the force has been raised; in 1940 there were 1,133 literate constables representing a percentage of 45.6 against 643 in 1931. The number of police-stations in charge of sub-inspectors has increased from 55 to 71 and of police-posts in charge of head-constables from 39 to 50. A prosecution staff has been created consisting of inspectors and sub-inspectors, the former being specially enlisted graduates in law, to strengthen the agency entrusted with this part of the department's work. The total strength of the force has been slightly reduced but the terms of service have been improved. Expenditure has increased from Rs. 1,258,000 to Rs. 1,289,000. Crime has increased slightly under most classes but there has been a welcome fall in cases of dacoity from 385 in 1932 to 19 in 1940; the figures for 1932 were abnormal owing to the disturbed conditions throughout the country.

42. **Age Distribution.**—Having discussed the various aspects of life and conditions in the State it will be profitable to see how the population is distributed by age groups. These are given in considerable detail in Imperial Table VII and its subsidiaries. As the notes to the tables make clear, the tendency for the numbers in the various age-groups to decrease after a certain stage is more regular on this occasion than at the previous Census. In 1931 the decrease commenced after the group 0-5; at this Census the decrease commences after the age group 5-10. The percentage of older people to the total population is a little higher in 1941 than it was in 1931. The increase in the age groups from 35-40 upwards is 13.7 per cent. against an increase of 10.3 per cent. for the whole population. This shows a tendency towards a prolongation of life in the older groups. The notes to Table VII, with special reference to Subsidiary V, mention the preference shown by those being censused, and by enumerators when they have to make a guess, for certain numbers, particularly those ending with 0 or 5. The Assam Census Report for 1931 in discussing this feature quotes from the report of Mr. H. G. W. Meikle, Actuary to the Government of India, entitled "Report on the Age Distribution and Rates of Mortality deduced from the Indian Census returns of 1921 and previous enumerations" and published in 1926 by the Government of India Press, Calcutta. The passage referred to reads as follows:—

"If an enumerator had to guess the ages of a lot of old men of about age 80 he would enter most as aged 60, 70, 75, 80, 85, 90, 100 or possibly even 120. It would be absurd if he were to guess many as aged either 77, 79, 81, 83 etc. At the youngest ages, say under 8, there is little preference shown for any particular age other than 5. At ages between 8 and 24 the preference is for even numbers and for age 15. Any one guessing the age of children aged about 10 would unconsciously enter more at 8, 10, 12 etc., than at 7, 9, 11, 13 etc. At ages 20 and over the largest numbers are found at each of the decennial ages. In this way 0 is much the most popular digit. The next most popular digit is 5".

The preference for round numbers in India is obviously due to the fact that a large proportion of the population does not know its own age. In addition, we get errors as a result of deliberate understatement or overstatement for various reasons. In dividing the population into age groups provision is made by a method known as 'smoothing' to overcome this feature of the age returns, as far as possible, but it must be recognised that our age returns are not accurate. However, since the idiosyncracy referred to has been a feature common to every Census previously taken too, and as it is well known to all actuaries and those studying our age tables, the error they contain does not destroy their value.

Experts in demography place great importance on the distribution of the population in certain main age groups; these are 0-15, 15-45 and all over 45. It is obvious that these three groups represent respectively the parents of the future, the present re-productive elements, and those who have passed the reproductive ages. The question has, of course, special reference to the females in these particular groups. The female is obviously much more important in questions relating to race reproduction than the male and the reproductive capacities of the latter are spread over a much longer age period. To be progressive, in a demographic sense, 40 per cent. of a country's population should be in the age group 0-15; less than 33 per cent. is considered to indicate a stationary position and a country is said to be regressive with less than 20 per cent. in this group. The relative figures for the Jammu and Kashmir State at this Census show 39.5 per cent. of the males in this group, 40.7 per cent. of the females, and 40.1 per cent. of the whole population. The figures for the main communities are Sikhs 44.7 per cent., Muslims 40 per cent., Hindus 37 per cent. and Buddhists 30.5 per cent. On the basis of these figures the Sikhs and Muslims are progressive, the Hindus hovering half way between a state of being progressive and stationary and the Buddhists a little less than stationary. At the 1931 Census the percentages for this group were slightly higher for males, females and the whole population. The re-productive groups 15-30 and 30-45 also have an important bearing on the increase to be expected in 1951. If we compare the figures in these groups with those for 1931 we find that the percentages in the group 15-30 at this Census are slightly below those for 1931 in all three cases—males, females and total population. In the age group 30-45 the position is slightly different; the figures for males, females and total are respectively 18.7 per cent., 18.1 per cent. and 18.5 per cent. in 1941 against 19 per cent., 17.5 per cent. and 18.3 per cent. in 1931. Our group 5-10 at this Census contains a larger number of the population than any other five year group; the largest group in 1931 was the 0-5 group. The 5-10 group at this Census also shows a bigger percentage of females to males than in 1931; all the females of the 1941 age group 5-10 will have entered the re-productive group 15-45 before the 1951 Census. It is not intended to make any predictions but the view may be hazarded that with other factors equal the percentage increase in the population at the 1951 Census will exceed that for 1941. An increase in excess of 10.3 per cent. is no light matter and is bound to strain our resources to the utmost. If the means of subsistence do not increase to a similar extent then the various checks to population will operate with increased force to correct the position. We need not examine the age groups for 45 and over closely. It will suffice to record that the percentages for the groups 45-60 and 60 and over in every case exceed those for 1931; longevity has increased.

43. **Sex.**—In demography at any rate the females of the species are more important than the males. The number of females per thousand males of the total population at this Census was 888 against 881 in 1931, 890 in 1921 and 887 in 1911. It is not proposed to go into further details here. These and other sex ratios are given in the subsidiary tables following Imperial Table VII. The predominance of males throughout India has been the subject of much discussion in the past. In the countries of Western Europe females are usually in excess and from time to time the accuracy of Indian sex statistics has been impugned on this account. It must be assumed that such critics are not conversant with social conditions in India. In the Indian Census Report for 1911 Sir Edward Gait in refuting criticisms of the kind referred to pointed out that social conditions in India were entirely different from those obtaining in Europe, that in Europe boys and girls have an equal chance whereas in India boys frequently receive greater attention during the earlier years of their lives. In India girls are usually given in marriage at an early age and on this account are exposed to greater dangers at the time of child birth than those normal in the case of mothers of more mature age. These conditions still obtain today in spite of the great advances made. Any one with any knowledge of India knows that the female, up to the age of 20 at any rate, is exposed to far greater risks than the male. What is true of India is true of the Jammu and Kashmir State in this respect. During the last fifteen years, in particular, reformers have been working to get the age of marriage postponed, both for boys and girls, until they have reached a more mature age. Infant Marriage Acts have been passed throughout India and the government of the Jammu and Kashmir State was one of the earliest to pass such legislation. The minimum legal marriage age for girls is now 14 and for boys 18. But the education and enlightenment of the mass of the people on this subject is likely to have far more practical effect than legislation. The tendency amongst educated classes today is to postpone the marriage of both their boys and girls to a more mature age. The standard of midwifery and the treatment of maternity cases have improved much in the last two decades. The full effect of these changes will not be apparent at once but it is probable that the ratio of females per thousand males from now on will show a steady improvement in the State until the ratio approaches that for the whole of India which, in 1931, was 940. The subject is one not likely to be neglected by the demologist and it is perhaps better left to him.

44. **Civil Condition.**—Imperial Table VII and its subsidiaries, especially subsidiaries viii, ix and x, give details on the subject of civil condition, that is to say the unmarried, married or widowed state of all elements of the population at all ages. Those not conversant with conditions in India must realise that the word 'married' does not mean the same in India as it does in western countries. In the latter it is synonymous with cohabitation; in India, and the same applies to the Jammu and Kashmir State, the so-called infant marriages mean nothing of the sort. These infant marriages are more in the nature of irrevocable betrothals. Normally, the girl wife

remains in the home of her husband's parents except for short intervals when she returns to her old home to see her parents. It is not until after the age of puberty that cohabitation between the young bride and bridegroom usually occurs. The Infant Marriage Act passed in 1929 prohibits the marriage of girls below the age of 14 but the tables show that at the time of the Census there were over 4,000 married girls and over 600 widowed girls in the age groups 0-15 and over 1,000 married girls in the age group 0-10. Many of these girls may be in the last year of the group but it would seem that infant marriage continues in spite of the Act. There were 99 married girls in the 0-5 group in 1931 so there have been many marriages of girls under 14 since the Act was passed. However, the number of married girls in the age group 0-15 is well below the figure for 1931. The proportion of unmarried, married and widowed may be accepted as correct but the statistics relating to civil condition by age are, of course, subject to the same defects as the age tables. The attitude to marriage in India is entirely different to that obtaining in western countries and this fact must be appreciated before any attempt is made to study the figures relating to civil condition in India, much less to discuss them or compare them with western countries. In India, and in the Jammu and Kashmir State, it is the aim of all parents belonging to the main communities to get their children married as early as possible and it is the aim of all to beget children as soon as the parties to a marriage have reached the age of puberty. In particular, the Hindu male must marry and obtain a son as early as possible to perform his funeral rites; a Hindu maiden, unmarried at an age considered suitable by local Hindu Society, is a creature pitied or derided by others of her community but seldom approved. It must however be recognised that many of the less conservative and more progressive elements appreciate the advantage of postponing the marriage of their daughters until an age when they are physically and mentally fit to endure the strain of pregnancy and childbirth. Amongst Muslims too early marriage is usual. Sikhs usually do not marry until the age of puberty; Buddhists usually postpone marriage later than any other of the main communities. Although the tendency is growing amongst the educated classes to postpone marriage to a later age, the immediate effect of the passing of the Infant Marriage Act was to cause a rush of infant marriages before the Act came into force. A later effect has probably been to over-state the ages of brides under the legal age for marriage. With or without the Act the tendency is towards later marriage, especially in the case of the boy, but it is too soon yet to gauge the effect of legislation or public opinion on this subject. By the next Census some changes in civil condition amongst the early age groups should become apparent. There should be no married females under the age of 14 and it would be well worth-while to produce a table showing the number of married boys and girls for each year up to the age of 18. India will always be a country of early marriages and for many obvious reasons it is well that this should be so; the reduction in the number of infant marriages, as distinct from marriage between young people, will probably be more influenced by the spread of education and a change in outlook rather than by legislation.

45. **Education.**—Reference has already been made to the recommendations of the Unemployment Commission for the appointment of a committee of educationists to consider and report on the educational system. The Committee appointed went into the subject very thoroughly and as previously mentioned submitted their report in 1939. They advocated many changes; the most important was the recommendation to introduce what is termed Basic Education, that is to say, the essential minimum of education—which is to centre round appropriate forms of craft work—required to equip any person for intelligent citizenship. It was considered that the full course of basic education should extend over a period of seven years and gradually replace the old system of Primary Education which extends over a period of five years. The Committee gave the opinion that a period of five years primary education was insufficient for the attainment of literacy and that most boys whose education was discontinued after completion of the primary course of education relapsed into illiteracy.

Considerable educational progress has been made during the decade. The physical features of the country do not facilitate the spread of education. Many of those living some distance from the towns are ignorant of and indifferent towards the benefits of education. In 1929 the educational machinery of the State was reorganised. The posts of Director of Education and Chief Inspectress of Girls Schools were created to coordinate and control all educational activities. The former post was reduced in 1931 as an act of retrenchment but was restored in 1932. At the same time the post of Special Inspector for Muslim Education was created to stimulate greater interest in education amongst Muslims.

The aim of His Highness' Government is the provision, in due course, of a primary school for boys in every village with a population of over 500, the steady expansion of primary schools for girls and the opening of an increasing number of Middle and High Schools for both sexes. The number of institutions for both boys and girls has increased considerably and the number of scholars in proportion. Expenditure has increased on boys schools from nearly Rs. 14 lacs to a little under Rs. 18 lacs and on girls schools from just over Rs. 2¼ lacs to over Rs. 3½ lacs. The systematic training of school teachers has been taken in hand and, on an average, ten graduate teachers have been deputed at Government expense annually for training in the B. T. class in the Training Colleges of British India. Scholarship grants have been increased and special scholarships granted for communities which are educationally backward; under this scheme Muslims, Rajputs, Harijans Sikhs and students from the Frontier Districts have benefited chiefly. In 1930 compulsory education was introduced in the cities of Jammu and Srinagar and in the towns of Mirpur, Udhampur, Baramulla and Sopore. To improve supervision the number of educational divisions each under an Assistant Inspector was increased. Special attention has been given to education in the backward Frontier Districts. To implement some of the recommendations contained in the interim report of the Educational Re-organisation Committee (1938), His Highness' Government sanctioned an extra grant of Rs. 130,000. The particular items provided for by this grant were a Teachers' Training School at Srinagar, the opening of Basic Schools at Jammu and Srinagar, Adult Education, Refresher courses for teachers, increased staff in educational offices, the provision of adult libraries, in cities, towns and villages the publication of adult readers and the construction of school buildings. The Adult Education movement was still in its infancy at the time of the Census and it is too early to estimate the extent of its success. It is reported that at the end of the decade 3,457 adult literacy centres had been opened throughout the State and that over 60,000 male adults were under instruction. To see what effect the campaign to remove adult illiteracy has on the percentage of literacy in the State we must wait until the Census in 1951. Girls education and the Technical Schools have been placed under the Director of Education to bring all educational activities under one control. Progress during the decade in various directions has been steady; the importance of an efficient educational organisation has been realised and the ever increasing provision of funds indicates the determination of His Highness' Government to maintain a progressive and liberal educational policy.

46. **Literacy.**—The total number of persons recorded as literate at the 1931 Census was 123,386 excluding Gilgit Agency; of these 114,321 were males and 9,065 females. The percentage of literacy in 1931 works out at 5.9 for males and .5 for females. It was the realisation of this educational backwardness that gave birth to the movement to accelerate educational expansion. The interest of the masses has been quickened and the value of education realised to a greater extent than previously. The standard of literacy for Census purposes is as low as it can be if the word is to have any real meaning. Any person who can read a simple letter in any language and write a simple reply is deemed to be literate. We have to depend a good deal on the enumerator's interpretation of our definition and, simple as the test is, it is probable that the Census figures exaggerate the extent of literacy rather than the reverse. However, the standard of education of our average enumerator is not deteriorating from one Census to another and we may assume that the enumerator's standard for showing a person as literate in 1941 was higher than in 1931. As in 1931, no one below the age of 5 is shown as literate in the tables whatever may have been recorded in the case of infant prodigies in the Census record. The 1941 figures for literates show a big advance for both males and females. Special reference is necessary to the literacy figures for Buddhists as a community and for Ladakh as a district. The figures for 1941 show an improvement on those for 1931 but it is thought that for neither Census do they reflect the true position. A high percentage of Buddhists over five years of age is reported to be literate in their own language, Bodhi or Bhotia; some local officials and travellers have put the figure as high as 90 per cent. amongst adults. It would seem that the Census agency in Ladakh—there are few Buddhists in the State outside Ladakh—at this and previous Censuses has not recognised literacy in Bodhi as literacy at all for the purposes of the Census. This, of course, is entirely wrong and is a matter for special attention at the Census in 1951. There is no need to go into all the details of literacy here; the figures are given in Imperial Table XI and its subsidiaries.

47. **Sabhas, Societies and the Press.**—There appears to be no previous record of the Sabhas or Societies in the State. Many of them are active for a short time and then fade out of existence through lack of interest or support. In all they numbered 435 in the spring of 1941. Since then

some of those listed will probably have become defunct whilst others will have come into existence. Of the total, 125 may be classed as social, 258 religious and 52 political.

The local Press has made a big advance during the decade. The first newspaper was registered in 1924 figures are not available of the number in circulation in 1931 but in the spring of 1941 there were 44. Some last for a short time only; others are published at long and uncertain intervals but a fair number are issued punctually and regularly. Most of them are published in Hindustani, in both Persian and Devanagri script, chiefly the former; a few are published in English. The standard of journalism is improving. Circulation figures are not available but the copies of papers purchased are to be counted in hundreds not thousands. The free expression of a variety of opinions is all to the good but there are so many newspapers for the comparatively small newspaper-reading public that most of them hover between life and death.

48. **Archæology.**—The State is rich in places of archæological interest; these consist chiefly of the ruins of ancient mosques and temples. Excavations were restricted in the early years of the decade owing to lack of funds due to the re-actions of the world trade depression of 1929 onwards but during the latter half work was resumed and discoveries of interest to the student of archæology were made at Martand and Gilgit.

49. **Languages and Scripts.**—The chief languages in use in the State are Kashmiri, Dogri and Punjabi; Hindustani is the language most commonly used as a subsidiary for conversation between the different elements of the population having a different mothertongue. English is spoken well by a large proportion of the educated classes. The area in which each language is used and the extent to which it is used are given in great detail in Imperial Table XII and its subsidiaries. It is only necessary here to say that the figures for Hindustani are inflated as the result of the Urdu-Hindi controversy. Propaganda was carried on during the Census by the adherents of both parties to the dispute with the result that many Hindus gave Hindi as their mother tongue and many Muslims gave Urdu quite contrary to the facts in the great majority of cases. The dispute is largely political and so to keep politics out of the Census it was decided to lump Hindi and Urdu together as Hindustani. There are few people in the State who can rightly claim Hindi or Urdu as their mothertongue. The real dispute is in the use of script. The old indigenous script of Kashmir is called Sharada. As a popular script it enjoyed reputation far and wide for over a thousand years. Almost all the inscriptions in Sanskrit incised on stones whether at Martanda or other monumental places are written in the same. The birch bark manuscripts, nay even the paper ones used to be copied in the same script before the advent of the Devanagri. That in most common use now and in the near past is the Persian script; the Devanagri script is that in which Hindi as opposed to Urdu is usually written and it is the script in which Sanskrit is written. The Hindu element of the population is naturally anxious that the script should not be allowed to go into disuse or a knowledge of it denied to their children. To meet the demands of the two main communities in the State His Highness' Government issued orders towards the end of 1940 that the common medium of instruction in schools in future would be simple Urdu and that the Persian and Devanagri scripts would both be taught and used. Students have been given the option of choosing either of the two scripts for reading and writing. Thus in future Students in Schools will be taught either the Persian or the Devanagri script at the option instead of only one script is Persian being taught to all.

50. **The Population Problem.**—The population problem in India has been discussed by students of demography from one Census to another and it may be presumed that this occasion will be no exception. In his book entitled 'The population problem in India', the revised edition of which was published in 1934, P. K. Wattal quotes the following from page 145 of the official report 'India in 1930-31':—

> "An advance of 10.6 per cent. in ten years is in itself startling enough, but it becomes vastly more so when it represents an addition of 34,000,000 persons to the country's population".

He gives the following from Dr. Hutton's All India report on the 1931 Census:—

> "this increase is from most points of view a cause for alarm rather than satisfaction".

Wattal also quotes Major General A. J. H. Russell as saying in 1927:—

> "the population of India is very near its saturation point, and for all practical purposes, it may be taken as proved that India as a whole is already over populated".

That was with reference to the 1921 Census when the population was 319,000,000 including

Burma which is not included in the figures for 1941. What then is to be said about the All-India increase of 15 per cent. in the decade 1931-41 and an actual increase of over 50,000,000 persons bringing the total to 388,800,000 (excluding Burma). The percentage increase of population is getting higher each decade and at each Census this naturally involves a higher actual increase of persons. The All-India population has increased by about 70,000,000 (excluding Burma) in two decades or say, in one generation. It is clear that the dangers to which Wattal referred have increased and the necessity for applying the remedies which he advocated becomes more urgent. The increase in the Jammu and Kashmir State was 9.8 per cent. in 1931 and 10.3 per cent. for 1941, against 10.6 per cent. and 15 per cent. respectively for All India, that is to say, an increase of 701,098 actual persons in one generation or just over 21 per cent. The position at first sight is not so serious for the Jammu and Kashmir State as for India as a whole but it must be remembered that the Jammu and Kashmir State is still almost entirely agricultural whereas India, although still mainly agricultural, is being rapidly industrialised in many areas. If an increase of 10.6 per cent. for All-India in 1931 gave the experts cause for alarm then an increase of 10.3 per cent. for Jammu and Kashmir in 1941 is equally, if not more, alarming. Wattal, discussing the 1931 figures, says:—

> "India today is the most populous country in the world, China not excepted. It is well known that agriculture can not support so dense a population as industry, per unit of space. Notwithstanding this, India, a predominantly agricultural country, with a density of 195 persons per square mile, is supporting a larger population per square mile than the highly industrialised continent of Europe with a mean density of 127, or the United States of America with a density of 41".

This statement has more force in 1941 than it had previously. The density in the Jammu and Kashmir State rose from 43 in 1931 to 48 in 1941 but if we leave out the enormous areas of the Jammu and Kashmir State which are uncultivable and uninhabitable and take areas such as the Jammu and Anantnag Districts we get a density exceeding the figure for All-India in 1931 and if we base the density figures on cultivated areas only we get figures exceeding 1,600 persons per square mile in several purely agricultural areas. Put this way the seriousness of the problem is more easily reaslised.

51. **The Malthus Theory.**—Population, according to Malthus, has an inherent tendency to multiply beyond the means of subsistence. From time to time economists of western countries suggest that the Malthusian theory no longer applies to the conditions of today. Comparisons are made between the low birth rate and the low increase of population in recent decades in countries of Europe and America and the high rate of increase in the production of food. It seems possible that in rejecting Malthus's dicta as out of date sufficient weight is not given to the extensive use of modern contraceptives as a check to population in western countries on the one hand and the defective distribution of the world's food stuffs on the other. It is all very well to say that world food production is in excess of world demand and that large quantities are surplus but the fact remains that whilst surpluses are rotting in some areas there are millions of persons suffering from want, undernourishment and semi-starvation in others. Mal-distribution of food stuffs and mal-distribution of purchasing power are the real problems and it is to these that attention should be given rather than to attempts to prove that the Malthus theory of population no longer stands. In any case, we are concerned with the population of India in general and of the Jammu and Kashmir State in particular, not with that of Europe and America. Let us examine the Malthus theory. It has been stated hundreds of times but bears repetition. It is lucidly discussed in the book "Population—Today's question" by McCleary from which these details have been taken. Malthus formulated his principle of population in three propositions:—

(i) Population is necessarily limited by the means of subsistence.

(ii) Population invariably increases where the means of subsistence increase unless prevented by some very powerful and obvious checks.

(iii) These checks, and the checks which repress the superior power of population, and keep its effects on a level with the means of subsistence, are all resolvable into moral restraint, misery and vice.

Malthus affirmed that the power of population to increase is infinitely greater than the power in the earth to produce subsistence for men and that population, when unchecked, increases in geometrical ratio whilst subsistence only increases in an arithmetrical ratio. He held that the effects of these two unequal powers must be kept equal and that the checks on population constantly operating could all be fairly resolved into moral restraint, misery and vice. Misery, he thought, was an absolutely necessary consequence; vice he was not so sure about. He classed the checks to population under two heads—positive and preventive. He declared the positive checks to be extremely various and pointed out that they included every cause, whether arising from misery or vice, which in any degree contributes to reduce the length of human life. The positive checks therefore include unwholesome occupations, severe labour, exposure to inclement weather, poverty, bad nursing, life in large towns, excesses of all kinds, epidemics, diseases, wars and famines. Amongst the preventive checks he specified "promiscuous intercourse, unnatural passions, violations of the marriage bed and improper arts to conceal the consequences of irregular connections"; these he classed as vice. The one preventive check he did not class as 'vice' he termed 'moral restraint'.

The geometrical ratio he had in mind was not any ratio but a particular ratio, *i. e.*, doubling every twenty-five years, and it was the ratio that would operate, not in any population, but in an unchecked population. His arithmetrical ratio was also a particular ratio and he regarded it as a maximum. He did not himself think it would be possible to increase the means of subsistence every twenty-five years by a quantity equal to that produced at the time he was writing, but he assumed that it would be possible in order not to overstate his case.

The popular idea of Malthus is that he prophesied that, if population went on increasing, dreadful things would happen at some future time. But the essence of his teaching is that the tendency of population to outpace the means of subsistence is, and always has been, constantly operating and is causing dreadful things, misery and vice, here and now, and has always done so. Some critics say that Malthus did not allow for variations in what he called "the passion between the sexes". It has been contended that intellectual development and the increasing diversity of interests in modern civilised communities tend to diminish sexual feeling to such an extent as to constitute an effective cheek on population. But even if we recognise this tendency it is to be doubted whether it will even attain such proportions as to upset the Malthus theory.

Malthus regarded birth control as a form of vice and he would probably contend, if he could revisit the earth, that the success of modern methods of birth control in bringing down the birth rate in western countries supports his principle of population. He was of opinion that if it were possible for each married couple to limit by a wish the number of their children, there would be reason to fear that the indolence of the human race would be very greatly increased and that the population of individual countries would never reach its natural and proper extent. Malthus's view that control of births is 'vice' makes his position secure. It must, however, be remembered that modern methods of contraception bear no comparison with methods of birth control used in the days of Malthus when to bring about an abortion was probably the most common method. Modern contraceptive methods are so effective when correctly applied that they may well produce the results forecasted by Malthus in his hypothetical case of the married couple's wish. But we are concerned with India, not Europe. The methods of contraception now practised in western countries are practically unknown in India except in the cities; even where these methods are known the facilities for using them are limited and the cost beyond the means of the masses.

The conditions in India today in general, and in the Jammu and Kashmir State in particular, except amongst the more sophisticated elements of the population, more closely resemble the conditions in Europe in the time of Malthus than present day conditions in Europe and the Malthusian theory applies with full force to our population problems. The geometrical and arithmetrical ratios discussed by Malthus have been ridiculed by some but as Wattal puts it "they occupy the same place in demography as the conception of the economic man in political economy or the Euclidean point in geometry".

52. **Modern Methods of Birth Control.**—Modern methods of birth control have indubitably brought about a big decrease in the birth rate in western countries. If we accept Malthus's view that all birth control must be classed as 'vice', then his position is not upset by what has happened to the birth rate in western countries in the last fifty years. The contraceptive methods now practised were not known and outside practical consideration in the time when Malthus lived. If he were alive today he would probably approve of them; if the contrary is assumed then we must add

contraception to the three checks given by Malthus and his theory stands. McCleary attributes to Mr. J. M. Keynes the dictum that every country should determine what size of population is most expedient and set about getting it. This is a sound suggestion but to implement it is a different matter. Malthus's first proposition is that population is limited by the means of subsistence; his second that population will increase if the means of subsistence increases unless prevented by powerful checks; his third that the checks consist of moral restraint, misery and vice; in view of what has been said above we will add a fourth check—Contraception.

53. **Jammu and Kashmir State today.**—Let us consider the population question with special reference to the Jammu and Kashmir State. In the past twenty years much has been done by His Highness' Government to improve agriculture and develop industries. The means of subsistence have been increased in many ways. Medical facilities have been improved, epidemics are being controlled with an efficiency not achieved in the past. We may assume with confidence that the efforts of His Highness' Government will be continuous and that agricultural and industrial development will continue to increase the means of subsistence but there is a limit and the problem becomes more difficult year by year. For some time to come the means of subsistence can be increased by providing better roads and communications to facilitate movement, reduce transport costs and improve the means of distribution of foodstuffs and other commodities whether grown in the country or imported. The cultivable and cultivated areas can be increased by the extension of existing irrigation canals and the construction of new ones. The land under cultivation can be made to produce more by the use of better methods, selected seeds and manures and by the consolidation of holdings. Reduction in the number of useless cattle will make it possible to maintain well a smaller number of better quality animals for both ploughing and milking and thus make for better farming and an improved diet resulting from an increased supply of milk products. An improvement in the breed of sheep will give an increased wool crop and increase the means of subsistence obtainable from this cottage industry. The development of industries dependent on the extensive forest areas can be expanded and the mineral deposits found in many districts of the State, Reasi in particular, can be exploited and new industries started. The silk industry may be extended, the tourist traffic encouraged and new wealth and fresh means of subsistence created in every direction. But we can not get away from Malthus's law. However fast the means of subsistence increase, the population will keep pace. In fact, it is only the increased facilities and the increasing means of subsistence that have made possible the large increase of population in the last two decades. The expansion of this or that industry and the creation of new ones are not cures for poverty and unemployment in the long run because we cannot get away from the operation of Malthus's law that the greater the means of subsistence the larger the population in the absence of powerful checks. Admittedly, those at present unemployed, and fit to work in any new spheres of employment that may be created and thrown open to them, will benefit but they will be followed by larger numbers of unemployed in the future as soon as any slump or check to expansion of trade occurs. It would be well to recognise the fact that for a country which is predominantly agricultural the population of the Jammu and Kashmir State has already reached a dangerously high level on the basis of cultivated area. In the absence of a railway to serve the heart of the country and good motor roads to reach the more remote areas quick relief of food shortages, occasioned by local failure or partial failure of crops, is difficult and the nearer we get to saturation point for population the more difficult it will become. Although agriculture will continue for some time to provide increased means of subsistence greater reliance will have to be placed on industries in the future. The country cannot stand still; it must either continue to make progress and provide the means of subsistence adequate to support the increasing population brought into being by a continuous increase of the means of subsistence over a long period or retrogression will set in. As soon as there is a check in the provision of the means of subsistence Malthus's population checks, which are always operating, will come into play with greater force. Moral restraint as a factor will probably remain the same—at least for a time. Misery and vice as classed by Malthus will increase. As a result of more efficient administration and the activities of beneficent departments some of the positive checks which control population have lost power in the last two decades, and are still losing power thus partly accounting for, it is reasonable to assume, a higher increase of population than in the previous decade. Working conditions are being improved, hours of labour are being reduced, epidemics are being controlled with greater efficiency, diseases which

previously caused death are being cured more frequently, nursing of children has improved, maternity treatment is better. With many of the positive checks to population being weakened by the increase of knowledge and application of scientific methods the function of reducing an excessive population is likely to be thrown on to other checks, some positive others preventive; most of the latter have been classed by Malthus as vice. Migration is, of course, a remedy for over-population in any particular area and thousands of subjects of the State go to the Punjab every winter in search of employment but such migrations are mostly temporary. Most classes in the State are loath to leave their homes except for limited periods. But even if large numbers were willing to migrate, where can they go with any hope of finding the means of livelihood and a permanent home except in a comparatively few cases. The State is not the only place suffering from pressure of population. India as a whole was considered over-populated twenty years ago; since then there has been an enormous increase. We see on every side countries, provinces and states adopting what may be called a nationalistic policy in the matter of immigration and employment. This does not assist adjustment by migration, that is to say, by the transfer of large numbers of people from over-populated areas to others not so thickly populated. With the increasing nationalistic tendencies noticeable in the last decade everywhere, migration by those willing to become emigrants has been made more difficult. If the barriers are broken down everywhere conditions may become easier but this does not look likely at present. We are therefore thrown back on Malthus's checks and it seems that the most powerful of the positive checks in the future will be misery in the form of poverty, want and semi-starvation leading to weakness, susceptibility to disease and premature death. What of the other checks listed by Malthus—moral restraint and vice? We cannot assess the amount of moral restraint being exercised now or likely to be exercised in the future. Judging by the tendency in the past towards early marriage, which is now controlled by law, and the large families common everywhere, it is not a very powerful check. Vice in the Malthusian sense we may expect to increase as a check in proportion to the weakening of other checks and the extent of over population.

54. **A Remedy.**—In these circumstances why should we not let our new check—contraception—play its part; in other words why not encourage birth control by the use of contraceptives as distinct from birth control after conception. The latter is rightly classed as 'vice'; contraception is not vice. This view has the support of thousands of religious and reputable persons. In the case of India, of which the Jammu and Kashmir State is essentially a part, the high death rate will only be reduced when the high birth rate is reduced. The waste of life from infantile mortality and child-birth at present is considerable. There are thousands of cases in which pregnancy takes place at the known risk of life to the mother. In thousands of families more children are not wanted; they cannot be properly clothed, fed and educated and yet they follow one after another in monotonous regularity to live a life of difficulty, handicapped from the beginning, and a source of pain and grief to all concerned. Surely, it is better to utilise the knowledge which science has placed within our reach. If the law of life and population is harsh why should we not soften it as far as we can. For the great majority of the population of the State there seem to be no religious grounds for objection to the use of contraceptives. Admittedly, the use of contraceptives is beyond the knowledge of the great majority of the people and beyond their means but the case for the use of contraceptive methods is beyond dispute if it is accepted that it does not run counter to religious teaching. It would not be possible to make the service available to all in the beginning but it is suggested that the opening of clinics in Jammu and Srinagar and in the larger towns be considered. It is unnecessary to go into details here; suffice it to say that the service should be conducted by a discreet and sympathetic staff. Service and advice should be free in certain circumstances and a fee charged to those in a position to pay. We should make good use of the knowledge we are fortunate enough to possess and give relief to untold numbers by some mitigation of the unrelenting laws of population.

A note on the medical aspect of the decade 1931-40 by Colonel Sir Ram Nath Chopra, Kt., C. I. E., I. M. S., (Retd.), Director of Medical Services, His Highness' Government, Jammu and Kashmir.

INTRODUCTORY.

To prepare a comprehensive note on the conditions of the decade (1931-40) from the Medical and Public Health points of view is no easy task. The reasons are not far to seek. Much relevant data is needed and this is very difficult to obtain. Attempts were made to collect as many facts and figures as possible from the vital statistics available and this note is the result. In spite of its shortcomings it contains much valuable information.

The subject is dealt with under the following headings:—

(1) Vital Statistics.

(2) Epidemics and Important Diseases.

(3) Venereal Diseases.

(4) Dietetics.

(5) General Sanitation.

(6) Birth Control.

(7) Conclusions.

(1) Vital Statistics.

The importance of Vital Statistics cannot be denied. They are compiled from records which are maintained in the urban areas of the Provinces of Jammu and Kashmir by the Municipal authorities and in the rural areas by the Police Department. The village chowkidar regularly visits the thana or police chowki once, twice or four times a month, and more frequently, according to the distance of the village from the thana or the police chowki, and reports the births and deaths of his own village to the Police Officer, who in turn makes these entries in his register, which is the ultimate official record. The chowkidar, if literate—generally he is not—makes the entries in his book himself; otherwise he is supposed to get the information entered by any available literate person in the village, generally the village shopkeeper, school teacher, numberdar or patwari. The entries are then attested by the numberdar and taken to the thana for entry in the concerned register. Births and deaths are rarely missed. Not being conversant with the nature of diseases the chowkidar is apt to make mistakes regarding the cause of death. However, in the case of certain diseases like plague, small-pox, diarrhœas and dysentery, cholera (if prevalent in epidemic form), tuberculosis of the lung (if associated with typical symptoms of prolonged fever, cough and wasting), measles, puerperal deaths, still births, asthma, injuries, senility and probably pneumonia, his report is generally accurate. "Fevers" is a heading under which he can often hide his ignorance of the actual cause of death—and he is not to be blamed for that. In the localities where malaria is rampant, the main bulk of deaths caused by fevers is attributable to malaria, especially so when such deaths occur during the malarial season. This fact is demonstrated by the figures given in Table 5 which show a very high incidence of deaths on account of fevers in the Districts of Jammu, Kathua, Reasi, Udhampur, Mirpur and Muzaffarabad—all notorious as heavy endemic and epidemic foci of malaria.

The record of deaths due to tuberculosis of the lungs probably represents an underestimate as the disease is not easily recognisable by a layman. Perusal of the records shows deaths recorded as due to 'fever' and cough with a duration of over six months; such are most likely cases of tuberculosis of the lungs. Mistakes as to the cause of death, apart from the diseases mentioned above, are liable in the recording of the deaths of children and infants.

The object of stating at length the above facts is to show that the records of vital statistics cannot be considered inaccurate because of the original source from which they emanate though mistakes are apt to occur regarding the cause of death. The fact that a certain percentage of births and deaths may not be recorded cannot be ignored but for practical purposes the data are quite reliable.

The births and deaths for Kashmir Province inclusive of Srinagar city and those for Jammu Province inclusive of Jammu city are given annually for the decade in Table No. 1. The figures for Kashmir Province by districts are given in Table No. 2 (a) and those for districts of the Jammu Province in Table No. 2. From a perusal of these tables it will be evident that the number of births everywhere exceeds the number of deaths except in Kashmir Province in 1935. The following points are worth noting:—

(i) In Kashmir Province the year 1936 shows the least number of deaths (34,958) and the year 1935 the maximum number (47,467). By far the worst year is 1935 as the number of deaths has exceeded the births. This was almost certainly due to a heavy epidemic of cholera which raged throughout the Valley during the summer of that year, and was responsible for 4 449 deaths. But for this epidemic the death rate would have been appreciably lower. 1940 is easily the best year; the number of births is 55,902 and deaths 38,580, *i. e.*, an excess of 17,322 births over deaths. Except for a small outbreak of small-pox in Kashmir Valley, Muzaffarabad District and Astore, which was very easily controlled, the year was quite healthy. 1936 was next best with an excess of 14,667. The death rate was high in 1933. This was apparently due to small-pox and typhus epidemics the former causing 237 deaths. In 1937 an epidemic of malaria visited tehsils Muzaffarabad, Uri and Karnah, causing a large number of deaths. In the subsequent year (1938) the birth rate was low and the death rate high. The latter was partly attributable to another epidemic of cholera in the Valley resulting in 287 deaths. The lower birth rate in this year could partly be accounted for by the malaria epidemic in the previous year. Taken as a whole there was a definite excess of births over deaths in the decade.

(ii) The figures for Jammu Province present a much better out-look than those for Kashmir. In 1934 a bad epidemic of plague broke out; it was especially virulent in the Jammu District. The deaths from plague alone were 1,157. The decrease of births in this year can be explained by the fact that plague appears to show a special predilection for females of child bearing age. An attack of the disease generally destroys the fœtus and often the mother and a consequent reduction in the recorded number of live births during the year of the epidemic is bound to occur. Plague also visited the Jammu District in 1933 with 783 deaths (Table No. 4). The high rate in the year 1935 is attributable to an epidemic of malaria which occurred in the province especially in the districts of Rajouri, Kathua and Jammu. On the whole, the excess of births over deaths is greater in the Jammu Province than in the Kashmir Province; 1936 and 1938 are the best years, the preponderance of births over deaths being 24,907 and 25,012 respectively. In this connection it may be mentioned that after a fall in the birth rate in 1934 there was an appreciable rise in subsequent years. That is what usually happens after a severe plague epidemic. In the first succeeding year, owing to the reduction in the number of child bearing women, the birth rate is not quite normal but in the second subsequent year it reaches a normal level.

(iii) The figures for Ladakh District are self-explanatory. In 1931 the birth and death rates are 2,083 and 2,045 respectively—almost equal. In later years a slight excess in births is noticeable so that, after a decade, in 1940 the figures are 2,364 births and 2,043 deaths. The reasons for a low birth rate in this districf are:—

(a) The country is very mountainous and contains vast desert and treeless tracts at altitudes from 12,000 to 18,000 ft. above sea level.

(b) Rainfall is very scanty—the average is 5.7" and crops are poor.

(c) Only 0.3 per cent. of the area is fit for cultivation.

(d) The Small-pox epidemic in 1937 in Skardu Tehsil cost more than 1,000 lives before it could be brought under control.

(e) A virulent malaria epidemic which resulted in more than 500 deaths visited the district.

(f) Buddhists, who live in Ladakh Tehsil and parts of Kargil, are polyandrous; only one man in the family marries. The other brothers do not marry as there are not enough women to go round and they have not the means to support a wife and family.

(g) A fair number of the residents of Skardu and Kargil Tehsils migrate to Kashmir and the plains of British India before the onset of winter every year and a number of them do not return for considerable periods.

(2) EPIDEMICS AND IMPORTANT DISEASES.

A. Plague.—(i) The Punjab was infected with plague in 1898 and the Jammu and Kashmir State in 1901. The disease was wholly confined to the Jammu Province and especially to the Jammu District, which is in close proximity to the Sialkot District of the Punjab.

A perusal of Table No. 3 will show that the number of deaths during the four decades was 40,905. The same table will show that the number of deaths caused by plague in the State for each of the four decades was 23,840 in 1901-10, 9,134 in 1911-20, 5,251 in 1921-30 and 2,680 in 1931-40. For details of the decade 1931-40 reference may be made to Table No. 4. Within a period of 30 years, the death rate has fallen from 23,840 to 2,680. This is decidedly a big drop. In fact, during 1934 the number of deaths was 1,157, in 1935 it was 7, in 1936 it was 2 and in 1937 it was 1 only. Since then no case has been reported.

From the behaviour of the disease in the past, one may be permitted to conclude, pending further investigations, that plague exhibits a long term periodicity. During the actual plague epochs, the disease exhibits no well defined periodicity but tends to recur at intervals whose minimum duration is two years and whose maximum is variable.

(ii) The problem presented by the prevention of plague offers formidable difficulties. Although there has not been a single case of plague in the Jammu District, the endemic centre for plague in the State, since 1937, it would be very unwise to assert that epidemics will not recur again. No radical change in the habits and customs of the people can be expected in the near future whilst the rehousing of the population presents unsurmountable difficulties. Above all, not only is the rat almost a domestic animal living in the closest association with man but, by reason both of its number and its highly prolific reproductive capacity, no appreciable reduction of rat infestation can be expected in spite of all the efforts that are being made to destroy this pest.

Nevertheless, much can be done by measures designed to exclude rats permanently from the habitations of man by prompt evacuation of houses upon the appearance of rat plague, by inoculation of contacts, by rat proofing of grain-stores and, last but not least, by carrying out intensive rat destruction during the "off-season" in endemic foci with the object of reducing the number of centres whence infection will be disseminated during the next plague season and thus hastening the arrival of the time when the "immunity" factor will exceed the "infection" factor, and plagne, both in man and rat, will spontaneously disappear.

An anti-plague-scheme, based upon lines somewhat similar to those outlined above, was started in May 1934, the worst plague year in the decade, in the Jammu Province and was operating till June 1939, a period of five years, at a cost of about Rs. 1,69,500 to the Government.

B. Cholera.—The Kashmir Valley has always had epidemics of cholera. The disease is not endemic here but, once cases are imported into the valley, it spreads like wild fire, especially because of the innumerable waterways traversing the length and breadth of the valley. The record of the past five decades has been given in Table No. 3. The number of deaths in the decade 1891-1900 is 21,712; in 1901-1910, 17,118; in 1911-20, 18,064; in 1921-30, 19,857 and in the decade 1931-40 it has fallen to the lowest level in 50 years, *viz.*, 5,582. As in the case of plague, this indicates an achievement worthy of praise. There was an epidemic in the summer of 1935 with 4,449 deaths in the valley but the disease during this year was controlled with an efficiency that is unique in the medical history of the State. Mass anti-cholera inoculations were performed within a very short period. The total number of inoculations was 1,306,273 and this work was speedily carried out in every nook and corner of the valley. About Rs. 105,000 were spent on this work alone; the results were very satisfactory and only 4,449 deaths occurred. In the majority of cases a single dose of 1 c. c. was thought to be sufficient to confer immunity; it was not found practicable to give the customary two injections. It was a gigantic experiment in anti-cholera inoculation in the State and proved highly effective. During the last decade there were three minor epidemics, apart from the one discussed above, in 1931 (Kashmir), in 1938 (Jammu Province) and in 1938 (Kashmir); these were not of any great importance and were soon brought under control. The provision of a clean water supply has been undertaken in many parts of the State in this decade and this has proved a great help in lowering the incidence of cholera. Tables No. 3 and No. 5 give the number of deaths from cholera in this decade. The number of deaths for each year of the decade is not available.

C. Small-pox.—Kashmir Province and the Frontier Districts are the worst sufferers from this disease as is shown in Table 5. The total number of deaths for the last three decades is shown in Table 3 and is as follows:—

In 1911-20, 16,405; in 1921-30, 15,546 and in 1931-40, 13,135 deaths. There has been a decided decrease in the number of deaths during the course of the last 30 years though this decrease is small and not as satisfactory as it ought to have been, especially when the highly effective weapon of vaccination is in our hands. The reasons which might account for this are:—

(i) A spirit of apathy and evasion towards vaccination prevailed among a section of the population. Even in places like Jammu and Srinagar where vaccination is compulsory, parents manage somehow to evade vaccination. The Health Officer, Jammu has observed that some children even upto the age of 12-15 are not vaccinated.

(ii) The geography of the country makes vaccinating campaigns in the mofussil difficult. The area is extensive and mountainous; villages are scattered and their population spread about at considerable distances; vaccinators can only go out once or twice a year and, if a child is somehow missed in that particular year, its vaccination will be postponed till the subsequent year. To make matters worse, weather conditions are frequently adverse and the access of the vaccinators to distant and isolated places becomes more difficult on account of rain or snow. Many places are only accessible to the vaccination staff during the six months of the summer. The Frontier Districts of Ladakh and Astore, and the Tehsils Kishtwar, Ramban and Reasi suffer particularly due to adverse geographical and weather conditions.

For the decade under review, the annual death figures for each year are not available. Yet the following resume of the small-pox epidemics will give an insight into the state of affairs. The years 1931 and 1932 were uneventful. In 1933 there was an epidemic in the Kashmir Province, resulting in 237 deaths. In 1934 an epidemic broke out in the Ladakh and Gilgit Districts with 56 and 220 deaths respectively; in 1935 there was another epidemic in the Hunza and Nagar illaqas of the Gilgit Agency; 1936 saw another epidemic in the Kashmir Province with 241 deaths; in 1937 Ladakh District was very seriously affected by a virulent small-pox epidemic resulting in more than 1,000 deaths. Many of the deaths had already occurred before medical aid could come to the rescue and control the spread of the disease. Here, as has been stated above, the climatic and geographical conditions of the district were greatly responsible for thwarting preventive efforts. In the same year a smaller epidemic broke out in the Mirpur District of the Jammu Province with 65 deaths. In 1940 an epidemic threatened the Kashmir Province, particularly Muzaffarabad District, but measures were speedily adopted and the disease was brought under control.

Table No. 8 represents the number of vaccinations, both primary and re-vaccinations, performed in the State during the decade under review. It will be seen that in 1933 primary vaccinations reached the high figure of 137,198 as compared to 74,789 in 1931 on account of the small-pox epidemic in Kashmir. In 1937 the number of vaccinations again went as high as 136,006 as this was an epidemic year. The Vaccination Department were alarmed by this epidemic and redoubled their efforts as is evident from the very large number of subsequent vaccinations, the best year being 1939 with 167,609 primary operations and 127,271 re-vaccinations. In 1940, 140,877 primary vaccinations and 58,363 re-vaccinations were performed. On the whole the progress of vaccination has been maintained and it is hoped that the small-pox scourge will dwindle to a minimum and the consequent deaths, disfigurement and blindness will be eliminated. There is no doubt that already much has been accomplished in this connection.

D. Fevers.—Table No. 5 gives the total number of deaths due to fevers of all kinds in the State for the decade 1931-40 as 209,825. The population of the Jammu District according to the 1931 Census was 336,766 and the number of deaths totals 45,466. The deaths per year in this district are as follows:—

Year.		District.	No. of deaths.
1931	..	.. Jammu	4,871
1932	..	.. ,,	4,943
1933	..	.. ,,	4.944
1934	..	.. ,,	6,013
1935	..	.. ,,	4.547
1936	..	.. ,,	3,840
1937	..	.. ,,	4,043
1938	..	.. ,,	4,236
1939	..	.. ,,	3 986
1940	..	.. ,,	4,043
		Total ..	45,466

From a perusal of these figures, it is clear that the average number of deaths in a year comes to 13.47 per 1,000. It will be seen that the number of deaths was high in 1934 (6,013); during this year the incidence of plague was large. Reasi comes next with a total of 30,829 deaths and then follows Kathua District (30,717).

Before discussing the incidence of fevers during the decade, certain facts are to be borne in mind.

(i) As pointed out in the beginning, the death reporter (Village Chowkidar) is apt to conceal his ignorance of the actual cause of death in the simple word 'fever', in Hindustani 'Bukhar'. In malaria infected localities like Ranbirsinghpura, Kathua, Rajouri, Bhimber, Muzaffarabad, Uri, Ramnagar, Udhampur and Ramban, all endemic foci of malaria, deaths from fevers, in the majority of cases, are attributable to malaria, especially when such deaths are reported during the malarial season and also during its aftermath.

(ii) Other diseases like enteric fever, malta fever, seven day fever, influenza, tuberculosis and pneumonia, to which the relatives or the Chowkidar are unable to affix a name, will all conveniently be placed under the one single heading of "Fever".

(iii) (a) In the Kashmir Valley, where malaria is non-existent, the incidence of fevers, due to typhoid, para-typhoid and the dysentery group is fairly high on account of bad sanitary conditions.

(b) Malta fever appears to be quite common in Kashmir but it is very seldom that this disease is properly diagnosed in the valley, much less so in other parts of the State, because of want of facilities for diagnosis. This disease is often mistaken for enteric fever.

(c) Acute rheumatic fever is commonly met with in the valley, frequently resulting in a damaged heart, and this may be the reason for finding so many cases of heart disease in Kashmir. This is also included under the head of 'Fever'.

(d) Tuberculosis which is prevalent in Kashmir may be classed as 'Fever'.

(e) Typhus, outbreaks of which are frequently met with in Kashmir, is sometimes included under 'Fever'.

(iv) Acute tonsilitis, other streptococcal infections and pyrexias, where diagnosis may not be established, are usually labelled as 'Fever'.

In view of the above, it is not surprising that deaths on account of 'Fevers' are extraordinarily high. All considered, the fact remains that fevers are taking a heavy toll of life.

With regard to malaria nothing substantial has been done so far. Cases of malaria have been found in places like Skardu, Kishtwar, Padar and Bhadrawah even though the altitude is high. It is also quite common in Ramban, Udhampur, Reasi, Mirpur and Poonch. There were epidemics of malaria in the Jammu Province during the years 1932, 1935 and 1936 and in 1937 in the Kashmir Province in tehsils Muzaffarabad, Uri and Karnah. In 1938-39 malaria was again prevalent in Skardu Tehsil. But apart from these exacerbations, which come off and on, the seasonal prevalence in all the endemic foci of the disease is well known. The Government spends large sums of money annually on purchase of quinine which is freely distributed to people throughout the State. Beyond that measure, nothing else has been done which could technically be termed a preventive measure for control of malaria on a big and scientific basis. It is hoped the next decade will be more fortunate in this respect.

E. Typhoid and Para-typhoid.—Typhoid and Para-typhoid fevers commonly occur throughout the State. Attempts are on foot to give the people pure water to drink and general sanitation is being improved but in this field, although a lot has been done, much remains to be accomplished.

F. Typhus.—Typhus may conveniently be placed amongst 'fevers' and in village returns it is usually placed in that category. It is only when it appears in the form of an epidemic that it attracts notice. During the decade under review, typhus was responsible for 465 deaths out of which 457 occurred in Baramulla District, 7 in Muzaffarabad District and one in Astore; this appears to be an underestimate. In 1931 it broke out in an epidemic form in Gilgit and in 1933 in the Kashmir Valley; again in 1936 in Bandipur with 17 deaths. In 1937 it was prevalent in an epidemic form in the districts of Baramulla and Anantnag.

G. Tuberculosis of the Lungs.—Table 9, compiled from the returns of all the hospitals and dispensaries in the State, indicates the incidence of cases.

Table 5 shows that the number of deaths during the decade was 15,300. Anantnag District is by far the worst with 5,317 deaths, with an average of 531.7 deaths per year or a rate of 0.54 per 1,000. Srinagar City is badly affected with a death rate of about 1.65 per 1,000 per annum. Similarly, Udhampur and Jammu Districts are bad. On going through the records of Jammu District, it transpired that the Jammu Tehsil and Ranbirsinghpura Tehsil recorded many more deaths from tuberculosis than Samba or Akhnoor. In any case Kashmir is far worse in this respect than Jammu.

The Anti-tuberculosis Campaign was started in 1929 with the patronage extended by His Late Majesty King George V and the grant of a considerable sum of money from Their Majesties' Jubilee Fund and by the generosity of His Highness' Government. Owing to the personal interest taken by the Ruler of the State considerable progress has been made in the expansion of this work.

The Tuberculosis Department is under a specialist. There are five institutions at present—two Tuberculosis dispensaries, one each in Srinagar and in Jammu, one sanatorium at Tangmarg and two hospitals for advanced cases, one in Jammu and the other at Srinagar. In addition to the above there is also a small sanatorium at Batote.

Tangmarg Sanatorium can accommodate 100 beds and is equipped with an X-Ray plant; up-to-date treatment is being carried out there. The average annual expenditure for upkeep is between Rs. 50,000 and Rs. 60,000.

In spite of all these laudable efforts tuberculosis appears to be on the increase. This may be due either to the actual increase of the disease or to the fact that cases are being added which hitherto remained unindentified and are now coming to light with the help of better methods of diagnosis.

With an up-to-date Tuberculosis Department as a separate unit, striving hard to fight the disease, there is every prospect that the incidence of tuberculosis will now decline.

Other tubercular diseases, such as tuberculosis of the glands, bones, and joints, abdominal tuberculosis and tuberculosis of the skin are also quite common. The number of cases recorded at various dispensaries has been shown in Table 9. It will be seen that the incidence is on the increase in both provinces.

H. Pneumonias.—The figures for deaths in the decade are available only for Jammu and Srinagar Cities and for Jammu and Mirpur Districts. Jammu District shows a large number of deaths as compared with Mirpur. The incidence of cases in both provinces shows a slow rise during the last four years of the decade. The total number of deaths recorded in the Jammu District is 10,438 as is shown in Table 6.

I. Maternal Mortality.—The figures for maternal deaths in the decade are available only for Jammu and Srinagar Cities and for Jammu District; they are given in Table 6. It has been observed from the figures for the Jammu District that these deaths are not so common in that area as in the urban areas of Jammu and Srinagar. In Srinagar the average death rate is 17.6 per thousand of births. In Jammu City it is about 16·9 per 1,000. The maternal mortality rate in Jammu District is about 2 per thousand live births. This appears to be somewhat underestimated. Women welfare Centres at Jammu and Srinagar are doing very useful work in this connection. In these centres expectant mothers are advised in matters concerning mother-craft and care of babies by a Lady Doctor and a Health Visitor. The mothers and babies attend centres where ante-natal and post-natal instructions are given. The Health Visitor also visits women in their houses and instructs them. She also attends to confinements wherever necessary, free of charge. The centres also train women as 'Dais' who, after completion of their training, are examined by a board and, if declared successful, are granted a license to conduct normal cases of labour.

J. Infantile Mortality.—(Table 6). The death of infants below one year seems to be quite common in rural as well as urban areas, particularly the latter. It is note-worthy that infant mortality has steadily increased in the decade, so much so that in 1940 the figures for Srinagar City were as high as 1,358, a rate of 195.6 per thousand live births. In Jammu District the average death rate per thousand births was about 10 which appears to be an underestimate.

Frequency of pregnancy has a very direct bearing on maternal and infantile mortality. Early marriage followed by early consummation, and in consequence by early maternity, leads to high infant and maternal mortality. Even if the mother is lucky to escape death, she often in such cases suffers from chronic ill-health, invalidism and allied troubles. Repeated pregnancies occurring at very short intervals are liable to prove a source of many ailments like anæmia, tuberculosis, etc. The remedy lies in aiming at fewer and better babies, reduction in the incidence of immature maternity and general improvement in the standard of living and social conditions.

The causes of infantile mortality are infantile debility, respiratory diseases, convulsions, diarrhoea and dysentery.

K. Injuries.—The number of deaths due to injuries during the decade was 3,572. This includes accidental deaths of all kinds in the way of drowning, falls, murders, snake bites, suicides, burns etc. In rural areas drowning in wells, ponds and rivers is quite common. Snake bites are quite common in Jammu Province, especially in the districts of Jammu, Mirpur and Kathua. For instance, in the former the number of deaths from snake bites was 122. Taken as a whole, the incidence of deaths by injuries is not at all high. Table 5 gives details of all the districts.

L. Diseases of the digestive system.—(Table 9). With a view to gauge the extent of digestive diseases in the State figures for cases of dyspepsia were collected from the returns of all the dispensaries. It is interesting to note that Kashmir Province, and especially the Kashmir Valley, is responsible for a large number of such cases. It will be seen that the number of such cases who attended the hospitals was in no year less than 45,000. There was a progressive increase in numbers from the year 1932 to 1937; since the latter year the figure has gone down very slightly but it has not gone down below 50,000.

Jammu Province has a low incidence yet it is surprising to note that in 1939 the number of cases went up to above 60,000; fortunately numbers declined again to just above 41,000 in the following year.

The factors conducive to dyspepsia may be summarised as below:—

(a) Diet.—The people in Kashmir Valley live on rice which is now largely polished and which has a low vitamin content. Raw green vegetables are sparingly taken or none at all. Fruits are seldom if ever taken. The consumption of milk and its products is an exception rather than a rule. Very small quantities of milk are taken with salted tea which is a decoction of green tea-leaves and is the universal beverage of the people.

(b) The big rice meals to which they are accustomed lead to a dilated stomach and ultimately to dyspepsia.

(c) Bad oral hygiene.

M. Helminthiasis.—Ascaris infestation is almost universal in Kashmir. This is generally due to bad sanitation and improper disposal of human excreta. Fresh night soil is used as a manure and is sold as such by the Srinagar Municipality to cultivators who use it in vegetable gardens. Tape-worm infestation is rather uncommon.

N. Ankylostomiasis.—Ankylostomiasis is often seen in Jammu Province. During the decade 1,092 stools, suspected to contain the ova of Ankylostoma, were examined in the Chemical Laboratory Jammu out of which 234 were positive.

In areas of the Jammu Province where there is a scarcity of water, and people are obliged to drink water from tanks and ponds, Guinea-worm is quite common.

O. Leprosy.—(Table 9). In India it has been found that there is strikingly close relationship between rainfall and humidity and Leprosy incidence. The relatively high Indian Leprosy rates of 0.5 to 1 or more per mille are met with in the wet areas of Assam, Bengal, Orissa, Eastern

Central Provinces, the Himalayas, and the very wet east coast of India, the last area extending up into Deccan and Berar. On the other hand, rates of under 0.15 per mille are met with in the very dry, hot N. W. Punjab, Rajputana, Sind and in central Madras.

The explanation of these facts, suggested by Rogers, is that dry heat is inimical to the survival of lepra bacillus outside the body whilst moist heat would favour this and also may act through the numerous insects' bites in hot humid climates producing minute lesions of the surface epithelium, affording entrance to just those layers of the dermal tissues where the Lepra bacillus flourishes best.

The incidence of leprosy in the State is as follows:—

During the years 1931 and 1938 the number of leprosy cases in Kashmir exceeded 500 per year; in 1932 it was about 800 and in the years 1933, 1936 and 1940 it exceeded 300 in each year. Obviously, the population of lepers is far more in Kashmir than in Jammu where the maximum figure was below two hundred in 1933. The figures have been taken from the annual returns of cases of leprosy who attended the dispensaries for treatment.

The accuracy of the above figures is disputable unless a proper census is taken of the number of lepers residing in the State. An investigation into the various factors which are instrumental in the spread of the disease is desirable and is going to be taken up.

(3) Venereal Diseases.

Table 9 gives the number of cases of syphilis and gonorrhoea which attended the dispensaries of the State for treatment. Only a very small percentage of these cases appear to have been diagnosed by proper laboratory methods; the diagnosis in the majority of these cases is almost entirely symptomatic. The total number of Kahn's Serological Tests performed in the Chemical Laboratory Jammu during the decade is 1,554 out of which 782 were found positive for syphilis. It would appear that the incidence of gonorrhoea is comparatively much lower than that of syphilis.

The Government has three Venereal Dispensaries operating in Ramnagar Tehsil where it is feared that the incidence of Venereal diseases has been rather high. The first such dispensary was started in 1929 and work has been going on ever since. By comparing the population figures of Ramnagar Tehsil an excess of 4,410 has been found in the present Census; the actual population in 1931 was 55,666 and that for 1941 60,076. This shows that the anti-venereal treatment has proved its efficacy in this area. The dispensaries were placed in this area because of the fact that the population was believed to have declined on account of the prevalence of these diseases. An intensive campaign in the affected areas is under contemplation.

(4) Dietetics.

As stated elsewhere Kashmir is a rice growing province and rice is thus the staple food in the valley. In the hilly areas, maize appears to be the chief article of diet. Rice is taken with green vegetables fried in small quantities of oil. Meat and eggs are very seldom taken and the same is the case with fruit and milk. In Jammu Province the staple food is barley, wheat or maize; rice is taken by a section of the population which appears to be very small. Rice is grown in Ranbirsinghpura Tehsil and there forms the main portion of the diet. It appears that the dietary standard is comparatively higher in Jammu than in Kashmir.

Proteins, fats, fruits, green vegetables and vitamins appear very sparingly in the dietary of the people of the State. It is only the well-to-do, a very small percentage of the population, who can afford, perhaps, to take a balanced diet. The poor cannot for want of means.

To get an insight into the state of nutrition of the people, figures have been collected for dental caries from the returns of the dispensaries. There is a steady rise in the number of cases of dental caries every year.

Rickets and Osteomalacia (in women) are often met within the Kashmir Valley. The frequency with which Caesarian sections are performed on pregnant women in Kashmir is well known; this is due to rickety pelvis and osteomalacia. It is indirectly responsible for the increase in the number of maternal and infantile deaths.

Pellagra is also met with in certain parts of Kashmir. True Beri Beri does not appear to exist in Kashmir although milled and polished rice is the staple food in urban areas. Yet it is a fact that manifestations of partial avitaminosis (Vitamin B) are often observed. The years 1933 and 1940 show quite a high incidence of a scurvy like condition. During winter in Kashmir fruits and vegetables containing vitamin are unobtainable.

(5) General Sanitation.

It is safe to assert that sanitation has greatly improved during this decade as compared to former decades. Apart from Jammu and Srinagar Municipalities, there are now 25 Town Area Committees; they are located at all District headquarters, important Tehsil headquarters and certain hill stations. This has improved the sanitation of these places. Pure water supply, paving of lanes and streets, laying of proper drains, general cleanliness of the area, improvement of housing, proper disposal of refuse and excreta and sanitary control of articles of food, are the main headings under which improvements have been effected. The details of sanitary work done in the rural areas by the Rural Development Department during the decade have been given in Table 7.

(6) Birth Control.

Despite the illiteracy and ignorance of the masses in the State, it may be permissible to observe that families with a high fertility rate do resent the increased number of children of their families especially when means are lacking to feed so many mouths. Mothers particularly in such cases often seek advice to help them to postpone the arrival of another baby for a considerable period. To achieve this they try all sorts of quack remedies. Prolonged lactation, which in a certain number of cases does help, is often resorted to. A belief, although unfounded, that there may be a "safe period" when the chances of conception are negligible, does exist in the minds of these people.

At the same time educated people do often resort to methods of birth control which, practised in a half hearted and unscientific manner, are often associated with failure. It is, therefore, quite correct to say that birth control methods, which could seriously affect the population figures, are not practised by the people in this country.

(7) Conclusions.

(i) The manner in which vital statistics are collected, if not ideal, is not wholly unsatisfactory.

(ii) Births show a clear preponderance over deaths in the decade despite the various epidemics, diseases and several adverse economic factors.

(iii) The decade has been, on the whole, exceptionally fortunate regarding epidemics. A comparison with past decades reveals a great decline in the number of deaths from plague and cholera and to a smaller extent from small-pox. In fact, plague has been non-existent since 1937. The control of the cholera epidemic in 1935 was a unique instance of what preventive medicine can accomplish. Much has been done to decrease small-pox. Efforts to overcome diseases in general have gone on steadily and have met with a considerable amount of success.

(iv) Malaria is still prevalent and epidemics of this disease occur frequently. A survey has been recently made by experts and preventive measures are being worked out.

(v) Tuberculosis, although still on the increase, is being tackled with ever increasing zeal. With an improvement in the social and economic conditions of the people the present efforts will bring greater success in the control of this disease.

(vi) Infantile mortality and maternal deaths are still on the increase. The state of affairs might have been worse but for the preventive measures adopted.

(vii) Leprosy is still rife in certain areas. A survey is going to be undertaken and preventive measures worked out.

(viii) The venereal dispensaries have done very useful work in fighting the venereal diseases. A campaign on a large scale against venereal diseases in affected areas is under contemplation.

(ix) The question of nutrition and dietetics is not one which can easily be solved unless the economic condition of the population as a whole is improved. The public should be educated in a manner that will bring home to them the principles and advantages of a balanced diet and a hygienic mode of living. The starting of a schcol of medical services is advised. A nutrition survey of the State is being contemplated.

(x) Much has been achieved in the direction of improvement of sanitation in general and the rate at which both rural and urban areas are progressing in this direction augurs well for the future of this country.

(xi) It is not out of place to mention that the construction of two new big modern hospitals, one in Jammu and the other in Srinagar is a matter of great satisfaction ; in the near future they will serve as important centres of healing for the suffering humanity of the State.

TABLE No. I

Vital Statistics, Jammu & Kashmir State

Year		Jammu Province		Kashmir Province	
		Births	Deaths	Births	Deaths
1931	..	40202	25077	46847	35430
1932	..	40615	27311	44944	35324
1933	..	46155	33045	43092	35648
1934	..	40053	31404	46533	36392
1935	..	45401	34206	46650	47467
1936	..	51846	26939	49625	34958
1937	..	50103	30042	51330	42552
1938	..	49127	24115	46509	43220
1939	..	46708	31620	43716	36875
1940	..	49070	30772	55902	38580
Total	..	**459280**	**294531**	**475148**	**386446**

TABLE No. 2

VITAL STATISTICS BY DISTRICTS OF THE JAMMU PROVINCE

Year.		Jammu District		Mirpur District		Kathua District		Reasi District		Udhampur District		Jammu City	
		Births	Deaths	Births	Deaths	Births	Deaths	Births	Deaths	Births	Deaths	Births	Deaths
1931	..	9450	7322	8451	5226	6342	4209	6422	3251	8325	4201	1212	868
1932	..	9726	8452	8321	5263	6321	4368	6466	2997	8625	5359	1156	872
1933	..	12322	10398	9976	6222	7342	5371	6851	3221	8464	6932	1200	901
1934	..	11209	9352	9799	6642	4426	4965	7212	3092	6201	6364	1206	989
1935	..	13251	9992	10452	6841	5322	5022	6231	3490	8711	7965	1434	896
1936	..	14381	7372	11928	5791	6632	3968	6872	4225	10496	4840	1537	743
1937	..	13739	7288	10255	6984	6627	4274	7979	4774	9809	5989	1694	733
1938	..	13691	6626	9998	5922	6502	3209	7681	3594	9615	3885	1640	879
1939	..	12631	9388	9996	6891	6502	4377	7591	4699	8360	5467	1628	798
1940	..	13334	9356	10252	6909	6961	4225	7525	4007	9256	5501	1742	774
Total	..	**123734**	**85546**	**99428**	**62691**	**62977**	**43988**	**70830**	**37350**	**87862**	**56503**	**14449**	**8453**

TABLE No. 2 (*a*)

Vital Statistics by Districts of the Kashmir Province and Ladakh

Year		Anantnag District		Baramulla District		Muzaffarabad District		Srinagar City		Ladakh District		Total	
		Births	Deaths	Births	Deaths	Births	Deaths	Births	Deaths	Births	Deaths	Births	Deaths
1931	..	17979	14331	15006	11492	7318	4564	4461	2998	2083	2045	46847	35430
1932	..	18200	13936	14821	12208	5419	4414	3996	2603	2508	2163	44944	35324
1933	..	16828	14053	13224	10184	5353	4013	5262	5044	2425	2354	43092	35648
1934	..	21583	17076	10735	8433	5545	4531	6476	4235	2194	2117	46533	36392
1935	..	20553	24394	10902	10510	5653	5131	6674	4662	2868	2770	46650	47467
1936	..	22852	16847	11826	7610	5912	4147	6230	4041	2805	2313	49625	34958
1937	..	24793	20563	11974	9248	5224	5030	6024	4281	3315	3430	51330	42552
1938	..	20161	19186	12196	10519	5157	5608	5693	4674	3302	3233	46509	43220
1939	..	18987	14587	11352	10030	4259	5233	5923	4174	3195	2851	43716	36875
1940	..	26714	17776	13700	9498	6184	4473	6940	4790	2364	2043	55902	38580
										Grand Total	..	**475148**	**386446**

Note.—The total number of still-births recorded for the decade for Anantnag, Baramulla and Muzaffarabad Districts is 3621.

TABLE No. 3

STATEMENT SHOWING THE NUMBER OF DEATHS IN THE JAMMU AND KASHMIR STATE FROM CHOLERA, SMALL-POX AND PLAGUE FOR THE FIVE DECADES FROM 1891 TO 1940

Disease.	1891-1900.	1901-1910	1911-1920	1921-1930	1931-1940
Cholera	21712	17118	18064	19857	5582
Small-pox	Records not available	Records not available	16405	15546	13135
Plague	Do.	do. 23840	9134	5251	2680

NOTE.—(a) Cholera. Mostly in the Kashmir Province.
(b) Small-pox. Major number of deaths in the Kashmir Province.
(c) Plague. Almost wholly confined to the Jammu Province, particularly to the Jammu District, which forms an endemic area of this disease.

TABLE No 4

Plague deaths in the Jammu and Kashmir State during the decade 1931-40 shown by years

Year			Jammu District	Jammu City	Kathua	Mirpur	Reasi	Anantnag	Baramulla	Srinagar	Total
1931	..	..	227	6							233
1932	..	..	466	31							497
1933	..	..	751	30	2						783
1934	..	..	1020	118	5			14			1157
1935	..	..	7								7
1936	..	..	2								2
1937	..	..	1								1
1938	..	..									
1939	..	..									
1940	..	..									
Total	..	..	**2474**	**185**	**7**			**14**			**2680**

TABLE No. 5

DEATHS FROM PRINCIPAL DISEASES IN THE JAMMU & KASHMIR STATE DURING THE DECADE 1931-1940

District	Cholera	Small-pox	Plague	Fevers	Tuberculosis	Injuries
Jammu District	290	1661	2474	45466	1885	640
Jammu City	21	156	185	1492	650	250
Mirpur District	7	1243	Nil	18563	355	56
Kathua District	188	420	7	30717	549	166
Reasi District	Nil	500	Nil	30829	461	859
Udhampur District	569	1037	Nil	25277	2121	507
Srinagar City	157	1550	Nil	12513	2898	380
Anantnag District	2849	3331	14	20664	5317	416
Baramulla District	1511	977	Nil	4793	683	188
Muzaffarabad District	Nil	924	Nil	16200	250	35
Astore District	Nil	280	Nil	1526	6	25
Ladakh District	Nil	1056	Nil	1785	125	50
Total ..	**5582**	**13135**	**2680**	**209825**	**15300**	**3572**

TABLE No. 6

DEATHS FROM SOME OF THE PRINCIPAL CAUSES TAKEN AS A SAMPLE FOR THE DECADE 1931-40 IN THE JAMMU DISTRICT, JAMMU CITY, SRINAGAR CITY AND MIRPUR DISTRICT

	Infant Mortality	Maternal Deaths	Pneumonias	Measles
Jammu City	2156	245	1285	190
Srinagar City	8487	951	5307 ..	41
Jammu District	1222	229	10438	585
Mirpur District	Not available	Not available	1650 ..	Not available
Total	**11865**	**1425**	**18680** ..	**816**

TABLE No. 7

SANITARY IMPROVEMENT WORK IN RURAL AREAS IN JAMMU AND KASHMIR STATE DURING THE LAST DECADE

Nature of Improvement	Works executed.	No.
1. Water Supply	Construction and improvement of wells	100
	Construction and improvement of ponds, springs and tanks etc.	200
	Construction of reservoirs	7
2. Pavements and drainage	Constructions, repairs and pavement of roads	75
	Constructions and repairs of lanes	30
	Constructions and repairs of ghats, bunds, etc.	38
	Construction of culverts	298
	Construction and repairs to drains	21
	Construction and repairs to bridges	5
3. Disposal of Excreta	Construction and repairs of bathing places	94
	Construction and repairs of latrines	116
	Dung pits constructed	3846
4. Housing improvement	Improvement of houses such as ventilations, white washing and draining etc.	3746
5. Medical aid	Medical aid rendered such as first aid dressing, distribution ot quinine etc.	243286 persons.

TABLE No. 8

Total Number of Vaccinations in the Jammu and Kashmir State by years

Year	Primary Vaccinations	Re-vaccinations
1931	74789	9722
1932	117410	16537
1933	137198	67218
1934	118955	36506
1935	104498	28505
1936	118537	54420
1937	136006	46270
1938	134165	77644
1939	167609	127271
1940	140877	58363

TABLE No. 9

Incidence of Diseases in both the Provinces

Year	Dyspepsia		Cholera		Dental Caries	
	Jammu	Kashmir	Jammu	Kashmir	Jammu	Kashmir
1931	27700	45200	6	290	550	690
1932	25425	53200	37	7	460	1350
1933	27540	45000	30	Nil	325	1580
1934	27700	49025	Nil	Nil	1725	4225
1935	29540	53050	71	10868	2525	5210
1936	30000	56005	125	Nil	2530	5900
1937	32520	59006	Nil	Nil	850	6425
1938	35820	55021	37	678	3180	9185
1939	65000	56042	Nil	1	1470	6580
1940	41540	52005	67	17	6650	6726

TABLE No. 9—CONTD

Year	Gonorrhoea		Syphilis		Leprosy		T. B. Lungs		Other T. B. Diseases	
	Kashmir	Jammu	Kashmir	Jammu	Kashmir	Jammu	Kashmir	Jammu	Kashmir	Jammu
1931	3325	2595	6812	7050	519	145	1552	581	810	672
1932	2758	2226	6425	4325	798	98	842	421	976	638
1933	3472	2453	7060	6925	386	192	1109	533	101	590
1934	3151	1227	8212	2927	210	56	665	522	565	685
1935	3525	2180	8660	5860	335	105	2872	518	660	685
1936	4112	2754	5550	5890	325	168	845	615	885	656
1937	3980	3225	5960	5792	78	135	1082	1082	1005	716
1938	3476	3090	5676	4280	525	108	1995	748	785	715
1939	3250	3176	5526	5112	98	162	1638	905	822	812
1940	2790	3480	4091	6982	342	115	1588	940	855	856

Census of India 1941

VOL. XXII

JAMMU AND KASHMIR

Part II

TABLES.

IMPERIAL TABLE I AND ITS SUBSIDIARIES.

Area, Houses and Population.

NOTES.

1. The area of the State and its districts remains the same as in 1931 except that the Gilgit District shown in 1931 with an area of 3112 sq. miles has been split into the two districts Astore and Gilgit (Leased Area); the joint area of these is the same as that shown for Gilgit in 1931.

2. (a) The districts Baramulla and Anantnag correspond to the districts designated "Baramulla District (including Langet) or Kashmir North" and "Srinagar District (including City) or Kashmir South" respectively in the 1931 tables. There is no change in the area of either.

(b) The Jammu District includes Jammy City and the Anantnag District includes Srinagar City.

(c) In 1931 the district now designated Gilgit Agency was shown as 'Frontier Illaqas'; there is no change in boundaries or area.

3. The Natural Divisions given in Subsidiary Table III and elsewhere in the tables comprise exactly the same areas as in 1931; the administrative units forming each such division are given in Subsidiary Table IV.

4. The population of the three villages of Karloop, Raipur and Kothar, together constituting the Karloop Jagir which is under the administration of the Pconch Jagir, was included with the population of the Jammu District in 1921 and 1931. On this occasion the population of the villages Karloop and Raipur, together totalling 876, has been included in the population of the Jammu Tehsil of the Jammu District and of village Kothar, totalling 992, in the Ramnagar Tehsil of the Udhampur District because the villages mentioned are actually located in the Tehsils and districts named.

5. The population of cantonments, shown separately in Imperial Tables III, IV and V, is included in the districts within which they are situated. Included in the figures for the Jammu Cantonment are those members of the State forces who at the time of the census were serving overseas; they totalled 320. Troops belonging to the State Military Forces serving in British India at the time of the census were enumerated in the areas in which they were stationed at the time of the census and are not included in the figures for Jammu and Kashmir. They numbered 1520.

6. The population of tehsils, which together make up the population of the districts shown in this table, is given separately in State Table I which follows Imperial Table XVI. The population of the villages in each tehsil is given separately in Part III of the report the title of which is 'Village Tables and Housing Statistics'. Part III has been published for local issue only.

7. For the purpose of the census in British India a 'Town' means every municipality, cantonment or continuous collection of houses which has urban characteristics or which is rich in historic association or constitutes an important trade centre with a population of more than 5000 persons. In these tables we have followed past practice in the State and have shown a number of places as towns with a population of less than 5000 and in some cases lacking urban characteristics. The places so included, which do not comply with the usual standard, have local historic associations or importance. There is only one change in the list of towns compared with 1931. Gilgit Cantonment has ceased to exist. Nowshera Cantonment has been created since 1931.

8. A 'village' for the purpose of these tables is a well recognised area with definite boundaries for revenue assessment purposes. Hamlets have not been treated as separate villages; they are included with the village within the area of which they are situated. The number of villages shown in the table is 8740 against 8903 shown in the corresponding table for 1931. Some villages shown in

1931 have ceased to exist altogether ; others shown separately in 1931 have ceased to exist as separate villages. A ' House ' for the purpose of these tables is any building, boat, tent, cave etc., in which any person or persons were found at the time of the census to reside alone or with others as a separate commensal unit.

10. On the basis of the classification of towns adopted for this table and in Imperial Tables III, IV and V the urban/rural ratio is 11.49 : 100 but if the standard definition be adopted *viz.*, places with a population exceeding 5000, the ratio works out at 8.82 : 100.

11. The figures for rainfall given in column 8 of Subsidiary Table I are for 1940 and represent the averages calculated from the figures available for the different stations in each district as supplied by the Meteorological Reporter to His Highness' Government. In a country with such diverse conditions in parts of every district such figures can at best only be approximate for any particular district as a whole.

12. The figures given in Subsidiary Table I are all based on data supplied by the Revenue Department of His Highness' Government except in the case of density and rainfall.

13. The figures given in Subsidiary I for ' Net cultivated ' area represent the gross cultivated area less the double cropped area ; fallows are not included. The ' gross cultivated ' area is represented by the ' net cultivated ' area plus the double cropped area. For the purpose of this table ' cultivable area ' is the area in any district deemed to be fit and available for cultivation.

14. Column 21 of Subsidiary I represents the balance of the area under crops not covered by columns 9 to 20. ' Kharaaba ' means the area under crops not maturing or harvested. This column also covers crops for which details are lacking or not covered by column 14.

15. (a) For Subsidiary II the tehsil was taken as the unit. The density per square mile having been calculated for each tehsil in each ' Natural Division ', the tehsils were classified according to the groups shown in the table and the collective area in square miles and the collective population (000 omitted) of each density group calculated.

The percentage figures show the ratio that the area and population to which they refer bear to the total area and population respectively of each Natural Division.

(b) There are no tehsils in the State with a density exceeding 750 persons per square mile.

16. (a) Subsidiary III shows the number of persons per 1000 houses and the number of houses per 100 square miles whereas the corresponding subsidiary table in 1931 shows the number of persons per house and the number of houses per square mile. The figures relating to previous censuses have been adjusted accordingly.

(b) The figures for 1901 are incomplete. Where blanks are shown it indicates that correct figures are not available.

17. The figures for 1901 in Subsidiary IV are lacking to the extent shown by the blanks.

18. Tabulation in British India and in many states was restricted owing to the war with the result that Imperial Table VI has not been produced for such areas. In these circumstances the proportion of the sexes in Subsidiary IV cannot be given for the ' natural ' population.

IMPERIAL TABLE I

I—AREA, HOUSES

District or State	Area in square miles	Towns	Villages	Occupied Houses		
				Total	In Towns	In Villages
1	2	3	4	5	6	7
JAMMU AND KASHMIR STATE	**84471**	**39**	**8740**	**764424**	**67983**	**696441**
JAMMU PROVINCE	**12378**	**21**	**4533**	**400226**	**25339**	**374887**
(a) Total Districts	**10656**	**20**	**4004**	**319141**	**23739**	**295402**
Jammu	1147	5	1165	88263	12974	75289
Kathua	1023	3	563	37598	2605	34993
Udhampur	5070	4	926	55947	2591	53356
Reasi	1789	3	648	48502	1251	47251
Mirpur	1627	5	702	88831	4318	84513
(b) Total Jagirs	**1722**	**1**	**529**	**81085**	**1600**	**79485**
Chenani Jagir	95		46	2562		2562
Poonch Jagir	1627	1	483	78523	1600	76923
KASHMIR PROVINCE	**8539**	**15**	**3518**	**298829**	**39815**	**259014**
Baramulla	3317	4	1370	106573	4936	101637
Anantnag	2814	9	1380	145473	33853	111620
Muzaffarabad	2408	2	768	46783	1026	45757
FRONTIER DISTRICTS	**63554**	**3**	**689**	**65369**	**2829**	**62540**
Ladakh	45762	2	468	46255	1863	44392
Astore	1632		39	2506		2506
Gilgit (Leased Area)	1480	1	45	3787	966	2821
Gilgit Agency	14680		137	12821		12821

Population								
Persons			Males			Females		
Total	Urban	Rural	Total	Urban	Rural	Total	Urban	Rural
8	*9*	*10*	*11*	*12*	*13*	*14*	*15*	*16*
4021616	**414435**	**3607181**	**2129872**	**231382**	**1898490**	**1891744**	**183053**	**1708691**
1981433	**123536**	**1857897**	**1034410**	**72045**	**962365**	**947023**	**51491**	**895532**
1547809	**114928**	**1432881**	**814016**	**67094**	**746922**	**733793**	**47834**	**685959**
431362	67682	363680	233976	41099	192877	197386	26583	170803
177672	10935	166737	94134	6032	88102	83538	4903	78635
294217	13332	280885	153608	7237	146371	140009	6095	134514
257903	6276	251627	135502	3510	131992	122401	2766	119635
386655	16703	369952	196796	9216	187580	189859	7487	182372
433624	**8608**	**425016**	**220394**	**4951**	**215443**	**213230**	**3657**	**209573**
11796		11796	6475		6475	5321		5321
421828	8608	413220	213919	4951	208968	207909	3657	204252
1728705	**280319**	**1448386**	**934738**	**153332**	**781406**	**793967**	**126987**	**666980**
612428	31563	580865	330050	17647	312403	282378	13916	268462
851606	242904	608702	463571	132275	331296	388035	110629	277406
264671	5852	258819	141117	3410	137707	123554	2442	121112
311478	**10580**	**300898**	**160724**	**6005**	**154719**	**150754**	**4575**	**146179**
195431	5909	189522	98478	3187	95291	96953	2722	94231
17026		17026	8948		8948	8078		8078
22495	4671	17824	12471	2818	9653	10024	1853	8171
76526		76526	40827		40827	35699		35699

I—(i) DENSITY, WATER-

District or State	Density	Percentage of total area: Cultivable	Percentage of total area: Net cultivated	Percentage of cultivable area: Net cultivated	Percentage of cultivable area: Double cropped	Percentage of cultivated area irrigated	Rainfall
1	2	3	4	5	6	7	8
JAMMU AND KASHMIR STATE ..	**48**	**5.6**	**4.9**	**86.8**	**14.8**	**35.1**	**28.45**
JAMMU PROVINCE	**160**	**17.7**	**14.9**	**85.2**	**22.3**	**16.1**	**44.17**
(a) Total Districts	**145**	**16.3**	**14.2**	**87.6**	**24.0**	**17.1**	**38.69**
Jammu	376	38.5	33.2	86.3	22.4	31.4	29.04
Kathua	174	26.3	23.3	88.6	23.4	25.1	49.04
Udhampur	58	6.3	5.3	83.5	27.3	18.3	40.99
Reasi	144	13.9	12.9	92.9	26.2	10.4	44.71
Mirpur	238	27.9	24.5	88.1	22.3	1.6	29.67
(b) Total Jagirs	**252**	**26.1**	**19.5**	**74.7**	**14.7**	**11.0**	**49.65**
Chenani Jagir	124	27.1	12.3	45.3	18.3	22.7	47.48
Poonch Jagir	259	26	20	77.1	14	8.8	51.83
KASHMIR PROVINCE	**202**	**19.0**	**17.0**	**89.1**	**5.1**	**52.2**	**32.45**
Baramulla	185	21.1	19.8	93.8	4.1	48.3	28.87
Anantnag	303	25.6	21.1	82.5	7.2	66.3	30.32
Muzaffarabad	110	8.4	8.2	96.7	1	22.4	38.17
FRONTIER DISTRICTS	**5**	**.4**	**.3**	**84.0**	**14.6**	**100**	**8.74**
Ladakh	4	.3	.3	89.7	16.7	100	10.6
Astore	10	.6	.6	92.6	14.8	100	10
Gilgit (Leased Area)	15	1.7	1	55.4	5.1	100	5.61
Gilgit Agency*	5						

*No information is available.

Percentage of gross cultivated area under												
Rice	Wheat	Barley	Bajra	Maize	Other food crops including Pulses	Oil-seeds	Spices	Sugarcane	Fibres	Dyes and tanning material	Drugs and Narcotics	Miscellaneous including Kharaaba
9	10	11	12	13	14	15	16	17	18	19	20	21
19.3	**19.5**	**2.2**	**3.9**	**29.6**	**10.7**	**5.2**	**.3**	**.3**	**1.1**	**.01**	**.3**	**7.59**
10.2	**27.7**	**3.3**	**6.8**	**28.8**	**11.2**	**2.7**	**.2**	**.5**	**1.7**	**.01**	**.3**	**6.59**
10.7	**29.9**	**3.8**	**7.8**	**22.8**	**12.3**	**3.0**	**.2**	**.5**	**1.9**	**.01**	**.3**	**6.79**
16.5	39.2	3.6	9.9	8.9	12.9	2.3	.2	1.4	2.6	.02	.4	2.08
21.5	28.7	3.8	7.7	15.9	8.9	6	.3	.9	2.5	.01	.4	3.39
10	18	10.8	.03	30.7	17.3	4.3	.3	.1	.6	.02	.4	1.45
9.4	27.2	1.4	.5	50.8	5.9	2.9	.3	.2	.8	.01	.2	.39
.3	33.2	.5	16	14.2	14.5	1	.1		2.6	.01	.2	17.39
7	**14.3**	**.7**	**1.1**	**56.8**	**4.4**	**1.1**	**.1**		**.2**			**14.3**
4.3	11.7	7		51.5	12.6	8.2	.4	.8	.2		.8	2.5
6.7	14.1	.4	1.4	57.6	3.7	.8	.1		.3			14.9
34.9	**7.2**	**.7**		**33.7**	**5.1**	**9.4**	**.5**	**.01**	**.4**		**.3**	**7.79**
34.2	10.8	.4		33.2	8.1	10.7	.2		.3		.1	2.0
45.8	4.5	1		20.2	3.1	11.2	1		.5		.7	12.0
8.1	4.7	.9		83.1	2	.7	.03	.01	.03			.43
.2	**20.4**	**.6**		**3.3**	**53.4**	**.6**	**.1**		**.01**		**.1**	**21.29**
	18.6			.3	55.7	.7	.1				.1	24.5
	18.2			9.6	60						.2	12.0
2.3	35.8	6		22.4	30.7	.1			.1		.1	2.5

I—(ii) AREA AND POPULATION (000 OMITTED), ACTUAL AND PERCENTAGE, BY TEHSIL DENSITY

Natural Division	TEHSILS WITH DENSITY													
	Under 100		100-150		150-200		200-300		300-450		450-600		600-750	
	Area	Population	Area	Population	Area	Population	Area	Population	Area	Population	Area	Population	Area	Population
1	2	3	4	5	6	7	8	9	10	11	12	13	14	15
JAMMU AND KASHMIR STATE	68470 81.05	475 11.85	5427 6.42	663 16.49	2934 3.47	536 13.32	4248 5.06	1046 26.02	2889 3.42	1047 26.03	346 .40	157 3.89	157 .18	97 2.40
I. The Sub-montane and Semi-mountainous Tract ..							1566 60.02	388 47.63	540 20.69	173 21.22	346 13.26	157 19.23	157 6.03	97 11.92
II. The Outer Hills	3574 36.58	105 9.02	3188 32.63	388 33.26	1380 14.15	252 21.60	958 9.80	212 18.19	669 6.84	209 17.93				
III. The Jhelum Valley ..	1342 15.71	59 3.40	2239 26.22	275 15.90	1554 18.19	284 16.43	1724 20.18	446 25.79	1680 19.70	665 38.48				
IV. The Indus Valley	63554 100	311 100												

I—(iii) PERSONS PER 1,000 HOUSES AND HOUSES PER 100 SQUARE MILES.

Natural Division	Persons per 1,000 houses					Houses per 100 square miles				
	1941	1931	1921	1911	1901	1941	1931	1921	1911	1901
1	2	3	4	5	6	7	8	9	10	11
JAMMU & KASHMIR STATE	**5261**	**5000**	**6000**	**6000**	**6000**	**905**	**800**	**700**	**600**	**600**
I. The Sub-montane and Semi-mountainous Tract ..	4660	4000	4000	5000		6697	5900	5600	5200	
II. The Outer Hills ..	5177	5000	5000	6000		2308	2000	1900	1700	
III. The Jhelum Valley ..	5785	6000	6000	7000	8000	3500	3100	2600	2300	1900
IV. The Indus Valley ..	4762	5000	6000	6000	6000	103	100	100	100	

I—(iv) PROPORTION OF SEXES BY NATURAL DIVISIONS AND DISTRICTS

Natural Division and District	Females per 1,000 males				
	1941	1931	1921	1911	1901
1	2	3	4	5	6
JAMMU & KASHMIR STATE	**888**	**881**	**890**	**887**	**884**
I. The Sub-montane and Semi-mountainous Tract ..	**887**	**864**	**884**	**846**	
Jammu District	844	825	883	808	
Kathua District (Jasmergarh and Kathua Tehsils only)	865	827	827	820	
Mirpur District (Mirpur and Bhimber Tehsils only)	967	936	901	913	
II. The Outer Hills	**936**	**905**	**925**	**916**	
Kathua District (Basohli Tehsil only) ..	922	941	931	911	
Mirpur District (Kotli Tehsil only)	958	888	995	235	
Udhampur District	915	903	896	894	
Reasi District	903	895	894	897	
Chenani Jagir	822	842			
Poonch Jagir	972	950	940	926	895
III. The Jhelum Valley	**849**	**852**	**857**	**872**	**676**
Baramulla District	856	857	863	884	877
Anantnag District	837	842	848	864	
Muzaffarabad District	876	881	869	871	854
IV. The Indus Valley	**938**	**940**	**956**	**978**	**933**
Ladakh District	985	1000	1011	1002	
Astore District	903 }	778	808	859	
Gilgit (Leased Area)	804 }				
Gilgit Agency	874	882	874		

IMPERIAL TABLE II AND ITS SUBSIDIARIES

Variation in Population during Fifty Years

1. The figures for this table for periods previous to 1941 have been taken from the corresponding table published with the 1931 report. From 1911 onwards all the figures required are available. The figures for 1891 and 1901 are missing for many districts and there is no alternative but to leave the relative spaces blank.

2. For the purpose of this table the populations of Astore and Gilgit (Leased Area) have been added together for comparison with the old Gilgit District, since the population figures for these districts separately are not available for censuses previous to 1941.

3. The figures shown for Udhampur for 1891 and 1901 represent the population of the Bhadrawah Jagir only. The Udhampur District was reconstituted during the decade 1901-1910 and the figures shown for 1911 are the earliest correct figures for the district available. The figures for 1891 and 1901 referred to might well have been omitted but as they were shown in 1931 it was thought better to show them again and explain to what area they relate.

4. Where the figures for 1901 are not available for the main table they are naturally lacking for Subsidiary (i) too and the relative spaces have had to be left blank here also.

5. The percentage variations shown in Subsidiary (I) all represent increases except in the few cases where a minus sign is given.

6. Natural Divisions I and II together constitute the Jammu Province—the figures for which are given below :—

PERCENTAGE VARIATION

1931 to 1941	1921 to 1931	1911 to 1921	1901 to 1911	1901 to 1941
10.8	9.0	2.7	5.3	30.2

DENSITY

1941	1931	1921	1911	1901
160	144	135	128	122

7. The figures for density in Astore and Gilgit (Leased Area) are given separately for 1941 ; the figures for periods previous to this are for the two combined, *i. e.*, for the old Gilgit District.

8. In Subsidiary (ii) entries against Astore have only been made in columns 2, 3 and 6 ; there are no Vital Statistics returns available for this area previous to the decade 1931-41. Columns 4, 5 and 7 have been left blank because the population figures are not available for Astore separately previous to 1941.

9. (a) The figures in columns 4 and 5 of Subsidiary II were calculated after excluding the births and deaths in Astore District and after exclusion of the 1931 population of the districts Astore, Gilgit (Leased Area) and Gilgit Agency.

(b) The total increase of population (254542) shown in column 6 includes the figures for Astore but the total shown in column 7 (355772) excludes the population of Astore, Gilgit (Leased Area) and Gilgit Agency.

10. (a) It is usual to show the figures given in columns 6 and 7 with 000 omitted but since our figures are small it was decided to give the figures fully.

(b) All variations shown in columns 6 and 7 represent increases except the one case where a minus sign has been given.

II—VARIATION IN POPULATION DURING FIFTY YEARS

Year.	Persons	Variation	Net Variation 1891-1941	Males	Variation	Females	Variation
1	2	3	4	5	6	7	8
JAMMU AND KASHMIR STATE							
1891	**2543952**			1353229		1190723	
1901	**2905578**	+ 361626		1542057	+ 188828	1363521	+ 172798
1911	**3158126**	+ 252548		1674367	+ 132310	1483759	+ 120238
1921	**3320518**	+ 162392		1757122	+ 82755	1563396	+ 79637
1931	**3646243**	+ 325725		1938338	+ 181216	1707905	+ 144509
1941	**4021616**	+ 375373	+ 1477664	2129872	+ 191534	1891744	+ 183839
JAMMU PROVINCE							
1891	**1434686**			767864		666822	
1901	**1516450**	+ 81704		805415	+ 37551	711035	+ 44213
1911	**1597865**	+ 81415		846790	+ 41375	751075	+ 40040
1921	**1640259**	+ 42394		859619	+ 12829	780640	+ 29565
1931	**1788441**	+ 148182		942815	+ 83196	845626	+ 64986
1941	**1981433**	+ 192992	+ 546747	1034410	+ 91595	947023	+ 101397
(a) **TOTAL DISTRICTS**							
1891	**1166078**			625919		540159	
1901	**1211962**	+ 45884		644736	+ 18817	567226	+ 27067
1911	**1252883**	+ 40921		667546	+ 22810	585337	+ 18111
1921	**1277858**	+ 24975		672546	+ 5000	605312	+ 19975
1931	**1390132**	+ 112274		738267	+ 65721	651865	+ 46553
1941	**1547809**	+ 157677	+ 381731	814016	+ 75749	733793	+ 81928
JAMMU (INCLUDING CITY)							
1891							
1901							
1911	**329283**			181979		147304	
1921	**337544**	+ 8261		184071	+ 2092	153473	+ 6169
1931	**375240**	+ 37696		205719	+ 21648	169521	+ 16048
1941	**431362**	+ 56122		233976	+ 28257	197386	+ 27865
KATHUA							
1891	**151518**			81434		70084	
1901	**154213**	+ 2695		82391	+ 957	71822	+ 1738
1911	**151802**	— 2411		81375	— 1016	70427	— 1395
1921	**154209**	+ 2407		82467	+ 1092	71742	+ 1315
1931	**161232**	+ 7023		85993	+ 3526	75239	+ 3497
1941	**177672**	+ 16440	+ 26154	94134	+ 8141	83538	+ 8299
UDHAMPUR							
1891	**32433**						
1901	**34311**	+ 1878					
1911	**242648**	+ 208337		127178		115470	
1921	**245255**	+ 2607		128637	+ 1459	116618	+ 1148
1931	**273668**	+ 28413		143514	+ 14877	130154	+ 13536
1941	**294217**	+ 20549	+ 261784	153608	+ 10094	140609	+ 10455
REASI							
1891							
1901							
1911	**205912**			108571		97341	
1921	**223652**	+ 17740		118094	+ 9523	105558	+ 8217
1931	**235245**	+ 11593		124210	+ 6116	111035	+ 5477
1941	**257903**	+ 22658		135502	+ 11292	122401	+ 11366

II—VARIATION IN POPULATION DURING FIFTY YEARS—CONTD.

Year	Persons	Variation	Net Variation 1891-1941	Males	Variation	Females	Variation
1	2	3	4	5	6	7	8
			MIRPUR				
1891							
1901							
1911	**323238**			168443		154795	
1921	**317198**	— 6040		159277	— 9166	157921	+ 3126
1931	**344747**	+ 27549		178831	+ 19554	165916	+ 7995
1941	**386655**	+ 41908		196796	+ 17965	189859	+ 23943
			(*b*) **TOTAL JAGIRS**				
1891	**268608**			141945		126663	
1901	**304488**	+ 35880		160679	+ 18734	143809	+ 17146
1911	**344982**	+ 40494		179244	+ 18565	165738	+ 21929
1921	**362401**	+ 17419		187073	+ 7829	175328	+ 9590
1931	**398309**	+ 35908		204548	+ 17475	193761	+ 18433
1941	**433624**	+ 35315	+ 165016	220394	+ 15846	213230	+ 19469
			CHENANI JAGIR				
1891							
1901							
1911	**10589**			5674		4915	
1921	**10620**	+ 31		5725	+ 51	4895	— 20
1931	**10925**	+ 305		5930	+ 205	4995	+ 100
1941	**11796**	+ 871		6475	+ 545	5321	+ 326
			POONCH JAGIR				
1891	**268608**			141945		126663	
1901	**304488**	+ 35880		160679	+ 18734	143809	+ 17146
1911	**334393**	+ 29905		173570	+ 12891	160823	+ 17014
1921	**351781**	+ 17388		181348	+ 7778	170433	+ 9610
1931	**387384**	+ 35603		198618	+ 17270	188766	+ 18333
1941	**421828**	+ 34444	+ 153220	213919	+ 15301	207909	+ 19143
			KASHMIR PROVINCE				
1891	**949041**			502345		446696	
1901	**1157394**	+ 208353		616887	+ 114542	540507	+ 93811
1911	**1295201**	+ 137807		691780	+ 74893	603421	+ 62914
1921	**1407086**	+ 111885		757824	+ 66044	649262	+ 45841
1931	**1569218**	+ 162132		847022	+ 89198	722196	+ 72934
1941	**1728705**	+ 159487	+ 779664	934738	+ 87716	793967	+ 71771
			BARAMULLA				
1891							
1901							
1911	**460515**			244488		216027	
1921	**502216**	+ 41701		269538	+ 25050	232678	+ 16651
1931	**559828**	+ 57612		301397	+ 31859	258431	+ 25753
1941	**612428**	+ 52600		330050	+ 28653	282378	+ 23947
			ANANTNAG (INCLUDING SRINAGAR CITY)				
1891						384777	
1901						463038	
1911	**639481**			342984		296497	— 166541
1921	**688761**	+ 49280		372606	+ 29622	316155	+ 19658
1931	**771943**	+ 83182		419190	+ 46584	352753	+ 36598
1941	**851606**	+ 79663		463571	+ 44381	388035	+ 35282

II—VARIATION IN POPULATION DURING FIFTY YEARS—CONTD.

Year	Persons	Variation	Net Variation 1891-1941	Males	Variation	Females	Variation
1	2	3	4	5	6	7	8
MUZAFFARABAD							
1891	**134800**			72881		61919	
1901	**168198**	+ 33398		90729	+ 17848	77469	+ 15550
1911	**195205**	+ 27007		104308	+ 13579	90897	+ 13428
1921	**216109**	+ 20904		115680	+ 11372	100429	+ 9532
1931	**237447**	+ 21338		126435	+ 10755	111012	+ 10583
1941	**264671**	+ 27224	+ 129871	141117	+ 14682	123554	+ 12542
FRONTIER DISTRICTS							
1891	**160225**			83020		77205	
1901	**231734**	+ 71509		119755	+ 36735	111979	+ 34774
1911	**265060**	+ 33326		135797	+ 16042	129263	+ 17284
1921	**273173**	+ 8113		139679	+ 3882	133494	+ 4231
1931	**288584**	+ 15411		148501	+ 8822	140083	+ 6589
1941	**311478**	+ 22894	+ 151253	160724	+ 12223	150754	+ 10671
LADAKH							
1891							
1901							
1911	**186656**			93220		93436	
1921	**183476**	− 3180		91258	− 1962	92218	− 1218
1931	**192138**	+ 8662		96259	+ 5001	95879	+ 3661
1941	**195431**	+ 3293		98478	+ 2219	96953	+ 1074
ASTORE AND GILGIT (LEASED AREA)							
1891							
1901							
1911	**23969**			13299		10670	
1921	**28706**	+ 4737		15880	+ 2581	12826	+ 2156
1931	**31902**	+ 3196		17752	+ 1872	14150	+ 1324
1941	**39521**	+ 7619		21419	+ 3667	18102	+ 3952
GILGIT AGENCY							
1891							
1901							
1911	**54435**			29278		25157	
1921	**60991**	+ 6556		32541	+ 3263	28450	+ 3293
1931	**64544**	+ 3553		34490	+ 1949	30054	+ 1604
1941	**76526**	+ 11982		40827	+ 6337	35699	+ 5645

II— (i) VARIATION AND DENSITY

Natural Division and District	Percentage variation					Density				
	1931 to 1941	1921 to 1931	1911 to 1921	1901 to 1911	1901 to 1941	1941	1931	1921	1911	1901
1	2	3	4	5	6	7	8	9	10	11
JAMMU & KASHMIR STATE	**10.3**	**9.8**	**5.1**	**8.7**	**38.4**	**48**	**43**	**39**	**37**	**34**
I. Sub-montane and Semi-mountainous Tract ..	**14.3**	**9.9**	**1**			**312**	**273**	**248**	**235**	
Jammu District ..	15.0	12.0	2.5		25.4	376	327	292	280	
Kathua District (Jasmergarh & Kathua Tehsils only) ..	12.4	7.4	2.6	1.5		262	233	210	211	208
Mirpur District (Mirpur & Bhimber Tehsils only) ..	13.9	7.7	− 1.8			262	230	215	196	
II. The Outer Hills ..	**8.4**	**8.5**	**3.8**			**119**	**110**	**104**	**98**	
Kathua District (Basohli Tehsil only)	7.0	.8	.2	− 5.3		115	108	109	113	119
Mirpur District (Kotli Tehsil only)	8	9.0	− 1.9			193	179	175	161	
Udhampur District ..	7.5	11.2	1.2		3.6	58	54	50	49	
Reasi District	9.6	4.7	8.6			144	131	123	110	
Poonch Jagir	8.9	10.1	5.2	9.8	38.5	259	238	216	203	185
Chenani Jagir	8	2.9	.3			124	115	111		
III. The Jhelum Valley (Kashmir Province)	**10.2**	**11.5**	**8.6**	**11.9**	**49.4**	**202**	**184**	**165**	**154**	**137**
Baramulla District ..	9.4	11.4	9.1			185	169	151	130	
Anantnag District ..	10.3	12.1	7.7			303	274	245	228	
Muzaffarabad District ..	11.5	9.9	10.7	16.0	57.2	110	99	90	94	81
IV. The Indus Valley (Frontier Districts)	**7.9**	**5.6**	**3.1**	**14.2**	**37.3**	**5**	**5**	**4**	**4**	**4**
Ladakh District ..	1.7	4.7	− 1.7		17.7	4	4	4	4	
Astore District .. }	23.9	11.1	19.8			10 }	10	9	8	
Gilgit (Leased Area) .. }						15 }				
Gilgit Agency	18.5	5.8	12.0			5	4	4	4	

II—(ii) POPULATION VARIATION ACCORDING TO {CENSUS / VITAL STATISTICS}

District	1931-41 Births	1931-41 Deaths	Per 1,000 of 1931 population Births	Per 1,000 of 1931 population Deaths	Column 2 minus 3	1941 minus 1931 (census)
1	2	3	4	5	6	7
Total ..	**1009037**	**754495**	**284**	**213**	**254542**	**355772**
Jammu	138183	93999	342	251	44184	56122
Kathua	62977	43988	390	273	18989	16440
Udhampur	87862	56503	321	206	31359	20549
Reasi	70830	37350	301	159	33480	22658
Mirpur	99428	62691	288	182	36737	41908
Chenani Jagir	2118	2496	194	229	— 378	871
Poonch Jagir	70034	69282	181	179	752	34444
Baramulla	125736	99732	225	178	26004	52600
Anantnag	266329	214251	345	278	52078	79663
Muzaffarabad	56024	47144	236	156	8880	27224
Ladakh	27059	25310	141	132	1740	3293
Astore	2457	1740			717	
Gilgit (Leased Area)*						
Gilgit Agency*						

*Vital Statistics figures for Gilgit Leased Area and Gilgit Agency are not available.

IMPERIAL TABLE III AND ITS SUBSIDIARIES

Towns and Villages Classified by Population

1. The definition of a town and of a village for census purposes has been given in the notes to Table I.

2. Variations in the number of towns and villages as compared with 1931 have been referred to in the notes to Table I.

3. Some places classified as towns consist of two or more villages. For the purposes of this table such villages have been taken together as one unit which has been classified according to the aggregate population of the several villages constituting the town. For instance, the two villages Baharyan and Udhampur together constitute Udhampur Town; in this table they are treated as one town and not as two separate villages.

4. The 'Floating population' given in column 22 refers to the population living in boats which has not been included in the population of any village; all other 'floating population' has been included in the total of the village within the limits of which it was enumerated. For instance, under columns 20, 21, and 22 the entries against Anantnag District are 201278 and 9515. Columns 20 and 21 refer to Srinagar City the full population of which is 207787 consisting of 201278 persons living in houses and 6509 persons living in boats. The remaining 3006 persons out of 9515 shown in column 22 are those living in boats within the Anantnag District but outside the limits of Srinagar City. Full details have been given for local information in Part III of the report—Village Tables.

5. Subsidiary I is similar to the table produced on page 90 of Part I of the 1931 report except for a minor difference. In 1931 the figures were given by Natural Divisions and Districts; on this occasion we give them by Natural Divisions only.

III—TOWNS AND VILLAGES

(N=Number

District or State	Total number of inhabited towns and villages	P	Under 500 N	Under 500 P	500-1000 N	500-1000 P	1000-2000 N	1000-2000 P
1	2	3	4	5	6	7	8	9
JAMMU & KASHMIR STATE ..	**8779**	**4021616**	**6495**	**1366381**	**1485**	**1028708**	**631**	**850465**
JAMMU PROVINCE ..	**4554**	**1981433**	**3401**	**670228**	**715**	**496599**	**332**	**452209**
(a) Total Districts ..	**4024**	**1547809**	**3158**	**606487**	**581**	**402071**	**222**	**300488**
Jammu	1170	431362	991	196282	120	82536	43	56328
Kathua	566	177672	465	86550	78	53571	19	24591
Udhampur	930	294217	756	133593	132	88763	32	44122
Reasi	651	257903	482	94548	119	83683	41	55401
Mirpur	707	386655	464	95514	132	93518	87	120046
(b) Total Jagirs ..	**530**	**433624**	**243**	**63741**	**134**	**94528**	**110**	**151721**
Chenani Jagir	46	11796	41	7423	3	2101	2	2272
Poonch Jagir	484	421828	202	56318	131	92427	108	149449
KASHMIR PROVINCE ..	**3533**	**1728705**	**2603**	**579400**	**634**	**437716**	**245**	**327309**
Baramulla	1374	612428	1021	233302	228	158225	108	148045
Anantnag	1389	851606	976	221337	279	193600	104	137570
Muzaffarabad	770	264671	606	124761	127	85891	33	41694
FRONTIER DISTRICTS ..	**692**	**311478**	**491**	**116753**	**136**	**94393**	**54**	**70947**
Ladakh	470	195431	349	80351	86	58896	28	38135
Astore	39	17026	25	5633	11	7764	3	3629
Gilgit (Leased Area)	46	22495	32	9130	9	7417	5	5948
Gilgit Agency	137	76526	85	21639	30	20316	18	23235

CLASSIFIED BY POPULATION

P=Population)

2000-5000		5000-10000		10000-20000		20000-50000		50000-100000		100000 & over		Floating population unclassed
N	P	N	P	N	P	N	P	N	P	N	P	
10	*11*	*12*	*13*	*14*	*15*	*16*	*17*	*18*	*19*	*20*	*21*	*22*
154	**411153**	**9**	**64103**	**3**	**37239**			**1**	**50379**	**1**	**201278**	**11910**
98	**261399**	**7**	**50619**					**1**	**50379**			
56	**146373**	**6**	**42011**					**1**	**50379**			
14	37369	1	8468					1	50379			
3	7374	1	5586									
10	27739											
8	18697	1	5574									
21	55194	3	22383									
42	**115026**	**1**	**8608**									
42	115026	1	8608									
45	**120369**	**2**	**13484**	**3**	**37239**					**1**	**201278**	**11910**
14	38305	1	6902	2	25254							2395
27	69739	1	6582	1	11985					1	201278	9515
4	12325											
11	**29385**											
7	**18049**											
4	**11336**											

III—(i) DISTRIBUTION OF THE POPULATION

Natural Division	Population per Town	Population per Village	Number per 1000 in Towns	Number per 1000 in Villages
1	2	3	4	5
JAMMU AND KASHMIR STATE	**10627**	**413**	**103**	**897**
I. The Sub-montane and Semi-mountainous Tract	7515	350	111	889
II. The Outer Hills	3707	460	29	971
III. The Jhelum Valley	18688	412	162	838
IV. The Indus Valley	3527	437	34	966

BETWEEN TOWNS AND VILLAGES

Number per 1000 of urban population in towns with a population of				Number per 1000 of rural population in villages with a population of			
20000 and over	10000 to 20000	5000 to 10000	Under 5000	5000 and over	2000 to 5000	500 to 2000	Under 500
6	*7*	*8*	*9*	*10*	*11*	*12*	*13*
623	**88**	**75**	**214**	**11**	**91**	**519**	**379**
559		251	190	19	91	443	447
		258	742	5	137	552	306
741	130		129	14	60	526	400
			1000		63	549	388

IMPERIAL TABLE IV AND ITS SUBSIDIARIES

Towns Classified by Population with Variations since 1891

NOTES

1. There are 39 places classed as towns which is the same as in 1931. There is one change. Gilgit Cantonment has ceased to exist. Nowshera Cantonment was created during the decade 1931-40.

2. There was no town in class II in 1931; on this occasion there is no town in class III; Jammu City has gone up into class II. Baramulla is now in class IV and Jammu Cantonment in class V; in 1931 these two places were in class V and VI respectively.

3. (a) Jammu City shows a large increase in population; this is partly due to increased trade and development and partly to the extension of the municipal boundaries. The area of the city which was one square mile in 1931 has been shown as two square miles on this occasion *vide* State Table I. The Palace area, which is on the borders of the municipality, was included with the city for census purposes.

(b) Baramulla town has been extended by bringing adjacent villages within the limits of the Town Area.

(c) The figures in brackets denote the number of towns in each class.

4. (a) Totals have been given for each class; class totals do not appear in the corresponding table for 1931.

(b) Where figures are not available the relative spaces have been left blank throughout the table.

5. (a) As there is no town in class III the spaces pertaining to 1941 in Subsidiary (i) have been left blank for this class.

(b) As Jammu City is shown in class II for the first time the spaces pertaining to decades previous to 1931-41 have been left blank.

6. The standard definition of a city for census purposes is a town with a population of not less than 100000. Srinagar is the only place in the State which satisfies this definition. Jammu has been included in Subsidiary (ii) owing to its historic and political importance. This is in accordance with past procedure.

7. The figures in column 3 denote density per square mile and those in column 4 the number of persons born outside State territories.

8. The standard form for Subsidiary (ii) requires percentage variations to be shown for each decade from 1881-91 onwards. The figures for 1881-91 are not available; consequently the table gives variations from 1891 onwards and for 1891-41.

IV—TOWNS CLASSIFIED BY POPULATION WITH VARIATIONS SINCE 1891

Town	State, District, etc.	Persons	Variation	Net Variation 1891-1941	Males	Variation	Females	Variation
1	2	3	4	5	6	7	8	9
GRAND TOTAL								
1891..	..	192537						
1901..	..	158748	− 33789					
1911..	..	266659	+ 107911		148300		118359	
1921..	..	282056	+ 15397		156720	+ 8420	125336	+ 6977
1931..	..	341883	+ 59827		191768	+ 35048	150115	+ 24779
1941..	..	414435	+ 72552	+ 221898	231382	+ 39614	183053	+ 32938
CLASS I—100000 AND OVER (1)								
1891..	..	118960						
1901..	..	122618	+ 3658					
1911..	..	124240	+ 1622		66994		57246	
1921..	..	139520	+ 15280		75152	+ 8158	64368	+ 7122
1931..	..	173573	+ 34053		94793	+ 19641	78780	+ 14412
1941..	..	207787	+ 34214	+ 88827	112460	+ 17667	95327	+ 16547
Srinagar	.. Anantnag							
1891..	..	118960						
1901..	..	122618	+ 3658					
1911..	..	124240	+ 1622		66994		57246	
1921..	..	139520	+ 15280		75152	+ 8158	64368	+ 7122
1931..	..	173573	+ 34053		94793	+ 19641	78780	+ 14412
1941..	..	207787	+ 34214	+ 88827	112460	+ 17667	95327	+ 16547
CLASS II—50000 TO 100000 (1)								
1891..	..	34542						
1901..	..	36130	+ 1588					
1911..	..	31726	− 4404		19362		12364	
1921..	..	31506	− 220		19121	− 241	12385	+ 21
1931..	..	38613	+ 7107		23361	+ 4240	15252	+ 2867
1941..	..	50379	+ 11766	+ 15837	29817	+ 6456	20562	+ 5310
Jammu	.. Jammu							
1891..	..	34542						
1901..	..	36130	+ 1588					
1911..	..	31726	− 4404		19362		12364	
1921	..	31506	− 220		19121	− 241	12385	+ 21
1931..	..	38613	+ 7107		23361	+ 4240	15252	+ 2867
1941..	..	50379	+ 11766	+ 15837	29817	+ 6456	20562	+ 5310
CLASS IV—10000 TO 20000 (3)								
1891..	..	24293						
1901..	..							
1911..	..	24132			12988		11144	
1921..	..	24732	+ 600		13604	+ 616	11128	− 16
1931..	..	28604	+ 3872		15839	+ 2235	12765	+ 1637
1941..	..	36479	+ 7875	+ 12186	20423	+ 4584	16056	+ 3291
Baramulla	.. Baramulla							
1891..	..	5656						
1901..	..							
1911..	..	6599			3586		3013	
1921..	..	6744	+ 145		3691	+ 105	3053	+ 40
1931..	..	6886	+ 142		3780	+ 89	3106	+ 53
1941..	..	12724	+ 5838	+ 7068	7133	+ 3353	5591	+ 2485

IV—TOWNS CLASSIFIED BY POPULATION WITH VARIATIONS SINCE 1891—CONTD.

Town	State, District, etc.	Persons	Variation	Net Variation 1891-1941	Males	Variation	Females	Variation
1	2	3	4	5	6	7	8	9
Anantnag	.. Anantnag							
1891..	..	**10227**						
1901..	..							
1911..	..	**9019**			4937		4082	
1921..	..	**9464**	+ 445		5303	+ 366	4161	+ 79
1931..	..	**10736**	+ 1272		6103	+ 800	4633	+ 472
1941..	..	**11985**	+ 1249	+ 1758	6723	+ 620	5262	+ 629
Sopur	.. Baramulla							
1891..	..	**8410**						
1901..	..							
1911..	..	**8514**			4465		4049	
1921..	..	**8524**	+ 10		4610	+ 145	3914	— 135
1931..	..	**10982**	+ 2458		5956	+ 1346	5026	+ 1112
1941..	..	**11770**	+ 788	+ 3360	6567	+ 611	5203	+ 177
CLASS V—5000 TO 10000 (4)								
1891..	..	**14742**						
1901..	..							
1911..	..	**22645**			**13958**		**8687**	
1921..	..	**21557**	**— 1088**		**12869**	**— 1089**	**8688**	+ 1
1931..	..	**24850**	**+ 3293**		**15374**	**+ 2505**	**9476**	**+ 788**
1941..	..	**31218**	**+ 6368**	**+ 16476**	**19157**	**+ 3783**	**12061**	**+ 2535**
Poonch	.. Poonch Jagir							
1891..	..	**7489**						
1901..	..							
1911..	..	**7564**			4662		2902	
1921..	..	**7026**	— 538		4103	— 559	2923	+ 21
1931..	..	**8152**	+ 1126		4906	+ 803	3246	+ 323
1941..	..	**8608**	+ 456	+ 1119	4951	+ 45	3657	+ 411
Mirpur	.. Mirpur							
1891..	..	**7253**						
1901..	..							
1911..	..	**6640**			3441		3190	
1921..	..	**6490**	— 150		3251	— 190	3239	+ 40
1931..	..	**7274**	+ 784		3840	+ 589	3434	+ 195
1941..	..	**8556**	+ 1282	+ 1303	4538	+ 698	4018	+ 584
Jammu Cantonment	Jammu							
1891..	..							
1901..	..							
1911..	..	**3201**			2847		354	
1921..	..	**2969**	— 232		2567	— 280	402	+ 48
1931..	..	**4181**	+ 1212		3626	+ 1059	555	+ 153
1941..	..	**8468**	+ 4287		6552	+ 2926	1916	+ 1361
Kathua	.. Kathua							
1891..	..							
1901..	..							
1911..	..	**5240**			3008		2232	
1921..	..	**5072**	— 168		2948	— 60	2124	— 108
1931..	..	**5243**	+ 171		3002	+ 54	2241	+ 117
1941..	..	**5586**	+ 343		3116	+ 114	2470	+ 229

IV—TOWNS CLASSIFIED BY POPULATION WITH VARIATIONS SINCE 1891—CONTD.

Town	State, District, etc.	Persons	Variation	Net Variation 1891-1941	Males	Variation	Females	Variation
1	2	3	4	5	6	7	8	9
CLASS VI—UNDER 5000 (30)								
1891..	..							
1901..	..							
1911..	..	**63916**			**34998**		**28918**	
1921..	..	**64741**	**+ 825**		**35974**	**+ 976**	**28767**	**− 151**
1931..	..	**76243**	**+ 11502**		**42401**	**+ 6427**	**33842**	**+ 5075**
1941..	..	**88572**	**+ 12329**		**49525**	**+ 7124**	**39047**	**+ 5205**
Gilgit	.. Gilgit							
1891..	..							
1901..	..							
1911..	..	**3562**			2301		1261	
1921..	..	**4393**	+ 831		2947	+ 646	1446	+ 185
1931..	..	**4474**	+ 81		2848	− 99	1626	+ 180
1941..	..	**4671**	+ 197		2818	− 30	1853	+ 227
Udhampur	.. Udhampur							
1891..	..							
1901..								
1911..	..	**2360**			1311		1049	
1921..	..	**2390**	+ 30		1373	+ 62	1017	− 32
1931..	..	**3633**	+ 1243		2065	+ 692	1568	+ 551
1941..	..	**4666**	+ 1033		2644	+ 579	2022	+ 454
Muzaffarabad	.. Muzaffarabad							
1891..	..							
1901..	..							
1911..	..	**3462**			2015		1474	
1921..	..	**3579**	+ 117		2131	+ 116	1448	+ 1
1931..	..	**4236**	+ 657		2506	+ 375	1730	+ 282
1941..	..	**4571**	+ 335		2609	+ 103	1962	+ 232
Bijbihara	.. Anantnag							
1891..	..							
1901..	..							
1911..	..	**4424**			2360		2064	
1921..	..	**4270**	− 154		2311	− 49	1959	− 105
1931..	..	**4438**	+ 168		2462	+ 151	1976	+ 17
1941..	..	**4532**	+ 94		2481	+ 19	2051	+ 75
Pampur	.. Anantnag							
1891..	..							
1901..	..							
1911..	..	**3348**			1851		1497	
1921..	..	**3494**	+ 146		1941	+ 90	1553	+ 56
1931..	..	**3869**	+ 375		2114	+ 173	1755	+ 202
1941..	..	**4446**	+ 577		2471	+ 357	1975	+ 220
Shopyan	.. Anantnag							
1891..	..							
1901..	..							
1911..	..	**2114**			1161		953	
1921..	..	**2236**	+ 122		1223	+ 62	1013	+ 60
1931..	..	**2217**	− 19		1187	− 36	1030	+ 17
1941..	..	**4359**	+ 2142		2346	+ 1159	2013	+ 983

IV—TOWNS CLASSIFIED BY POPULATION WITH VARIATIONS SINCE 1891—CONTD.

Town	State, District, etc.	Persons	Variation	Net Variation 1891-1941	Males	Variation	Females	Variation
1	2	3	4	5	6	7	8	9
Charar Sharif ..	Baramulla							
1891.. ..								
1901.. ..								
1911.. ..		**3380**			1853		1527	
1921.. ..		**3342**	− 38		1894	+ 41	1448	− 79
1931.. ..		**3784**	+ 442		2136	+ 242	1648	+ 200
1941.. ..		**4037**	+ 253		2253	+ 117	1784	+ 136
Machha Bhawan	Anantnag							
1891.. ..								
1901.. ..								
1911.. ..								
1921.. ..								
1931.. ..		**3016**			1603		1413	
1941.. ..		**3487**	+ 471		1955	+ 352	1532	+ 119
Akhnur ..	Jammu							
1891.. ..								
1901.. ..								
1911.. ..		**3033**			1550		1483	
1921.. ..		**2905**	− 128		1496	− 54	1409	− 74
1931.. ..		**3007**	+ 102		1608	+ 112	1399	− 10
1941..		**3398**	+ 391		1799	+ 191	1599	+ 200
Leh	Ladakh							
1891.. ..								
1901.. ..								
1911.. ..		**2895**			1464		1431	
1921.. ..		**2401**	− 494		1182	− 282	1219	− 122
1931.. ..		**3093**	+ 692		1571	+ 389	1522	+ 303
1941.. ..		**3372**	+ 279		1814	+ 243	1558	+ 36
Samba ..	Jammu							
1891.. ..								
1901.. ..								
1911.. ..		**2307**			1210		1097	
1921.. ..		**2418**	+ 111		1263	+ 53	1155	+ 58
1931.. ..		**2917**	+ 499		1524	+ 261	1393	+ 238
1941.. ..		**3287**	+ 370		1718	+ 194	1569	+ 176
Kishtwar ..	Udhampur							
1891.. ..								
1901.. ..								
1911.. ..		**2378**			1277		1101	
1921.. ..		**2546**	+ 168		1396	+ 119	1150	+ 49
1931.. ..		**3335**	+ 789		1874	+ 478	1461	+ 311
1941.. ..		**3235**	− 100		1759	− 115	1476	+ 15
Pattan ..	Baramulla							
1891.. ..								
1901.. ..								
1911.. ..		**1903**			1018		885	
1921.. ..		**2243**	+ 340		1236	+ 218	1007	+ 122
1931.. ..		**2691**	+ 448		1485	+ 249	1206	+ 199
1941..		**3032**	+ 341		1694	+ 209	1338	+ 132

IV—TOWNS CLASSIFIED BY POPULATION WITH VARIATIONS SINCE 1891— CONTD.

Town	State, District, etc.	Persons	Variation	Net Variation 1891-1941	Males	Variation	Females	Variation
1	2	3	4	5	6	7	8	9
Bhadrawah	.. Udhampur							
1891..	..							
1901..	..							
1911..	..	2563			1348		1215	
1921..	..	2603	+ 40		1369	+ 21	1234	+ 19
1931..	..	2895	+ 292		1538	+ 169	1357	+ 123
1941..	..	2989	+ 94		1549	+ 11	1440	+ 83
Parol	.. Kathua							
1891..	..							
1901..	..							
1911..	..	1678			917		761	
1921..	..	2158	+ 480		1209	+ 292	949	+ 188
1931..	..	3016	+ 858		1661	+ 452	1355	+ 406
1941..	..	2966	− 50		1613	− 48	1353	− 2
Reasi	.. Reasi							
1891..	..							
1901..	..							
1911..	..	1905			1062		843	
1921..	..	1940	+ 35		1073	+ 11	867	+ 24
1931..	..	2106	+ 106		1193	+ 120	913	+ 46
1941..	..	2822	+ 716		1584	+ 391	1238	+ 325
Kotli	.. Mirpur							
1891..	..							
1901..	..							
1911..	..	1584			825		759	
1921..	..	1563	− 21		813	− 12	750	− 9
1931..	..	1537	− 26		807	− 6	730	− 20
1941..	..	2761	+ 1224		1460	+ 653	1301	+ 571
Manawar	.. Mirpur							
1891..	..							
1901..	..							
1911..	..	2057			1142		915	
1921..	..	1966	− 91		1078	− 64	888	− 27
1931..	..	2120	+ 154		1133	+ 55	987	+ 99
1941..	..	2580	+ 460		1369	+ 236	1211	+ 224
Skardu	.. Ladakh							
1891..	..							
1901..	..							
1911..	..	2197			1137		1060	
1921..	..	2282	+ 85		1246	+ 109	1036	− 24
1931..	..	2417	+ 135		1343	+ 97	1074	+ 38
1941..	..	2537	+ 120		1373	+ 30	1164	+ 90
Rampur Rajouri	Reasi							
1891..	..							
1901..	..							
1911..	..	2192			1203		989	
1921..	..	2253	+ 61		1214	+ 11	1039	+ 50
1931..	..	2164	− 89		1225	+ 11	939	− 100
1941..	..	2449	+ 285		1387	+ 162	1062	+ 123

IV—TOWNS CLASSIFIED BY POPULATION WITH VARIATIONS SINCE 1891—CONTD.

Town	State, District, etc.	Persons	Variation	Net Variation 1891-1941	Males	Variation	Females	Variation
1	2	3	4	5	6	7	8	9
Ramnagar ..	Udhampur							
1891.. ..								
1901.. ..								
1911.. ..		**2073**			1107		966	
1921.. ..		**1977**	— 96		1061	— 46	916	— 50
1931.. ..		**1904**	— 73		1029	— 32	875	— 41
1941.. ..		**2442**	+ 538		1285	+ 256	1157	+ 282
Basohli ..	Kathua							
1891.. ..								
1901.. ..								
1911.. ..		**1954**			1003		951	
1921.. ..		**1914**	— 40		979	— 24	935	— 16
1931.. ..		**2092**	+ 178		1094	+ 115	998	+ 63
1941.. ..		**2383**	+ 291		1303	+ 209	1080	+ 82
Daru ..	Anantnag							
1891.. ..								
1901.. ..								
1911.. ..		**2202**			1157		1045	
1921.. ..		**2177**	— 25		1163	+ 6	1014	— 31
1931.. ..		**2252**	+ 75		1192	+ 29	1060	+ 46
1941.. ..		**2280**	+ 28		1222	+ 30	1058	— 2
Verinag ..	Anantnag							
1891.. ..								
1901.. ..								
1911.. ..		**2095**			1063		1032	
1921.. ..		**2156**	+ 61		1103	+ 40	1053	+ 21
1931.. ..		**2134**	— 22		1045	— 58	1089	+ 36
1941.. ..		**2219**	+ 85		1116	+ 71	1103	+ 14
Bhimbar ..	Mirpur							
1891.. ..								
1901.. ..								
1911.. ..		**1438**			777		661	
1921.. ..		**1709**	+ 271		931	+ 154	778	+ 117
1931.. ..		**2020**	+ 311		1121	+ 190	899	+ 121
1941.. ..		**2194**	+ 174		1243	+ 122	951	+ 52
Sri Ranbirsinghpura.	Jammu							
1891.. ..								
1901.. ..								
1911.. ..		**1336**			761		575	
1921.. ..		**1611**	+ 275		890	+ 129	721	+ 146
1931.. ..		**2080**	+ 469		1198	+ 308	882	+ 161
1941.. ..		**2150**	+ 70		1213	+ 15	937	+ 55
Badamibagh Cantonment.	Anantnag							
1891.. ..								
1901.. ..								
1911.. ..		**2104**			1384		720	
1921.. ..		**2215**	+ 111		1452	+ 68	763	+ 43
1931.. ..		**886**	— 1329		725	— 727	161	— 602
1941.. ..		**1809**	+ 923		1501	+ 776	308	+ 147

IV—TOWNS CLASSIFIED BY POPULATION WITH VARIATIONS SINCE 1891—CONCLD.

Town	State, District, etc.	Persons	Variation	Net Variation 1891-1941	Males	Variation	Females	Variation
1	2	3	4	5	6	7	8	9
Uri (Pirasthan) ..	Muzaffarabad							
1891..	..							
1901..	..							
1911..	..	**544**			298		246	
1921..	..							
1931..	..	**960**			619		341	
1941..	..	**1281**	+ 321		801	+ 182	480	+ 139
Katra	.. Reasi							
1891..	..							
1901..	..							
1911..	..	**828**			443		385	
1921..	..							
1931..	..	**950**			495		455	
1941..	..	**1005**	+ 55		539	+ 44	466	+ 11
Nowshera Cantonment.	Mirpur							
1891..	..							
1901..	..							
1911..	..							
1921..	..							
1931..	..							
1941..	..	**612**			606		6	

IV—(i) TOWNS CLASSIFIED BY POPULATION

Class of town	Towns of each class in 1941	Proportion to total urban population	Females per 1,000 males	Variation per cent. in the class totals					
				1931 to 1941	1921 to 1931	1911 to 1921	1901 to 1911	1891 to 1901	1891 to 1941
1	2	3	4	5	6	7	8	9	10
JAMMU AND KASHMIR STATE.	**39**	**100**	**791**	**21.2**	**17.3**	**– 3.1**	**89.5**	**– 19.7**	**115.2**
I. 100,000 and over ..	1	50.1	848	19.7	22.5	12.2	3	3.1	74.7
II. 50,000-100,000 ..	1	12.2	690	30.5					45.8
III. 20,000-50,000 ..					22.5	– .7	– 12.2	4.6	
IV. 10,000-20,000 ..	3	8.8	786	27.5	100				50.2
V. 5,000-10,000 ..	4	7.5	629	25.6	— 44.1	– 4.7			111.8
VI. Under 5,000 ..	30	21.4	788	16.2	16.8	– 24.1			

IV—(ii) CITIES—CHIEF FIGURES

City	Population 1941	Density	Females per 1,000 Males	Foreign born per 1,000	Literates per 1,000		Percentage Variation					
					M	F	1931-41	1921-31	1911-21	1901-11	1891-1901	1891-41
1	2	3	4	5	6	7	8	9	10	11	12	13
I. Jammu ..	50379	25190	690	155	517	345	30.4	22.5	— .7	— 12.2	4.6	45.8
II. Srinagar	207787	18890	848	8	297	86	19.7	22.4	12.2	3	3.1	74.7

IMPERIAL TABLE V AND ITS SUBSIDIARIES

Towns arranged Territorially with Population by Communities

NOTES

1. The districts Chenani Jagir, Astore and Gilgit Agency do not appear in this table as they contain no towns.

2. Details of the communities shown will be found in the notes to Imperial Table XIII.

3. The details of 'Others' shown in columns 17 and 18 are as follows —

	Males	Females
Total	1112	1062
Anglo-Indians	3	3
Other Non-Indian Christians	144	154
Parsees	9	7
Buddhists	951	889
Jews	2	7
Others	3	2

4. The detail of the civil and military population enumerated in cantonments is given below :—

Cantonments.	Population: Military P	M	F	Civil P	M	F
Jammu Cantonment	3925	3925	..	4543	2627	1916
Badami Bagh Cantonment	1192	1192	..	617	309	308
Nowshera Cantonment	511	511	..	101	95	6
Total	5628	5628	..	5261	3031	2230

5. In 1931, *vide* para. 65 of the 1931 Census Report—Part I, there were ten towns in the Natural Divisions designated Sub-montane and Outer Hills respectively, fifteen in the Jhelum Valley and four in the Indus Valley. On this occasion there are eleven places shown as towns in the Sub-montane Division (Nowshera Cantonment having been included) and three in the Indus Valley (Gilgit Cantonment having ceased to exist). There is no change in the Jhelum Valley and Indus Valley Divisions.

6. The only places in the State having true urban characteristics are the two cities—Jammu and Srinagar. Jammu Cantonment, Mirpur, Poonch, Sopur, Baramulla and Anantnag have semi-urban characteristics.

7. Subsidiary (i) corresponds to the table shown on page 91 of the 1931 Census Report—Part I except that on this occasion we give the figures for Natural Divisions only. Column 8—Others—covers the communities of which details have been given in note 3 above.

V—TOWNS ARRANGED TERRITORIALLY

District or State	Town, Municipality, Suburb, Cantonment, etc.	Population		Hindus			
				Scheduled castes		Others	
		M	F	M	F	M	F
1	2	3	4	5	6	7	8
JAMMU & KASHMIR STATE ..		**231382**	**183053**	**1052**	**848**	**71392**	**51856**
JAMMU PROVINCE ..		**72045**	**51491**	**1034**	**839**	**40924**	**28660**
Jammu		**41099**	**26583**	**776**	**597**	**24498**	**15550**
Jammu City	Municipality ..	29817	20562	566	429	17237	12332
Jammu Cantonment ..	Cantonment ..	6552	1916	61	24	4910	1197
Akhnur	T. A. C.	1799	1599	68	62	832	775
Samba	Do.	1718	1569	47	61	973	824
Sri Ranbirsinghpura ..	Do.	1213	937	34	21	546	422
Kathua		**6032**	**4903**	**105**	**74**	**3985**	**3162**
Kathua	T. A. C.	3116	2470	34	25	1975	1504
Parol		1013	1353	61	47	972	812
Bosohli		1303	1080	10	2	1038	846
Udhampur		**7237**	**6095**	**57**	**85**	**4052**	**3393**
Udhampur	T. A. C.	2644	2022	52	48	1950	1558
Kishtwar	Do.	1759	1476			504	405
Bhadrawah	Do.	1549	1440	1	33	479	409
Ramnagar		1285	1157	4	4	1119	1021
Reasi		**3510**	**2766**	**74**	**66**	**1974**	**1648**
Rampur Rajouri	T. A. C.	1387	1062			689	534
Reasi	Do.	1584	1238	55	55	859	731
Katra	Do.	539	466	19	11	426	383
Mirpur		**9216**	**7487**	**22**	**15**	**4959**	**3782**
Mirpur	T. A. C.	4538	4018			2365	2054
Manawar		1369	1211	15	12	493	461
Bhimber	T. A. C.	1243	951	4	3	641	485
Kotli	Do.	1460	1301			896	782
Nowshera	Cantonment ..	606	6	3		564	
POONCH JAGIR		**4951**	**3657**		**2**	**1456**	**1125**
Poonch	Municipality ..	4951	3657		2	1456	1125
KASHMIR PROVINCE ..		**153332**	**126987**	**18**	**9**	**30132**	**23124**
Baramulla		**17647**	**13916**	**1**		**1993**	**1361**
Sopur	T. A. C.	6567	5203	1		628	439
Baramulla	Do.	7133	5591			1293	879
Charar Sharif		2253	1784			6	
Pattan		1604	1338			66	43

T. A. C. = Town Area Committee
M. = Males
F. = Females

WITH POPULATION BY COMMUNITIES

Muslims		Indian Christians		Jains		Sikhs		Others	
M	F	M	F	M	F	M	F	M	F
9	*10*	*11*	*12*	*13*	*14*	*15*	*16*	*17*	*18*
151622	**125105**	**928**	**799**	**425**	**378**	**4851**	**3005**	**1112**	**1062**
25958	**18847**	**807**	**681**	**417**	**377**	**2887**	**2074**	**18**	**13**
13211	**8533**	**648**	**560**	**416**	**372**	**1537**	**960**	**13**	**11**
9751	6169	517	440	412	372	1322	813	12	7
1383	571	61	51	4		132	69	1	4
852	712	9	7			38	43		
633	613	39	42			26	29		
592	468	22	20			19	6		
1832	**1573**	**74**	**70**			**36**	**24**		
1031	888	44	30			32	23		
560	466	20	28						
241	219	10	12			4	1		
3057	**2573**	**40**	**21**	**1**	**5**	**28**	**18**	**2**	
602	389	20	12	1	2	19	13		
1250	1066					5	5		
1064	998					3		2	
141	120	20	9		3	1			
1388	**1003**	**11**	**5**			**63**	**44**		
673	507					25	21		
653	444					17	8		
62	52	11	5			21	15		
3317	**2901**	**34**	**25**			**883**	**763**	**1**	**1**
1690	1512					483	452		
555	479	16	13			290	246		
518	405	18	12			61	45	1	1
518	499					46	20		
36	6					3			
3153	**2264**					**340**	**265**	**2**	**1**
3153	2264					340	265	2	1
121087	**102734**	**74**	**82**	**8**	**1**	**1858**	**878**	**155**	**159**
15374	**12400**	**18**	**21**			**241**	**108**	**20**	**26**
5905	4761					30		3	3
5627	4576	18	21			178	92	17	23
2246	1784					1			
1596	1279					32	16		

V—TOWNS ARRANGED TERRITORIALLY

District or State	Town, Municipality, Suburb, Cantonment, etc.	Population		Hindus			
				Scheduled castes		Others	
		M	F	M	F	M	F
1	2	3	4	5	6	7	8
Anantnag ..		**132275**	**110629**	**17**	**9**	**27188**	**21059**
Srinagar City	Municipality	112460	95327	17	9	23870	19130
Anantnag	T. A. C.	6723	5262			1025	793
Bijbihara	Do.	2481	2051			230	178
Pampur..		2471	1975			71	41
Machha Bhawan		1955	1532			530	406
Duru ..		1222	1058			27	9
Shopian..	T. A. C.	2346	2013			341	197
Verinag		1116	1103			196	153
Badami Bagh	Cantonment	1501	308			833	152
Muzaffarabad		**3410**	**2442**			**951**	**704**
Muzaffarabad	T. A. C.	2609	1962			730	575
Uri (Pirasthan)	Do.	801	480			221	129
FRONTIER DISTRICTS		**6005**	**4575**			**336**	**72**
Ladakh ..		**3187**	**2722**			**290**	**51**
Leh ..		1814	1558			200	16
Skardu ..		1373	1164			90	35
Gilgit ..		**2318**	**1853**			**46**	**21**
Gilgit ..		2818	1853			46	21

T. A. C.=Town Area Committee.
M=Males.
F=Females.

WITH POPULATION BY COMMUNITIES—CONCLD.

Muslims		Indian Christians		Jains		Sikhs		Others	
M	F	M	F	M	F	M	F	M	F
9	*10*	*11*	*12*	*13*	*14*	*15*	*16*	*17*	*18*
103536	**88773**	**56**	**61**	**8**	**1**	**1335**	**594**	**135**	**132**
87439	75531	50	55	8	1	943	469	133	132
5058	4493	2				38	6		
2247	1870					2	3	2	
2400	1934								
1300	1077					65	49		
1195	1049								
1990	1811					15	5		
920	950								
327	88	4	6			272	62		
2177	**1561**					**282**	**176**		**1**
1717	1279					162	108		
460	282					120	68		1
4577	**3524**	**47**	**36**			**106**	**53**	**939**	**890**
1850	**1717**	**45**	**36**			**63**	**28**	**939**	**890**
625	612	45	36			5	4	939	890
1225	1105					58	24		
2727	**1807**	**2**				**43**	**25**		
2727	1807	2				43	25		

V—(i) NUMBER PER 1,000 OF THE TOTAL POPULATION AND OF EACH MAIN COMMUNITY WHO LIVE IN TOWNS

Natural Division	Number per 1000 who live in towns						
	Population	Hindus	Muslims	Indian Christians	Sikhs	Jains	Others
1	2	3	4	5	6	7	8
JAMMU & KASHMIR STATE	**103**	**153**	**89**	**561**	**119**	**882**	**53**
I. The Sub-montane and Semi-mountainous Tract ..	111	143	72	554	204	880	277
II. The Outer Hills	29	49	18	430	45	1000	8
III. The Jhelum Valley ..	162	623	139	754	101	1000	791
IV The Indus Valley ..	34	544	30	542	525		46

V—(ii) COMMUNITIES OF URBAN AND RURAL POPULATION

Natural Division	Per 10000 of urban population						Per 10000 of rural population					
	Hindus	Muslims	Indian Christians	Sikhs	Jains	Others	Hindus	Muslims	Indian Christians	Sikhs	Jains	Others
1	2	3	4	5	6	7	8		10	11	12	13
I. The Sub-montane & Semi-mountainous Tract ..	5983	3315	154	458	87	3	4459	5301	15	223	1	1
II. The Outer Hills ..	5248	4471	30	248	2	1	2898	6941	1	154		6
III. The Jhelum Valley	1901	7984	6	98		11	223	9608		168		1
IV. The Indus Valley	386	7657	78	150		1729	11	8707	2	5		1275

TABLE VI AND ITS SUBSIDIARIES

Birthplace

NOTES

1. This table has been produced in two parts. Part I gives details by districts; Part II gives the details separately for the two cities—Jammu and Srinagar.

2. In section B of the table (Countries in Asia beyond India) under sub-section (ii), (Outside British Dominions) against the heading ELSEWHERE, the entry is 266. The detail of this entry is as follows :—

	Persons	Males	Females
Total ..	266	135	131
Badakhshan	2	1	1
Iraq	27	7	20
Kashgar	2	2	
Persia	1	1	
Syria	1	.	1
Samarkand	1	1	
Tibet	3	2	1
Turkey	1		1
Turkistan	12	6	6
Wakkan	202	107	95
Yarkand	14	8	6

3. When this table was being compiled the fact that Bihar and Orissa are now separate provinces was overlooked and the figures were amalgamated under one head as in 1931. When the error was detected it was not considered necessary to extract the figures separately in view of the small number involved (18 persons) and the fact that the two provinces were classed together in 1931. Similarly, the figures for Deccan States, Gujrat States and the States of the Western India Agency have not been given separately but classed together under the comprehensive heading 'Bombay States' as in 1931. Since the total number of persons involved in this case is only 3 the failure to give the figures separately is of no importance.

4. The table shows that out of a total population of 4021616 persons, 3882028 or 96.53 per cent. were born in the district where they were enumerated, 75069 or 1.87 per cent. were born elsewhere in the State and 64519 or 1.60 per cent. were born outside the State.

5. (a) Subsidiary (i) shows that the figures for immigrants at this census are 64519 against 64196 in 1931; the increase is negligible.

(b) The correct figures for emigrants cannot be given because tabulation throughout British India, and in the majority of the States, was restricted owing to the war. To arrive at the 'natural population' given in column 5 we have adopted for 1941 the figures for emigrants in 1931. This is in accordance with a suggestion received from the Census Commissioner for India. There is no reason to believe this figure is far wide of the mark; the true figures for 1941 probably exceed slightly those for 1931.

(c) The corresponding table on page 72 of the 1931 Report—Part I gives the figures by natural divisions and districts; on this occasion the figures have been given for the State as a whole only.

(d) It is usual to show such tables with 000 omitted, we have shown actuals.

(e) The percentage variation at 10.20 compares with 10 shown in 1931 but as the figures for emigrants for 1931 have been adopted for 1941 the comparison is of little value.

6. (a) Subsidiary (ii) has been prepared by districts. The corresponding table on page 111 of the 1931 Report —Part I gives the figures by natural divisions as well as districts.

(b) The totals shown for the whole State in columns 2, 3 and 4 represent the sum of the totals shown for Jammu Province, Kashmir Province and Frontier Districts in columns 5, 6 and 7 as well as the totals in columns 2 , 3 and 4.

(c) The corresponding table on page 111 of the 1931 Report—Part I cannot be compared fully with the table produced on this occasion. In the 1931 table the district components do not in some cases correctly add up to agree with the provincial and natural division totals.

7. (a) The standard form for Subsidiary (iii) is designed to show the distribution of emigrants from the State to places throughout India.

Since tabulation in British India was restricted, ***vide*** note 5 (b) above, it is not possible to produce this subsidiary at all because the figures from which it must be prepared can not be obtained from most of the Provinces and States of India owing to the restricted tabulation in those areas.

(b) The numbers of persons born and enumerated in the State are given in columns 2, 3 and 4 of the main table against item 1 ; they are 3957097, 2103941 and 1853156 for persons, males and females respectively.

(c) The great majority of emigrants from the State go to the Punjab and the North Western Frontier Province as labourers. This migration is almost entirely seasonal. The movement outwards commences in the late autumn and back to the State in the early spring. A considerable number of men from the Jammu Province are recruited for the army in British India ; this movement is of a semi-permanent nature. Men in fairly large numbers leave the Poonch and Mirpur Districts in particular in search of employment as domestic servants, seamen and traders. This movement also is of a semi-permanent nature.

8. (a) The standard form for Subsidiary (iv) is designed to show the variations in both immigration and emigration between 1931 and 1941 and the difference between immigration and emigration in 1931 and 1941. But as tabulation in British India and in most of the States was restricted it is impossible to show the figures for emigrants. To have repeated the 1931 figures for emigrants as done in the case of Subsidiary (i) would have been useless. We have therefore given the figures for immigrants only and omitted columns 5 to 9 of the standard form.

(b) The names of Provinces and States from which there are no immigrants have been omitted.

(c) In the corresponding table on page 113 of the 1931 Report—Part I Burma was shown. As Burma is no longer a part of India it has been omitted from this subsidiary table on this occasion.

(d) Variations shown represent an increase unless a minus sign has been given.

(e) It will be noticed that the great majority of immigrants to the State come from the adjacent Punjab and North Western Frontier Provinces.

9. A 1/50 random sample was extracted from the record and tabulated for comparison with the full table. The figures have been given for the whole State and not by districts as the latter would require too much space. The sample table comes immediately after Subsidiary (iv). The population of Gilgit Agency is not included in the sample because the record for that area, totalling 76526 slips, was tabulated in the North Western Frontier Province and was not available. The population of the State less Gilgit Agency is 3945090. The sample slips totalled 78901 ; multiplied by 50 this gives a total of 3945050 or an 'error' of 40.

The sample is reasonably representative for large totals but not for heads against which the entries are small. The sample table has been produced only for the purpose of comparison with actuals and for the information of those interested in the value of sampling for such purposes.

NOTE :—P stands for Persons, M for Males and F for Females.

IMPERIAL TABLE VI

VI—BIRTHPLACE (PART

District, State, Province or Country where born	Population of Province or State			District Jammu		
	P	M	F	P	M	F
	2	3	4	5	6	7
A—BORN IN INDIA						
I—DISTRICTS WITHIN THE STATE ..	**3957097**	**2103941**	**1853156**	**400139**	**222716**	**177423**
(i) **District of Enumeration**	**3882028**	**2067298**	**1814730**	**381572**	**213061**	**168511**
(ii) **Other Districts**	**75069**	**36643**	**38426**	**18567**	**9655**	**8912**
II—PROVINCES OR STATES IN INDIA BEYOND THE STATE	**61809**	**24205**	**37604**	**30441**	**10708**	**19733**
(a) **Provinces and States adjacent to the State**	**60235**	**23418**	**36817**	**29667**	**10381**	**19286**
(i) **British Territory**	**58748**	**22827**	**35921**	**29547**	**10327**	**19220**
North-West Frontier Province ..	**6545**	4069	2476	**337**	219	118
Punjab	**52203**	18758	33445	**29210**	10108	19102
(ii) **States**	**1487**	**591**	**896**	**120**	**54**	**66**
North-West FrontPier rovince States ..	**873**	338	535	**2**	2	
Bhawalpur	**11**	9	2	**8**	8	
Chamba	**481**	178	303	**25**	3	22
Bilaspur	**4**		4	**3**		3
Jind	**18**	10	8	**16**	8	8
Kapurthala	**36**	19	17	**25**	13	12
Mandi	**2**	1	1	**2**	1	1
Nabha	**8**	5	3	**4**	1	3
Patiala	**52**	30	22	**34**	18	16
Suket	**2**	1	1	**1**		1
(b) **Other Provinces and States in India** ..	**1385**	**692**	**693**	**742**	**304**	**438**
(i) **British Territory**	**603**	**338**	**265**	**153**	**75**	**78**
Ajmer-Merwara	**2**	1	1			
Assam	**9**	6	3			
Baluchistan	**72**	32	40	**23**	4	19
Bengal	**72**	37	35	**26**	16	10
Behar and Orissa	**18**	14	4	**3**	3	
Bombay	**65**	37	28	**26**	15	11
C. P. & Berar	**22**	10	12	**7**	3	4
Delhi	**74**	34	40	**25**	10	15
Madras	**50**	29	21	**18**	8	10
Sind	**59**	31	28	**15**	11	4
U. P. of Agra & Oudh	**160**	107	53	**10**	5	5
(ii) **States**	**782**	**354**	**428**	**539**	**229**	**360**
Baroda	**6**	3	3	**4**	1	3
Bombay States	**3**	1	2			
C. I. Agency	**7**	3	4			
Gwalior	**18**	17	1	**13**	12	1
Hyderabad	**28**	11	17	**5**	4	1
Mysore	**9**	8	1	**1**	1	
Rajputana Agency	**134**	87	47	**106**	63	43
U. P. States	**577**	224	353	**460**	148	312

I—DISTRICTS)

WHERE ENUMERATED								
Kathua			Udhampur			Reasi		
P	M	F	P	M	F	P	M	F
8	*9*	*10*	*11*	*12*	*13*	*14*	*15*	*16*
168047	**90721**	**77326**	**293013**	**152888**	**140125**	**257239**	**135109**	**122130**
160990	**87332**	**73658**	**285234**	**149298**	**135936**	**246979**	**130670**	**116309**
7057	**3389**	**3668**	**7779**	**3590**	**4189**	**10260**	**4439**	**5821**
9553	**3357**	**6198**	**1164**	**686**	**478**	**647**	**380**	**267**
9520	**3336**	**6184**	**1114**	**647**	**467**	**618**	**359**	**259**
9184	**3208**	**5976**	**988**	**592**	**396**	**613**	**357**	**256**
			40	39	1	**162**	82	80
9184	3208	5976	**948**	553	395	**451**	275	176
336	**128**	**208**	**126**	**55**	**71**	**5**	**2**	**3**
			14	9	5			
326	121	205	**111**	45	66	**1**		1
1		1						
1	1							
3	2	1						
3	3							
2	1	1	**1**	1		**4**	2	2
33	**19**	**14**	**47**	**36**	**11**	**26**	**20**	**6**
21	**13**	**8**	**36**	**28**	**8**	**20**	**14**	**6**
1		1						
6	5	1	**2**	1	1	**1**	1	
1		1	**4**	2	2	**4**	1	3
1	1					**4**	3	1
1		1	**1**	1				
			3	3				
3	1	2				**2**	1	1
			4	4				
2	1	1						
6	5	1	**22**	17	5	**9**	8	1
12	**6**	**6**	**11**	**8**	**3**	**6**	**6**	
						1	1	
			1	1				
2	2					**2**	2	
3		3	**3**	1	2			
1	1		**3**	3		**3**	3	
6	3	3	**4**	3	1			

VI—BIRTHPLACE (PART

District, State, Province or Country where born	DISTRICT — Mirpur P	Mirpur M	Mirpur F	Chenani Jagir P	Chenani Jagir M	Chenani Jagir F
1	*17*	*18*	*19*	*20*	*21*	*22*
A—BORN IN INDIA—CONTD.						
I—DISTRICTS WITHIN THE STATE ..	**377813**	**194522**	**183291**	**11684**	**6389**	**5295**
(i) District of Enumeration	**371639**	**192554**	**179085**	**9212**	**5040**	**4172**
(ii) Other Districts	**6174**	**1968**	**4206**	**2472**	**1349**	**1123**
II—PROVINCES OR STATES IN INDIA BEYOND THE STATE	**8800**	**2252**	**6548**	**89**	**63**	**26**
(a) Provinces & States adjacent to the State ..	**8515**	**2118**	**6397**	**82**	**59**	**23**
(i) British Territory	**8505**	**2113**	**6392**	**63**	**49**	**14**
North-West Frontier Province ..	**82**	51	31	**5**	4	1
Punjab	**8423**	2062	6361	**58**	45	13
(ii) States	**10**	**5**	**5**	**19**	**10**	**9**
North-West Frontier Province States ..						
Bahawalpur	**2**		2			
Chamba				**17**	8	9
Bilaspur						
Jind	**1**	1				
Kapurthala	**1**		1			
Mandi						
Nabha	**1**	1				
Patiala	**5**	3	2	**1**	1	
Suket				**1**	1	
(b) Other Provinces & States in India ..	**199**	**112**	**87**	**5**	**3**	**2**
(i) British Territory	**98**	**48**	**50**	**5**	**3**	**2**
Ajmer-Merwara						
Assam	**4**	3	1			
Baluchistan	**20**	12	8			
Bengal	**5**	1	4			
Bihar & Orissa	**4**	4				
Bombay	**11**	7	4			
C. P. & Berar	**4**		4			
Delhi	**18**	10	8	**1**		1
Madras	**2**		2			
Sind	**29**	11	18			
U. P. of Agra & Oudh	**1**		1	**4**	3	1
(ii) States	**101**	**64**	**37**			
Baroda						
Bombay States						
C. I. Agency						
Gwalior	**1**	1				
Hyderabad	**10**	4	6			
Mysore	**3**	2	1			
Rajputana Agency	**5**	4	1			
U. P. States	**82**	53	29			

I—DISTRICTS)—CONTD.

WHERE ENURMERATED—(CONTD).

Poonch Jagir			Baramulla			Anantnag		
P	M	F	P	M	F	P	M	F
23	24	25	26	27	28	29	30	31
420964	213421	207543	610937	329174	281763	848333	461555	386778
418977	212578	206399	604475	326001	278474	838714	456293	382421
1987	843	1144	6462	3173	3289	9619	5262	4357
859	496	363	1442	859	583	2784	1773	1011
830	478	352	1394	828	566	2547	1634	913
822	470	352	1393	828	565	2536	1626	910
60	37	23	911	558	353	768	434	334
762	433	329	482	270	212	1768	1192	576
8	8		1		1	11	8	3
7	7		1		1	1	1	
1	1							
						6	4	2
						4	3	1
23	13	10	43	28	15	218	121	97
10	7	3	40	26	14	191	102	89
						1	1	
1	1		1	1		2		2
						10	1	9
3	3		1		1	22	10	12
2	1	1				4	2	2
1		1	1	1		24	13	11
2	2		1		1	5	2	3
			5	1	4	18	9	9
1		1	5	2	3	17	14	3
			4	3	1	7	3	4
			22	18	4	81	47	3
13	6	7	3	2	1	27	19	8
2		2				1	1	
						5	3	2
1		1	1		1	4	1	3
						5	5	
10	6	4	2	2		12	9	3

VI—BIRTHPLACE (PART

DISTRICT

District, State, Province or Country where born	Muzaffarabad			Ladakh		
	P	M	F	P	M	F
1	32	33	34	35	36	37
A—BORN IN INDIA—CONTD.						
I—DISTRICTS WITHIN THE STATE ..	262932	140135	122797	195145	98273	96872
(i) District of Enumeration	259964	138459	121505	194642	97874	96768
(ii) Other Districts	2968	1676	1292	503	399	104
II—PROVINCES OR STATES IN INDIA BEYOND THE STATE	1717	970	747	159	110	49
(a) Provinces & States adjacent to the State ..	1681	943	738	158	110	48
(i) British Territory..	1678	940	738	157	110	47
North-West Frontier Province ..	1133	586	547	1	1	
Punjab	545	354	191	156	109	47
(ii) States	3	3		1		1
North-West Frontier Province States ..	1	1				
Bahawalpur						
Chamba	1	1				
Bilaspur						
Jind						
Kapurthala				1		1
Mandi						
Nabha						
Patiala	1	1				
Suket						
(b) Other Provinces & States in India ..	18	17	1	1		1
(i) British Territory..	9	8	1	1		1
Ajmer-Merwara						
Assam						
Baluchistan						
Bengal	2	2				
Bihar & Orissa..						
Bombay						
C. P. & Berar						
Delhi	1	1				
Madras	1		1			
Sind	2	2				
U. P. of Agra & Oudh	3	3		1		1
(ii) States	9	9				
Baroda						
Bombay States						
C. I. Agency						
Gwalior						
Hyderabad	1	1				
Mysore						
Rajputana Agency	1	1				
U. P. States	7	7				

I—DISTRICTS)—CONTD.

WHERE ENUMERATED—(CONTD.)

Astore			Gilgit (Leased Area)			Gilgit Agency		
P	M	F	P	M	F	P	M	F
38	*39*	*40*	*41*	*42*	*43*	*44*	*45*	*46*
16803	8802	8001	19305	10420	8885	74743	39816	34927
16085	8315	7770	18845	10042	8803	74700	39781	34919
718	487	231	460	378	82	43	35	8
223	146	77	2418	1543	875	1511	862	649
211	136	75	2400	1533	867	1498	856	642
174	112	62	2400	1533	867	688	562	126
147	95	52	2271	1447	824	628	516	112
27	17	10	129	86	43	60	46	14
37	24	13				810	294	516
37	24	13				810	294	516
10	8	2	18	10	8	2	1	1
10	8	2	7	5	2	2	1	1
			1	1				
10	8	2						
			3	2	1	1		1
			1	1				
			2	1	1			
						1	1	
			11	5	6			
			2		2			
			1	1				
			8	4	4			

VI—BIRTHPLACE (PART

District, State, Province or Country where born	Population of Province or State			District Jammu		
	P	M	F	P	M	F
1	2	3	4	5	6	7
A—BORN IN INDIA—CONCLD.						
(c) French & Portuguese Settlements ..	**22**	**19**	**3**			
(d) India, unspecified	**167**	**76**	**91**	**32**	**23**	**9**
TOTAL A ..	*4018906*	*2128146*	*1890760*	*430580*	*233424*	*197156*
B—COUNTRIES IN ASIA BEYOND INDIA						
(i) Within British Dominions	**48**	**19**	**29**	**8**	**4**	**4**
Burma	**43**	16	27	**8**	4	4
Ceylon	**3**	2	1			
Straits Settlements & Malaya ..	**2**	1	1			
Elsewhere						
(ii) Outside British Dominions	**1536**	**1037**	**499**	**727**	**530**	**197**
Afghanistan	**273**	179	94	**52**	47	5
China	**101**	75	26			
Nepal	**896**	648	248	**675**	483	192
Elsewhere	**266**	135	131			
(iii) Asia, unspecified	**741**	**484**	**257**	**4**	**3**	**1**
TOTAL B ..	*2325*	*1540*	*785*	*739*	*537*	*202*
C—COUNTRIES IN EUROPE						
(i) United Kingdom & North Ireland	**249**	123	126	**25**	12	13
(ii) Eire	**6**	2	4			
(iii) British possessions in Europe ..	**1**	1				
(iv) Continental Europe	**78**	46	32			
(v) Europe, unspecified	**12**	3	9	**1**		1
TOTAL C ..	*346*	*175*	*171*	*26*	*12*	*14*
D—COUNTRIES IN AFRICA						
(i) Within British Dominions	**6**		**6**	**6**		**6**
Kenya (British East Africa) ..	**6**		6	**6**		6
Mauritius						
Union of South Africa						
Zanzibar						
Elsewhere						
(ii) Outside British Dominions						
Mozambique						
Elsewhere						
(iii) Africa, unspecified	**15**	**7**	**8**	**8**	**2**	**6**
TOTAL D ..	*21*	*7*	*14*	*14*	*2*	*12*

I—DISTRICTS)—CONTD.

WHERE ENUMERATED—(CONTD).

Kathua			Udhampur			Reasi		
P	M	F	P	M	F	P	M	F
8	9	10	11	12	13	14	15	16
2	2		3	3		3	1	2
177602	94078	83524	294177	153574	140603	257886	135489	122397
5	3	2				2		2
4	3	1				2		2
1		1						
64	53	11	32	29	3	13	11	2
7	7		1	1		2	1	1
1	1		5	5				
56	45	11	26	23	3	11	10	1
1		1						
70	56	14	32	29	3	15	11	4
			4	2	2	2	2	
			1	1				
			5	3	2	2	2	
			3	2	1			
			3	2	1			

VI—BIRTHPLACE (PART

DISTRICT

District, State, Province or Country where born	Mirpur P	Mirpur M	Mirpur F	Chenani Jagir P	Chenani Jagir M	Chenani Jagir F
1	17	18	19	20	21	22
A—BORN IN INDIA—CONCLD..						
(c) French & Portuguese Settlements ..						
(d) India, unspecified	**86**	**22**	**64**	**2**	**1**	**1**
TOTAL A ..	*386613*	*196774*	*189839*	*11773*	*6452*	*5321*
B—COUNTRIES IN ASIA BEYOND INDIA						
(i) Within British Dominions	**21**	**7**	**14**			
Burma	**20**	6	14			
Ceylon						
Straits Settlements & Malaya ..	**1**	1				
Elsewhere						
(ii) Outside British Dominions	**13**	**12**	**1**	**23**	**23**	
Afghanistan	**5**	4	1	**9**	9	
China	**6**	6				
Nepal	**2**	2		**14**	14	
Elsewhere						
(iii) Asia, unspecified	**1**	**1**				
TOTAL B ..	*35*	*20*	*15*	*23*	*23*	
C—COUNTRIES IN EUROPE						
(i) United Kingdom & North Ireland	**3**		3			
(ii) Eire						
(iii) British possessions in Europe ..						
(iv) Continental Europe						
(v) Europe, unspecified						
TOTAL C ..	*3*		*3*			
D—COUNTRIES IN AFRICA						
(i) Within British Dominions						
Kenya (British East Africa) ..						
Mauritius						
Union of South Africa						
Zanzibar						
Elsewhere						
(ii) Outside British Dominions						
Mozambique						
Elsewhere						
(iii) Africa, unspecified	**2**	**1**	**1**			
TOTAL D ..	*2*	*1*	*1*			

I—DISTRICTS)—CONTD.

WHERE ENUMERATED—(CONTD).

Poonch Jagir			Baramulla			Anantnag		
P	M	F	P	M	F	P	M	F
23	*24*	*25*	*26*	*27*	*28*	*29*	*30*	*31*
			4	**2**	**2**	**18**	**17**	**1**
6	**5**	**1**	**1**	**1**		**1**	**1**	
421823	*213917*	*207906*	*612379*	*330033*	*282346*	*851117*	*463328*	*387789*
1		**1**				**8**	**4**	**4**
1		1				**5**	2	3
						3	2	1
2	**1**	**1**	**11**	**9**	**2**	**251**	**125**	**126**
1	1		**5**	4	1	**112**	45	67
			1	1		**2**	2	
			5	4	1	**99**	62	37
1		1				**38**	16	22
			1		**1**			
3	*1*	*2*	*12*	*9*	*3*	*259*	*129*	*130*
2	1	1	**5**	2	3	**191**	98	93
			6	2	4			
			17	1	16	**24**	14	10
			6	2	4	**4**		4
2	*1*	*1*	*34*	*7*	*27*	*219*	*112*	*107*
			1	**1**		**1**	**1**	
			1	*1*		*1*	*1*	

VI—BIRTHPLACE (PART

District, State, Province or Country where born	District: Muzaffarabad P	Muzaffarabad M	Muzaffarabad F	Ladakh P	Ladakh M	Ladakh F
1	32	33	34	35	36	37
A.—BORN IN INDIA—CONCLD.						
(c) French & Portuguese Settlements ..						
(d) India, unspecified	**18**	**10**	**8**			
TOTAL A ..	*264649*	*141105*	*123544*	*195304*	*98383*	*96921*
B—COUNTRIES IN ASIA BEYOND INDIA						
(i) Within British Dominions	**2**	**1**	**1**			
Burma	**2**	1	1			
Ceylon						
Straits Settlements & Malaya ..						
Elsewhere						
(ii) Outside British Dominions	**15**	**11**	**4**	**83**	**61**	**22**
Afghanistan	**7**	7		**8**	6	2
China				**74**	54	20
Nepal	**4**	4		**1**	1	
Elsewhere	**4**		4			
(iii) Asia, unspecified				**2**		**2**
TOTAL B ..	*17*	*12*	*5*	*85*	*61*	*24*
C—COUNTRIES IN EUROPE						
(i) United Kingdom & North Ireland	**5**		**5**	**4**	1	3
(ii) Eire						
(iii) British possessions in Europe ..				**1**	1	
(iv) Continental Europe				**36**	31	5
(v) Europe, unspecified						
TOTAL C ..	*5*		*5*	*41*	*33*	*8*
D—COUNTRIES IN AFRICA						
(i) Within British Dominions						
Kenya (British East Africa) ..						
Mauritius						
Union of South Africa						
Zanzibar						
Elsewhere						
Outside British Dominions						
Mozambique						
Elsewhere						
(iii) Africa, unspecified						
TOTAL D ..						

I—DISTRICTS)—Contd.

WHERE ENUMERATED—(CONTD.)

Astore			Gilgit (Leased Area)			Gilgit Agency		
P	M	F	P	M	F	P	M	F
38	*39*	*40*	*41*	*42*	*43*	*44*	*45*	*46*
2	**2**					**11**	**5**	**6**
17026	*8948*	*8078*	*21723*	*11963*	*9760*	*76254*	*40678*	*35576*
			1		**1**			
			1		1			
			30	**23**	**7**	**272**	**149**	**123**
			27	23	4	**37**	24	13
						12	6	6
			3		3			
						223	119	104
			732	**480**	**252**			
			763	*503*	*260*	*272*	*149*	*123*
			8	5	3			
			1		1			
			9	*5*	*4*			

VI—BIRTHPLACE (PART

District, State, Province or Country where born	Population of Province or State			District — Jammu		
	P	M	F	P	M	F
1	2	3	4	5	6	7
E—COUNTRIES IN AMERICA						
(i) Within British Dominions	**5**	**1**	**4**			
Canada	5	1	4			
Elsewhere						
(ii) Outside British Dominions	**1**		**1**			
United States	1		1			
Elsewhere						
(iii) America, unspecified	**6**	**1**	**5**	**3**	**1**	**2**
TOTAL E ..	*12*	*2*	*10*	*3*	*1*	*2*
F—COUNTRIES IN AUSTRALASIA						
(i) Within British Dominions	**1**	**1**				
Australia						
New Zealand	1	1				
Other British possessions in Australasia						
(ii) Outside British Dominions						
(iii) Australasia, unspecified	**4**		**4**			
TOTAL F ..	*5*	*1*	*4*			
G—AT SEA	**1**	**1**				
TOTAL G ..	*1*	*1*				
TOTAL RETURNED ..	*4021616*	*2129872*	*1891744*	*431362*	*233976*	*197386*
Birthplace not returned						
TOTAL POPULATION ..	*4021616*	*2129872*	*1891744*	*431362*	*233976*	*197386*

—DISTRICTS).—CONTD.

WHERE ENUMERATED—(CONTD.)

Kathua			Udhampur			Reasi		
P	M	F	P	M	F	P	M	F
8	9	10	11	12	13	14	15	16
177672	94134	83538	294217	153608	140609	257903	135502	122401
177672	94134	83538	294217	153608	140609	257903	135502	122401

VI—BIRTHPLACE (PART

District, State, Province or Country where born	District: Mirpur P	M	F	Chenani Jagir P	M	F
1	17	18	19	20	21	22
E—COUNTRIES IN AMERICA						
(i) Within British Dominions						
Canada						
Elsewhere						
(ii) Outside British Dominions						
United States						
Elsewhere						
(iii) America, unspecified						
TOTAL E						
F—COUNTRIES IN AUSTRALASIA						
(i) Within British Dominions						
Australia						
New Zealand						
Other British possessions in Australasia						
(ii) Outside British Dominions						
(iii) Australasia, unspecified	1		1			
TOTAL F	1		1			
G—AT SEA	1	1				
TOTAL G	1	1				
TOTAL RETURNED	386655	196796	189859	11796	6475	5321
Birthplace not returned						
TOTAL POPULATION	386655	196796	189859	11796	6475	5321

I—DISTRICTS)—Contd.

WHERE ENUMERATED—(CONTD.)

Poonch Jagir			Baaramulla			Anantnag		
P	M	F	P	M	F	P	M	F
23	24	25	26	27	28	29	30	31
			1		1	4	1	3
			1		1	4	1	3
						1		1
						1		1
			1		1	2		2
			2		2	7	1	6
						3		3
						3		3
421828	213919	207909	612428	330050	282378	851606	463571	388035
421828	213919	207909	612428	330050	282378	851606	463571	388035

VI—BIRTHPLACE (PART

District, State, Province or country where born	DISTRICT					
	Muzaffarabad			Ladakh		
	P	M	F	P	M	F
1	32	33	34	35	36	37
E—COUNTRIES IN AMERICA						
(i) Within British Dominions						
Canada						
Elsewhere						
(ii) Outside British Dominions						
United States						
Elsewhere						
(iii) America, unspecified						
TOTAL E ..						
F—COUNTRIES IN AUSTRALASIA						
(i) Within British Dominions				1	1	
Australia				1	1	
New Zealand						
Other British possessions in Australasia						
(ii) Outside British Dominions						
(iii) Australasia, unspecified						
TOTAL F ..				1	1	
G—AT SEA						
TOTAL G ..						
TOTAL RETURNED ..	264671	141117	123554	194531	98478	96953
Birthplace not returned						
TOTAL POPULATION ..	264671	141117	123554	195431	98478	96953

I—DISTRICTS)—CONCLD.

WHERE ENUMERATED—(CONCLD.)

Astore			Gilgit (Leased Area)			Gilgit Agency		
P	M	F	P	M	F	P	M	F
38	39	40	41	42	43	44	45	46
17026	8948	8078	22495	12471	10024	76526	40827	35699
17026	8948	8078	22495	12471	10024	76526	40827	35699

VI—BIRTHPLACE (PART II—CITIES)

District, State, Province or Country where born	Population of Cities			City where enumerated: Jammu			City where enumerated: Srinagar		
	P	M	F	P	M	F	P	M	F
1	*2*	*3*	*4*	*5*	*6*	*7*	*8*	*9*	*10*
A—BORN IN INDIA									
I—DISTRICTS WITHIN THE STATE	**248670**	**137229**	**111441**	**42592**	**25758**	**16834**	**206078**	**111471**	**94607**
(i) District of Enumeration ..	**238121**	**130157**	**107964**	**35529**	**20859**	**14670**	**202592**	**109298**	**93294**
(ii) Other Districts	**10549**	**7072**	**3477**	**7063**	**4899**	**2164**	**3486**	**2173**	**1313**
II—PROVINCES OR STATES IN INDIA BEYOND THE STATE	**9028**	**4798**	**4230**	**7645**	**3984**	**3661**	**1383**	**814**	**569**
(a) Provinces & States adjacent to the State	**8201**	**4431**	**3770**	**7022**	**3740**	**3282**	**1179**	**691**	**488**
(i) British Territory ..	**8122**	**4389**	**3733**	**6952**	**3705**	**3247**	**1170**	**684**	**486**
N. W. F. Province ..	**368**	241	127	**237**	161	76	**131**	80	51
Punjab	**7754**	4148	3606	**6715**	3544	3171	**1039**	604	435
(ii) States	**79**	**42**	**37**	**70**	**35**	**35**	**9**	**7**	**2**
N. W. F. P. States ..	**1**	1					**1**	1	
Bahawalpur ..	**4**	4		**4**	4				
Chamba	**6**	2	4	**6**	2	4			
Bilaspur									
Jind	**9**	5	4	**9**	5	4			
Kapurthala ..	**27**	15	12	**21**	11	10	**6**	4	2
Mandi	**1**		1	**1**		1			
Nabha	**3**		3	**3**		3			
Patiala	**27**	15	12	**25**	13	12	**2**	2	
Suket	**1**		1	**1**		1			
(b) Other Provinces & States in India	**789**	**334**	**455**	**604**	**229**	**375**	**185**	**105**	**80**
(i) British Territory ..	**257**	**139**	**118**	**93**	**48**	**45**	**164**	**91**	**73**
Ajmer-Merwara ..	**1**	1					**1**	1	
Assam	**2**		2				**2**		2
Baluchistan ..	**9**		9				**9**		9
Bengal	**35**	20	15	**18**	10	8	**17**	10	7
Bihar & Orissa ..	**3**	2	1				**3**	2	1
Bombay	**44**	25	19	**22**	14	8	**22**	11	11
C. P. & Berar ..	**9**	3	6	**4**	1	3	**5**	2	3
Delhi	**37**	16	21	**20**	7	13	**17**	9	8
Madras	**31**	19	12	**18**	8	10	**13**	11	2
Sind	**16**	9	7	**10**	7	3	**6**	2	4
U. P. of Agra & Oudh..	**70**	44	26	**1**	1		**69**	43	26
(ii) States	**532**	**195**	**337**	**511**	**181**	**330**	**21**	**14**	**7**
Baroda	**3**		3	**3**		3			
Bombay States ..									
C. I. Agency ..	**4**	3	1				**4**	3	1
Gwalior	**12**	11	1	**12**	11	1			
Hyderabad ..	**8**	4	4	**4**	3	1	**4**	1	3
Mysore	**4**	4		**1**	1		**3**	3	
Rajputana Agency ..	**106**	67	39	**96**	60	36	**10**	7	3
U. P. States ..	**395**	106	289	**395**	106	289			

VI—BIRTHPLACE (PART II—CITIES)—CONTD.

District, State., Province or Country where born	Population of Cities			City where enumerated — Jammu			City where enumerated — Srinagar		
	P	M	F	P	M	F	P	M	F
1	2	3	4	5	6	7	8	9	10
A—BORN IN INDIA—CONCLD.									
(c) French, Portuguese Settlements	**18**	**17**	**1**				**18**	**17**	**1**
(d) India, unspecified ..	**20**	**16**	**4**	**19**	**15**	**4**	**1**	**1**	
TOTAL A ..	*257698*	*142027*	*115671*	*50237*	*29742*	*20495*	*207461*	*112285*	*95176*
B—COUNTRIES IN ASIA BEYOND INDIA.									
(i) Within British Dominions ..	**10**	**4**	**6**	**6**	**3**	**3**	**4**	**1**	**3**
Burma	**10**	4	6	**6**	3	3	**4**	1	3
Ceylon ..									
Straits Settlements and Malaya ..									
Elsewhere ..									
(ii) Outside British Dominions ..	**240**	**137**	**103**	**118**	**68**	**50**	**122**	**69**	**53**
Afghanistan ..	**25**	24	1	**22**	22		**3**	2	1
China	**2**	2					**2**	2	
Nepal	**177**	97	80	**96**	46	50	**81**	51	30
Elsewhere ..	**36**	14	22				**36**	14	22
(iii) Asia, unspecified ..									
Total B ..	*250*	*141*	*109*	*124*	*71*	*53*	*126*	*70*	*56*
C—COUNTRIES IN EUROPE									
(i) United Kingdom and North Ireland ..	**177**	91	86	**10**	2	8	**167**	89	78
(ii) Eire ..									
(iii) British possessions in Europe ..									
(iv) Continental Europe	**24**	14	10				**24**	14	10
(v) Europe, unspecified									
TOTAL C ..	*201*	*105*	*96*	*10*	*2*	*8*	*191*	*103*	*88*
D—COUNTRIES IN AFRICA									
(i) Within British Dominions ..									
Kenya (British East Africa)									
Mauritius									
Union of South Africa ..									
Zanzibar									
Elsewhere ..									
(ii) Outside British Dominions ..									
Mozambique ..									
Elsewhere ..									
(iii) Africa, unspecified ..	**9**	**3**	**6**	**8**	**2**	**6**	**1**	**1**	
TOTAL D ..	*9*	*3*	*6*	*8*	*2*	*6*	*1*	*1*	

VI—BIRTHPLACE (PART II—CITIES)—CONCLD.

District, State, Province or Country where born	Population of Cities			City where enumerated: Jammu			Srinagar		
	P	M	F	P	M	F	P	M	F
1	2	3	4	5	6	7	8	9	10
E—COUNTRIES IN AMERICA									
(i) Within British Dominions ..	**4**	**1**	**3**				**4**	**1**	**3**
Canada	4	1	3				4	1	3
Elsewhere ..									
(ii) Outside British Dominions ..									
United States ..									
Elsewhere ..									
(iii) America, unspecified ..	**2**		**2**				**2**		**2**
TOTAL E ..	*6*	*1*	*5*				*6*	*1*	*5*
F—COUNTRIES IN AUSTRALASIA									
(i) Within British Dominions ..									
Australia									
New Zealand ..									
Other British possessions in Australasia ..									
(ii) Outside British Dominions ..									
(iii) Australasia, unspecified ..	**2**		**2**				**2**		**2**
TOTAL F ..	*2*		*2*				*2*		*2*
G—AT SEA									
TOTAL G ..									
TOTAL RETURNED ..	*258166*	*142277*	*115889*	*50379*	*29817*	*20562*	*207787*	*112460*	*95327*
Birthplace not returned ..									
TOTAL POPULATION ..	*258166*	*142277*	*115889*	*50379*	*29817*	*20562*	*207787*	*112460*	*95327*

VI—(i) VARIATION IN NATURAL POPULATION

State	1941 Recorded population	1941 Immigrants	1941 Emigrants	1941 Natural population (2+4—3)	1931 Recorded population	1931 Immigrants	1931 Emigrants	1931 Natural population (6+8—7)	Percentage variation (1931—1941)
1	2	3	4	5	6	7	8	9	10
Jammu & Kashmir State ..	4021616	64519	94448	4051545	3646243	64196	94448	3676495*	10.20

* This total is wrongly shown as 3675495 in the corresponding table in 1931.

VI—(ii) IMMIGRATION

Natural division and district where enumerated	Born in: District or State			Other parts of the State			Adjacent province or State			Other parts of India			Beyond India		
	P	M	F	P	M	F	P	M	F	P	M	F	P	M	F
1	2	3	4	5	6	7	8	9	10	11	12	13	14	15	16
JAMMU & KASHMIR STATE ..	**3957097**	**2103941**	**1853156**				**60235**	**23418**	**36817**	**1574**	**787**	**787**	**2710**	**1726**	**984**
Jammu Province ..	**1874603**	**990533**	**884070**	**54296**	**25233**	**29063**	**50346**	**17378**	**32968**	**1209**	**564**	**645**	**979**	**702**	**277**
(A) TOTAL DISTRICTS ..	*1446414*	*772915*	*673499*	*49837*	*23041*	*26796*	*49434*	*16841*	*32593*	*1173*	*542*	*631*	*951*	*677*	*274*
Jammu ..	381572	213061	168511	18567	9655	8912	29667	10381	19286	774	327	447	782	552	230
Kathua ..	160990	87332	73658	7057	3389	3668	9520	3336	6184	35	21	14	70	56	14
Udhampur ..	285234	149298	135936	7779	3590	4189	1114	647	467	50	39	11	40	34	6
Reasi	246979	130670	116309	10260	4439	5821	618	359	259	29	21	8	17	13	4
Mirpur	371639	192554	179085	6174	1968	4206	8515	2118	6397	285	134	151	42	22	20
(B) TOTAL JAGIRS ..	*428189*	*217618*	*210571*	*4459*	*2192*	*2267*	*912*	*537*	*375*	*36*	*22*	*14*	*28*	*25*	*3*
Chenani Jagir ..	9212	5040	4172	2472	1349	1123	82	59	23	7	4	3	23	23	
Poonch Jagir ..	418977	212578	206399	1987	843	1144	830	478	352	29	18	11	5	2	3
Kashmir Province ..	**1703153**	**920753**	**782400**	**19049**	**10111**	**8938**	**5622**	**3405**	**2217**	**321**	**197**	**124**	**560**	**272**	**288**
Baramulla ..	604475	326001	278474	6462	3173	3289	1394	828	566	48	31	17	49	17	32
Anantnag ..	838714	456293	382421	9619	5262	4357	2547	1634	913	237	139	98	489	243	246
Muzaffarabad ..	259964	138459	121505	2968	1676	1292	1681	943	738	36	27	9	22	12	10
Frontier Districts ..	**304272**	**156012**	**148260**	**1724**	**1299**	**425**	**4267**	**2635**	**1632**	**44**	**26**	**18**	**1171**	**752**	**419**
Ladakh ..	194642	97874	96768	503	399	104	158	110	48	1		1	127	95	32
Astore	16085	8315	7770	718	487	231	211	136	75	12	10	2			
Gilgit Leased Area ..	18845	10042	8803	460	378	82	2400	1533	867	18	10	8	772	508	264
Gilgit Agency ..	74700	39781	34919	43	35	8	1498	856	642	13	6	7	272	149	123

VI—(iv) IMMIGRATION INTO THE STATE FROM OTHER PARTS OF INDIA

Province	Immigration 1941	Immigration 1931	Immigration Variation
1	2	3	4
TOTAL	*61809*	*61033*	*776*
British India Proxinces	59768	60090	− 322
Ajmer-Merwara	2	6	− 4
Assam	9	7	2
Bihar & Orissa	18	23	− 5
Baluchistan	72	93	− 21
Bengal	72	111	− 39
Bombay	65	180	− 115
Central Provinces & Berar	22	45	− 23
Delhi	74	83	− 9
Madras	50	33	17
North Western Frontier Province	6545	6384	161
Punjab	52203	52366	− 163
Sind	59		59
United Provinces	577	759	− 182
States and Agencies	1852	926	926
Bombay States	3	19	− 16
Baroda State	6	22	− 16
Central India Agency	7	11	− 4
Gwalior	18	22	− 4
Hyderabad	28	19	9
Mysore	9	2	7
North Western Frontier Province States	873	88	785
Punjab States			
Bhawalpur	11		
Bilaspur	4		
Chamba	481		
Jind	18		
Kapurthala	36	668	− 54
Mandi	2		
Nabha	8		
Patiala	52		
Suket	2		
Sikim State		2	—
Rajputana Agency	134	64	
United Provinces States	160	9	151
Foreign Territories	22	17	5
Goa & French Possessions	22	17	5
India, unspecified	167		167
India, unspecified	167		167

IMPERIAL TABLE VI—BIRTHPLACE

1/50 SAMPLE

Comparative Results

Born in	Population of State as per 1/50 sample			50 times 1/50 sample—Population			Actual population vide Table VI		
	P	M	F	P	M	F	P	M	F
1	2	3	4	5	6	7	8	9	10
A. INDIA									
I. WITHIN THE STATE ..	**77522**	**41144**	**36378**	**3876100**	**2057200**	**1818900**	**3882354**	**2064125**	**1818229**
(i) District of Enumeration	**75510**	40115	35395	**3775500**	2005750	1769750	**3807328**	2027517	1779811
(ii) Other Districts ..	**2012**	1029	983	**100600**	51450	49150	**75026**	36608	38418
II. PROVINCES AND STATES IN INDIA BEYOND THE STATE ..	**1322**	**591**	**731**	**66100**	**29550**	**36550**	**60298**	**23343**	**36955**
(a) Provinces & States adjacent to State ..	**1281**	**564**	**717**	**64050**	**28200**	**35850**	**58737**	**22562**	**36175**
(i) British Territory ..	**1260**	549	711	**63000**	27450	35550	**58060**	22265	35795
(ii) States ..	**21**	15	6	**1050**	750	300	**677**	297	380
(b) Other Provinces & States in India ..	**40**	**27**	**13**	**2000**	**1350**	**650**	**1383**	**691**	**692**
(i) British Territory ..	**28**	18	10	**1400**	900	500	**601**	337	264
(ii) States ..	**12**	9	3	**600**	450	150	**782**	354	428
(c) French & Portuguese Settlements ..							**22**	**19**	**3**
(d) India, Unspecified ..	**1**		**1**	**50**		**50**	**156**	**71**	**85**
TOTAL A ..	*78844*	*41735*	*37109*	*3942200*	*2086750*	*1855450*	*3942652*	*2087468*	*1855184*
B. COUNTRIES IN ASIA BEYOND INDIA ..	**44**	**32**	**12**	**2200**	**1600**	**600**	**2053**	**1391**	**662**
C. COUNTRIES IN EUROPE ..	**10**	**6**	**4**	**500**	**300**	**200**	**346**	**175**	**171**
D. COUNTRIES IN AFRICA ..	**2**		**2**	**100**		**100**	**21**	**7**	**14**
E. COUNTRIES IN AMERICA ..	**1**		**1**	**50**		**50**	**12**	**2**	**10**
F. COUNTRIES IN AUSTRALASIA ..							**5**	**1**	**4**
G. AT SEA							**1**	**1**	
TOTAL POPULATION ..	*78901**	*41773*	*37128*	*3945050**	*2088650*	*1856400*	*3945090**	*2089045*	*1856045*

*Population of Gilgit Agency not included.

TABLE VII AND ITS SUBSIDIARIES

Age and Civil Condition

NOTES

1. The title of the table is slightly different to the corresponding table in 1931; the word 'sex' has been omitted as all important tables give sex details.

2. The table is in four parts; the corresponding table in 1931 was in three parts. The present table gives the figures for the whole State and for Provinces separately; in 1931 these were both included in the first part.

3. (i) In Part I the figures are given for the whole State separately for the communities shown in Table XIII.

(ii) Part II presents the details by provinces for the four main communities only; all other communities are shown under 'Others'.

(iii) Part III gives the same details as Part II but by districts instead of provinces.

(iv) Part IV gives details for the two cities separately in two parts :—

(a) for the total population of each city and

(b) for all communities as shown in Table XIII.

4. The figures for Gilgit Agency were not made available for age groups by communities. The whole population of the Gilgit Agency has, therefore, been treated as Muslim. There are only 99 persons belonging to other communities. The total Muslims shown in this table will naturally exceed those shown in Table XIII by 99. This does not of course affect the total population but it affects the other communities concerned to the extent of the numbers involved; they are Hindus 74, Sikhs 21 and Christians 4, *vide* the detail for Gilgit Agency given in Table XIII.

5. The figures shown under 'Widowed' include those shown as 'Divorced' in the record. Hindus shown by enumerators as divorced were treated as married persons temporarily separated or deserted. The divorced persons included belong to the Muslim, Christian and Buddhist communities. The detail of these is as follows :—

	Persons	Males	Females
Total Population	13987	5742	8245
Muslim	13560	5641	7919
Christian	5	2	3
Buddhist	422	99	323

6. Scheduled Castes are included with Hindus. 'Others' in Part I refer to those similarly shown in Table XIII.

7. To facilitate comparison between the numbers in the various age groups in 1931 and 1941 respectively a table has been prepared which is given below :—

Comparative Age Table for Total Population

Age.		Persons		Males		Females	
		1941	1931	1941	1931	1941	1931
TOTAL	..	*4021616*	*3646243*	*2129872*	*1938338*	*1891744*	*1707905*
0-1	..	82786	115930	41645	58323	41141	57607
1-2	..	98375	118293	49194	59284	49181	59009
2-3	..	112273	117890	56803	59099	55470	58791
3-4	..	122932	115806	61269	58525	61663	57281
4-5	..	118253	111623	60127	56700	58126	54923
TOTAL 0-5	..	*534619*	*579542*	*269038*	*291931*	*265581*	*287611*
5-10	..	587147	469120	308754	253182	278393	215938
10-15	..	489922	429988	263250	234021	226672	195967
15-20	..	406613	350597	214310	178694	192303	171903
20-25	..	376837	364687	191418	182673	185419	182012
25-30	..	343494	323912	175343	167877	168151	156035
30-35	..	306182	287468	161927	156681	144255	130787
35-40	..	252315	215654	135836	120001	116479	95653
40-45	..	183360	164794	101377	91981	81983	72813
45-50		158091	127624	88648	72028	69443	55596
50-55	..	113837	101362	65457	57413	48380	43949
55-60	..	95500	76945	54948	43698	40552	33245
60-65	..	64988	64878	37366	36427	27622	28451
65-70	..	41194	31348	23299	18084	17895	13264
70 and over	..	67517	58326	38901	33645	28616	24681
TOTAL 5 AND OVER	..	*3486997*	*3066701*	*1860834*	*1646407*	*1626163*	*1420294*

8. Certain features of the comparative table given above may be noted :—

(i) In the group 0-5 there is a decrease in 1941 ; for the age 0-1 this exceeds 28 per cent. The decrease is also large in groups 1-2 and 2-3 but in groups 3-4 and 4-5 an increase is shown and this increase continues for all higher age groups.

(ii) In 1931 there was no age group in which females exceeded males. At this census the females in group 3-4 out-number males by 394. The numbers of females per 1000 in this group for the three census years 1921, 1931 and 1941 are 983, 966 and 1006 respectively. In all other groups males exceed females.

(iii) The age group 0-5 shows a decrease of nearly 8 per cent. compared with 1931 but the group 5-10 shows an increase of over 25 per cent. The latter is the highest increase in any age group at this census ; in 1931 the highest increase was in group 0-5.

(iv) The table for 1941 shows a more regular tendency than in 1931. In 1931 the group 0-5 contained the largest number for any one group ; the numbers in the following 5 year groups decreased until the group 20-25 which showed a sudden rise ; thereafter all groups up to 70 showed a steady decrease in numbers. In 1941 from and including the group 5-10 the decrease is regular.

(v) In 1931 the total for all ages in groups 35-40 and above was 840931 ; in 1941 it was 976802 an increase of 135871 or 13·7 per cent. against 10.3 per cent. for all ages. This indicates a very definite tendency. The increase in all the groups within this range is marked except in the age group 60-65.

9. Some details may be noted concerning the percentage increase in the number of females in the different age groups in 1931 and in 1941.

(i) Age-group 5-10 .. .. 29 per cent. increase in 1941 against a decrease of 9 per cent. in 1931.

(ii) Age-group 10-15 .. .. 15 per cent. increase in 1941 against 18 per cent. increase in 1931.

(iii) Age-group 15-20 .. .. 12 per cent. increase in 1941 against 18 per cent. increase in 1931.

10. (i) At this census 2026892 of the total population are included in the age groups 15-50 out of 4021616 against 1834736 out of 3646243 in 1931. The percentage works out at 50.4 for 1941 and 50.3 for 1931.

A country is said to be progressive if 40 per cent. of its population is included in the age group 0-15, stationary if the percentage in this group is not more than 33 per cent. and regressive if it is not more than 20 per cent. In this table the number included in the group 0-15 is 1611688 which is a fraction over 40 per cent. of the total population.

(ii) In the case of Hindus the number in age group 0-15 is 37 per cent., for Muslims it is over 40 per cent. and for Sikhs it is 44.7 per cent. of the populations of their respective communities. In the case of the Buddhists the number constitutes 30.5 per cent. of the total of the community.

11. **Subsidiary (i)** :—

(i) The figures for years previous to 1941 have been taken from the 1931 report. Where figures are not available spaces have been left blank.

(ii) The figures are for Natural Divisions; they have been given separately for Jammu Province to facilitate comparison with 1931.

(iii) The mean ages given in this table and in Subsidiary (ii) have been calculated by the same method as in 1931. The table below gives the basis of our calculations :—

Age groups (Class-intervals).	Mid-values of the class intervals.	Persons (frequency distribution).	Deviation from arbitrary value.	Products (3 × 4).
1	2	3	4	5
0-5	2	1263	— 9	— 11367
5-10	7	1449	— 8	— 11592
10-15	12	1236	— 7	— 8652
15-20	17	1006	— 6	— 6036
20-25	22	899	— 5	— 4495
25-30	27	823	— 4	— 3292
30-35	32	760	— 3	— 2280
35-40	37	638	— 2	— 1276
40-45	42	476	— 1	— 476
45-50	47	420	0	— 49466
50-55	52	307	1	307
55-60	57	258	2	516
60-65	62	175	3	525
65-70	67	109	4	436
70-75	72	31	5	150
75-80	77	30	6	180
80-85	82	30	7	210
85-90	87	30	8	240
90-95	92	30	9	270
95-100	97	30	10	300
TOTAL		10000		3134

$$\begin{array}{r} -49466 \\ 3134 \\ \hline -46332 \end{array} \qquad \frac{-46332}{10000} = -4.6332$$

multiplying —4.6332 by 5 we get—23.1660 *i.e.*, —23.17 which when subtracted from 47 (the mid-year of the middle age group 45-50) gives 23.83 as the mean age.

12. **Subsidiary (ii)** :—

The table deals with the four main communities only as in the corresponding table for 1931. There is a decrease in the mean age of Hindu females and of Sikhs, both males and females, in 1941 as compared with 1931 ; in all other cases the mean age shows an increase.

13. **Susbsidiary (iii)** :—

(i) The table has been prepared by province and community. The figures for periods previous to 1941 have been taken from subsidiary V (a) to Imperial Table VII for 1931.

(ii) It will be observed that there is a decrease of children per 100 of persons aged 15-40 in the case of Muslims and Buddhists as compared with 1931. There is a decrease in children per 100 married females aged 15-40 in the case of Hindus only.

(iii) There are no entries for Buddhists under the Kashmir Province because only ten Buddhists were enumerated in this area and they were all over ten years of age.

(iv) In that part of the table showing persons over 60 per 100 of the population aged 15-40, it will be seen that the figures for Hindus and Buddhists exceed considerably those for Muslims and Sikhs. In the last part of the table it will be noticed that whilst the figures for married females aged 15-40 per 100 females of all ages are the same in 1941 as in 1931 there is a fall in the ratio in the case of Muslims and Buddhists.

14. **Subsidiary (iv)** :—

(i) This table has been prepared by provinces as in 1931 to facilitate comparison of figures.

(ii) All variations shown represent an increase except where a minus sign has been given.

(iii) The increase variation for all ages shows a fall as compared with 1931 but figures for the latter were affected by the phenomenal increase of the population for every age group in the Frontier Districts for which Gilgit [now divided into Astore and Gilgit (Leased Area)] and Frontier Illaqas (Gilgit Agency) were responsible —Ladakh showed no such phenomenal increase in 1931. The increase variation for the Frontier Districts has fallen back to what may be considered a normal figure. The phenomenal increase variation for 'Gilgit' and 'Frontier Illaqas' (Gilgit Agency) in 1931 must be attributed to special factors—probably defective enumeration in 1921.

15. **Subsidiary (v)** :—

(i) This table constitutes a new feature in the census reports for this State.

(ii) The area chosen for the selection of one lac enumeration slips of each sex for the purposes of this table was Srinagar City. As there were not quite enough females in Srinagar for the purpose the remaining 5000 slips were taken from Khas Tehsil (Anantnag District) in which tehsil Srinagar is situated.

(iii) The tendency for persons to give ages ending with 0 or 5 is brought out very clearly in this table from age 20 onwards. This is noticeable at every census in every province and state throughout India.

Another peculiar feature brought out by this table is that after the age 20 the odd numbers 1, 3, 7 and 9 are looked upon with least favour by those being censused ; this is not so in every case but it is so in sufficient cases to be noticeable. Thirty is the age common to the largest number of persons, both male and female.

16. **Subsidiary VI** :—

(i) In the age group 3-4 for the total population the females outnumber the males ; this was not the case for any age group in 1931.

(ii) In the important age group 0-30 Hindu females per 1000 males show an increase from 919 in 1931 to 936 in 1941.

(iii) For All-ages Hindus and Muslims have shown an improved proportion of females but both are still below the proportion for Sikhs and Buddhists; the latter are the same as in 1931 whilst the proportion in the case of Sikhs has fallen from 923 to 895. The proportion for Sikhs in the important group 0-30 has fallen to 947 from 970 in 1931.

17. **Subsidiary VII** :—

The table has been prepared for provinces.

18. **Subsidiary VIII** :—

The age groups and communities are the same as in 1931. The totals under each category have been given for both males and females in addition to the figures under each age group.

19. **Subsidiary IX** :—

(i) The table has been prepared by provinces instead of natural divisions to facilitate comparison with 1931.

(ii) It is to be remembered, as stated in note 5 above, that those Hindus shown as divorced, both male and female, were not treated as such for the purposes of Table VII and its subsidiaries.

(iii) The Infant Marriage Act in force in the State prohibits the marriage of boys below the age of 18 and of girls below the age of 14. It is probable that this law is frequently broken secretly in a number of cases. As a result some under age persons may have been shown as unmarried when they were in fact married or their ages may have been advanced to an age over the permissible marriage age.

20. **Subsidiary X** :—

(i) This table has been prepared by provinces to facilitate comparison with 1931.

(ii) As the few Buddhists recorded in the Kashmir Province were all males no entries appear in this table against Buddhists under 'Kashmir Province'.

21. **Fertility Tables** :—

(i) For the purpose of these tables Jammu District (excluding Jammu City) and Ladakh District were selected for rural areas and Jammu City was taken as the Urban area. The communities selected were Hindu, Muslim and Sikh for Jammu District and Jammu City and Muslim and Buddhist for Ladakh District. The selection was influenced by the fact that the three main communities are fairly represented in the Jammu District and in Jammu City and are living under the same conditions. To include the fourth main community, Buddhists, Ladakh was selected so that comparison could be made between the Muslim and Buddhist women of that area. It is important to note that polyandry is practised by the Buddhists and polygamy to some extent by the Muslims. As true urban conditions only obtain in the State in the two cities—Jammu and Srinagar—it was suitable to select one of these. As the communities are more evenly represented in Jammu that city was chosen in preference to Srinagar for the purposes of our tables.

(ii) The tables are based on questions 6, 7 and 8 of the census questionnaire—age, number of children born to a married woman and the number surviving and a mother's age at the time of the birth of her first child.

(iii) It must be stated that questions 7 and 8 were badly answered and that the tables cannot be regarded as representative of the true position; at best they are an indication of conditions. They will serve for comparison if similar figures are produced at a future date. The tables produced are numbered I, II and V; this is because the full set of tables suggested by the Census Commissioner for India ran from I to V. The material for tables III and IV was so defective as not to be worth presentation.

(iv) Averages have been shown to two decimal places and the proportion to survivors per 1000 born to the nearest whole number.

(v) The Census Commissioner for India expressed the wish that information should be collected on other aspects of the subject not covered by the census questionnaire but this did not prove feasible. It seems quite clear that, in this State at any rate, little reliable data connected with fertility problems will be collected except through the agency of a special investigation carried out under the control of Medical Officers by trained investigators—preferably women.

(vi) The tables produced for Jammu District show that a fair proportion of women are married at the age of 14 and below in all three communities, that children are born to Hindu and Muslim mothers from the age of 12, and in the case of Sikhs from the age of 16, and that the smaller the number of children in any family the larger the percentage of survivors.

According to the tables for Jammu District and City 40 is the highest age of a mother at the time of the birth of her first child.

(vii) There is no marked difference between the figures for the rural and urban areas of the Jammu District.

(viii) Table II for the Ladakh District shows a number of women to have been well over 40 at the time of the birth of the first child; the highest age given is 58. This indicates the unreliable nature of the information collected on this subject by means of the census.

22. **One-in-fifty Sample :—**

(i) The table has been produced to illustrate the difference in the results obtained from tabulation of the whole record and those from a 1/50 sample. The table will be found immediately after the Fertility tables at the end of the subsidiaries to Table VII.

(ii) The figures are given for the whole State for the main age groups and for the main communities for the age groups 0-5, 5-30 and 30 and over only.

(iii) The smaller the unit the less favourable the comparison with the full table. This is to be expected.

(iv) The sample does not include the population of the Gilgit Agency as the record for that district was not sorted and tabulated in the State.

NOTE —P stands for Persons, M for Males and F for Females.

VII—AGE AND CIVIL CONDITION (PART I—STATE SUMMARY)

JAMMU AND KASHMIR STATE

Community and Age	Population P	Population M	Population F	Unmarried P	Unmarried M	Unmarried F	Married P	Married M	Married F	Widowed P	Widowed M	Widowed F
1	2	3	4	5	6	7	8	9	10	11	12	13
Total Population	**4021616**	**2129872**	**1891744**	**1992481**	**1177045**	**815436**	**1734733**	**842515**	**892218**	**294402**	**110312**	**184090**
0-1 ..	**82786**	41645	41141	**82785**	41645	41140				**1**		1
1-2 ..	**98375**	49194	49181	**98363**	49191	49172	**10**	2	8	**2**	1	1
2-3 ..	**112273**	56803	55470	**112256**	56796	55460	**8**	4	4	**9**	3	6
3-4 ..	**122932**	61269	61663	**122914**	61263	61651	**14**	4	10	**4**	2	2
4-5 ..	**118253**	60127	58126	**118223**	60119	58104	**21**	7	14	**9**	1	8
TOTAL 0-5 ..	*534619*	*269038*	*265581*	*534541*	*269014*	*265527*	*53*	*17*	*36*	*25*	*7*	*18*
5-10 ..	**587147**	308754	278393	**585874**	308565	277309	**1200**	164	1036	**73**	25	48
10-15 ..	**489922**	263250	226672	**444690**	257713	186977	**44478**	5346	39132	**754**	191	563
15-20 ..	**406613**	214310	192303	**240615**	170812	69803	**162217**	42261	119956	**3781**	1237	2544
20-25 ..	**376837**	191418	185419	**96104**	87028	9076	**271702**	100314	171388	**9031**	4076	4955
25-30 ..	**343494**	175343	168151	**41811**	39284	2527	**287245**	129009	158236	**14438**	7050	7388
30-35 ..	**306182**	161927	144255	**18340**	17032	1308	**267126**	135274	131852	**20716**	9621	11095
35-40 ..	**252315**	135836	116479	**10010**	9192	818	**215189**	115666	99523	**27116**	10978	16138
40-45 ..	**183360**	101377	81983	**5875**	5350	525	**149017**	85509	63508	**28468**	10518	17950
45-50 ..	**158091**	88648	69443	**4541**	4085	456	**117642**	72626	45016	**35908**	11937	23971
50-55 ..	**113837**	65457	48380	**3111**	2782	329	**78881**	52002	26879	**31845**	10673	21172
55-60 ..	**95500**	54948	40552	**2385**	2124	261	**57335**	41082	16253	**35780**	11742	24038
60-65 ..	**64988**	37366	27622	**1664**	1483	181	**35918**	26666	9252	**27406**	9217	18189
65-70 ..	**41194**	23299	17895	**1089**	948	141	**19845**	15141	4704	**20260**	7210	13050
70 and over ..	**67517**	38901	28616	**1831**	1633	198	**26885**	21438	5447	**38801**	15830	22971
TOTAL ..	*3486997*	*1860834*	*1626163*	*1457940*	*908031*	*549909*	*1734680*	*842498*	*892182*	*294377*	*110305*	*184072*
Hindu	**809091**	**430638**	**378453**	**389007**	**39022**	**149985**	**332871**	**163731**	**169140**	**87213**	**27885**	**59328**
0-1 ..	**16811**	8516	8295	**16811**	8516	8295						
1-2 ..	**18165**	9088	9077	**18165**	9088	9077						
2-3 ..	**20767**	10445	10322	**20767**	10445	10322						
3-4 ..	**22366**	11287	11079	**22366**	11287	11079						
4-5 ..	**22028**	11190	10838	**22028**	11190	10838						
TOTAL 0-5 ..	*100137*	*50526*	*49611*	*100137*	*50526*	*49611*						
5-10 ..	**108972**	56857	52115	**108919**	56847	52072	**51**	9	42	**2**	1	1
10-15 ..	**91851**	47857	43994	**82291**	47383	34908	**9437**	443	8994	**123**	31	92
15-20 ..	**76960**	39880	37080	**46044**	34167	11877	**30150**	5510	24640	**766**	203	563
20-25 ..	**72817**	37541	35276	**21351**	20571	780	**49250**	16299	32951	**2216**	671	1545
25-30 ..	**67611**	35041	32570	**11251**	11042	209	**52422**	22714	29708	**3938**	1285	2653
30-35 ..	**62150**	33314	28836	**5992**	5877	115	**50022**	25477	24545	**6136**	1960	4176
35-40 ..	**52865**	28949	23916	**3677**	3599	78	**41133**	22974	18159	**8055**	2376	5679
40-45 ..	**40802**	23122	17680	**2445**	2301	54	**29659**	18124	11535	**8698**	2607	6091
45-50 ..	**36821**	21127	15694	**2049**	1989	60	**23855**	15876	7979	**10917**	3262	7655
50-55 ..	**27624**	16302	11322	**1502**	1441	61	**16526**	11810	4716	**9596**	3051	6545
55-60 ..	**23947**	13707	10240	**1158**	1108	50	**12172**	9314	2858	**10617**	3285	7332
60-65 ..	**17194**	9960	7234	**786**	759	27	**8012**	6415	1597	**8396**	2786	5610
65-70 ..	**11551**	6696	4855	**546**	511	35	**4641**	3925	716	**6364**	2260	4104
70 and over ..	**17789**	9759	8030	**859**	811	48	**5541**	4841	700	**11389**	4107	7282
TOTAL ..	*708954*	*380112*	*328842*	*288870*	*188496*	*100374*	*332871*	*163731*	*169140*	*87213*	*27885*	*59328*

VII—AGE AND CIVIL CONDITION (PART I—STATE SUMMARY)—Contd.

Community and Age	Population			Unmarried			Married			Widowed		
	P	M	F	P	M	F	P	M	F	P	M	F
1	2	3	4	5	6	7	8	9	10	11	12	13
Muslim	**3101346**	**1641763**	**1459583**	**1546087**	**906242**	**639845**	**1355551**	**655694**	**699857**	**199708**	**79827**	**119881**
0-1 ..	**63755**	31971	31784	**63754**	31971	31783				**1**		1
1-2 ..	**77543**	38821	38722	**77531**	38818	38713	**10**	2	8	**2**	1	1
2-3 ..	**88591**	44868	43723	**88574**	44861	43713	**8**	4	4	**9**	3	6
3-4 ..	**97162**	48279	48883	**97144**	48273	48871	**14**	4	10	**4**	2	2
4-5 ..	**93132**	47299	45833	**93192**	47291	45811	**21**	7	14	**9**	1	8
Total 0-5 ..	*420183*	*211238*	*208945*	*420105*	*211214*	*208891*	*53*	*17*	*36*	*25*	*7*	*18*
5-10 ..	**462034**	243504	218530	**460888**	243330	217558	**1076**	150	926	**70**	24	46
10-15 ..	**384645**	208445	176200	**350131**	203570	146561	**33893**	4717	29176	**621**	158	463
15-20 ..	**318275**	168778	149497	**187427**	132321	55106	**127916**	35446	92470	**2932**	1011	1921
20-25 ..	**294122**	149070	145052	**71631**	64374	7257	**215879**	81365	134514	**6612**	3331	3281
25-30 ..	**267313**	136022	131291	**29096**	27248	1848	**227990**	103112	124878	**10227**	5662	4565
30-35 ..	**236408**	124690	111718	**11571**	10653	918	**210652**	106514	104138	**14185**	7523	6662
35-40 ..	**192883**	103391	89492	**5790**	5250	540	**168615**	89725	78890	**18478**	8416	10062
40-45 ..	**137296**	75398	61898	**3012**	2679	333	**115148**	65011	50137	**19136**	7708	11428
45-50 ..	**116599**	64946	51653	**2150**	1866	284	**90270**	54668	35602	**24179**	8412	15767
50-55 ..	**82456**	47067	35389	**1335**	1161	174	**59680**	38555	21125	**21441**	7351	14090
55-60 ..	**68306**	39464	28842	**1000**	877	123	**43082**	30450	12632	**24224**	8137	16087
60-65 ..	**45441**	26148	19293	**704**	615	89	**26527**	19372	7155	**18210**	6161	12049
65-70 ..	**27924**	15707	12217	**417**	359	58	**14302**	10650	3652	**13205**	4698	8507
70 and over ..	**47461**	27895	19566	**830**	725	105	**20468**	15942	4526	**26163**	11228	14935
Total ..	*2681163*	*1430525*	*1250638*	*1125982*	*695028*	*430954*	*1355498*	*655677*	*699821*	*199683*	*79820*	*119863*
Christian	**3505**	**1886**	**1619**	**1904**	**1071**	**833**	**1417**	**741**	**676**	**184**	**74**	**110**
0-1 ..	**106**	55	51	**106**	55	51						
1-2 ..	**89**	43	46	**89**	43	46						
2-3 ..	**89**	46	43	**89**	46	43						
3-4 ..	**123**	64	59	**123**	64	59						
4-5 ..	**94**	51	43	**94**	51	43						
Total 0-5 ..	*501*	*259*	*242*	*501*	*259*	*242*						
5-10 ..	**568**	303	265	**568**	303	265						
10-15 ..	**401**	230	171	**387**	227	160	**14**	3	11			
15-20 ..	**289**	160	129	**184**	123	61	**102**	35	67	**3**	2	1
20-25 ..	**311**	149	162	**95**	68	27	**208**	77	131	**8**	4	4
25-30 ..	**312**	156	156	**55**	36	19	**250**	117	133	**7**	3	4
30-35 ..	**255**	142	113	**33**	19	14	**215**	118	97	**7**	5	2
35-40 ..	**215**	124	91	**22**	10	12	**173**	102	71	**20**	12	8
40-45 ..	**155**	91	64	**15**	9	6	**122**	73	49	**19**	10	9
45-50 ..	**143**	80	63	**11**	6	5	**112**	67	45	**20**	7	13
50-55 ..	**99**	55	44	**8**	4	4	**72**	46	26	**19**	5	14
55-60 ..	**94**	54	40	**10**	3	7	**60**	44	16	**24**	7	17
60-65 ..	**67**	30	37	**7**	1	6	**40**	24	16	**20**	5	15
65-70 ..	**39**	20	19	**4**	1	3	**22**	13	9	**13**	6	7
70 and over ..	**55**	32	23	**4**	2	2	**27**	22	5	**24**	8	16
Total ..	*3004*	*1627*	*1377*	*1403*	*812*	*591*	*1417*	*741*	*676*	*184*	*74*	*110*

VII—AGE AND CIVIL CONDITION (PART I—STATE SUMMARY)—Contd.

Community and Age		Population			Unmarried			Married			Widowed		
		P	M	F	P	M	F	P	M	F	P	M	F
1		2	3	4	5	6	7	8	9	10	11	12	13
Jain		**910**	**490**	**420**	**487**	**290**	**197**	**333**	**168**	**165**	**90**	**32**	**58**
	0-1 ..	**30**	14	16	**30**	14	16						
	1-2 ..	**25**	8	17	**25**	8	17						
	2-3 ..	**31**	19	12	**31**	19	12						
	3-4 ..	**30**	16	14	**30**	16	14						
	4-5 ..	**33**	22	11	**33**	22	11						
	Total 0-5 ..	*149*	*79*	*70*	*149*	*79*	*70*						
	5-10 ..	**132**	72	60	**131**	72	59	**1**		1			
	10-15 ..	**98**	53	45	**97**	53	44	**1**		1			
	15-20 ..	**82**	38	44	**53**	33	20	**27**	4	23	**2**	1	1
	20-25 ..	**77**	37	40	**21**	17	4	**54**	20	34	**2**		2
	25-30 ..	**71**	38	33	**9**	9		**59**	27	32	**3**	2	1
	30-35 ..	**63**	34	29	**6**	6		**52**	25	27	**5**	3	2
	35-40 ..	**52**	34	18	**5**	5		**41**	26	15	**6**	3	3
	40-45 ..	**40**	25	15	**4**	4		**29**	18	11	**7**	3	4
	45-50 ..	**40**	22	18	**3**	3		**25**	16	9	**12**	3	9
	50-55 ..	**28**	18	10	**4**	4		**16**	12	4	**8**	2	6
	55-60 ..	**32**	17	15	**3**	3		**13**	9	4	**16**	5	11
	60-65 ..	**23**	9	14	**1**	1		**9**	6	3	**13**	2	11
	65-70 ..	**10**	5	5	**1**	1		**4**	3	1	**5**	1	4
	70 and over ..	**13**	9	4				**2**	2		**11**	7	4
	Total ..	*761*	*411*	*350*	*338*	*211*	*127*	*333*	*168*	*165*	*90*	*32*	*58*
Sikh		**65882**	**34764**	**31118**	**34984**	**20428**	**14556**	**26775**	**12919**	**13856**	**4123**	**1417**	**2706**
	0-1 ..	**1614**	826	788	**1614**	826	788						
	1-2 ..	**1957**	947	1010	**1957**	947	1010						
	2-3 ..	**2066**	1050	1016	**2066**	1050	1016						
	3-4 ..	**2240**	1102	1138	**2240**	1102	1138						
	4-5 ..	**2190**	1166	1024	**2190**	1166	1024						
	Total 0-5 ..	*10067*	*5091*	*4976*	*10067*	*5091*	*4976*						
	5-10 ..	**10693**	5668	5025	**10625**	5665	4960	**67**	3	64	**1**		1
	10-15 ..	**8733**	4641	4092	**7785**	4547	3238	**940**	92	848	**8**	2	6
	15-20 ..	**6817**	3445	3372	**3942**	2777	1165	**2834**	655	2179	**41**	13	28
	20-25 ..	**5778**	2819	2959	**1356**	1230	126	**4314**	1544	2770	**108**	45	63
	25-30 ..	**5026**	2535	2491	**572**	551	21	**4291**	1918	2373	**163**	66	97
	30-35 ..	**4498**	2367	2131	**254**	223	31	**3972**	2049	1923	**272**	95	177
	35-40 ..	**3625**	1967	1658	**134**	113	21	**3102**	1738	1364	**389**	116	273
	40-45 ..	**2692**	1512	1180	**86**	78	8	**2189**	1308	881	**417**	126	291
	45-50 ..	**2312**	1364	948	**57**	52	5	**1760**	1154	606	**495**	158	337
	50-55 ..	**1688**	1011	677	**32**	29	3	**1185**	827	358	**471**	155	316
	55-60 ..	**1357**	796	561	**24**	23	1	**833**	610	223	**500**	163	337
	60-65 ..	**941**	555	386	**15**	15		**541**	415	126	**385**	125	260
	65-70 ..	**655**	374	281	**15**	14	1	**321**	249	72	**319**	111	208
	70 and over ..	**1000**	[illegible]	381	**20**	20		**426**	357	69	**554**	242	312
	Total ..	*55815*	*29673*	*26142*	*24917*	*15337*	*9580*	*26775*	*12919*	*13856*	*4123*	*1417*	*2706*

VII—AGE AND CIVIL CONDITION (PART I—STATE SUMMARY)—Contd.

Community and Age	Population			Unmarried			Married			Widowed		
	P	M	F	P	M	F	P	M	F	P	M	F
1	2	3	4	5	6	7	8	9	10	11	12	13
Parsee	**29**	**17**	**12**	**16**	**9**	**7**	**10**	**5**	**5**	[illegible]	[illegible]	
0-1 ..	**4**	1	3	**4**	1	3						
1-2 ..	**1**	1		**1**	[illegible]							
2-3 ..												
3-4 ..	**1**		1	**1**		1						
4-5 ..	**1**	1		**1**	1							
Total 0-5 ..	*7*	*3*	*4*	*7*	*3*	*4*						
5-10 ..	**5**	2	3	**5**	2	3						
10-15 ..	**1**	1		**1**	1							
15-20 ..	**5**	3	2	**1**	1		**4**	2	2			
20-25 ..	**1**	1		**1**	1							
25-30 ..	**5**	3	2	**1**	1		**4**	2	2			
30-35 ..	**2**	1	1				**1**		1			
35-40 ..												
40-45 ..	**1**	1					**1**	1				
45-50 ..	**1**	1								**1**	1	
50-55 ..												
55-60 ..												
60-65 ..												
65-70 ..												
70 and over ..	**1**	1								**1**	1	
Total ..	*22*	*14*	*8*	*9*	*6*	*3*	*10*	*5*	*5*	*3*	*3*	
Buddhist	**40696**	**20268**	**20428**	**19907**	**9956**	**9951**	**17720**	**9243**	**8477**	**3069**	**1069**	**2000**
0-1 ..	**457**	262	195	**457**	262	195						
1-2 ..	**585**	284	301	**585**	284	301						
2-3 ..	**722**	373	349	**722**	373	349						
3-4 ..	**1007**	520	487	**1007**	520	487						
4-5 ..	**772**	398	374	**772**	398	374						
Total 0-5 ..	*3543*	*1837*	*1706*	*3543*	*1837*	*1706*						
5-10 ..	**4713**	2340	2373	**4708**	2338	2370	**5**	2	3			
10-15 ..	**4178**	2019	2159	**3986**	1928	2058	**190**	91	99	**2**		2
15-20 ..	**4169**	2001	2168	**2959**	1386	1573	**1173**	608	565	**37**	7	30
20-25 ..	**3718**	1797	1921	**1646**	765	881	**1987**	1007	980	**85**	25	60
25-30 ..	**3148**	1544	1604	**824**	395	429	**2224**	1117	1107	**100**	32	68
30-35 ..	**2799**	1376	1423	**483**	253	230	**2206**	1089	1117	**110**	34	76
35-40 ..	**2666**	1369	1297	**381**	215	166	**2118**	1099	1019	**167**	55	112
40-45 ..	**2369**	1224	1145	**312**	189	123	**1866**	971	895	**191**	64	127
45-50 ..	**2170**	1106	1064	**271**	169	102	**1616**	844	772	**283**	93	190
50-55 ..	**1937**	1003	934	**230**	143	87	**1399**	752	647	**308**	108	200
55-60 ..	**1760**	910	850	**190**	110	80	**1173**	655	518	**397**	145	252
60-65 ..	**1319**	663	656	**151**	92	59	**787**	433	354	**381**	138	243
65-70 ..	**1014**	497	517	**106**	62	44	**555**	301	254	**353**	134	219
70 and over ..	**1193**	582	611	**117**	74	43	**421**	274	147	**655**	234	421
Total ..	*37153*	*18431*	*18722*	*16364*	*8119*	*8245*	*17720*	*9243*	*8477*	*3069*	*1069*	*2000*

VII--AGE AND CIVIL CONDITION (PART I—STATE SUMMARY)—CONTD.

Community and Age	Population			Unmarried			Married			Widowed		
	P	M	F	P	M	F	P	M	F	M	M	F
1	2	3	3	4	5	7	8	9	10	11	12	13
Jew	**11**	**2**	**9**	**6**	**1**	5	**4**	**1**	3	**1**		**1**
0-1 ..												
1-2 ..												
2-3 ..												
3-4 ..												
4-5 ..												
TOTAL 0-5 ..												
5-10 ..												
10-15 ..	1		1	1		1						
15-20 ..												
20-25 ..	1		1	1		1						
25-30 ..	2	1	1	2	1	1						
30-35 ..												
35-40 ..	3		3	1		1	2		2			
40-45 ..	1		1	1		1						
45-50 ..												
50-55 ..												
55-60 ..	2		2				1		1	1		1
60-65 ..	1	1					1	1				
65-70 ..												
70 and over ..												
TOTAL ..	*11*	*2*	*9*	*6*	*1*	*5*	*4*	*1*	*3*	*1*		*1*
Tribes	**51**	**29**	**22**	**31**	**19**	**12**	**17**	**9**	**8**	**3**	**1**	**2**
0-1 ..	1		1	1		1						
1-2 ..	4	2	2	4	2	2						
2-3 ..	2	2		2	2							
3-4 ..	1	1		1	1							
4-5 ..	1		1	1		1						
TOTAL 0-5 ..	*9*	5	*4*	*9*	*5*	*4*						
5-10 ..	10	6	4	10	6	4						
10-15 ..	6	2	4	6	2	4						
15-20 ..	4	3	1	2	2		2	1	1			
20-25 ..	4	3	1	2	2		2	1	1			
25-30 ..	3	1	2				3	1	2			
30-35 ..	5	3	2	1	1		4	2	2			
35-40 ..	5	2	3				4	2	2	1		1
40-45 ..	1	1					1	1				
45-50 ..	1	1					1	1				
50-55 ..												
55-60 ..												
60-65 ..												
65-70 ..												
70 abd over ..	3	2	1	1	1					2	1	1
TOTAL ..	*42*	*24*	*18*	*22*	*14*	*8*	*17*	*9*	*8*	*3*	*1*	*2*

VII—AGE AND CIVIL CONDITION (PART I—STATE SUMMARY)—CONCLD.

Community and Age		Population			Unmarried			Married			Widowed		
		P	M	F	P	M	F	P	M	F	P	M	F
1		2	3	4	5	6	7	8	9	10	11	12	13
Others		**95**	**15**	**80**	**52**	**7**	**45**	**35**	**4**	**31**	**8**	**4**	**4**
	0-1 ..	**8**		8	**8**		8						
	1-2 ..	**6**		6	**6**		6						
	2-3 ..	**5**		5	**5**		5						
	3-4 ..	**2**		2	**2**		2						
	4-5 ..	**2**		2	**2**		2						
	TOTAL 0-5 ..	*23*		*23*	*23*		*23*						
	5-10 ..	**20**	2	18	**20**	2	18						
	10-15 ..	**8**	2	6	**5**	2	3	**3**		3			
	15-20 ..	**12**	2	10	**3**	2	1	**9**		9			
	20-25 ..	**8**	1	7				**8**	1	7			
	25-30 ..	**3**	2	1	**1**	1		**2**	1	1			
	30-35 ..	**2**		2				**2**		2			
	35-40 ..	**1**		1				**1**		1			
	40-45 ..	**2**	2					**2**	2				
	45-50 ..	**4**	1	3				**3**		3	**1**	1	
	50-55 ..	**5**	1	4				**3**		3	**2**	1	1
	55-60 ..	**2**		2				**1**		1	**1**		1
	60-65 ..	**2**		2				**1**		1	**1**		1
	65-70 ..	**1**		1							**1**		1
	70 and over ..	**2**	2								**2**	2	
	TOTAL ..	*72*	*15*	*57*	*29*	*7*	*22*	*35*	*4*	*31*	*8*	*4*	*4*

VII—AGE AND CIVIL CONDITION (PART II—PROVINCES)

Community	Age	Population P	Population M	Population F	Unmarried P	Unmarried M	Unmarried F	Married P	Married M	Married F	Widowed P	Widowed M	Widowed F
1		*2*	*3*	*4*	*5*	*6*	*7*	*8*	*9*	*10*	*11*	*12*	*13*
JAMMU PROVINCE													
Total Population		**1981433**	**1034410**	**947023**	**995545**	**585841**	**409704**	**815918**	**390531**	**425387**	**169970**	**58038**	**111932**
	0-1 ..	**41406**	20642	20764	**41406**	20642	20764						
	1-2 ..	**49127**	24491	24636	**49127**	24491	24636						
	2-3 ..	**55879**	28052	27827	**55879**	28052	27827						
	3-4 ..	**60102**	30015	30087	**60102**	30015	30087						
	4-5 ..	**60090**	30555	29535	**60090**	30555	29535						
	TOTAL 0-5 ..	*266604*	*133755*	*132849*	*266604*	*133755*	*132849*						
	5-10 ..	**294549**	153711	140838	**294443**	153690	140753	**100**	20	80	**6**	1	5
	10-15 ..	**242653**	128767	113886	**222193**	127125	95073	**20166**	1573	18593	**289**	69	220
	15-20 ..	**191913**	98854	93059	**118451**	83503	34948	**71658**	14797	56861	**1804**	554	1250
	20-25 ..	**174318**	85871	88447	**46398**	42603	3795	**123166**	41323	81843	**4754**	1045	2809
	25-30 ..	**161418**	79826	81592	**20976**	20188	788	**132532**	56245	76287	**7910**	3393	4517
	30-35 ..	**147655**	76178	71477	**9582**	9169	413	**126260**	62342	63918	**11813**	4667	7146
	35-40 ..	**121815**	64205	57610	**5179**	4916	263	**101516**	54142	47374	**15120**	5147	9973
	40-45 ..	**88418**	48205	40213	**3077**	2903	174	**69620**	40218	29402	**15721**	5084	10637
	45-50 ..	**79728**	44112	35616	**2519**	2347	172	**56768**	35636	21132	**20441**	6129	14312
	50-55 ..	**58730**	33667	25063	**1802**	1675	127	**39121**	26378	12743	**17807**	5614	12193
	55-60 ..	**51897**	29562	22335	**1436**	1334	102	**29579**	21741	7838	**20882**	6487	14395
	60-65 ..	**36654**	20965	15689	**1018**	943	75	**19210**	14693	4517	**16426**	5329	11097
	65-70 ..	**24498**	13923	10575	**719**	647	72	**11155**	8855	2300	**12624**	4421	8203
	70 and over ..	**40583**	22809	17774	**1143**	1043	100	**15067**	12568	2499	**24373**	9198	15175
	TOTAL ..	*1714829*	*900655*	*814174*	*728941*	*452086*	*276855*	*815918*	*390531*	*425387*	*169970*	*58038*	*111932*
Hindu		**722835**	**381745**	**341090**	**343772**	**210029**	**133743**	**299683**	**146441**	**153242**	**79380**	**25275**	**54105**
	0-1 ..	**15367**	7734	7633	**15367**	7734	7633						
	1-2 ..	**16415**	8211	8204	**16415**	8211	8204						
	2-3 ..	**18610**	9298	9312	**18610**	9298	9312						
	3-4 ..	**19993**	10112	9881	**19993**	10112	9881						
	4-5 ..	**19630**	9964	9666	**19630**	9964	9666						
	TOTAL 0-5 ..	*90015*	*45319*	*44696*	*90015*	*45319*	*44696*						
	5-10 ..	**97043**	50655	46388	**96994**	50645	46349	**47**	9	38	**2**	1	1
	10-15 ..	**81870**	42577	39293	**73004**	42129	30875	**8753**	419	8334	**113**	29	84
	15-20 ..	**68560**	35156	33404	**40475**	30001	10474	**27386**	4966	22420	**699**	189	510
	20-25 ..	**64397**	32606	31791	**18226**	17552	674	**44151**	14436	29715	**2020**	618	1402
	25-30 ..	**59578**	30287	29291	**9356**	9167	189	**46650**	19953	26697	**3572**	1167	2405
	30-35 ..	**55125**	29074	26051	**4919**	4816	103	**44651**	22495	22156	**5555**	1763	3792
	35-40 ..	**46978**	25334	21644	**3009**	2939	70	**36709**	20278	16431	**7260**	2117	5143
	40-45 ..	**36117**	20220	15897	**1976**	1927	49	**26400**	16001	10399	**7741**	2292	5449
	45-50 ..	**33003**	18799	14204	**1665**	1609	56	**21559**	14301	7258	**9779**	2889	6890
	50-55 ..	**24798**	14573	10225	**1228**	1172	56	**14990**	10700	4290	**8580**	2701	5879
	55-60 ..	**21793**	12450	9343	**957**	912	45	**11213**	8574	2639	**9623**	2964	6659
	60-65 ..	**15793**	9148	6645	**669**	644	25	**7468**	5963	1505	**7656**	2541	5115
	65-70 ..	**10803**	6264	4539	**486**	451	35	**4385**	3701	684	**5932**	2112	3820
	70 and over ..	**16962**	9283	7679	**793**	746	47	**5321**	4645	676	**10848**	3892	6956
	TOTAL ..	*632820*	*336426*	*296394*	*253757*	*164710*	*89047*	*299683*	*146441*	*153242*	*79380*	*25275*	*54105*

VII—AGE AND CIVIL CONDITION (PART II—PROVINCES)—CONTD.

JAMMU PROVINCE—contd.

Community and Age	Population P	Population M	Population F	Unmarried P	Unmarried M	Unmarried F	Married P	Married M	Married F	Widowed P	Widowed M	Widowed F
1	2	3	4	5	6	7	8	9	10	11	12	13
Muslim	**1215676**	**630318**	**585358**	**628971**	**362648**	**266323**	**499081**	**235880**	**263201**	**87624**	**31790**	**55834**
0-1 ..	**24995**	12373	12622	**24995**	12373	12622						
1-2 ..	**31446**	15683	15763	**31446**	15683	15763						
2-3 ..	**35941**	18072	17869	**35941**	18072	17869						
3-4 ..	**38654**	19159	19495	**38654**	19159	19495						
4-5 ..	**39024**	19802	19222	**39024**	19802	19222						
TOTAL 0-5 ..	*170060*	*85089*	*84971*	*170060*	*85089*	*84971*						
5-10 ..	**190415**	99348	91067	**190377**	99337	91040	**34**	11	23	**4**		4
10-15 ..	**155183**	83212	71971	**144079**	82061	62018	**10929**	1112	9817	**175**	39	136
15-20 ..	**119175**	61603	57572	**75500**	51797	23703	**42592**	9451	33141	**1083**	355	728
20-25 ..	**106417**	51654	54763	**27385**	24347	3038	**76377**	26011	50366	**2655**	1296	1359
25-30 ..	**98709**	48049	50660	**11271**	10685	586	**83207**	35177	48030	**4231**	2187	2044
30-35 ..	**89590**	45625	43965	**4494**	4205	289	**79017**	38578	40439	**6079**	2842	3237
35-40 ..	**72402**	37559	34843	**2077**	1896	181	**62743**	32720	30023	**7582**	2943	4639
40-45 ..	**50472**	26952	23520	**1038**	915	123	**41760**	23340	18420	**7674**	2697	4977
45-50 ..	**45096**	24368	20728	**807**	693	114	**33997**	20543	13454	**10292**	3132	7160
50-55 ..	**32733**	18386	14347	**539**	471	68	**23296**	15097	8199	**8898**	2818	6080
55-60 ..	**29108**	16538	12570	**456**	401	55	**17762**	12729	5033	**10890**	3408	7482
60-65 ..	**20176**	11425	8751	**338**	288	50	**11365**	8442	2923	**8473**	2695	5778
65-70 ..	**13245**	7408	5837	**219**	185	34	**6554**	4989	1565	**6472**	2234	4238
70 and over ..	**22895**	13102	9793	**331**	278	53	**9448**	7680	1768	**13116**	5144	7972
TOTAL ..	*1045616*	*545229*	*500387*	*458911*	*277559*	*181352*	*499081*	*235880*	*263201*	*87624*	*31790*	*55834*
Sikh	**38566**	**20036**	**18530**	**20543**	**11889**	**8654**	**15338**	**7299**	**8039**	**2685**	**848**	**1837**
0-1 ..	**891**	462	429	**891**	462	429						
1-2 ..	**1147**	545	602	**1147**	545	602						
2-3 ..	**1210**	620	590	**1210**	620	590						
3-4 ..	**1295**	656	639	**1295**	656	639						
4-5 ..	**1314**	718	596	**1314**	718	596						
TOTAL 0-5 ..	*5857*	*3001*	*2856*	*5857*	*3001*	*2856*						
5-10 ..	**6399**	3363	3036	**6381**	3363	3018	**18**		18			
10-15 ..	**5105**	2721	2384	**4654**	2688	1966	**450**	32	418	**1**	1	
15-20 ..	**3745**	1878	1867	**2248**	1556	692	**1483**	317	1166	**14**	5	9
20-25 ..	**3107**	1420	1687	**695**	626	69	**2345**	768	1577	**67**	26	41
25-30 ..	**2757**	1290	1467	**307**	295	12	**2353**	962	1391	**97**	33	64
30-35 ..	**2634**	1309	1325	**148**	128	20	**2320**	1128	1192	**166**	53	113
35-40 ..	**2206**	1166	1040	**82**	70	12	**1868**	1023	845	**256**	73	183
40-45 ..	**1659**	931	728	**51**	49	2	**1331**	804	527	**277**	78	199
45-50 ..	**1455**	844	611	**37**	35	2	**1084**	714	370	**334**	95	239
50-55 ..	**1053**	622	431	**27**	24	3	**735**	514	221	**291**	84	207
55-60 ..	**881**	509	372	**18**	17	1	**534**	392	142	**329**	100	229
60-65 ..	**619**	363	256	**10**	10		**341**	266	75	**268**	87	181
65-70 ..	**413**	232	181	**11**	10	1	**200**	154	46	**202**	68	134
70 and over ..	**676**	387	289	**17**	17		**276**	225	51	**383**	145	238
TOTAL ..	*32709*	*17035*	*15674*	*14686*	*8888*	*5798*	*15338*	*7299*	*8039*	*2685*	*848*	*1837*

VII—AGE AND CIVIL CONDITION (PART II—PROVINCES)—CONTD.

JAMMU PROVINCE—concld.

Community and Age	Population P	Population M	Population F	Unmarried P	Unmarried M	Unmarried F	Married P	Married M	Married F	Widowed P	Widowed M	Widowed F
1	2	3	4	5	6	7	8	9	10	11	12	13
Buddhist	**522**	**247**	**275**	**230**	**108**	**122**	**255**	**123**	**132**	**37**	**16**	**21**
0-1 ..	**16**	9	7	**16**	9	7						
1-2 ..	**4**	1	3	**4**	1	3						
2-3 ..	**5**	2	3	**5**	2	3						
3-4 ..	**14**	10	4	**14**	10	4						
4-5 ..	**6**	4	2	**6**	4	2						
TOTAL 0-5 ..	*45*	*26*	*19*	*45*	*26*	*19*						
5-10 ..	**66**	23	43	**66**	23	43						
10-15 ..	**72**	28	44	**56**	21	35	**16**	7	9			
15-20 ..	**102**	45	57	**38**	18	20	**61**	25	36	**3**	2	1
20-25 ..	**49**	24	25	**14**	9	5	**33**	14	19	**2**	1	1
25-30 ..	**41**	23	18	**4**	4		**35**	18	17	**2**	1	1
30-35 ..	**34**	15	19	**1**	1		**33**	14	19			
35-40 ..	**17**	13	4	**1**	1		**14**	11	3	**2**	1	1
40-45 ..	**18**	7	11	**2**	2		**11**	1	10	**5**	4	1
45-50 ..	**23**	14	9	**2**	2		**16**	11	5	**5**	1	4
50-55 ..	**37**	21	16	**1**	1		**24**	17	7	**12**	3	9
55-60 ..	**18**	8	10				**12**	5	7	**6**	3	3
60-65 ..												
65-70 ..												
70 and over ..												
TOTAL ..	*477*	*221*	*256*	*185*	*82*	*103*	*255*	*123*	*132*	*37*	*16*	*21*
Others	**3834**	**2064**	**1770**	**2029**	**1167**	**862**	**1561**	**788**	**773**	**244**	**109**	**135**
0-1 ..	**137**	64	73	**137**	64	73						
1-2 ..	**115**	51	64	**115**	51	64						
2-3 ..	**113**	60	53	**113**	60	53						
3-4 ..	**146**	78	68	**146**	78	68						
4-5 ..	**116**	67	49	**116**	67	49						
TOTAL 0-5 ..	*627*	*320*	*307*	*627*	*320*	*307*						
5-10 ..	**626**	322	304	**625**	322	303	**1**		1			
10-15 ..	**423**	229	194	**405**	226	179	**18**	3	15			
15-20 ..	**331**	172	159	**190**	131	59	**136**	38	98	**5**	3	2
20-25 ..	**348**	167	181	**78**	69	9	**260**	94	166	**10**	4	6
25-30 ..	**333**	177	156	**38**	37	1	**287**	135	152	**8**	5	3
30-35 ..	**272**	155	117	**20**	19	1	**239**	127	112	**13**	9	4
35-40 ..	**212**	133	79	**10**	10		**182**	110	72	**20**	13	7
40-45 ..	**152**	95	57	**10**	10		**118**	72	46	**24**	13	11
45-50 ..	**151**	87	64	**8**	8		**112**	67	45	**31**	12	19
50-55 ..	**109**	65	44	**7**	7		**76**	50	26	**26**	8	18
55-60 ..	**97**	57	40	**5**	4	1	**58**	41	17	**34**	12	22
60-65 ..	**66**	29	37	**1**	1		**36**	22	14	**29**	6	23
65-70 ..	**37**	19	18	**3**	1	2	**16**	11	5	**18**	7	11
70 and over ..	**50**	37	13	**2**	2		**22**	18	4	**26**	17	9
TOTAL ..	*3207*	*1744*	*1463*	*1402*	*847*	*555*	*1561*	*788*	*773*	*244*	*109*	*135*

VII—AGE AND CIVIL CONDITION (PART II—PROVINCES)—CONTD.

KASHMIR PROVINCE

Community and Age	Population P	Population M	Population F	Unmarried P	Unmarried M	Unmarried F	Married P	Married M	Married F	Widowed P	Widowed M	Widowed F
1	2	3	4	5	6	7	8	9	10	11	12	13
Total Population	**1728705**	**934738**	**793967**	**844574**	**505779**	**338795**	**779338**	**382297**	**397041**	**104793**	**46662**	**58131**
0-1 ..	**36877**	18713	18164	**36877**	18713	18164						
1-2 ..	**42019**	21269	20750	**42019**	21269	20750						
2-3 ..	**47231**	24125	23106	**47231**	24125	23106						
3-4 ..	**52761**	26261	26500	**52761**	26261	26500						
4-5 ..	**49394**	25091	24303	**49394**	25091	24303						
TOTAL 0-5 ..	*228282*	*115459*	*112823*	*228282*	*115459*	*112823*						
5-10 ..	**248319**	131927	116392	**247569**	131845	115724	**729**	78	651	**21**	4	17
10-15 ..	**211132**	114652	96480	**189742**	111932	77810	**21033**	2645	18388	**357**	75	282
15-20 ..	**183813**	98700	85113	**103235**	75339	27896	**78969**	22823	56146	**1609**	538	1071
20-25 ..	**173516**	91124	82392	**41377**	38500	2877	**128525**	50787	77738	**3614**	1837	1777
25-30 ..	**157135**	82421	74714	**17303**	16612	696	**134166**	62544	71622	**5661**	3265	2396
30-35 ..	**135052**	74034	61018	**7023**	6705	318	**120190**	62784	57406	**7839**	4545	3294
35-40 ..	**112273**	62402	49871	**3753**	3556	197	**97966**	53383	44583	**10554**	5463	5091
40-45 ..	**81515**	45911	35604	**2137**	2014	123	**68125**	38846	29279	**11253**	5051	6202
45-50 ..	**64942**	37709	27233	**1479**	1368	111	**49955**	30983	18972	**13508**	5358	8150
50-55 ..	**44503**	26427	18076	**924**	851	73	**31658**	21036	10622	**11921**	4540	7381
55-60 ..	**33845**	20620	13225	**640**	586	54	**21062**	15412	5650	**12143**	4622	7521
60-65 ..	**21398**	13173	8225	**417**	382	35	**12290**	9366	2924	**8691**	3425	5266
65-70 ..	**12795**	7466	5329	**231**	214	17	**6260**	4893	1367	**6304**	2359	3945
70 and over ..	**20185**	12713	7472	**457**	416	41	**8410**	6717	1693	**11318**	5580	5738
TOTAL ..	*1500423*	*819279*	*681144*	*616292*	*390320*	*225972*	*779338*	*382297*	*397041*	*104793*	*46662*	*58131*
Hindu	**85580**	**48388**	**37192**	**44953**	**28794**	**16159**	**32802**	**16988**	**15814**	**7825**	**2606**	**5219**
0-1 ..	**1428**	773	655	**1428**	773	655						
1-2 ..	**1734**	866	868	**1734**	866	868						
2-3 ..	**2143**	1142	1001	**2143**	1142	1001						
3-4 ..	**2356**	1170	1186	**2356**	1170	1186						
4-5 ..	**2381**	1214	1167	**2381**	1214	1167						
TOTAL 0-5 ..	*10042*	*5165*	*4877*	*10042*	*5165*	*4877*						
5-10 ..	**11860**	6161	5699	**11856**	6161	5695	**4**		4			
10-15 ..	**9945**	5260	4685	**9253**	5234	4019	**682**	24	658	**10**	2	8
15-20 ..	**8368**	4704	3664	**5548**	4148	1400	**2753**	542	2211	**67**	14	53
20-25 ..	**8353**	4890	3463	**3101**	2995	106	**5056**	1842	3214	**196**	53	143
25-30 ..	**7903**	4648	3255	**1867**	1847	20	**5671**	2684	2987	**365**	117	248
30-35 ..	**6903**	4135	2768	**1059**	1047	12	**5265**	2893	2372	**579**	195	384
35-40 ..	**5819**	3555	2264	**664**	656	8	**4362**	2641	1721	**793**	258	535
40-45 ..	**4651**	2872	1779	**467**	462	5	**3228**	2095	1133	**956**	315	641
45-50 ..	**3799**	2309	1490	**382**	378	4	**2279**	1558	721	**1138**	373	765
50-55 ..	**2817**	1720	1097	**273**	268	5	**1528**	1102	426	**1016**	350	666
55-60 ..	**2150**	1254	896	**200**	195	5	**957**	738	219	**993**	321	672
60-65 ..	**1397**	808	589	**116**	114	2	**541**	449	92	**740**	245	495
65-70 ..	**748**	432	316	**60**	60		**256**	224	32	**432**	148	284
70 and over ..	**825**	475	350	**65**	64	1	**220**	196	24	**540**	215	325
TOTAL ..	*75538*	*43223*	*32315*	*34911*	*23629*	*11282*	*32802*	*16988*	*15814*	*7825*	*2606*	*5219*

VII—AGE AND CIVIL CONDITION (PART II—PROVINCES)—Contd.

KASHMIR PROVINCE—contd.

Community and Age	Population P	Population M	Population F	Unmarried P	Unmarried M	Unmarried F	Married P	Married M	Married F	Widowed P	Widowed M	Widowed F
1	2	3	4	5	6	7	8	9	10	11	12	13
Muslim	**1615478**	**871499**	**743979**	**784952**	**468356**	**316596**	**735038**	**359662**	**375376**	**95488**	**43481**	**52007**
0-1 ..	**34730**	17580	17150	**34730**	17580	17150						
1-2 ..	**39477**	20003	19474	**39477**	20003	19474						
2-3 ..	**44231**	22553	21678	**44231**	22553	21678						
3-4 ..	**49465**	24647	24818	**49465**	24647	24818						
4-5 ..	**46135**	23429	22706	**46135**	23429	22706						
Total 0-5 ..	*214038*	*108212*	*105826*	*214038*	*108212*	*105826*						
5-10 ..	**232122**	123438	108684	**231426**	123359	108067	**676**	75	601	**20**	4	16
10-15 ..	**197513**	107443	90076	**177316**	104809	72507	**19863**	2562	17301	**340**	72	268
15-20 ..	**172356**	92421	89935	**95972**	69961	26011	**74869**	21944	52925	**1515**	516	999
20-25 ..	**162482**	84832	77650	**37588**	34893	2695	**121517**	48174	73343	**3377**	1765	1612
25-30 ..	**146945**	76529	70416	**15150**	14501	649	**126566**	58913	67653	**5229**	3115	2114
30-35 ..	**126269**	68843	57426	**5839**	5557	282	**113276**	58978	54298	**7154**	4308	2846
35-40 ..	**104992**	58033	46959	**3020**	2853	167	**92350**	50020	42330	**9622**	5160	4462
40-45 ..	**75798**	42443	33355	**1625**	1520	105	**64018**	36235	27783	**10155**	4688	5467
45-50 ..	**60265**	34870	25395	**1071**	972	99	**46987**	28977	18010	**12207**	4921	7286
50-55 ..	**41038**	24316	16722	**641**	577	64	**29675**	19620	10055	**10722**	4119	6603
55-60 ..	**31190**	19068	12122	**426**	383	43	**19793**	14447	5346	**10971**	4238	6733
60-65 ..	**19656**	12165	7491	**289**	262	27	**11538**	8762	2776	**7829**	3141	4688
65-70 ..	**11795**	6888	4907	**165**	149	16	**5876**	4571	1305	**5754**	2168	3586
70 and over ..	**19013**	11998	7015	**386**	348	38	**8034**	6384	1650	**10593**	5266	5327
Total ..	*1401440*	*763287*	*638153*	*570914*	*360144*	*210770*	*735038*	*359662*	*375376*	*95488*	*43481*	*52007*
Sikh	**27034**	**14557**	**12477**	**14284**	**8443**	**5841**	**11313**	**5545**	**5768**	**1437**	**569**	**868**
0-1 ..	**710**	356	354	**710**	356	354						
1-2 ..	**800**	397	403	**800**	397	403						
2-3 ..	**846**	424	422	**846**	424	422						
3-4 ..	**933**	442	491	**933**	442	491						
4-5 ..	**867**	443	424	**867**	443	424						
Total 0-5 ..	**4156**	**2062**	**2094**	**4156**	**2062**	**2094**						
5-10 ..	**4248**	2277	1971	**4198**	2274	1924	**49**	3	46	**1**		1
10-15 ..	**3596**	1901	1695	**3101**	1841	1260	**488**	59	429	**7**	1	6
15-20 ..	**3044**	1550	1494	**1676**	1207	469	**1341**	335	1006	**27**	8	19
20-25 ..	**2640**	1384	1256	**653**	597	56	**1946**	768	1178	**41**	19	22
25-30 ..	**2239**	1226	1013	**264**	255	9	**1909**	938	971	**66**	33	33
30-35 ..	**1838**	1039	799	**106**	95	11	**1626**	902	724	**106**	42	64
35-40 ..	**1407**	791	616	**52**	43	9	**1222**	705	517	**133**	43	90
40-45 ..	**1026**	576	450	**35**	29	6	**851**	499	352	**140**	48	92
45-50 ..	**849**	515	334	**20**	17	3	**669**	435	234	**160**	63	97
50-55 ..	**631**	386	245	**5**	5		**446**	310	136	**180**	71	109
55-60 ..	**474**	286	188	**6**	6		**297**	217	80	**171**	63	108
60-65 ..	**321**	191	130	**5**	5		**199**	148	51	**117**	38	79
65-70 ..	**242**	142	100	**4**	4		**121**	95	26	**117**	43	74
70 and over ..	**323**	231	92	**3**	3		**149**	131	18	**171**	97	74
Total ..	*22878*	*12495*	*10383*	*10128*	*6381*	*3747*	*11313*	*5545*	*5768*	*1437*	*569*	*868*

VII—AGE AND CIVIL CONDITION (PART II—PROVINCES)—CONTD.

KASHMIR PROVINCE—concld.

Community and Age		Population P	Population M	Population F	Unmarried P	Unmarried M	Unmarried F	Married P	Married M	Married F	Widowed P	Widowed M	Widowed F
1		*2*	*3*	*4*	*5*	*6*	*7*	*8*	*9*	*10*	*11*	*12*	*13*
Buddhist		**10**	**10**		**7**	**7**		**2**	**2**		**1**	**1**	
	0-1 ..												
	1-2 ..												
	2-3 ..												
	3-4 ..												
	4-5 ..												
	TOTAL 0-5 ..												
	5-10 ..												
	10-15 ..	**1**	1		**1**	1							
	15-20 ..	**2**	2		**2**	2							
	20-25 ..	**3**	3		**3**	3							
	25-30 ..	**1**	1		**1**	1							
	30-35 ..												
	35-40 ..	**2**	2					**2**	2				
	40-45 ..												
	45-50 ..	**1**	1								**1**	1	
	50-55 ..												
	55-60 ..												
	60-65 ..												
	65-70 ..												
	70 and over ..												
	TOTAL ..	*10*	*10*		*7*	*7*		*2*	*2*		*1*	*1*	
Others		**603**	**284**	**319**	**378**	**179**	**199**	**183**	**100**	**83**	**42**	**5**	**37**
	0-1 ..	**9**	4	5	**9**	4	5						
	1-2 ..	**8**	3	5	**8**	3	5						
	2-3 ..	**11**	6	5	**11**	6	5						
	3-4 ..	**7**	2	5	**7**	2	5						
	4-5 ..	**11**	5	6	**11**	5	6						
	TOTAL 0-5 ..	*46*	*20*	*26*	*46*	*20*	*26*						
	5-10 ..	**89**	51	38	**89**	51	38						
	10-15 ..	**71**	47	24	**71**	47	24						
	15-20 ..	**43**	23	20	**37**	21	16	**6**	2	4			
	20-25 ..	**38**	15	23	**32**	12	20	**6**	3	3			
	25-30 ..	**47**	17	30	**26**	8	18	**20**	9	11	**1**		1
	30-35 ..	**42**	17	25	**19**	6	13	**23**	11	12			
	35-40 ..	**53**	21	32	**17**	4	13	**30**	15	15	**6**	2	4
	40-45 ..	**40**	20	20	**10**	3	7	**28**	17	11	**2**		2
	45-50 ..	**28**	14	14	**6**	1	5	**20**	13	7	**2**		2
	50-55 ..	**17**	5	12	**5**	1	4	**9**	4	5	**3**		3
	55-60 ..	**31**	12	19	**8**	2	6	**15**	10	5	**8**		8
	60-65 ..	**24**	9	15	**7**	1	6	**12**	7	5	**5**	1	4
	65-70 ..	**10**	4	6	**2**	1	1	**7**	3	4	**1**		1
	70 and over ..	**24**	9	15	**3**	1	2	**7**	6	1	**14**	2	12
	TOTAL ..	*557*	*264*	*293*	*332*	*159*	*173*	*183*	*100*	*83*	*42*	*5*	*37*

VII—AGE AND CIVIL CONDITION (PART II—PROVINCES)—Contd.

FRONTIER DISTRICTS

Community and Age		Population P	Population M	Population F	Unmarried P	Unmarried M	Unmarried F	Married P	Married M	Married F	Widowed P	Widowed M	Widowed F
1		2	3	4	5	6	7	8	9	10	11	12	13
Total Population		**311478**	**160724**	**150754**	**152362**	**85425**	**66937**	**139477**	**69687**	**69790**	**19639**	**5612**	**14027**
	0-1	**4503**	2290	2213	**4502**	2290	2212				**1**		1
	1-2	**7229**	3434	3795	**7217**	3431	3786	**10**	2	8	**2**	1	1
	2-3	**9163**	4626	4537	**9146**	4619	4527	**8**	4	4	**9**	3	6
	3-4	**10069**	4993	5076	**10051**	4987	5064	**14**	4	10	**4**	2	2
	4-5	**8769**	4481	4288	**8739**	4473	4266	**21**	7	14	**9**	1	8
	Total 0-5	*39733*	*19824*	*19909*	*39655*	*19800*	*19855*	*53*	*17*	*36*	*25*	*7*	*18*
	5-10	**44279**	23116	21163	**43862**	23030	20832	**371**	66	305	**46**	20	26
	10-15	**36137**	19831	16306	**32750**	18656	14094	**3279**	1128	2151	**108**	47	61
	15-20	**30887**	16756	14131	**18929**	11970	6959	**11590**	4641	6949	**368**	145	223
	20-25	**29003**	14423	14580	**8329**	5925	2404	**20011**	8204	11807	**663**	294	369
	25-30	**24941**	13096	11845	**3527**	2484	1043	**20547**	10220	10327	**867**	392	475
	30-35	**23475**	11715	11760	**1735**	1158	577	**20676**	10148	10528	**1064**	409	655
	35-40	**18227**	9229	8998	**1078**	720	358	**15707**	8141	7566	**1442**	368	1074
	40-45	**13427**	7261	6166	**661**	433	228	**11272**	6445	4827	**1494**	383	1111
	45-50	**13421**	6827	6594	**543**	370	173	**10919**	6007	4912	**1959**	450	1509
	50-55	**10604**	5363	5241	**385**	256	129	**8102**	4588	3514	**2117**	519	1598
	55-60	**9758**	4766	4992	**309**	204	105	**6694**	3929	2765	**2755**	633	2122
	60-65	**6936**	3228	3708	**229**	158	71	**4418**	2607	1811	**2289**	463	1826
	65-70	**3901**	1910	1991	**139**	87	52	**2430**	1393	1037	**1332**	430	902
	70 and over	**6749**	3379	3370	**231**	174	57	**3408**	2153	1255	**3110**	1052	2038
	Total	*271745*	*140900*	*130845*	*112707*	*65625*	*47082*	*139424*	*69670*	*69754*	*19614*	*5605*	*14009*
Hindu		**676**	**505**	**171**	**282**	**199**	**83**	**386**	**302**	**84**	**8**	**4**	**4**
	0-1	**16**	9	7	**16**	9	7						
	1-2	**16**	11	5	**16**	11	5						
	2-3	**14**	5	9	**14**	5	9						
	3-4	**17**	5	12	**17**	5	12						
	4-5	**17**	12	5	**17**	12	5						
	Total 0-5	*80*	*42*	*38*	*80*	*42*	*38*						
	5-10	**69**	41	28	**69**	41	28						
	10-15	**36**	20	16	**34**	20	14	**2**		2			
	15-20	**32**	20	12	**21**	18	3	**11**	2	9			
	20-25	**67**	45	22	**24**	24		**43**	21	22			
	25-30	**130**	106	24	**28**	28		**101**	77	24	**1**	1	
	30-35	**122**	105	17	**14**	14		**106**	89	17	**2**	2	
	35-40	**68**	60	8	**4**	4		**62**	55	7	**2**	1	1
	40-45	**34**	30	4	**2**	2		**31**	28	3	**1**		1
	45-50	**19**	19		**2**	2		**17**	17				
	50-55	**9**	9		**1**	1		**8**	8		**1**		1
	55-60	**4**	3	1	**1**	1		**2**	2		**1**		1
	60-65	**4**	4		**1**	1		**3**	3				
	65-70												
	70 and over	**2**	1	1	**1**	1					**1**		1
	Total	*596*	*463*	*133*	*202*	*157*	*45*	*386*	*302*	*84*	*8*	*4*	*4*

VII—AGE AND CIVIL CONDITION (PART II—PROVINCES)—Contd.

Community and Age	Population			Unmarried			Married			Widowed		
	P	M	F	P	M	F	P	M	F	P	M	F
1	2	3	4	5	6	7	8	9	10	11	12	13
FRONTIER DISTRICTS—contd.												
Muslim	**270192**	**139946**	**130246**	**132164**	**75238**	**56926**	**121432**	**60152**	**61280**	**16596**	**4556**	**12040**
0-1 ..	4030	2018	2012	4029	2018	2011				1		1
1-2 ..	6620	3135	3485	6608	3132	3476	10	2	8	2	1	1
2-3 ..	8419	4243	4176	8402	4236	4166	8	4	4	9	3	6
3-4 ..	9043	4473	4570	9025	4467	4558	14	4	10	4	2	2
4-5 ..	7973	4068	3905	7943	4060	3883	21	7	14	9	1	8
Total 0-5 ..	*36085*	*17937*	*18148*	*36007*	*17913*	*18094*	*53*	*17*	*36*	*25*	*7*	*18*
5-10 ..	39497	20718	18779	39085	20634	18451	366	64	302	46	20	26
10-15 ..	31943	17790	14153	28736	16700	12036	3101	1043	2058	106	47	59
15-20 ..	26744	14754	11990	15955	10563	5392	10455	4051	6404	334	140	194
20-25 ..	25233	12584	12639	6658	5134	1524	17985	7180	10805	580	270	310
25-30 ..	21659	11444	10215	2675	2062	613	18217	9022	9195	767	360	407
30-35 ..	20549	10222	10327	1238	891	347	18359	8958	9401	952	373	579
35-40 ..	15489	7799	7690	693	501	192	13522	6985	6537	1274	313	961
40-45 ..	11026	6003	5023	349	244	105	9370	5436	3934	1307	323	984
45-50 ..	11238	5708	5530	272	201	71	9286	5148	4138	1680	359	1321
50-55 ..	8685	4365	4320	155	113	42	6709	3838	2871	1821	414	1407
55-60 ..	8008	3858	4150	118	93	25	5527	3274	2253	2363	491	1872
60-65 ..	5609	2558	3051	77	65	12	3624	2168	1456	1908	325	1583
65-70 ..	2884	1411	1473	33	25	8	1872	1090	782	979	296	683
70 and over ..	5553	2795	2758	113	99	14	2986	1878	1108	2454	818	1636
Total ..	*234107*	*122009*	*112098*	*96157*	*57325*	*38832*	*121379*	*60135*	*61244*	*16571*	*4549*	*12022*
Sikh	**282**	**171**	**111**	**157**	**96**	**61**	**124**	**75**	**49**	**1**		**1**
0-1 ..	13	8	5	13	8	5						
1-2 ..	10	5	5	10	5	5						
2-3 ..	10	6	4	10	6	4						
3-4 ..	12	4	8	12	4	8						
4-5 ..	9	5	4	9	5	4						
Total 0-5 ..	*54*	*28*	*26*	*54*	*28*	*26*						
5-10 ..	46	28	18	46	28	18						
10-15 ..	32	19	13	30	18	12	2	1	1			
15-20 ..	28	17	11	18	14	4	10	3	7			
20-25 ..	31	15	16	8	7	1	23	8	15			
25-30 ..	30	19	11	1	1		29	18	11			
30-35 ..	26	19	7				26	19	7			
35-40 ..	12	10	2				12	10	2			
40-45 ..	7	5	2				7	5	2			
45-50 ..	8	5	3				7	5	2	1		1
50-55 ..	4	3	1				4	3	1			
55-60 ..	2	1	1				2	1	1			
60-65 ..	1	1					1	1				
65-70 ..												
70 and over ..	1	1					1	1				
Total ..	*228*	*143*	*85*	*103*	*68*	*35*	*124*	*75*	*49*	*1*		*1*

VII—AGE AND CIVIL CONDITION (PART II—PROVINCES)—CONCLD.

Community and Age		Population			Unmarried			Married			Widowed		
		P	M	F	P	M	F	P	M	F	P	M	F
1		2	3	4	5	6	7	8	9	10	11	12	13
FRONTIER DISTRICTS—concld.													
Buddhist		**40164**	**20011**	**20153**	**19670**	**9841**	**9829**	**17463**	**9118**	**8345**	**3031**	**1052**	**1979**
0-1	..	**441**	253	188	**441**	253	188						
1-2	..	**581**	283	298	**581**	283	298						
2-3	..	**717**	371	346	**717**	371	346						
3-4	..	**993**	510	483	**993**	510	483						
4-5	..	**766**	394	372	**766**	394	372						
TOTAL 0-5	..	*3498*	*1811*	*1687*	*3498*	*1811*	*1687*						
5-10	..	**4747**	2317	2330	**4642**	2315	2327	**5**	2	3			
10-15	..	**4105**	1990	2115	**3929**	1906	2023	**174**	84	90	**2**		2
15-20	..	**4065**	1954	2111	**2919**	1366	1553	**1112**	583	529	**34**	5	29
20-25	..	**3666**	1770	1896	**1629**	753	876	**1954**	993	961	**83**	24	59
25-30	..	**3106**	1520	1586	**819**	390	429	**2189**	1099	1090	**98**	31	67
30-35	..	**2765**	1361	1404	**482**	252	230	**2173**	1075	1098	**110**	34	76
35-40	..	**2647**	1354	1293	**380**	214	166	**2102**	1086	1016	**165**	54	111
40-45	..	**2351**	1217	1134	**310**	187	123	**1855**	970	885	**186**	60	126
45-50	..	**2146**	1091	1055	**269**	167	102	**1600**	833	767	**277**	91	186
50-55	..	**1900**	982	918	**229**	142	87	**1375**	735	640	**296**	105	191
55-60	..	**1742**	902	840	**190**	110	80	**1161**	650	511	**391**	142	249
60-65	..	**1319**	663	656	**151**	92	59	**787**	433	354	**381**	138	243
65-70	..	**1014**	497	517	**106**	62	44	**555**	301	254	**353**	134	219
70 and over	..	**1193**	582	611	**117**	74	43	**421**	274	147	**655**	234	421
TOTAL	..	*36666*	*18200*	*18466*	*16172*	*8030*	*8142*	*17463*	*9118*	*8345*	*3031*	*1052*	*1979*
Others		**164**	**91**	**73**	**89**	**51**	**38**	**72**	**40**	**32**	**3**		**3**
0-1	..	**3**	2	1	**3**	2	1						
1-2	..	**2**		2	**2**		2						
2-3	..	**3**	1	2	**3**	1	2						
3-4	..	**4**	1	3	**4**	1	3						
4-5	..	**4**	2	2	**4**	2	2						
TOTAL 0-5	..	*16*	*6*	*10*	*16*	*6*	*10*						
5-10	..	**20**	12	8	**20**	12	8						
10-15	..	**21**	12	9	**21**	12	9						
15-20	..	**18**	11	7	**16**	9	7	**2**	2				
20-25	..	**16**	9	7	**10**	7	3	**6**	2	4			
25-30	..	**16**	7	9	**4**	3	1	**11**	4	7	**1**		1
30-35	..	**13**	8	5	**1**	1		**12**	7	5			
35-40	..	**11**	6	5	**1**	1		**9**	5	4	**1**		1
40-45	..	**9**	6	3				**9**	6	3			
45-50	..	**10**	4	6				**9**	4	5	**1**		1
50-55	..	**6**	4	2				**6**	4	2			
55-60	..	**2**	2					**2**	2				
60-65	..	**3**	2	1				**3**	2	1			
65-70	..	**3**	2	1				**3**	2	1			
70 and over	..												
TOTAL	..	*148*	*85*	*63*	*73*	*45*	*28*	*72*	*40*	*32*	*3*		*3*

VII—AGE AND CIVIL CONDITION (PART III—DISTRICTS)

JAMMU

Community and Age		Population P	Population M	Population F	Unmarried P	Unmarried M	Unmarried F	Married P	Married M	Married F	Widowed P	Widowed M	Widowed F
1		2	3	4	5	6	7	8	9	10	11	12	13
		431362	**233976**	**197386**	**214812**	**129788**	**85024**	**177349**	**89368**	**87981**	**39201**	**14820**	**24381**
	0-1	**10301**	5118	5183	**10301**	5118	5183						
	1-2	**10892**	5474	5418	**10892**	5474	5418						
	2-3	**12451**	6369	6082	**12451**	6369	6082						
	3-4	**12874**	6569	6305	**12874**	6569	6305						
	4-5	**12800**	6618	6182	**12800**	6618	6182						
Total Population	TOTAL 0-5	*59318*	*30148*	*29170*	*59318*	*30148*	*29170*						
	5-10	**60885**	32287	28598	**60810**	32272	28538	**73**	15	58	**2**		2
	10-15	**51239**	27063	24176	**45921**	26653	19268	**5249**	388	4861	**69**	22	47
	15-20	**42688**	22933	19755	**25946**	18925	7021	**16360**	3859	12501	**382**	149	233
	20-30	**74142**	39490	34652	**15952**	15166	786	**55507**	23134	32373	**2683**	1190	1493
	30-40	**58452**	32353	26099	**3654**	3527	127	**48665**	26447	22218	**6133**	2379	3754
	40-50	**37813**	21885	15928	**1540**	1500	40	**27735**	17424	10311	**8538**	2961	5577
	50-60	**24689**	14648	10041	**888**	844	44	**14654**	10583	4071	**9147**	3221	5926
	60 and over	**22136**	13169	8967	**783**	753	30	**9106**	7518	1588	**12247**	4898	7349
	TOTAL	*372044*	*203828*	*168216*	*155494*	*99640*	*55854*	*177349*	*89368*	*87981*	*39201*	*14820*	*24381*
		248173	**134637**	**113536**	**121518**	**74806**	**46712**	**101958**	**51248**	**50710**	**24697**	**8583**	**16114**
	0-1	**5853**	2913	2940	**5853**	2913	2940						
	1-2	**6062**	3000	3062	**6062**	3000	3062						
	2-3	**6956**	3557	3399	**6956**	3557	3399						
	3-4	**7067**	3623	3444	**7067**	3623	3444						
	4-5	**7093**	3668	3425	**7093**	3668	3425						
Hindu	TOTAL 0-5	*33031*	*16761*	*16270*	*33031*	*16761*	*16270*						
	5-10	**34079**	18250	15829	**34047**	18243	15804	**31**	7	24	**1**		1
	10-15	**28790**	15227	13563	**25589**	15047	10542	**3163**	168	2995	**38**	12	26
	15-20	**24312**	13143	11169	**14768**	11097	3671	**9332**	1975	7357	**212**	71	141
	20-30	**42312**	22359	19953	**9417**	9114	303	**31258**	12658	18600	**1637**	587	1050
	30-40	**34238**	18680	15558	**2331**	2283	48	**27978**	15134	12844	**3929**	1263	2666
	40-50	**22809**	13226	9583	**1108**	1091	17	**16234**	10423	5811	**5467**	1712	3755
	50-60	**15078**	8959	6119	**648**	612	36	**8594**	6364	2230	**5836**	1983	3853
	60 and over	**13524**	8032	5492	**579**	558	21	**5368**	4519	849	**7577**	2955	4622
	TOTAL	*215142*	*117876*	*97266*	*88487*	*58045*	*30442*	*101958*	*51248*	*50710*	*24697*	*8583*	*16114*
		170739	**92578**	**78211**	**86590**	**51052**	**35538**	**70562**	**35629**	**34933**	**13637**	**5897**	**7740**
	0-1	**4103**	2024	2079	**4103**	2024	2079						
	1-2	**4458**	2277	2181	**4458**	2277	2181						
	2-3	**5121**	2613	2508	**5121**	2613	2508						
	3-4	**5383**	2731	2652	**5383**	2731	2652						
	4-5	**5276**	2718	2558	**5276**	2718	2558						
Muslim	TOTAL 0-5	*24341*	*12363*	*11978*	*24341*	*12363*	*11978*						
	5-10	**24875**	13055	11820	**24850**	13047	11803	**24**	8	16	**1**		1
	10-15	**20905**	11007	9898	**18909**	10782	8127	**1965**	215	1750	**31**	10	21
	15-20	**17142**	9155	7987	**10393**	7289	3104	**6592**	1796	4796	**157**	70	87
	20-30	**29826**	16093	13733	**6099**	5668	431	**22739**	9849	12890	**988**	576	412
	30-40	**22638**	12737	9901	**1210**	1154	56	**19348**	10525	8823	**2080**	1058	1022
	40-50	**14041**	8064	5977	**390**	367	23	**10763**	6516	4247	**2888**	1181	1707
	50-60	**8966**	5294	3672	**215**	207	8	**5649**	3919	1730	**3102**	1168	1934
	60 and over	**8055**	4810	3245	**183**	175	8	**3482**	2801	681	**4390**	1834	2556
	TOTAL	*146448*	*80215*	*66233*	*622 9*	*38689*	*23560*	*70562*	*35629*	*34933*	*13637*	*5897*	*7740*

VII—AGE AND CIVIL CONDITION (PART III--DISTRICTS)—CONTD.

Community and Age			Population			Unmarried			Married			Widowed	
			P	M	F	P	M	F	P	M	F	P	M	F
1			2	3	4	5	6	7	8	9	10	11	12	13
							JAMMU—concld.							
			9151	**4980**	**4171**	**4973**	**2910**	**2063**	**3520**	**1819**	**1701**	**658**	**251**	**407**
	0-1	..	**227**	121	106	**227**	121	106						
	1-2	..	**285**	152	133	**285**	152	133						
	2-3	..	**283**	149	134	**283**	149	134						
	3-4	..	**294**	145	149	**294**	145	149						
	4-5	..	**330**	175	155	**330**	175	155						
Sikh	TOTAL 0-5	..	*1419*	*742*	*677*	*1419*	*742*	*677*						
	5-10	..	**1407**	704	703	**1390**	704	686	**17**		17			
	10-15	..	**1179**	627	552	**1069**	624	445	**110**	3	107			
	15-20	..	**953**	486	467	**617**	426	191	**328**	55	273	**8**	5	3
	20-30	..	**1431**	748	683	**336**	294	42	**1053**	435	618	**42**	19	23
	30-40	..	**1156**	686	470	**88**	66	22	**973**	580	393	**95**	40	55
	40-50	..	**707**	441	266	**24**	24		**544**	367	177	**139**	50	89
	50-60	..	**474**	292	182	**14**	14		**304**	226	78	**156**	52	104
	60 and over	..	**425**	254	171	**16**	16		**191**	153	38	**218**	85	133
	TOTAL	..	*7732*	*4238*	*3494*	*3554*	*2168*	*1386*	*3520*	*1819*	*1701*	*658*	*251*	*407*
			2	**2**		**1**	**1**		**1**	**1**				
	0-1	..												
	1-2	..												
	2-3	..												
	3-4	..												
	4-5	..												
Buddhist	TOTAL 0-5	..												
	5-10	..												
	10-15	..												
	15-20	..												
	20-30	..												
	30-40	..	**2**	2		**1**	1		**1**	1				
	40-50	..												
	50-60	..												
	60 and over	..												
	TOTAL	..	*2*	*2*		*1*	*1*		*1*	*1*				
			3247	**1779**	**1468**	**1730**	**1019**	**711**	**1308**	**671**	**637**	**209**	**89**	**120**
	0-1	..	**118**	60	58	**118**	60	58						
	1-2	..	**87**	45	42	**87**	45	42						
	2-3	..	**91**	50	41	**91**	50	41						
	3-4	..	**130**	70	60	**130**	70	60						
	4-5	..	**101**	57	44	**101**	57	44						
Others	TOTAL 0-5	..	*527*	*282*	*245*	*527*	*282*	*245*						
	5-10	..	**524**	278	246	**523**	278	245	**1**		1			
	10-15	..	**365**	202	163	**354**	200	154	**11**	2	9			
	15-20	..	**281**	149	132	**168**	113	55	**108**	33	75	**5**	3	2
	20-30	..	**573**	290	283	**100**	90	10	**457**	192	265	**16**	8	8
	30-40	..	**418**	248	170	**24**	23	1	**365**	207	158	**29**	18	11
	40-50	..	**256**	154	102	**18**	18		**194**	118	76	**44**	18	26
	50-60	..	**171**	103	68	**11**	11		**107**	74	33	**53**	18	35
	60 and over	..	**132**	73	59	**5**	4	1	**65**	45	20	**62**	24	38
	TOTAL	..	*2720*	*1497*	*1223*	*1203*	*737*	*466*	*1308*	*671*	*637*	*209*	*89*	*120*

VII—AGE AND CIVIL CONDITION (PART III—DISTRICTS)—Contd.

Community and Age		Population P	Population M	Population F	Unmarried P	Unmarried M	Unmarried F	Married P	Married M	Married F	Widowed P	Widowed M	Widowed F
1		2	3	4	5	6	7	8	9	10	11	12	13
						KATHUA							
Total Population		**177672**	**94134**	**83538**	**86378**	**52352**	**34026**	**72273**	**35265**	**37008**	**19021**	**6517**	**12504**
	0-1	**3263**	1636	1627	**3263**	1636	1627						
	1-2	**4262**	2198	2064	**4262**	2198	2064						
	2-3	**4902**	2435	2467	**4902**	2435	2467						
	3-4	**5117**	2585	2532	**5117**	2585	2532						
	4-5	**4899**	2479	2420	**4899**	2479	2420						
	Total 0-5	*22443*	*11333*	*11110*	*22443*	*11333*	*11110*						
	5-10	**24798**	13044	11754	**24797**	13043	11754	**1**	1				
	10-15	**20616**	10744	9872	**18722**	10669	8053	**1874**	71	1803	**20**	4	16
	15-20	**17302**	8909	8393	**10515**	7695	2820	**6643**	1178	5465	**144**	36	108
	20-30	**31829**	16444	15385	**7018**	6828	190	**23326**	9046	14280	**1485**	570	915
	30-40	**24628**	13338	11290	**1600**	1572	28	**19783**	10584	9199	**3245**	1182	2063
	40-50	**15906**	8933	6973	**616**	599	17	**11028**	6976	4052	**4262**	1358	2904
	50-60	**10576**	6109	4467	**361**	340	21	**5931**	4374	1557	**4284**	1395	2889
	60 and over	**9574**	5280	4294	**306**	273	33	**3687**	3035	652	**5581**	1972	3609
	Total	*155229*	*82801*	*72428*	*63935*	*41019*	*22916*	*72273*	*35265*	*37008*	*19021*	*6517*	*12504*
Hindu		**131823**	**69448**	**62375**	**63109**	**38770**	**24339**	**53171**	**25701**	**27470**	**15543**	**4977**	**10566**
	0-1	**2338**	1162	1176	**2338**	1162	1176						
	1-2	**3027**	1583	1444	**3027**	1583	1444						
	2-3	**3513**	1745	1768	**3513**	1745	1768						
	3-4	**3626**	1817	1809	**3626**	1817	1809						
	4-5	**3511**	1800	1711	**3511**	1800	1711						
	Total 0-5	*16015*	*8107*	*7908*	*16015*	*8107*	*7908*						
	5-10	**17821**	9400	8421	**17821**	9400	8421						
	10-15	**14859**	7707	7152	**13482**	7676	5806	**1365**	30	1335	**12**	1	11
	15-20	**12624**	6433	6191	**7675**	5686	1989	**4845**	731	4114	**104**	16	88
	20-30	**23574**	11994	11580	**5582**	5457	125	**16839**	6157	10682	**1153**	380	773
	30-40	**18657**	10001	8656	**1391**	1366	25	**14582**	7764	6818	**2684**	871	1813
	40-50	**12374**	6905	5469	**545**	529	16	**8294**	5322	2972	**3535**	1054	2481
	50-60	**8371**	4780	3591	**317**	299	18	**4522**	3386	1136	**3532**	1095	2437
	60 and over	**7528**	4121	3407	**281**	250	31	**2724**	2311	413	**4523**	1560	2963
	Total	*115808*	*61341*	*54467*	*47094*	*30663*	*16431*	*53171*	*25701*	*27470*	*15543*	*4977*	*10566*
Muslim		**45214**	**24355**	**20859**	**22931**	**13398**	**9533**	**18854**	**9444**	**9410**	**3429**	**1513**	**1916**
	0-1	**919**	472	447	**919**	472	447						
	1-2	**1217**	610	607	**1217**	610	607						
	2-3	**1365**	681	684	**1365**	681	684						
	3-4	**1473**	758	715	**1473**	758	715						
	4-5	**1372**	670	702	**1372**	670	702						
	Total 0-5	*6346*	*3191*	*3155*	*6346*	*3191*	*3155*						
	5-10	**6869**	3591	3278	**6868**	3590	3278	**1**	1				
	10-15	**5676**	3001	2675	**5165**	2957	2208	**503**	41	462	**8**	3	5
	15-20	**4615**	2443	2172	**2800**	1980	820	**1776**	443	1333	**39**	20	19
	20-30	**8140**	4395	3745	**1412**	1348	64	**6402**	2859	3543	**326**	188	138
	30-40	**5894**	3287	2607	**204**	201	3	**5138**	2783	2355	**552**	303	249
	40-50	**3478**	1994	1484	**70**	69	1	**2692**	1627	1065	**716**	298	418
	50-60	**2171**	1306	865	**42**	40	2	**1390**	974	416	**739**	292	447
	60 and over	**2025**	1147	878	**24**	22	2	**952**	716	236	**1049**	409	640
	Total	*38868*	*21164*	*17704*	*16585*	*10207*	*6378*	*18854*	*9444*	*9410*	*3429*	*1513*	*1916*

VII—AGE AND CIVIL CONDITION (PART III—DISTRICTS)—Contd.

Community and Age		Population P	Population M	Population F	Unmarried P	Unmarried M	Unmarried F	Married P	Married M	Married F	Widowed P	Widowed M	Widowed F
1		2	3	4	5	6	7	8	9	10	11	12	13
						KATHUA—concld.							
Sikh		**431**	**228**	**203**	**233**	**131**	**102**	**163**	**77**	**86**	**35**	**20**	**15**
	0-1 ..	**2**		2	**2**		2						
	1-2 ..	**11**	5	6	**11**	5	6						
	2-3 ..	**17**	6	11	**17**	6	11						
	3-4 ..	**11**	7	4	**11**	7	4						
	4-5 ..	**12**	6	6	**12**	6	6						
	Total 0-5 ..	*53*	*24*	*29*	*53*	*24*	*29*						
	5-10 ..	**70**	37	33	**70**	37	33						
	10-15 ..	**58**	26	32	**54**	26	28	**4**		4			
	15-20 ..	**51**	24	27	**33**	22	11	**17**	2	15	**1**		1
	20-30	**75**	33	42	**17**	16	1	**54**	16	38	**4**	1	3
	30-40 ..	**50**	33	17	**3**	3		**41**	25	16	**6**	5	1
	40-50 ..	**37**	25	12	**1**	1		**29**	20	9	**7**	4	3
	50-60 ..	**23**	17	6	**1**	1		**12**	9	3	**10**	7	3
	60 and over ..	**14**	9	5	**1**	1		**6**	5	1	**7**	3	4
	Total ..	*378*	*204*	*174*	*180*	*107*	*73*	*163*	*77*	*86*	*35*	*20*	*15*
Others		**204**	**103**	**101**	**105**	**53**	**52**	**85**	**43**	**42**	**14**	**7**	**7**
	0-1 ..	**4**	2	2	**4**	2	2						
	1-2 ..	**7**		7	**7**		7						
	2-3 ..	**7**	3	4	**7**	3	4						
	3-4 ..	**7**	3	4	**7**	3	4						
	4-5 ..	**4**	3	1	**4**	3	1						
	Total 0-5 ..	*29*	*11*	*18*	*29*	*11*	*18*						
	5-10 ..	**38**	16	22	**38**	16	22						
	10-15 ..	**23**	10	13	**21**	10	11	**2**		2			
	15-20 ..	**12**	9	3	**7**	7		**5**	2	3			
	20-30 ..	**40**	22	18	**7**	7		**31**	14	17	**2**	1	1
	30-40 ..	**27**	17	10	**2**	2		**22**	12	10	**3**	3	
	40-50 ..	**17**	9	8				**13**	7	6	**4**	2	2
	50-60 ..	**11**	6	5	**1**		1	**7**	5	2	**3**	1	2
	60 and over ..	**7**	3	4				**5**	3	2	**2**		2
	Total ..	*175*	*92*	*83*	*76*	*42*	*34*	*85*	*43*	*42*	*14*	*7*	*7*
						UDHAMPUR							
Total Population		**294217**	**153608**	**140609**	**140859**	**83494**	**57365**	**125339**	**60897**	**64442**	**28019**	**9217**	**18802**
	0-1 ..	**6218**	3119	3099	**6218**	3119	3099						
	1-2 ..	**6154**	3031	3123	**6154**	3031	3123						
	2-3 ..	**7461**	3711	3750	**7461**	3711	3750						
	3-4 ..	**8473**	4252	4221	**8473**	4252	4221						
	4-5 ..	**8153**	4076	4077	**8153**	4076	4077						
	Total 0-5 ..	*36459*	*18189*	*18270*	*36459*	*18189*	*18270*						
	5-10 ..	**40104**	20456	19648	**40102**	20455	19647	**2**	1	1			
	10-15 ..	**33293**	17171	16122	**30715**	17081	13634	**2549**	83	2466	**29**	7	22
	15-20 ..	**27851**	14195	13656	**16944**	12155	4789	**10625**	1968	8657	**282**	72	210
	20-30 ..	**51849**	25743	26106	**11045**	10324	721	**38634**	14673	23961	**2170**	746	1424
	30-40 ..	**43129**	23417	19712	**3038**	2917	121	**35678**	18919	16759	**4413**	1581	2832
	40-50 ..	**27222**	15331	11891	**1246**	1170	76	**20021**	12214	7807	**5955**	1947	4008
	50-60 ..	**17695**	9977	7718	**699**	657	42	**10780**	7430	3350	**6216**	1890	4326
	60 and over ..	**16615**	9129	7486	**611**	546	65	**7050**	5609	1441	**8954**	2974	5980
	Total ..	*257758*	*135419*	*122339*	*104400*	*65305*	*39095*	*125339*	*60897*	*64442*	*28019*	*9217*	*18802*

VII—AGE AND CIVIL CONDITION (PART III—DISTRICTS)—CONTD.

Community and Age		Population			Unmarried			Married			Widowed		
		P	M	F	P	M	F	P	M	F	P	M	F
1		2	3	4	5	6	7	8	9	10	11	12	13
UDHAMPUR—contd.													
		164820	**85179**	**79641**	**74795**	**45482**	**29313**	**70858**	**3418?**	**36674**	**19167**	**5513**	**13654**
	0-1 ..	**3463**	1804	1659	**3463**	1804	1659						
	1-2 ..	**3242**	1581	1661	**3242**	1581	1661						
	2-3 ..	**3849**	1840	2009	**3849**	1840	2009						
	3-4 ..	**4423**	2235	2188	**4423**	2235	2188						
	4-5 ..	**4286**	2120	2166	**4286**	2120	2166						
Hindu	TOTAL 0-5 ..	*19263*	*9580*	*9683*	*19263*	*9580*	*9683*						
	5-10 ..	**20825**	10567	10258	**20823**	10566	10257	**2**	1	1			
	10-15 ..	**17633**	9080	8553	**15774**	9041	6733	**1838**	33	1805	**21**	6	15
	15-20 ..	**15228**	7483	7745	**8621**	6388	2233	**6437**	1063	5374	**170**	32	138
	20-30 ..	**29030**	14326	14764	**6168**	5931	237	**21518**	8017	13501	**1404**	378	1026
	30-40 ..	**24328**	12915	11413	**2108**	2046	62	**19146**	10017	9129	**3074**	852	2222
	40-50 ..	**16688**	9250	7438	**974**	933	41	**11467**	7120	4347	**4247**	1197	3050
	50-60 ..	**11123**	6285	4838	**569**	541	28	**6265**	4528	1737	**4289**	1216	3073
	60 and over ..	**10642**	5693	4949	**495**	456	39	**4185**	3505	780	**5962**	1832	4130
	TOTAL ..	*145557*	*75599*	*69958*	*55532*	*35902*	*19630*	*70858*	*34184*	*36674*	*19167*	*5513*	*13654*
		128327	**67878**	**60449**	**65573**	**37750**	**27823**	**53967**	**26454**	**27513**	**8787**	**3674**	**5113**
	0-1 ..	**2731**	1305	1426	**2731**	1305	1426						
	1-2 ..	**2892**	1441	1451	**2892**	1441	1451						
	2-3 ..	**3585**	1860	1725	**3585**	1860	1725						
	3-4 ..	**4026**	2001	2025	**4026**	2001	2025						
	4-5 ..	**3840**	1941	1899	**3840**	1941	1899						
Muslim	TOTAL 0-5 ..	*17074*	*8548*	*8526*	*17074*	*8548*	*8526*						
	5-10 ..	**19135**	9825	9310	**19135**	9825	9310						
	10-15 ..	**15529**	8032	7497	**14832**	7988	6844	**689**	43	646	**8**	1	7
	15-20 ..	**12466**	6637	5829	**8255**	5725	2530	**4102**	874	3228	**109**	38	71
	20-30 ..	**22571**	11316	11255	**4843**	4364	479	**16970**	6589	10381	**758**	363	395
	30-40 ..	**18683**	10433	8250	**925**	866	59	**16424**	8841	7583	**1334**	726	608
	40-50 ..	**10443**	6034	4409	**266**	231	35	**8485**	5061	3424	**1692**	742	950
	50-60 ..	**6485**	3640	2845	**128**	114	14	**4452**	2860	1592	**1905**	666	1239
	60 and over ..	**5941**	3413	2528	**115**	89	26	**2845**	2186	659	**2981**	1138	1843
	TOTAL ..	*111253*	*59330*	*51923*	*48499*	*29202*	*19297*	*53967*	*26454*	*27513*	*8787*	*3674*	*5113*
		445	**243**	**202**	**212**	**120**	**92**	**210**	**112**	**98**	**23**	**11**	**12**
	0-1 ..	**5**	1	4	**5**	1	4						
	1-2 ..	**9**	4	5	**9**	4	5						
	2-3 ..	**17**	5	12	**17**	5	12						
	3-4 ..	**9**	5	4	**9**	5	4						
	4-5	**16**	7	9	**16**	7	9						
Sikh	TOTAL 0-5 ..	*56*	*22*	*34*	*56*	*22*	*34*						
	5-10 ..	**64**	32	32	**64**	32	32						
	10-15 ..	**52**	27	25	**47**	27	20	**5**		5			
	15-20 ..	**46**	25	21	**26**	20	6	**20**	5	15			
	20-30 ..	**74**	44	30	**13**	13		**57**	28	29	**4**	3	1
	30-40 ..	**56**	33	23	**2**	2		**52**	30	22	**2**	1	1
	40-50 ..	**42**	22	20	**2**	2		**35**	17	18	**5**	3	2
	50-60 ..	**27**	18	9	**1**	1		**22**	15	7	**4**	2	2
	60 and over ..	**28**	20	8	**1**	1		**19**	17	2	**8**	2	6
	TOTAL ..	*389*	*221*	*168*	*156*	*98*	*58*	*210*	*112*	*98*	*23*	*11*	*12*

VII—AGE AND CIVIL CONDITION (PART III—DISTRICTS)—CONTD.

Community and Age		Population P	Population M	Population F	Unmarried P	Unmarried M	Unmarried F	Married P	Married M	Married F	Widowed P	Widowed M	Widowed F
1		2	3	4	5	6	7	8	9	10	11	12	13
UDHAMPUR—concld.													
Buddhist		**520**	**245**	**275**	**229**	**107**	**122**	**254**	**122**	**132**	**37**	**16**	**21**
	0-1 ..	**16**	9	7	**16**	9	7						
	1-2 ..	**4**	1	3	**4**	1	3						
	2-3 ..	**5**	2	3	**5**	2	3						
	3-4 ..	**14**	10	4	**14**	10	4						
	4-5 ..	**6**	4	2	**6**	4	2						
	TOTAL 0-5 ..	*45*	*26*	*19*	*45*	*26*	*19*						
	5-10 ..	**66**	23	43	**66**	23	43						
	10-15 ..	**72**	28	44	**56**	21	35	**16**	7	9			
	15-20 ..	**102**	45	57	**38**	18	20	**61**	25	36	**3**	2	1
	20-30 ..	**90**	47	43	**18**	13	5	**68**	32	36	**4**	2	2
	30-40 ..	**49**	26	23	**1**	1		**46**	24	22	**2**	1	1
	40-50 ..	**41**	21	20	**4**	4		**27**	12	15	**10**	5	5
	50-60 ..	**55**	29	26	**1**	1		**36**	22	14	**18**	6	12
	60 and over ..												
	TOTAL ..	*475*	*219*	*256*	*184*	*81*	*103*	*254*	*122*	*132*	*37*	*16*	*21*
Others		**105**	**63**	**42**	**50**	**35**	**15**	**50**	**25**	**25**	**5**	**3**	**2**
	0-1 ..	**3**		3	**3**		3						
	1-2 ..	**7**	4	3	**7**	4	3						
	2-3 ..	**5**	4	1	**5**	4	1						
	3-4 ..	**1**	1		**1**	1							
	4-5 ..	**5**	4	1	**5**	4	1						
	TOTAL 0-5 ..	*21*	*13*	*8*	*21*	*13*	*8*						
	5-10 ..	**14**	9	5	**14**	9	5						
	10-15 ..	**7**	4	3	**6**	4	2	**1**		1			
	15-20 ..	**9**	5	4	**4**	4		**5**	1	4			
	20-30 ..	**24**	10	14	**3**	3		**21**	7	14			
	30-40 ..	**13**	10	3	**2**	2		**10**	7	3	**1**	1	
	40-50 ..	**8**	4	4				**7**	4	3	**1**		1
	50-60 ..	**5**	5					**5**	5				
	60 and over ..	**4**	3	1				**1**	1		**3**	2	1
	TOTAL ..	*84*	*50*	*34*	*29*	*22*	*7*	*50*	*25*	*25*	*5*	*3*	*2*
REASI													
Total Population		**257903**	**135502**	**122401**	**128925**	**76160**	**52765**	**107062**	**51697**	**55365**	**21916**	**7645**	**14271**
	0-1 ..	**5125**	2624	2 01	**5125**	2624	2501						
	1-2 ..	**6456**	3198	3258	**6456**	3198	3258						
	2-3 ..	**7535**	3789	3746	**7535**	3789	3746						
	3-4 ..	**7912**	3931	3981	**7912**	3931	3981						
	4-5 ..	**7745**	3993	3752	**7745**	3993	3752						
	TOTAL 0-5 ..	*34773*	*17535*	*17238*	*34773*	*17535*	*17238*						
	5-10 ..	**38237**	19901	18336	**38232**	19901	18331	**5**		5			
	10-15 ..	**31588**	16790	14798	**28833**	16552	12281	**2699**	229	2470	**56**	9	47
	15-20 ..	**25374**	12808	12476	**14928**	10509	4329	**10135**	2199	7936	**311**	100	211
	20-30 ..	**44603**	22088	22515	**8432**	7989	443	**34210**	13225	20985	**1961**	874	1087
	30-40 ..	**35176**	18714	16462	**2059**	1995	64	**29472**	15325	14147	**3645**	1394	2251
	40-50 ..	**21147**	11921	9226	**791**	757	34	**15898**	9720	6178	**4458**	1444	3014
	50-60 ..	**13838**	8074	5764	**438**	410	28	**8590**	6163	2427	**4810**	1501	3309
	60 and over ..	**13167**	7581	5586	**439**	422	17	**6053**	4836	1217	**6675**	2323	4352
	TOTAL ..	*223130*	*117967*	*105163*	*94152*	*58625*	*35527*	*107062*	*51697*	*55365*	*21916*	*7645*	*14271*

VII—AGE AND CIVIL CONDITION (PART III—DISTRICTS)—Contd.

Community and Age		Population P	Population M	Population F	Unmarried P	Unmarried M	Unmarried F	Married P	Married M	Married F	Widowed P	Widowed M	Widowed F
1		*2*	*3*	*4*	*5*	*6*	*7*	*8*	*9*	*10*	*11*	*12*	*13*
REASI—contd.													
		80725	**42211**	**38514**	**36287**	**22476**	**13811**	**33755**	**16456**	**17299**	**10683**	**3279**	**7404**
	0-1 ..	**1674**	807	867	**1674**	807	867						
	1-2 ..	**1594**	766	828	**1594**	766	828						
	2-3 ..	**1703**	853	850	**1703**	853	850						
	3-4 ..	**1983**	977	1006	**1983**	977	1006						
	4-5 ..	**1912**	976	936	**1912**	976	936						
Hindu	Total 0-5 ..	*8866*	*4379*	*4487*	*8866*	*4379*	*4487*						
	5-10 ..	**9762**	4956	4806	**9760**	4956	4804	**2**		2			
	10-15 ..	**8755**	4441	4314	**7603**	4301	3302	**1125**	134	991	27	6	21
	15-20 ..	**7564**	3754	3810	**4143**	3071	1072	**3282**	633	2649	**139**	50	89
	20-30 ..	**14091**	7037	7054	**3340**	3259	81	**9927**	3515	6412	**824**	263	561
	30-40 ..	**12061**	6386	5675	**1263**	1239	24	**8991**	4631	4360	**1807**	516	1291
	40-50 ..	**8211**	4645	3566	**616**	594	22	**5274**	3390	1884	**2321**	661	1660
	50-60 ..	**5680**	3315	2365	**348**	335	13	**2950**	2268	682	**2382**	712	1670
	60 and over ..	**5735**	3298	2437	**348**	342	6	**2204**	1885	319	**3183**	1071	2112
	Total ..	*71859*	*37832*	*34027*	*27421*	*18097*	*9324*	*33755*	*16456*	*17299*	*10683*	*3279*	*7404*
		175539	**92412**	**83127**	**91806**	**53179**	**38627**	**72650**	**34919**	**37731**	**11083**	**4314**	**6769**
	0-1 ..	**3411**	1794	1617	**3411**	1794	1617						
	1-2 ..	**4824**	2412	2412	**4824**	2412	2412						
	2-3 ..	**5782**	2906	2876	**5782**	2906	2876						
	3-4 ..	**5879**	2928	2951	**5879**	2928	2951						
	4-5 ..	**5778**	2985	2793	**5778**	2985	2793						
Muslim	Total 0-5 ..	*25674*	*13025*	*12649*	*25674*	*13025*	*12649*						
	5-10 ..	**28230**	14816	13414	**28227**	14816	13411	**3**		3			
	10-15 ..	**22638**	12242	10396	**21047**	12145	8902	**1562**	94	1468	**29**	3	26
	15-20 ..	**17646**	9054	8592	**10685**	7456	3229	**6790**	1548	5242	**171**	50	121
	20-30 ..	**30228**	14914	15314	**5042**	4682	360	**24063**	9626	14437	**1123**	606	517
	30-40 ..	**22906**	12225	10681	**783**	743	40	**20308**	10612	9696	**1815**	870	945
	40-50 ..	**12776**	7176	5600	**171**	159	12	**10507**	6247	4260	**2098**	770	1328
	50-60 ..	**8075**	4711	3364	**87**	73	14	**5589**	3858	1731	**2399**	780	1619
	60 and over ..	**7366**	4249	3117	**90**	80	10	**3828**	2934	894	**3448**	1235	2213
	Total ..	*149865*	*79387*	*70478*	*66132*	*40154*	*25978*	*72650*	*34919*	*37731*	*11083*	*4314*	*6769*
		1541	**823**	**718**	**777**	**475**	**302**	**..617**	**299**	**318**	**147**	**49**	**98**
	0-1 ..	**37**	23	14	**37**	23	14						
	1-2 ..	**34**	20	14	**34**	20	14						
	2-3 ..	**48**	29	19	**48**	29	19						
	3-4 ..	**48**	25	23	**48**	25	23						
	4-5 ..	**52**	30	22	**52**	30	22						
Sikh	Total 0-5 ..	*219*	*127*	*92*	*219*	*127*	*92*						
	5-10 ..	**227**	117	110	**227**	117	110						
	10-15 ..	**184**	101	83	**172**	100	72	**12**	1	11			
	15-20 ..	**154**	86	68	**94**	69	25	**59**	17	42	**1**		1
	20-30 ..	**266**	126	140	**46**	44	2	**207**	78	129	**13**	4	9
	30-40 ..	**197**	96	101	**12**	12		**162**	76	86	**23**	8	15
	40-50 ..	**151**	92	59	**4**	4		**110**	77	33	**37**	11	26
	50-60 ..	**79**	45	34	**3**	2	1	**47**	34	13	**29**	9	20
	60 and over ..	**64**	33	31				**20**	16	4	**44**	17	27
	Total ..	*1322*	*696*	*626*	*558*	*348*	*210*	*617*	*299*	*318*	*147*	*49*	*98*

VII—AGE AND CIVIL CONDITION (PART III—DISTRICTS)—CONTD.

Community and Age		Population P	Population M	Population F	Unmarried P	Unmarried M	Unmarried F	Married P	Married M	Married F	Widowed P	Widowed M	Widowed F
1		2	3	4	5	6	7	8	9	10	11	12	13
REASI —concld.													
		98	**56**	**42**	**55**	**30**	**25**	**40**	**23**	**17**	**3**	**3**	
	0-1 ..	**3**		3	**3**		3						
	1-2 ..	**4**		4	**4**		4						
	2-3 ..	**2**	1	1	**2**	1	1						
	3-4 ..	**2**	1	1	**2**	1	1						
	4-5 ..	**3**	2	1	**3**	2	1						
Others	TOTAL 0-5 ..	*14*	*4*	*10*	*14*	*4*	*10*						
	5-10	**18**	12	6	**18**	12	6						
	10-15 ..	**11**	6	5	**11**	6	5						
	15-20 ..	**10**	4	6	**6**	3	3	**4**	1	3			
	20-30 ..	**18**	11	7	**4**	4		**13**	6	7			
	30-40 ..	**12**	7	5	**1**	1		**11**	6	5	**1**	1	
	40-50 ..	**9**	8	1				**7**	6	1			
	50-60 ..	**4**	3	1				**4**	3	1	**2**	2	
	60 and over ..	**2**	1	1	**1**		1	**1**	1				
	TOTAL ..	*84*	*52*	*32*	*41*	*26*	*15*	*40*	*23*	*17*	*3*	*3*	
MIRPUR													
		386655	**196796**	**189859**	**197912**	**114061**	**83851**	**155951**	**71852**	**84099**	**32792**	**10883**	**21909**
	0-1 ..	**7415**	3634	3781	**7415**	3634	3781						
	1-2 ..	**9726**	4813	4913	**9726**	4813	4913						
	2-3 ..	**10753**	5463	5290	**10753**	5463	5290						
	3-4 ..	**12543**	6301	6242	**12543**	6301	6242						
	4-5 ..	**12433**	6308	6125	**12433**	6308	6125						
Total Population	TOTAL 0-5 ..	*52870*	*26519*	*26351*	*52870*	*26519*	*26351*						
	5-10 ..	**60981**	31958	29023	**60971**	31958	29013	**10**		10			
	10-15 ..	**48166**	25480	22686	**44701**	25234	19467	**3436**	242	3194	**29**	4	25
	15-20 ..	**35363**	17654	17709	**22727**	15205	7522	**12396**	2398	9998	**240**	51	189
	20-30 ..	**60712**	28551	32161	**12212**	11074	1138	**46587**	16599	29988	**1913**	878	1035
	30-40 ..	**49505**	23977	25528	**2505**	2363	142	**42702**	20061	22641	**4298**	1553	2745
	40 50 ..	**32727**	16850	15877	**871**	785	86	**25273**	14204	11069	**6583**	1861	4722
	50-60 ..	**23176**	12901	10275	**578**	513	65	**14907**	10022	4885	**7691**	2366	5325
	60 and over ..	**23155**	12906	10249	**477**	410	67	**10640**	8326	2314	**12038**	4170	7868
	TOTAL ..	*333785*	*170277*	*163508*	*145042*	*87542*	*57500*	*155951*	*71852*	*84099*	*32792*	*10883*	*21909*
		63576	**32983**	**30593**	**31170**	**18423**	**12747**	**26592**	**12678**	**13914**	**5814**	**1882**	**3932**
	0-1 ..	**1375**	705	670	**1375**	705	670						
	1-2 ..	**1654**	851	803	**1654**	851	803						
	2-3 ..	**1698**	883	815	**1698**	883	815						
	3-4 ..	**1983**	1020	963	**1983**	1020	963						
	4-5 ..	**1861**	940	921	**1861**	940	921						
Hindu	TOTAL 0-5 ..	*8571*	*4399*	*4172*	*8571*	*4399*	*4172*						
	5-10 ..	**9417**	4863	4554	**9408**	4863	4545	**9**		9			
	10-15 ..	**7608**	3907	3701	**6802**	3882	2920	**799**	25	774	**7**		7
	15-20 ..	**5652**	2755	2897	**3381**	2364	1017	**2239**	387	1852	**32**	4	28
	20-30 ..	**9455**	4593	4862	**1909**	1837	72	**7240**	2659	4581	**306**	97	209
	30-40 ..	**8191**	4128	4063	**508**	506	2	**6983**	3418	3565	**700**	204	496
	40-50 ..	**6032**	3297	2735	**250**	245	5	**4615**	2731	1884	**1167**	321	846
	50-60 ..	**4346**	2518	1828	**198**	194	4	**2752**	1890	862	**1396**	434	962
	60 and over ..	**4304**	2523	1781	**143**	133	10	**1955**	1568	387	**2206**	822	1384
	TOTAL ..	*55005*	*28584*	*26421*	*22599*	*14024*	*8575*	*26592*	*12678*	*13914*	*5814*	*1882*	*3932*

VII—AGE AND CIVIL CONDITION (PART III—DISTRICTS)—Contd.

MIRPUR—concld.

Community and Age		Population P	Population M	Population F	Unmarried P	Unmarried M	Unmarried F	Married P	Married M	Married F	Widowed P	Widowed M	Widowed F
1		2	3	4	5	6	7	8	9	10	11	12	13
		310880	**157536**	**153344**	**160317**	**91875**	**68442**	**124346**	**56888**	**67458**	**26217**	**8773**	**17444**
	0-1 ..	**5758**	2767	2991	**5758**	2767	2991						
	1-2 ..	**7723**	3807	3916	**7723**	3807	3916						
	2-3 ..	**8680**	4371	4309	**8680**	4371	4309						
	3-4 ..	**10136**	5070	5066	**10136**	5070	5066						
	4-5 ..	**10165**	5142	5023	**10165**	5142	5023						
Muslim	Total 0-5 ..	*42462*	*21157*	*21305*	*42462*	*21157*	*21305*						
	5-10 ..	**49471**	25963	23508	**49470**	25963	23507	**1**		1			
	10-15 ..	**38905**	20670	18235	**36404**	20469	15935	**2480**	198	2282	**21**	3	18
	15-20 ..	**28570**	14335	14235	**18671**	12367	6304	**9692**	1921	7771	**207**	47	160
	20-30 ..	**49633**	23278	26355	**10080**	9024	1056	**37974**	13480	24494	**1579**	774	805
	30-40 ..	**39908**	19189	20719	**1947**	1807	140	**34445**	16056	18389	**3516**	1326	2190
	40-50 ..	**25656**	12974	12682	**597**	517	80	**19791**	10963	8828	**5268**	1494	3774
	50-60 ..	**18143**	9984	8159	**365**	306	59	**11651**	7792	3859	**6127**	1886	4241
	60 and over ..	**18132**	9986	8146	**321**	265	56	**8312**	6478	1834	**9499**	3243	6256
	Total ..	*268418*	*136379*	*132039*	*117855*	*70718*	*47137*	*124346*	*56888*	*67458*	*26217*	*8773*	*17444*
		12111	**6227**	**5884**	**6384**	**3738**	**2646**	**4972**	**2265**	**2707**	**755**	**224**	**531**
	0-1 ..	**280**	160	120	**280**	160	120						
	1-2 ..	**345**	153	192	**345**	153	192						
	2-3 ..	**372**	207	165	**372**	207	165						
	3-4 ..	**420**	208	212	**420**	208	212						
	4-5 ..	**406**	225	181	**406**	225	181						
Sikh	Total 0-5 ..	*1823*	*953*	*870*	*1823*	*953*	*870*						
	5-10 ..	**2079**	1126	953	**2079**	1126	953						
	10-15 ..	**1644**	898	746	**1487**	879	608	**156**	18	138	**1**	1	
	15-20 ..	**1133**	560	573	**672**	471	201	**460**	89	371	**1**		1
	20-30 ..	**1608**	671	937	**222**	212	10	**1358**	452	906	**28**	7	21
	30-40 ..	**1395**	654	741	**49**	49		**1264**	582	682	**82**	23	59
	40-50 ..	**1031**	574	457	**24**	23	1	**862**	507	355	**145**	44	101
	50-60 ..	**682**	397	285	**15**	13	2	**500**	338	162	**167**	46	121
	60 and over ..	**716**	394	322	**13**	12	1	**372**	279	93	**331**	103	228
	Total ..	*10288*	*5274*	*5014*	*4561*	*2785*	*1776*	*4972*	*2265*	*2707*	*755*	*224*	*531*
		88	**50**	**38**	**41**	**25**	**16**	**41**	**21**	**20**	**6**	**4**	**2**
	0-1 ..	**2**	2		**2**	2							
	1-2 ..	**4**	2	2	**4**	2	2						
	2-3 ..	**3**	2	1	**3**	2	1						
	3-4 ..	**4**	3	1	**4**	3	1						
	4-5 ..	**1**	1		**1**	1							
Others	Total 0-5 ..	*14*	*10*	*4*	*14*	*10*	*4*						
	5-10 ..	**14**	6	8	**14**	6	8						
	10-15 ..	**9**	5	4	**8**	4	4	**1**	1				
	15-20 ..	**8**	4	4	**3**	3		**5**	1	4			
	20-30 ..	**16**	9	7	**1**	1		**15**	8	7			
	30-40 ..	**11**	6	5	**1**	1		**10**	5	5			
	40-50 ..	**8**	5	3				**5**	3	2	**3**	2	1
	50-60 ..	**5**	2	3				**4**	2	2	**1**		1
	60 and over ..	**3**	3					**1**	1		**2**	2	
	Total ..	*74*	*40*	*34*	*27*	*15*	*12*	*41*	*21*	*20*	*6*	*4*	*2*

VII—AGE AND CIVIL CONDITION (PART III—DISTRICTS)—CONTD.

CHENANI JAGIR

Community and Age		Population P	Population M	Population F	Unmarried P	Unmarried M	Unmarried F	Married P	Married M	Married F	Widowed P	Widowed M	Widowed F
1		2	3	4	5	6	7	8	9	10	11	12	13
Total Population		**11796**	**6475**	**5321**	**5032**	**3213**	**1819**	**5348**	**2821**	**2527**	**1416**	**441**	**975**
	0-1 ..	**202**	98	104	**202**	98	104						
	1-2 ..	**208**	86	122	**208**	86	122						
	2-3 ..	**246**	122	124	**246**	122	124						
	3-4 ..	**272**	129	143	**272**	129	143						
	4-5 ..	**250**	115	135	**250**	115	135						
	TOTAL 0-5 ..	*1178*	*550*	*628*	*1178*	*550*	*628*						
	5-10 ..	**1368**	674	694	**1366**	674	692	**2**		2			
	10-15 ..	**1257**	669	588	**1032**	647	385	**220**	21	199	**5**	1	4
	15-20 ..	**1212**	665	547	**607**	509	98	**582**	150	432	**23**	6	17
	20-30 ..	**2380**	1377	1003	**515**	504	11	**1741**	828	913	**124**	45	79
	30-40 ..	**1795**	1028	767	**169**	165	4	**1371**	774	597	**255**	89	166
	40-50 ..	**1121**	647	474	**71**	70	1	**749**	489	260	**301**	88	213
	50-60 ..	**749**	457	292	**48**	48		**411**	323	88	**290**	86	204
	60 and over ..	**736**	408	328	**46**	46		**272**	236	36	**418**	126	292
	TOTAL ..	*10618*	*5925*	*4693*	*3854*	*2663*	*1191*	*5348*	*2821*	*2527*	*1416*	*441*	*975*
Hindu		**9581**	**4975**	**4606**	**4060**	**2546**	**1514**	**4254**	**2065**	**2189**	**1267**	**364**	**903**
	0-1 ..	**168**	83	85	**168**	83	85						
	1-2 ..	**168**	71	97	**168**	71	97						
	2-3 ..	**205**	101	104	**205**	101	104						
	3-4 ..	**228**	108	120	**228**	108	120						
	4-5 ..	**203**	98	105	**203**	98	105						
	TOTAL 0-5 ..	*972*	*461*	*511*	*972*	*461*	*511*						
	5-10 ..	**1169**	576	593	**1167**	576	591	**2**		2			
	10-15 ..	**1032**	531	501	**833**	514	319	**196**	16	180	**3**	1	2
	15-20 ..	**930**	453	477	**430**	351	79	**481**	97	384	**19**	5	14
	20-30 ..	**1758**	899	859	**353**	344	9	**1297**	523	774	**108**	32	76
	30-40 ..	**1431**	749	682	**148**	144	4	**1061**	539	522	**222**	66	156
	40-50 ..	**976**	549	427	**66**	65	1	**630**	408	222	**280**	76	204
	50-60 ..	**656**	397	259	**46**	46		**349**	278	71	**261**	73	188
	60 and over ..	**657**	360	297	**45**	45		**238**	204	34	**374**	111	263
	TOTAL ..	*8609*	*4514*	*4095*	*3088*	*2085*	*1003*	*4254*	*2065*	*2189*	*1267*	*364*	*903*
Muslim		**2205**	**1491**	**714**	**969**	**664**	**305**	**1088**	**751**	**337**	**148**	**76**	**72**
	0-1 ..	**34**	15	19	**34**	15	19						
	1-2 ..	**40**	15	25	**40**	15	25						
	2-3 ..	**40**	20	20	**40**	20	20						
	3-4 ..	**44**	21	23	**44**	21	23						
	4-5 ..	**47**	17	30	**47**	17	30						
	TOTAL 0-5 ..	*205*	*88*	*117*	*205*	*88*	*117*						
	5-10 ..	**198**	97	101	**198**	97	101						
	10-15 ..	**225**	138	87	**199**	133	66	**24**	5	19	**2**		2
	15-20 ..	**281**	212	69	**177**	158	19	**100**	53	47	**4**	1	3
	20-30 ..	**618**	474	144	**162**	160	2	**440**	301	139	**16**	13	3
	30-40 ..	**363**	278	85	**21**	21		**309**	234	75	**33**	23	10
	40-50 ..	**145**	98	47	**5**	5		**119**	81	38	**21**	12	9
	50-60 ..	**92**	59	33	**2**	2		**62**	45	17	**28**	12	16
	60 and over ..	**78**	47	31				**34**	32	2	**44**	15	29
	TOTAL ..	*2000*	*1403*	*597*	*764*	*576*	*188*	*1088*	*751*	*337*	*148*	*76*	*72*

VII—AGE AND CIVIL CONDITION (PART III—DISTRICTS)—CONTD.

Community and Age		Population P	Population M	Population F	Unmarried P	Unmarried M	Unmarried F	Married P	Married M	Married F	Widowed P	Widowed M	Widowed F
1		2	3	4	5	6	7	8	9	10	11	12	13
CHENANI JAGIR—concld.													
		10	**9**	**1**	**3**	**3**		**6**	**5**	**1**	**1**	**1**	
	0-1												
	1-2												
	2-3	**1**	1		**1**	1							
	3-4												
	4-5												
Sikh	TOTAL 0-5	*1*	*1*		*1*	*1*							
	5-10	**1**	1		**1**	1							
	10-15												
	15-20	**1**		1				**1**		1			
	20-30	**4**	4					**4**	4				
	30-40	**1**	1					**1**	1				
	40-50												
	50-60	**1**	1								**1**	1	
	60 and over	**1**	1		**1**	1							
	TOTAL	*9*	*8*	*1*	*2*	*2*		*6*	*5*	*1*	*1*	*1*	
POONCH JAGIR													
		421828	**213919**	**207909**	**221626**	**126772**	**94854**	**172596**	**78631**	**93965**	**27606**	**8516**	**19090**
	0-1	**8882**	4413	4469	**8882**	4413	4469						
	1-2	**11429**	5691	5738	**11429**	5691	5738						
	2-3	**12531**	6163	6368	**12531**	6163	6368						
	3-4	**12911**	6248	6663	**12911**	6248	6663						
	4-5	**13810**	6966	6844	**13810**	6966	6844						
Total Population	TOTAL 0-5	*59563*	*29481*	*30082*	*59563*	*29481*	*30082*						
	5-10	**68176**	35391	32785	**68165**	35387	32778	**7**	3	4	**4**	1	3
	10-15	**56494**	30850	25644	**52274**	30289	21985	**4139**	539	3600	**81**	22	59
	15-20	**42123**	21600	20523	**26784**	18415	8369	**14917**	3045	11872	**422**	140	282
	20-30	**70221**	32004	38217	**12199**	10905	1294	**55693**	20063	35630	**2329**	1036	1293
	30-40	**56785**	27556	29229	**1736**	1546	190	**50105**	24374	24731	**4944**	1636	3308
	40-50	**32210**	16750	15460	**461**	369	92	**25684**	14827	10857	**6065**	1554	4511
	50-60	**19904**	11063	8841	**226**	197	29	**13427**	9224	4203	**6251**	1642	4609
	60 and over	**16352**	9224	7128	**218**	183	35	**8624**	6556	2068	**7510**	2485	5025
	TOTAL	*362265*	*184438*	*177827*	*162063*	*97291*	*64772*	*172596*	*78631*	*93965*	*27606*	*8516*	*19090*
		24137	**12312**	**11825**	**12833**	**7526**	**5307**	**9095**	**4109**	**4986**	**2209**	**677**	**1532**
	0-1	**496**	260	236	**496**	260	236						
	1-2	**668**	359	309	**668**	359	309						
	2-3	**686**	319	367	**686**	319	367						
	3-4	**683**	332	351	**683**	332	351						
	4-5	**764**	362	402	**764**	362	402						
Hindu	TOTAL 0-5	*3297*	*1632*	*1665*	*3297*	*1632*	*1665*						
	5-10	**3970**	2043	1927	**3968**	2041	1927	**1**	1		**1**	1	
	10-15	**3193**	1684	1509	**2921**	1668	1253	**267**	13	254	**5**	3	2
	15-20	**2250**	1135	1115	**1457**	1044	413	**770**	80	690	**23**	11	12
	20-30	**3695**	1685	2010	**813**	777	36	**2722**	860	1862	**160**	48	112
	30-40	**3197**	1549	1648	**179**	171	8	**2619**	1270	1349	**399**	108	291
	40-50	**2030**	1147	883	**82**	79	3	**1445**	908	537	**503**	160	343
	50-60	**1337**	769	568	**59**	57	2	**771**	560	211	**507**	152	355
	60 and over	**1168**	668	500	**57**	57		**500**	417	83	**611**	194	417
	TOTAL	*20840*	*10680*	*10160*	*9536*	*5894*	*3642*	*9095*	*4109*	*4986*	*2209*	*677*	*1532*

VII—AGE AND CIVIL CONDITION (PART III—DISTRICTS —CONTD.

POONCH JAGIR—concld.

Community and Age		Population P	Population M	Population F	Unmarried P	Unmarried M	Unmarried F	Married P	Married M	Married F	Widowed P	Widowed M	Widowed F
1		2	3	4	5	6	7	8	9	10	11	12	13
		382722	**194068**	**188654**	**200785**	**114730**	**86055**	**157614**	**71795**	**85819**	**24323**	**7543**	**16780**
	0-1 ..	**8039**	3996	4043	**8039**	3996	4043						
	1-2 ..	**10292**	5121	5171	**10292**	5121	5171						
	2-3 ..	**11368**	5621	5747	**11368**	5621	5747						
	3-4 ..	**11713**	5650	6063	**11713**	5650	6063						
	4-5 ..	**12546**	6329	6217	**12546**	6329	6217						
Muslim	TOTAL 0-5 ..	*53958*	*26717*	*27241*	*53958*	*26717*	*27241*						
	5-10 ..	**61637**	32001	29636	**61629**	31999	29630	**5**	2	3	**3**		3
	10-15 ..	**51305**	28122	23183	**47523**	27587	19936	**3706**	516	3190	**76**	19	57
	15-20 ..	**38455**	19767	18688	**24519**	16822	7097	**13540**	2816	10724	**396**	129	267
	20-30 ..	**64110**	29233	34877	**11018**	9786	1232	**50996**	18484	32512	**2096**	963	1133
	30-40 ..	**51600**	25035	26565	**1481**	1309	172	**45788**	22247	23541	**4331**	1479	2852
	40-50 ..	**29029**	14980	14049	**346**	260	86	**23400**	13388	10012	**5283**	1332	3951
	50-60 ..	**17909**	9930	7979	**156**	130	26	**12265**	8378	3887	**5488**	1422	4066
	60 and over ..	**14719**	8283	6436	**155**	120	35	**7914**	5964	1950	**6650**	2199	4451
	TOTAL ..	*328764*	*167351*	*161413*	*146827*	*88013*	*58814*	*157614*	*71795*	*85819*	*24323*	*7543*	*16780*
		14877	**7526**	**7351**	**7961**	**4512**	**3449**	**5850**	**2722**	**3128**	**1066**	**292**	**774**
	0-1 ..	**340**	157	183	**340**	157	183						
	1-2 ..	**463**	211	252	**463**	211	252						
	2-3 ..	**472**	223	249	**472**	223	249						
	3-4 ..	**513**	266	247	**513**	266	247						
	4-5 ..	**498**	275	223	**498**	275	223						
Sikh	TOTAL 0-5 ..	*2286*	*1132*	*1154*	*2286*	*1132*	*1154*						
	5-10 ..	**2551**	1346	1205	**2550**	1346	1204	**1**		1			
	10-15 ..	**1988**	1042	946	**1825**	1032	793	**163**	10	153			
	15-20 ..	**1407**	697	710	**806**	548	258	**598**	149	449	**3**		3
	20-30 ..	**2406**	1084	1322	**368**	342	26	**1965**	717	1248	**73**	25	48
	30-40 ..	**1985**	972	1013	**76**	66	10	**1695**	857	838	**214**	49	165
	40-50 ..	**1146**	621	525	**33**	30	3	**835**	530	305	**278**	61	217
	50-60 ..	**648**	361	287	**11**	10	1	**384**	284	100	**253**	67	186
	60 and over ..	**460**	271	189	**6**	6		**209**	175	34	**245**	90	155
	TOTAL ..	*12591*	*6394*	*6197*	*5675*	*3380*	*2295*	*5850*	*2722*	*3128*	*1066*	*292*	*774*
		92	**13**	**79**	**47**	**4**	**43**	**37**	**5**	**32**	**8**	**4**	**4**
	0-1 ..	**7**		7	**7**		7						
	1-2 ..	**6**		6	**6**		6						
	2-3 ..	**5**		5	**5**		5						
	3-4 ..	**2**		2	**2**		2						
	4-5 ..	**2**		2	**2**		2						
Others	TOTAL 0-5 ..	*22*		*22*	*22*		*22*						
	5-10 ..	**18**	1	17	**18**	1	17						
	10-15 ..	**8**	2	6	**5**	2	3	**3**		3			
	15-20 ..	**11**	1	10	**2**	1	1	**9**		9			
	20-30 ..	**10**	2	8				**10**	2	8			
	30-40 ..	**3**		3				**3**		3			
	40-50 ..	**5**	2	3				**4**	1	3	**1**	1	
	50-60 ..	**10**	3	7				**7**	2	5	**3**	1	2
	60 and over ..	**5**	2	3				**1**		1	**4**	2	2
	TOTAL ..	*10*	*13*	*57*	*25*	*4*	*21*	*37*	*5*	*32*	*8*	*4*	*4*

VII—AGE AND CIVIL CONDITION (PART III—DISTRICTS)—Contd.

BARAMULLA

Community and Age		Population P	Population M	Population F	Unmarried P	Unmarried M	Unmarried F	Married P	Married M	Married F	Widowed P	Widowed M	Widowed F
1		2	3	4	5	6	7	8	9	10	11	12	13
Total Population		**612428**	**330050**	**282378**	**291170**	**173654**	**117516**	**285324**	**139007**	**146317**	**35934**	**17389**	**18545**
	0-1	**13546**	6951	6595	**13546**	6951	6595						
	1-2	**14663**	7377	7286	**14663**	7377	7286						
	2-3	**16665**	8371	8294	**16665**	8371	8294						
	3-4	**19085**	9445	9640	**19085**	9445	9640						
	4-5	**16991**	8654	8337	**16991**	8654	8337						
	Total 0-5	*80950*	*40798*	*40152*	*80950*	*40798*	*40152*						
	5-10	**86098**	46498	39600	**86086**	46493	39593	**12**	5	7			
	10-15	**72168**	39554	32614	**65213**	38717	26496	**6857**	818	6039	**98**	19	79
	15-20	**65972**	35400	30572	**36183**	26478	9705	**29269**	8736	20533	**520**	186	334
	20-30	**119614**	61130	58484	**18425**	17217	1208	**97976**	41978	55998	**3213**	1935	1278
	30-40	**89133**	48267	40866	**2849**	2633	216	**80279**	42122	38157	**6005**	3512	2493
	40-50	**52249**	29711	22538	**853**	767	86	**43046**	25211	17835	**8350**	3733	4617
	50-60	**27203**	16717	10486	**337**	308	29	**18799**	13026	5773	**8067**	3383	4684
	60 and over	**19041**	11975	7066	**274**	243	31	**9086**	7111	1975	**9681**	4621	5060
	Total	*531478*	*289252*	*242226*	*210220*	*132856*	*77364*	*285324*	*139007*	*146317*	*35934*	*17389*	*18545*
Hindu		**12919**	**7579**	**5340**	**7005**	**4590**	**2415**	**4748**	**2517**	**2231**	**1166**	**472**	**694**
	0-1	**263**	128	135	**263**	128	135						
	1-2	**241**	120	121	**241**	120	121						
	2-3	**324**	183	141	**324**	183	141						
	3-4	**353**	165	188	**353**	165	188						
	4-5	**347**	180	167	**347**	180	167						
	Total 0-5	*1528*	*776*	*752*	*1528*	*776*	*752*						
	5-10	**1799**	928	871	**1799**	928	871						
	10-15	**1428**	771	657	**1337**	766	571	**89**	4	85	**2**	1	1
	15-20	**1211**	705	506	**838**	638	200	**363**	65	298	**10**	2	8
	20-30	**2379**	1420	959	**834**	814	20	**1470**	583	887	**75**	23	52
	30-40	**1961**	1244	717	**371**	370	1	**1411**	802	609	**179**	72	107
	40-50	**1350**	908	442	**161**	161		**873**	621	252	**316**	126	190
	50-60	**770**	510	260	**93**	93		**375**	290	85	**302**	127	175
	60 and over	**493**	317	176	**44**	44		**167**	152	15	**282**	121	161
	Total	*11391*	*6803*	*4588*	*5477*	*3814*	*1663*	*4748*	*2517*	*2231*	*1166*	*472*	*694*
Muslim		**590936**	**317983**	**272953**	**279661**	**166445**	**113216**	**276906**	**134778**	**142128**	**34369**	**16760**	**17609**
	0-1	**13060**	6706	6354	**13060**	6706	6354						
	1-2	**14162**	7127	7035	**14162**	7127	7035						
	2-3	**16048**	8041	8007	**16048**	8041	8007						
	3-4	**18416**	9135	9281	**18416**	9135	9281						
	4-5	**16361**	8333	8028	**16361**	8333	8028						
	Total 0-5	**78047**	**39342**	**38705**	**78047**	**39342**	**38705**						
	5-10	**82938**	44834	38104	**82928**	44830	38098	**10**	4	6			
	10-15	**69649**	38188	31461	**62916**	37378	25538	**6638**	792	5846	**95**	18	77
	15-20	**63827**	34190	29637	**34840**	25459	9381	**28482**	8548	19934	**505**	183	322
	20-30	**115718**	58982	56736	**17374**	16203	1171	**95228**	40878	54350	**3116**	1901	1215
	30-40	**86109**	46485	39624	**2425**	2232	193	**77914**	40828	37086	**5770**	3425	2345
	40-50	**50296**	28465	21831	**668**	593	75	**41686**	24300	17386	**7942**	3572	4370
	50-60	**26090**	16005	10085	**237**	212	25	**18186**	12577	5609	**7667**	3216	4451
	60 and over	**18262**	11492	6770	**226**	196	30	**8762**	6851	1911	**9274**	4445	4829
	Total	*512889*	*278641*	*234248*	*201614*	*127103*	*74511*	*276906*	*134778*	*142128*	*34369*	*16760*	*17609*

VII—AGE AND CIVIL CONDITION (PART III—DISTRICTS,—CONTD.

BARAMULLA—concld.

Community and Age		Population			Unmarried			Married			Widowed		
		P	M	F	P	M	F	P	M	F	P	M	F
1		2	3	4	5	6	7	8	9	10	11	12	13
Sikh		**8458**	**4433**	**4025**	**4422**	**2583**	**1839**	**3639**	**1694**	**1945**	**397**	**156**	**241**
	0-1 ..	**222**	116	106	**222**	116	106						
	1-2 ..	**259**	130	129	**259**	130	129						
	2-3 ..	**290**	145	145	**290**	145	145						
	3-4 ..	**314**	144	170	**314**	144	170						
	4-5 ..	**280**	139	141	**280**	139	141						
	TOTAL 0-5 ..	*1365*	*674*	*691*	*1365*	*674*	*691*						
	5-10 ..	**1349**	731	618	**1347**	730	617	**2**	1	1			
	10-15 ..	**1079**	587	492	**948**	565	383	**130**	22	108	**1**		1
	15-20 ..	**922**	499	423	**494**	375	119	**423**	123	300	**5**	1	4
	20-30 ..	**1495**	718	777	**201**	192	9	**1272**	515	757	**22**	11	11
	30-40 ..	**1039**	527	512	**42**	29	13	**941**	483	458	**56**	15	41
	40-50 ..	**592**	334	258	**19**	12	7	**482**	287	195	**91**	35	56
	50-60 ..	**335**	200	135	**3**	3		**234**	157	77	**98**	40	58
	60 and over ..	**282**	163	119	**3**	3		**155**	106	49	**124**	54	70
	TOTAL ..	*7093*	*3759*	*3334*	*3057*	*1909*	*1148*	*3639*	*1694*	*1945*	*397*	*156*	*241*
Buddhist		**1**	**1**					**1**	**1**				
	0-1 ..												
	1-2 ..												
	2-3 ..												
	3-4 ..												
	4-5 ..												
	TOTAL 0-5 ..												
	5-10 ..												
	10-15 ..												
	15-20 ..												
	20-30 ..												
	30-40 ..	**1**	1					**1**	1				
	40-50 ..												
	50-60 ..												
	60 and over ..												
	TOTAL ..	*1*	*1*					*1*	*1*				
Others		**114**	**54**	**60**	**82**	**36**	**46**	**30**	**17**	**13**	**2**	**1**	**1**
	0-1 ..	**1**	1		**1**	1							
	1-2 ..	**1**		1	**1**		1						
	2-3 ..	**3**	2	1	**3**	2	1						
	3-4 ..	**2**	1	1	**2**	1	1						
	4-5 ..	**3**	2	1	**3**	2	1						
	TOTAL 0-5 ..	*10*	*6*	*4*	*10*	*6*	*4*						
	5-10 ..	**12**	5	7	**12**	5	7						
	10-15 ..	**12**	8	4	**12**	8	4						
	15-20 ..	**12**	6	6	**11**	6	5	**1**		1			
	20-30 ..	**22**	10	12	**16**	8	8	**6**	2	4			
	30-40 ..	**23**	10	13	**11**	2	9	**12**	8	4			
	40-50 ..	**11**	4	7	**5**	1	4	**5**	3	2	**1**		1
	50-60 ..	**8**	2	6	**4**		4	**4**	2	2			
	60 and over ..	**4**	3	1	**1**		1	**2**	2		**1**	1	
	TOTAL ..	*104*	*48*	*56*	*72*	*30*	*42*	*30*	*17*	*13*	*2*	*1*	*1*

VII—AGE AND CIVIL CONDITION (PART III—DISTRICTS)—CONTD.

ANANTNAG

Community	Age		Population P	Population M	Population F	Unmarried P	Unmarried M	Unmarried F	Married P	Married M	Married F	Widowed P	Widowed M	Widowed F
1			2	3	4	5	6	7	8	9	10	11	12	13
			851606	**463571**	**388035**	**415084**	**250759**	**164325**	**382284**	**189059**	**193225**	**54238**	**23753**	**30485**
	0-1	..	**17104**	8700	8404	**17104**	8700	8404						
	1-2	..	**20038**	10077	9961	**20038**	10077	9961						
	2-3	..	**22579**	11687	10892	**22579**	11687	10892						
	3-4	..	**24978**	12464	12514	**24978**	12464	12514						
	4-5	..	**23793**	12059	11734	**23793**	12059	11734						
Total Population	Total 0-5	..	*108492*	*54987*	*53505*	*108492*	*54987*	*53505*						
	5-10	..	**120247**	63506	56741	**120208**	63499	56709	**28**	7	21	**11**		11
	10-15	..	**103539**	56118	47421	**93746**	55042	38704	**9644**	1054	8590	**149**	22	127
	15-20	..	**89488**	48452	41036	**51025**	37539	13486	**37756**	10711	27045	**707**	202	505
	20-30	..	**162374**	86634	75740	**30865**	29427	1438	**127184**	54913	72271	**4325**	2294	2031
	30-40	..	**125616**	70699	54917	**6628**	6414	214	**109154**	58876	50278	**9834**	5409	4425
	40-50	..	**76183**	43802	32381	**2403**	2276	127	**60102**	35728	24374	**13678**	5798	7880
	50-60	..	**39613**	23628	15985	**1068**	979	89	**25688**	17878	7810	**12857**	4771	8086
	60 and over	..	**26054**	15745	10309	**649**	596	53	**12728**	9892	2836	**12677**	5257	7420
	Total	..	*743114*	*408584*	*334530*	*306592*	*195772*	*110820*	*382284*	*189059*	*193225*	*54238*	*23753*	*30485*
			66815	**37470**	**29345**	**34912**	**22360**	**12552**	**25731**	**13185**	**12546**	**6172**	**1925**	**4247**
	0-1	..	**1052**	584	468	**1052**	584	468						
	1-2	..	**1362**	679	683	**1362**	679	683						
	2-3	..	**1652**	877	775	**1652**	877	775						
	3-4	..	**1826**	923	903	**1826**	923	903						
	4-5	..	**1859**	940	919	**1859**	940	919						
Hindu	Total 0-5	..	*7751*	*4003*	*3748*	*7751*	*4003*	*3748*						
	5-10	..	**9165**	4775	4390	**9161**	4775	4386	**4**		4			
	10-15	..	**7834**	4122	3712	**7274**	4105	3169	**552**	16	536	**8**	1	7
	15-20	..	**6621**	3704	2917	**4360**	3249	1111	**2212**	450	1762	**49**	5	44
	20-30	..	**12767**	7471	5296	**3880**	3781	99	**8468**	3590	4878	**419**	100	319
	30-40	..	**9853**	5866	3987	**1270**	1252	18	**7492**	4281	3211	**1091**	333	758
	40-50	..	**6599**	3935	2664	**655**	646	9	**4268**	2766	1502	**1676**	523	1153
	50-60	..	**3938**	2300	1638	**369**	359	10	**1964**	1436	528	**1605**	505	1100
	60 and over	..	**2287**	1294	993	**192**	190	2	**771**	646	125	**1324**	458	866
	Total	..	*59064*	*33467*	*25597*	*27161*	*18357*	*8804*	*25731*	*13185*	*12546*	*6172*	*1925*	*4247*
			778684	**422619**	**356065**	**377030**	**226490**	**150540**	**353889**	**174422**	**179467**	**47765**	**21707**	**26058**
	0-1	..	**15901**	8049	7852	**15901**	8049	7852						
	1-2	..	**18521**	9335	9186	**18521**	9335	9186						
	2-3	..	**20745**	10713	10032	**20745**	10713	10032						
	3-4	..	**22954**	11446	11508	**22954**	11446	11508						
	4-5	..	**21770**	11031	10739	**21770**	11031	10739						
Muslim	Tota2 0-5	..	*99891*	*50574*	*49317*	*99891*	*50574*	*49317*						
	5-10	..	**110222**	58255	51967	**110191**	58250	51941	**21**	5	16	**10**		10
	10-15	..	**94964**	51558	43406	**85829**	50536	35293	**8997**	1002	7995	**138**	20	118
	15-20	..	**82167**	44339	37828	**46302**	34016	12286	**35215**	10130	25085	**650**	193	457
	20-30	..	**148309**	78378	69931	**26675**	25377	1298	**117757**	50822	66935	**3877**	2179	1698
	30-40	..	**114965**	64349	50616	**5282**	5103	179	**100999**	54197	46802	**8684**	5049	3635
	40-50	..	**69146**	39619	29527	**1728**	1618	110	**55476**	32752	22724	**11942**	5249	6693
	50-60	..	**35437**	21195	14242	**688**	615	73	**23557**	16333	7224	**11192**	4247	6945
	60 and over	..	**23583**	14352	9231	**444**	401	43	**11867**	9181	2686	**11272**	4770	6502
	Total	..	*678793*	*372045*	*306748*	*2777139*	*175916*	*101223*	*353889*	*174422*	*179467*	*47765*	*21707*	*26058*

VII—AGE AND CIVIL CONDITION (PART III—DISTRICTS)—CONTD.

ANANTNAG—concld.

Community	Age	Population P	Population M	Population F	Unmarried P	Unmarried M	Unmarried F	Married P	Married M	Married F	Widowed P	Widowed M	Widowed F
1		2	3	4	5	6	7	8	9	10	11	12	13
		5654	**3260**	**2394**	**2879**	**1775**	**1104**	**2513**	**1369**	**1144**	**262**	**116**	**146**
	0-1 ..	**144**	65	79	**144**	65	79						
	1-2 ..	**148**	60	88	**148**	60	88						
	2-3 ..	**174**	93	81	**174**	93	81						
	3-4 ..	**195**	94	101	**195**	94	101						
	4-5 ..	**158**	86	72	**158**	86	72						
Sikh	TOTAL 0-5 ..	*819*	*398*	*421*	*819*	*398*	*421*						
	5-10 ..	**797**	436	361	**793**	434	359	**3**	2	1	**1**		1
	10-15 ..	**690**	402	288	**592**	365	227	**95**	36	59	**3**	1	2
	15-20 ..	**672**	393	279	**340**	260	80	**324**	129	195	**8**	4	4
	20-30 ..	**1238**	761	477	**268**	254	14	**941**	492	449	**29**	15	14
	30-40 ..	**728**	455	273	**53**	51	2	**622**	379	243	**53**	25	28
	40-50 ..	**381**	217	164	**10**	9	1	**315**	183	132	**56**	25	31
	50-60 ..	**199**	118	81	**2**	2		**147**	97	50	**50**	19	31
	60 and over ..	**130**	80	50	**2**	2		**66**	51	15	**62**	27	35
	TOTAL ..	*4835*	*2862*	*1973*	*2060*	*1377*	*683*	*2513*	*1369*	*1144*	*262*	*116*	*146*
		9	**9**		**7**	**7**		**1**	**1**		**1**	**1**	
	0-1 ..												
	1-2 ..												
	2-3 ..												
	3-4 ..												
	4-5 ..												
Buddhist	TOTAL 0-5 ..												
	5-10 ..												
	10-15 ..	**1**	1		**1**	1							
	15-20 ..	**2**	2		**2**	2							
	20-30 ..	**4**	4		**4**	4							
	30-40 ..	**1**	1					**1**	1				
	40-50 ..	**1**	1	-							**1**	1	
	50-60 ..												
	60 and over ..												
	TOTAL ..	*9*	*9*		*7*	*7*		*1*	*1*		*1*	*1*	
		444	**213**	**231**	**256**	**127**	**129**	**150**	**82**	**68**	**38**	**4**	**34**
	0-1 ..	**7**	2	5	**7**	2	5						
	1-2 ..	**7**	3	4	**7**	3	4						
	2-3 ..	**8**	4	4	**8**	4	4						
	3-4 ..	**3**	1	2	**3**	1	2						
	4-5 ..	**6**	2	4	**6**	2	4						
Others	TOTAL 0-5 ..	*31*	*12*	*19*	*31*	*12*	*19*						
	5-10 ..	**63**	40	23	**63**	40	23						
	10-15 ..	**50**	35	15	**50**	35	15						
	15-20 ..	**26**	14	12	**21**	12	9	**5**	2	3			
	20-30 ..	**56**	20	36	**38**	11	27	**18**	9	9			
	30-40 ..	**69**	28	41	**23**	8	15	**40**	18	22	**6**	2	4
	40-50 ..	**56**	30	26	**10**	3	7	**43**	27	16	**3**		3
	50-60 ..	**39**	15	24	**9**	3	6	**20**	12	8	**10**		10
	60 and over ..	**54**	19	35	**11**	3	8	**24**	14	10	**19**	2	17
	TOTAL ..	*413*	*201*	*212*	*225*	*115*	*110*	*150*	*82*	*68*	*38*	*4*	*34*

VII—AGE AND CIVIL CONDITION (PART I.I—DISTRICTS)—CONTD.

Community	and Age	Population			Unmarried			Married			Widowed		
		P	M	F	P	M	F	P	M	F	P	M	F
	1	*2*	*3*	*4*	*5*	*6*	*7*	*8*	*9*	*10*	*11*	*12*	*13*
						MUZAFFARABAD							
		264671	**141117**	**123554**	**138320**	**81366**	**56954**	**111730**	**54231**	**57499**	**14621**	**5520**	**9101**
	0-1 ..	**6227**	3062	3165	**6227**	3062	3165						
	1-2 ..	**7318**	3815	3503	**7318**	3815	3503						
	2-3 ..	**7987**	4067	3920	**7987**	4067	3920						
	3-4 ..	**8698**	4352	4346	**8698**	4352	4346						
	4-5 ..	**8610**	4378	4232	**8610**	4378	4232						
Total Population	TOTAL 0-5 ..	*38840*	*19674*	*19166*	*38840*	*19674*	*19166*						
	5-10 ..	**41974**	21923	20051	**41275**	21853	19422	**689**	66	623	**10**	4	6
	10-15 ..	**35425**	18980	16445	**30783**	18173	12610	**4532**	773	3759	**110**	34	76
	15-20 ..	**28353**	14848	13505	**16027**	11322	4705	**11944**	3376	8568	**382**	150	232
	20-30 ..	**48663**	25781	22882	**9395**	8468	927	**37531**	16440	21091	**1737**	873	864
	30-40 ..	**32576**	17470	15106	**1299**	1214	85	**28723**	15159	13554	**2554**	1087	1467
	40-50 ..	**18025**	10107	7918	**360**	339	21	**14932**	8890	6042	**2733**	878	1855
	50-60 ..	**11532**	6702	4830	**159**	150	9	**8233**	5544	2689	**3140**	1008	2132
	60 and over ..	**9283**	5632	3651	**182**	173	9	**5146**	3973	1173	**3955**	1486	2469
	TOTAL ..	*225831*	*121443*	*104388*	*99480*	*61692*	*37788*	*111730*	*54231*	*57499*	*14621*	*5520*	*9101*
		5846	**3339**	**2507**	**3036**	**1844**	**1192**	**2323**	**1286**	**1037**	**487**	**209**	**278**
	0-1 ..	**113**	61	52	**113**	61	52						
	1-2 ..	**131**	67	64	**131**	67	64						
	2-3 ..	**167**	82	85	**167**	82	85						
	3-4 ..	**177**	82	95	**177**	82	95						
	4-5 ..	**175**	94	81	**175**	94	81						
Hindu	TOTAL 0-5 ..	*763*	*386*	*377*	*763*	*386*	*377*						
	5-10 ..	**896**	458	438	**896**	458	438						
	10-15 ..	**683**	367	316	**642**	363	279	**41**	4	37			
	15-20 ..	**536**	295	241	**350**	261	89	**178**	27	151	**8**	7	1
	20-30 ..	**1110**	647	463	**254**	247	7	**789**	353	436	**67**	47	20
	30-40 ..	**908**	580	328	**82**	81	1	**724**	451	273	**102**	48	54
	40-50 ..	**501**	338	163	**33**	33		**366**	266	100	**102**	39	63
	50-60 ..	**259**	164	95	**11**	11		**146**	114	32	**102**	39	63
	60 and over ..	**190**	104	86	**5**	4	1	**79**	71	8	**106**	29	77
	TOTAL ..	*5083*	*2953*	*2130*	*2273*	*1458*	*815*	*2323*	*1286*	*1037*	*487*	*209*	*278*
		245858	**130897**	**114961**	**128261**	**75421**	**52840**	**104243**	**50462**	**53781**	**13354**	**5014**	**8340**
	0-1 ..	**5769**	2825	2944	**5769**	2825	2944						
	1-2 ..	**6794**	3541	3253	**6794**	3541	3253						
	2-3 ..	**7438**	3799	3639	**7438**	3799	3639						
	3-4 ..	**8095**	4066	4029	**8095**	4066	4029						
	4-5 ..	**8004**	4065	3039	**8004**	4065	3939						
Muslim	TOTAL 0-5 ..	*36100*	*18296*	*17804*	*36100*	*18296*	*17804*						
	5-10 ..	**38962**	20349	18613	**38307**	20279	18028	**645**	66	579	**10**	4	6
	10-15 ..	**32906**	17697	15209	**28571**	16895	11676	**4228**	768	3460	**107**	34	73
	15-20 ..	**26362**	13892	12470	**14830**	10486	4344	**11172**	3266	7906	**360**	140	220
	20-30 ..	**45400**	24001	21399	**8689**	7814	875	**35098**	15387	19711	**1613**	800	813
	30-40 ..	**30187**	16042	14145	**1152**	1075	77	**26713**	13973	12740	**2322**	994	1328
	40-50 ..	**16621**	9229	7392	**300**	281	19	**13843**	8160	5683	**2478**	788	1690
	50-60 ..	**10701**	6184	4517	**142**	133	9	**7725**	5157	2568	**2834**	894	1940
	60 and over ..	**8619**	5207	3412	**170**	162	8	**4819**	3685	1134	**3630**	1360	2270
	TOTAL ..	*209758*	*112601*	*97157*	*92161*	*57125*	*35036*	*104243*	*50462*	*53781*	*13354*	*5014*	*8340*

VII—AGE AND CIVIL CONDITION (PART III—DISTRICTS)—CONTD.

Community and Age		Population			Unmarried			Married			Widowed		
		P	M	F	P	M	F	P	M	F	P	M	F
1		2	3	4	5	6	7	8	9	10	11	12	13
MUZAFFARABAD—concld.													
		12922	**6864**	**6058**	**6983**	**4085**	**2898**	**5161**	**2482**	**2679**	**778**	**297**	**481**
	0-1	**344**	175	169	**344**	175	169						
	1-2	**393**	207	186	**393**	207	186						
	2-3	**382**	186	196	**382**	186	196						
	3-4	**424**	204	220	**424**	204	220						
	4-5	**429**	218	211	**429**	218	211						
Sikh	TOTAL 0-5	*1972*	*990*	*982*	*1972*	*990*	*982*						
	5-10	**2102**	1110	992	**2058**	1110	948	**44**		44			
	10-15	**1827**	912	915	**1561**	911	650	**263**	1	262			
	15-20	**1450**	658	792	**842**	572	270	**594**	83	511	**3**		3
	20-30	**2146**	1131	1015	**448**	406	42	**1642**	699	943	**14**	3	11
	30-40	**1478**	848	630	**63**	58	5	**1285**	745	540	**56**	26	30
	40-50	**902**	540	362	**26**	25	1	**723**	464	259	**130**	45	85
	50-60	**571**	354	217	**6**	6		**362**	273	89	**153**	51	102
	60 and over	**474**	321	153	**7**	7		**248**	217	31	**203**	75	128
											219	97	122
	TOTAL	*10950*	*5874*	*5076*	*5011*	*3095*	*1916*	*5161*	*2482*	*2679*	*778*	*297*	*481*
		45	**17**	**28**	**40**	**16**	**24**	**3**	**1**	**2**	**2**		**2**
	0-1	**1**	1		**1**	1							
	1-2												
	2-3												
	3-4	**2**		2	**2**		2						
	4-5	**2**	1	1	**2**	1	1						
Others	TOTAL 0-5	*5*	*2*	*3*	*5*	*2*	*3*						
	5-10	**14**	6	8	**14**	6	8						
	10-15	**9**	4	5	**9**	4	5						
	15-20	**5**	3	2	**5**	3	2						
	20-30	**7**	2	5	**4**	1	3	**2**	1	1	**1**		1
	30-40	**3**		3	**2**		2	**1**		1			
	40-50	**1**		1	**1**		1						
	50-60	**1**		1									
	60 and over										**1**		1
	TOTAL	*40*	*15*	*25*	*35*	*14*	*21*	*3*	*1*	*2*	*2*		*2*
LADAKH													
		195431	**98478**	**96953**	**93200**	**50588**	**42612**	**87840**	**43943**	**43897**	**14391**	**3947**	**10444**
	0-1	**2904**	1473	1431	**2904**	1473	1431						
	1-2	**4302**	2004	2298	**4302**	2004	2298						
	2-3	**5393**	2850	2543	**5393**	2850	2543						
	3-4	**5679**	2823	2856	**5679**	2823	2856						
	4-5	**4651**	2311	2340	**4651**	2311	2340						
Total Population	TOTAL 0-5	*22929*	*11461*	*11468*	*22929*	*11461*	*11468*						
	5-10	**24227**	12662	11565	**24212**	12653	11559	**15**	9	6			
	10-15	**21961**	11738	10223	**20759**	11026	9733	**1156**	692	464	**46**	20	26
	15-20	**19707**	10807	8900	**13265**	7620	5645	**6204**	3095	3109	**238**	92	146
	20-30	**34079**	17233	16846	**8365**	5532	2833	**24715**	11260	13455	**999**	441	558
	30-40	**25878**	12374	13504	**1838**	1150	688	**22415**	10742	11673	**1625**	482	1143
	40-50	**18360**	9322	9038	**837**	525	312	**15019**	8193	6826	**2504**	604	1900
	50-60	**15093**	7053	8040	**554**	344	210	**10755**	5852	4903	**3784**	857	2027
	60 and over	**13197**	5828	7369	**441**	277	164	**7561**	4100	3461	**5195**	1451	3744
	TOTAL	*172502*	*87017*	*85485*	*70271*	*39127*	*31144*	*87840*	*43943*	*43897*	*14391*	*3947*	*10444*

VII—AGE AND CIVIL CONDITION (PART III—DISTRICTS)—Contd.

Community and Age		Population P	Population M	Population F	Unmarried P	Unmarried M	Unmarried F	Married P	Married M	Married F	Widowed P	Widowed M	Widowed F
1		2	3	4	5	6	7	8	9	10	11	12	13
LADAKH—contd.													
		455	**361**	**94**	**170**	**124**	**46**	**283**	**236**	**47**	**2**	**1**	**1**
	0-1 ..	**9**	6	3	**9**	6	3						
	1-2 ..	**6**	5	1	**6**	5	1						
	2-3 ..	**7**	2	5	**7**	2	5						
	3-4 ..	**12**	3	9	**12**	3	9						
	4-5 ..	**12**	7	5	**12**	7	5						
Hindu	Total 0-5 ..	*46*	*23*	*23*	*46*	*23*	*23*						
	5-10 ..	**39**	24	15	**39**	24	15						
	10-15 ..	**18**	11	7	**18**	11	7						
	15-20 ..	**16**	12	4	**11**	10	1	**5**	2	3			
	20-30 ..	**141**	113	28	**35**	35		**106**	78	28			
	30-40 ..	**150**	136	14	**16**	16		**133**	119	14	**1**	1	
	40-50 ..	**37**	35	2	**4**	4		**33**	31	2			
	50-60 ..	**8**	7	1	**1**	1		**6**	6		**1**		1
	60 and over ..												
	Total ..	*409*	*338*	*71*	*124*	*101*	*23*	*283*	*236*	*47*	*2*	*1*	*1*
		154492	**77925**	**76567**	**73182**	**40520**	**32662**	**69954**	**34511**	**35443**	**11356**	**2894**	**8462**
	0-1 ..	**2442**	1207	1235	**2442**	1207	1235						
	1-2 ..	**3708**	1712	1996	**3708**	1712	1996						
	2-3 ..	**4660**	2474	2186	**4660**	2474	2186						
	3-4 ..	**4662**	2308	2354	**4662**	2308	2354						
	4-5 ..	**3862**	1905	1957	**3862**	1905	1957						
Muslim	Total 0-5 ..	*19334*	*9606*	*9728*	*19334*	*9606*	*9728*						
	5-10 ..	**19495**	10291	9204	**19485**	10284	9201	**10**	7	3			
	10-15 ..	**17798**	9713	8085	**16774**	9086	7688	**980**	607	373	**44**	20	24
	15-20 ..	**15590**	8819	6771	**10308**	6226	4082	**5078**	2506	2572	**204**	87	117
	20-30 ..	**27103**	13797	13306	**5866**	4343	1523	**20419**	9068	11351	**818**	386	432
	30-40 ..	**20275**	9498	10777	**960**	668	292	**17967**	8437	9530	**1348**	393	955
	40-50 ..	**13801**	6965	6836	**254**	167	87	**11507**	6345	5162	**2040**	453	1587
	50-60 ..	**11431**	5154	6277	**134**	91	43	**8201**	4453	3748	**3096**	610	2486
	60 and over ..	**9665**	4082	5583	**67**	49	18	**5792**	3088	2704	**3806**	945	2861
	Total ..	*135158*	*68319*	*66839*	*53848*	*30914*	*22934*	*69954*	*34511*	*35443*	*11356*	*2894*	*8462*
		182	**107**	**75**	**103**	**62**	**41**	**79**	**45**	**34**			
	0-1 ..	**11**	6	5	**11**	6	5						
	1-2 ..	**6**	4	2	**6**	4	2						
	2-3 ..	**7**	3	4	**7**	3	4						
	3-4 ..	**8**	1	7	**8**	1	7						
	4-5 ..	**7**	3	4	**7**	3	4						
Sikh	Total 0-5 ..	*39*	*17*	*22*	*39*	*17*	*22*						
	5-10 ..	**29**	20	9	**29**	20	9						
	10-15 ..	**20**	12	8	**18**	11	7	**2**	1	1			
	15-20 ..	**18**	11	7	**11**	9	2	**7**	2	5			
	20-30 ..	**42**	23	19	**6**	5	1	**36**	18	18			
	30-40 ..	**23**	17	6				**23**	17	6			
	40-50 ..	**7**	5	2				**7**	5	2			
	50-60 ..	**4**	2	2				**4**	2	2			
	Total ..	*143*	*90*	*53*	*64*	*45*	*19*	*79*	*45*	*34*			

VII—AGE AND CIVIL CONDITION (PART III—DISTRICTS)—Contd.

Community and Age		Population			Unmarried			Married			Widowed		
		P	M	F	P	M	F	P	M	F	P	M	F
1		2	3	4	5	6	7	8	9	10	11	12	13
						LADAKH—concld.							
		40164	**20011**	**20153**	**19670**	**9841**	**9829**	**17463**	**9118**	**8345**	**3031**	**1052**	**1979**
	0-1 ..	**441**	253	188	**441**	253	188						
	1-2 ..	**581**	283	298	**581**	283	298						
	2-3 ..	**717**	371	346	**717**	371	346						
	3-4 ..	**993**	510	483	**993**	510	483						
	4-5 ..	**766**	394	372	**766**	394	372						
Buddhist	Total 0-5 ..	*3498*	*1811*	*1687*	*3498*	*1811*	*1687*						
	5-10 ..	**4647**	2317	2330	**4642**	2315	2327	**5**	2	3			
	10-15 ..	**4105**	1990	2115	**3929**	1906	2023	**174**	84	90	**2**		2
	15-20 ..	**4065**	1954	2111	**2919**	1366	1553	**1112**	583	529	**34**	5	29
	20-30 ..	**6772**	3290	3482	**2448**	1143	1305	**4143**	2092	2051	**181**	55	126
	30-40 ..	**5412**	2715	2697	**862**	466	396	**4275**	2161	2114	**275**	88	187
	40-50 ..	**4497**	2308	2189	**579**	354	225	**3455**	1803	1652	**463**	151	312
	50-60 ..	**3642**	1884	1758	**419**	252	167	**2536**	1385	1151	**687**	247	440
	60 and over ..	**3526**	1742	1784	**374**	228	146	**1763**	1008	755	**1389**	506	883
	Total ..	*36666*	*18200*	*18466*	*16172*	*8030*	*8142*	*17463*	*9118*	*8345*	*3031*	*1052*	*1979*
		138	**74**	**64**	**75**	**41**	**34**	**61**	**33**	**28**	**2**		**2**
	0-1 ..	**1**	1		**1**	1							
	1-2 ..	**1**		1	**1**		1						
	2-3 ..	**2**		2	**2**		2						
	3-4 ..	**4**	1	3	**4**	1	3						
	4-5 ..	**4**	2	2	**4**	2	2						
Others	Total 0-5 ..	*12*	*4*	*8*	*12*	*4*	*8*						
	5-10 ..	**17**	10	7	**17**	10	7						
	10-15 ..	**20**	12	8	**20**	12	8						
	15-20 ..	**18**	11	7	**16**	9	7	**2**	2				
	20-30 ..	**21**	10	11	**10**	6	4	**11**	4	7			
	30-40 ..	**18**	8	10				**17**	8	9			
	40-50 ..	**18**	9	9				**17**	9	8	**1**		1
	50-60 ..	**8**	6	2				**8**	6	2	**1**		1
	60 and over ..	**6**	4	2				6	4	2			
	Total ..	*126*	*70*	*56*	*63*	*37*	*26*	*61*	*33*	*28*	*2*		*2*
						ASTORE							
		17026	**8948**	**8078**	**9308**	**5157**	**4151**	**7172**	**3648**	**3524**	**546**	**143**	**403**
	0-1 ..	**174**	88	86	**174**	88	86						
	1-2 ..	**508**	249	259	**508**	249	259						
	2-3 ..	**625**	306	319	**625**	306	319						
	3-4 ..	**725**	354	371	**725**	354	371						
	4-5 ..	**587**	314	273	**587**	314	273						
Total Population	Total 0-5 ..	*2619*	*1311*	*1308*	*2619*	*1311*	*1308*						
	5-10 ..	**3050**	1593	1457	**3050**	1593	1457						
	10-15 ..	**2010**	1079	931	**1947**	1065	882	**61**	14	47	**2**		2
	15-20 ..	**1507**	789	718	**1044**	654	390	**455**	132	323	**8**	3	5
	20-30 ..	**2935**	1516	1419	**539**	446	93	**2337**	1056	1281	**59**	14	45
	30-40 ..	**2404**	1261	1143	**84**	67	17	**2238**	1165	1073	**82**	29	53
	40-50 ..	**1066**	558	508	**17**	13	4	**964**	531	433	**85**	14	71
	50-60 ..	**781**	429	352	**5**	5		**655**	405	250	**121**	19	102
	60 and over ..	**654**	412	242	**3**	3		**462**	345	117	**189**	64	125
	Total ..	*14407*	*7637*	*6770*	*6689*	*3846*	*2843*	*7172*	*3648*	*3524*	*546*	*143*	*403*

VII—AGE AND CIVIL CONDITION (PART III—DISTRICTS)—Contd.

ASTORE—contd.

Community and Age		Population P	Population M	Population F	Unmarried P	Unmarried M	Unmarried F	Married P	Married M	Married F	Widowed P	Widowed M	Widowed F
1		2	3	4	5	6	7	8	9	10	11	12	13
Hindu		**113**	**72**	**41**	**56**	**35**	**21**	**54**	**37**	**17**	**3**		**3**
	0-1 ..	**3**	3		**3**	3							
	1-2 ..	**8**	5	3	**8**	5	3						
	2-3 ..	**4**	1	3	**4**	1	3						
	3-4 ..	**1**		1	**1**		1						
	4-5 ..	**3**	3		**3**	3							
	Total 0-5 ..	*19*	*12*	*7*	*19*	*12*	*7*						
	5-10 ..	**15**	6	9	**15**	6	9						
	10-15 ..	**8**	4	4	**8**	4	4						
	15-20 ..	**7**	4	3	**5**	4	1	**2**		2			
	20-30 ..	**26**	17	9	**9**	9		**17**	8	9			
	30-40 ..	**20**	13	7				**19**	13	6	**1**		1
	40-50 ..	**12**	11	1				**11**	11		**1**		1
	50-60 ..	**3**	3					**3**	3		**1**		
	60 and over ..	**3**	2	1				**2**	2		**1**		1
	Total ..	*94*	*60*	*34*	*37*	*23*	*14*	*54*	*37*	*17*	*3*		*3*
Muslim		**16878**	**8852**	**8026**	**9238**	**5112**	**4126**	**7098**	**3597**	**3501**	**542**	**143**	**399**
	0-1 ..	**169**	83	86	**169**	83	86						
	1-2 ..	**499**	243	256	**499**	243	256						
	2-3 ..	**620**	304	316	**620**	304	316						
	3-4 ..	**723**	353	370	**723**	353	370						
	4-5 ..	**584**	311	273	**584**	311	273						
	Total 0-5 ..	*2595*	*1294*	*1301*	*2595*	*1294*	*1301*						
	5-10 ..	**3030**	1585	1445	**3030**	1585	1445						
	10-15 ..	**2000**	1074	926	**1937**	1060	877	**61**	14	47	**2**		2
	15-20 ..	**1497**	783	714	**1038**	649	389	**451**	131	320	**8**	3	5
	20-30 ..	**2899**	1493	1406	**529**	436	93	**2311**	1043	1268	**59**	14	45
	30-40 ..	**2378**	1243	1135	**84**	67	17	**2213**	1147	1066	**81**	29	52
	40-50 ..	**1051**	545	506	**17**	13	4	**951**	518	433	**83**	14	69
	50-60 ..	**778**	426	352	**5**	5		**652**	402	250	**121**	19	102
	60 and over ..	**650**	409	241	**3**	3		**459**	342	117	**188**	64	124
	Total ..	*14283*	*7558*	*6725*	*6643*	*3818*	*2825*	*7098*	*3597*	*3501*	*542*	*143*	*399*
Sikh		**30**	**20**	**10**	**12**	**8**	**4**	**17**	**12**	**5**	**1**		**1**
	0-1 ..	**1**	1		**1**	1							
	1-2 ..	**1**	1		**1**	1							
	2-3 ..	**1**	1		**1**	1							
	3-4 ..	**1**	1		**1**	1							
	4-5 ..												
	Total 0-5 ..	*4*	*4*		*4*	*4*							
	5-10 ..	**4**	1	3	**4**	1	3						
	10-15 ..	**2**	1	1	**2**	1	1						
	15-20 ..	**3**	2	1	**1**	1		**2**	1	1			
	20-30 ..	**8**	5	3	**1**	1		**7**	4	3			
	30-40 ..	**5**	4	1				**5**	4	1			
	40-50 ..	**3**	2	1				**2**	2		**1**		1
	50-60 ..												
	60 and over ..	**1**	1					**1**	1				
	Total ..	*26*	*16*	*10*	*8*	*4*	*4*	*17*	*12*	*5*	*1*		*1*

VII—AGE AND CIVIL CONDITION (PART III—DISTRICTS)—Contd.

Community and Age		Population			Unmarried			Married			Widowed		
		P	M	F	P	M	F	P	M	F	P	M	F
1		*2*	*3*	*4*	*5*	*6*	*7*	*8*	*9*	*10*	*11*	*12*	*13*
ASTORE—concld.													
		5	**4**	**1**	**2**	**2**		**3**	**2**	**1**			
	0-1 ..	**1**	1		**1**	1							
	1-2 ..												
	2-3 ..												
	3-4 ..												
	4-5 ..												
Others	Total 0-5 ..	*1*	*1*		*1*	*1*							
	5-10 ..	**1**	1		**1**	1							
	10-15 ..												
	15-20 ..												
	20-30 ..	**2**	1	1				**2**	1	1			
	30-40 ..	**1**	1					**1**	1				
	40-50 ..												
	50-60 ..												
	60 and over ..												
	Total ..	*4*	*3*	*1*	*1*	*1*		*3*	*2*	*1*			
GILGIT (LEASED AREA)													
		22495	**12471**	**10024**	**11632**	**7021**	**4611**	**9515**	**4897**	**4618**	**1348**	**553**	**795**
	0-1 ..	**645**	314	331	**645**	314	331						
	1-2 ..	**557**	279	278	**557**	279	278						
	2-3 ..	**705**	357	348	**705**	357	348						
	3-4 ..	**711**	339	372	**711**	339	372						
	4-5 ..	**713**	368	345	**713**	368	345						
Total Population	Total 0-5 ..	*3331*	*1657*	*1674*	*3331*	*1657*	*1674*						
	5-10 ..	**3295**	1750	1545	**3271**	1750	1521	**22**		22	**2**		2
	10-15 ..	**2688**	1485	1203	**2374**	1437	937	**301**	43	258	**13**	5	8
	15-20 ..	**2228**	1267	961	**1356**	1013	343	**836**	241	595	**36**	13	23
	20-30 ..	**4261**	2384	1877	**978**	878	100	**3109**	1408	1701	**174**	98	76
	30-40 ..	**3236**	1840	1396	**233**	208	25	**2752**	1511	1241	**251**	121	130
	40-50 ..	**1475**	861	614	**56**	50	6	**1197**	735	462	**222**	76	146
	50-60 ..	**1091**	666	425	**21**	19	2	**797**	558	239	**273**	89	184
	60 and over ..	**890**	561	329	**12**	9	3	**501**	401	100	**377**	151	226
	Total ..	*19164*	*10814*	*8350*	*8301*	*5364*	*2937*	*9515*	*4897*	*4618*	*1348*	*553*	*795*
		108	**72**	**36**	**56**	**40**	**16**	**49**	**29**	**20**	**3**	**3**	
	0-1 ..	**4**		4	**4**		4						
	1-2 ..	**2**	1	1	**2**	1	1						
	2-3 ..	**3**	2	1	**3**	2	1						
	3-4 ..	**4**	2	2	**4**	2	2						
	4-5 ..	**2**	2		**2**	2							
Hindu	Total 0-5 ..	*15*	*7*	*8*	*15*	*7*	*8*						
	5-10 ..	**15**	11	4	**15**	11	4						
	10-15 ..	**10**	5	5	**8**	5	3	**2**		2			
	15-20 ..	**9**	4	5	**5**	4	1	**4**		4			
	20-30 ..	**30**	21	9	**8**	8		**21**	12	9	**1**	1	
	30-40 ..	**20**	16	4	**2**	2		**16**	12	4	**2**	2	
	40-50 ..	**4**	3	1				**4**	3	1			
	50-60 ..	**2**	2		**1**	1		**1**	1				
	60 and over ..	**3**	3		**2**	2		**1**	1				
	Total ..	*93*	*65*	*28*	*41*	*33*	*8*	*49*	*29*	*20*	*3*	*3*	

VII—AGE AND CIVIL CONDITION (PART III—DISTRICTS)—Contd.

Community and Age		Population			Unmarried			Married			Widowed		
		P	M	F	P	M	F	P	N	F	P	M	F
1		2	3	4	5	6	7	8	9	10	11	12	13
GILGIT (LEASED AREA)—contd.													
		22296	**12342**	**9954**	**11522**	**6947**	**4575**	**9430**	**4845**	**4585**	**1344**	**550**	**794**
	0-1 ..	**639**	313	326	**639**	313	326						
	1-2 ..	**551**	278	273	**551**	278	273						
	2-3 ..	**699**	352	347	**699**	352	347						
	3-4 ..	**704**	335	369	**704**	335	369						
	4-5 ..	**709**	364	345	**709**	364	345						
Muslim	Total 0-5 ..	*3302*	*1642*	*1660*	*3302*	*1642*	*1660*						
	5-10 ..	**3265**	1731	1534	**3241**	1731	1510	**22**		22	**2**		2
	10-15 ..	**2667**	1474	1193	**2355**	1426	929	**299**	43	256	**13**	5	8
	15-20 ..	**2212**	1259	953	**1345**	1005	340	**831**	241	590	**36**	13	23
	20-30 ..	**4211**	2352	1859	**964**	864	100	**3075**	1391	1684	**172**	97	75
	30-40 ..	**3201**	1811	1390	**229**	204	25	**2723**	1488	1235	**249**	119	130
	40-50 ..	**1465**	854	611	**56**	50	6	**1187**	728	459	**222**	76	146
	50-60 ..	**1087**	662	425	**20**	18	2	**794**	555	239	**273**	89	184
	60 and over ..	**886**	557	329	**10**	7	3	**499**	399	100	**377**	151	226
	Total ..	*18904*	*10700*	*8294*	*8220*	*5305*	*2915*	*9430*	*4845*	*4585*	*1344*	*550*	*794*
		70	**44**	**26**	**42**	**26**	**16**	**28**	**18**	**10**			
	0-1 ..	**1**	1		**1**	1							
	1-2 ..	**3**		3	**3**		3						
	2-3 ..	**2**	2		**2**	2							
	3-4 ..	**3**	2	1	**3**	2	1						
	4-5 ..	**2**	2		**2**	2							
Sikh	Total 0-5 ..	*11*	*7*	*4*	*11*	*7*	*4*						
	5-10 ..	**13**	7	6	**13**	7	6						
	10-15 ..	**10**	6	4	**10**	6	4	**1**		1			
	15-20 ..	**7**	4	3	**6**	4	2	**9**	4	5			
	20-30 ..	**11**	6	5	**2**	2		**10**	8	2			
	30-40 ..	**10**	8	2				**5**	3	2			
	40-50 ..	**5**	3	2				**2**	2				
	50-60 ..	**2**	2					**1**	1				
	60 and over ..	**1**	1										
	Total ..	*59*	*37*	*22*	*31*	*19*	*12*	*28*	*18*	*10*			
		21	**13**	**8**	**12**	**8**	**4**	**8**	**5**	**3**	**1**		**1**
	0-1 ..	**1**		1	**1**		1						
	1-2 ..	**1**		1	**1**		1						
	2-3 ..	**1**	1		**1**	1							
	3-4 ..												
	4-5 ..												
Others	Total 0-5 ..	*3*	*1*	*2*	*3*	*1*	*2*						
	5-10 ..	**2**	1	1	**2**	1	1						
	10-15 ..	**1**		1	**1**		1						
	15-20 ..	**9**	5	4	**4**	4		**4**	1	3	**1**		1
	20-30 ..	**5**	5		**2**	2		**3**	3				
	30-40 ..	**1**	1					**1**	1				
	40-50 ..												
	50-60 ..												
	60 and over ..												
	Total ..	*18*	*12*	*6*	*9*	*7*	*2*	*8*	*5*	*3*	*1*		*1*

VII—AGE AND CIVIL CONDITION (PART III—DISTRICTS)—Concld.

Community and Age		Population			Unmarried			Married			Widowed		
		P	M	F	P	M	F	P	M	F	P	M	F
1		*2*	*3*	*4*	*5*	*6*	*7*	*8*	*9*	*10*	*11*	*12*	*13*
GILGIT AGENCY													
		76526	**40827**	**35699**	**38222**	**22659**	**15563**	**34950**	**17199**	**17751**	**3354**	**969**	**2385**
	0-1 ..	**780**	415	365	**779**	415	364				**1**		1
	1-2 ..	**1862**	902	960	**1850**	899	951	**10**	2	8	**2**	1	1
	2-3 ..	**2440**	1113	1327	**2423**	1106	1317	**8**	4	4	**9**	3	6
	3-4 ..	**2954**	1477	1477	**2936**	1471	1465	**14**	4	10	**4**	2	2
	4-5 ..	**2818**	1488	1330	**2788**	1480	1308	**21**	7	14	**9**	1	8
Total Population	Total 0-5 ..	*10854*	*5395*	*5459*	*10776*	*5371*	*5405*	*53*	*17*	*36*	*25*	*7*	*18*
	5-10 ..	**13707**	7111	6596	**13329**	7034	6295	**334**	57	277	**44**	20	24
	10-15 ..	**9478**	5529	3949	**7670**	5128	2542	**1761**	379	1382	**47**	22	25
	15-20 ..	**7445**	3893	3552	**3264**	2683	581	**4095**	1173	2922	**86**	37	49
	20-30 ..	**12669**	6386	6283	**1974**	1553	421	**10397**	4700	5697	**298**	133	165
	30-40 ..	**10184**	5469	4715	**658**	453	205	**8978**	4871	4107	**548**	145	403
	40-50 ..	**5947**	3347	2600	**294**	215	79	**5011**	2993	2018	**642**	139	503
	50-60 ..	**3397**	1981	1416	**114**	92	22	**2589**	1702	887	**694**	187	507
	60 and over ..	**2845**	1716	1129	**143**	130	13	**1732**	1307	425	**970**	279	691
	Total ..	*65672*	*35432*	*30240*	*27446*	*17288*	*10158*	*34897*	*17182*	*17715*	*3329*	*962*	*2367*
		76526	**40827**	**35699**	**38222**	**22659**	**15563**	**34950**	**17199**	**17751**	**3354**	**969**	**2385**
	0-1 ..	**780**	415	365	**779**	415	364				**1**		1
	1-2 ..	**1862**	902	960	**1850**	899	951	**10**	2	8	**2**	1	1
	2-3 ..	**2440**	1113	1327	**2423**	1106	1317	**8**	4	4	**9**	3	6
	3-4 ..	**2954**	1477	1477	**2936**	1471	1465	**14**	4	10	**4**	2	2
	4-5 ..	**2818**	1488	1330	**2788**	1480	1308	**21**	7	14	**9**	1	8
Muslim	Total 0-5 ..	*10854*	*5395*	*5459*	*10776*	*5371*	*5405*	*53*	*17*	*36*	*25*	*7*	*18*
	5-10 ..	**13707**	7111	6596	**13329**	7034	6295	**334**	57	277	**44**	20	24
	10-15 ..	**9478**	5529	3949	**7670**	5128	2542	**1761**	379	1382	**47**	22	25
	15-20 ..	**7445**	3893	3552	**3264**	2683	581	**4095**	1173	2922	**86**	37	49
	20-30 ..	**12669**	6386	6283	**1974**	1553	421	**10397**	4700	5697	**298**	133	165
	30-40 ..	**10184**	5469	4715	**658**	453	205	**8978**	4871	4107	**548**	145	403
	40-50 ..	**5947**	3347	2600	**294**	215	79	**5011**	2993	2018	**642**	139	503
	50-60 ..	**3397**	1981	1416	**114**	92	22	**2589**	1702	887	**694**	187	507
	60 and over ..	**2845**	1716	1129	**143**	130	13	**1732**	1307	425	**970**	279	691
	Total ..	*65672*	*35432*	*30240*	*27446*	*17288*	*10158*	*34897*	*17182*	*17715*	*3329*	*962*	*2367*

VII—AGE AND CIVIL CONDITION (PART IV—CITIES).

JAMMU

A—Total Population

Community and Age		Population P	Population M	Population F	Unmarried P	Unmarried M	Unmarried F	Married P	Married M	Married F	Widowed P	Widowed M	Widowed F
1		2	3	4	5	6	7	8	9	10	11	12	13
		50379	29818	20561	25567	16397	9170	20804	11884	8920	4008	1537	2471
	0-1 ..	1314	709	605	1314	709	605						
	1-2 ..	1195	610	585	1195	610	585						
	2-3 ..	1219	642	577	1219	642	577						
	3-4 ..	1318	669	649	1318	669	649						
	4-5 ..	1391	719	672	1391	719	672						
Total Population	TOTAL 0-5 ..	6437	3349	3088	6437	3349	3088						
	5-10 ..	6103	3276	2827	6087	3276	2811	16		16			
	10-15 ..	5550	3148	2402	5213	3120	2093	322	19	303	15	9	6
	15-20 ..	5479	3315	2164	3798	2864	934	1607	398	1209	74	53	21
	20-30 ..	10244	6366	3878	2936	2751	185	6936	3412	3524	372	203	169
	30-40 ..	7239	4559	2680	602	575	27	5993	3735	2258	643	248	395
	40-50 ..	4516	2864	1652	268	259	9	3345	2302	1043	904	304	600
	50-60 ..	2606	1607	999	122	111	11	1608	1201	407	876	295	581
	60 and over ..	2205	1334	871	104	92	12	977	817	160	1124	425	699
	TOTAL ..	43942	26469	17473	19130	13048	6082	20804	11884	8920	4008	1537	2471
B—Communities													
		30564	17803	12761	15176	9817	5359	12733	7070	5663	2655	916	1739
	0-1 ..	803	456	347	803	456	347						
	1-2 ..	706	349	357	706	349	357						
	2-3 ..	734	388	346	734	388	346						
	3-4 ..	767	394	373	767	394	373						
	4-5 ..	798	406	392	798	406	392						
Hindu	TOTAL 0-5 ..	3808	1993	1815	3808	1993	1815						
	5-10 ..	3634	1961	1673	3634	1961	1673						
	10-15 ..	3318	1897	1421	3117	1879	1238	193	11	182	8	7	1
	15-20 ..	3293	1998	1295	2257	1738	519	994	228	766	42	32	10
	20-30 ..	6101	3653	2448	1696	1621	75	4177	1927	2250	228	105	123
	30-40 ..	4420	2661	1759	347	337	10	3632	2188	1444	441	136	305
	40-50 ..	2907	1798	1109	170	164	6	2122	1455	667	615	179	436
	50-60 ..	1719	1026	693	76	65	11	1033	769	264	610	192	418
	60 and over ..	1364	816	548	71	59	12	582	492	90	711	265	446
	TOTAL ..	26756	15810	10946	11368	7824	3544	12733	7070	5663	2655	916	1739
		15920	9751	6169	8391	5321	3070	6463	3926	2537	1066	504	562
	0-1 ..	380	182	198	380	182	198						
	1-2 ..	395	207	188	395	207	188						
	2-3 ..	391	203	188	391	203	188						
	3-4 ..	428	205	223	428	205	223						
	4-5 ..	458	234	224	458	234	224						
Muslim	TOTAL 0-5 ..	2052	1031	1021	2052	1031	1021						
	5-10 ..	1937	1032	905	1935	1032	903	2		2			
	10-15 ..	1780	1010	770	1694	1001	693	79	7	72	7	2	5
	15-20 ..	1780	1112	668	1292	948	344	462	147	315	26	17	9
	20-30 ..	3395	2271	1124	1058	968	90	2218	1219	999	119	84	35
	30-40 ..	2299	1543	756	217	201	16	1924	1255	669	158	87	71
	40-50 ..	1309	867	442	81	78	3	999	688	311	229	101	128
	50-60 ..	704	465	239	35	35		464	348	116	205	82	123
	60 and over ..	664	420	244	27	27		315	262	53	322	131	191
	TOTAL ..	13868	8720	5148	6339	4290	2049	6463	3926	2537	1066	504	562

VII—AGE AND CIVIL CONDITION (PART IV—CITIES)—CONTD.

Community and Age	Population			Unmarried			Married			Widowed		
	P	M	F	P	M	F	P	M	F	P	M	F
1	2	3	4	5	6	7	8	9	10	11	12	13
JAMMU—contd.												
	962	**519**	**443**	**512**	**298**	**214**	**395**	**198**	**197**	**55**	**23**	**32**
0-1 ..	**39**	20	19	**39**	20	19						
1-2 ..	**25**	13	12	**25**	13	12						
2-3 ..	**25**	14	11	**25**	14	11						
3-4 ..	**49**	27	22	**49**	27	22						
4-5 ..	**28**	16	12	**28**	16	12						
Christian TOTAL 0-5 ..	*166*	*90*	*76*	*166*	*90*	*76*						
5-10 ..	**158**	84	74	**158**	84	74						
10-15 ..	**110**	59	51	**104**	58	46	**6**	1	5			
15-20 ..	**83**	41	42	**45**	31	14	**36**	9	27	**2**	1	1
20-30 ..	**193**	94	99	**25**	22	3	**162**	69	93	**6**	3	3
30-40 ..	**122**	74	48	**8**	7	1	**105**	62	43	**9**	5	4
40-50 ..	**63**	37	26	**3**	3		**47**	28	19	**13**	6	7
50-60 ..	**32**	19	13	**2**	2		**21**	15	6	**9**	2	7
60 and over ..	**35**	21	14	**1**	1		**18**	14	4	**16**	6	10
TOTAL ..	*796*	*429*	*367*	*346*	*208*	*138*	*395*	*198*	*197*	*55*	*23*	*32*
	784	**412**	**372**	**416**	**240**	**176**	**288**	**144**	**144**	**80**	**28**	**52**
0-1 ..	**25**	13	12	**25**	13	12						
1-2 ..	**20**	7	13	**20**	7	13						
2-3 ..	**23**	13	10	**23**	13	10						
3-4 ..	**26**	13	13	**26**	13	13						
4-5 ..	**26**	17	9	**26**	17	9						
Jain TOTAL 0-5 ..	*120*	*63*	*57*	*120*	*63*	*57*						
5-10 ..	**114**	60	54	**113**	60	53	**1**		1			
10-15 ..	**89**	46	43	**88**	46	42	**1**		1			
15-20 ..	**72**	32	40	**48**	28	20	**22**	3	19	**2**	1	1
20-30 ..	**126**	63	63	**25**	21	4	**96**	40	56	**5**	2	3
30-40 ..	**99**	58	41	**8**	8		**82**	45	37	**9**	5	4
40-50 ..	**67**	37	30	**6**	6		**46**	27	19	**15**	4	11
50-60 ..	**54**	32	22	**6**	6		**27**	20	7	**21**	6	15
60 and over ..	**43**	21	22	**2**	2		**13**	9	4	**28**	10	18
TOTAL ..	*664*	*349*	*315*	*296*	*177*	*119*	*288*	*144*	*144*	*80*	*28*	*52*
	2135	**1322**	**813**	**1064**	**715**	**349**	**919**	**541**	**378**	**152**	**66**	**86**
0-1 ..	**66**	37	29	**66**	37	29						
1-2 ..	**49**	34	15	**49**	34	15						
2-3 ..	**46**	24	22	**46**	24	22						
3-4 ..	**47**	30	17	**47**	30	17						
4-5 ..	**80**	45	35	**80**	45	35						
Sikh TOTAL 0-5 ..	*288*	*170*	*118*	*288*	*170*	*118*						
5 10 ..	**259**	139	120	**246**	139	107	**13**		13			
10-15 ..	**252**	135	117	**209**	135	74	**43**		43			
15-20 ..	**250**	131	119	**155**	118	37	**93**	11	82	**2**	2	
20-30 ..	**425**	282	143	**130**	117	13	**281**	156	125	**14**	9	5
30-40 ..	**295**	219	76	**22**	22		**247**	182	65	**26**	15	11
40-50 ..	**170**	125	45	**8**	8		**130**	103	27	**32**	14	18
50·60 ..	**97**	65	32	**3**	3		**63**	49	14	**31**	13	18
60 and over ..	**99**	56	43	**3**	3		**49**	40	9	**47**	13	34
TOTAL ..	*1847*	*1152*	*695*	*776*	*545*	*231*	*919*	*541*	*378*	*152*	*66*	*86*

VII—AGE AND CIVIL CONDITION (PART IV—CITIES)—Contd.

Community and Age		Population			Unmarried			Married			Widowed		
		P	M	F	P	M	F	P	M	F	P	M	F
1		2	3	4	5	6	7	8	9	10	11	12	13
JAMMU—concld.													
Parsee		**10**	**7**	**3**	**6**	**4**	**2**	**4**	**3**	**1**			
0-1	..	1	1		1	1							
1-2	..												
2-3	..												
3-4	..	1		1	1		1						
4-5	..	1	1		1	1							
Total 0-5	..	*3*	*2*	*1*	*3*	*2*	*1*						
5-10	..	1		1	1		1						
10-15	..	1	1		1	1							
15-20	..												
20-30	..	3	2	1	1	1		2	1	1			
30-40	..	2	2					2	2				
40-50	..												
50-60	..												
60 and over	..												
Total	..	*7*	*5*	*2*	*3*	*2*	*1*	*4*	*3*	*1*			
Buddhist		**1**	**1**					**1**	**1**				
0-1	..												
1-2	..												
2-3	..												
3-4	..												
4-5	..												
Total 0-5	..												
5-10	..												
10-15	..												
15-20	..												
20-30	..												
30-40	..	1	1					1	1				
40-50	..												
50-60	..												
60 and over	..												
Total	..	*1*	*1*					*1*	*1*				
Others		**3**	**3**		**2**	**2**		**1**	**1**				
0-1	..												
1-2	..												
2-3	..												
3-4	..												
4-5	..												
Total 0-5	..												
5-10	..												
10-15	..												
15-20	..	1	1		1	1							
20-30	..	1	1		1	1			1				
30-40	..	1	1					1					
40-50	..												
50-60	..												
60 and over	..												
Total	..	*3*	*3*		*2*	*2*		*1*	*1*				

VII—AGE AND CIVIL CONDITION (PART IV—CITIES)—Contd.

SRINAGAR

A—Total Population

Community and Age		Population P	Population M	Population F	Unmarried P	Unmarried M	Unmarried F	Married P	Married M	Married F	Widowed P	Widowed M	Widowed F
1		2	3	4	5	6	7	8	9	10	11	12	13
		207787	**112460**	**95327**	**109273**	**65672**	**43601**	**86893**	**43808**	**43085**	**11621**	**2980**	**8641**
	0-1	**3177**	1701	1476	**3177**	1701	1476						
	1-2	**4385**	2223	2162	**4385**	2223	2162						
	2-3	**5234**	2687	2547	**5234**	2687	2547						
	3-4	**6172**	3059	3113	**6172**	3059	3113						
	4-5	**6140**	3031	3109	**6140**	3031	3109						
Total Population	Total 0-5	*25108*	*12701*	*12407*	*25108*	*12701*	*12407*						
	5-10	**31899**	15984	15915	**31891**	15983	15908	**8**	1	7			
	10-15	**27182**	14126	13056	**24983**	13988	10995	**2174**	138	2036	**25**		25
	15-20	**22343**	12086	10257	**14036**	10289	3747	**8143**	1786	6357	**164**	11	153
	20-30	**39500**	21346	18154	**9468**	9024	444	**29100**	12103	16997	**932**	219	713
	30-40	**29229**	16809	12420	**2334**	2279	55	**24896**	13944	10952	**1999**	586	1413
	40-50	**18016**	10835	7181	**903**	885	18	**14036**	9183	4853	**3077**	767	2310
	50-60	**9540**	5729	3811	**394**	378	16	**6089**	4615	1474	**3057**	736	2321
	60 and over	**4970**	2844	2126	**156**	145	11	**2447**	2038	409	**2367**	661	1706
	Total	*182679*	*99759*	*82920*	*84165*	*52971*	*31194*	*86893*	*43808*	*43085*	*11621*	*2980*	*8641*

B—Communities.

Community and Age		Population P	Population M	Population F	Unmarried P	Unmarried M	Unmarried F	Married P	Married M	Married F	Widowed P	Widowed M	Widowed F
		43026	**23887**	**19139**	**22824**	**14514**	**8310**	**16537**	**8392**	**8145**	**3665**	**981**	**2684**
	0-1	**575**	312	263	**575**	312	263						
	1-2	**892**	457	435	**892**	457	435						
	2-3	**1075**	602	473	**1075**	602	473						
	3-4	**1208**	626	582	**1208**	626	582						
	4-5	**1252**	633	619	**1252**	633	619						
Hindu	Total 0-5	*5002*	*2630*	*2372*	*5002*	*2630*	*2372*						
	5-10	**6250**	3201	3049	**6247**	3201	3046	**3**		3			
	10-15	**5237**	2740	2497	**4858**	2727	2131	**373**	13	360	**6**		6
	15-20	**4417**	2498	1919	**2853**	2163	690	**1534**	335	1199	**30**		30
	20-30	**8147**	4701	3446	**2376**	2330	46	**5508**	2326	3182	**263**	45	218
	30-40	**6140**	3604	2536	**792**	777	15	**4706**	2655	2051	**642**	172	470
	40-50	**4104**	2446	1658	**415**	410	5	**2707**	1764	943	**982**	272	710
	50-60	**2474**	1422	1052	**206**	201	5	**1266**	937	329	**1002**	284	718
	60 and over	**1255**	645	610	**75**	75		**440**	362	78	**740**	208	532
	Total	*38024*	*21257*	*16767*	*17822*	*11884*	*5938*	*16537*	*8392*	*8145*	*3665*	*981*	*2684*
		162970	**87439**	**75531**	**85545**	**50597**	**34948**	**69548**	**34868**	**34680**	**7877**	**1974**	**5903**
	0-1	**2570**	1376	1194	**2570**	1376	1194						
	1-2	**3464**	1755	1709	**3464**	1755	1709						
	2-3	**4118**	2064	2054	**4118**	2064	2054						
	3-4	**4926**	2415	2511	**4926**	2415	2511						
	4-5	**4855**	2381	2474	**4855**	2381	2474						
Muslim	Total 0-5	*19933*	*9991*	*9942*	*19933*	*9991*	*9942*						
	5-10	**25436**	12659	12777	**25431**	12658	12773	**5**	1	4			
	10-15	**21746**	11263	10483	**19933**	11138	8795	**1794**	125	1669	**19**		19
	15-20	**17719**	9451	8268	**11040**	8018	3022	**6545**	1422	5123	**134**	11	123
	20-30	**30947**	16353	14594	**6968**	6599	369	**23313**	9581	13732	**666**	173	493
	30-40	**22796**	13010	9786	**1509**	1482	27	**19947**	11120	8827	**1340**	408	932
	40-50	**13765**	8288	5477	**477**	469	8	**11205**	7329	3876	**2083**	490	1593
	50-60	**6985**	4261	2724	**180**	174	6	**4771**	3641	1130	**2034**	446	1588
	60 and over	**3643**	2163	1480	**74**	68	6	**1968**	1649	319	**1601**	446	1155
	Total	*143037*	*77448*	*65589*	*65612*	*40606*	*25006*	*60548*	*34868*	*34680*	*7877*	*1974*	*5[illegible]*

VII—AGE AND CIVIL CONDITION (PART IV—CITIES)—CONTD.

SRINAGAR—contd.

Community and Age	Population P	Population M	Population F	Unmarried P	Unmarried M	Unmarried F	Married P	Married M	Married F	Widowed P	Widowed M	Widowed F
1	2	3	4	5	6	7	8	9	10	11	12	13
	346	**171**	**175**	**204**	**105**	**99**	**114**	**64**	**50**	**28**	**2**	**26**
0-1 ..	**6**	2	4	**6**	2	4						
1-2 ..	**5**	2	3	**5**	2	3						
2-3 ..	**5**	1	4	**5**	1	4						
3-4 ..	**1**		1	**1**		1						
4-5 ..	**6**	2	4	**6**	2	4						
Christian TOTAL 0-5 ..	*23*	*7*	*16*	*23*	*7*	*16*						
5-10 ..	**53**	37	16	**53**	37	16						
10-15 ..	**44**	31	13	**44**	31	13						
15-20 ..	**18**	9	9	**17**	9	8	**1**		1			
20-30 ..	**39**	11	28	**28**	6	22	**11**	5	6			
30-40 ..	**53**	23	30	**17**	7	10	**32**	15	17	**4**	1	3
40-50 ..	**46**	27	19	**7**	3	4	**36**	24	12	**3**		3
50-60 ..	**30**	12	18	**8**	3	5	**15**	9	6	**7**		7
60 and over ..	**40**	14	26	**7**	2	5	**19**	11	8	**14**	1	13
TOTAL ..	*323*	*164*	*159*	*181*	*98*	*83*	*114*	*64*	*50*	*28*	*2*	*26*
	9	**8**	**1**	**5**	**5**		**4**	**3**	**1**			
0-1 ..												
1-2 ..	**1**	1		**1**	1							
2-3 ..	**2**	2		**2**	2							
3-4 ..												
4-5 ..												
Jain TOTAL 0-5 ..	*3*	*3*		*3*	*3*							
5-10 ..												
10-15 ..												
15-20 ..	**3**	2	1	**1**	1		**2**	1	1			
20-30 ..	**2**	2		**1**	1		**1**	1				
30-40 ..												
40-50 ..	**1**	1					**1**	1				
50-60 ..												
60 and over ..												
TOTAL ..	*6*	*5*	*1*	*2*	*2*		*4*	*3*	*1*			
	1412	**943**	**469**	**678**	**442**	**236**	**685**	**479**	**206**	**49**	**22**	**27**
0-1 ..	**25**	11	14	**25**	11	14						
1-2 ..	**23**	8	15	**23**	8	15						
2-3 ..	**34**	18	16	**34**	18	16						
3-4 ..	**37**	18	19	**37**	18	19						
4-5 ..	**27**	15	12	**27**	15	12						
Sikh TOTAL 0-5 ..	*146*	*70*	*76*	*146*	*70*	*76*						
5-10 ..	**157**	87	70	**157**	87	70						
10-15 ..	**154**	91	63	**147**	91	56	**7**		7			
15-20 ..	**184**	124	60	**123**	96	27	**61**	28	33			
20-30 ..	**357**	273	84	**87**	82	5	**267**	190	77	**3**	1	2
30-40 ..	**237**	172	65	**15**	13	2	**209**	154	55	**13**	5	8
40-50 ..	**98**	72	26	**3**	3		**86**	64	22	**9**	5	4
50-60 ..	**49**	34	15				**36**	28	8	**13**	6	7
60 and over ..	**30**	20	10				**19**	15	4	**11**	5	6
TOTAL ..	*1266*	*873*	*393*	*532*	*372*	*160*	*685*	*479*	*206*	*49*	*22*	*27*

VII—AGE AND CIVIL CONDITION (PART IV—CITIES)—CONTD.

Community and Age	Population P	Population M	Population F	Unmarried P	Unmarried M	Unmarried F	Married P	Married M	Married F	Widowed P	Widowed M	Widowed F
1	2	3	4	5	6	7	8	9	10	11	12	13
SRINAGAR—contd.												
	6	**3**	**3**	**3**	**1**	**2**	**2**	**1**	**1**	**1**	**1**	
0-1 ..												
1-2 ..												
2-3 ..												
3-4 ..												
4-5 ..												
Parsee TOTAL 0-5 ..												
5-10 ..	**2**		2	**2**		2						
10-15 ..												
15-20 ..												
20-30 ..	**1**	1		**1**	1							
30-40 ..	**1**		1				**1**		1			
40-50 ..	**1**	1					**1**	1				
50-60 ..												
60 and over ..	**1**	1								**1**	1	
TOTAL ..	*6*	*3*	*3*	*3*	*1*	*2*	*2*	*1*	*1*	*1*	*1*	
	7	**7**		**7**	**7**							
0-1 ..												
1-2 ..												
2-3 ..												
3-4 ..												
4-5 ..												
Buddhist TOTAL 0-5 ..												
5-10 ..												
10-15 ..	**1**	1		**1**	1							
15-20 ..	**2**	2		**2**	2							
20-30 ..	**4**	4		**4**	4							
30-40 ..												
40-50 ..												
50-60 ..												
60 and over ..												
TOTAL ..	*7*	*7*		*7*	*7*							
	9	**2**	**7**	**5**	**1**	**4**	**3**	**1**	**2**	**1**		**1**
0-1 ..												
1-2 ..												
2-3 ..												
3-4 ..												
4-5 ..												
Jews TOTAL 0-5 ..												
5-10 ..												
10-15 ..												
15-20 ..												
20-30 ..	**3**	1	2	**3**	1	2						
30-40 ..	**2**		2	**1**		1	**1**		1			
40-50 ..	**1**		1	**1**		1						
50-60 ..	**2**		2				**1**		1	**1**		1
60 and over ..	**1**	1					**1**	1				
TOTAL ..	*9*	*2*	*7*	*5*	*1*	*4*	*3*	*1*	*2*	*1*		*1*

VII—AGE AND CIVIL CONDITION (PART IV—CITIES)—CONCLD.

Community and Age	Population P	Population M	Population F	Unmarried P	Unmarried M	Unmarried F	Married P	Married M	Married F	Widowed P	Widowed M	Widowed F
1	2	3	4	5	6	7	8	9	10	11	12	13
SRINAGAR—concld.												
	2		**2**	**2**		**2**						
0-1 ..	1		1	1		1						
1-2 ..												
2-3 ..												
3-4 ..												
4-5 ..												
Others TOTAL 0-5 ..	*1*		*1*	*1*		*1*						
5-10 ..	1		1	1		1						
10-15 ..												
15-20 ..												
20-30 ..												
30-40 ..												
40-50 ..												
50-60 ..												
60 and over ..												
TOTAL ..	*1*		*1*	*1*		*1*						

VII—(i) AGE DISTRIBUTION OF 10000 OF EACH SEX IN THE STATE AND EACH NATURAL DIVISION.

Age		1941 M	1941 F	1931 M	1931 F	1921 M	1921 F	1911 M	1911 F	1901 M	1901 F
1		*2*	*3*	*4*	*5*	*6*	*7*	*8*	*9*	*10*	*11*
JAMMU AND KASHMIR STATE											
0-1	..	196	217	301	337	307	336	432	477	353	392
1-2	..	230	260	305	345	189	207	111	119	154	158
2-3	..	267	293	304	344	260	293	264	293	282	321
3-4	..	288	326	302	335	329	363	318	353	301	348
4-5	..	282	308	292	321	301	328	305	328	294	320
TOTAL 0-5	..	*1263*	*1404*	*1504*	*1682*	*1386*	*1527*	*1430*	*1570*	*1384*	*1539*
5-10	..	1449	1472	1306	1264	1503	1542	1444	1511	1449	1505
10-15	..	1236	1198	1207	1147	1209	1077	1169	1062	1230	1116
15-20	..	1006	1017	922	1006	833	862	870	876	833	816
20-25	..	899	980	942	1065	740	908	800	919	708	832
25-30	..	823	889	866	913	795	880	785	837	763	818
30-35	..	760	763	808	766	832	799	791	783	861	830
35-40	..	638	616	619	561	572	502	555	506	600	532
40-45	..	476	433	474	426	556	560	596	612	654	644
45-50	..	420	367	376	325	322	275	331	284	331	300
50-55	..	307	256	296	257	436	388	440	398	450	384
55-60	..	258	213	225	194	149	105	135	102	132	120
60-65	..	175	146	187	166	337	203	346	301		
65-70	..	109	95	93	77	70	50	73	50	605	564
70 and over	..	181	151	173	144	260	232	235	189		
Mean age	..	**23.83**	**22.66**	**23.6**	**23.05**	**25**	**24**	**25**	**23**	**21**	**24**
I THE SUB-MONTANE & SEMI-MOUNTAINOUS TRACT											
0-5	..	1299	1440	1457	1677	1287	1440	1234	1380		
5-10	..	1462	1475	1264	1237	1468	1513	1348	1436		
10-15	..	1193	1212	1177	1159	1219	1081	1194	1049		
15-20	..	944	973	917	967	776	816	826	824		
20-40	..	2932	3048	3105	3074	2813	2904	3045	3128		
40-60	..	1560	1347	1514	1367	1644	1558	1656	1582		
60 and over	..	610	505	566	499	793	688	697	601		
Mean age	..	**25.90**	**24·43**			**28**	**27**	**24**	**21**		
II THE OUTER HILLS											
0-5	..	1288	1377	1283	1712	1385	1463	1411	1517		
5-10	..	1503	1495	1322	1246	1530	1527	1419	1417		
10-15	..	1282	1197	1228	1128	1216	1071	1163	1053		
15-20	..	964	990	903	1022	810	879	826	884		
20-40	..	2978	3234	3094	3243	2778	3034	2895	3044		
40-60	..	1464	1268	1368	1209	1496	1332	1528	1413		
60 and over	..	521	439	502	440	785	684	755	611		
Mean age	..	**24.91**	**24.99**			**27**	**26**	**26**	**22**		
JAMMU PROVINCE											
0-5	..	1293	1403	1519	1684	1345	1453	1339	1463	1247	1361
5-10	..	1486	1487	1304	1252	1505	1524	1390	1461	1339	1425
10-15	..	1246	1203	1206	1137	1217	1075	1176	1053	1234	1150
15-20	..	956	983	909	995	798	854	826	860	855	858
20-40	..	2958	3158	3089	3191	2792	2983	2957	3077	2984	3047
40-60	..	1503	1301	1439	1276	1555	1426	1581	1479	1661	1523
60 and over	..	558	465	534	465	788	685	731	607	660	636
Mean age	..	**25.27**	**24.13**	**24.65**	**24.0**	**26**	**25**	**24**	**21**	**31**	**21**

VII—(i) AGE DISTRIBUTION OF 10000 OF EACH SEX IN THE STATE AND EACH NATURAL DIVISION—CONCLD.

Age		1941		1931		1921		1911		1901	
		M	F	M	M	M	F	M	M	M	F
1		*2*	*3*	*4*	*5*	*6*	*7*	*8*	*9*	*10*	*11*
III THE JHELUM VALLEY (KASHMIR PROVINCE)											
0-5	..	1235	1421	1509	1704	1434	1626	1537	1705	1616	1835
5-10	..	1411	1466	1327	1294	1530	1608	1512	1598	1637	1668
10-15	..	1227	1215	1215	1178	1243	1086	1182	1100	1252	1115
15-20	..	1055	1073	948	1059	850	875	917	907	817	784
20-40	..	3317	3375	3392	3432	3106	3219	2890	2987	2730	2858
40-60	..	1398	1185	1261	1068	1341	1195	1421	1296	1436	1329
60 and over	..	357	265	348	267	519	391	541	407	513	411
Mean age	..	**24.30**	**22.76**	**23**	**22**	**24**	**23**	**25**	**23**	**19**	**19**
IV THE INDUS VALLEY (FRONTIER DISTRICTS)											
0-5	..	1233	1321	1469	1598	1377	1450	1452	1561	1115	1234
5-10	..	1439	1405	1265	1199	1305	1269	1426	1366	1226	1234
10-15	..	1234	1082	1154	1050	1118	1042	1025	910	940	883
15-20	..	1042	937	857	859	997	841	916	811	761	695
20-40	..	3015	3130	3202	3326	2917	3059	2996	3150	3603	3546
40-60	..	1507	1525	1485	1416	1434	1424	1411	1361	1603	1555
60 and over	..	530	600	568	556	752	896	774	841	719	853
Mean age	..	**25.33**	**25.95**	**25.3**	**25.05**	**26**	**27**	**23**	**26**	**26**	**27**

VII—(ii) AGE DISTRIBUTION OF 10000 OF EACH SEX BY MAIN COMMUNITY

Community and Age	1941		1931		1921		1911		1901	
	M	F	M	F	M	F	M	F	M	F
1	2	3	4	5	6	7	8	9	10	11
Hindu										
0-5 ..	1173	1311	1316	1536	1142	1289	1115	1268	1066	1215
5-10 ..	1320	1377	1155	1158	1268	1406	1169	1383	1186	1325
10-15 ..	1111	1163	1084	1091	1117	998	1091	961	1167	989
15-20 ..	926	980	903	985	811	854	826	857	822	814
20-40 ..	3131	3184	3126	3210	3050	3068	3210	3216	3263	3261
40-60 ..	1724	1452	1823	1779	1799	1624	1790	1660	1803	1636
60 and over ..	615	533	593	541	813	761	799	705	693	760
Mean age ..	**27.00**	**24.73**	**26.85**	**25.2**	**23**	**27**	**27**	**26**	**28**	**26**
Muslim										
0-5 ..	1286	1429	1552	1725	1458	1597	1532	1665	1498	1458
5-10 ..	1476	1488	1347	1294	1575	1586	1530	1567	1541	1569
10-15 ..	1267	1210	1242	1165	1239	1101	1196	1094	1254	1158
15-20 ..	1030	1025	930	1014	838	863	883	882	835	816
20-40 ..	3131	3276	3241	3341	2906	3104	2845	2997	2820	2936
40-60 ..	1384	1220	1276	1119	1363	1236	1409	1308	1483	1381
60 and over ..	426	352	412	342	621	313	605	487	509	487
Mean age ..	**24.28**	**23.27**	**23.5**	**22.5**	**25**	**24**	**24**	**22**	**24**	**23**
Sikh										
0-5 ..	1464	1599	1756	1885	1516	1653	1491	1633	1381	1628
5-10 ..	1630	1615	1456	1334	1640	1669	1552	1648	1462	1500
10-15 ..	1335	1315	1265	1173	1241	1094	1209	1096	1206	1058
15-20 ..	991	1084	845	1029	716	926	902	884	886	884
20-40 ..	2786	2969	2928	3132	2839	2857	2837	3006	2892	2967
40-60 ..	1347	1082	1315	1037	1409	1312	1437	1281	1553	1402
60 and over ..	447	336	435	360	639	501	572	452	621	561
Mean age ..	**23.39**	**20.88**	**23.6**	**21.85**	**25**	**23**	**24**	**22**	**25**	**25**
Buddhist										
0-5 ..	906	835	1085	1165	933	1002	895	1013	774	810
5-10 ..	1155	1162	1046	1041	950	997	1114	1108	1111	1071
10-15 ..	996	1057	950	974	915	913	899	881	929	904
15-20 ..	987	1061	780	815	1057	871	860	859	871	818
20-40 ..	3003	3057	3060	3035	3062	2684	3097	3007	3183	2855
40-60 ..	2093	1955	2105	2052	2045	2067	2058	2083	2015	1957
60 and over ..	860	873	974	918	1038	1466	1077	1049	1117	1585
Mean age ..	**30.22**	**30·00**	**29.9**	**29.45**	**31**	**32**	**30**	**30**	**30**	**32**

VII—(iii) PROPORTION OF (A) CHILDREN UNDER 10 AND OF (B) MARRIED FEMALAS AGED 15-40

Province and community	CHILDREN (BOTH SEXES) PER 100									
	Persons aged 15-40					Married females aged 15-40				
	1941	1931	1921	1911	1901	1941	1931	1921	1911	1901
1	*2*	*3*	*4*	*5*	*6*	*7*	*8*	*9*	*10*	*11*
JAMMU & KASHMIR STATE										
All Communities ..	**67**	**70**	**77**	**77**	**77**	**179**	**166**	**183**	**183**	**190**
Hindu ..	63	62	65	60	58	161	170	167	157	152
Muslim ..	67	69	81	90	84	165	162	187	191	203
Sikh ..	81	72	88	83	78	196	185	199	195	192
Buddhist ..	50	56	51	53	49	172	167	202	170	154
JAMMU PROVINCE										
All Communities ..	**70**	**70**	**78**	**73**	**69**	**172**	**168**	**185**	**178**	**175**
Hindu ..	64	63	67	60	59	159	159	167	156	150
Muslim ..	74	74	86	82	78	178	173	196	192	193
Sikh ..	84	82	84	79	69	198	186	192	191	176
Buddhist ..	45	59	42	61	40	118	134	111	127	139
KASHMIR PROVINCE										
All Communities ..	**63**	**66**	**77**	**82**	**94**	**155**	**154**	**181**	**189**	**213**
Hindu ..	58	57	56	61	61	175	163	159	168	169
Muslim ..	62	66	78	83	96	154	154	181	190	215
Sikh ..	75	87	93	88	88	191	182	208	200	208
Buddhist ..										
FRONTIER DISTRICTS										
All communities ..	**66**		**69**	**74**	**56**	**178**		**179**	**185**	**169**
Hindu ..	36		16	8	3	189		179	151	100
Muslim ..	69		74	81	58	178		175	188	171
Sikh ..	79		40	21	8	238		250	140	50
Buddhist ..	50		51	53	50	173		204	152	157

PERSONS OVER 60 TO THOSE AGED 15-40;

PER 100 FEMALAS; FOR TOTAL POPULATION AND IN CERTAIN COMMUNITIES.

Persons over 60 per 100 aged 15-40										Married females aged 15-40 per 100 females of all ages				
1941		1931		1921		1911		1901						
M	F	M	F	M	F	M	F	M	F	1941	1931	1921	1911	1901
12	*13*	*14*	*15*	*16*	*17*	*18*	*19*	*20*	*21*	*22*	*23*	*24*	*25*	*26*
11	**9**	**19**	**21**	**18**	**15**	**17**	**14**	**17**	**15**	**36**	**38**	**35**	**34**	**33**
15	12	26	29	21	19	20	17	17	18	34	34	33	34	34
10	8	17	19	17	13	19	13	16	13	37	39	35	35	33
11	8	20	20	18	13	15	12	16	15	34	34	34	35	35
22	21	48	48	25	41	27	27	28	43	23	26	19	24	24
14	**11**	**24**	**25**	**23**	**20**	**21**	**18**	**18**	**19**	**35**	**36**	**33**	**34**	**33**
16	13	27	30	22	17	19	14	17	14	34	35	33	34	32
13	10	22	22	19	15	13	13	18	15	34	36	34	34	35
14	10	23	22	22	15	27	15	22	30	33	35	34	35	25
		31	28	13	9	14	10	14	11	35	35	37	36	34
8	**6**	**13**	**15**	**11**	**11**	**13**	**12**	**13**	**14**	**32**	**41**	**35**	**34**	**34**
8	8	14	19	13	9	14	10	15	11	33	34	37	36	34
8	6	13	14	16	11	14	9	15	14	39	40	35	36	35
9	6	18	19							35	39			
13	**15**			**19**	**23**	**20**	**21**	**16**	**20**	**31**		**31**	**32**	**29**
1	2			1	2	1	2		4	46		44	52	55
11	14			18	19	20	20	15	17	32		33	33	30
3								4		38		24	42	24
22	21			25	42	27	27	28	46	23		19	27	24

VII—(iv) PERCENTAGE VARIATION IN POPULATION BY AGE

Province	Period	All ages	0-10	10-15	15-40	40-60	60 and over
1	2	3	4	5	6	7	8
JAMMU AND KASHMIR STATE	**1931-1941**	**10.3**	**7.0**	**13.9**	**9.3**	**17.0**	**12.4**
	1921-1931	**11.9**	**8.2**	**15.0**	**22.9**	**3.2**	**— 24.0**
	1911-1921	**5.1**	**5.1**	**7.7**	**4.9**	**1.2**	**9.1**
JAMMU PROVINCE	1931-1941	10.8	9.4	15.5	8.9	14.2	13.5
	1921-1931	9.0	7.5	11.4	20.3	— .03	— 11.5
	1911-1921	2.7	5.8	5.5	— 1.3	.005	12.8
KASHMIR PROVINCE	1931-1941	10.2	4.5	12.2	10.1	21.8	11.5
	1921-1931	11.5	4.9	15.9	20.3	2.7	— 24.1
	1911-1921	8.6	5.9	9.6	13.5	1.8	4.4
FRONTIER DISTRICTS	1931-1941	7.9	5.3	13.5	6.5	12.4	8.9
	1921-1931	36.0	39.0	38.9	43.0	33.8	— 7.5
	1911-1921	3.2	6.0	12.4	.2	7.2	2.7

VII—(v) ACTUAL AGES RETURNED BY 100000 OF EACH SEX IN SRINAGAR CITY 1941

Age		M	F	Age	M	F	Age	M	F	Age	M	F
0	..	1477	1500	30	4747	4958	60	1565	1517	90	16	25
1	..	1974	2216	31	396	261	61	47	43	91	2	4
2	..	2415	2648	32	1473	1169	62	104	78	92	1	1
3	..	2680	3222	33	741	524	63	63	31	93		
4	..	2698	3176	34	665	535	64	60	68	94		
5	..	3125	3543	35	4058	3696	65	462	349	95	3	4
6	..	3006	3635	36	929	658	66	46	31	96	3	
7	..	2800	3488	37	699	428	67	34	19	97		1
8	..	2984	3429	38	956	709	68	40	20	98	1	1
9	..	2455	2977	39	248	206	69	14	8	99		1
10	..	3088	3326	40	4292	3998	70	378	424	100	9	6
11	..	1907	2452	41	231	122	71	10	6	101	1	1
12	..	3245	3344	42	762	464	72	19	23	102		
13	..	1846	2215	43	331	188	73	10	8	103		
14	..	2316	2441	44	339	208	74	3	3	104		
15	..	2439	2315	45	2926	2343	75	227	268	105	1	
16	..	2187	1922	46	346	230	76	9	7	106	1	
17	..	1512	1352	47	268	191	77	6	8	107	1	
18	..	2842	2721	48	502	343	78	11	4	108		
19	..	1284	1171	49	117	81	79	2	4	109		
20	..	3294	3722	50	2891	2626	80	120	119	110	2	
21	..	1098	855	51	122	75	81	3	3	111	1	
22	..	2272	2246	52	387	211	82	4	7	128	1	
23	..	1101	938	53	196	101	83					
24	..	1515	1541	54	178	130	84	4	3			
25	..	4014	4523	55	1339	1055	85	14	20			
26	..	1178	1085	56	207	129	86	1	1			
27	..	1063	1016	57	171	76	87	10				
28	..	1664	1586	58	150	86	88	1	1			
29	..	452	430	59	62	41	89					

VII– (vi) FEMALES PER 1000 MALES

Age			Total population				Hindus			
			1941	1931	1921	1911	1941	1931	1921	1911
1			*2*	*3*	*4*	*5*	*6*	*7*	*8*	*9*
TOTAL ALL AGES	..	..	*888*	*881*	*890*	*887*	*878*	*873*	*872*	*853*
TOTAL 0-30	..	..	*926*	*924*	*935*	*924*	*936*	*919*	*918*	*895*
0-1	..	..	987	983	975	980	974	987	971	965
1-2	..	..	999	995	973	955	998	997	910	945
2-3	..	..	977	995	1001	982	988	983	991	984
3-4	..	..	1006	966	983	986	982	996	1052	982
4-5	..	..	967	965	970	952	968	1063	977	962
TOTAL 0-5	..	..	*987*	*983*	*980*	*974*	*982*	1019	*984*	*970*
5-10	..	..	901	854	913	928	916	867	967	973
10-15	..	..	861	838	792	806	919	860	779	751
15-20	..		897	961	921	892	929	944	918	885
20-25	..	..	968	995	1093	1018	939	946	989	917
25-30	..	..	959	929	986	945	929	882	882	874
TOTAL 30 AND OVER	..	..	*813*	*790*	*807*	*816*	*784*	*788*	*804*	*790*
30-40	..	..	875	816	825	849	847	807	819	809
40-50	..	..	797	780	853	856	754	775	810	819
50-60	..	..	738	762	751	769	718	741	756	749
60 and over	..	..	744	750	767	733	762	1083	816	753

BY MAIN COMMUNITIES AND AGE

Muslims				Sikhs				Buddhists			
1941	1931	1921	1911	1941	1931	1921	1911	1941	1931	1921	1911
10	*11*	*12*	*13*	*14*	*15*	*16*	*17*	*18*	*19*	*20*	*21*
889	*882*	*894*	*896*	*805*	*923*	*901*	*853*	*1008*	*1008*	*1000*	*999*
922	*923*	*939*	*931*	*947*	*970*	*946*	*895*	*1034*	*1029*	*1011*	*1014*
994	989	974	985	954	938	916	854	745	975	1045	1100
997	979	987	956	1066	1005	927	804	1059	1000	1043	1238
974	996	1006	979	967	1002	895	1000	936	1163	1101	1155
1013	979	968	985	1032	958	1052	1027	937	1163	1026	1074
969	956	965	948	878	1038	1106	950	940	1073	1187	1157
989	*983*	*979*	*974*	*977*	*986*	*982*	*932*	*929*	*1072*	*1075*	*1130*
897	847	900	917	891	750	912	897	1014	1005	1050	993
845	828	794	819	882	883	792	773	1069	1022	999	979
886	964	921	894	977	1154	1164	836	1083	1039	825	999
973	1007	1124	1050	1050	1500	1028	1032	1069	1026	1033	1000
965	946	1018	972	982	1001	922	930	1039	1004	1147	921
819	*790*	*805*	*823*	*776*	*750*	*812*	*769*	*973*	*889*	*988*	*981*
882	822	829	862	874	830●	833	819	991	976	675	981
809	783	855	868	740	771	880	807	948	966	990	1011
742	1042	742	773	685	738	776	687	933	1002	1039	1011
732	726	738	720	677	748	706	673	1024	985	1418	974

VII—(vii) FEMALES PER 1000 MALES BY MAIN

Community and Province	All ages	0-5	0-1	1-2	2-3	3-4	4-5
1	2	3	4	5	6	7	8
JAMMU PROVINCE							
All Communities	**915**	**985**	1006	1006	992	1002	966
Hindu	**893**	**986**	987	999	1001	977	970
Muslim	**929**	**998**	1020	1005	988	1017	971
Sikh	**924**	**952**	929	1104	951	974	830
Buddhist	**1113**	**731**	777	3000	1500	400	500
KASHMIR PROVINCE							
All Communities	**849**	**977**	971	975	957	1009	968
Hindu	**768**	**944**	847	1002	876	1013	961
Muslim	**854**	**977**	981	973	961	1006	969
Sikh	**884**	**1015**	994	1015	995	1111	957
Buddhist							
FRONTIER DISTRICTS							
All Communities	**938**	**1004**	966	1105	981	1017	957
Hindu	**339**	**905**	778	454	1800	2400	417
Muslim	**931**	**1011**	997	1112	984	1022	960
Sikh	**649**	**929**	825	1000	667	2000	800
Buddhist	**1007**	**931**	743	1053	932	947	944

COMMUNITIES, AGE AND PROVINCE

Age										
0-30	5-10	10-15	15-20	20-25	25-30	30 and over	30-40	40-50	50-60	60 and over
9	*10*	*11*	*12*	*13*	*14*	*15*	*16*	*17*	*18*	*19*
956	916	884	941	1030	1021	**838**	919	822	749	763
950	916	922	950	975	966	**801**	876	771	740	764
958	916	866	934	1060	1054	**865**	911	862	771	763
972	903	876	994	1188	1137	**822**	955	754	709	739
1219	1870	1586	1267	1042	787	**886**	821	852	896	
895	881	841	862	904	906	**752**	813	752	665	630
831	925	891	779	708	700	**657**	654	630	670	731
898	880	838	865	915	920	**758**	822	759	664	625
916	885	892	964	908	826	**711**	773	719	644	571
915	916	826	843	1004	904	**984**	991	906	1010	1065
511	683	800	600	489	226	**134**	151	81	83	200
902	906	796	813	1004	893	**991**	1000	901	1030	1076
754	643	684	647	1067	579	**356**	310	500	500	
1032	1006	1063	1080	1071	1043	**974**	993	948	933	1024

VII—(viii) DISTRIBUTION BY CIVIL CONDITION OF 1000 OF EACH SEX, COMMUNITY AND AGE

Community	Sex and Age	Unmarried					Married					Widowed				
		1941	1931	1921	1911	1901	1941	1931	1921	1911	1901	1941	1931	1921	1911	1901
1	*2*	*3*	*4*	*5*	*6*	*7*	*8*	*9*	*10*	*11*	*12*	*13*	*14*	*15*	*16*	*17*
All Communities	**Males*** ..	**553**					**396**					**51**				
	0-5 ..	1000	1000	998	999	997			2	1	3					
	5-10 ..	1000	982	986	989	989		18	13	11	11			1		
	10-15 ..	980	948	915	918	922	19	51	82	80	76	1	1	3	2	2
	15-20 ..	798	678	710	697	716	197	309	280	294	273	5	13	10	9	11
	20-40 ..	218	200	206	212	231	739	717	737	739	728	43	83	57	49	41
	40-60 ..	46	39	60	52	62	810	735	792	817	828	144	226	148	131	110
	60 and over ..	41	31	47	40	42	634	609	627	664	712	325	360	326	296	246
	Females* ..	**431**					**472**					**97**				
	0-5 ..	1000	1000	996	998	995			4	2	5					
	5-10 ..	996	957	947	949	952	4	42	50	49	46		1	3	2	2
	10-15 ..	823	778	655	635	645	174	217	336	357	346	3	5	9	8	9
	15-20 ..	363	179	162	143	176	624	800	812	828	795	13	21	26	29	29
	20-40 ..	22	20	28	20	35	913	905	891	894	878	65	75	81	86	87
	40-60 ..	6	6	15	7	7	632	584	618	629	646	362	410	367	364	347
	60 and over ..	6	5	8	10	10	262	217	224	248	272	732	778	768	742	718
Hindu	**Males*** ..	**554**					**382**					**64**				
	0-5 ..	1000	1000	999	999	998			1	1	2					
	5-10 ..	1000	966	986	988	987		33	13	11	12		1	1	1	1
	10-15 ..	1000	938	925	927	923		60	72	71	74		2	3	2	3
	15-20 ..	858	737	742	744	721	137	251	248	246	269	5	12	10	10	10
	20-40 ..	306	310	297	301	316	650	628	637	636	635	44	62	66	63	49
	40-60	94	105	120	111	126	742	691	700	716	726	164	204	180	173	143
	60 and over ..	75	77	92	80	87	577	560	573	592	586	348	363	335	328	327
	Females* ..	**396**					**447**					**157**				
	0-5 ..	1000	999	994	996	995		1	5	4	5			1		
	5-10 ..	1000	928	893	894	913		69	98	102	85		3	9	4	4
	10-15 ..	794	708	501	469	491	204	280	477	512	490	2	12	22	19	19
	15-20 ..	320	120	65	72	68	665	835	885	876	879	15	45	50	52	53
	20-40 ..	9	12	9	10	10	874	828	822	815	824	117	160	169	175	166
	40-60 ..	4	3	4	5	3	493	440	467	472	466	503	557	529	523	531
	60 and over ..	5	2	3	7	2	150	131	136	170	152	845	867	861	823	846
Muslim	**Males*** ..	**552**					**399**					**49**				
	0-5 ..	1000	1000	998	999	997			2	1	3					
	5-10 ..	1000	985	986	990	990		15	13	10	10			1		
	10-15 ..	977	949	913	916	922	22	50	84	82	76	1	1	3	2	2
	15-20 ..	785	661	702	684	715	209	328	288	307	273	6	11	10	9	12
	20-40 ..	209	183	180	182	199	743	759	766	774	764	48	58	54	44	37
	40-60 ..	29	24	37	28	36	832	823	825	856	869	139	153	138	116	95
	60 and over ..	24	12	31	22	21	659	629	648	694	762	317	395	321	284	217
	Females* ..	**438**					**480**					**82**				
	0-5 ..	1000	1000	997	998	995			3	2	5					
	5-10 ..	996	963	960	962	962	4	36	39	37	37		1	1	1	1
	10-15 ..	832	791	690	672	682	165	205	304	323	312	3	4	6	5	6
	15-20 ..	368	188	180	154	202	619	796	800	823	776	13	16	20	23	22
	20-40 ..	22	19	29	20	42	927	925	913	921	898	51	56	58	59	60
	40-60 ..	5	5	16	7	7	673	628	670	684	711	322	367	314	309	282
	60 and over ..	5	5	8	9	9	300	242	260	273	323	695	753	732	718	663

*Similar figures previous to 1941 are not available.

VII—(viii) DISTRIBUTION BY CIVIL CONDITION OF 1000 OF EACH SEX, COMMUNITY AND AGE.—CONCLD.

Community	Sex and Age	Unmarried					Married					Widowed				
		1941	1931	1921	1911	1901	1941	1931	1921	1911	1901	1941	1931	1921	1911	1901
1	2	3	4	5	6	7	8	9	10	11	12	13	14	15	16	17
Sikh	**Males*** ..	**587**					**372**					**41**				
	0-5 ..	1000	999	1000	999	998		1		1	2					
	5-10 ..	1000	987	996	992	993		12	4	7	7		1		1	
	10-15 ..	980	964	943	956	963	20	35	55	42	36		1	2	2	1
	15-20 ..	807	683	746	765	762	190	305	243	228	234	3	12	11	7	4
	20-40 ..	217	176	205	212	236	750	770	748	749	733	33	54	47	39	31
	40-60 ..	40	32	44	56	59	832	812	821	818	839	128	156	135	126	102
	60 and over ..	25	29	35	39	49	665	614	641	684	708	310	357	324	277	248
	Females*	**468**					**445**					**87**				
	0-5 ..	1000	999	998	998	998		1	2	2	2					
	5-10 ..	988	958	955	958	972	12	40	44	40	26		2	1	2	2
	10-15 ..	789	774	660	650	715	210	220	335	344	277	1	6	5	6	8
	15-20 ..	345	171	81	84	99	646	810	903	900	879	9	19	16	16	22
	20-40 ..	22	15	18	16	13	912	908	905	902	913	66	77	77	87	74
	40-60 ..	5	12	24	9	4	615	584	596	585	662	380	414	380	406	334
	60 and over ..		1	25	18	2	255	186	195	198	326	745	813	780	784	672
Buddhist	**Males*** ..	**491**					**456**					**53**				
	0-5 ..	1000	1000	1000	983	990				17	9					1
	5-10 ..	1000	1000	991	924	958			9	74	41				2	1
	10-15 ..	955	986	906	816	821	45	13	92	180	177		1	2	4	2
	15-20 ..	693	582	661	580	638	304	404	334	411	347	3	14	5	9	15
	20-40 ..	267	214	223	211	216	708	748	743	759	699	25	38	34	30	115
	40-60 ..	144	120	123	135	135	759	770	794	788	773	97	110	83	77	92
	60 and over ..	130	101	102	121	165	579	586	585	579	705	291	313	313	300	130
	Females* ..	**487**					**415**					**98**				
	0-5 ..	1000	1000	998	998	991			2	2	8					1
	5-10 ..	999	999	997	987	957	1	1	2	11	43			1	2	
	10-15 ..	955	971	954	944	889	45	26	46	54	99		3		2	12
	15-20 ..	726	633	787	719	668	261	342	205	275	319	13	25	8	6	13
	20-40 ..	273	222	286	214	181	676	714	649	730	766	51	64	65	56	53
	40-60 ..	98	76	107	68	163	710	702	685	726	728	192	222	208	206	209
	60 and over ..	82	52	63	78	115	423	440	198	436	405	495	508	739	486	480

*Similar figures previous to 1941 are not available.

VII—(ix) DISTRIBUTION BY CIVIL CONDITION OF 1000 OF

MALES

Province & Community	All ages			0-5			5-10			10-15			15-40			40 and over		
	U	M	W	U	M	W	U	M	W	U	M	W	U	M	W	U	M	W
1	2	3	4	5	6	7	8	9	10	11	12	13	14	15	16	17	18	19
JAMMU AND KASHMIR STATE																		
All Communities ..	553	396	51	1000			1000			980	19	1	368	595	37	44	768	188
Hindu ..	554	382	64	1000			1000			1000			431	532	37	90	698	212
Muslim ..	552	399	49	1000			1000			977	22	1	352	610	38	28	791	181
Sikh ..	587	372	41	1000			1000			980	20		373	601	26	37	790	173
Buddhist ..	491	456	53	1000			1000			955	45		373	608	19	140	707	153
JAMMU PROVINCE																		
All Communties ..	567	377	56	1000			1000			987	13		395	567	38	51	751	198
Hindu ..	550	384	66	1000			1000			990	10		424	538	38	82	705	213
Muslim ..	576	374	50	1000			1000			987	13		379	582	39	27	786	187
Sikh ..	594	364	42	1000			1000			989	11		380	593	27	42	788	170
Buddhist ..	438	498	64	1000			1000			750	250		275	683	42	100	680	220
KASHMIR PROVINCE																		
All Communities ..	541	409	50	1000			1000			977	23		345	617	38	35	777	188
Hindu ..	593	353	54	1000			1000			1000			489	482	29	156	645	199
Muslim ..	537	412	51	1000			1000			976	24		335	626	39	27	785	188
Sikh ..	587	384	29	1000			999	1		969	31		368	610	22	30	790	180
Buddhist ..	700	200	100							1000			750	250				1000
FRONTIER DISTRICTS																		
All Communities ..	534	432	34	1000			998	2		941	57	2	342	634	24	52	828	120
Hindu ..	394	598	8	1000			1000			1000			262	726	12	121	879	
Muslim ..	537	430	33	1000			997	3		937	59	4	337	637	26	31	856	113
Sikh ..	561	439		1000			1000			1000			275	725			1000	
Buddhist ..	492	455	53	1000			1000			957	43		373	608	19	140	708	152

U=Unmarried.
M=Married.
W=Widowed.

EACH SEX AND AGE BY PROVINCE AND COMMUNITY

Females																	
All Ages			0-5			5-10			10-15			15-40			40 and over		
U	M	W	U	M	W	U	M	W	U	M	W	U	M	W	U	M	W
20	21	22	23	24	25	26	27	28	29	30	31	32	33	34	35	36	37
431	472	97	1000			996	4		823	174	3	103	845	52	6	544	450
396	447	157	1000			1000			794	204	2	81	827	92	4	401	595
438	480	82	1000			996	4		832	165	3	105	853	42	5	590	405
468	445	87	1000			988	12		789	210	1	110	841	49	4	529	467
487	415	98	1000			999	1		955	45		405	544	51	95	618	287
433	449	118	1000			1000			834	164	2	102	833	65	4	483	513
392	450	158	1000			1000			784	214	2	81	826	93	4	401	595
455	450	95	1000			1000			862	136	2	116	834	50	5	538	457
467	434	99	1000			994	6		824	176		110	835	55	3	499	498
443	480	77	1000			1000			795	205		203	765	32		631	369
424	503	73	1000			994	6		807	190	3	90	871	39	3	613	384
432	427	141	1000			1000			858	140	2	101	809	90	3	406	591
425	505	70	1000			995	5		805	192	3	90	875	35	4	625	371
466	462	72	1000			977	23		743	253	4	107	849	44	6	583	411
445	463	92	998	2		987	12	1	867	129	4	185	769	46	25	619	356
480	487	33	1000			1000			875	125		37	951	12		500	500
440	467	93	998	2		980	16	4	852	144	4	153	801	46	10	630	360
550	441	9	1000			1000			923	77		106	894			857	143
488	414	98	1000			999	1		958	42		390	569	41	94	621	285

VII—(x) SEX-RATIO BY CIVIL CONDITION, AGE, COMMUNITY AND PROVINCE

FEMALES PER 1000 MALES

Province and Community	All Ages			0-10			10-15			15-40			40 and over		
	U	M	W	U	M	W	U	M	W	U	M	W	U	M	W
1	2	3	4	5	6	7	8	9	10	11	12	13	14	15	16
JAMMU AND KASHMIR STATE															
All Communities ..	693	1059	1669	940	5923	2062	726	7320	2948	258	1303	1277	114	543	1833
Hindu ..	627	1033	2127	947	4667	1000	737	20302	2968	174	1398	225	37	428	2089
Muslim ..	706	1067	1502	938	576	2065	720	6185	293	274	1285	1021	15	575	1729
Sikh ..	713	1073	1910	923	21333		712	9217	3000	279	1342	1905	78	475	1908
Buddhist ..	999	917	1871	976	1500		1067	1038		1088	973	2261	641	848	1803
JAMMU PROVINCE															
All Communities ..	70	109	1929	952	4000	5000	748	1182	3188	25	1426	1636	75	502	2035
Hindu ..	669	1046	2144	948	4222	1000	732	1989	2897	179	1430	2264	42	430	2102
Muslim ..	734	1112	175	954	209		756	8828	3487	299	1423	1248	154	553	1974
Sikh ..	728	1101	2166	923			731	13062		31	1470	2158	56	467	2172
Buddhist ..	1111	1073	1312	1265			1667	1286		757	1146	800		852	1545
KASHMIR PROVINCE															
All Communities ..	670	1039	1246	924	8346	4250	695	6952	376	227	1219	87	78	554	1429
Hindu ..	561	931	2003	934			768	27417	4000	145	1179	2140	14	416	1956
Muslim ..	676	9044	1196	924	8013	4000	692	6753	3722	241	123	810	93	566	139
Sikh ..	692	1040	1526	927	15333		684	7271	6000	252	1205	1575	13	489	1496
Buddhist ..															
FRONTIER DISTRICTS															
All Communities ..	784	1001	2499	950	4108	1630	755	1907	1298	510	115	1739	485	742	2747
Hindu ..	422	278	1000	795			700			34	324	250		52	
Muslim ..	743	1018	2643	948	4173	1630	73	1973	1255	421	117	1683	330	725	3135
Sikh ..	635	653		786			667	1000		227	724			375	
Buddhist ..	998	915	1881	973	1500		1061	1071		1093	98	232	645	848	1809

U=Unmarried.
M=Married.
W=Widowed.

FERTILITY TABLES

DISTRICT—Jammu (excluding City)
COMMUNITY—Hindu

I—Size of family and present age of married woman

Age	No. of married women	Total No. of children born	Average	Total No. of children surviving	Proportion of survivors to 1000 born
1	2	3	4	5	6
12 ..	313	1	.01	1	1000
13 ..	332	10	.03	7	700
14 ..	1003	1		1	1000
15 ..	519	23	.04	18	783
16 ..	1732	581	.34	425	732
17 ..	895	435	.49	258	593
18 ..	1950	1234	.63	846	686
19 ..	894	754	.84	704	934
20 ..	2698	2654	.98	1909	719
21 ..	755	1002	1.33	595	594
22 ..	1894	2890	1.53	2032	703
23 ..	976	2111	2.16	1349	639
24 ..	1317	3048	2.31	2086	684
25 ..	3135	7395	2.36	6108	826
26 ..	1282	3400	2.72	2674	766
27 ..	1273	2672	2.10	2009	752
28 ..	1583	5611	3.54	4184	746
29 ..	592	1567	2.65	1131	722
30 ..	3635	9427	2.59	5809	616
31 ..	274	1058	3.86	650	614
32 ..	1738	6394	3.68	3104	485
33 ..	574	1771	3.09	1312	741
34 ..	630	2508	3.98	1917	764
35 ..	2320	8426	3.63	6471	768
36 ..	917	3236	3.53	2330	720
37 ..	315	887	2.82	622	701
38 ..	400	2523	6.31	1696	672
39 ..	151	818	5.42	658	804
40 ..	1611	7287	4.52	5323	730
41 ..	225	1046	4.65	759	726
42 ..	462	1951	4.22	1420	728
43 ..	195	859	4.41	626	729
44 ..	175	850	4.86	616	725
45 ..	1301	6731	5.17	5344	794
46 ..	165	999	6.05	671	672
47 ..	71	220	3.10	137	623
48 ..	342	1497	4.38	905	605
49 ..	87	618	7.10	387	626
50 ..	1315	5861	4.46	4005	683
51 ..	84	256	3.05	152	594
52 ..	130	722	5.55	486	673
53 ..	24	31	1.29	16	516
54 ..	28	94	3.36	79	840
55 ..	486	2713	5.58	1384	510
56 ..	78	225	2.88	190	844
57 ..	39	425	10.90	122	287
58 ..	75	420	5.60	248	590
59 ..	32	201	6.28	123	612
60 ..	493	2319	4.70	1377	594
TOTAL ..	*41515*	*107852*	*2.60*	*75276*	*698*

DISTRICT—Jammu (excluding City)
COMMUNITY—Muslim

I—Size of family and present age of married woman—contd.

Age		No. of married women	Total No. of children born	Average	Total No. of children surviving	Proportion of survivors to 1000 born
1		2	3	4	5	6
12	..	77	2	.03	2	1000
13	..	93	1	.01	1	1000
14	..	585	4	.01	4	1000
15	..	624	15	.02	15	1000
16	..	1161	100	.09	74	740
17	..	561	145	.26	109	752
18	..	2101	1229	.58	840	683
19	..	576	447	.78	412	922
20	..	2126	1329	.63	1120	843
21	..	249	178	.71	138	775
22	..	1328	1218	.92	545	447
23	..	506	743	1.47	380	511
24	..	803	1008	1.26	692	687
25	..	3113	3753	1.20	2208	588
26	..	875	1123	1.28	950	846
27	..	495	821	1.66	697	849
28	..	1377	2894	2.10	1874	648
29	..	406	658	1.62	507	771
30	..	2858	3468	1.21	2210	637
31	..	100	173	1.73	140	809
32	..	1019	2128	2.09	1559	733
33	..	292	521	1.78	333	639
34	..	312	694	2.22	576	830
35	..	2419	4485	1.85	3077	686
36	..	407	794	1.95	494	622
37	..	191	337	1.76	223	662
38	..	291	732	2.52	508	694
39	..	215	595	2.77	434	729
40	..	1980	5917	2.99	5437	919
41	..	140	477	3.40	328	688
42	..	262	933	3.56	624	669
43	..	175	630	3.60	409	649
44	..	150	749	4.99	538	718
45	..	1200	5259	4.38	3826	728
46		98	572	5.84	352	615
47	..	63	249	3.95	184	739
48	..	169	709	4.20	452	638
49	..	95	502	5.28	270	538
50	..	980	3939	4.02	2722	691
51	..	135	286	2.12	169	591
52	..	105	534	5.09	325	609
53	..	35	169	4.83	114	675
54	..	45	276	6.13	183	663
55	..	460	1619	3.52	1152	712
56	..	37	265	7.16	179	675
57	..	30	82	2.73	57	695
58	..	48	235	4.90	152	647
59	..	50	146	2.92	78	534
60	..	418	2318	5.55	1486	641
TOTAL	..	*31835*	*55461*	*1.74*	*39159*	*706*

FERTILITY TABLES—Contd.

District—Jammu (excluding City)
Community—Sikh

I—Size of family and present age of married woman—concld.

Age		No. of married women	Total No. of children born	Average	Total No. of children surviving	Proportion of survivors to 1000 born
1		2	3	4	5	6
12	..	1				
13	..	2				
14	..	14				
15	..	32				
16	..	30	2	.07	2	1000
17	..	23	5	.22	4	800
18	..	83	45	.54	34	756
19	..	33	28	.85	20	714
20	..	84	88	1.05	70	795
21	..	22	33	1.50	27	818
22	..	69	106	1.54	85	802
23	..	21	32	1.52	28	875
24	..	32	62	1.94	50	806
25	..	114	267	2.34	220	824
26	..	74	117	1.58	95	812
27	..	15	51	3.40	43	843
28	..	63	159	2.52	133	836
29	..	16	55	3.44	45	818
30	..	117	382	3.26	306	801
31	..	5	21	4.20	18	857
32	..	63	241	3.83	190	788
33	..	11	56	5.09	42	750
34	..	22	87	3.95	76	874
35	..	87	437	5.02	360	824
36	..	26	130	5.00	97	746
37	..	8	51	6.37	38	745
38	..	13	68	5.23	46	676
39	..	8	33	4.12	24	727
40	..	88	458	5.20	329	718
41	..	4	22	5.50	17	773
42	..	10	55	5.50	36	655
43	..	3	17	5.67	12	706
44	..	2	14	7.00	12	857
45	..	44	210	4.77	151	719
46	..	5	31	6.20	23	742
48	..	11	57	5.18	43	754
49	..	2	16	8.00	10	625
50	..	49	223	4.55	140	628
54	..	2	11	5.50	8	727
55	..	14	78	5.57	49	628
56	..	1	5	5.00	5	1000
60	..	25	114	4.56	83	728
Total	..	*1348*	*3867*	*2.87*	*2971*	*768*

FERTILITY TABLES—CONTD.

DISTRICT—Jammu (excluding City)
COMMUNITY—Hindu

II—Size of family by age of mother at birth of first child

Age at birth of first child	No. of married women	Total No. of children born	Average	Total No. of children surviving	Proportion of survivors to 1000 born
1	2	3	4	5	6
12 ..	7	18	2.57	15	833
13 ..	26	82	3.14	78	951
14 ..	2324	6197	2.67	4258	687
15	2780	10760	3.90	7628	709
16 ..	4136	10083	2.44	7698	763
17 ..	2756	9715	3.53	5123	527
18 ..	3862	13341	3.45	8848	663
19 ..	2111	10441	4.95	8014	768
20 ..	1120	11157	9.96	8191	734
21 ..	1064	11205	10.53	9742	869
22 ..	744	6775	9.10	3403	502
23 ..	861	8191	9.40	5545	677
24 ..	605	4516	7.46	3523	780
25 ..	774	3315	4.28	1716	512
26 ..	58	362	6.24	247	682
27 ..	46	484	10.52	379	784
28 ..	63	199	3.16	165	830
29 ..	22	293	13.32	208	710
30 ..	41	187	4.56	116	620
31 ..	9	98	10.89	77	786
32 ..	24	154	6.42	116	753
33 ..	18	32	1.78	22	688
34 ..	12	63	5.25	47	746
35 ..	7	76	10.86	49	645
36 ..	6	69	11.50	43	623
37 ..	6	15	2.50	10	667
38 ..	5	5	1.00	3	600
39 ..	3	8	2.67	5	625
40 ..	3	11	3.66	7	636
TOTAL ..	*23493*	*107852*	*4.59*	*75276*	*698*

FERTILITY TABLES—CONTD.

DISTRICT—Jammu (excluding City)
COMMUNITY—Muslim

II—Size of family by age of mother at birth of first child—contd.

Age at birth of first child	No. of married women	Total No. of children born	Average	Total No. of children surviving	Proportion of survivors to 1000 born
1	2	3	4	5	6
12 ..	17	99	5.82	70	707
13 ..	114	437	3.83	288	659
14 ..	817	2209	2.70	1507	682
15 ..	1418	3762	2.65	2518	669
16 ..	2286	7981	3.49	4855	608
17 ..	2488	7463	3.00	4986	668
18 ..	2427	7394	3.05	6250	845
19 ..	1665	6172	3.70	4231	686
20 ..	1539	6108	3.97	4201	688
21 ..	762	2677	3.51	1846	690
22 ..	758	2698	3.56	2007	740
23 ..	568	1676	2.95	1302	777
24 ..	431	1365	3.17	986	722
25 ..	442	1513	3.42	1098	720
26 ..	252	969	3.85	747	771
27 ..	229	800	3.49	560	700
28 ..	87	273	3.14	209	766
29 ..	71	219	3.08	178	813
30 ..	188	655	3.48	496	757
31 ..	103	316	3.06	256	810
32 ..	82	223	2.72	198	888
33 ..	44	112	2.55	93	830
34 ..	41	91	2.22	72	791
35 ..	52	90	1.73	72	800
36 ..	26	57	2.19	50	877
37 ..	33	64	1.94	53	828
38 ..	5	9	1.80	8	889
39 ..	9	16	1.78	12	750
40 ..	13	13	1.00	10	769
TOTAL ..	*16967*	*55461*	*3.27*	*39159*	*706*

FERTILITY TABLES—CONTD.

DISTRICT—Jammu (excluding City)
COMMUNITY—Sikh

II—Size of family by age of mother at birth of first child—concld.

Age at birth of first child		No. of married women	Total No. of children born	Average	Total No. of children surviving	Proportion of survivors to 1000 born
1		2	3	4	5	6
15	..	197	745	3.78	585	785
16	..	294	1072	3.65	823	768
17	..	229	779	3.40	596	765
18	..	181	589	3.25	457	776
19	..	133	478	3.59	352	736
20	..	58	176	3.03	138	784
21	..	2	11	5.50	8	727
22	..	1	9	9.00	6	667
23	..	1	8	8.00	6	750
TOTAL	..	*1096*	*3867*	*3.53*	*2971*	*768*

FERTILITY TABLES—CONTD.

DISTRICT—Jammu (excluding City)
COMMUNITY—Hindu

V—Number of children born and surviving

No. of children born		Number of children surviving													
		1	2	3	4	5	6	7	8	9	10	11	12	13	14
1		2	3	4	5	6	7	8	9	10	11	12	13	14	15
1	5954	5262													
2	9120	2267	6500												
3	15333	1772	1494	5961											
4	13676	513	820	3801	3492										
5	14210	188	720	3018	2852	3005									
6	14220	1759	1320	801	1896	1265	2904								
7	11473	2141	1048	498	1116	1385	1992	1792							
8	4984	1509	546	117	276	310	348	210	112						
9	10656	2003	24	162	216	355	558	413	280	378					
10	3900	806	56	72	120	265	186	301	272	225	100				
11	2167	449	78	24	16	145	84	147	152	243	410	33			
12	816	6	28	12	188	30	6	84	96	63	60	22	12		
13	741	80	82	60	20	35	72	49	48	63	90	22	12		
14	602	10	8	33	20	20	42	49	72	54	70	11			14
TOTAL ..	*107852*	*18815*	*12724*	*14559*	*10212*	*6815*	*6192*	*3045*	*1032*	*1026*	*730*	*88*	*24*		*14*

FERTILITY TABLES—CONTD.

DISTRICT—Jammu (excluding City)
COMMUNITY—Muslim

V—Number of children born and surviving—contd.

No. of children born		Number of children surviving										
		1	2	3	4	5	6	7	8	9	10	11
1		*2*	*3*	*4*	*5*	*6*	*7*	*8*	*9*	*10*	*11*	*12*
1	4331	3959										
2	4054	866	2722									
3	6174	358	1792	2856								
4	8304	189	1560	1878	2728							
5	7925	180	520	705	1808	2565						
6	8016	39	186	1461	1224	1495	2058					
7	6167	117	284	243	452	745	654	609				
8	4184	9	40	108	348	365	396	182	536			
9	2907	4	18	51	132	235	396	336	216	63		
10	1540	1	6	24	48	105	84	175	208	72	40	
11	770	1	4	12	32	30	54	98	96	27	20	
12	780		6	9	20	50	60	49	72	90	20	
13	221					5	12	7	48	36		11
14	56				4			7			10	11
15												
16	32							7				
TOTAL ..	*55461*	*5723*	*6938*	*7347*	*6796*	*5595*	*3714*	*1470*	*1176*	*288*	*90*	*22*

FERTILITY TABLES—CONTD.

DISTRICT—Jammu (excluding City)
COMMUNITY—Sikh

V—Number of children born and surviving—concld.

No. of children born		Number of children surviving							
		1	2	3	4	5	6	7	8
1		*2*	*3*	*4*	*5*	*6*	*7*	*8*	*9*
1	253	217							
2	388	36	282						
3	507	21	90	312					
4	540	7	48	108	272				
5	500	7	8	69	100	210			
6	630		16	39	92	130	204		
7	560	2	10	36	52	85	132	77	
8	408	1	6	3	28	85	42	84	24
9	81					5	24	7	
TOTAL ..	*3867*	*291*	*460*	*567*	*544*	*515*	*402*	*168*	*24*

FERTILITY TABLES—CONTD.

DISTRICT—Jammu City
COMMUNITY—Hindu

I—Size of family and present age of married woman

Age	No. of married women	Total No. of children born	Average	Total No. of children surviving	Proportion of survivors to 1000 born
1	2	3	4	5	6
12 ..	1				
13 ..	2				
14 ..	13				
15 ..	92	10	.11	6	600
16 ..	161	34	.21	27	794
17 ..	127	86	.68	67	779
18 ..	294	196	.67	158	806
19 ..	161	128	.80	103	805
20 ..	401	515	1.28	436	847
21 ..	92	165	1.80	132	800
22 ..	300	337	1.80	446	831
23 ..	156	311	2.00	249	801
24 ..	177	401	2.30	339	845
25 ..	500	1298	2.60	949	731
26 ..	162	502	3.10	369	735
27 ..	152	435	2.90	335	770
28 ..	194	640	3.30	471	736
29 ..	46	168	3.70	136	810
30 ..	396	1145	2.89	823	719
31 ..	160	439	2.74	319	727
32 ..	194	526	2.71	356	677
33 ..	105	309	2.94	216	699
34 ..	115	332	2.89	209	630
35 ..	149	818	5.49	500	611
36 ..	116	451	3.89	233	517
37 ..	105	350	3.30	188	537
38 ..	80	271	3.40	229	845
39 ..	95	365	3.84	312	855
40 ..	237	946	3.95	498	526
41 ..	30	181	6.03	99	547
42 ..	53	349	6.60	210	602
43 ..	23	126	5.48	76	603
44 ..	46	118	2.60	113	958
45 ..	164	1104	6.73	532	482
46 ..	22	64	2.90	57	891
47 ..	42	89	2.12	72	809
48 ..	52	127	2.44	120	945
49 ..	23	44	1.91	36	818
50 ..	114	954	8.37	547	573
51 ..	14	40	2.86	36	900
52 ..	24	97	4.04	85	876
53 ..	17	78	4.59	62	795
54 ..	11	40	3.64	35	875
55 ..	51	178	3.50	108	607
56 ..	18	124	6.89	44	355
57 ..	11	83	7.55	41	494
58 ..	12	121	10.08	69	570
59 ..	17	108	6.35	78	722
60 ..	23	176	7.60	84	477
TOTAL ..	*5550*	*15579*	*2.30*	*10610*	*681*

FERTILITY TABLES—CONTD.

DISTRICT—Jammu City
COMMUNITY—Muslim

I—Size of family and present age of married woman—contd.

Age		No. of married women	Total No. of children born	Average	Total No. of children surviving	Proportion of survivors to 1000 born
1		2	3	4	5	6
14	..	27	19	.70	17	895
15	..	42	34	.80	30	882
16	..	46	40	.87	33	825
17	..	109	100	.92	80	800
18	..	98	100	1.02	73	730
19	..	91	80	.88	62	775
20	..	86	109	1.27	83	761
21	..	61	100	1.64	66	660
22	..	201	381	1.90	331	868
23	..	158	252	1.60	226	897
24	..	101	206	2.04	167	811
25	..	47	72	1.53	58	806
26	..	55	139	2.53	96	691
27	..	133	335	2.52	270	806
28	..	148	387	2.61	331	855
29	..	102	252	2.47	157	623
30	..	91	268	2.95	232	866
31	..	88	273	3.10	191	700
32	..	90	430	4.78	298	693
33	..	43	181	4.21	127	702
34	..	51	224	4.40	158	705
35	..	132	375	2.84	234	624
36	..	17	37	2.18	14	378
37	..	67	184	2.75	109	592
38	..	53	189	3.57	121	640
39	..	48	150	3.13	132	880
40	..	35	80	2.30	61	762
41	..	42	152	3.62	100	658
42	..	20	121	6.05	76	628
43	..	6	36	6.00	32	889
44	..	8	66	8.25	63	955
45	..	98	562	5.73	356	633
46	..	7	40	5.71	28	700
47	..	10	36	3.60	34	944
48	..	12	78	6.50	60	769
49	..	3	20	6.67	11	550
50	..	95	414	4.36	328	792
51	..	15	75	5.00	70	933
52	..	5	35	7.00	26	743
53	..	4	26	6.50	24	923
54	..	4	24	6.00	22	917
55	..	20	82	4.10	74	902
56	..	3	24	8.00	24	1000
57	..	2	18	9.00	18	1000
58	..	1	7	7.00	6	857
59	..	10	42	4.20	42	1000
60	..	47	169	3.60	104	615
TOTAL	..	2632	7024	2.67	5255	748

FERTILITY TABLES—CONTD.

DISTRICT—Jammu City
COMMUNITY—Sikh

I—Size of family and present age of married woman—concld.

Age	No. of married women	Total No. of children born	Average	Total No. of children surviving	Proportion of survivors to 1000 born
1	2	3	4	5	6
15 ..	3	3	1.00	3	1000
16 ..	18	6	.33	6	1000
17 ..	18	7	.39	7	1000
18 ..	16	7	.44	4	571
19 ..	11	5	.45	3	600
20 ..	9	4	.44	2	500
21 ..	5	2	.40	1	500
22 ..	13	6	.46	4	667
23 ..	12	6	.50	4	667
24 ..	28	23	.82	17	739
25 ..	24	27	1.12	24	889
26 ..	19	34	1.79	16	471
27 ..	5	12	2.40	4	333
28 ..	11	25	2.27	13	520
29 ..	9	19	2.11	9	474
30 ..	18	52	2.89	27	519
31 ..	13	65	5.00	34	523
32 ..	9	40	4.44	12	300
33 ..	11	54	4.91	14	259
34 ..	16	90	5.62	33	367
35 ..	14	79	5.64	28	354
36 ..	2	21	10.50	13	619
37 ..	5	29	5.80	22	759
38 ..	3	24	8.00	15	625
39 ..	4	34	8.50	18	529
40 ..	5	29	5.80	18	621
41 ..	12	60	5.00	37	617
42 ..	3	33	11.00	12	364
43 ..	5	24	4.80	18	750
44 ..	8	31	3.87	20	645
45 ..	4	26	6.50	23	885
46 ..	1	4	4.00	4	1000
47 ..	1	4	4.00	4	1000
48 ..	1	4	4.00	4	1000
49 ..	2	9	4.50	8	889
50 ..	2	6	3.00	6	1000
51 ..	2	13	6.50	10	769
52 ..	3	18	6.00	15	833
53 ..	5	31	6.20	18	581
54 ..	4	19	4.75	16	842
55 ..	1	9	9.00	8	889
56 ..	1	5	5.00	4	800
57 ..	1	7	7.00	6	857
58 ..	2	15	7.50	13	867
59 ..	3	14	4.67	13	929
60 ..	1	8	8.00	6	750
TOTAL ..	*363*	*1043*	*2.87*	*596*	*571*

FERTILITY TABLES—CONTD.

DISTRICT—Jammu City
COMMUNITY—Hindu

II—Size of family by age of mother at birth of first child

Age at birth of first child	No. of married women	Total No. of children born	Average	Total No. of children surviving	Proportion of survivors to 1000 born
1	2	3	4	5	6
13 ..	5	24	4.80	18	750
14 ..	320	750	2.34	723	964
15 ..	570	2519	4.42	1548	615
16 ..	611	3862	6.32	2691	697
17 ..	450	794	1.76	221	278
18 ..	481	2815	5.85	2331	828
19 ..	312	1500	4.81	950	633
20 ..	339	1244	3.67	959	771
21 ..	133	548	4.12	359	655
22 ..	83	293	3.53	165	563
23 ..	32	287	8.97	155	540
24 ..	47	224	4.77	95	424
25 ..	64	370	5.78	193	522
26 ..	5	50	10.00	6	120
27 ..	26	66	2.54	48	727
28 ..	5	33	6.60	16	485
29 ..	22	86	3.91	48	558
30 ..	14	24	1.71	18	750
31 ..	14	72	5.14	53	736
32 ..	2	2	1.00	1	500
34 ..	1	1	1.00	1	1000
35 ..	2	5	2.50	3	600
36 ..	5	9	1.80	7	778
39 ..	1	1	1.00	1	1000
TOTAL ..	*3544*	*15579*	*4.00*	*10610*	*681*

FERTILITY TABLES—CONTD.

DISTRICT—Jammu City
COMMUNITY—Muslim

II—Size of family by age of mother at birth of first child—contd.

Age at birth of first child	No. of married women	Total No. of children born	Average	Total No. of children surviving	Proportion of survivors to 1000 born
1	2	3	4	5	6
13 ..	40	65	1.63	57	877
14 ..	82	680	8.29	511	751
15 ..	302	1094	3.62	816	746
16 ..	298	1095	3.34	734	670
17 ..	248	811	3.27	620	764
18 ..	105	702	3.42	600	855
19 ..	142	471	3.32	351	745
20 ..	189	762	4.03	538	706
21 ..	83	248	2.99	210	847
22 ..	65	224	3.45	166	741
23 ..	80	230	2.88	171	743
24 ..	37	103	3.05	84	816
25 ..	69	189	2.74	134	709
26	22	31	1.41	24	774
27 ..	29	60	2.07	39	650
28 ..	16	47	2.94	38	809
29 ..	10	20	2.00	13	650
30 ..	23	76	3.30	67	882
31 ..	5	6	1.20	5	833
32 ..	4	10	2.50	8	800
33 ..	14	41	2.93	26	634
35 ..	7	16	2.29	11	688
36 ..	7	13	1.86	11	846
37 ..	14	24	1.71	16	667
38 ..	1	1	1.00	1	1000
39 ..	5	5	1.00	4	800
TOTAL ..	1997	7024	3.52	5255	748

FERTILITY TABLES—Contd.

District—Jammu City
Community—Sikh

II—Size of family by age of mother at birth of first child—concld.

Age at birth of first child	No. of married women	Total No. of children born	Average	Total No. of children surviving	Proportion of survivors to 1000 born
1	2	3	4	5	6
14 ..	6	25	4·17	17	680
15 ..	26	105	4·04	63	600
16 ..	64	367	5·73	185	504
17 ..	44	211	4·80	101	479
18 ..	36	164	4·56	103	628
19 ..	15	62	4·13	38	613
20 ..	4	31	7·75	22	710
21 ..	10	57	5·70	48	842
27 ..	1	7	7·00	6	857
29 ..	2	14	7·00	13	929
Total ..	*208*	*1043*	*5·01*	*596*	*571*

FERTILITY TABLES—Contd.

District—Jammu City
Community—Hindu

V—Number of children born and surviving

No. of children born		Number of children surviving										
		1	2	3	4	5	6	7	8	9	10	11
1		*2*	*3*	*4*	*5*	*6*	*7*	*8*	*9*	*10*	*11*	*12*
1	669	557										
2	1462	210	876									
3	1545	56	464	546								
4	1736	36	212	345	816							
5	1810	20	86	210	340	555						
6	1734	19	74	153	240	265						
7	1386	21	32	87	156	315	474					
8	1352	8	32	72	104	115	210	238				
9	702	6		21	36	50	204	147	184			
10	570	2	4	9	20	35	78	154	112	54		
							66	63	72	36	30	
11	737	6	16	12	24	45		70	72	45	10	
12	264	1	6		8	15	78	28	40	27	10	
13	507		14	6	16	30	12	28	56	18	20	
14	336	1		9	4	5	36	28	24	36	10	
15	375		8		12	20	24	35	24	18	50	22
16	128	1										
17	136			15			6	7	8			11
18	90				4	5		7	8	36	10	11
19	19			3			6		16	9	10	11
20	21									9		11
Total ..	*15579*	*944*	*1824*	*1488*	*1780*	*1455*	*1194*	*805*	*616*	*288*	*150*	*66*

FERTILITY TABLES—CONTD.

DISTRICT—Jammu City
COMMUNITY—Muslim

V—Number of children born and surviving—contd.

No. of children born		Number of children surviving									
		1	2	3	4	5	6	7	8	9	10
1		2	3	4	5	6	7	8	9	10	11
1	613	574									
2	684	89	254								
3	903	36	236	414							
4	764	7	78	195	292						
5	1055	9	36	102	412	440					
6	858		16	54	124	195	276				
7	808	6	22	42	60	120	186	140			
8	456		6	3	44	50	54	91	64		
9	387		2	6	28	35	48	49	56	36	
10	270		4	6	8	5	24	35	32	18	40
11	77				4		6	7	8		20
12	60				4		6	14			10
14	14					5					
15	15							7			
TOTAL ..	7024	721	654	822	976	855	600	343	160	54	70

FERTILITY TABLES—CONTD.

DISTRICT—Jammu City
COMMUNITY—Sikh

V—Number of children born and surviving—concld.

No. of children born		Number of children surviving								
		1	2	3	4	5	6	7	8	9
1		2	3	4	5	6	7	8	9	10
1	61	47								
2	32	3	26							
3	33		6	12						
4	108	6	10	21	20					
5	80		8	12	12	25				
6	84		6	3	16	15	12			
7	154		4	18	16	20	24	14		
8	184		6	12	16	10	36	14	16	
9	144		8	18	8		12	7		9
10	30			3		5	6			
11	121			9	16	10	6	7		
12	12					5				
TOTAL ..	1043	57	74	108	104	90	96	42	16	9.

FERTILITY TABLES—CONTD.

DISTRICT—Ladakh
COMMUNITY—Muslim

I—Size of family and present age of married woman

Age	No. of married women	Total No. of children born	Average	Total No. of children surviving	Proportion of survivors to 1000 born
1	2	3	4	5	6
12 ..	31	2	.06	1	500
13 ..	20	2	.10	2	1000
14 ..	142	11	.08	8	727
15 ..	143	10	.07	8	800
16 ..	383	24	.06	20	833
17 ..	326	29	.09	17	586
18 ..	1571	499	.32	237	475
19 ..	356	102	.29	84	824
20 ..	1450	591	.41	496	839
21 ..	268	136	.51	102	750
22 ..	800	695	.87	527	758
23 ..	282	258	.91	245	950
24 ..	4116	5702	1.39	4136	725
25 ..	498	789	1.58	591	749
26 ..	625	1241	1.99	1186	956
27 ..	375	706	1.88	556	788
28 ..	578	1446	2.50	924	639
29 ..	245	590	2.41	369	625
30 ..	2872	5492	1.91	4058	739
31 ..	192	599	3.12	387	646
32 ..	486	1576	3.24	881	559
33 ..	184	612	3.33	408	667
34 ..	471	1481	3.14	807	545
35 ..	271	966	3.56	707	732
36 ..	5512	15487	2.81	9891	639
37 ..	190	762	4.01	538	706
38 ..	343	1327	3.87	918	692
39 ..	308	1411	4.58	901	639
40 ..	476	1662	3.49	1078	649
41 ..	176	577	3.28	391	675
42 ..	1341	3849	2.87	3166	823
43 ..	129	451	3.50	313	694
44 ..	210	558	2.66	352	631
45 ..	180	497	2.76	347	698
46 ..	196	519	2.65	356	686
47 ..	72	188	2.61	138	734
48 ..	3024	12954	4.28	9305	718
49 ..	81	295	3.64	214	725
50 ..	268	1019	3.80	658	646
51 ..	110	364	3.31	114	313
52 ..	188	985	5.24	592	601
53 ..	107	576	5.38	329	571
54 ..	522	2758	5.28	1699	616
55 ..	75	441	5.88	249	565
56 ..	89	440	4.94	245	557
57 ..	40	135	3.37	82	607
58 ..	88	377	4.28	239	634
59 ..	[illegible]	182	5.06	112	615
60 ..	1428	6724	4.71	3673	546
TOTAL ..	*31874*	*78097*	*2.45*	*52657*	*674*

FERTILITY TABLES—Contd.

District—Ladakh
Community—Buddhist

I—Size of family and present age of married woman—concld.

Age	No. of married women	Total No. of children born	Average	Total No. of children surviving	Proportion of survivors to 1000 born
1	2	3	4	5	6
13 ..	1				
14 ..	9				
15 ..	20	1	.05	1	1000
16 ..	24	1	.04	1	1000
17 ..	70	1	.01	1	1000
18 ..	86	6	.07	5	833
19 ..	110	23	.20	18	782
20 ..	170	49	.29	38	776
21 ..	138	70	.51	44	628
22 ..	143	86	.60	65	756
23 ..	159	78	.49	74	949
24 ..	247	159	.64	125	786
25 ..	373	415	1.11	357	860
26 ..	142	186	1.31	160	860
27 ..	147	190	1.29	172	905
28 ..	167	175	1.05	165	943
29 ..	168	295	1.76	268	908
30 ..	395	706	1.79	632	895
31 ..	171	294	1.72	271	922
32 ..	225	194	.86	174	897
33 ..	179	584	3.26	484	829
34 ..	172	480	2.79	381	794
35 ..	249	763	3.06	627	822
36 ..	277	835	3.01	733	878
37 ..	232	590	2.54	524	888
38 ..	208	628	3.02	570	908
39 ..	153	358	2.34	331	925
40 ..	278	538	1.94	489	909
41 ..	209	486	2.33	457	940
42 ..	174	254	1.46	231	909
43 ..	130	368	2.83	310	842
44 ..	140	233	1.66	220	944
45 ..	200	418	2.09	386	923
46 ..	129	413	3.20	379	918
47 ..	153	295	1.93	247	837
48 ..	218	445	2.04	370	831
49 ..	146	355	2.43	307	865
50 ..	188	681	3.62	377	554
51 ..	85	274	3.22	203	741
52 ..	114	341	2.99	244	716
53 ..	108	206	1.97	158	767
54 ..	98	352	3.59	325	923
55 ..	129	415	3.22	354	853
56 ..	102	389	3.81	278	714
57 ..	100	356	3.56	267	750
58 ..	95	335	3.53	246	734
59 ..	64	243	3.80	180	741
60 ..	181	670	3.72	499	745
Total ..	*7476*	*15234*	2.04	*12748*	*837*

FERTILITY TABLES—CONTD.

DISTRICT—Ladakh
COMMUNITY—Muslim

II—Size of family by age of mother at birth of first child

Age at birth of first child	No. of married women	Total No. of children born	Average	Total No. of children surviving	Proportion of survivors to 1000 born
1	2	3	4	5	6
10 ..	1	2	2.00	1	500
11 ..	3	12	4.00	11	917
12 ..	83	335	4.04	224	669
13 ..	152	565	3.72	337	596
14 ..	385	1294	3.36	817	631
15 ..	882	2862	3.24	1927	673
16 ..	1207	4132	3.42	2787	674
17 ..	1656	3788	2.29	3312	874
18 ..	3589	12943	3.61	8994	695
19 ..	2227	6630	2.98	4263	643
20 ..	3161	11371	3.60	5702	501
21 ..	1344	3702	2.75	2722	735
22 ..	1419	4386	3.09	3298	752
23	742	1999	2.69	1487	744
24 ..	4057	15851	3.91	11049	697
25 ..	642	1890	2.94	1316	696
26 ..	436	1229	2.82	885	720
27 ..	301	865	2.87	657	760
28 ..	296	942	3.18	469	498
29 ..	140	304	2.17	243	799
30 ..	325	987	3.04	696	705
31 ..	86	181	2.10	147	812
32 ..	69	206	2.99	156	757
33 ..	39	95	2.44	72	958
34 ..	67	169	2.52	111	657
35 ..	83	213	2.57	158	742
36 ..	228	649	2.85	471	726
37 ..	64	233	3.64	156	670
38 ..	30	49	1.63	36	735
39 ..	42	67	1.60	56	836
40 ..	20	59	2.95	42	712
41 ..	1	1	1.00	1	1000
42 ..	6	19	3.17	14	737
43 ..	2	3	1.50	3	1000
44 ..	1	4	4.00	2	500
48 ..	4	6	1.50	4	667
49 ..	1	1	1.00	1	1000
50 ..	1	1	1.00	1	1000
54 ..	1	2	2.00	2	1000
55 ..	1	1	1.00	1	1000
56 ..	12	46	3.83	23	500
58 ..	2	3	1.50	3	1000
TOTAL ..	*23808*	*78097*	*3.28*	*52657*	*674*

FERTILITY TABLES—Contd.

District—Ladakh
Community—Buddhist

II—Size of family by age of mother at birth of first child—concld.

Age at birth of first child	No. of married women	Total No. of children born	Average	Total No. of children surviving	Proportion of survivors to 1000 born
1	2	3	4	5	6
12 ..	3	14	4.67	12	857
13 ..	74	217	2.93	202	931
14 ..	119	381	3.21	321	843
15 ..	182	623	3.42	555	891
16 ..	206	737	3.58	617	837
17 ..	240	868	3.62	761	877
18 ..	345	1052	3.05	835	794
19 ..	350	1090	3.11	908	833
20 ..	533	1529	2.87	1331	871
21 ..	402	1222	3.04	972	795
22 ..	384	1102	2.87	931	845
23 ..	322	929	2.89	807	869
24 ..	362	1093	3.02	834	763
25 ..	460	1373	2.98	1076	783
26 ..	191	547	2.86	466	852
27 ..	132	347	2.63	287	827
28 ..	156	429	2.75	366	853
29 ..	125	244	1.95	222	910
30 ..	122	345	2.83	289	838
31 ..	64	112	1.75	98	875
32 ..	36	122	3.39	94	770
33 ..	50	151	3.02	136	901
34 ..	53	132	2.49	117	886
35 ..	54	180	3.33	158	878
36 ..	38	119	3.13	98	824
37 ..	37	102	2.76	94	922
38 ..	25	83	3.32	75	904
39 ..	1	7	7.00	7	1000
40 ..	3	7	2.33	5	714
41 ..	18	65	3.61	65	1000
42 ..	2	3	1.50	2	667
43 ..	1	1	1.00	1	1000
48 ..	1	6	6.00	4	667
52 ..	1	2	2.00	2	1000
Total ..	5092	15234	2.99	12748	837

FERTILITY TABLES—CONTD.

DISTRICT—Ladakh
COMMUNITY—Muslim

V—Number of children born and surviving

No. of children born		Number of children surviving 1	2	3	4	5	6	7	8	9	10
1		2	3	4	5	6	7	8	9	10	11
1	9816	9726									
2	13914	2044	11400								
3	14262	1515	4620	5054							
4	11496	515	2100	2124	3500						
5	9010	270	1420	888	2812	1025					
6	7032	148	150	95	176	575	150				
7	5187	150	118	60	128		20	120			
8	4432	250	70	81	15	5		20	199		
9	1674	131	58	34		5				116	
10	550	75	52	14	118	90			30		20
11	462	35	20	6	50		10	8		6	
12	156	95	15	10		5			15		
13	78	8	10		40		8			4	
14	28	11	15								
TOTAL ..	78097	14973	20048	8366	6839	1705	188	148	244	126	20

FERTILITY TABLES—CONCLD.

DISTRICT—Ladakh
COMMUNITY—Buddhist

V—Number of children born and surviving—concld.

No. of children born		Number of children surviving 1	2	3	4	5	6	7	8	9	10	11
1		2	3	4	5	6	7	8	9	10	11	12
1	1225	1172										
2	2050	169	1594									
3	2175	54	268	1539								
4	2348	20	120	363	1468							
5	2415	9	52	261	376	1285						
6	2124		20	99	224	270	1122					
7	1155	2	6	24	84	135	198	476				
8	752	1	4	9	40	45	96	161	208			
9	486		2	6	8	15	12	35	80	225		
10	270					15	12	35	16	27	110	
11	209			3			6		8	9	130	11
12	12						6					
13	13			3								
TOTAL ..	15234	1427	2066	2307	2200	1765	1452	707	312	261	240	11

IMPERIAL TABLE VII—

1/50

Comparative

Community and Age			Population* in 1/50 sample P	M	F	Population* 50 times 1/50 sample P	M	F
1			2	3	4	5	6	7
Total Population	..	..	**78901**	**41773**	**37128**	**3945050**	**2088650**	**1856400**
0-1	..	..	1861	964	897	93050	48200	44850
1-2	..	..	2001	1028	973	100050	51400	48650
2-3	..	..	2105	1133	972	105250	56650	48600
3-4	..	..	2464	1283	1181	123200	64150	59050
4-5	..	..	2309	1206	1103	115450	60300	55150
	Total 0-5	..	*10740*	*5614*	*5126*	*537000*	*280700*	*256300*
5-10	..	..	11026	5769	5257	551300	288450	262850
10-15	..	..	9282	4956	4326	464100	247800	216300
15-20	..	..	7813	4075	3738	390650	203750	186900
20-25	..	..	7106	3568	3538	355300	178400	176900
25-30	..	..	6672	3333	3339	333600	166650	166950
30-35	..	..	5937	3118	2819	296850	155900	140950
35-40	..	..	5002	2692	2310	250100	134600	115500
40-45	..	..	3694	2026	1668	184700	101300	83400
45-50	..	..	3277	1816	1461	163850	90800	73050
50-55	..	..	2411	1388	1023	120550	69400	51150
55-60	..	..	2036	1179	857	101800	58950	42850
60-65	..	..	1476	841	635	73800	42050	31750
65-70	..	..	948	550	398	47400	27500	19900
70 and over	..	..	1481	848	633	74050	42400	31650
	Total	..	*68161*	*36159*	*32002*	*3408050*	*1807950*	*1600100*
Hindu	..	..	**16203**	**8603**	**7600**	**810150**	**430150**	**380000**
0-5		..	2078	1074	1004	103900	53700	50200
5-30	..	..	8052	4182	3870	402600	209100	193500
30 and over	..	..	6073	3347	2726	303650	167350	136300
Muslim	..	..	**60444**	**31995**	**28449**	**3022200**	**1599750**	**1422450**
0-5		..	8391	4415	3976	419550	220750	198800
5-30	..	..	32687	16900	15787	1634350	845000	789350
30 and over	..	..	19366	10680	8686	968300	534000	434300
Sikh	..	..	**1338**	**713**	**625**	**66900**	**35650**	**31250**
0-5	..	..	183	82	101	9150	4100	5050
5-30	..	..	721	399	322	36050	19950	16100
30 and over	..	..	434	232	202	21700	11600	10100
Buddhist	..	..	**809**	**401**	**408**	**40450**	**20050**	**20400**
0-5	..	..	76	36	40	3800	1800	2000
5-30	..	..	374	185	189	18700	9250	9450
30 and over	..	..	359	180	179	17950	9000	8950

*Population of Gilgit Agency not included.

AGE AND CIVIL CONDITION

SAMPLE

Results

						Unmarried*					
Actual figures *vide* Table VII			in 1/50 sample			50 times 1/50 sample			Actual figures *vide* Table VII		
P	M	P	P	M	F	P	M	F	P	M	F
8	*9*	*10*	*11*	*12*	*13*	*14*	*15*	*16*	*17*	*18*	*19*
3945090	**2089045**	**1856045**	**38658**	**22618**	**16040**	**1932900**	**1130900**	**802000**	**1954259**	**1154386**	**799873**
82006	41230	40776	1861	964	897	93050	48200	44850	82006	41230	40776
96513	48292	48221	2001	1028	973	100050	51400	48650	96513	48292	48221
109833	55690	54143	2105	1133	972	105250	56650	48600	109833	55690	54143
119978	59792	60186	2464	1283	1181	123200	64150	59050	119978	59792	60186
115435	58639	56796	2309	1206	1103	115450	60300	55150	115435	58639	56796
523765	*263643*	*260122*	*10740*	*5614*	*5126*	*537000*	*280700*	*256300*	*523765*	*263643*	*260122*
573440	301643	271797	11005	5758	5247	550250	287900	262350	572545	301531	271014
480444	257721	222723	8278	4760	3518	413900	238000	175900	437020	252585	184435
399168	210417	188751	4535	3129	1406	226750	156450	70300	237351	168129	69222
370541	188207	182334	1848	1555	293	92400	77750	14650	94696	85877	8819
337121	172168	164953	892	760	132	44600	38000	6600	41245	38882	2363
300907	159143	141764	459	360	99	22950	18000	4950	17963	16778	1185
247406	133151	114255	288	204	84	14400	10200	4200	9729	8993	736
179797	99401	80396	170	134	36	8500	6700	1300	5689	5220	469
155707	87277	68430	135	107	28	6750	5350	1400	4433	4000	433
112134	64490	47644	86	67	19	4300	3350	950	3062	2744	318
93806	53934	39872	56	44	12	2800	2200	600	2320	2070	250
63821	36670	27151	56	41	15	2800	2050	750	1617	1442	175
40596	22956	17640	37	30	7	1850	1500	350	1071	933	138
66437	38224	28213	73	55	18	3650	2750	900	1753	1559	194
3421325	*1825402*	*1595923*	*27918*	*17004*	*10914*	*1395900*	*850200*	*545700*	*1430494*	*890743*	*539751*
809091	**430638**	**378453**	**7663**	**4677**	**2986**	**383150**	**233850**	**149300**	**389007**	**239022**	**149985**
100137	50526	49611	2078	1074	1004	103900	53700	50200	100137	50526	49611
418211	217176	201035	5166	3225	1941	258300	161250	97050	269856	170010	99846
290743	162936	127807	419	378	41	20950	18900	2050	19014	18486	528
3024820	**1600936**	**1423884**	**29901**	**17333**	**12568**	**1495050**	**866650**	**628400**	**1507865**	**883583**	**624282**
409329	205843	203486	8391	4415	3976	419550	220750	198800	409329	205843	203486
1683090	882900	800190	20621	12284	8337	1031050	614200	416850	1072936	654445	418491
932401	512193	420208	889	634	255	44450	31700	12750	25600	23295	2305
65882	**34764**	**31118**	**660**	**392**	**268**	**33000**	**19600**	**13400**	**34984**	**20428**	**14556**
10067	5091	4976	183	82	101	9150	4100	5050	10067	5091	4976
37047	19108	17939	460	297	163	23000	14850	8150	24280	14770	9510
18768	10565	8203	17	13	4	850	650	200	637	567	70
40696	**20268**	**20428**	**383**	**190**	**193**	**19150**	**9500**	**9650**	**19907**	**9956**	**9951**
3543	1837	1706	76	36	40	3800	1800	2000	3543	1837	1706
19926	9701	10225	275	138	137	13750	6900	6850	14123	6812	7311
17227	8730	8497	32	16	16	1600	800	800	2241	1307	934

IMPERIAL TABLE VII—

1/50

Comparative

Community and Age			Married*					
			In 1/50 sample			50 times 1/50 sample		
			P	M	F	P	M	F
1			20	21	22	23	24	25
Total Population ..		..	**34147**	**16725**	**17422**	**1707350**	**836250**	**871100**
0-1	..	..						
1-2	..	..						
2-3	..	..						
3-4	..	..						
4-5		..						
TOTAL 0-5		..						
5-10	..	..	17	8	9	850	400	450
10-15	..	..	989	190	799	49450	9500	39950
15-20	..	..	3187	908	2279	159350	45400	113950
20-25	..	..	5046	1912	3134	252300	95600	156700
25-30	..	..	5474	2421	3053	273700	121050	1 2650
30-35	..	..	5057	2553	2504	252850	127650	125200
35-40	..	..	4148	2250	1898	207400	112500	94900
40-45	..	..	2937	1656	1281	146850	82800	64050
45-50	..	..	2396	1439	957	119800	71950	47850
50-55	..	..	1692	1080	612	84600	54000	30600
55-60	..	..	1245	878	367	62250	43900	18350
60-65	..	..	844	600	244	42200	30000	12200
65-70	..	..	501	366	135	25050	18300	6750
70 and over	..	..	614	464	150	30700	23200	7500
TOTAL		..	*34147*	*16725*	*17422*	*1707350*	*836250*	*871100*
Hindu	..	..	**6852**	**3339**	**3513**	**342600**	**166950**	**175650**
0-5	..	..						
5-30	..	..	2745	899	1846	137250	44950	92300
30 and over	..	..	4107	2440	1667	205350	122000	83350
Muslim	..	..	**26299**	**12872**	**13427**	**1314950**	**643600**	**671350**
0-5	..	..						
5-30	..	..	11594	4378	7216	579700	218900	360800
30 and over	..	..	14705	8494	6211	735250	424700	310550
Sikh	..	..	**568**	**286**	**282**	**28400**	**14300**	**14100**
0-5	..	..						
5-30	..	..	253	101	152	12650	5050	7600
30 and over	..	..	315	185	130	15750	9250	6500
Buddhist		..	**380**	**197**	**183**	**19000**	**9850**	**9150**
0-5	..	..						
5-30	..	..	94	46	48	4700	2300	2400
30 and over	..	..	286	151	135	14300	7550	6750

*Population of Gilgit Agency not included.

AGE AND CIVIL CONDITION – CONCLD.

SAMPLE

Results. concld.

			Widowed*								
Actual figures vide Table VII			In 1/50 sample			50 times 1/50 sample			Actual figures vide Table VII		
P	M	F	P	M	F	P	M	F	P	M	F
26	*27*	*28*	*29*	*30*	*31*	*32*	*33*	*34*	*35*	*36*	*37*
1699783	**825316**	**874467**	**6096**	**2430**	**3666**	**304800**	**121500**	**183300**	**291048**	**109343**	**181705**
866	107	759	4	3	1	200	150	50	29	5	24
42717	4967	37750	15	6	9	750	300	450	707	169	538
158122	41088	117034	91	38	53	4550	1900	2650	3695	1200	2495
266929	98312	168617	212	101	111	[illegible]0600	5050	5550	8916	4018	4898
281621	126311	155310	306	152	154	[illegible]5300	7600	7700	14255	6975	7280
262438	132813	129625	421	205	216	21050	10250	10800	20506	9552	10954
210899	113256	97643	566	238	328	28300	11900	16400	26778	10902	15876
145969	83733	62236	587	236	351	29350	11800	17550	28139	10448	17691
115679	71409	44270	746	270	476	37300	13500	23800	35595	11868	23727
77508	51147	26361	633	241	392	31650	12050	19600	31564	10599	20966
56119	40235	15884	735	257	478	36750	12850	23900	35367	11629	23738
35132	26095	9037	576	200	376	28800	10000	18800	27072	9133	17939
19473	14869	4604	410	154	250	20500	7700	12800	20052	7154	12898
26311	20974	5337	794	329	405	39700	16450	23250	38373	15691	22682
1699783	*825316*	*874467*	*6096*	*2430*	*3666*	*304800*	*121500*	*183300*	*291048*	*109343*	*181705*
332871	**163731**	**169140**	**1688**	**587**	**1101**	**84400**	**29350**	**55050**	**87213**	**27885**	**59328**
141310	44975	96335	141	58	83	7050	2900	4150	7045	2191	4854
191561	118756	72805	1547	529	1018	77350	26450	50900	80168	25694	54474
1320601	**638495**	**682106**	**4244**	**1790**	**2454**	**212200**	**89500**	**122700**	**196354**	**78858**	**117496**
590167	218481	371686	472	238	234	23600	11900	11700	19987	9974	10013
730434	420014	310420	3772	1552	2220	188600	77600	111000	176367	68884	107483
26775	**12919**	**13856**	**110**	**35**	**75**	**5500**	**1750**	**3750**	**4123**	**1417**	**2706**
12446	4212	8232	8	1	7	400	50	350	321	126	195
14329	8707	5622	102	34	68	5100	1700	3400	3802	1291	2511
17720	**9243**	**8477**	**46**	**14**	**32**	**2300**	**700**	**1600**	**3069**	**1069**	**2000**
5579	2825	2754	5	1	4	250	50	200	224	64	160
12141	6418	5723	41	13	28	2050	650	1400	2845	1005	1840

TABLE VIII

Means of Livelihood

NOTES

1. This table corresponds to Table X of the 1931 report. As the Census Commissioner for India anticipated in the compilation instructions, this table proved the most difficult to compile. The questions on which it is based also proved beyond the capabilities of the majority of our enumerators and the answers recorded were very defective. The results are most unsatisfactory and the table must be declared useless for statistical purposes. For these reasons Part II of the table giving the details by districts has not been produced ; it would be waste of paper and printing to do so.

2. The table is based on the answers to census questions 9, 10 and 14 which read as follows :—

(9) Are you wholly or partly dependent on any one else ?

(10) If so, give means of livelihood of persons on whom dependent.

(14) Give your means of livelihood in order of importance.

At the 1931 Census the relative questions 9, 10 and 11 were to the following effect :—

(9) Enter clearly whether the person enumerated is an earner or dependent.

(10) Enter the principal occupation of persons engaged in trade or in any profession either directly or through their servants.

(11) Enter in this column any occupation which the person enumerated follows at any time of the year in addition to his principal occupation.

3. In 1931 the total population was divided into earners, working dependents and non-working dependents. The figures recorded were :—

Total Population	Earners		Working dependents		Non-working dependents	
	M	F	M	F	M	F
3646243	752104	56045	221997	895159	964237	756701

At this census there were five classes instead of 3 *viz.* :—

P—With this as Principal means of livelihood without subsidiary.

PS—With this as Principal means of livelihood with some other as subsidiary.

S—With this as subsidiary.

PD—This as means of livelihood of those partly dependent.

TD—Total dependents on those with this means of livelihood; this figure includes partly dependents.

The total population as shown at the top of the table is made up of the totals of the columns P, PS and TD. The table does not include figures for the population of the Gilgit Agency (76526).

4. The number of classified means of livelihood at this census was 236 against 195 in 1931. Groups against which there are no entries have not been shown in the table.

5. Having stated in para. 1 above that the table produced is useless for statistical purposes it is unnecessary to go into the defects in detail but some instances may be given :—

(i) Group 27. A total of 52 persons have been recorded as dependent on this M/L. It is known that thousands are partly dependent on bee-keeping.

(ii) Group 28. A total of 231 persons has been shown as dependent on the rearing of silk-worms and only 2986 persons with this as a subsidiary M/L. It is known that over 60000 persons rear silkworms as a subsidiary occupation.

(iii) Group 86. A total of 65 persons has been shown as dependent on the manufacture of matches, fireworks and explosives whereas there is a prosperous match factory at Baramulla in the Kashmir Province and it is known that many others manufacture fireworks and explosives.

(iv) Group 122. A total of 84 persons is shown as dependent on the making, assembling or repairing of motor vehicles and cycles, eleven of whom are shown as engaged in this work as their principal M/L. There are numerous motor and cycle repair shops throughout the towns of the State and the numbers dependent on this trade in one way or another must run into some thousands.

These examples have been given to show that the table does not present a correct picture of the facts. These defects are due to three causes :—

(a) Defective answers given by those censused.

(b) Defective work by some enumerators due to carelessness or ignorance or both.

(c) Defective work by sorters and compilers.

6. As already remarked it would be waste of paper and printing to re-produce Part II giving details by districts. Even though defective, Part I—Summary for the State—has some value in spite of its defects. It gives a general idea of trades and occupations followed in the State and gives totals for each M/L for comparison with the figures for 1931 and those to be produced at the next census.

7. The grand totals for PS and S in the table should have been the same, that is to say, the total of column 5 should be the same as that in column 7 and column 6 should be the same as column 8, if the table were correctly prepared, although the components making these totals will not agree. This error is obviously due to defective compilation. The defect was detected after it was realised the table was useless for statistical purposes any how and in the interests of economy it was not considered worth-while to retain staff to work on a table which was in any case worthless for statistical purposes.

8. It must be recognised that the questions on which this table is based are not easy for an educated person to answer correctly. Whatever may have been the experience elsewhere they were too difficult for good results in this State. In 43154 slips the questions were not answered at all or the answers were such as to be useless for the purposes of the table. Scrutiny of the relative table produced in 1931 discloses the fact that the figures given therein for many occupations are not in accordance with known facts.

9. As the main table is so defective no attempt has been made to re-produce figures for the 1/50 sample or to prepare subsidiary tables.

NOTE.—P stands for Persons, M for Males and F for Females.

VIII—PART I—MEANS OF LIVELIHOOD—GENERAL TABLE—STATE SUMMARY

P	.. 742110
PS	.. 356926
TD	.. 2846054
Population	.. 3945090

Group No.	Means of Livelihood	P		PS		S		PD	TD
		M	F	M	F	M	F	P	P
1	*2*	*3*	*4*	*5*	*6*	*7*	*8*	*9*	*10*
	TOTAL ..	*709212*	*32898*	*351143*	*5783*	*213271*	*4632*	*319134*	*2846054*
	CLASS A—PRODUCTION OF RAW MATERIALS	**559713**	**23033**	**308712**	**3954**	**119820**	**2307**	**177114**	**2340371**
	Sub-class I—Exploitation of Animals and Vegetation	**559656**	**23033**	**308695**	**3952**	**119789**	**2307**	**177012**	**2340135**
	Order 1—Pasture and Agriculture ..	**558829**	**23025**	**308398**	**3952**	**118935**	**2303**	**176195**	**2336598**
	(a) Cultivation	**547510**	**22604**	**304793**	**3852**	**105714**	**2164**	**166614**	**2300357**
1	Non-cultivating proprietors taking rent in money or kind	178126	11285	189174	1260	35846	579	43090	1241953
2	*Bat.i* share-croppers	21546	492	8013	99	11572	204	8846	63539
3	Estate Agents and Managers of owners ..	22	3	22	1	343		14	463
4	Estate Agents and Managers of Government	6		1		39			15
5	Rent collectors, clerks etc.	121		43		449	6	186	328
6	Cultivating owners	196327	5178	65861	1036	29029	424	59196	313785
7	Tenant cultivators	139442	4799	39155	1378	19180	389	48183	648244
8	Agricultural labourers	11920	847	2524	78	9256	562	7099	32030
	(b) Cultivation of special crops, fruit, etc. (Planters, managers, clerks, and labourers)	**1330**	**64**	**303**	**4**	**416**	**4**	**845**	**4725**
18	Market gardeners, flower and fruit growers ..	1330	64	303	4	416	4	845	4725
	(c) Forestry	**1611**	**5**	**718**	**2**	**4374**	**5**	**1261**	**5556**
19	Forest officers, rangers, guards, etc. ..	1345	3	680		397		366	4901
20	Woodcutters and charcoal burners ..	161	2	10	2	3388	3	630	512
21	Collectors of forest produce	105		28		589	2	265	143
	(d) Stock raising	**8343**	**352**	**2454**	**94**	**5447**	**128**	**7280**	**25842**
23	Breeders and keepers of cattle and buffaloes for milk production	1458	36	719	5	591	103	1061	4203
24	Breeders and keepers of cattle and buffaloes for other purposes	1831	104	366	22	721	5	1167	5888
25	Herdsmen, shepherds and breeders of other animals	5054	212	1369	67	4135	20	5052	15751
	(e) Raising of small animals and insects	**35**		**130**		**2984**	**2**	**195**	**118**
27	Birds, bees, etc.	7						1	45
28	Silkworms	28		130		2984	2	194	73
	Order 2—Fishing and Hunting ..	**827**	**8**	**297**		**854**	**4**	**817**	**3537**
30	Fishing and Pearling	770	8	294		788	4	799	3331
31	Hunting	57		3		66		18	206

VIII—PART I—MEANS OF LIVELIHOOD—GENERAL TABLE—STATE SUMMARY—Contd.

Group No.	Means of Livelihood	P		PS		S		PD	TD
		M	F	M	F	M	F	P	P
1	2	3	4	5	6	7	8	9	10
	CLASS A—PRODUCTION OF RAW MATERIALS—contd.								
	Sub-class II—Exploitation of Minerals ..	**57**		**17**	**2**	**31**		**102**	**236**
	Order 3—Metallic Minerals ..	**55**		**17**	**2**	**28**		**102**	**208**
32	Gold	49		16	2	28		98	121
33	Iron	6		1					33
37	Other metallic minerals							4	54
	Order 4—Non-metallic Minerals ..	**2**				**3**			**28**
44	Other non-metallic minerals	2				3			28
	CLASS B—PREPARATION AND SUPPLY OF MATERIAL SUBSTANCES ..	**85091**	**5772**	**24898**	**1244**	**61225**	**1919**	**130016**	**286509**
	Sub-class III—Industry	**57692**	**5219**	**17782**	**1185**	**39820**	**1566**	**122638**	**191568**
	Order 5—Textiles	**7341**	**4169**	**2236**	**1048**	**8316**	**1129**	**107453**	**32938**
45	Cotton ginning, cleaning and pressing ..	189	6	54		311		32	453
46	Cotton spinning	734	2389	260	695	854	695	50801	10390
47	Cotton sizing and weaving	1349	420	786	26	2293	24	1830	5960
49	Jute spinning and weaving	131	170	48	4	140	30	2363	1274
50	Rope, twine and string	232		72		70		56	429
51	Hemp and flax spinning and weaving ..	57	2	12		100		43	300
52	Other fibres (coconut, aloes, straw, linseed) ..						1	71	
53	Wool carding and spinning	265	972	46	308	360	310	37658	2055
54	Wool weaving	1834	67	448	13	2607	59	3387	5387
55	Woollen carpet weaving	668	1	224	1	213	3	158	1882
56	Silk spinning and weaving	421	10	128		352		139	1037
58	Dyeing and bleaching, preparation and sponging of textiles	639	7	81	1	306		121	1611
59	Calico printing	31		8				6	77
60	Hosiery works	55	11	8		150		60	250
61	Lace, crepe, embroideries, fringes, etc., and insufficiently described textile industries ..	736	114	61		560	7	10728	1833
	Order 6—Hides, skins and hard materials from the animal kingdom ..	**4902**	**72**	**2010**	**35**	**4549**	**72**	**1483**	**16682**
62	Tanners, curriers, leather dressers and leather dyers, etc.	259		52		397		31	860
63	Makers of leather articles such as trunks, water bags, saddlery and harness, etc., excluding boots and shoes	212		34		231		9	1447
64	Boots, shoes, sandal and clog makers ..	3838	72	1823	35	3755	72	1356	13727
65	Furriers and persons occupied with feathers and bristles ; brush makers	572		95		156		86	589
66	Bone, ivory, horn, shell, etc., workers except buttons	21		6		10		1	59
	Order 7—Wood	**6216**	**157**	**2880**	**24**	**6623**	**35**	**3249**	**21167**
67	Sawyers	433	1	1122		1607		533	3612
68	Carpenters, turners and joiners	3825	1	1320		3724	6	999	12632
69	Veneer and plywood makers	6				2			16
70	Match Veneer and splint makers ..	71		8		9		6	122
71	Basket makers and other industries of woody materials, including leaves, and thatchers and builders working with bamboo, reeds or similar materials	1881	15	430	24	1281	29	1711	4785

VIII—PART I—MEANS OF LIVELIHOOD—GENERAL TABLE—STATE SUMMARY—CONTD.

Group No.	Means of Livelihood	P M	P F	PS M	PS F	S M	S F	PD P	TD P
1	2	3	4	5	6	7	8	9	10
	CLASS B—PREPARATION AND SUPPLY OF MATERIAL SUBSTANCES—contd.								
	Sub-Class III—Industry—contd.								
	Order 8—Metals	**3380**	**15**	**1161**	**1**	**2655**	**21**	**819**	**10795**
72	Smelting, forging and rolling of iron and other metals	82		51		18		5	124
73	Makers of arms, guns, etc.	8		2		29		4	29
74	Blacksmiths, other workers in iron, makers of implements other than cutlers .. .	2563	12	1015	1	1672	18	599	8089
76	Workers in brass, copper, bronze and bell metal	482	1	51		851		123	1794
77	Workers in other metals(except precious metals)	245	2	42		85	3	88	759
	Order 9—Ceramics	**2861**	**94**	**81**	**23**	**1829**	**51**	**476**	**12907**
79	Potters and makers of earthenware ..	2620	91	3	21	1715	47	335	11488
80	Brick makers	200	2	50		34		87	640
82	Makers of porcelain and crockery ..	23	1	17		28	4	52	98
84	Makers of glass bangles, glass beads and necklaces, glass earstuds, etc.	3		4		52			519
85	Other workers in ceramics (mosaic, tile, plaster of Paris, mica, alabaster etc., works) ..	15		7	2			2	162
	Order 10—Chemical products properly so called and analogous ..	**1913**	**41**	**824**	**9**	**1895**	**27**	**618**	**6851**
86	Manufacture of matches, fireworks and other explosives	11				6		2	54
87	Manufacture of aerated and mineral waters and ice	33	4	6	3	2	5		97
88	Manufacture and refining of vegetable and hydrogenerated oils	1513	30	734	5	1830	19	512	5069
89	Manufacture and refining of mineral oils ..	127	7	21	1	40		46	649
90	Others (soap, candles, perfumes and toilet goods, etc.)	95		5		3		7	72
91	Manufacture of dyes, paints, colours, varnishes and inks	15				6	1	1	42
92	Manufacture of chemicals, drugs and other pharmaceutical goods	10		3				3	52
93	Manufacture of paper, cardboard and papier mache	107		51		5		47	729
94	Manufacture of shellac and lac products ..	2		4		3	2		87
	Order 11—Food Industries ..	**6887**	**155**	**1772**	**28**	**4058**	**91**	**1605**	**20320**
95	Rice pounders and huskers and flour grinders millers of cereals and pulses	1456	93	502	13	2410	31	441	3966
96	Grain parchers, etc.	31	2	4		8		47	555
97	Bakers and biscuit makers	2433	28	394	5	529	18	536	6627
98	Butchers	1303		225		415	1	229	4177
101	Sweatmeat, and condiment makers ..	649	19	201	2	79	30	84	1876
102	Butter, cheese and ghee makers	949	13	443	8	611	11	249	3009
105	Manufacturers of tobacco	48				6		4	70
106	Manufacturers of opium, ganja, etc. ..	18		2				11	40
107	Others			1				4	
	Order 12—Industries of dress and the toilet	**17505**	**399**	**5379**	**16**	**7813**	**103**	**5492**	**49230**
108	Tailors, milliners, dressmakers and darners ..	7479	208	3028	4	3689	80	2331	19075
109	Embroiderers, hat, cap and turban makers ..	5165	3	942	1	26		1815	15430
110	Other industries pertaining to dress (garters, belts, buttons, umbrellas, canes etc.) ..	1							1
111	Washing and cleaning ..	1666	187	326	11	752	23	573	4798
112	Barbers, hairdressers and wig-makers ..	3182		1076		3346		773	9894
113	Other industries connected with the toilet (tattooers, shampooers and bath houses etc.)	12	1	7					32

Group No.	Means of Livelihood.	P M	P F	PS M	PS F	S M	S F	PD P	TD P
1	2	3	4	5	6	7	8	9	10
	CLASS B—PREPARATION AND SUPPLY OF MATERIAL SUBSTANCES—contd.								
	Sub-class III—Industry—concld.								
	Order 13—Furniture Industries ..	**13**		**2**				**1**	**70**
114	Cabinet makers, carriage painters, etc. ..	13		2				1	70
	Order 14—Building Industries ..	**2832**	**2**	**509**		**1015**	**11**	**571**	**7377**
116	Lime burners and cement workers ..	4				1		1	6
117	Excavators and well sinkers ..	321		76		145	1	126	716
118	Stone cutters and dressers ..	355		118		92	2	91	905
119	Brick layers and masons	1310	2	187		519	6	250	3633
120	Builders (other than buildings made of bamboo or similar materials)	622		99		256	2	101	1324
121	House decorators, painters and plumbers ..	220		29		2		2	793
	Order 15—Construction of means of transport	**11**						**2**	**73**
122	Persons engaged in making, assembling or repairing motor vehicles or cycles ..	11						2	73
	Order 16—Production and transmission of physical force ..	**154**		**46**	**1**	**21**		**1**	**402**
125	Heat, light, electricity, motive power etc., gas works and electric light and power ..	144		38	1	21		1	325
126	Electrical Engineers ..	10		8					77
	Order 17—Miscellaneous and undefined Industries ..	**3677**	**115**	**882**		**1046**	**26**	**868**	**12766**
127	Printers, lithographers and engravers ..	97		118		30		47	615
128	Bookbinders and stichers	57		3				5	164
129	Makers of musical instruments ..	10		3		3			25
130	Makers of watches, clocks, optical, photographic and mathematical instruments, etc.	91		13		11		14	620
131	Workers in precious stones	154		14		13		49	492
132	Workers in precious metals, makers of jewellery and ornaments, enamellers, gilders etc. ..	2824	7	666		827	8	611	9073
133	Film producers			1					
134	Toy, kite, cage, fishing tackle, etc., makers, taxidermists, etc.	7							34
136	Scavenging	437	108	64		162	18	142	1733
	Sub-class IV—Transport	**6977**	**141**	**2274**	**12**	**8208**	**85**	**2148**	**21702**
	Order 18—Transport by air ..	**4**		**1**					**19**
137	Persons concerned with aerodromes and aeroplanes	4		1					19

VIII—PART I—MEANS OF LIVELIHOOD—GENERAL TABLE—STATE SUMMARY—CONTD.

Group No.	Means of Livelihood	P M	P F	PS M	PS F	S M	S F	PD P	TD P
1	2	3	4	5	6	7	8	9	10
	CLASS B—PREPARATION AND SUPPLY OF MATERIAL SUBSTANCES—contd.								
	Sub-class IV—Transport—concld.								
	Order 19—Transport by water	**1839**	**106**	**348**		**548**	**8**	**576**	**7142**
138	Ship-owners, boat-owners and their employees, officers, mariners etc. Ship brokers boat-men and towmen	1499	103	251		419	8	493	5781
139	Persons (other than labourers) employed in harbours, docks, rivers and canals, including pilots	48		26		4		8	493
140	Labourers employed on harbours, docks, rivers and canals	292	3	71		125		75	868
	Order 20—Transport by road ..	**4427**	**33**	**1884**	**12**	**7210**	**76**	**1482**	**11402**
141	Persons (other than labourers) employed on the construction and maintenance of roads and bridges	155		58		663	4	44	564
142	Labourers employed on roads and bridges ..	1187	12	881	11	1964	38	535	2406
143	Owners, managers and employees (excluding personal servants) connected with mechanically driven vehicles (including trams) ..	610		205		96		36	1685
144	Owners, managers and employees (excluding personal servants) connected with other vehicles	808	11	138		714	14	189	2121
145	Palki, etc., bearers and owners		1	27		11		11	51
146	Pack elephant, camel, mule, ass and bullock, owners and drivers	1644	5	571		3707	20	608	4413
147	Porters and messengers	23	4	4	1	55		59	162
	Order 21—Transport by rail ..	**167**	**2**	**32**		**108**	**1**	**46**	**823**
148	Railway employees of all kinds other than coolies	64		21		34		13	403
149	Labourers employed on railway construction and maintenance, and coolies, and porters employed on railway premises	103	2	11		74	1	33	420
	Order 22—Post Office, Telegraph and Telephone Services ..	**540**		**9**		**342**		**44**	**2316**
150	Post Office, Telegraph, Telephone and Wireless services	540		9		342		44	2316
	Sub-class V—Trade ..	**20422**	**412**	**4842**	**47**	**13197**	**268**	**5230**	**73239**
	Order 23—Banks, establishments of credit, exchange and insurance ..	**1316**	**27**	**534**	**13**	**1357**	**47**	**163**	**5395**
151	Officers, employees, etc., of joint stock banks and co-operative banks	309		81		47		19	1201
152	Munims, agents or employees of indigenous banking firms	81	2	7		39		8	312
153	Individua' moneylenders	915	25	438	13	1261	47	135	3715
154	Exchange and insurance agents, money changers and brokers and their employees ..	11		8		10		1	167
	Order 24—Brokerage commission and export	**147**		**27**		**5**		**4**	**508**
155	Brokers, commission agents, commercial travellers, warehouse owners and employees ..	147		27		5		4	508

VIII—PART I—MEANS OF LIVELIHOOD—GENERAL TABLE—STATE SUMMARY—Contd.

Group No.	Means of Livelihood	P M	P F	PS M	PS F	S M	S F	PD P	TD P
1	2	3	4	5	6	7	8	9	10
	CLASS B—PREPARATION AND SUPPLY OF MATERIAL SUBSTANCES—contd.								
	Sub-class V—Trade—contd.								
	Order 25—Trade in textiles ..	**970**	**9**	**10**		**382**	**7**	**272**	**7832**
156	Trade in piece-goods, wool, cotton, Jute, silk, hair and other textiles	970	9	10		382	7	272	7832
	Order 26—Trade in skins, leather and furs	**118**	**1**	**25**		**92**	**28**	**24**	**966**
157	Trade in hides, skins, leather, furs. feathers, horn, etc. and the articles made from these	118	1	25		92	28	24	966
	Order 27—Trade in wood ..	**108**	**4**	**76**		**422**		**56**	**2045**
158	Trade in wood (not fire-wood)	89	4	73		420		55	1971
159	Trade in bark, bamboos, canes, thatches and other forest produce	19		3		2		1	74
	Order 28—Trade in metals ..	**53**		**5**		**35**		**18**	**194**
160	Trade in metals, machinery knives, tools, etc.	53		5		35		18	194
	Order 29—Trade in pottery, bricks and tiles ..	**26**	**4**	**35**	**2**	**134**	**2**	**16**	**318**
161	Trade in pottery, bricks and tiles	26	4	35	2	134	2	16	318
	Order 30—Trade in chemical products ..	72	**3**	48	**1**	32		**16**	**1033**
162	Drugs, dyes, paints, petroleum, kerosine, explosive etc.	72	3	48	1	32		16	1033
	Order 31—Hotels, cafes, restaurants, etc.	**520**	**9**	**56**	**4**	**101**	**2**	**47**	**836**
163	Vendors of wine, liquors, aerated waters and ice	165	4	13	4	7	1	7	266
164	Owners and managers of hotels, cook-shops, sarais etc., (and employees)	324	5	39		53	1	27	523
165	Hawkers of drink anf food stuffs ..	31		4		41		13	47
	Order 32—Other trade in food stuffs ..	9759	278	1778	9	5785	136	2593	30172
166	Dealers in unprepared grain, seeds and pulses	123	4	80		189		38	600
167	Dealers in floor (ata, etc.) and prepared grain and pulses	1513	26	233	5	781	4	243	4026
168	Dealers in sweatmeats, sugar and spices ..	2512	24	23	2	1651	20	646	9011
169	Dealers in dairy products, eggs and poultry ..	2038	28	639	1	1500	86	443	5639
170	Dealers in animals for food	359		16		37		83	627
171	Dealers in fodder for animals	315	4	41	1	179	6	119	1248
172	Dealers in fruits and vegetables	1261	65	194		716	6	397	3778
173	Dealers in other food stuffs	1464	124	522		482	4	556	4473
174	Dealers in tobacco	110		24		129		15	526
175	Dealers in opium	3	1	2					20
176	Dealers in Ganja . ..	61	2	4		121	10	53	224

VIII—PART I—MEANS OF LIVELIHOOD—GENERAL TABLE—STATE SUMMARY—CONTD.

Group No.	Means of Livelihood	P M	P F	PS M	PS F	S M	S F	PD P	TD P
1	2	3	4	5	6	7	8	9	10
	CLASS B—PREPARATION AND SUPPLY OF MATERIAL SUBSTANCES—concld.								
	Sub-class V—Trade—contd.								
	Order 33—Trade in clothing and toilet articles	**139**		**5**		**83**	**1**	**9**	**1030**
177	Trade in ready-made-clothing and other articles of dress and the toilet (hats, umbrellas, socks, ready-made shoes, perfumes, etc.)	139		5		83	1	9	1030
	Order 34—Trade in furniture ..	**107**		**9**		**11**		**9**	**357**
178	Trade in furniture, carpets, curtains and bedding	85		9		11		6	239
179	Hardware, cooking utensils, porcelain, crockery glassware, bottles, articles for gardening, etc.	22						3	118
	Order 35—Trade in building materials ..	**20**		**5**		**20**			**33**
180	Trade in building materials (other than bricks, tiles, and woody materials)	20		5		20			33
	Order 36—Trade in means of transport	**377**	**5**	**79**		**414**	**3**	**82**	**854**
181	Dealers and hirers of mechanical, transport, motors, cycles, etc.	33		5		18			85
182	Dealers and hirers of other carriages, carts, boats, etc.	13		10				5	80
183	Dealers and hirers of elephants, camels, horses, cattle, asses, mules, etc.	331	5	64		396	3	77	689
	Order 37—Trade in fuel ..	**382**	**36**			**491**	**7**	**246**	**1609**
184	Dealers in firewood, charcoal, coal, cowdung, etc.	382	36			491	7	246	1609
	Order 38—Trade in articles of luxury and those pertaining to letters and the arts and sciences ..	**547**	**2**	**133**	**1**	**104**		**121**	**2039**
185	Dealers in precious stones, jewellery (real and imitation), clocks, optical instruments, etc.	236		29				5	494
186	Dealers in common bangles, bead neklaces, fans, small articles, toys, hunting and fishing tackle, flowers, etc.	182	2	72		88		88	1174
187	Publishers, booksellers, stationers, dealers in music, pictures, musical instruments, wireless sets and curiosities	125		29	1	13		25	348
188	Film distributors	4		3		3		3	23
	Order 39—Trade of other sorts .	**5761**	**34**	**2017**	**17**	**3729**	**35**	**1554**	**18018**
189	Dealers in rags, stable refuse, etc. ..	16		2		1		3	147
190	General storekeepers and shopkeepers otherwise unspecified	4524	23	1879	16	3386	31	1263	14935
191	Itinerant traders, pedlars, and hawkers (of other than food, etc.)	651	5	106	1	191	2	112	1687
192	Other trades (including farmers of pounds, tools and markets)	570	6	30		151	2	176	1249

VIII—PART I—MEANS OF LIVELIHOOD—GENERAL TABLE—STATE SUMMARY—Contd.

Group No.	Means of Livelihood	P M	P F	PS M	PS F	S M	S F	PD P	TD P
1	2	3	4	5	6	7	8	9	10
	CLASS C—PUBLIC ADMINISTRATION AND LIBERAL ARTS ..	**29443**	**1006**	**12289**	**251**	**13649**	**91**	**3563**	**90526**
	Sub-class VI—Public Force	**7341**		**5248**	**5**	**2876**	**5**	**591**	**19130**
	Order 40—Army	**3792**		**3570**		**1075**		**159**	**9610**
193	Army (Imperial)	1917		1923		202		4	936
194	Army (Indian States)	1875		1647		873		155	8674
	Order 43—Police	**3549**		**1678**	**5**	**1801**	**5**	**432**	**9520**
197	Police	2745		1143		674	4	197	6382
198	Village watchmen	804		535	5	1127	1	235	3138
	Sub-class VII—Public Administration ..	**9996**	**108**	**2898**	**5**	**4408**	**16**	**815**	**32060**
	Order 44—Public Administration ..	**9996**	**108**	**2898**	**5**	**4408**	**16**	**815**	**32060**
199	Servants of the State (*i. e.*, of the Imperial British India or Provincial Governments) ..	2182	28	461	4	601	7	215	6407
200	Servants of Indian States ..	5832	19	1551		859	1	336	19780
202	Municipal and other local (not village) service	1119	60	175	1	184	1	70	2802
203	Village officials and servants other than watchmen	863	1	711		2764	7	194	3071
	Sub-class VIII—Professions and Liberal Arts	**12106**	**898**	**4143**	**241**	**6365**	**70**	**2157**	**39336**
	Order 45—Religion	**6160**	**156**	**2167**	**227**	**4494**	**59**	**1320**	**19710**
204	Priests, ministers, etc.	4477	70	1719	207	3563	37	984	14364
205	Monks, nuns, religious mendicants ..	250	14	62	10	222	2	35	653
206	Other religious workers	1093	67	292	10	576	14	274	3370
207	Servants in religious edifices, burial and burning grounds, pilgrim conductors, circumcisors, etc.	340	5	94		133	6	27	1323
	Order 46—Law	**816**		**483**		**126**		**54**	**2941**
208	Lawyers of all kinds including Qazis, Law Agents and Mukhtiars	405		100		32		29	1428
209	Lawyers' clerks, petition-writers, etc. ..	411		383		94		25	1513
	Order 47—Medicine	**1372**	**179**	**335**	**3**	**690**	**5**	**208**	**4950**
210	Registered medical practitioners including oculists	363	14	83	1	128	1	36	1441
211	Other persons practising the healing arts without being registered	535	3	144		487	4	109	1875
212	Dentists	18	6	4		6			89
213	Midwives, vaccinators, compounders, nurses, masseurs, etc.	402	156	93	2	65		59	1357
214	Veterinary Surgeons	54		11		4		4	188
	Order 48—Instruction	**3168**	**558**	**1037**	**9**	**566**	**3**	**456**	**10176**
215	Professors and teachers of all kinds ..	2949	523	986	9	474	2	415	9367
216	Clerks and servants connected with education	219	35	51		92	1	41	809

VIII—PART I—MEANS OF LIVELIHOOD—GENERAL TABLE—STATE SUMMARY—Contd.

Group No.	Means of Livelihood	P M	P F	PS M	PS F	S M	S F	PD P	TD P
1	2	3	4	5	6	7	8	9	10
	CLASS C—PUBLIC ADMINISTRATION AND LIBERAL ARTS—concld.								
	Sub-class VIII—Professions and Liberal Arts—concld.								
	Order 49—Letters, arts and sciences (other than 44)) ..	**590**	**5**	**121**	**2**	**489**	**3**	**119**	**1559**
217	Public scribes, stenographers, etc. ..	40		18	2	5		1	104
218	Architects, surveyors, engineers, and their employees (not being State servants) ..	23		3		6		2	63
219	Authors, editors, journalists and photographers	107		16		3		15	244
200	Artists, sculptors and image-makers ..	17	1	1		6		2	75
221	Scientists (astronomers, botanists, etc.) ..	8		7		4		1	74
222	Horscope casters, astrologers, fortune-tellers, wizards, witches and mediums ..	81		7		160		5	232
223	Musicians (composers and performers other than military), actors, dancers etc. ..	259	3	63		287		86	654
224	Managers and employees of places of public entertainment, race courses, societies, clubs	22				5			41
225	Conjurors, acrobats, recitors, exhibitors of curiosities and wild animals etc. ..	33	1	6		13	3	7	72
	CLASS D—MISCELLANEOUS ..	**34965**	**3087**	**5244**	**334**	**18577**	**315**	**8441**	**128648**
	Sub-class IX—Persons living on their income	**2629**	**163**	**322**	**1**	**6144**	**122**	**298**	**10951**
	Order 50—Persons living principally on their income ..	**2629**	**163**	**322**	**1**	**6144**	**122**	**298**	**10951**
226	Proprietors (other than of agricultural land) fund and scholarships holders and pensioners	2629	163	322	1	6144	122	298	10951
	Sub-class X—Domestic Service, ..	**11129**	**1316**	**1651**	**123**	**2630**	**80**	**3237**	**15975**
	Order 51—Domestic Service ..	**11129**	**1316**	**1651**	**123**	**2630**	**80**	**3237**	**15975**
227	Private motor-drivers and cleaners ..	378		49		152		93	1494
228	Other domestic service	10751	1316	1602	123	2478	80	3144	14481
	Sub-class XI—Insufficiently described occupation	**16480**	**771**	**3222**	**57**	**8940**	**92**	**3975**	**41567**
	Order 52—General terms which do not indicate a definite occupation ..	**16480**	**771**	**3222**	**57**	**8940**	**92**	**3975**	**41567**
229	Manufacturers, businessmen and contractors otherwise unspecified	2930	29	669	6	1175	54	557	8962
230	Cashiers, accountants, book-keepers, clerks, and other employees in unspecified offices and warehouses and shops	3070	51	422	1	478	4	402	5920
231	Mechanics otherwise unspecified	121	132	4		8	1	41	750
232	Labourers and workmen otherwise unspecified	10350	559	2127	50	7279	33	2975	25935
	Sub-class XII—Unproductive	**4727**	**837**	**49**	**153**	**863**	**21**	**931**	**60155**
	Order 53—Inmates of jails, asylums and alms houses	**270**	**2**	**19**		**1**		**20**	**2402**
233	Inmates of jails, asylums and alms houses ..	270	2	19		1		20	2402

VIII—PART I—MEANS OF LIVELIHOOD—GENERAL TABLE—STATE SUMMARY—Concld.

Group No.	Means of Livelihood	P M	P F	PS M	PS F	S M	S F	PD P	TD P
1	2	3	4	5	6	7	8	9	10
	CLASS D—MISCELLANEOUS.—concld.								
	Sub-class XII—Unproductive—concld.								
	Order 54—Beggars, vagrants ..	**4357**	**835**	**30**	**41**	**862**	**19**	**911**	**14543**
234	Beggars and vagrants	4357	835	30	41	862	19	911	14543
	Order 55—Other unclassified non-productive industries ..	**100**			**112**		**2**		**43210**
235	Other unclassified non-productive industries	100			112		2		56
236	Enumeration slips without clear answer to the questions on which the table is based ..								43154

Note.—No figures for Gilgit Agency were available for this Table.

IMPERIAL TABLE IX

Industry

NOTES

1. No Imperial Table was compiled for Industry at the 1931 Census; the corresponding table in the 1931 report is State Table VI. The table now compiled and produced does not give a correct picture of Industry in the State and it should not be used for statistical purposes.

2. The industries have been classified in accordance with the lists received from the Census Commissioner for India; those against which there were no entries have been omitted from the table

3. The table is based on the answers to census questions Nos. 14 and 16 which read as follows:—

14. What is your means of livelihood?

16. If you are employed by someone else what is his business?

These questions were very poorly answered; in many cases they were not answered at all. The response was also poor to the special enquiries made in 1931 and State Table VI for 1931 is also unreliable for statistical purposes. Some specific reasons may be given for declaring the present table useless for statistical purposes.

(i) Sixteen industries shown in the table for 1931 do not appear in the present table at all although they are all known to exist. For instance: cotton-printing, papier machie, lime works, toy factories, hydro-electric works, waterworks, and tent factories.

(ii) The figures given against all industries are ridiculously small. Under 'Textiles' the total population employed in the silk industry is shown as 515 and in wool carding, spinning and weaving 82; we know that thousands are employed in these industries.

The figures under 'Wood' are equally ridiculous. The extraction of timber is one of the biggest industries in the State and provides employment for thousands; the total for all categories is shown as 135.

(iii) Under group III 8 persons are shown as rearing silk worms; we know that over 60,000 persons are so employed.

(iv) Many industries are not shown at all such as :—
Group V—mines and quarries—stone quarries are numerous; group VI—Textiles—none are shown as employed in rope-making. Under group VII none are shown under Taxidermy although there are a number of taxidermists in Srinagar City. Under group XI four persons are shown as employed in making matches, one as a supervisor and three as clerks; there are no operatives shown at all. Santonin extraction is not shown at all. There are factories at Baramulla both for the manufacture of matches and the extraction of santonin. Sufficient examples have been given to justify condemnation of the table.

4. It would have saved space and printing to have omitted this table altogether but it was thought better to produce it if only to show how bad it is so that the subject may receive special attention at the next census. It is doubted, however, if the census agency is suitable for getting reliable detailed information regarding industries.

NOTE.—P stands for Persons, M for Males and F for Females.

IX—INDUSTRY

Industry	Total population engaged			Directional, Supervising and Clerical Staff: Managers		Supervising & Technical		Clerical			Welfare, Doctors, Compounders, Schoolmasters etc.		Operatives: Child (less than 15)		Youth (15-16)		Adult (17 & over)	
				Indian	Other	Indian	Other	Indian	Other		Indian	Other						
	P	M	F						M	F			M	F	M	F	M	F
1	*2*	*3*	*4*	*5*	*6*	*7*	*8*	*9*	*10*	*11*	*12*	*13*	*14*	*15*	*16*	*17*	*18*	*19*
I—Agricultural, pastoral, dairy and farm produce	**16**	**15**	**1**	**9***											**1**		**6**	
Dairying ..	**14**	13	1	9*											1		4	
Poultry Farms ..	**2**	2															2	
III—Raising of small animals and insects ..	**8**	**8**															**8**	
Silkworms ..	**8**	8															8	
VI—Textiles ..	**984**	**979**	**5**	**11**		**19**		**84**	**1**				**31**		**137**		**696**	**5**
Cotton spinning and weaving ..	**24**	24		1				3					1		3		16	
Cotton carpet weaving	**2**	2		1													1	
Wool carding, spinning and weaving..	**82**	82				2		26					1		2		51	
Woollen carpet weaving ..	**204**	204		1				5	1				7		77		113	
Silk ..	**515**	510	5	7		15		50							5		433	5
Lace and Embroidery	**154**	154		1		2							22		50		79	
Shawl and fringe weaving ..	**2**	2															2	
Hosiery ..	**1**	1															1	
VII—Hides, skins and hard materials from the animal kingdom ..	**15**	**15**		**2**				**1**					**1**				**11**	
Tanneries ..	**2**	2						1									1	
Leather and leather dyeing ..	**4**	4		2													2	
Boots and shoes ..	**9**	9											1				8	
VIII—Wood ..	**253**	**253**		**15**	**1**	**15**	**1**	**88**					**1**		**2**		**130**	
Extraction of timber and timber yards..	**135**	135		5	1	4		81							1		43	
Furniture ..	**12**	12		5											1		6	
Match veneer and splint making	**78**	78		1		10	1	7					1				58	
Sawmills ..	**9**	9															9	
Willow works ..	**16**	16		4		1											11	
Cane and baskets ..	**3**	3															3	
IX—Metals ..	**19**	**19**		**1**		**2**		**1**							**1**		**14**	
Iron and steel ..	**7**	7						1							1		4	
Steel trunks ..	**1**	1															1	
Brass, copper, bronze, tin and bell metal	**1**	1															1	
Jewellery and ornaments of gold and silver	**10**	10				2											8	
X—Ceramics ..	**1**	**1**															**1**	
Bricks ..	**1**	1															1	

*Includes 1 female.

IX—INDUSTRY—CONTD.

Industry	Total population engaged			Directional, Supervising and Clerical Staff: Managers		Supervising & Technical		Clerical			Welfare, Doctors, Compounders, Schoolmasters etc.		Operatives: Child (less than 15)		Youth (15 16)		Adult (17 & over)	
				Indian	Other	Indian	Other	Indian	Other		Indian	Other						
	P	M	F						M	F			M	F	M	F	M	F
1	2	3	4	5	6	7	8	9	10	11	12	13	14	15	16	17	18	19
XI—Chemical products, properly so called and analogous ..	**100**	**100**		**6**		**9**	**1**	**15**							**2**		**67**	
Matches ..	**4**	4				1		3										
Aerated water ..	**9**	9															9	
Oil Mills ..	**16**	16				1	1	5									9	
Manufacture and refining of mineral oils ..	**12**	12													1		11	
Resin and Turpentine	**35**	35				7		6									22	
Paint and varnish ..	**19**	19		2											1		16	
Soap ..	**3**	3		3														
Chemicals, drugs, antiseptics and pharmaceutical works generally ..	**2**	2		1				1										
XII—Food ..	**81**	**81**		**22**		**1**							**1**		**22**		**35**	
Rice pounding and husking ..	**26**	26													12		14	
Flour grinding ..	**9**	9		1									1		1		6	
Biscuits ..	**1**	1															1	
Bakeries, Confectioneries, etc. ..	**39**	39		20											8		11	
Slaughter houses ..	**2**	2													1		1	
Fruit canning, fruit juice, etc. ..	**4**	4		1		1											2	
XIII—Narcotics ..	**3**	**3**				**1**		**1**									**1**	
Tobacco, snuff, biris and cigarettes ..	**3**	3				1		1									1	
XIV—Dress and Toilet ..	**306**	**305**	**1**	**7**		**2**		**1**					**34**		**41**		**220**	**1**
Tailoring ..	**133**	132	1	7		2							4		6		113	1
Hats and caps ..	**171**	171						1					29		35		106	
Re-dyeing and cleaning ..	**2**	2											1				1	
XV—Building ..	**145**	**145**		**1**		**14**		**6**					**2**		**1**		**121**	
Stone and marble ..	**3**	3															3	
Cement and concrete	**142**	142		1		14		6					2		1		118	
XVI—Construction assembly and repair of means of transport ..	**137**	**137**		**6**		**9**		**2**							**3**		**117**	
Bicycles ..	**4**	4		2				1									1	
Motor cars ..	**99**	99		4				1									94	
Railways ..	**34**	34				9									3		22	

IX—INDUSTRY—Concld.

Industry	Total population engaged			Directional, Supervising and Clerical Staff: Managers		Supervising & Technical		Clerical			Welfare, Doctors, Compounders, Schoolmasters etc.		Operatives: Child (less than 15)		Youth (15 16)		Adult (17 & over)	
				Indian	Other	Indian	Other	Indian	Other		Indian	Other						
	P	M	F						M	F			M	F	M	F	M	F
1	2	3	4	5	6	7	8	9	10	11	12	13	14	15	16	17	18	19
XVII—Production and Transmission of physical energy ..	**172**	**172**						**135**									**37**	
Telephone ..	**148**	148						117									31	
Telegraph ..	**24**	24						18									6	
XVIII—Electrical ..	**6**	**6**				**3**											**3**	
Electric Fans ..	**3**	3															3	
Electric fittings ..	**3**	3				3												
XIX—Stationery ..	**1**	**1**													**1**			
Ink ..	**1**	1													1			
XX—Miscellaneous and undefined ..	**28**	**27**	**1**	1*		**3**	**2**								**4**		**18**	
Printing and binding	**17**	17				3	2								3		11	
Photo, lithography & map producing ..	**4**	4															2	
Cinema film production ..	**5**	5															5	
Games and sports articles ..	**2**	1	1	1*											1			
XXI—Transport, mechanically driven vehicles ..	**70**	**70**		**61**		**1**		**4**									**4**	
Motor transport ..	**70**	70		61		1		4									4	

*Female.

IMPERIAL TABLE X

(i) Unemployment by age and locality for less or more than one year.

(ii) Educated unemployment.

NOTES

---

1. The corresponding table in the 1931 report was Imperial Table XII. On this occasion the information is presented in a different form. In 1931 figures were given for "Educated unemployment" only.

2. The total 'Educated unemployed' shown in 1931 was 289; on this occasion the figures given in Part II total 3837 including 200 persons with degrees.

3. The figures shown in the present tables cannot be regarded as giving a true picture of the actual position; they must be regarded as an under-statement. The uneducated classes are seldom entirely unemployed for long in the real meaning of the term; labour in the State is not organised and many in this class are under-employed rather than unemployed.

(ii) The figures shown for 'Educated unemployed' are far nearer the facts than those given in 1931 but it is probable the actual figures when the census was taken were nearer 5000 than 3837; it is thought that many actually unemployed have not so declared themselves.

4. Of the total 'Educated unemployed' 2675 or 70 per cent. belong to the Kashmir Province and 1069 or 28 per cent. to the Jammu Province. The maximum amount of educated unemployment in any district is found in Anantnag with 2066 or 54 per cent. of the total for the whole State. Srinagar City is situated in this district and contributes largely to the big percentage shown; the actual numbers for Srinagar are 1391 or more than 36 per cent. of the total for the whole State. The figures for Jammu City present a big contrast; only 133 educated persons belonging to Jammu City are shown as unemployed.

5. The table does not include the population of the Gilgit Agency. The figures were not compiled for that area but it may be stated that educated unemployment is negligible.

X—(i) UNEMPLOYMENT BY AGE AND LOCALITY FOR LESS ("LESS") OR MORE ("MORE") THAN ONE YEAR

District or State		Total unemployed	Age 16-20 Less	Age 16-20 More	Age 21-25 Less	Age 21-25 More	Age 26-30 Less	Age 26-30 More	Age 31-35 Less	Age 31-35 More	Age 36-40 Less	Age 36-40 More
1		*2*	*3*	*4*	*5*	*6*	*7*	*8*	*9*	*10*	*11*	*12*
JAMMU AND KASHMIR STATE	..	**5640**	**1016**	**1667**	**470**	**1394**	**195**	**546**	**73**	**168**	**40**	**71**
JAMMU PROVINCE	..	**1610**	**338**	**563**	**123**	**338**	**53**	**122**	**7**	**37**	**9**	**20**
(A) TOTAL DISTRICTS	..	*1145*	*259*	*391*	*78*	*257*	*35*	*88*	*6*	*18*	*5*	*8*
Jammu	..	**436**	93	143	33	102	19	36	1	5	2	2
Kathua	..	**50**	7	18	5	13	1	4	1	1		
Udhampur	..	**229**	36	101	14	54	8	11	2	2	1	
Reasi	..	**42**	9	15	1	9		4		4		
Mirpur	..	**388**	114	114	25	79	7	33	2	6	2	6
(B) **Total Jagirs**	..	*465*	*79*	*172*	*45*	*81*	*18*	*34*	*1*	*19*	*4*	*12*
Chenani Jagir	..	**1**				1						
Poonch Jagir	..	**464**	79	172	45	80	18	34	1	19	4	12
KASHMIR PROVINCE	..	**3860**	**621**	**1059**	**334**	**1034**	**133**	**411**	**65**	**123**	**30**	**50**
Baramulla	..	**1305**	341	259	125	262	91	111	36	45	21	14
Anantnag	..	**2244**	236	714	161	691	34	274	23	69	9	33
Muzaffarabad	..	**311**	44	86	48	81	8	26	6	9		3
FRONTIER DISTRICTS	..	**170**	**57**	**45**	**13**	**22**	**9**	**13**	**1**	**8**	**1**	**1**
Ladakh	..	**58**	26	12	2	7	5	2		2	1	1
Astore	..	**28**	5	10	5	5		1		2		
Gilgit (Leased Area)	..	**84**	26	23	6	10	4	10	1	4		
Gilgit Agency*	..											

*NOTE—Information for Gilgit Agency is not available.

X—(ii) EDUCATED UNEMPLOYMENT

Standard of Education	Total unemployed	Age 16-20	21-25	26-30	31-35	36-40
1	2	3	4	5	6	7
JAMMU AND KASHMIR STATE						
Literates	**1014**	559	267	130	41	17
Middle School	**1070**	564	352	101	36	17
Matriculates or S. L. C. ..	**1298**	557	549	143	34	15
Intermediate in Arts or Science	**255**	73	143	36	2	1
Degrees—						
Indian—						
Graduate in Arts or Science	**172**	30	105	36	1	
Post Graduate in Arts or Science	**8**		5	3		
Teaching	**1**		1			
Engineering ..						
Agriculture ..						
Veterinary ..	**2**		2			
Commerce ..						
Legal	**4**		2	2		
Medical	**1**		1			
Other (*e.g.* oriental) ..	**12**	2	7	2	1	
British ..						
American ..						
Continental ..						
Other Foreign ..						
JAMMU PROVINCE						
Literates	**463**	286	93	63	14	7
Middle School	**282**	188	75	15	3	1
Matriculates or S. L. C.	**245**	134	85	26		
Intermediate in Arts or Science	**30**	9	14	5	2	
Degrees— ..						
Indian—						
Graduate in Arts or Science	**34**	5	22	7		
Post Graduate in Arts or Science	**5**		4	1		
Teaching	**1**		1			
Legal	**2**		1	1		
Medical	**1**		1			
Other (*e.g.* oriental ..	**6**	1	4	1		
(a) Total Districts						
Literates	**280**	176	51	41	9	3
Middle School	**237**	160	62	12	3	
Matriculates or S. L. C. ..	**219**	116	78	25		
Intermediate in Arts or Science	**26**	8	13	3	2	
Degrees—						
Indian—						
Graduate in Arts or Science	**32**	5	22	5		
Post Graduate in Arts or Science	**4**		3	1		
Teaching	**1**		1			
Legal	**2**		1	1		
Other (*e.g.* oriental) ..	**5**	1	3	1		
JAMMU						
Literates	**76**	58	5	11	1	1
Middle School	**83**	53	24	5	1	
Matriculates or S. L. C. ..	**135**	67	50	18		
Intermediate in Arts or Science	**19**	7	9	2	1	

X—(ii) EDUCATED UNEMPLOYMENT—Contd.

Standard of Education	Total unemployed	Age 16-20	21-25	26-30	31-35	36-10
1	2	3	4	5	6	7
JAMMU—concld.						
Degrees—						
Indian—						
Graduate in Arts or Science ..	**28**	5	18	5		
Post Graduate in Arts or Science	**4**		3	1		
Teaching	**1**		1			
Legal	**1**		1			
Other (e.g. oriental) ..	**3**		2	1		
KATHUA						
Literates	**20**	10	6	3	1	
Middle School	**14**	9	4		1	
Matriculates or S. L. C. ..	**12**	5	6	1		
Intermediate in Arts or Science	**1**		1			
Degrees—						
Indian—						
Other (e.g. oriental) ..	**1**		1			
UDHAMPUR						
Literates	**56**	36	14	5		1
Middle School	**47**	31	11	4	1	
Matriculates or S. L. C. ..	**28**	13	11	4		
Intermediate in Arts or Science	**3**		3			
Degrees—						
Indian—						
Graduate in Arts or Science	**1**		1			
REASI						
Literates	**21**	8	4	5	4	
Middle School	**16**	12	3	1		
Matriculates or S. L. C. ..	**4**	3	1			
Degrees—						
Indian—						
Other (e.g. oriental) ..	**1**	1				
MIRPUR						
Literates	**107**	64	22	17	3	1
Middle School	**77**	55	20	2		
Matriculates or S. L. C. ..	**40**	28	10	2		
Intermediate in Arts or Science	**3**	1		1	1	
Degrees—						
Indian—						
Graduate in Arts or Science ..	**3**		3			
Legal	**1**			1		
(b) Total Jagirs						
Literates	**183**	110	42	22	5	4
Middle School ..	**45**	28	13	3		1
Matriculates or S. L. C. ..	**26**	18	7	1		
Intermediate in Arts or Science	**4**	1	1	2		

X—(ii) EDUCATED UNEMPLOYMENT—Contd.

Standard of Education	Total unemployed	Age				
		16-20	21-25	26-30	39-35	36-40
1	2	3	4	5	6	7
(b) Total Jagirs—concld.						
Degrees —						
Indian—						
Graduates in Arts or Science ..	2			2		
Post Graduate in Arts or Science	1		1			
Medical	1		1			
Other (*e.g.* oriental) ..	1		1			
CHENANI JAGIR						
Matriculates or S. L. C. ..	1		1			
POONCH JAGIR						
Literates	183	110	42	22	5	4
Middle School ..	45	28	13	3		1
Matriculates or S. L . C. ..	25	18	6	1		
Intermediate in Arts or Science	4	1	1	2		
Degrees—						
Indian—						
Graduate in Arts or Science ..	2			2		
Post Graduate in Arts or Science ..	1		1			
Medical ..	1		1			
Other (*e.g.* oriental) ..	1		1			
KASHMIR PPOVINCE						
Literates	499	235	171	61	24	8
Middle School	751	351	270	81	33	16
Matriculates or S. L. C. ..	1049	421	462	117	34	15
Intermediate in Arts or Science	225	64	129	31		1
Degrees-						
Indian—						
Graduate in Arts or Science ..	138	25	83	29	1	
Post Graduate in Arts or Science ..	3		1	2		
Veterinary	2		2			
Legal	2		1	1		
Other (*e.g.* oriental) ..	6	1	3	1	1	
BARAMULLA						
Literates	168	81	48	28	10	1
Middle School	130	57	56	10	5	2
Matriculates or S. L. C. ..	127	46	62	13	5	1
Intermediate in Arts or Science	6	5	1			
Degrees —						
Indian—						
Graduate in Arts or Science ..	5	1	4			
Other (*e.g.* oriental) ..	1		1			

X—(ii) EDUCATED UNEMPLOYMENT—CONTD.

Standard of Education	Total unemployed	Age 16-20	21-25	26-30	31-35	36-40
1	2	3	4	5	6	7
ANANTNAG						
Literates	**251**	114	93	24	13	7
Middle School	**568**	266	194	66	28	14
Matriculates or S. L .C. ..	**896**	364	388	103	27	14
Intermediate in Arts or Science	**214**	59	125	29		1
Degrees —						
Indian—						
Graduate in Arts or Science ..	**129**	23	78	27	1	
Post Graduate in Arts or Science ..	**3**		1	2		
Veterinary	**2**		2			
Legal	**2**		1	1		
Other (*e.g.* oriental) ..	**1**		1			
MUZAFFARABAD						
Literates	**80**	40	30	9	1	
Middle School	**53**	28	20	5		
Matriculates or S. L. C. ..	**26**	11	12	1	2	
Intermediate in Arts or Science	**5**		3	2		
Degrees—						
Indian—						
Graduate in Arts or Science ..	4	1	1	2		
Other (*e.g.* oriental) ..	4	1	1	1	1	
FRONTIER DISTRICTS						
Literates	**52**	38	3	6	3	2
Middle School	**37**	25	7	5		
Matriculates or S. L. C. ..	**4**	2	2			
LADAKH						
Literates	**38**	29	2	3	2	2
Middle School	**19**	9	6	4		
ASTORE						
Literates	**6**	4	1		1	
Middle School	**7**	5	1	1		
Matriculates or S. L. C. ..	**4**	2	2			
GILGIT (LEASED AREA)						
Literates	**8**	5		3		
Middle School ..	**11**	11				
GILGIT AGENCY						
JAMMU CITY						
Literates	**8**	7		1		
Middle School ..	**19**	13	4	1	1	
Matriculates or S. L. C. ..	**67**	30	26	11		
Intermediate in Arts or Science	**14**	6	6	1	1	

X—(ii) EDUCATED UNEMPLOYMENT—CONCLD.

Standard of Education	Total unemployed	Age 16-20	21-25	26-30	31-35	36-40
1	2	3	4	5	6	7
JAMMU CITY—concld.						
Degrees—						
Indian—						
Graduate in Arts or Science ..	**20**	2	14	4		
Post Graduate in Arts or Science	**3**		2	1		
Legal	1		1			
Other (e.g. oriental) ..	**1**		1			
SRINAGAR CITY						
Literates	**79**	25	45	5	3	1
Middle School	**266**	124	90	36	9	7
Matriculates or S. L. C. ..	**729**	291	316	91	22	9
Intermediate in Arts or Science	**188**	51	109	27		1
Degrees—						
Indian—						
Graduate in Arts or Science ..	**122**	22	73	26	1	
Post Graduate in Arts or Science	**2**			2		
Veterinary ..	**2**		2	1		
Legal	**2**		1			
Other (e. g. oriental) ..	**1**		1			

NOTE.—No figures for Gilgit Agency are available.

IMPERIAL TABLE XI AND ITS SUBSIDIARIES

Literacy by Community and Age

NOTES

1. The corresponding table in the 1931 Report is Imperial Table XIII. On that occasion the table was in three parts. The present table is in four parts; the figures for the whole State and for Provinces are given separately whereas in 1931 they were given together in Part I.

2. This table does not include the population of the Gilgit Agency (76526). The figures for that area were not compiled for this table. It may be stated that the standard of literacy in the Gilgit Agency is low actually and also in comparison with other districts in the State.

3. (i) All persons below 5 years of age are treated as illiterate as in 1931 but whereas in 1931 the age group 0-5 was shown in the table on this occasion it has been omitted as redundant.

(ii) In the 1931 table the last age group shown was for 20 and over; in the present table those aged 20 and over are split up into three groups.

(iii) The totals for 'Scheduled Castes' and 'Hindus' in column 3 of the table are shown as 133498 and 575456 respectively. These totals exclude the age group 0-5; inclusive of the age group 0-5 the totals will not agree with the totals in Table XIII but with those given in Table XIV. The reason is that 39072 Arya Samajists of Scheduled Castes origin were shown with 'Other Hindus' in Table XIII and with Scheduled Castes in Table XIV. Thus the total number of persons with Scheduled Castes origin is 152536 as shown in Table XIV and not 113464 as shown in Table XIII. When the defect in Table XIII was detected it was thought better to explain the position in the notes to the tables rather than to reconstruct Table XIII.

4. Those shown as literate in English in columns 12, 13 and 14 of the table are also included in the figures for literates given in columns 6, 7 and 8.

5. The figures for Christians have been shown under one head and not under four different heads. Practically all European Christians may be considered literate; the numbers of those describing themselves as Anglo-Indians at the census was negligible.

6. The census questions provided for an answer with regard to the script of literacy and the record was sorted for local comment. Owing to the script controversy, which was going on at the time of the census, the answers given were not in accordance with fact and are useless as a basis for discussion. They have been ignored because to use them would only give rise to misunderstanding.

7. (i) The total literates in the State excluding Gilgit Agency, are 238384 at this census representing 6.9 per cent. of the total population over five years of age given in the table (3421325), against 123386 (excluding Gilgit Agency) in 1931. The figure for Frontier Illaqas (Gilgit Agency) in 1931 was only 499.

(ii) In 1941 we have 47615 literate in English (excluding Gilgit Agency) against 19455 (excluding Gilgit Agency) in 1931. There were only 14 persons literate in English in the Gilgit Agency in 1931.

(iii) There are 202976 literate males at this census out of a total male population, over 5 years of age, of 1825402 (excluding Gilgit Agency) against 114321 (excluding Gilgit Agency) in 1931. The percentage for 1941 is 11.1. There were 486 literate males in the Gilgit Agency in 1931.

(iv) There are 35408 literate females at this census out of a total female population, over 5 years of age, of 1595923 (excluding Gilgit Agency) against 9065 (excluding Gilgit Agency) in 1931. The percentage for 1941 is 2.2. There were 13 literate females in the Gilgit Agency in 1931.

8. The figures for literacy given for the Buddhist community in this table and for the Ladakh District, where nearly all the Buddhists in the State live, are not reliable. Information received from reliable travellers, which has been confirmed by the District Census Officer, is to the effect that about 90 per cent. of adult Buddhists are literate in their own language—Boddhi or Bhotia of Ladakh which is a dialect of the Tibetan language. It seems clear that the local census agency considered, erroneously, that literacy in Bhotia did not count.

9. (i) There are 126819 literates in the Jammu Province giving a percentage of 7.4 to the total of the population of the province over 5 years of age (1714829).

(ii) Similar figures for the Kashmir Province are 105238 literates out of 1500423, giving 7 per cent.

(iii) In the Frontier Districts (excluding Gilgit Agency) there are 6327 literates out of 206073 which gives 3 per cent.

(iv) For the two cities the figures for the two main communities are :—

Place	Community	Persons	Literates	Percentage
Jammu	Hindu	26756	15163	56.6
	Muslim	13868	5580	40.2
Srinagar	Hindu	38024	23040	60.5
	Muslim	143037	17497	12.2

(v) The percentages of literacy for the main communities for the whole population over 5 years of age excluding Gilgit Agency are as follows :—

Community	Persons	Literates	Percentage
Muslims	2615491	110692	4
Hindus (including Scheduled Castes)	708954	106877	15
Sikhs	55815	17765	32
Buddhists	37153	1920	5
Scheduled Castes (Separately)	133498	2036	1.5

The figures for Buddhists are subject to the remarks wih respect to this community in para. 8 above.

10. **Subsidiary (i)**—

The proportion of literates per 10,000 of the population aged 5 and over was 409 in 1931.

11. **Subsidiary (ii)**—

(a) The figures are best for Jammu District followed by Anantnag. Ladakh makes the poorest showing but the remarks in para. 8 must be taken into consideration.

(b) Of the two cities the figures for Jammu are the better both as regards proportion of literates as well as for literate females.

(c) The progress of literacy is shown in the following table :—

	Literate per 1000		
	1941	1931	1921
State	70	41	26
Jammu Province	74	49	27
Kashmir Province ..	70	35	26
Frontier Districts (excluding Gilgit Agency)	31	25	19

12. **Subsidiary (iii)**—

(a) As there are no literacy figures available for Gilgit Agency the columns against this district have been left blank.

(b) The blanks under the Buddhist community against many districts mean that there are no Buddhists in such districts.

(c) The figures given in the corresponding table for 1931 are per thousand of the community population and not per ten thousand as shown at this census.

13. **Subsidiary (iv)**—

(a) Where there are blank spaces it is to be understood no figures are available.

(b) The figures for literacy in English in Anantnag District, which includes Srinagar City, are easily the best. This has been the case in previous censuses too.

(c) Jammu District which includes Jammu City, shows the best figures for females literate in English.

14. **Subsidiary (v)**—

(a) This subsidiary clearly shows the marked improvement in the decade 1931-41 as compared with 1921-31.

(b) The Chenani Jagir shows a fall from 120 per 1000 literates in 1931 to 68 per 1000 in 1941. Unfortunately, figures for 1921 are not available for comparison. The Chenani Jagir is backward educationally compared with all other districts in the Jammu and Kashmir Provinces and it seems obvious that the 1931 figures were inflated due to some unknown cause.

15. **Subsidiary (vi)**—

(a) The figures given in this table are based on data supplied by the Director of Education for 1941 and 1931 with the exception of those for Poonch Jagir, Gilgit (Leased Area) and Gilgit Agency. The data for Poonch Jagir was supplied by the Administrator, Poonch Jagir and for Gilgit (Leased Area) and Gilgit Agency by the Assistant Political Agent Gilgit.

(b) The figures given in the text of the 1931 Report and in the marginal table referring to the subject do not agree. The figures given for 1931 in the present report are based on information supplied by the Director of Education.

16. **Subsidiary (vii)**—

Persons shown as able to read only have been treated as partly literate; they have not been included in the tables with literates. This information has been produced in the form of a subsidiary because the subject is of local interest.

17. (i) Information is given below showing the number of newspapers in the State and the number of printing presses in 1931 and 1941. The information was obtained from the Publicity Department of the Chief Secretariat.

News papers and Printing presses—

(a) Newspapers during 1931 and 1941.

	1931 Number	1941 Number
Jammu & Kashmir State	1	44
Jammu Province	1	24
Kashmir Province		20
Frontier Districts		

(b) Printing Presses during 1931 and 1941.

	1931 Number	1941 Number
Jammu & Kashmir State	8	37
Jammu Province	4	22
Kashmir Province	4	15
Frontier Districts		

(ii) The first newspaper was published in the State in 1924 and the first press installed in 1912.

(iii) Local newspapers are mostly printed in the Persian (Urdu) script; a few are in English (Roman) and Hindi (Devanagri) scripts.

(iv) The circulation of newspapers is not known.

(v) No details are available regarding the publication of non-educational books in the State. The number is few but is increasing.

18. A 1/50 sample was extracted for this table. The comparative results are shown as a subsidiary. The table is confined to two age groups 5-30 and 30 and over for the main communities. To give greater detail did not seem necessary.

NOTE.—P stands for Persons, M for Males and F for Females.

XI—LITERACY BY COMMUNITY AND AGE (PART I—STATE SUMMARY)

Community	Age	Population: Total P	Total M	Total F	Literate P	Literate M	Literate F	Illiterate P	Illiterate M	Illiterate F	Literate in English P	Literate in English M	Literate in English F
1	2	3	4	5	6	7	8	9	10	11	12	13	14
JAMMU AND KASHMIR STATE													
Total Population	..	*3421325*	*1825402*	*1595923*	*238384*	*202976*	*35408*	*3182941*	*1622426*	*1560515*	*47615*	*45254*	*2361*
	5-10 ..	**573440**	301643	271797	**16489**	11924	4565	**556951**	289719	267232	**442**	374	68
	10-15 ..	**480444**	257721	222723	**36003**	28450	7553	**444441**	229271	215170	**5548**	5027	521
	15-20 ..	**399168**	210417	188751	**38127**	31442	6685	**361041**	178975	182066	**9787**	9080	707
	20-30 ..	**707662**	360375	347287	**60017**	51227	8790	**647645**	309148	338497	**16536**	15861	675
	30-50 ..	**883817**	478972	404845	**65670**	59158	6512	**818147**	419814	398333	**13127**	12816	311
	50 and over	**376794**	216274	160520	**22078**	20775	1303	**354716**	195499	159217	**2175**	2096	79
Scheduled Castes	..	*133498*	*71328*	*62170*	*2036*	*1827*	*209*	*131462*	*69501*	*61961*	*107*	*101*	*6*
	5-10 ..	**20542**	10622	9920	**128**	107	21	**20414**	10515	9899	**1**	1	
	10-15 ..	**17436**	9055	8381	**356**	310	46	**17080**	8745	8335	**15**	13	2
	15-20 ..	**14847**	7598	7249	**366**	328	38	**14481**	7270	7211	**32**	30	2
	20-30 ..	**27096**	13849	13247	**535**	479	56	**26561**	13370	13191	**45**	43	2
	30-50 ..	**35833**	19796	16087	**505**	463	42	**35378**	19333	16045	**12**	12	
	50 and over	**17694**	10408	7286	**146**	140	6	**17548**	10268	7280	**2**	2	
Hindu	..	*575456*	*308784*	*266672*	*104841*	*84310*	*20531*	*470615*	*224474*	*246141*	*28247*	*27051*	*1196*
	5-10 ..	**88430**	46235	42195	**7926**	5117	2809	**80504**	41118	39386	**275**	234	41
	10-15 ..	**74415**	38802	35613	**14613**	10355	4258	**59802**	28447	31355	**2800**	2502	298
	15-20 ..	**62113**	32282	29831	**14793**	11108	3685	**47320**	21174	26146	**4875**	4498	377
	20-30 ..	**113332**	58733	54599	**25311**	20178	5133	**88021**	38555	49466	**9401**	9071	330
	30-50 ..	**156755**	86716	70039	**30967**	27052	3915	**125788**	59664	66124	**9300**	9157	143
	50 and over	**80411**	46016	34395	**11231**	10500	731	**69180**	35516	33664	**1596**	1589	7
Muslim	..	*2615491*	*1395093*	*1220398*	*110692*	*101051*	*9641*	*2504799*	*1294042*	*1210757*	*16467*	*15697*	*770*
	5-10 ..	**448327**	236393	211934	**6954**	5727	1227	**441373**	230666	210707	**93**	82	11
	10-15 ..	**375167**	202916	172251	**18072**	15744	2328	**357095**	187172	169923	**2393**	2216	177
	15-20 ..	**310830**	164885	145945	**20036**	17937	2099	**290794**	146948	143846	**4317**	4048	269
	20-30 ..	**548766**	278706	270060	**29202**	26927	2275	**519564**	251779	267785	**6207**	5962	245
	30-50 ..	**667055**	359609	307446	**28168**	26711	1457	**638837**	332898	305989	**3107**	3044	63
	50 and over	**265346**	152584	112762	**8260**	8005	255	**257086**	144579	112507	**350**	345	5
Christian		*3004*	*1627*	*1377*	*656*	*367*	*289*	*2348*	*1260*	*1088*	*472*	*227*	*245*
	5-10 ..	**568**	303	265	**71**	46	25	**497**	257	240	**42**	32	10
	10-15 ..	**401**	230	171	**79**	56	23	**322**	174	148	**47**	33	14
	15-20 ..	**289**	160	129	**61**	38	23	**228**	122	106	**31**	15	16
	20-30 ..	**623**	305	318	**118**	58	60	**505**	247	258	**88**	34	54
	30-50 ..	**769**	438	331	**205**	115	90	**564**	323	241	**159**	75	84
	50 and over	**354**	191	163	**122**	54	68	**232**	137	95	**105**	38	67
Jain	..	*761*	*411*	*350*	*450*	*272*	*178*	*311*	*139*	*172*	*95*	*88*	*7*
	5-10 ..	**132**	72	60	**34**	17	17	**98**	55	43	**1**	1	
	10-15 ..	**98**	53	45	**66**	32	34	**32**	21	11	**11**	9	2
	15-20 ..	**82**	38	44	**73**	34	39	**9**	4	5	**20**	18	2
	20-30 ..	**148**	75	73	**107**	65	42	**41**	10	31	**33**	31	2
	30-50 ..	**195**	115	80	**121**	85	36	**74**	30	44	**21**	20	1
	50 and over	**106**	58	48	**49**	39	10	**57**	19	38	**9**	9	

XI—LITERACY BY COMMUNITY AND AGE (PART I—STATE SUMMARY)—Concld.

Community	Age	Population											
		Total			Literate			Illiterate			Literate in English		
		P	M	F	P	M	F	P	M	F	P	M	F
1	2	3	4	5	6	7	8	9	10	11	12	13	14
Sikh	..	55815	29673	26142	17765	13240	4525	38050	16433	21617	2195	2071	124
	5-10 ..	**10693**	5668	5025	**1365**	905	460	**9328**	4763	4565	**27**	24	3
	10-15 ..	**8733**	4641	4092	**2771**	1910	861	**5962**	2731	3231	**278**	251	27
	15-20 ..	**6817**	3445	3372	**2672**	1874	798	**4145**	1571	2574	**508**	468	40
	20-30 ..	**10804**	5354	5450	**4346**	3129	1217	**6458**	2225	4233	**753**	714	39
	30-50 ..	**13127**	7210	5917	**4888**	3929	959	**8239**	3281	4958	**518**	503	15
	50 and over	**5641**	3355	2286	**1723**	1493	230	**3918**	1862	2056	**111**	111	
Parsee	..	22	14	8	12	7	5	10	7	3	11	7	4
	5-10 ..	**5**	2	3	**3**		3	**2**	2		**2**		2
	10-15 ..	**1**	1		**1**	1					**1**	1	
	15-20 ..	**5**	3	2				**5**	3	2			
	20-30 ..	**6**	4	2	**3**	2	1	**3**	2	1	**3**	2	1
	30-50 ..	**4**	3	1	**4**	3	1				**4**	3	1
	50 and over	**1**	1		**1**	1					**1**	1	
Buddhist	..	37153	18431	18722	1920	1898	22	35233	16533	18700	11	10	1
	5-10 ..	**4713**	2340	2373	**7**	5	2	**4706**	2335	2371			
	10-15 ..	**4178**	2019	2159	**44**	42	2	**4134**	1977	2157	**2**	2	
	15-20 ..	**4169**	2001	2168	**126**	123	3	**4043**	1878	2165	**4**	3	1
	20-30 ..	**6866**	3341	3525	**392**	388	4	**6474**	2953	3521	**3**	3	
	30-50 ..	**10004**	5075	4929	**808**	800	8	**9196**	4275	4921	**2**	2	
	50 and over	**7223**	3655	3568	**543**	540	3	**6680**	3115	3565			
Jew	..	11	2	9	9	2	7	2		2	9	2	7
	5-10 ..												
	10-15 ..	**1**		1	**1**		1				**1**		1
	15-20 ..												
	20-30 ..	**3**	1	2	**3**	1	2				**3**	1	2
	30-50 ..	**4**		4	**4**		4				**4**		4
	50 and over	**3**	1	2	**1**	1		**2**		2	**1**	1	
Tribes	..	42	24	18	2	2		40	22	18			
	5-10 ..	**10**	6	4				**10**	6	4			
	10-15 ..	**6**	2	4				**6**	2	4			
	15-20 ..	**4**	3	1				**4**	3	1			
	20-30 ..	**7**	4	3				**7**	4	3			
	30-50 ..	**12**	7	5				**12**	7	5			
	50 and over	**3**	2	1	**2**	2		**1**		1			
Others	..	72	15	57	1		1	71	15	56	1		1
	5-10 ..	**20**	2	18	**1**		1	**19**	2	17	**1**		1
	10-15 ..	**8**	2	6				**8**	2	6			
	15-20 ..	**12**	2	10				**12**	2	10			
	20-30 ..	**11**	3	8				**11**	3	8			
	30-50 ..	**9**	3	6				**9**	3	6			
	50 and over	**12**	3	9				**12**	3	9			

XI—LITERACY BY COMMUNITY AND AGE (PART II—PROVINCES)

Community	Age	Population: Total P	Total M	Total F	Literate P	Literate M	Literate F	Illiterate P	Illiterate M	Illiterate F	Literate in English P	Literate in English M	Literate in English F
1	2	3	4	5	6	7	8	9	10	11	12	13	14
JAMMU PROVINCE													
Total Population	..	*1714829*	*900655*	*814174*	*126819*	*105371*	*21448*	*1588010*	*795284*	*792726*	*18555*	*17542*	*1013*
	5-10 ..	**294549**	153711	140838	**8985**	6501	2484	**285564**	147210	138354	**119**	96	23
	10-15 ..	**242653**	128767	113886	**19691**	15427	4264	**222962**	113340	109622	**2396**	2173	223
	15-20 ..	**191913**	98854	93059	**19781**	15829	3952	**172132**	83025	89107	**3987**	3660	327
	20-30 ..	**335736**	165697	170039	**30030**	24560	5470	**305706**	141137	164569	**6117**	5799	318
	30-50 ..	**437616**	232700	204916	**35561**	31180	4381	**402055**	201520	200535	**4976**	4861	115
	50 and over	**212362**	120926	91436	**12771**	11874	897	**199591**	109052	90539	**960**	953	7
Scheduled Castes	..	*133456*	*71300*	*62156*	*2026*	*1818*	*208*	*131430*	*69482*	*61948*	*106*	*100*	*6*
	5-10 ..	**20533**	10617	9916	**128**	107	21	**20405**	10510	9895	**1**	1	
	10-15 ..	**17431**	9052	8379	**354**	308	46	**17077**	8744	8333	**14**	12	2
	15-20 ..	**14842**	7594	7248	**365**	327	38	**14477**	7267	7210	**32**	30	2
	20-30 ..	**27088**	13843	13245	**532**	477	55	**26556**	13366	13190	**45**	43	2
	30-50 ..	**35871**	19789	16082	**502**	460	42	**35369**	19329	16040	**12**	12	
	50 and over	**17691**	10405	7286	**145**	139	6	**17546**	10266	7280	**2**	2	
Hindu	..	*499364*	*265126*	*234238*	*65231*	*52192*	*13039*	*434133*	*212934*	*221199*	*11604*	*10964*	*640*
	5-10 ..	**76510**	40038	36472	**4634**	3090	1544	**71876**	36948	34928	**64**	45	19
	10-15 ..	**64439**	33525	30914	**9215**	6700	2515	**55224**	26825	28399	**1195**	1045	150
	15-20 ..	**53718**	27562	26156	**9419**	7096	2323	**44299**	20466	23833	**2228**	2025	203
	20-30 ..	**96887**	49050	47837	**15208**	11866	3342	**81679**	37184	44495	**3877**	3696	181
	30-50 ..	**135352**	73638	61714	**19224**	16476	2748	**116128**	57162	58966	**3561**	3477	84
	50 and over	**72458**	41313	31145	**7531**	6964	567	**64927**	34349	30578	**679**	676	3
Muslim	..	*1045616*	*545229*	*500387*	*50073*	*44305*	*5768*	*995543*	*500924*	*494619*	*5596*	*5330*	*266*
	5-10 ..	**190415**	99348	91067	**3478**	2809	669	**186937**	96539	90398	**35**	34	1
	10-15 ..	**155183**	83212	71971	**8682**	7410	1272	**146501**	75802	70699	**1037**	985	52
	15-20 ..	**119175**	61603	57572	**8642**	7465	1177	**110533**	54138	56395	**1481**	1388	93
	20-30 ..	**205126**	99703	105423	**12132**	10716	1416	**192994**	88987	104007	**1808**	1710	98
	30-50 ..	**257560**	134504	123056	**13065**	12016	1049	**244495**	122488	122007	**1067**	1045	22
	50 and over	**118157**	66859	51298	**4074**	3889	185	**114083**	62970	51113	**168**	168	
Christian	.	*2342*	*1299*	*1043*	*141*	*102*	*39*	*2201*	*1197*	*1004*	*69*	*43*	*26*
	5-10 ..	**466**	242	224	**12**	6	6	**454**	236	218	**2**		2
	10-15 ..	**312**	172	140	**16**	12	4	**296**	160	136	**4**	2	2
	15-20 ..	**233**	130	103	**21**	15	6	**212**	115	97	**8**	4	4
	20-30 ..	**517**	264	253	**34**	22	12	**483**	242	241	**19**	10	9
	30-50 ..	**575**	347	228	**42**	36	6	**533**	311	222	**24**	19	5
	50 and over	**239**	144	95	**16**	11	5	**223**	133	90	**12**	8	4
Jain	..	*755*	*406*	*349*	*444*	*267*	*177*	*311*	*139*	*172*	*89*	*83*	*6*
	5-10 ..	**132**	72	60	**34**	17	17	**98**	55	43	**1**	1	
	10-15 ..	**98**	53	45	**66**	32	34	**32**	21	11	**11**	9	2
	15-20 ..	**79**	36	43	**70**	32	38	**9**	4	5	**17**	16	1
	20-30 ..	**146**	73	73	**105**	63	42	**41**	10	31	**31**	29	2
	30-50 ..	**194**	114	80	**120**	84	36	**74**	30	44	**20**	19	1
	50 and over	**106**	58	48	**49**	39	10	**57**	19	38	**9**	9	

XI—LITERACY BY COMMUNITY AND AGE (PART II—PROVINCES)—CONTD.

Community / Age	Population: Total P	M	F	Literate P	M	F	Illiterate P	M	F	Literate in English P	M	F
1 / 2	3	4	5	6	7	8	9	10	11	12	13	14
JAMMU PROVINCE—concld.												
SIKH ..	*32709*	*17035*	*15674*	*8893*	*6678*	*2215*	*23816*	*10357*	*13459*	*1086*	*1018*	*68*
5-10 ..	**6399**	3363	3036	**698**	472	226	**5701**	2891	2810	**16**	15	1
10-15 ..	**5105**	2721	2384	**1357**	964	393	**3748**	1757	1991	**134**	119	15
15-20 ..	**3745**	1878	1867	**1264**	894	370	**2481**	984	1497	**221**	197	24
20-30 ..	**5864**	2710	3154	**2016**	1414	602	**3848**	1296	2552	**335**	310	25
30-50 ..	**7954**	4250	3704	**2606**	2106	500	**5348**	2144	3204	**290**	287	3
50 and over	**3642**	2113	1529	**952**	828	124	**2690**	1285	1405	**90**	90	
PARSEE	*16*	*11*	*5*	*6*	*4*	*2*	*10*	*7*	*3*	*5*	*4*	*1*
5-10 ..	**3**	2	1	**1**		1	**2**	2				
10-15 ..	**1**	1		**1**	1					**1**	1	
15-20 ..	**5**	3	2				**5**	3	2			
20-30 ..	**5**	3	2	**2**	1	1	**3**	2	1	**2**	1	1
30-50 ..	**2**	2		**2**	2					**2**	2	
50 and over												
BUDDHIST ..	*477*	*221*	*256*	*3*	*3*		*474*	*218*	*256*			
5-10 ..	**66**	23	43				**66**	23	43			
10-1 ..	**72**	28	44				**72**	28	44			
15-20 ..	**102**	45	57				**102**	45	57			
20-30 ..	**90**	47	43	**1**	1		**89**	46	43			
30-50 ..	**92**	49	43				**92**	49	43			
50 and over	**55**	29	26	**2**	2		**53**	27	26			
TRIBES ..	**23**	*13*	*10*	*2*	*2*		*21*	*11*	*10*			
5-10 ..	**6**	4	2				**6**	4	2			
10-15 ..	**4**	1	3				**4**	1	3			
15-20 ..	**2**	1	1				**2**	1	1			
20-30 ..	**2**	1	1				**2**	1	1			
30-50 ..	**7**	4	3				**7**	4	3			
50 and over	**2**	2		**2**	2							
OTHERS	*71*	*15*	*56*				*71*	*15*	*56*			
5-10 ..	**19**	2	17				**19**	2	17			
10-15 ..	**8**	2	6				**8**	2	6			
15-20 ..	**12**	2	10				**12**	2	10			
20-30 ..	**11**	3	8				**11**	3	8			
30-50 ..	**9**	3	6				**9**	3	6			
50 and over	**12**	3	9				**12**	3	9			
KASHMIR PROVINCE												
TOTAL POPULATION ..	*1500423*	*819279*	*681144*	*105238*	*91556*	*13682*	*1395185*	*727723*	*667462*	*28555*	*27240*	*1315*
5-10 ..	**248319**	131927	116392	**7302**	5254	2048	**241017**	126673	114344	**319**	275	44
10-15 ..	**211132**	114652	96480	**15765**	12527	3238	**195367**	102125	93242	**3130**	2833	297
15-20 ..	**183813**	98700	85113	**17611**	14929	2682	**166202**	83771	82431	**5738**	5362	376
20-30 ..	**330651**	173545	157106	**28296**	25066	3230	**302355**	148479	153876	**10208**	9865	43
30-50 ..	**393782**	220056	173726	**27975**	25886	2089	**365807**	194170	171637	**7964**	7774	190
50 and over	**132726**	80399	52327	**8289**	7894	395	**124437**	72505	51932	**1196**	1131	65

XI—LITERACY BY COMMUNITY AND AGE (PART II—PROVINCES)—CONTD.

KASHMIR PROVINCE—contd.

Community	Age	Population: Total P	Total M	Total F	Literate P	Literate M	Literate F	Illiterate P	Illiterate M	Illiterate F	Literate in English P	Literate in English M	Literate in English F
1	2	3	4	5	6	7	8	9	10	11	12	13	14
SCHEDULED CASTES ..	..	*42*	*28*	*14*	*10*	*9*	*1*	*32*	*19*	*13*	*1*	*1*	
	5-10 ..	**9**	5	4				**9**	5	4			
	10-15 ..	**5**	3	2	**2**	2		**3**	1	2	**1**	1	
	15-20 ..	**5**	4	1	**1**	1		**4**	3	1			
	20-30 ..	**8**	6	2	**3**	2	1	**5**	4	1			
	30-50 ..	**12**	7	5	**3**	3		**9**	4	5			
	50 and over	**3**	3		**1**	1		**2**	2				
HINDU ..	..	*75496*	*43195*	*32301*	*39269*	*31830*	*7439*	*36227*	*11365*	*24862*	*16519*	*15966*	*553*
	5-10 ..	**11851**	6156	5695	**3268**	2012	1256	**8583**	4144	4439	**210**	188	22
	10-15 ..	**9940**	5257	4683	**5373**	3638	1735	**4567**	1619	2948	**1601**	1453	148
	15-20 ..	**8363**	4700	3663	**5353**	4000	1353	**3010**	700	2310	**2643**	2471	172
	20-30 ..	**16248**	9532	6716	**9990**	8221	1769	**6258**	1311	4947	**5494**	5346	148
	30-50 ..	**21160**	12864	8296	**11594**	10432	1162	**9566**	2432	7134	**5660**	5601	59
	50 and over	**7934**	4686	3248	**3691**	3527	164	**4243**	1159	3084	**911**	907	4
MUSLIM ..	..	*1401440*	*763287*	*638153*	*56757*	*53035*	*3722*	*1344683*	*710252*	*634431*	*10565*	*10069*	*496*
	5-10 ..	**232122**	123438	108684	**3313**	2774	539	**228809**	120664	108145	**56**	46	10
	10-15 ..	**197519**	107443	90076	**8936**	7913	1023	**188583**	99530	89053	**1342**	1217	125
	15-20 ..	**172356**	92421	79935	**10834**	9944	890	**161522**	82477	79045	**2787**	2611	176
	20-30 ..	**309427**	161361	148066	**15943**	15130	813	**293484**	146231	147253	**4251**	4108	143
	30-50 ..	**367324**	204189	163135	**13995**	13603	392	**353329**	190586	162743	**1956**	1916	40
	50 and over	**122692**	74435	48257	**3736**	3671	65	**118956**	70764	48192	**173**	171	2
CHRISTIAN ..	..	*516*	*245*	*271*	*427*	*205*	*222*	*89*	*40*	*49*	*369*	*170*	*199*
	5-10 ..	**83**	50	33	**58**	40	18	**25**	10	15	**39**	32	7
	10-15 ..	**68**	46	22	**53**	38	15	**15**	8	7	**42**	31	11
	15-20 ..	**38**	19	19	**28**	14	14	**10**	5	5	**22**	11	11
	20-30 ..	**74**	25	49	**63**	22	41	**11**	3	8	**55**	18	37
	30-50 ..	**152**	68	84	**132**	58	74	**20**	10	10	**122**	48	74
	50 and over	**101**	37	64	**93**	33	60	**8**	4	4	**89**	30	59
JAIN ..	..	*6*	*5*	*1*	*6*	*5*	*1*				*6*	*5*	*1*
	5-10 ..												
	10-15 ..												
	15-20 ..	**3**	2	1	**3**	2	1				**3**	2	1
	20-30 ..	**2**	2		**2**	2					**2**	2	
	30-50 ..	**1**	1		**1**	1					**1**	1	
	50 and over												
SIKH ..	..	*22878*	*12495*	*10383*	*8750*	*6464*	*2286*	*14128*	*6031*	*8097*	*1077*	*1022*	*55*
	5-10 ..	**4248**	2277	1971	**660**	428	232	**3588**	1849	1739	**11**	9	2
	10-15 ..	**3596**	1901	1695	**1399**	935	464	**2197**	966	1231	**142**	130	12
	15-20 ..	**3044**	1550	1494	**1391**	967	424	**1653**	583	1070	**282**	266	16
	20-30 ..	**4879**	2610	2269	**2290**	1686	604	**2589**	924	1665	**402**	386	13
	30-50 ..	**5120**	2921	2199	**2244**	1788	456	**2876**	1133	1743	**219**	207	12
	50 and over	**1991**	1236	755	**766**	660	106	**1225**	576	649	**21**	21	

XI—LITERACY BY COMMUNITY AND AGE (PART II—PROVINCES)—Contd.

Community	Age	Population: Total P	Total M	Total F	Literate P	Literate M	Literate F	Illiterate P	Illiterate M	Illiterate F	Literate in English P	Literate in English M	Literate in English F
1	2	3	4	5	6	7	8	9	10	11	12	13	14
KASHMIR PROVINCE—concld.													
Buddhist	..	10	10		3	3		7	7		2	2	
	5-10 ..												
	10-15 ..	1	1		1	1					1	1	
	15-20 ..	2	2		1	1		1	1		1	1	
	20-30 ..	4	4		1	1		3	3				
	30-50 ..	3	3					3	3				
	50 and over												
Parsee	..	6	3	3	6	3	3				6	3	3
	5-10 ..	2		2	2		2				2		2
	10-15 ..												
	15-20 ..												
	20-30 ..	1	1		1	1					1	1	
	30-50 ..	2	1	1	2	1	1				2	1	1
	50 and over	1	1		1	1					1	1	
Jew	..	11	2	9	9	2	7	2		2	9	2	7
	5-10 ..												
	10-15 ..	1		1	1		1				1		1
	15-20 ..												
	20-30 ..	3	1	2	3	1	2				3	1	2
	30-50 ..	4		4	4		4				4		4
	50 and over	3	1	2	1	1		2		2	1	1	
Tribes	..	17	9	8				17	9	8			
	5-10 ..	3	1	2				3	1	2			
	10-15 ..	2	1	1				2	1	1			
	15-20 ..	2	2					2	2				
	20-30 ..	5	3	2				5	3	2			
	30-50 ..	4	2	2				4	2	2			
	50 and over	1		1				1		1			
Others ..	..	1		1	1		1				1		1
	5-10 ..	1		1	1		1				1		1
	10-15 ..												
	15-20 ..												
	20-30 ..												
	30-50 ..												
	50 and over												
FRONTIER DISTRICTS													
Total Population	..	206073	105468	100605	6327	6049	278	199746	99419	100327	505	472	33
	5-10 ..	30572	16005	14567	202	169	33	30370	15836	14534	4	3	1
	10-15 ..	26659	14302	12357	547	496	51	26112	13806	12306	22	21	1
	15-20 ..	23442	12863	10579	735	684	51	22707	12179	10528	62	58	4
	20-30 ..	41275	21133	20142	1691	1601	90	39584	19532	20052	211	197	14
	30-50 ..	52419	26216	26203	2134	2092	42	50285	24124	26161	187	181	6
	50 and over	31706	14949	16757	1018	1007	11	30688	13942	16746	19	12	7

XI—LITERACY BY COMMUNITY AND AGE (PART II—PROVINCES)—Concld.

Community	Age	Population											
		Total			Literate			Illiterate			Literate in English		
		P	M	F	P	M	F	P	M	F	P	M	F
1	2	3	4	5	6	7	8	9	10	11	12	13	15
		FRONTIER DISTRICTS—concld.											
Hindu	..	*596*	*463*	*133*	*341*	*288*	*53*	*255*	*175*	*80*	*124*	*121*	*3*
	5-10 ..	**69**	41	28	**24**	15	9	**45**	26	19	**1**	1	
	10-15 ..	**36**	20	16	**25**	17	8	**11**	3	8	**4**	4	
	15-20 ..	**32**	20	12	**21**	12	9	**11**	8	3	**4**	2	2
	20-30 ..	**197**	151	46	**113**	91	22	**84**	60	24	**30**	29	1
	30-50 ..	**243**	214	29	**149**	144	5	**94**	70	24	**79**	79	
	50 and over	**19**	17	2	**9**	9		**10**	8	2	**6**	6	
Muslim	..	*168435*	*86577*	*81858*	*3862*	*3711*	*151*	*164573*	*82866*	*81707*	*306*	*298*	*8*
	5-10 ..	**25790**	13607	12183	**163**	144	19	**25627**	13463	12164	**2**	2	
	10-15 ..	**22465**	12261	10204	**454**	421	33	**22011**	11840	10171	**14**	14	
	15-20 ..	**19299**	10861	8438	**560**	528	32	**18739**	10333	8406	**49**	49	
	20-30 ..	**34213**	17642	16571	**1127**	1081	46	**33086**	16561	16525	**148**	144	4
	30-50 ..	**42171**	20916	21255	**1108**	1092	16	**41063**	19824	21239	**84**	83	1
	50 and over	**24497**	11290	13207	**450**	445	5	**24047**	10845	13202	**9**	6	3
Christian	..	*146*	*83*	*63*	*88*	*60*	*28*	*58*	*23*	*35*	*34*	*14*	*20*
	5-10 ..	**19**	11	8	**1**		1	**18**	11	7	**1**		1
	10-15 ..	**21**	12	9	**10**	6	4	**11**	6	5	**1**		1
	15-20 ..	**18**	11	7	**12**	9	3	**6**	2	4	**1**		1
	20-30 ..	**32**	16	16	**21**	14	7	**11**	2	9	**14**	6	8
	30-50 ..	**42**	23	19	**31**	21	10	**11**	2	9	**13**	8	5
	50 and over	**14**	10	4	**13**	10	3	**1**		1	**4**		4
Sikh	..	*228*	*143*	*85*	*122*	*98*	*24*	*106*	*45*	*61*	*32*	*31*	*1*
	5-10 ..	**46**	28	18	**7**	5	2	**39**	23	16			
	10-15 ..	**32**	19	13	**15**	11	4	**17**	8	9	**2**	2	
	15-20 ..	**28**	17	11	**17**	13	4	**11**	4	7	**5**	5	
	20-30 ..	**61**	34	27	**40**	29	11	**21**	5	16	**16**	15	1
	30-50 ..	**53**	39	14	**38**	35	3	**15**	4	11	**9**	9	
	50 and over	**8**	6	2	**5**	5		**3**	1	2			
Buddhist	..	*36666*	*18200*	*18466*	*1914*	*1892*	*22*	*34752*	*16308*	*18444*	*9*	*8*	*1*
	5-10 ..	**4647**	2317	2330	**7**	5	2	**4640**	2312	2328			
	10-15 ..	**4105**	1990	2115	**43**	41	2	**4062**	1949	2113	**1**	1	
	15-20 ..	**4065**	1954	2111	**125**	122	3	**3940**	1832	2108	**3**	2	1
	20-30 ..	**6772**	3290	3482	**390**	386	4	**6382**	2904	3478	**3**	3	
	30-50 ..	**9909**	5023	4886	**808**	800	8	**9101**	4223	4878	**2**	2	
	50 and over	**7168**	3626	3542	**541**	538	3	**6627**	3088	3539			
Tribes	..	*2*	*2*					*2*	*2*				
	5-10 ..	**1**	1					**1**	1				
	10-15 ..												
	15-20 ..												
	20-30 ..												
	30-50 ..	**1**	1					**1**	1				
	50 and over												

XI—LITERACY BY COMMUNITY AND AGE (PART III—DISTRICTS)

Community	Age	Population: Total P	Total M	Total F	Literate P	Literate M	Literate F	Illiterate P	Illiterate M	Illiterate F	Literate in English P	Literate in English M	Literate in English F
1	2	3	4	5	6	7	8	9	10	11	12	13	14
JAMMU													
TOTAL POPULATION	..	*372044*	*203828*	*168216*	*43760*	*34150*	*9610*	*328284*	*169678*	*158606*	*10215*	*9416*	*799*
	5-10 ..	**60885**	32287	28598	**3092**	2009	1083	**57793**	30278	27515	**63**	45	18
	10-15 ..	**51239**	27063	24176	**6355**	4499	1856	**44884**	22564	22320	**1085**	903	182
	15-20 ..	**42688**	22933	19755	**6963**	5192	1771	**35725**	17741	17984	**2139**	1876	263
	20-30 ..	**74142**	39490	34652	**10963**	8433	2535	**63174**	31057	32117	**3421**	3178	243
	30-50 ..	**96265**	54238	42027	**11919**	9966	1953	**84346**	44272	40074	**2833**	2745	88
	50 and over	**46825**	27817	19008	**4463**	4051	412	**42362**	23766	18596	**674**	669	5
HINDU	..	*215142*	*117876*	*97266*	*30182*	*23560*	*6622*	*184960*	*94316*	*90644*	*7188*	*6692*	*496*
	5-10 ..	**34079**	18250	15829	**2104**	1314	790	**31975**	16936	15039	**39**	23	16
	10-15 ..	**28790**	15227	13563	**4151**	2910	1241	**24639**	12317	12322	**714**	591	123
	15-20 ..	**24312**	13143	11169	**4609**	3449	1160	**19703**	9694	10009	**1437**	1276	161
	20-30 ..	**42312**	22359	19953	**7509**	5761	1748	**34803**	16598	18205	**2369**	2236	133
	30-50 ..	**57047**	31906	25141	**8485**	7093	1392	**48562**	24813	23749	**2127**	2066	61
	50 and over	**28602**	16991	11611	**3324**	3033	291	**25278**	13958	11320	**502**	500	2
MUSLIM	..	*146448*	*80215*	*66233*	*11015*	*8713*	*2302*	*135433*	*71502*	*63931*	*2461*	*2240*	*221*
	5-10 ..	**24875**	13055	11820	**814**	574	240	**24061**	12481	11580	**17**	17	
	10-15 ..	**20905**	11007	9898	**1868**	1362	506	**19037**	9645	9392	**313**	269	44
	15-20 ..	**17142**	9155	7987	**2006**	1516	490	**15136**	7639	7497	**594**	514	80
	20-30 ..	**29826**	16093	13733	**2832**	2236	596	**26994**	13857	13137	**858**	779	79
	30-50 ..	**36679**	20801	15878	**2643**	2244	399	**34036**	18557	15479	**563**	545	18
	50 and over	**17021**	10104	6917	**852**	781	71	**16169**	9323	6846	**116**	116	
CHRISTIAN	..	*1927*	*1065*	*862*	*111*	*77*	*34*	*1816*	*988*	*828*	*57*	*32*	*25*
	5-10 ..	**383**	200	183	**11**	6	5	**372**	194	178	**2**		2
	10-15 ..	**262**	147	115	**14**	10	4	**248**	137	111	**4**	2	2
	15-20 ..	**195**	108	87	**15**	10	5	**180**	98	82	**7**	3	4
	20-30 ..	**421**	212	209	**28**	17	11	**393**	195	198	**17**	8	9
	30-50 ..	**471**	282	189	**32**	27	5	**439**	255	184	**18**	13	5
	50 and over	**195**	116	79	**11**	7	4	**184**	109	75	**9**	6	3
SIKH	..	*7732*	*4238*	*3494*	*2004*	*1528*	*476*	*5728*	*2710*	*3018*	*416*	*366*	*50*
	5-10 ..	**1407**	704	703	**128**	98	30	**1279**	606	673	**4**	4	
	10-15 ..	**1179**	627	552	**255**	184	71	**924**	443	481	**42**	31	11
	15-20 ..	**953**	486	467	**264**	185	79	**689**	301	388	**84**	67	17
	20-30 ..	**1431**	748	683	**494**	355	139	**937**	393	544	**144**	125	19
	30-50 ..	**1363**	1127	736	**638**	517	121	**1225**	610	615	**104**	101	3
	50 and over	**899**	546	353	**225**	189	36	**674**	357	317	**38**	38	
JAIN	..	*751*	*405*	*346*	*440*	*266*	*174*	*311*	*139*	*172*	*88*	*82*	*6*
	5-10 ..	**132**	72	60	**34**	17	17	**98**	55	43	**1**	1	
	10-15 ..	**98**	53	45	**66**	32	34	**32**	21	11	**11**	9	2
	15-20 ..	**78**	36	42	**69**	32	37	**9**	4	5	**17**	16	1
	20-30 ..	**144**	73	71	**103**	63	40	**41**	10	31	**31**	29	2
	30-50 ..	**193**	113	80	**119**	83	36	**74**	30	44	**19**	18	1
	50 and over	**106**	58	48	**49**	39	10	**57**	19	38	**9**	9	

XI—LITERACY BY COMMUNITY AND AGE (PART III—DISTRICTS)—Contd.

Community	Age	Population: Total P	Total M	Total F	Literate P	Literate M	Literate F	Illiterate P	Illiterate M	Illiterate F	Literate in English P	Literate in English M	Literate in English F
1	2	3	4	5	6	7	8	9	10	11	12	13	14
JAMMU—concld.													
Parsee	..	16	11	5	6	4	2	10	7	3	5	4	1
	5-10 ..	3	2	1	1		1	2	2				
	10-15 ..	1	1		1	1					1	1	
	15-20 ..	5	3	2				5	3	2			
	20-30 ..	5	3	2	2	1	1	3	2	1	2	1	1
	30-50 ..	2	2		2	2					2	2	
Buddhist	..	2	2					2	2				
	5-10 ..												
	10-15 ..												
	15-20 ..												
	20-30 ..												
	30-50 ..	2	2					2	2				
	50 and over												
Tribes	..	23	13	10	2	2		21	11	10			
	5-10	6	4	2				6	4	2			
	10-15 ..	4	1	3				4	1	3			
	15-20 ..	2	1	1				2	1	1			
	20-30 ..	2	1	1				2	1	1			
	30-50 ..	7	4	3				7	4	3			
	50 and over	2	2		2	2							
Others	..	3	3					3	3				
	5-10 ..												
	10-15 ..												
	15-20 ..	1	1					1	1				
	20-30 ..	1	1					1	1				
	30-50 ..	1	1					1	1				
	50 and over												
KATHUA													
Total Population	..	155229	82801	72428	9631	8426	1205	145598	74375	71223	1013	988	25
	5-10 ..	24798	13044	11754	690	550	140	24108	12494	11614	3	2	1
	10-15 ..	20616	10744	9872	1504	1256	248	19112	9488	9624	126	121	5
	15-20 ..	17302	8909	8393	1470	1224	246	15832	7685	8147	217	210	7
	20-30 ..	31829	16444	15385	2267	1041	326	29562	14503	15059	383	374	9
	30-50 ..	40534	22271	18263	2740	2525	215	37794	19746	18048	255	252	3
	50 and over	20150	11389	8761	960	930	30	19190	10459	8731	29	29	
Hindu	..	115808	61341	54467	8145	7090	1055	107663	54251	53412	842	824	18
	5-10 ..	17821	9400	8421	588	464	124	17233	8936	8297	1	1	
	10-15 ..	14859	7707	7152	1273	1049	224	13586	6658	6928	109	104	5
	15-20 ..	12624	6433	6191	1219	1007	212	11405	5426	5979	179	174	5
	20-30 ..	23574	11994	11580	1855	1578	277	21719	10416	11303	310	305	5
	30-50 ..	31031	16906	14125	2358	2169	189	28673	14737	13936	220	217	3
	50 and over	15899	8901	6998	852	823	29	15047	8078	6969	23	23	

XI—LITERACY BY COMMUNITY AND AGE (PART III—DISTRICTS)—CONTD.

Community	Age	Population: Total P	Total M	Total F	Literate P	Literate M	Literate F	Illiterate P	Illiterate M	Illiterate F	Literate in English P	Literate in English M	Literate in English F
1	2	3	4	5	6	7	8	9	10	11	12	13	14
						KATHUA—concld.							
MUSLIM	..	*38868*	*21164*	*17704*	*1430*	*1291*	*139*	*37438*	*19873*	*17565*	*152*	*149*	3
	5-10 ..	**6869**	3591	3278	**100**	86	14	**6769**	3505	3264	**1**	1	
	10-15 ..	**5676**	3001	2675	**226**	203	23	**5450**	2798	2652	**16**	16	
	15-20 ..	**4615**	2443	2172	**243**	210	33	**4372**	2233	2139	**34**	33	1
	20-30 ..	**8140**	4395	3745	**403**	358	45	**7737**	4037	3700	**68**	66	2
	30-50 ..	**9372**	5281	4091	**356**	332	24	**9016**	4949	4067	**28**	28	
	50 and over	**4196**	2453	1743	**102**	102		**4094**	2351	1743	**5**	5	
CHRISTIAN	..	*175*	*92*	*83*	*2*	*2*		*173*	*90*	*83*			
	5-10 ..	**38**	16	22				**38**	16	22			
	10-15 ..	**23**	10	13				**23**	10	13			
	15-20 ..	**12**	9	3				**12**	9	3			
	20-30 ..	**40**	22	18				**40**	22	18			
	30-50 ..	**44**	26	18	**2**	2		**42**	24	18			
	50 and over	**18**	9	9				**18**	9	9			
SIKH	..	*378*	*204*	*174*	*54*	*43*	*11*	*324*	*161*	*163*	*19*	*15*	4
	5-10 ..	**70**	37	33	**2**		2	**68**	37	31	**1**		1
	10-15 ..	**58**	26	32	**5**	4	1	**53**	22	31	**1**	1	
	15-20 ..	**51**	24	27	**8**	7	1	**43**	17	26	**4**	3	1
	20-30 ..	**75**	33	42	**9**	5	4	**66**	28	38	**5**	3	2
	30-50 ..	**87**	58	29	**24**	22	2	**63**	36	27	**7**	7	
	50 and over	**37**	26	11	**6**	5	1	**31**	21	10	**1**	1	
						UDHAMPUR							
TOTAL POPULATION	..	*257758*	*135419*	*122339*	*15201*	*13047*	*2154*	*242557*	*122372*	*120185*	*1648*	*1621*	*27*
	5-10 ..	**40104**	20456	19648	**1052**	788	264	**39052**	19668	19384	**12**	11	1
	10-15 ..	**33293**	17171	16122	**2190**	1757	433	**31103**	15414	15689	**164**	160	4
	15-20 ..	**27851**	14195	13656	**2148**	1769	379	**25703**	12426	13277	**284**	275	9
	20-30 ..	**51849**	25743	26106	**3526**	3004	522	**48323**	22739	25584	**619**	608	11
	30-50 ..	**70351**	38748	31603	**4595**	4153	442	**65756**	34595	31161	**524**	522	2
	50 and over	**34310**	19106	15204	**1690**	1576	114	**32620**	17530	15090	**45**	45	
HINDU	..	*145557*	*75599*	*69958*	*10544*	*8870*	*1674*	*135013*	*66729*	*68284*	*1177*	*1158*	*19*
	5-10 ..	**20825**	10567	10258	**711**	532	179	**20114**	10035	10079	**7**	6	1
	10-15 ..	**17633**	9080	8553	**1436**	1136	300	**16197**	7944	8253	**101**	98	3
	15-20 ..	**15228**	7483	7745	**1371**	1087	284	**13857**	6396	7461	**189**	183	6
	20-30 ..	**29090**	14326	14764	**2321**	1803	428	**26769**	12433	14336	**436**	429	7
	30-50 ..	**41016**	22165	18851	**3342**	2966	376	**37674**	19199	18475	**408**	406	2
	50 and over	**21765**	11978	9787	**1363**	1256	107	**20402**	10722	9680	**36**	36	
MUSLIM	..	*111253*	*59330*	*51923*	*4510*	*4060*	*450*	*106743*	*55270*	*51473*	*445*	*439*	6
	5-10 ..	**19135**	9825	9310	**332**	251	81	**18803**	9574	9229	**5**	5	
	10-15 ..	**15529**	8032	7497	**734**	605	129	**14795**	7427	7368	**60**	59	1
	15-20 ..	**12466**	6637	5829	**755**	665	90	**11711**	5972	5739	**93**	90	3
	20-30 ..	**22571**	11316	11255	**1166**	1081	85	**21405**	10235	11170	**174**	172	2
	30-50 ..	**29126**	16467	12659	**1215**	1157	58	**27911**	15310	12601	**105**	105	
	50 and over	**12426**	7053	5373	**308**	301	7	**12118**	6752	5366	**8**	8	

XI—LITERACY BY COMMUNITY AND AGE (PART III—DISTRICTS)—Contd.

Community	Age	Population: Total P	Total M	Total F	Literate P	Literate M	Literate F	Illiterate P	Illiterate M	Illiterate F	Literate in English P	Literate in English M	Literate in English F
1	2	3	4	5	6	7	8	9	10	11	12	13	14
UDHAMPUR—concld.													
Christian	..	79	48	31	15	13	2	64	35	29	5	5	
	5-10 ..	**31**	8	5				**13**	8	5			
	10-15 ..	**7**	4	3	**2**	2		**5**	2	3			
	15-20 ..	**8**	5	3	**3**	3		**5**	2	3			
	20-30 ..	**22**	10	12	**4**	3	1	**18**	7	11			
	30-50 ..	**20**	13	7	**4**	3	1	**16**	10	6	**2**	2	
	50 and over	**9**	8	1	**2**	2		**7**	6	1	**3**	3	
Jain	..	4	1	3	4	1	3				1	1	
	5-10 ..												
	10-15 ..												
	15-20 ..	**1**		1	**1**		1						
	20-30 ..	**2**		2	**2**		2						
	30-50 ..	**1**	1		**1**	1							
	50 and over										**1**	1	
Sikh	..	389	221	168	125	100	25	264	121	143	20	18	2
	5-10 ..	**64**	32	32	**9**	5	4	**55**	27	28			
	10-15 ..	**52**	27	25	**18**	14	4	**34**	13	21	**3**	3	
	15-20 ..	**46**	25	21	**18**	14	4	**28**	11	17	**2**	2	
	20-30 ..	**74**	44	30	**32**	26	6	**42**	18	24	**7**	5	2
	30-50 ..	**98**	55	43	**33**	26	7	**65**	29	36	**7**	7	
	50 and over	**55**	38	17	**15**	15		**40**	23	17	**1**	1	
Buddhist	..	475	219	256	3	3		472	216	256			
	5-10 ..	**66**	23	43				**66**	23	43			
	10-15 ..	**72**	28	44				**72**	28	44			
	15-20 ..	**102**	45	57				**102**	45	57			
	20-30 ..	**90**	47	43	**1**	1		**89**	46	43			
	30-50 ..	**90**	47	43				**90**	47	43			
	50 and over	**55**	29	26	**2**	2		**53**	27	26			
Others	..	1	1					1	1				
	5-10 ..	**1**	1					**1**	1				
	10-15 ..												
	15-20 ..												
	20-30 ..												
	30-50 ..												
	50 and over												
REASI													
Total Population	..	223130	117967	105163	9053	7852	1201	214077	110115	103962	558	548	10
	5-10 ..	**38237**	19901	18336	**525**	399	126	**37712**	19502	18210	**2**	2	
	10-15 ..	**31588**	16790	14798	**1258**	1017	241	**30330**	15773	14557	**32**	31	1
	15-20 ..	**25374**	12898	12476	**1330**	1079	251	**24044**	11819	12225	**77**	76	1
	20-30 ..	**44603**	22088	22515	**2125**	1813	312	**42478**	20275	22203	**191**	186	5
	30-50 ..	**56323**	30635	25688	**2768**	2535	233	**53555**	28100	25455	**227**	224	3
	50 and over	**27005**	15955	11350	**1047**	1009	38	**25958**	14646	11312	**29**	29	

XI—LITERACY BY COMMUNITY AND AGE (PART III—DISTRICTS)—Contd.

Community	Age	Population: Total P	Total M	Total F	Literate P	Literate M	Literate F	Illiterate P	Illiterate M	Illiterate F	Literate in English P	Literate in English M	Literate in English F
1	2	3	4	5	6	7	8	9	10	11	12	13	14
REASI—concld.													
Hindu	..	*71859*	*37832*	*34027*	*5008*	*4130*	*878*	*66851*	*33702*	*33149*	*390*	*383*	*7*
	5-10 ..	**9762**	4956	4806	**302**	208	94	**9460**	4748	4712			
	10-15 ..	**8755**	4441	4314	**657**	478	179	**8098**	3963	4135	**24**	23	1
	15-20 ..	**7564**	3754	3810	**684**	505	179	**6880**	3249	3631	**48**	47	1
	20-30 ..	**14091**	7037	7054	**1089**	868	221	**13002**	6169	6833	**111**	108	3
	30-50 ..	**20272**	11031	9241	**1604**	1431	173	**18668**	9600	9068	**183**	181	2
	50 and over	**11415**	6613	4802	**672**	640	32	**10743**	5973	4770	**24**	24	
Muslim	..	*149865*	*79387*	*70478*	*3717*	*3466*	*251*	*146148*	*75921*	*70227*	*150*	*147*	*3*
	5-10 ..	**28230**	14816	13414	**203**	178	25	**28027**	14638	13389	**2**	2	
	10-15 ..	**22638**	12242	10396	**554**	504	50	**22084**	11738	10346	**6**	6	
	15-20 ..	**17646**	9054	8592	**595**	537	58	**17051**	8517	8534	**27**	27	
	20-30 ..	**30228**	14914	15314	**957**	889	68	**29271**	14025	15246	**77**	75	2
	30-50 ..	**35682**	19401	16281	**1066**	1021	45	**34616**	18380	16236	**34**	33	1
	50 and over	**15441**	8960	6481	**342**	337	5	**15099**	8623	6476	**4**	4	
Christian	..	*84*	*52*	*32*	*3*	*3*		*81*	*49*	*32*	*2*	*2*	
	5-10 ..	**18**	12	6				**18**	12	6			
	10-15 ..	**11**	6	5				**11**	6	5			
	15-20 ..	**10**	4	6				**10**	4	6			
	20-30 ..	**18**	11	7				**18**	11	7			
	30-50 ..	**21**	15	6	**3**	3		**18**	12	6	**2**	2	
	50 and over	**6**	4	2				**6**	4	2			
Sikh	..	*1322*	*696*	*626*	*325*	*253*	*72*	*997*	*443*	*554*	*16*	*16*	
	5-10 ..	**227**	117	110	**20**	13	7	**207**	104	103			
	10-15 ..	**184**	101	83	**47**	35	12	**137**	66	71	**2**	2	
	15-20 ..	**154**	86	68	**51**	37	14	**103**	49	54	**2**	2	
	20-30 ..	**266**	126	140	**79**	56	23	**187**	70	117	**3**	3	
	30-50 ..	**348**	188	160	**95**	80	15	**253**	108	145	**8**	8	
	50 and over	**143**	78	65	**33**	32	1	**110**	46	64	**1**	1	
MIRPUR													
Total Population	..	*333785*	*170277*	*163508*	*25873*	*21439*	*4434*	*307912*	*148838*	*159074*	*3751*	*3638*	*113*
	5-10 ..	**60981**	31958	29023	**2272**	1726	546	**58709**	30232	28477	**29**	28	1
	10-15 ..	**48166**	25480	22686	**4916**	3953	963	**43250**	21527	21723	**831**	806	25
	15-20 ..	**35363**	17654	17709	**4247**	3426	821	**31116**	14228	16888	**991**	957	34
	20-30 ..	**60712**	28551	32161	**5283**	4280	1003	**55429**	24271	31158	**997**	961	36
	30-50 ..	**82232**	40827	41405	**6549**	5629	920	**75683**	35198	40485	**767**	751	16
	50 and over	**46331**	25807	20524	**2606**	2425	181	**43725**	23382	20343	**136**	135	1
Hindu	..	*55005*	*28584*	*26421*	*9113*	*6877*	*2236*	*45892*	*21707*	*24185*	*1554*	*1472*	*82*
	5-10 ..	**9417**	4863	4554	**791**	507	284	**8626**	4356	4270	**13**	12	1
	10-15 ..	**7608**	3907	3701	**1461**	988	473	**6147**	2919	3228	**201**	185	16
	15-20 ..	**5652**	2755	2897	**1301**	912	389	**4351**	1843	2508	**318**	294	24
	20-30 ..	**9455**	4593	4862	**1959**	1447	512	**7496**	3146	4350	**508**	481	27
	30-50 ..	**14223**	7425	6798	**2563**	2074	489	**11660**	5351	6309	**448**	435	13
	50 and over	**8650**	5041	3609	**1038**	949	89	**7612**	4092	3520	**66**	65	1

XI—LITERACY BY COMMUNITY AND AGE (PART III—DISTRICTS)—Contd.

Community	Age	Population: Total P	Total M	Total F	Literate P	Literate M	Literate F	Illiterate P	Illiterate M	Illiterate F	Literate in English P	Literate in English M	Literate in English F
1	2	3	4	5	6	7	8	9	10	11	12	13	14
MIRPUR—concld.													
Muslim	..	268418	136379	132039	13679	12319	1360	254739	124060	130679	1739	1719	20
	5-10 ..	49471	25963	23508	1194	1031	163	48277	24932	23345	5	5	
	10-15 ..	38905	20670	18235	2880	2561	319	36025	18109	17916	560	555	5
	15-20 ..	28570	14335	14235	2474	2189	285	26096	12146	13950	581	576	5
	20-30 ..	49633	23278	26355	2758	2453	305	46875	20825	26050	374	367	7
	30-50 ..	65564	32163	33401	3162	2915	247	62402	29248	33154	191	188	3
	50 and over	36275	19970	16305	1211	1170	41	35064	18800	16264	28	28	
Christian	..	74	40	34	7	5	2	67	35	32	2	2	
	5-10 ..	14	6	8	1		1	13	6	7			
	10-15 ..	9	5	4				9	5	4			
	15-20 ..	8	4	4	3	2	1	5	2	3	1	1	
	20-30 ..	16	9	7	2	2		14	7	7			
	30-50 ..	19	11	8	1	1		18	10	8	1	1	
	50 and over	8	5	3				8	5	3			
Sikh	..	10288	5274	5014	3074	2238	836	7214	3036	4178	456	445	11
	5-10 ..	2079	1126	953	286	188	98	1793	938	855	11	11	
	10-15 ..	1644	898	746	575	404	171	1069	494	575	70	66	4
	15-20 ..	1133	560	573	469	323	146	664	237	427	91	86	5
	20-30 ..	1608	671	937	564	378	186	1044	293	751	115	113	2
	30-50 ..	2426	1228	1198	823	639	184	1603	589	1014	127	127	
	50 and over	1398	791	607	357	306	51	1041	485	556	42	42	
CHENANI JAGIR													
Total Population	..	10618	5925	4693	388	369	19	10230	5556	4674	23	23	
	5-10 ..	1368	674	694	11	10	1	1357	664	693			
	10-15 ..	1257	669	588	38	34	4	1219	635	584			
	15-20 ..	1212	665	547	50	47	3	1162	618	544	2	2	
	20-30 ..	2380	1377	1003	109	102	7	2271	1275	996	10	10	
	30-50 ..	2916	1675	1241	125	121	4	2791	1554	1237	9	9	
	50 and over	1485	865	620	55	55		1430	810	620	2	2	
Hindu	..	8609	4514	4095	318	301	17	8291	4213	4078	21	21	
	5-10 ..	1169	576	593	9	8	1	1160	568	592			
	10-15 ..	1032	531	501	32	29	3	1000	502	498			
	15-20 ..	930	453	477	43	40	3	887	413	474	1	1	
	20-30 ..	1758	899	859	81	75	6	1677	824	853	10	10	
	30-50 ..	2407	1298	1109	105	101	4	2302	1197	1105	8	8	
	50 and over	1313	757	556	48	48		1265	709	556	2	2	
Muslim	..	2000	1403	597	66	64	2	1934	1339	595	2	2	
	5-10 ..	198	97	101	2	2		196	95	101			
	10-15 ..	225	138	87	6	5	1	219	133	86			
	15-20 ..	281	212	69	7	7		274	205	69	1	1	
	20-30 ..	618	474	144	25	24	1	593	450	143			
	30-50 ..	508	376	132	20	20		488	356	132	1	1	
	50 and over	170	106	64	6	6		164	100	64			

XI—LITERACY BY COMMUNITY AND AGE (PART III—DISTRICTS)—CONTD.

Community	Age	Population: Total P	M	F	Literate P	M	F	Illiterate P	M	F	Literate in English P	M	F
1	2	3	4	5	6	7	8	9	10	11	12	13	14
CHENANI JAGIR—concld.													
SIKH	..	*9*	*8*	*1*	*4*	*4*		*5*	*4*	*1*			
	5-10 ..	**1**	1					**1**	1				
	10-15 ..												
	15-20 ..	**1**		1				**1**		1			
	20-30 ..	**4**	4		**3**	3		**1**	1				
	30-50 ..	**1**	1					**1**	1				
	50 and over	**2**	2		**1**	1		**1**	1				
POONCH JAGIR													
TOTAL POPULATION	..	*362265*	*184438*	*177827*	*22913*	*20088*	*2825*	*339352*	*164350*	*175002*	*1347*	*1308*	*39*
	5-10 ..	**68176**	35391	32785	**1343**	1019	324	**66833**	34372	32461	**10**	8	2
	10-15 ..	**56494**	30850	25644	**3430**	2911	519	**53064**	27939	25125	**158**	152	6
	15-20 ..	**42123**	21600	20523	**3573**	3092	481	**38550**	18508	20042	**277**	264	13
	20-30 ..	**70221**	32004	38217	**5752**	4987	765	**64469**	27017	37452	**496**	482	14
	30-50 ..	**88995**	44306	44689	**6865**	6251	614	**82130**	38055	44075	**361**	358	3
	50 and over	**36256**	20287	15969	**1950**	1828	122	**34306**	18459	15847	**45**	44	1
HINDU	..	*20840*	*10680*	*10160*	*3947*	*3182*	*765*	*16893*	*7498*	*9395*	*538*	*514*	*24*
	5-10 ..	**3970**	2043	1927	**257**	164	93	**3713**	1879	1834	**5**	4	1
	10-15 ..	**3193**	1684	1509	**559**	418	141	**2634**	1266	1368	**60**	56	4
	15-20 ..	**2250**	1135	1115	**557**	423	134	**1693**	712	981	**88**	80	8
	20-30 ..	**3695**	1685	2010	**926**	721	205	**2769**	964	1805	**178**	170	8
	30-50 ..	**5227**	2696	2531	**1269**	1102	167	**3958**	1594	2364	**179**	176	3
	50 and over	**2505**	1437	1068	**379**	354	25	**2126**	1083	1043	**28**	28	
MUSLIM	..	*328764*	*167351*	*161413*	*15656*	*14392*	*1264*	*313108*	*152959*	*160149*	*647*	*634*	*13*
	5-10 ..	**61637**	32001	29636	**833**	687	146	**60804**	31314	29490	**5**	4	1
	10-15 ..	**51305**	28122	23183	**2414**	2170	244	**48891**	25952	22939	**82**	80	2
	15-20 ..	**38455**	19767	18688	**2562**	2341	221	**35893**	17426	18467	**151**	147	4
	20-30 ..	**64110**	29233	34877	**3991**	3675	316	**60119**	25558	34561	**257**	251	6
	30-50 ..	**80629**	40015	40614	**4603**	4327	276	**76026**	35688	40338	**145**	145	
	50 and over	**32628**	18213	14415	**1253**	1192	61	**31375**	17021	14354	**7**	7	
CHRISTIAN	..	*3*	*2*	*1*	*3*	*2*	*1*				*3*	*2*	*1*
	5-10 ..												
	10-15 ..												
	15-20 ..												
	20-30 ..												
	30-50 ..												
	50 and over	**3**	2	1	**3**	2	1				**3**	2	1
SIKH	..	*12591*	*6394*	*6197*	*3307*	*2512*	*795*	*9284*	*3882*	*5402*	*159*	*158*	*1*
	5-10 ..	**2551**	1346	1205	**253**	168	85	**2298**	1178	1120			
	10-15 ..	**1988**	1042	946	**457**	323	134	**1531**	719	812	**16**	16	
	15-20 ..	**1407**	697	710	**454**	328	126	**953**	369	584	**38**	37	1
	20-30 ..	**2406**	1084	1322	**835**	591	244	**1571**	493	1078	**61**	61	
	30-50 ..	**3131**	1593	1538	**993**	822	171	**2138**	771	1367	**37**	37	
	50 and over	**1108**	632	476	**315**	280	35	**793**	352	441	**7**	7	

XI—LITERACY BY COMMUNITY AND AGE (PART III—DISTRICTS)—Contd.

Community	Age	Population: Total P	Total M	Total F	Literate P	Literate M	Literate F	Illiterate P	Illiterate M	Illiterate F	Literate in English P	Literate in English M	Literate in English F
	2	3	4	5	6	7	8	9	10	11	12	13	14
POONCH JAGIR—concld.													
Others	..	*67*	*11*	*56*				*67*	*11*	*56*			
	5-10 ..	**18**	1	17				**18**	1	17			
	10-15 ..	**8**	2	6				**8**	2	6			
	15-20 ..	**11**	1	10				**11**	1	10			
	20-30 ..	**10**	2	8				**10**	2	8			
	30-50 ..	**8**	2	6				**8**	2	6			
	50 and over	**12**	3	9				**12**	3	9			
BARAMULLA													
Total Population	..	*531478*	*289252*	*242226*	*23827*	*21926*	*1901*	*507651*	*267326*	*240325*	*4104*	*4010*	*94*
	5-10 ..	**86098**	46498	39600	**1170**	927	243	**84928**	45571	39357	**18**	17	1
	10-15 ..	**72168**	39554	32614	**3135**	2707	428	**69033**	36847	32186	**334**	323	11
	15-20 ..	**65972**	35400	30572	**4148**	3757	391	**61824**	31643	30181	**869**	845	24
	20-30 ..	**119614**	61130	58484	**6767**	6288	479	**112847**	54842	58005	**1612**	1585	27
	30-50 ..	**141382**	77978	63404	**6640**	6336	304	**134742**	71642	63100	**1155**	1131	24
	50 and over	**46244**	28692	17552	**1967**	1911	56	**44277**	26781	17496	**116**	109	7
Hindu	..	*11391*	*6803*	*4588*	*5219*	*4690*	*529*	*6172*	*2113*	*4059*	*1803*	*1785*	*18*
	5-10 ..	**1799**	928	871	**306**	218	88	**1493**	710	783	**9**	8	1
	10-15 ..	**1428**	771	657	**560**	442	118	**868**	329	539	**87**	84	
	15-20 ..	**1211**	705	506	**658**	565	93	**553**	140	413	**243**	238	5
	20-30 ..	**2379**	1420	959	**1304**	1175	129	**1075**	245	830	**615**	608	7
	30-50 ..	**3311**	2152	1159	**1824**	1739	85	**1487**	413	1074	**756**	754	2
	50 and over	**1263**	827	436	**567**	551	16	**696**	276	420	**93**	93	
Muslim	..	*512889*	*278641*	*234248*	*15601*	*15097*	*504*	*497288*	*263544*	*233744*	*1827*	*1791*	*36*
	5-10 ..	**82938**	44834	38104	**607**	559	48	**82331**	44275	38056	**2**	2	
	10-15 ..	**69649**	38188	31461	**2079**	1953	126	**67570**	36235	31335	**180**	174	6
	15-20 ..	**63827**	34190	29637	**2997**	2867	130	**60830**	31323	29507	**506**	491	15
	20-30 ..	**115718**	58982	56736	**4714**	4582	132	**111004**	54400	56604	**839**	826	13
	30-50 ..	**136405**	74950	61455	**4044**	3983	61	**132361**	70967	61394	**291**	289	2
	50 and over	**44352**	27497	16855	**1160**	1153	7	**43192**	26344	16848	**9**	9	
Christian	..	*102*	*48*	*54*	*68*	*30*	*38*	*34*	*18*	*16*	*62*	*29*	*33*
	5-10 ..	**12**	5	7	**2**	2		**10**	3	7	**2**	2	
	10-15 ..	**11**	8	3	**2**	2		**9**	6	3	**2**	2	
	15-20 ..	**12**	6	6	**8**	4	4	**4**	2	2	**6**	4	2
	20-30 ..	**22**	10	12	**18**	9	9	**4**	1	3	**14**	8	6
	30-50 ..	**33**	14	19	**28**	10	18	**5**	4	1	**28**	10	18
	50 and over	**12**	5	7	**10**	3	7	**2**	2		**10**	3	7
Sikh	..	*7093*	*3759*	*3334*	*2937*	*2109*	*828*	*4156*	*1650*	*2506*	*410*	*405*	*5*
	5-10 ..	**1349**	731	618	**255**	148	107	**1094**	583	511	**5**	5	
	10-15 ..	**1079**	587	492	**493**	310	183	**586**	277	309	**64**	63	1
	15-20 ..	**922**	499	423	**485**	321	164	**437**	178	259	**114**	112	2
	20-30 ..	**1495**	718	777	**731**	522	209	**764**	196	568	**144**	143	1
	30-50 ..	**1631**	861	770	**743**	604	139	**888**	257	631	**79**	78	1
	50 and over	**617**	363	254	**230**	204	26	**387**	159	228	**4**	4	

XI—LITERACY BY COMMUNITY AND AGE (PART III—DISTRICTS)—Contd.

Community	Age	Population: Total P	Total M	Total F	Literate P	Literate M	Literate F	Illiterate P	Illiterate M	Illiterate F	Literate in English P	Literate in English M	Literate in English F
1	2	3	4	5	6	7	8	9	10	11	12	13	14
BARAMULLA—concld.													
Buddhist	..	*1*	*1*					*1*	*1*				
	5-10 ..												
	10-15 ..												
	15-20 ..												
	20-30 ..												
	30-50 ..	**1**	1					**1**	1				
	50 and over												
Jew	..	*2*		*2*	*2*		*2*				*2*		*2*
	5-10 ..												
	10-15 ..	**1**		1	**1**		1				**1**		1
	15-20 ..												
	20-30 ..												
	30-50 ..	**1**		1	**1**		1				**1**		1
	50 and over												
ANANTNAG													
Total Population	..	*743114*	*408584*	*334530*	*67606*	*58022*	*9584*	*675508*	*350562*	*324946*	*23080*	*21880*	*1200*
	5-10 ..	**120247**	63506	56741	**5125**	3584	1541	**115122**	59922	55200	**289**	247	42
	10-15 ..	**103539**	56118	47421	**10582**	8190	2392	**92957**	47928	45029	**2652**	2367	285
	15-20 ..	**89488**	48452	41036	**11433**	9500	1933	**78055**	38952	39103	**4598**	4249	349
	20-30 ..	**162374**	86634	75740	**17824**	15656	2168	**144550**	70978	73572	**8079**	7774	305
	30-50 ..	**201799**	114501	87298	**17537**	16208	1329	**184262**	98293	85969	**6418**	6257	161
	50 and over	**65667**	39373	26294	**5105**	4884	221	**60562**	34489	26073	**1044**	986	58
Hindu	..	*59064*	*33467*	*25597*	*31662*	*25441*	*6221*	*27402*	*8026*	*19376*	*14110*	*13580*	*530*
	5-10 ..	**9165**	4775	4390	**2734**	1670	1064	**6431**	3105	3326	**194**	174	20
	10-15 ..	**7834**	4122	3712	**4475**	2995	1480	**3359**	1127	2232	**1469**	1324	145
	15-20 ..	**6621**	3704	2917	**4396**	3249	1147	**2225**	455	1770	**2323**	2158	165
	20-30 ..	**12767**	7471	5296	**8082**	6611	1471	**4685**	860	3825	**4680**	4541	139
	30-50 ..	**16452**	9801	6651	**9029**	8092	937	**7423**	1709	5714	**4647**	4590	57
	50 and over	**6225**	3594	2631	**2946**	2824	122	**3279**	770	2509	**797**	793	4
Muslim	..	*678793*	*372045*	*306748*	*33771*	*30935*	*2836*	*645022*	*341110*	*303912*	*8266*	*7816*	*450*
	5-10 ..	**110222**	58255	51967	**2256**	1816	440	**107966**	56439	51527	**50**	40	10
	10-15 ..	**94964**	51558	43406	**5810**	4977	833	**89154**	46581	42573	**1102**	983	119
	15-20 ..	**82167**	44339	37828	**6707**	6012	695	**75460**	38327	37133	**2168**	2008	160
	20-30 ..	**148309**	78378	69931	**9127**	8550	577	**139182**	69828	69354	**3209**	3086	123
	30-50 ..	**184111**	103968	80143	**7930**	7672	258	**176181**	96296	79885	**1582**	1546	36
	50 and over	**59020**	35547	23473	**1941**	1908	33	**57079**	33639	23440	**155**	153	2
Christian	..	*374*	*182*	*192*	*330*	*162*	*168*	*44*	*20*	*24*	*301*	*140*	*161*
	5-10 ..	**57**	39	18	**44**	33	11	**13**	6	7	**37**	30	7
	10-15 ..	**48**	34	14	**43**	32	11	**5**	2	3	**40**	29	11
	15-20 ..	**21**	10	11	**18**	8	10	**3**	2	1	**16**	7	9
	20-30 ..	**45**	13	32	**41**	11	30	**4**	2	2	**38**	9	29
	30-50 ..	**115**	54	61	**101**	48	53	**14**	6	8	**91**	38	53
	50 and over	**88**	32	56	**83**	30	53	**5**	2	3	**79**	27	52

XI—LITERACY BY COMMUNITY AND AGE (PART III—DISTRICTS)—Contd.

Community	Age	Population: Total P	Total M	Total F	Literate P	Literate M	Literate F	Illiterate P	Illiterate M	Illiterate F	Literate in English P	Literate in English M	Literate in English F
1	2	3	4	5	6	7	8	9	10	11	12	13	14
						ANANTNAG—contd.							
Jain	..	6	5	1	6	5	1				6	5	1
	5-10 ..												
	10-15 ..												
	15-20 ..	**3**	2	1	**3**	2	1				**3**	2	1
	20-30 ..	**2**	2		**2**	2					**2**	2	
	30-50 ..	**1**	1		**1**	1					**1**	1	
	50 and over												
Sikh	..	4835	2862	1973	1820	1471	349	3015	1391	1624	381	332	49
	5-10 ..	**797**	436	361	**88**	65	23	**709**	371	338	**5**	3	2
	10-15 ..	**690**	402	288	**253**	185	68	**437**	217	220	**40**	30	10
	15-20 ..	**672**	393	279	**308**	228	80	**364**	165	199	**87**	73	14
	20-30 ..	**1238**	761	477	**567**	479	88	**671**	282	389	**146**	134	12
	30-50 ..	**1109**	672	437	**471**	394	77	**638**	278	360	**92**	81	11
	50 and over	**329**	198	131	**133**	120	13	**196**	78	118	**11**	11	
Parsee	..	6	3	3	6	3	3				6	3	3
	5-10 ..	**2**		2	**2**		2				**2**		2
	10-15 ..												
	15-20 ..												
	20-30 ..	**1**	1		**1**	1					**1**	1	
	30-50 ..	**2**	1	1	**2**	1	1				**2**	1	1
	50 and over	**1**	1		**1**	1					**1**	1	
Buddhist	..	9	9		3	3		6	6		2	2	
	5-10 ..												
	10-15 ..	**1**	1		**1**	1					**1**	1	
	15-20 ..	**2**	2		**1**	1		**1**	1		**1**	1	
	20-30 ..	**4**	4		**1**	1		**3**	3				
	30-50 ..	**2**	2					**2**	2				
	50 and over												
Jew	..	9	2	7	7	2	5	2		2	7	2	5
	5-10 ..												
	10-15 ..												
	15-20 ..												
	20-30 ..	**3**	1	2	**3**	1	2				**3**	1	2
	30-50 ..	**3**		3	**3**		3				**3**		3
	50 and over	**3**	1	2	**1**	1		**2**		2	**1**	1	
Tribes	..	17	9	8				17	9	8			
	5-10 ..	**3**	1	2				**3**	1	2			
	10-15 ..	**2**	1	1				**2**	1	1			
	15-20 ..	**2**	2					**2**	2				
	20-30 ..	**5**	3	2				**5**	3	2			
	30-50 ..	**4**	2	2				**4**	2	2			
	50 and over	**1**		1				**1**		1			

XI—LITERACY BY COMMUNITY AND AGE (PART III—DISTRICTS)—Contd.

Community	Age	Population: Total P	Total M	Total F	Literate P	Literate M	Literate F	Illiterate P	Illiterate M	Illiterate F	Literate in English P	Literate in English M	Literate in English F
1		3	4	5	6	7	8	9	10	11	12	13	14
ANANTNAG—concld.													
Others	..			1	1		1				1		1
	5-10 ..	**1**		1	**1**		1				**1**		1
	10-15 ..												
	15-20 ..												
	20-30 ..												
	30-50 ..												
	50 and over												
MUZAFFARABAD													
Total Population	..	*225831*	*121443*	*104388*	*13805*	*11608*	*2197*	*212026*	*109835*	*102191*	*1371*	*1350*	*21*
	5-10 ..	**41974**	21923	20051	**1007**	743	264	**40967**	21180	19787	**12**	11	1
	10-15 ..	**35425**	18980	16445	**2048**	1630	418	**33377**	17350	16027	**144**	143	1
	15-20 ..	**28353**	14848	13505	**2030**	1672	358	**26323**	13176	13147	**271**	268	3
	20-30 ..	**48663**	25781	22882	**3705**	3122	583	**44958**	22659	22299	**517**	506	11
	30-50 ..	**50601**	27577	23024	**3798**	3342	456	**46803**	24235	22568	**391**	386	5
	50 and over	**20815**	12334	8481	**1217**	1099	118	**19598**	11235	8363	**36**	36	
Hindu	..	*5083*	*2953*	*2130*	*2398*	*1708*	*690*	*2685*	*1245*	*1440*	*607*	*602*	*5*
	5-10 ..	**896**	458	438	**228**	124	104	**668**	334	334	**7**	6	1
	10-15 ..	**683**	367	316	**340**	203	137	**343**	164	179	**46**	46	
	15-20 ..	**536**	295	241	**300**	187	113	**236**	108	128	**77**	75	2
	20-30 ..	**1110**	647	463	**607**	437	170	**503**	210	293	**199**	197	2
	30-50 ..	**1409**	918	491	**744**	604	140	**665**	314	351	**257**	257	
	50 and over	**449**	268	181	**179**	153	26	**270**	115	155	**21**	21	
Muslim	..	*209758*	*112601*	*97157*	*7385*	*7003*	*382*	*202373*	*105598*	*96775*	*472*	*462*	*10*
	5-10 ..	**38962**	20349	18613	**450**	399	51	**38512**	19950	18562	**4**	4	
	10-15 ..	**32906**	17697	15209	**1047**	983	64	**31859**	16714	15145	**60**	60	
	15-20 ..	**26362**	13892	12470	**1130**	1065	65	**25232**	12827	12405	**113**	112	1
	20-30 ..	**45400**	24001	21399	**2102**	1998	104	**43298**	22003	21295	**203**	196	7
	30-50 ..	**46808**	25271	21537	**2021**	1948	73	**44787**	23323	21464	**83**	81	2
	50 and over	**19320**	11391	7929	**635**	610	25	**18685**	10781	7904	**9**	9	
Christian	..	*40*	*15*	*25*	*29*	*13*	*16*	*11*	*2*	*9*	*6*	*1*	*5*
	5-10	**14**	6	8	**12**	5	7	**2**	1	1			
	10-15 ..	**9**	4	5	**8**	4	4	**1**		1			
	15-20 ..	**5**	3	2	**2**	2		**3**	1	2			
	20-30 ..	**7**	2	5	**4**	2	2	**3**		3	**3**	1	2
	30-50 ..	**4**		4	**3**		3	**1**		1	**3**		3
	50 and over	**1**		1				**1**		1			
Sikh	..	*10950*	*5874*	*5076*	*3993*	*2884*	*1109*	*6957*	*2990*	*3967*	*286*	*285*	*1*
	5-10 ..	**2102**	1110	992	**317**	215	102	**1785**	895	890	**1**	1	
	10-15 ..	**1827**	912	915	**653**	440	213	**1174**	472	702	**38**	37	1
	15-20 ..	**1450**	658	792	**598**	418	180	**852**	240	612	**81**	81	
	20-30 ..	**2146**	1131	1015	**992**	685	307	**1154**	446	708	**112**	112	
	30-50 ..	**2380**	1388	992	**1030**	790	240	**1350**	598	752	**48**	48	
	50 and over	**1045**	675	370	**403**	336	67	**642**	339	303	**6**	6	

XI—LITERACY BY COMMUNITY AND AGE (PART III—DISTRICTS)—Contd.

Community	Age	Population: Total P	Total M	Total F	Literate P	Literate M	Literate F	Illiterate P	Illiterate M	Illiterate F	Literate in English P	Literate in English M	Literate in English F
1	2	3	4	5	6	7	8	9	10	10	12	13	14
						LADAKH							
Total Population	..	*172502*	*87017*	*85485*	*4592*	*4440*	*152*	*167910*	*82577*	*85333*	*261*	*236*	*25*
	5-10 ..	**24227**	12662	11565	**116**	98	18	**24111**	12564	11547	**1**	1	
	10-15 ..	**21961**	11738	10223	**327**	301	26	**21634**	11437	10197	**11**	11	
	15-20 ..	**19707**	10807	8900	**466**	441	25	**19241**	10366	8875	**34**	31	3
	20-30 ..	**34079**	17233	16846	**1127**	1082	45	**32952**	16151	16801	**99**	90	9
	30-50 ..	**44238**	21696	22542	**1677**	1649	28	**42561**	20047	22514	**105**	99	6
	50 and over	**28290**	12881	15409	**879**	869	10	**27411**	12012	15399	**11**	4	7
Hindu	..	*409*	*338*	*71*	*223*	*199*	*24*	*186*	*139*	*47*	*70*	*69*	*1*
	5-10 ..	**39**	24	15	**14**	11	3	**25**	13	12			
	10-15 ..	**18**	11	7	**12**	9	3	**6**	2	4	**1**	1	
	15-20 ..	**16**	12	4	**9**	6	3	**7**	6	1	**2**	1	1
	20-30 ..	**141**	113	28	**78**	66	12	**63**	47	16	**14**	14	
	30-50 ..	**187**	171	16	**107**	104	3	**80**	67	13	**51**	51	
	50 and over	**8**	7	1	**3**	3		**5**	4	1	**2**	2	
Muslim	..	*135158*	*68319*	*66839*	*2317*	*2246*	*71*	*132841*	*66073*	*66768*	*142*	*134*	*8*
	5-10 ..	**19495**	10291	9204	**93**	80	13	**19402**	10211	9191	**1**	1	
	10-15 ..	**17798**	9713	8085	**257**	240	17	**17541**	9473	8068	**8**	8	
	15-20 ..	**15590**	8819	6771	**311**	297	14	**15279**	8522	6757	**24**	24	
	20-30 ..	**27103**	13797	13306	**619**	601	18	**26484**	13196	13288	**64**	60	4
	30-50 ..	**34076**	16463	17613	**716**	711	5	**33360**	15752	17608	**40**	39	1
	50 and over	**21096**	9236	11860	**321**	317	4	**20775**	8919	11856	**5**	2	3
Christian	..	*126*	*70*	*56*	*74*	*51*	*23*	*52*	*19*	*33*	*20*	*5*	*15*
	5-10 ..	**17**	10	7				**17**	10	7			
	10-15 ..	**20**	12	8	**9**	6	3	**11**	6	5			
	15-20 ..	**18**	11	7	**12**	9	3	**6**	2	4	**1**		1
	20-30 ..	**21**	10	11	**14**	10	4	**7**		7	**7**	2	5
	30-50 ..	**36**	17	19	**26**	16	10	**10**	1	9	**8**	3	5
	50 and over	**14**	10	4	**13**	10	3	**1**		1	**4**		4
Sikh	..	*143*	*90*	*53*	*64*	*52*	*12*	*79*	*38*	*41*	*20*	*20*	
	5-10 ..	**29**	20	9	**2**	2		**27**	18	9			
	10-15 ..	**20**	12	8	**6**	5	1	**14**	7	7	**1**	1	
	15-20 ..	**13**	11	7	**9**	7	2	**9**	4	5	**4**	4	
	20-30 ..	**42**	23	19	**26**	19	7	**16**	4	12	**11**	11	
	30-50 ..	**30**	22	8	**20**	18	2	**10**	4	6	**4**	4	
	50 and over	**4**	2	2	**1**	1		**3**	1	2			
Buddhist	..	*36666*	*18200*	*18466*	*1914*	*1892*	*22*	*34752*	*16308*	*18444*	*9*	*8*	*1*
	5-10 ..	**4647**	2317	2330	**7**	5	2	**4640**	2312	2328			
	10-15 ..	**4105**	1990	2115	**43**	41	2	**4062**	1949	2113			
	15-20 ..	**4065**	1954	2111	**125**	122	3	**3940**	1832	2108	**1**	1	
	20-30 ..	**6772**	3290	3482	**390**	386	4	**6382**	2904	3478	**3**	2	1
	30-50 ..	**9909**	5023	4886	**808**	800	8	**9101**	4223	4878	**3**	3	
	50 and over	**7168**	3626	3542	**541**	538	3	**6627**	3088	3539	**2**	2	

XI—LITERACY BY COMMUNITY AND AGE (PART III—DISTRICTS)—Contd.

ASTORE

Community	Age	Total P	Total M	Total F	Literate P	Literate M	Literate F	Illiterate P	Illiterate M	Illiterate F	Literate in English P	Literate in English M	Literate in English F
1	2	3	4	5	6	7	8	9	10	11	12	13	14
Total Population	..	14407	7637	6770	573	539	34	13834	7098	6736	72	71	1
	5-10 ..	**3050**	1593	1457	**29**	24	5	**3021**	1569	1452	**1**	1	
	10-15 ..	**2010**	1079	931	**66**	61	5	**1944**	1018	926	**3**	3	
	15-20 ..	**1507**	789	718	**73**	67	6	**1434**	722	712	**5**	5	
	20-30 ..	**2935**	1516	1419	**198**	184	14	**2737**	1332	1405	**31**	30	1
	30-50 ..	**3470**	1819	1651	**160**	156	4	**3310**	1663	1647	**27**	27	
	50 and over	**1435**	841	594	**47**	47		**1388**	794	594	**5**	5	
Hindu	..	94	60	34	60	47	13	34	13	21	31	31	
	5-10 ..	**15**	6	9	**7**	3	4	**8**	3	5	**1**	1	
	10-15 ..	**8**	4	4	**6**	4	2	**2**		2	**2**	2	
	15-20 ..	**7**	4	3	**5**	3	2	**2**	1	1	**1**	1	
	20-30 ..	**26**	17	9	**13**	10	3	**13**	7	6	**7**	7	
	30-50 ..	**32**	24	8	**25**	23	2	**7**	1	6	**17**	17	
	50 and over	**6**	5	1	**4**	4		**2**	1	1	**3**	3	
Muslim	..	14283	7558	6725	493	476	17	13790	7082	6708	36	36	
	5-10 ..	**3030**	1585	1445	**21**	20	1	**3009**	1565	1444			
	10-15 ..	**2000**	1074	926	**59**	56	3	**1941**	1018	923	**1**	1	
	15-20 ..	**1497**	783	714	**66**	62	4	**1431**	721	710	**4**	4	
	20-30 ..	**2899**	1493	1406	**177**	169	8	**2722**	1324	1398	**21**	21	
	30-50 ..	**3429**	1788	1641	**128**	127	1	**3301**	1661	1640	**8**	8	
	50 and over	**1428**	835	593	**42**	42		**1386**	793	593	**2**	2	
Christian	..	3	2	1				3	2	1			
	5-10 ..	**1**	1					**1**	1				
	10-15 ..												
	15-20 ..												
	20-30 ..	**2**	1	1				**2**	1	1			
	30-50 ..												
	50 and over												
Sikh	..	26	16	10	20	16	4	6		6	5	4	1
	5-10 ..	**4**	1	3	**1**	1		**3**		3			
	10-15 ..	**2**	1	1	**1**	1		**1**		1			
	15-20 ..	**3**	2	1	**2**	2		**1**		1			
	20-30 ..	**8**	5	3	**8**	5	3				**3**	2	1
	30-50 ..	**8**	6	2	**7**	6	1	**1**		1	**2**	2	
	50 and over	**1**	1		**1**	1							
Tribes	..	1	1					1	1				
	5-10 ..												
	10-15 ..												
	15-20 ..												
	20-30 ..												
	30-50 ..	**1**	1					1	**1**				
	50 and over												

XI—LITERACY BY COMMUNITY AND AGE (PART III—DISTRICTS)—Concld.

Community	Age	Population: Total P	Total M	Total F	Literate P	Literate M	Literate F	Illiterate P	Illiterate M	Illiterate F	Literate in English P	Literate in English M	Literate in English F
1	2	3	4	5	6	7	8	9	10	11	12	13	14
GILGIT (LEASED AREA)													
Total Population		*19164*	*10814*	*8350*	*1162*	*1070*	*92*	*18002*	*9744*	*8258*	*172*	*165*	*7*
	5-10 ..	**3295**	1750	1545	**57**	47	10	**3238**	1703	1535	**2**	1	1
	10-15 ..	**2688**	1485	1203	**154**	134	20	**2534**	1351	1183	**8**	7	1
	15-20 ..	**2228**	1267	961	**196**	176	20	**2032**	1091	941	**23**	22	1
	20-30 ..	**4261**	2384	1877	**366**	335	31	**3895**	2049	1846	**81**	77	4
	30-50 ..	**4711**	2701	2010	**297**	287	10	**4414**	2414	2000	**55**	55	
	50 and over	**1981**	1227	754	**92**	91	1	**1889**	1136	753	**3**	3	
Hindu	..	*93*	*65*	*28*	*58*	*42*	*16*	*35*	*23*	*12*	*23*	*21*	*2*
	5-10 ..	**15**	11	4	**3**	1	2	**12**	10	2			
	10-15 ..	**10**	5	5	**7**	4	3	**3**	1	2	**1**	1	
	15-20 ..	**9**	4	5	**7**	3	4	**2**	1	1	**1**		1
	20-30 ..	**30**	21	9	**22**	15	7	**8**	6	2	**9**	8	1
	30-50 ..	**24**	19	5	**17**	17		**7**	2	5	**11**	11	
	50 and over	**5**	5		**2**	2		**3**	3		**1**	1	
Muslim	..	*18994*	*10700*	*8294*	*1052*	*989*	*63*	*17942*	*9711*	*8231*	*128*	*128*	
	5-10	**3265**	1731	1534	**49**	44	5	**3216**	1687	1529	**1**	1	
	10-15 ..	**2667**	1474	1193	**138**	125	13	**2529**	1349	1180	**5**	5	
	15-20 ..	**2212**	1259	953	**183**	169	14	**2029**	1090	939	**21**	21	
	20-30 ..	**4211**	2352	1859	**331**	311	20	**3880**	2041	1839	**63**	63	
	30-50 ..	**4666**	2665	2001	**264**	254	10	**4402**	2411	1991	**36**	36	
	50 and over	**1973**	1219	754	**87**	86	1	**1886**	1133	753	**2**	2	
Christian	..	*17*	*11*	*6*	*14*	*9*	*5*	*3*	*2*	*1*	*14*	*9*	*5*
	5-10 ..	**1**		1	**1**		1				**1**		1
	10-15 ..	**1**		1	**1**		1				**1**		1
	15-20 ..												
	20-30 ..	**9**	5	4	**7**	4	3	**2**	1	1	**7**	4	3
	30-50 ..	**6**	6		**5**	5		**1**	1		**5**	5	
	50 and over												
Sikh	..	*59*	*37*	*22*	*38*	*30*	*8*	*21*	*7*	*14*	*7*	*7*	
	5-10 ..	**13**	7	6	**4**	2	2	**9**	5	4			
	10-15 ..	**10**	6	4	**8**	5	3	**2**	1	1	**1**	1	
	15-20 ..	**7**	4	3	**6**	4	2	**1**		1	**1**	1	
	20-30 ..	**11**	6	5	**6**	5	1	**5**	1	4	**2**	2	
	30-50 ..	**15**	11	4	**11**	11		**4**		4	**3**	3	
	50 and over	**3**	3		**3**	3							
Tribes	..	*1*	*1*					*1*	*1*				
	5-10 ..	**1**	1					**1**	1				
	10-15 ..												
	15-20 ..												
	20-30 ..												
	30-50 ..												
	50 and over												

GILGIT AGENCY.
(Information not available.)

XI—LITERACY BY COMMUNITY AND AGE (PART IV—CITIES)

Community	Age	Population: Total P	Total M	Total F	Literate P	Literate M	Literate F	Illiterate P	Illiterate M	Illiterate F	Literate in English P	Literate in English M	Literate in English F
1	2	3	4	5	6	7	8	9	10	11	12	13	14
JAMMU													
TOTAL POPULATION	..	*43942*	*26469*	*17473*	*22412*	*15410*	*7002*	*21530*	*11059*	*10471*	*7378*	*6655*	*723*
	5-10 ..	**6103**	3276	2827	**1966**	1129	837	**4137**	2147	1990	**51**	37	14
	10-15 ..	**5550**	3148	2402	**3405**	2054	1351	**2145**	1094	1051	**835**	666	169
	15-20 ..	**5479**	3315	2164	**3543**	2309	1234	**1936**	1006	930	**1556**	1311	245
	20-30 ..	**10244**	6366	3878	**5693**	3921	1772	**4551**	2445	2106	**2376**	2160	215
	30-50 ..	**11755**	7423	4332	**5775**	4294	1481	**5980**	3129	2851	**1985**	1908	77
	50 and over	**4811**	2941	1870	**2030**	1703	327	**2781**	1238	1543	**575**	573	2
HINDU	..	*26756*	*15810*	*10946*	*15163*	*10374*	*4789*	*11593*	*5436*	*6157*	*5163*	*4707*	*456*
	5-10 ..	**3634**	1961	1673	**1340**	738	602	**2294**	1223	1071	**32**	18	14
	10-15 ..	**3318**	1897	1421	**2182**	1303	879	**1136**	594	542	**553**	437	116
	15-20 ..	**3293**	1998	1295	**2301**	1512	.789	**992**	486	506	**1058**	906	152
	20-30 ..	**6101**	3653	2448	**3801**	2594	1207	**2300**	1059	1241	**1617**	1498	119
	30-50 ..	**7327**	4459	2868	**4054**	2982	1072	**3273**	1477	1796	**1472**	1419	53
	50 and over	**3083**	1842	1241	**1485**	1245	240	**1598**	597	1001	**431**	429	2
MUSLIM	..	*13868*	*8720*	*5148*	*5580*	*3914*	*1666*	*8288*	*4806*	*3482*	*1768*	*1569*	*199*
	5-10 ..	**1937**	1032	905	**517**	322	195	**1420**	710	710	**16**	16	
	10-15 ..	**1780**	1010	770	**1007**	621	386	**773**	389	384	**232**	192	40
	15-20 ..	**1780**	1112	668	**1007**	659	348	**773**	453	320	**408**	336	72
	20-30 ..	**3395**	2271	1124	**1446**	1036	410	**1949**	1235	714	**604**	533	71
	30-50 ..	**3608**	2410	1198	**1228**	948	280	**2380**	1462	918	**411**	395	16
	50 and over	**1368**	885	483	**375**	328	47	**993**	557	436	**97**	97	
CHRISTIAN	..	*796*	*429*	*367*	*65*	*45*	*20*	*731*	*384*	*347*	*32*	*19*	*13*
	5-10 ..	**158**	84	74	**7**	5	2	**151**	79	72			
	10-15 ..	**110**	59	51	**9**	6	3	**101**	53	48	**2**	1	1
	15-20 ..	**83**	41	42	**10**	6	4	**73**	35	38	**6**	3	3
	20-30 ..	**193**	94	99	**18**	12	6	**175**	82	93	**11**	6	5
	30-50 ..	**185**	111	74	**17**	13	4	**168**	98	70	**11**	7	4
	50 and over	**67**	40	27	**4**	3	1	**66**	37	26	**2**	2	
JAIN	..	*664*	*349*	*315*	*437*	*263*	*174*	*227*	*86*	*141*	*86*	*80*	*6*
	5-10 ..	**114**	60	54	**34**	17	17	**80**	43	37	**1**	1	
	10-15 ..	**89**	46	43	**66**	32	34	**23**	14	9	**11**	9	2
	15-20 ..	**72**	32	40	**69**	32	37	**3**		3	**17**	16	1
	20-30 ..	**126**	63	63	**101**	61	40	**25**	2	23	**29**	27	2
	30-50 ..	**166**	95	71	**119**	83	36	**47**	12	35	**19**	18	1
	50 and over	**97**	53	44	**48**	38	10	**49**	15	34	**9**	9	
SIKH	..	*1847*	*1152*	*695*	*1161*	*810*	*351*	*686*	*342*	*344*	*324*	*276*	*48*
	5-10 ..	**259**	139	120	**67**	47	20	**192**	92	100	**2**	2	
	10-15 ..	**252**	135	117	**140**	91	49	**112**	44	68	**36**	26	10
	15-20 ..	**250**	131	119	**156**	100	56	**94**	31	63	**67**	50	17
	20-30 ..	**425**	282	143	**325**	217	108	**100**	65	35	**113**	95	18
	30-50 ..	**465**	344	121	**355**	266	89	**110**	78	32	**76**	73	3
	50 and over	**196**	121	75	**118**	89	29	**78**	32	46	**30**	30	

XI—LITERACY BY COMMUNITY AND AGE (PART IV—CITIES)—CONTD.

Community	Age	Population: Total P	Total M	Total F	Literate P	Literate M	Literate F	Illiterate P	Illiterate M	Illiterate F	Literate in English P	Literate in English M	Literate in English F
1	2	3	4	5	6	7	8	9	10	11	12	13	14
JAMMU—concld.													
PARSEE	..	*7*	*5*	*2*	*6*	*4*	*2*	*1*	*1*		*5*	*4*	*1*
	5-10 ..	**1**		1	**1**		1						
	10-15 ..	**1**	1		**1**	1					**1**	1	
	15-20 ..												
	20-30 ..	**3**	2	1	**2**	1	1	**1**	1		**2**	1	1
	30-50 ..	**2**	2		**2**	2					**2**	2	
	50 and over												
BUDDHIST	..	*1*	*1*						*1*				
	5-10 ..												
	10-15 ..												
	15-20 ..												
	20-30 ..												
	30-50 .	**1**	1					**1**	1				
	50 and over												
OTHERS	..	*3*	*3*					*3*	*3*				
	5-10 ..												
	10-15 ..												
	15-20 ..	**1**	1					**1**	1				
	20-30 ..	**1**	1					**1**	1				
	30-50 ..	**1**	1					**1**	1				
	50 and over												
SRINAGAR.													
TOTAL POPULATION	..	*182679*	*99759*	*82920*	*41556*	*33374*	*8182*	*141123*	*66385*	*74738*	*18682*	*17551*	*1131*
	5-10 ..	**31899**	15984	15915	**3946**	2594	1352	**27953**	13390	14563	**269**	230	39
	10-15 ..	**27182**	14126	13056	**7244**	5206	2038	**19938**	8920	11018	**2289**	2015	274
	15-20 ..	**22343**	12086	10257	**7124**	5500	1624	**15219**	6586	8633	**3675**	3339	336
	20-30 ..	**39500**	21346	18154	**10342**	8524	1818	**29158**	12822	16336	**6267**	5977	290
	30-50 ..	**47245**	27644	19601	**10031**	8871	1160	**37214**	18773	18441	**5248**	5103	145
	50 and over	**14510**	8573	5937	**2869**	2679	190	**11641**	5894	5747	**934**	887	47
HINDU	..	*38024*	*21257*	*16767*	*23040*	*17482*	*5558*	*14984*	*3775*	*11209*	*11788*	*11270*	*518*
	5-10 ..	**6250**	3201	3049	**2301**	1361	940	**3949**	1840	2109	**183**	165	18
	10-15 ..	**5237**	2740	2497	**3562**	2256	1306	**1675**	484	1191	**1304**	1162	142
	15-20 ..	**4417**	2498	1919	**3308**	2281	1027	**1109**	217	892	**1961**	1799	162
	20-30 ..	**8147**	4701	3446	**5724**	4422	1302	**2423**	279	2144	**3797**	3659	138
	30-50 ..	**10244**	6050	4194	**6222**	5354	868	**4022**	696	3326	**3825**	3771	54
	50 and over	**3729**	2067	1662	**1923**	1808	115	**1806**	259	1547	**718**	714	4
MUSLIM	..	*143037*	*77448*	*65589*	*17497*	*15174*	*2323*	*125540*	*62274*	*63266*	*6318*	*5900*	*418*
	5-10 ..	**25436**	12659	12777	**1562**	1174	388	**23874**	11485	12389	**41**	32	9
	10-15 ..	**21746**	11263	10483	**3547**	2857	690	**18199**	8406	9793	**913**	800	113
	15-20 ..	**7719**	9451	8268	**3668**	3115	553	**14051**	6336	7715	**1632**	1481	51
	20-30 ..	**30947**	16353	14594	**4356**	3900	456	**26591**	12453	14138	**2325**	2213	112
	30-50 ..	**36561**	21298	15263	**3522**	3314	208	**33039**	17984	15055	**1270**	1239	31
	50 and over	**10628**	6424	4204	**842**	814	28	**9786**	5610	4176	**137**	135	2

XI—LITERACY BY COMMUNITY AND AGE (PART IV—CITIES)—Contd.

Community	Age	Population: Total P	Total M	Total F	Literate P	Literate M	Literate F	Illiterate P	Illiterate M	Illiterate F	Literate in English P	Literate in English M	Literate in English F
1	2	3	4	5	7	7	8	9	10	11	12	13	14
						SRINAGAR—contd.							
Christian	..	323	164	159	294	152	148	29	12	17	275	138	137
	5-10 ..	53	37	16	42	32	10	11	5	6	37	30	7
	10-15 ..	44	31	13	40	30	10	4	1	3	39	29	10
	15-20 ..	18	9	9	16	7	9	2	2		15	7	8
	20-30 ..	39	11	28	36	10	26	3	1	2	34	8	26
	30-50 ..	99	50	49	92	47	45	7	3	4	82	37	45
	50 and over	70	26	44	68	26	42	2		2	68	27	41
Jain	..	6	5	1	6	5	1				6	5	1
	5-10 ..												
	10-15 ..												
	15-20 ..	3	2	1	3	2	1				3	2	1
	20-30 ..	2	2		2	2					2	2	
	30-50 ..	1	1		1	1					1	1	
	50 and over												
Sikh	..	1266	873	393	703	554	149	563	319	244	279	231	48
	5-10 ..	157	87	70	38	27	11	119	60	59	5	3	2
	10-15 ..	154	91	63	94	62	32	60	9	31	32	23	9
	15-20 ..	184	124	60	128	94	34	56	30	26	63	49	14
	20-30 ..	357	273	84	220	188	32	137	85	52	105	93	12
	30-50 ..	335	244	91	189	154	35	146	90	56	65	54	11
	50 and over	79	54	25	34	29	5	45	25	20	9	9	
Parsee	..	6	3	3	6	3	3				6	3	3
	5-10 ..	2		2	2		2				2		2
	10-15 ..												
	15-20 ..												
	20-30 ..	1	1		1	1					1	1	
	30-50 ..	2	1	1	2	1	1				2	1	1
	50 and over	1	1		1	1					1	1	
Buddhist	..	7	7		2	2		5	5		2	2	
	5-10 ..												
	10-15 ..	1	1		1	1					1	1	
	15-20 ..	2	2		1	1		1	1		1	1	
	20-30 ..	4	4					4	4				
	30-50 ..												
	50 and over												
Jew	..	9	2	7	7	2	5	2		2	7	2	5
	5-10 ..												
	10-15 ..												
	15-20 ..												
	20-30 ..	3	1	2	3	1	2				3	1	
	30-50 ..	3		3	3		3				3		2
	50 and over	3	1	2	1	1		2		2	1	1	3

XI—LITERACY BY COMMUNITY AND AGE (PART IV—CITIES)—Concld.

Community	Age	Population: Total P	Total M	Total F	Literate P	Literate M	Literate F	Illiterate P	Illiterate M	Illiterate F	Literate in English P	Literate in English M	Literate in English F
1	2	3	4	5	6	7	8	9	10	11	12	13	14
SRINAGAR—concld.													
Others	..	1		1	1		1				1		1
	5-10 ..	1		1	1		1				1		1
	10-15 ..												
	15-20 ..												
	20-30 ..												
	30-50 ..												
	50 and over												

XI—(i) LITERACY BY AGE,

Community	Literate								
	All ages (5 and over)			5-10		10-15		15-20	
	P	M	F	M	F	M	F	M	F
1	2	3	4	5	6	7	8	9	10
All communities ..	**697**	1112	222	395	168	1105	339	1494	354
Scheduled Castes ..	**153**	225	34	101	21	342	55	432	52
Other Hindu ..	**1822**	2730	770	1107	666	2669	1196	3441	1235
Muslim ..	**423**	724	79	242	58	776	135	1088	145
Christian ..	**2184**	2256	2099	1518	943	2435	1345	2375	1783
Jain ..	**5913**	6618	5086	2361	2833	6038	7556	8947	8864
Sikh ..	**3184**	4462	1731	1597	911	4115	2105	5440	2367
Parsee ..	**5455**	5000	6250		10000	10000			
Buddhist ..	**517**	1030	12	21	7	208	9	615	14
Jew ..	**8182**	10000	7778				10000		
Tribes ..	**476**	842							
Others ..	**139**		175		556				

NOTE.—Figures for Gilgit Agency are not available for this table.

SEX AND COMMUNITY

per 10000

20-30		30-50		50 and over		Illiterate per 10000			Literate in English per 10000		
M	F	M	F	M	F	F	M	F	P	M	F
11	*12*	*13*	*14*	*15*	*16*	*17*	*18*	*19*	*20*	*21*	*22*
1421	253	1235	161	961	81	**9303**	8888	9778	**139**	248	15
346	42	234	26	135	8	**9847**	9744	9966	**8**	14	1
3436	940	3110	559	2282	213	**8178**	7270	9230	**491**	875	45
)66	84	743	47	525	23	**9577**	9276	9921	**63**	113	0
1902	1887	2626	2719	2827	4172	**7816**	7744	7901	**1571**	1334	1779
8667	5753	7391	4300	6724	2083	**4087**	3382	4914	**1248**	2141	200
5844	2233	5449	1621	4450	1006	**6817**	5538	8269	**393**	698	47
5000	5000	10000	10000	10000		**4545**	5000	3750	**5000**	5000	5000
1161	11	1576	16	1478	8	**9483**	8970	9988	**3**	5	
10000	10000		10000	10000		**1818**		2222	**8182**	10000	7778
				10000		**9524**	9167	10000			
						9861	10000	9825			

XI—(ii) LITERACY BY AGE,

Natural Divison and District	Literate				
	All ages (5 and over)			5-10	
	Total	Males	Females	Males	Females
1	2	3	4	5	6
JAMMU AND KASHMIR STATE	**697**	**1112**	**222**	**395**	**168**
I. Sub-montane and Semi-mountainous Tract—					
Jammu District (including city)	**1176**	1675	571	622	379
Kathua District (Jasmergarh and Kathua Tehsils only)	**616**	1017	144	338	90
Mirpur District (Mirpur and Bhimbar Tehsils only)	**856**	1399	316	600	219
II. The Outer Hills—					
Kathua District (Bosohli Tehsil only)	**628**	1018	199	562	166
Mirpur District (Kotli Tehsil only)	**543**	911	159	394	111
Udhampur District	**590**	963	176	385	134
Reasi District	**406**	666	114	201	69
Chenani Jagir	**365**	623	40	150	14
Poonch Jagir	**632**	1089	159	288	99
JAMMU PROVINCE	**740**	**1170**	**263**	**422**	**176**
III. The Jhelum Valley (Kashmir Province)	**701**	**1118**	**201**	**398**	**176**
Baramulla District	**448**	758	78	199	61
Anantnag District	**910**	1420	287	564	272
Muzaffarabad District	**611**	956	210	339	132
IV. The Indus Valley (Frontier Districts)	**307**	**574**	**28**	**106**	**23**
Ladakh District	**266**	510	18	77	16
Gilgit (Leased Area)	**606**	989	110	269	65
Gilgit Agency*					
Cities					
Jammu	**5100**	5822	4007	3446	2960
Srinagar	**2275**	3345	987	1623	850

* Figures for Gilgit Agency are not available for this table.

per 10000									
10-15		15-20		20-30		30-50		50 and over	
Males	Females	Males	Females	Males	Females	Males	Females	Males	Females
7	*8*	*9*	*10*	*11*	*12*	*13*	*14*	*15*	*16*
1105	**339**	**1494**	**354**	**1421**	**253**	**1235**	**161**	**961**	**81**
1662	768	2264	896	2136	732	1837	465	1456	217
1163	215	1417	267	1154	199	1139	94	923	12
1773	492	2274	539	1651	366	1494	266	993	109
1180	314	1302	332	1220	229	1126	150	648	61
928	263	1188	285	1145	186	1091	114	766	22
1023	269	1246	278	1167	200	1072	140	825	75
606	163	836	201	821	139	827	91	645	33
508	68	707	55	741	70	722	32	636	
944	202	1430	234	1558	200	1411	137	901	77
1198	**374**	**1601**	**425**	**1482**	**322**	**1340**	**214**	**982**	**98**
1093	**335**	**1513**	**315**	**1444**	**206**	**1176**	**120**	**982**	**75**
584	131	1061	128	1029	82	813	48	666	32
1459	504	1961	471	1807	286	1416	152	1240	84
859	254	1126	265	1211	255	1212	198	891	139
347	**41**	**532**	**48**	**758**	**45**	**798**	**16**	**674**	**7**
256	25	408	28	628	27	760	12	675	6
902	166	1389	208	1405	165	1063	50	742	13
6525	5624	6965	5702	6159	4569	5785	3419	5791	1749
3685	1561	4550	1583	3993	1001	3209	592	3125	320

XI—(iii) LITERACY BY COMMUNITY, SEX AND LOCALITY

Natural Division and District	Literate per 10000: Hindus Males	Hindus Females	Muslims Males	Muslims Females	Sikhs Males	Sikhs Females	Buddhists Males	Buddhists Females
1	2	3	4	5	6	7	8	9
JAMMU AND KASHMIR STATE	**2000**	**548**	**616**	**66**	**3807**	**1454**	**936**	**11**
I. The Sub-montane and Semi-mountainous Tract ..	**1638**	**491**	**887**	**187**	**3307**	**1272**		
Jammu District ..	1750	557	941	296	3068	1141		
Kathua District (Jasmergarh and Kathua Tehsils only)	1050	146	539	89	1651	452		
Mirpur District (Mirpur and Bhimbar Tehsils only) ..	1912	658	899	117	3588	1408		
II. The Outer Hills ..	**1162**	**263**	**518**	**55**	**3363**	**1114**	**122**	
Kathua District (Basohli Tehsil only) ..	983	197	504	64	7000	5000		
Mirpur District (Kotli Tehsil only) ..	3233	1210	542	30	3641	1517		
Udhampur District ..	1041	210	598	74	4115	1238	122	
Reasi District ..	978	228	375	30	3074	1003		
Chenani Jagir ..	605	37	429	28	4444			
Poonch Jagir ..	2584	646	741	67	3338	1081		
III. The Jhelum Valley ..	**6580**	**2000**	**609**	**50**	**4440**	**1832**	**3000**	
Baramulla District ..	6188	991	475	18	4758	2057		
Anantnag District ..	6790	2120	732	80	4512	1458	3333	
Muzaffarabad ..	5115	2752	535	33	4202	1831		
IV. The Indus Valley ..	**5703**	**3099**	**374**	**16**	**5731**	**2162**	**945**	**11**
Ladakh District ..	5512	2553	288	9	4860	1600	945	11
Astore District ..	6528	3171	538	21	8000	4000		
Gilgit (Leased Area) ..	5833	4444	801	63	6818	3077		
Gilgit Agency ..								

TABLE XI.—(IV) LITERACY IN ENGLISH BY AGE, SEX AND LOCAILTY.

XI—(iv) LITERACY IN ENGLISH BY

PER 10000 OF

Natural Division and District	5-10		10-15		15-20		20-30	
	M	F	M	F	M	F	M	F
1	2	3	4	5	6	7	8	9
JAMMU AND KASHMIR STATE ..	**12**	**3**	**195**	**23**	**432**	**37**	**440**	**19**
I. The Sub-montane ansd Semi-mountainous Tract ..	**11**	**3**	**337**	**46**	**707**	**81**	**612**	**43**
Jammu District ..	14	6	334	75	818	133	805	70
Kathua District (Jasmergarh and Kathua Tehsils only) ..	1	1	99	6	231	14	229	8
Mirpur District (Mirpur and Bhimbar Tehsils only) ..	11		432	16	716	27	421	15
II. The Outer Hills ..	**2**		**57**	**2**	**134**	**4**	**161**	**3**
Kathua District (Basohli Tehsil only) ..	2		136	3	243		225	3
Mirpur District (Kotli Tehsil only)	2	1	56		150	2	140	2
Udhampur District ..	6		93	2	194	7	236	4
Reasi District ..	1		18	1	59	1	84	2
Chenani Jagir ..					30		73	
Poonch Jagir ..	2		49	1	122	6	159	4
JAMMU PROVINCE ..	**6**	**2**	**169**	**20**	**370**	**35**	**350**	**19**
III. The Jhelum Valley ..	**21**	**4**	**247**	**31**	**543**	**44**	**568**	**22**
Baramulla District ..	4		82	3	231	8	259	5
Anantnag District ..	39	7	422	60	877	85	897	40
Muzaffarabad District ..	5		75	1	180	2	196	5
IV. The Indus Valley ..	**2**	**1**	**15**	**1**	**45**	**4**	**93**	**7**
Ladakh District ..	1		9		29	3	52	5
Astore District ..	6		28		63		198	7
Gilgit (Leased Area) ..	6	6	47	8	174	10	323	21
Gilgit Agency ..								

AGE, SEX AND LOCALITY

POPULATION 1941

30-50 M	30-50 F	50 and over M	50 and over F	All ages M	All ages F	All ages 1931 M	1931 F	1921 M	1921 F	1911 M	1911 F
10	*11*	*12*	*13*	*14*	*15*	*16*	*17*	*18*	*19*	*20*	*21*
268	**8**	**97**	**5**	**248**	**15**	**113**	**6**				
369	**14**	**150**	**2**	**354**	**28**	**148**	**15**	**87**	**3**	**51**	**2**
506	21	241	3	462	47	211	28	135	6	80	3
121	3	36		121	5	62	2	34	1	13	
225	5	61	1	270	9	78	1	31	1	22	
95		**21**		**81**	**2**	**190**	**12**	**15**		**8**	
101		10		117	1	95		8		11	
81		25		73	1	30	1	9		6	
135	1	24		120	2	70	1	27		12	
73	1	18		47	1	14		8		3	
54		23		39		48					
81	1	22	1	71	2	37	1	12	1	9	1
209	**6**	**79**	**1**	**195**	**12**	**88**	**6**	**44**	**2**	**25**	**1**
353	**11**	**141**	**12**	**332**	**19**	**159**	**6**	**102**	**4**	**52**	**2**
145	4	38	4	139	4	57	2	32	1	16	
546	18	250	22	536	36	262	10	176	7	90	3
143	2	29		111	2	55	1	26	1	13	
69	**2**	**8**	**4**	**45**	**3**	**28**	**2**	**28**	**2**	**18**	**1**
46	3	3	5	27	3	22	2	14	1	11	
148		59		93	1}	94	6	102	7	76	4
204		24		152	8}	3	1				

XI—(v) PROGRES OF

Natural Division and District	Literate — All ages (10 and over) — Males 1941	1931	1921	1911	Females 1941	1931	1921	1911
1	2	3	4	5	6	7	8	9
JAMMU AND KASHMIR STATE ..	**123**	**79**	**54**	**53**	**23**	**7**	**3**	**2**
I. The Sub-montane and Semi-mountainous Tract	**157**	**124**	**75**	**74**	**45**	**20**	**7**	**4**
Jammu District	187	154	88	88	61	29	10	6
Kathuh District (Jasmergarh and Kathua Tehsils only) ..	111	83	133	62	12	5	1	1
Mirpur District (Mirpur and Bhimbar Tehsils only)	126	92	27	57	33	13		3
II. The Outer Hills	**105**	**85**	**41**	**39**	**17**	**8**	**3**	**1**
Kathua District (Basohli Tehsil only)	117	86	86	60	37	6	1	2
Mirpur District (Kotli Tehsil only)	87	67	37	32	14	7	1	1
Udhampur District ..	107	93	48	52	18	5	2	1
Reasi District	76	49	31	36	12	3	8	1
Poonch Jagir	128	66	31	27	17	4	2	1
Chenani Jagir	68	120			5	9		
III. The Jhelum Valley	**126**	**69**	**55**	**58**	**26**	**4**	**2**	**1**
Baramulla	87	44	33	36	8	1	1	
Anantnag	158	90	75	74	29	4	3	1
Muzaffarabad ..	109	58	44	38	23	5	4	1
IV. The Indus Valley	**66**	**46**	**42**	**41**	**28**	**2**	**2**	**1**
Ladakh District	58	46	35	35	2	1	1	1
Astore*	85	96	79	84	5	5	9	2
Gilgit (Leased Area)*	113				12			
Gilgit Agency†		20				1		

*Figures are not separately available for Astore and Gilgit (Leased Area) previous to 1941.
†No figures are available for Gilgit Agency or 1941 or for 1921 and 1911.

LITERACY SINCE 1911

per 1000

15-20								20 and over							
Males				Females				Males				Females			
1941	1931	1921	1911	1941	1931	1921	1911	1941	1931	1921	1911	1941	1931	1921	1911
10	*11*	*12*	*13*	*14*	*15*	*16*	*17*	*18*	*19*	*20*	*21*	*22*	*23*	*24*	*25*
147	**89**	**53**	**42**	**35**	**10**	**4**	**2**	**122**	**87**	**61**	**62**	**18**	**6**	**3**	**2**
167	**154**	**102**	**68**	**59**	**29**	**11**	**6**	**12**	**133**	**77**	**83**	**32**	**17**	**6**	**4**
141	197	135	81	71	42	17	10	121	161	85	98	42	25	8	5
142	9	66	43	27	8	1		110	90	69	70	12	5	2	1
227	106	56	57	54	18	8	4	136	102	66	64	26	1		3
121	**253**	**33**	**26**	**25**	**30**	**3**	**1**	**1**	**260**	**48**	**47**	**14**	**19**	**4**	**1**
130	79	78	48	33	9		2	114	95	98	1	16		1	2
117	64	20	26	29	11	1	2	104	77	46	37	13	5	1	1
125	98	31	28	28	6	2	1	104	102	56	62	15	4	2	1
8	44	2	22	20	5	5	1	78	57	37	43	10	3	10	1
143	75	30	24	23	5	3	1	135	74	36	31	15	3	2	1
71	85			5	13			71	137			4	10		
151	**77**	**53**	**42**	**32**	**5**	**2**	**1**	**122**	**75**	**60**	**65**	**15**	**3**	**3**	**1**
106	47	26	24	13	2	1	1	87	50	39	44	6	1	1	
196	104	78	[illegible]0	47	6	3		153	98	82	84	20	3	3	1
113	62	32	26	27	8	2	1	115	67	52	47	21	4	5	2
53	**41**	**25**	**24**	**5**	**2**	**2**		**75**	**5**	**52**	**51**	**2**	**2**	**2**	**1**
41	36	18	20	3	2	1		69	55	45	44	2	1	1	1
85 } 139 }	[illegible]7	65	52	8 } 2 }	6			93 } 113 }	108	92	102	5 } 9 }	5	6	2
	16				1				30						

XI—(vi) INSTITUTIONS AND SCHOLARS

	1941		1931		1921		1911	
	Institutions	Scholars	Institutions	Scholars	Institutions	Scholars	Institutions	Scholars
1	2	3	4	5	6	7	8	9
ALL KINDS ..	**1841**	**119075**	**1352**	**80439**	**938**	**38885**	**379**	**21194**
I. Boys' Institutions ..	**1600**	**101542**	**1212**	**71078**	**919**	**37192**	**379**	**21194**
Colleges ..	3	2196	2	902	2	441	2	125
State	2	2060	2	902	2	441	2	125
Aided	1	136						
Secondary Schools ..	136	35446	71	19452	44	9431	39	9232
State	108	35446	58	19452 (a)	36	8077		
Aided	28		13		8	1354		
Primary Schools	1129	55536	937	45649	322	15492	202	9448
State	1093	55536	901	45649 (a)	300	13869	202	9448
Aided	36		36		22	1623		
Maktabs and Pathshalas ..	168	4796	145	3834	51	1613 (b)		
Technical Schools ..	8	370	8	335	1	72		
Training Schools ..	1	101	4	106	3	48	1	19
Private Indigenous Schools ..	155	3097	45	800	219	4181	135	2370
Advanced ..	1	140						
Elementary	154	2957	45	800				
Schools for special instructions								
State and Private					277	5914		
II. Girls' Institutions	**241**	**17533**	**140**	**9361**	**19**	**1693**		
Secondary Schools ..	45	7429	19	3150	5	1004		
State	30	7429	11	3150	3	614		
Aided	15		8		2	390		
Primary Schools ..	186	9725	113	6004	11	689		
State	170	9725	97	6004	9	538		
Aided	16		16		2	151		
Maktabs and Pathshalas ..	8	338	8	207	3	(c)		
Training Schools (d) ..	2	41						

(a) Figures for Gilgit (Leased Area) and Gilgit Agency for 1931 which are not available are not included.
(b) Includes scholars in 3 girls pathshalas the number of which are not separately available.
(c) Scholars are not separately available and have been included with boy scholars.
(d) These are attached to high schools.

XI—(vii) PARTIAL LITERACY BY COMMUNITY AND AGE

Community	Age	Persons	Males	Females
1	2	3	4	5
JAMMU AND KASHMIR STATE				
Total Population	.. ..	**33500**	**24075**	**9425**
	5-10	3578	2397	1181
	10-15 ..	4900	3294	1606
	15-20 ..	4306	2822	1484
	20-30	7353	5012	2341
	30-50	9576	7344	2232
	50 and over ..	3787	3206	581
Scheduled Castes	.. ..	**284**	**238**	**46**
	5-10 ..	34	28	6
	10-15 ..	58	48	10
	15-20 ..	38	33	5
	20-30 ...	62	51	11
	30-50	73	60	13
	50 and over ..	19	18	1
Hindu	.. ..	**4418**	**2740**	**1678**
	5-10	842	452	390
	10-15	772	439	333
	15-20	464	247	217
	20-30	751	425	326
	30-50	1114	777	337
	50 and over ..	475	400	75
Muslim	..	**26561**	**19495**	**7066**
	5-10 ..	2494	1791	703
	10-15	3819	2651	1168
	15-20	3553	2371	1182
	20-30	6078	4221	1857
	30-50	7734	6023	1711
	50 and over ..	2883	2438	445
Sikh	.. ..	**1197**	**662**	**535**
	5-10	164	96	68
	10-15	186	100	86
	15-20	144	71	73
	20-30	251	117	134
	30-50	317	175	142
	50 and over ..	135	103	32
Christian	.. ..	**22**	**14**	**8**
	5-10	8	5	3
	10-15 ..	7	3	4
	15-20	2	1	1
	20-30	4	4	
	30-50	1	1	
	50 and over ..			
Buddhist	.. ..	**980**	**903**	**77**
	5-10	16	13	3
	10-15	50	48	2
	15-20	103	98	5
	20-30	205	193	12
	30-50	332	305	27
	50 and over ..	274	246	28

XI—(vii) PARTIAL LITERACY BY COMMUNITY AND AGE—CONCLD.

Community	Age	Persons	Males	Females
1	2	3	4	5
Jain	.. ..	**36**	**21**	**15**
	5-10	**20**	12	8
	10-15 ..	**8**	5	3
	15-20	**2**	1	1
	20-30	**1**		1
	30-50	**4**	2	2
	50 and over ..	**1**	1	
Tribes	.. ..	**2**	**2**	
	5-10			..
	10-15			
	15-20			
	20-30	**1**	1	
	30-50	**1**	1	
	50 and over ..			

IMPERIAL TABLE XI—COMPARATIVE RESULTS.

IMPERIAL

LITERACY BY

1/50

Comparative

Community and Age	Population: In 1/50 sample P	M	F	50 times 1/50 sample P	M	F
1	2	3	4	5	6	7
Total Population	**68160**	**36158**	**32002**	**3408000**	**1807900**	**1600100**
5-10	**11026**	5769	5257	551300	288450	262850
10-15	**9281**	4955	4326	464050	247750	216300
15-20	**7813**	4075	3738	390650	203750	186900
20-30	**13778**	6901	6877	688900	345050	343850
30-50	**17910**	9652	8258	895500	482600	412900
50 and over	**8352**	4806	3546	417600	240300	177300
Hindu	**12593**	**6657**	**5936**	**629650**	**332850**	**296800**
5-30	**7123**	3681	3442	356150	184050	172100
30 and over	**5470**	2976	2494	273500	148800	124700
Muslim	**52053**	**27580**	**24473**	**2602650**	**1379000**	**1223650**
5-30	**32687**	16900	15787	1634350	845000	789350
30 and over	**19366**	10680	8686	968300	534000	434300
Sikh	**1155**	**631**	**524**	**57750**	**31550**	**26200**
5-30	**721**	399	322	36050	19950	16100
30 and over	**434**	232	202	21700	11600	10100
Buddhist	**733**	**365**	**368**	**36650**	**18250**	**18400**
5-30	**374**	185	189	18700	9250	9450
30 and over	**359**	180	179	17950	9000	8950

TABLE XI

COMMUNITY AND AGE

SAMPLE

Results

			LITERATE								
Actual figures *vide* Table XI			In 1/50 sample			50 times 1/50 sample			Actual figires *vide* Table XI		
P	M	F	P	M	F	P	M	F	P	M	F
8	*9*	*10*	*11*	*12*	*13*	*14*	*15*	*16*	*17*	*18*	*19*
3421325	1825402	1595923	4921	4069	852	246050	203450	42600	238384	202976	35408
573440	301643	271797	344	233	111	17200	11650	5550	16489	11924	4565
480444	257721	222723	678	527	151	33900	26350	7550	36003	28450	7553
399168	210417	188751	726	584	142	36300	29200	7100	38127	31442	6685
707662	360375	347287	1249	1016	233	62450	50800	11650	60017	51227	8790
883817	478972	404845	1439	1261	178	71950	63050	8900	65670	59158	6512
376794	216274	160520	485	448	37	24250	22400	1850	22078	20775	1303
708954	380112	328842	2188	1719	469	109400	85950	23450	106877	86137	20740
418211	217176	201035	1261	897	364	63050	44850	18200	64028	47982	16046
290743	162936	127807	927	822	105	46350	41100	5250	42849	38155	4694
2615491	1395093	1220398	2324	2049	275	116200	102450	13750	110692	101051	9641
1683090	882900	800190	1497	1296	201	74850	64800	10050	74264	66335	7929
932401	512193	420208	827	753	74	41350	37650	3700	36428	34716	1712
55815	29673	26142	346	253	93	17300	12650	4650	17765	13240	4525
37047	19108	17939	215	152	63	10750	7600	3150	11154	7818	3336
18768	10565	8203	131	101	30	6550	5050	1500	6611	5422	1189
37153	18431	18722	35	33	2	1750	1650	100	1920	1898	22
19926	9701	10225	9	8	1	450	400	50	569	558	11
17227	8730	8497	26	25	1	1300	1250	50	1351	1340	11

IMPERIAL

LITERACY BY

1/50

Comparative

Community and Age		Illiterate: In 1/50 sample			Illiterate: 50 times 1/50 sample		
		P	M	F	P	M	F
1		*20*	*21*	*22*	*23*	*24*	*25*
Total Population	..	**63239**	**32089**	**31150**	**3161950**	**1604450**	**1557500**
5-10	..	**10682**	5536	5146	**534100**	276800	257300
10-15	..	**8603**	4428	4175	**430150**	221400	208750
15-20	..	**7087**	3491	3596	**354350**	174550	179800
20-30	..	**12529**	5885	6644	**626450**	294250	332200
30-50	..	**16471**	8391	8080	**823550**	419550	404000
50 and over	..	**7867**	4358	3509	**393350**	217900	175450
Hindu	..	**10405**	**4938**	**5467**	**520250**	**246900**	**273350**
5-30	..	**5862**	2784	3078	**293100**	139200	153900
30 and over	..	**4543**	2154	2389	**227150**	107700	119450
Muslim	..	**49729**	**25531**	**24198**	**2486450**	**1276550**	**1209900**
5-30	..	**31190**	15604	15586	**1559500**	780200	779300
30 and over	..	**18539**	9927	8612	**926950**	496350	430600
Sikh	..	**809**	**378**	**431**	**40450**	**18900**	**21550**
5-30	..	**506**	247	259	**25300**	12350	12950
30 and over	..	**303**	131	172	**15150**	6550	8600
Buddhist	..	**698**	**332**	**366**	**34900**	**16600**	**18300**
5-30		**365**	177	188	**18250**	8850	9400
30 and over	..	**333**	155	178	**16650**	7750	8900

TABLE XI

COMMUNITY AND AGE

SAMPLE

Results—concld.

			Literate in English								
Actual figures *vide* Table XI			In 1/50 sample			50 times 1/50 sample			Actual figures *vide* Table XI		
P	M	F	P	M	F	P	M	F	P	M	F
26	*27*	*28*	*29*	*30*	*31*	*32*	*33*	*34*	*35*	*36*	*37*
3182941	**1622426**	**1560515**	**907**	**840**	**67**	**45350**	**42000**	**3350**	**47615**	**45254**	**2361**
556951	280719	267232	**5**	4	1	**250**	200	50	**442**	374	68
444441	229271	215170	**84**	78	6	**4200**	3900	300	**5548**	5027	521
361041	178975	182066	**164**	152	12	**8200**	7600	600	**9787**	9080	707
647645	309148	338497	**315**	285	30	**15750**	14250	1500	**16536**	15861	675
818147	419814	398333	**278**	264	14	**13900**	13200	700	**13127**	12816	311
354716	195499	159217	**61**	57	4	**3050**	2850	200	**2175**	2096	79
602077	**293975**	**308102**	**532**	**506**	**26**	**26600**	**25300**	**1300**	**28354**	**27152**	**1202**
354183	169194	184989	**293**	272	21	**14650**	13600	1050	**17444**	16392	1052
247894	124781	123113	**239**	234	5	**11950**	11700	250	**10910**	10760	150
2504799	**1294042**	**1210757**	**326**	**299**	**27**	**16300**	**14950**	**1350**	**16467**	**15697**	**770**
1608826	816565	792261	**241**	221	20	**12050**	11050	1000	**13010**	12308	702
895973	77477	418496	**85**	78	7	**4250**	3900	350	**3457**	3389	68
38050	**16433**	**21617**	**34**	**28**	**6**	**1700**	**1400**	**300**	**2195**	**2071**	**124**
25893	11290	14593	**27**	23	4	**1350**	1150	200	**1566**	1457	109
12157	5143	7014	**7**	5	2	**350**	250	100	**629**	614	15
35233	**16533**	**18700**							**11**	**10**	**1**
19357	9143	10214							**9**	8	1
15876	7390	8486							**2**	2	

IMPERIAL TABLE XII AND ITS SUBSIDIARIES

Mothertongue

NOTES

1. The table is in two parts as was the corresponding table XV in 1931. It is based on the answers to census questions 18 and 19—Mothertongue and other Indian languages in common use.

2. Part I is the main table giving the various mothertongues spoken in the State and classified in accordance with the scheme of classification issued by the Census Commissioner for India. The mothertongues are given under three main heads :—

A. Languages of India.

B. Languages of other Asiatic countries and Africa.

C. European languages.

The method of presentation of the main table is slightly different to that adopted in 1931 and on this occasion four subsidiary languages have been given in Part II instead of three ; Hindustani, which includes both Hindi and Urdu, has been added. This language is of All-India interest as well as of local interest.

3. Part II is divided into sections A and B. The former shows the extent to which the four chief subsidiary languages are used and the latter the extent of Polylingualism ; in this case those speaking more than two languages, including their mothertongue.

4. An Appendix follows Part II (B) showing the classification of dialects adopted for the purposes of the table. The classification of these dialects, many of which are associated with local place names, is based partly on local knowledge and partly by reference to the 1931 Report.

5. (i) 'Hindi' and 'Urdu' have been combined and shown as Hindustani with the approval of the Census Commissioner for India.

(ii) The term 'Hindustani' replaces 'Western Hindi' in the classification shown in Part I (A). This has been done in consultation with the Census Commissioner for India to make the position of Hindustani quite clear.

6. Thirteen mothertongues have been shown in Part II of the table as against ten in 1931 ; those added are Bodhi, Kishtwari and Dardastani and they all refer to isolated areas.

7. (i) In Part II (A) the main language under which each mothertongue has been shown in Part I has been given in brackets. The method adopted in the classification of dialects has been referred to in note 4 above.

(ii) The languages selected as subsidiary languages for the purposes of this part of the table are those most in use.

(iii) The column "Total returning the mothertongue" has been added to the table to facilitate appreciation of the table.

8. The totals of the persons speaking the mothertongues shown in Part II (A) will not agree with the totals shown against the same mothertongues in Part I but with the totals against each given in the Appendix referred to in note 4 above. This is because Part I shows the total speaking the mothertongue inclusive of dialects whereas Part II (A) does not. Take Kashmiri as an example. Part I gives a total of 1549460 persons with this as mothertongue whereas Part II (A) shows 1512912

persons only. The difference, 36548, is accounted for by the total of those dialects grouped with Kashmiri in the Appendix. In Part I Dogri is included under Punjabi—columns 32-34—in accordance with the classification scheme for the languages of India, but in Part II (A) Dogri and Punjabi are rightly shown separately as it is a matter of particular local interest to do so ; it will be seen that more persons speak the dialect 'Dogri' than the main language 'Punjabi'.

9. **Subsidiary (i)**—

(a) This subsidiary has been prepared in accordance with the scheme issued by the Census Commissioner for India. The method of presentation of the corresponding table in 1931 was different ; for this reason figures are not available for columns 6 and 7 and they have been left blank.

(b) The word 'Dogri' in brackets against Punjabi is to indicate that the figures given includes Dogri with Punjabi as in the case of Part I of the table.

(c) Column 8 shows the localities where each language is chiefly spoken. Only the names of those Tehsils have been given against each where at least 10 per cent. of the population of the tehsil speaks the language. Where column 8 is blank it indicates that the language is not spoken by 10 per cent. of the population of any tehsil.

(d) The use of the Tibetan Group of languages is almost entirely confined to the Ladakh District.

(e) Shina and Burushaski are scarcely used except in the Astore, Gilgit (Leased Area) and Gilgit Agency Districts.

(f) Kashmiri is spoken widely from Karnah to Bhadrawah with a sprinkling of persons using it in Poonch, Uri and Reasi.

(g) Gojri, the language of the Gujjars, is included with Rajasthani. Pahari which is shown separately in the scheme, is closely connected with Gojari and is spoken in much the same areas.

(h) Dogri is the language most used in the Udhampur Kathua, Jammu and Chenani Jagir Districts.

10. **Subsidiary (ii)**—

(a) The languages selected for this table in 1931 were Dogri, Kashmiri, Punjabi, Gojari and Pahari. On this occasion we have excluded the last two named but included Hindustani ; the same languages are given as subsidiaries in Part II (A).

(b) The Table is besed on the figures given in Part II (A) for Dogri, Kashmiri and Punjabi and on Part I for Hindustani as the figures for the latter are not given in Part II (A).

(c) In 1931 the corresponding table was given by Natural Divisions. On this occasion the figures are given by Districts.

(d) This table brings out clearly the widespread use of 'Hindustani' as a subsidiary language.

11. **Subsidiary (iii)**—

(a) In 1931 the corresponding subsidiary table gave figures only for Kashmiris, Gujjars and Shins. On this occasion we have expanded the table to cover the elements inhabiting Ladakh.

(b) The figures given in columns 3 and 4 of the table against Balti, Gujjar, Kashmiri and Shin have been taken from Imperial Table XIV ; the tribe 'Kashmiri' includes Kashmiri

Pandits, Kashmiri Muslims, Hajjams, Hanjis, Sheikhs and Syeds of Kashmir Province the figures for all of which have been taken from Imperial Table XIV—Part III.

The figures for Buddhists have been taken from Imperial Table XIII and the figures given for Ladakhis are the population figures of Ladakh Tehsil shown in State Table I. The figures for ' tribe ' are necessarily approximate. The method adopted is the most accurate possible for the purposes of this table.

(c) The figures given in columns 5 to 8 are based on Table XII—Part II (A). In columns 5 and 6 are given those speaking the language as mothertongue without any subsidiary. The figures have been arrived at by subtracting the sum of the speakers of subsidiary languages from the total of those returning the language as mothertongue in Table XII—Part II (A).

(d) The totals shown in columns 7 and 8 have been obtained by adding up the number of persons under subsidiary languages under each particular mothertongue in table XII—Part II (A).

(e) This table also brings out the widespread use of Hindustani as a subsidiary language.

(f) Kashmiri and Shina have not only maintained their widespread use, *vide* columns 5 and 6 as compared with 1931 but shown an increase. The figures for Gojri, on the other hand, show a decrease or weakening in the use of the tribal language. These indications cannot be accepted as tendencies until confirmed by the figures for 1951.

NOTE.—P stands for Persons, M for Males and F for Females.

XII—PART I

A.—LANGUAGES

District or State		Population			Bhotia of Baltistan or Balti		
		P	M	F	P	M	F
1		2	3	4	5	6	7
JAMMU AND KASHMIR STATE	..	**4021616**	**2129872**	**1891744**	**134012**	**67787**	**66225**
Jammu Province	..	**1981433**	**1034410**	**947023**	**184**	**173**	**11**
(a) TOTAL DISTRICTS	..	*1547809*	*814016*	*733793*	*125*	*114*	*11*
Jammu	..	**431362**	233976	197386	**16**	14	2
Kathua	..	**177672**	94134	83538	**22**	21	1
Udhampur	..	**294217**	153608	140609	**86**	78	8
Reasi	..	**257903**	135502	122401			
Mirpur	..	**386655**	196796	189859	**1**	1	
(b) TOTAL JAGIRS	..	*433624*	*220394*	*213230*	*59*	*59*	
Chenani Jagir	..	**11796**	6475	5321	**59**	59	
Poonch Jagir	..	**421828**	213919	207909			
Kashmir Province	..	**1728705**	**934738**	**793967**	**352**	**320**	**32**
Baramulla	..	**612428**	330050	282378	**64**	32	32
Anantnag	..	**851606**	463571	388035	**209**	209	
Muzaffarabad	..	**264671**	141117	123554	**79**	79	
Frontier Districts	..	**311478**	**160724**	**150754**	**133476**	**67294**	**66182**
Ladakh	..	**195431**	98478	96953	**133163**	66994	66169
Astore	..	**17026**	8948	8078	**72**	59	13
Gilgit (Leased Area)	..	**22495**	12471	10024	**152**	152	
Gilgit Agency	..	**76526**	40827	35699	**89**	89	

(MOTHER TONGUE)

OF INDIA

Bhotia of Ladakh or Ladakhi			Bhotia of Tibet or Tibetan			Bhotia (Others)			Chitrali		
P	M	F	P	M	F	P	M	F	P	M	F
8	*9*	*10*	*11*	*12*	*13*	*14*	*15*	*16*	*17*	*18*	*19*
46953	**23253**	**23700**	**503**	**342**	**161**	**328**	**185**	**143**	**6425**	**3258**	**3167**
299	**135**	**164**	**145**	**143**	**2**	**284**	**156**	**128**	**1**	**1**	
299	*135*	*164*	*50*	*49*	*1*	*284*	*156*	*128*	*1*	*1*	
			1		1	**38**	36	2			
			49	49							
299	135	164				**246**	120	126	**1**	1	
			95	*94*	*1*						
			89	89							
			6	5	1						
230	**37**	**193**	**26**	**15**	**11**	**24**	**13**	**11**			
5	4	1									
221	31	190	**20**	12	8	**24**	13	11			
4	2	2	**6**	3	3						
46424	**23081**	**23343**	**332**	**184**	**148**	**20**	**16**	**4**	**6424**	**3257**	**3167**
46420	23080	23340	**317**	170	147						
3	1	2				**20**	16	4	**1**	1	
1		1	**15**	14	1						
									205	102	103
									6218	3154	3064

A.—LANGUAGES

District or State	Other Kafir Languages			Kohistani		
	P	M	F	P	M	F
1	20	21	22	23	24	25
JAMMU AND KASHMIR STATE ..	**4291**	**2278**	**2013**	**1160**	**638**	**522**
Jammu Province ..				**823**	**466**	**357**
(a) TOTAL DISTRICTS ..				*823*	*466*	*357*
Jammu ..				**537**	307	230
Kathua ..				**53**	25	28
Udhampur ..				**150**	90	60
Reasi ..				**83**	44	39
Mirpur ..						
(b) TOTAL JAGIRS ..						
Chenani Jagir ..						
Poonch Jagir ..						
Kashmir Province ..	**39**	**22**	**17**	**297**	**148**	**149**
Baramulla ..	**24**	16	8	**147**	78	69
Anantnag ..	**15**	6	9	**5**	2	3
Muzaffarabad ..				**145**	68	77
Frontier Districts ..	**4252**	**2256**	**1996**	**40**	**24**	**16**
Ladakh ..						
Astore ..						
Gilgit (Leased Area) ..				**35**	19	16
Gilgit Agency ..	**4252**	2256	1996	**5**	5	

(MOTHER TONGUE)—CONTD.

OF INDIA—contd.

Kashmiri			Shina			Panjabi			Rajasthani		
P	M	F	P	M	F	P	M	F	P	M	F
26	27	28	29	30	31	32	33	34	35	36	37
1549460	**837357**	**712103**	**84604**	**44716**	**39888**	**1075273**	**559439**	**515834**	**283741**	**150581**	**133160**
178390	**94810**	**83580**	**114**	**69**	**45**	**1000018**	**524660**	**475358**	**187980**	**98215**	**89765**
158863	*84232*	*74631*	*113*	*68*	*45*	*968690*	*508375*	*460315*	*140184*	*73848*	*66336*
2650	2037	613	**25**	23	2	**358309**	193396	164913	**40764**	21555	19209
2326	1171	1155				**156388**	82791	73597	**7664**	4091	3573
128668	68078	60590	**83**	40	43	**100882**	52692	48190	**23212**	11789	11423
25105	12871	12234				**96886**	49311	47575	**61806**	33037	28769
114	75	39	**5**	5		**256225**	130185	126040	**6738**	3376	3362
19527	*10578*	*8949*	*1*	*1*		*31328*	*16285*	*15043*	*47796*	*24367*	*23429*
798	627	171	**1**	1		**8695**	4517	4178	**482**	243	239
18729	9951	8778				**22633**	11768	10865	**47314**	24124	23190
1369573	**741603**	**627970**	**7888**	**4101**	**3787**	**73473**	**33677**	**39796**	**92392**	**50165**	**42227**
545032	293590	251442	**7785**	4033	3752	**12116**	6432	5684	**32759**	18108	14651
800524	435058	365466	**98**	63	35	**13194**	7802	5392	**26732**	14526	12206
24017	12955	11062	**5**	5		**48163**	19443	28720	**32901**	17531	15370
1497	**944**	**553**	**76602**	**40546**	**36056**	**1782**	**1102**	**680**	**3369**	**2201**	**1168**
1174	689	485	**13562**	6990	6572	**453**	362	91			
133	97	36	**16447**	8498	7949	**236**	199	37	**22**	14	8
171	140	31	**18217**	9755	8462	**238**	156	82	**771**	416	355
19	18	1	**28376**	15303	13073	**855**	385	470	**2576**	1771	805

XII—PART I

A.—LANGUAGES

District or State		Western Pahari			Pahari (Unspecified)			Tamil			Telugu		
		P	M	F	P	M	F	P	M	F	P	M	F
1		*38*	*39*	*40*	*41*	*42*	*43*	*44*	*45*	*46*	*47*	*48*	*49*
JAMMU AND KAHSMIR STATE		**531319**	**280165**	**251154**	**4**	**3**	**1**	**44**	**30**	**14**	**3**	**3**	
Jammu Province	..	**360870**	**183437**	**177433**				**23**	**13**	**10**	**1**	**1**	
(a) TOTAL DISTRICTS	..	*123288*	*63581*	*59707*				*23*	*13*	*10*	*1*	*1*	
Jammu	..	**63**	45	18				**22**	12	10			
Kathua	..	**4312**	2283	2029									
Udhampur	..	**38507**	19377	19130				1	1		**1**	1	
Reasi	..	**60628**	31621	29007									
Mirpur	..	**19778**	10255	9523									
(b) TOTAL JAGIRS	..	*237582*	*119856*	*117726*									
Chenani Jagir	..	**869**	497	372									
Poonch Jagir	..	**236713**	119359	117354									
Kashmir Province	..	**170432**	**96720**	**73712**	**4**	**3**	**1**	**21**	**17**	**4**	**2**	**2**	
Baramulla	..	**9681**	5174	4507	**4**	3	1	**5**	3	2			
Anantnag	..	**5156**	2752	2404				**15**	14	1	**2**	2	
Muzaffarabad	..	**155595**	88794	66801				**1**		1			
Frontier Districts	..	**17**	**8**	**9**									
Ladakh	..	**5**	2	3									
Astore	..	**12**	6	6									
Gilgit (Leased Area)	..												
Gilgit Agency	..												

(MOTHER TONGUE)—CONTD.

OF INDIA—contd.

Burmese			Lahnda or Western Panjabi			Sindhi			Marathi			Bengali			Eastern Hindi		
P	M	F	P	M	F	P	M	F	P	M	F	P	M	F	P	M	F
50	51	52	53	54	55	56	57	58	59	60	61	62	63	64	65	66	67
1		1	82993	42194	40799	3	2	1	17	7	10	52	36	17	7	1	6
			82975	42184	40791	1		1	8	2	6	26	19	7	7	1	6
			82973	42184	40789	1		1	8	2	6	25	18	7	7	1	6
			44	17	27				6	1	5	18	14	4	7	1	6
			41		41				1	1							
			1	1								1	1				
												2	1	1			
			82887	42166	40721	1		1	1		1	4	2	2			
			2		2							1	1				
			2		2							1	1				
1		1	8	3	5	2	2		9	5	4	23	15	8			
			1		1				2	2		8	5	3			
1		1	7	3	4				7	3	4	13	8	5			
						2	2					2	2				
			10	7	3							3	2	1			
			5	2	3												
			5	5								3	2	1			

A.—LANGUAGES

District or State	Gujrati			Hindustani			Naipali		
	P	M	F	P	M	F	P	M	F
1	*68*	*69*	*70*	*71*	*72*	*73*	*74*	*75*	*76*
JAMMU AND KASHMIR STATE ..	**191**	**113**	**78**	**178528**	**94868**	**83660**	**1467**	**957**	**510**
Jammu Province ..	**57**	**34**	**23**	**167368**	**88623**	**78745**	**1222**	**822**	**400**
(a) TOTAL DISTRICTS ..	*57*	*34*	*23*	*70188*	*39517*	*30671*	*1207*	*807*	*400*
Jammu ..	**57**	34	23	**27382**	15521	11861	**1037**	693	344
Kathua ..				**6689**	3620	3069	**118**	74	44
Udhampur ..				**1924**	1093	831	**39**	29	10
Reasi ..				**13331**	8575	4756	**13**	11	2
Mirpur ..				**20862**	10708	10154			
(b) TOTAL JAGIRS ..				*97180*	*49106*	*48074*	*15*	*15*	
Chenani Jagir ..				**773**	413	360	**15**	15	
Poonch Jagir ..				**96407**	48693	47714			
Kashmir Province ..	**71**	**43**	**28**	**10631**	**6027**	**4604**	**243**	**133**	**110**
Baramulla ..	**20**	11	9	**3907**	2097	1810	**8**	5	3
Anantnag ..	**51**	32	19	**3172**	1814	1358	**232**	125	107
Muzaffarabad ..				**3552**	2116	1436	**3**	3	
Frontier Districts ..	**63**	**36**	**27**	**529**	**218**	**311**	**2**	**2**	
Ladakh ..				**22**	18	4	**2**	2	
Astore ..				**5**	5				
Gilgit (Leased Area) ..	**1**	1		**110**	68	42			
Gilgit Agency ..	**62**	35	27	**392**	127	265			

(MOTHER TONGUE) – CONTD.

OF INDIA—contd.

Balochi			Pashto			Other Eranian Languages			Newari			Kanarese			Coorgi		
P	M	F	P	M	F	P	M	F	P	M	F	P	M	F	P	M	F
77	*78*	*79*	*80*	*81*	*82*	*83*	*84*	*85*	*86*	*87*	*88*	*89*	*90*	*91*	*92*	*93*	*94*
5	**3**	**2**	**4197**	**2554**	**1643**	**351**	**186**	**165**	**2**	**2**		**7**	**3**	**4**	**2**	**2**	
2	**1**	**1**	**523**	**370**	**153**	**21**	**12**	**9**							**2**	**2**	
2	*1*	*1*	*489*	*339*	*150*	*21*	*12*	*9*							*2*	*2*	
			303	213	90	**21**	12	9							**2**	2	
			9	8	1												
			106	74	32												
			47	29	18												
2	1	1	**24**	15	9												
			34	*31*	*3*												
			15	14	1												
			19	17	2												
1	**1**		**2419**	**1395**	**1024**	**23**	**13**	**10**	**2**	**2**		**7**	**3**	**4**			
			726	379	347												
1	1		**1511**	906	605	**18**	10	8	**2**	2		**7**	3	4			
			182	110	72	**5**	3	2									
2	1	1	**1255**	**789**	**466**	**307**	**161**	**146**									
			1	1		**2**	2										
			46	34	12	**1**	1										
2	1	1	**418**	275	143	**304**	158	146									
			790	479	311												

A.—LANGUAGES OF INDIA —concld.

District or State	Khowar			Konkani			Oriya			Burushaski		
	P	M	F	P	M	F	P	M	F	P	M	F
1	95	96	97	98	99	100	101	102	103	104	105	106
JAMMU AND KASHMIR STATE ..	**1487**	**892**	**595**	**1**		**1**	**7**	**7**		**33132**	**17424**	**15708**
Jammu Province ..							**7**	**7**				
(a) TOTAL DISTRICTS ..							7	7				
Jammu ..							7	7				
Kathua ..												
Udhampur ..												
Reasi ..												
Mirpur ..												
(b) TOTAL JAGIRS ..												
Chenani Jagir ..												
Poonch Jagir ..												
Kashmir Province ..				**1**		**1**				**3**	**3**	
Baramulla ..				1		1						
Anantnag ..										3	3	
Muzaffarabad ..												
Frontier Districts ..	**1487**	**892**	**595**							**33129**	**17421**	**15708**
Ladakh ..										244	122	122
Astore ..										22	12	10
Gilgit (Leased Area) ..	2	1	1							1732	1132	600
Gilgit Agency ..	1485	891	594							31131	16155	14976

(MOTHER TONGUE)—CONTD.

B.—LANGUAGES OF OTHER ASIATIC COUNTRIES AND AFRICA

Turkish			Chinese			Arabic			Persian			Japanese		
P	M	F	P	M	F	P	M	F	P	M	F	P	M	F
107	*108*	*109*	*110*	*111*	*112*	*113*	*114*	*115*	*116*	*117*	*118*	*119*	*120*	*121*
283	**188**	**95**	**1**	**1**		**9**	**5**	**4**	**309**	**179**	**130**	**1**	**1**	
1	**1**					**8**	**5**	**3**	**29**	**20**	**9**			
1	*1*					*7*	*5*	*2*	*28*	*20*	*8*			
									22	18	4			
									1	1				
1	1					**7**	5	2	**5**	1	4			
						1		1	1		1			
						1		1	**1**		1			
120	**69**	**51**	**1**	**1**		**1**		**1**	**15**	**11**	**4**	**1**	**1**	
66	17	19							3	2	1			
54	22	32	**1**	1		**1**		1	**8**	8		**1**	1	
									4	1	3			
162	**118**	**44**							**265**	**148**	**117**			
42	33	9							**7**	5	2			
									1		1			
73	46	27							**28**	23	5			
47	39	8							**229**	120	109			

XII—PART I

C— EUROPEAN

District or State		English P	English M	English F	Dutch P	Dutch M	Dutch F	Danish P	Danish M	Danish F	German P	German M	German F	French P	French M	French F
1		122	123	124	125	126	127	128	129	130	131	132	133	134	135	136
JAMMU AND KASHMIR STATE	..	**397**	**197**	**200**	**3**	**2**	**1**	**1**	**1**		**15**	**3**	**12**	**12**	**6**	**6**
Jammu Province	..	**44**	**28**	**16**												
(a) TOTAL DISTRICTS	..	*42*	*27*	*15*												
Jammu	..	**31**	18	13												
Kathua	..															
Udhampur	..	**9**	7	2												
Reasi	..	**2**	2													
Mirpur	..															
(b) TOTAL JAGIRS	..	*2*	*1*	*1*												
Chenani Jagir	..															
Poonch Jagir	..	**2**	1	1												
Kashmir Province	..	**330**	**156**	**174**	**3**	**2**	**1**	**1**	**1**		**15**	**3**	**12**	**6**	**3**	**3**
Baramulla	..	**47**	27	20							**5**		5	**4**	2	2
Anantnag	..	**278**	129	149	**3**	2	1	**1**	1		**10**	3	7	**2**	1	1
Muzaffarabad	..	**5**		5												
Frontier Districts	..	**23**	**13**	**10**										**6**	**3**	**3**
Ladakh	..	**6**	3	3										**6**	3	3
Astore	..															
Gilgit (Leased Area)	..	**17**	10	7												
Gilgit Agency	..															

(MOTHER TONGUE)—CONCLD.

LANGUAGES

Italian			Portuguese			Spanish			Swiss			Welsh			Slavonic (Russian) Polish & Others			Finnish		
P	M	F	P	M	F	P	M	F	P	M	F	P	F	F	P	M	F	P	M	F
137	138	139	140	141	142	143	144	145	146	147	148	149	150	151	152	153	154	155	156	157
3	.	3	2	1	1	2		2	1	1		3		3	2		2	2	1	1
3		3	2	1	1	2		2	1	1		3		3	2		2	2	1	1
3		3	1		1	2		2							2		2			
			1	1					1	1		3		3				2	1	1

District or State		Total returning the mother-tongue		Using a language subsidiary to Kashmiri: Subsidiary language Dogri		Subsidiary language Punjabi	
		M	F	M	F	M	F
1		2	3	4	5	6	7
JAMMU AND KASHMIR STATE	..	**818196**	**694716**	**3532**	**1469**	**2600**	**995**
Jammu Province	..	**75684**	**66200**	**3512**	**1462**	**1061**	**395**
(a) TOTAL DISTRICTS	..	*65109*	*57273*	*3480*	*1452*	*781*	*163*
Jammu	..	2016	610	108	27	231	29
Kathua	..	1171	1155	247	127	19	14
Udhampur	..	48996	43249	1287	704	450	102
Reasi	..	12852	12220	1838	594	72	17
Mirpur	..	74	39			9	1
(b) TOTAL JAGIRS	..	*10575*	*8927*	*32*	*10*	*280*	*232*
Chenani Jagir	..	624	149	32	10		
Poonch Jagir	..	9951	8778			280	232
Kashmir Province	..	**741571**	**627963**	**20**	**7**	**1537**	**600**
Baramulla	..	293590	251442			611	293
Anantnag	..	435028	365459	20	7	443	120
Muzaffarabad		12953	11062			483	187
Frontier Districts	..	**941**	**553**			**2**	
Ladakh	..	687	485			1	
Astore	..	96	36			1	
Gilgit (Leased Area)	..	140	31				
Gilgit Agency	..	18	1				

BILINGUALISM)

(Kashmiri) Subsidiary language Hindustani M	F	Total returning the mother-tongue M	F	Using a language subsidiary to Dogri (Punjabi): Subsidiary language Kashmiri M	F	Subsidiary language Punjabi M	F	Subsidiary language Hindustani M	F
8	*9*	*10*	*11*	*12*	*13*	*14*	*15*	*16*	*17*
72119	**14840**	**349730**	**310265**	**582**	**237**	**2898**	**1675**	**12125**	**7114**
8980	**4335**	**347691**	**309452**	**283**	**144**	**2834**	**1656**	**11438**	**7027**
4833	*1608*	*342843*	*304928*	*281*	*138*	*2814*	*1633*	*11227*	*6886*
865	114	150698	129410	121	5	1803	846	6515	3539
29	37	81235	71850	25	17	339	165	1601	807
3654	1236	51972	47710	114	107	459	542	1469	576
264	241	41583	40515	21	9	103	24	724	1345
21	10	17355	15443			110	56	918	619
4147	*2727*	*4848*	*4524*	*2*	*6*	*20*	*23*	*211*	*141*
15	4	4436	4154	2	4	2		50	13
4132	2723	412	370		2	18	23	161	128
62795	**10448**	**1818**	**807**	**299**	**93**	**61**	**19**	**479**	**85**
13000	1666	103	60	25	7	8	1	19	1
48746	8514	1676	728	273	86	50	16	439	79
1049	268	39	19	1		3	2	21	5
344	**57**	**221**	**6**			**3**		**208**	**2**
139	27	212	5			3		203	2
73	15	8	1					4	
132	15	1						1	

District or State		Total returning the mother-tongue		Using a language subsidiary to Punjabi (Punjabi) — Subsidiary language Kashmiri		Subsidiary language Dogri		Subsidiary language Hindustani	
		M	F	M	F	M	F	M	F
1		*18*	*19*	*20*	*21*	*22*	*23*	*24*	*25*
JAMMU AND KASHMIR STATE	..	**208995**	**204759**	**3007**	**2321**	**846**	**742**	**10628**	**5394**
Jammu Province	..	**176879**	**165752**	**69**	**20**	**837**	**733**	**7264**	**4280**
(a) Total Districts	..	*165458*	*155240*	*62*	*15*	*830*	*733*	*5973*	*3461*
Jammu	..	42694	35496	17	4	548	493	3011	1418
Kathua	..	1555	1744	5	8	39	35	75	62
Udhampur	..	673	467	2		45	38	145	94
Reasi	..	7706	6936	36	1	185	142	125	123
Mirpur	..	112830	110597	2	2	13	25	2617	1764
(b) Total Jagirs	..	*11421*	*10512*	*7*	*5*	*7*		*1291*	*819*
Chenani Jagir	..	65	17			7		18	10
Poonch Jagir	..	11356	10495	7	5			1273	809
Kashmir Province	..	**31241**	**38350**	**2937**	**2300**	**9**	**9**	**3123**	**1044**
Baramulla	..	6326	5622	1707	1357	1		801	286
Anantnag	..	5519	4027	1134	901	7	6	1429	437
Muzaffarabad	..	19396	28701	96	42	1	3	893	321
Frontier Districts	..	**875**	**657**	**1**	**1**			**241**	**70**
Ladakh	..	150	86					58	9
Astore	..	191	36	1	1			62	6
Gilgit (Leased Area)	..	154	82					121	55
Gilgit Agency	..	380	453						

BILINGUALISM—CONTD.

Total returning the mother-tongue		USING A LANGUAGE SUBSIDIARY TO PAHARI (WESTERN PAHARI)							
		Subsidiary language Kashmiri		Subsidiary language Dogri		Subsidiary language Punjabi		Subsidiary language Hindustani	
M	F	M	F	M	F	M	F	M	F
26	*27*	*28*	*29*	*30*	*31*	*32*	*33*	*34*	*35*
260371	**231813**	**1034**	**706**	**127**	**251**	**1134**	**881**	**18770**	**16336**
163654	**158103**	**140**	**127**	**125**	**250**	**1082**	**761**	**13802**	**13693**
43798	*40377*	*19*	*22*	*110*	*242*	*52*	*22*	*1850*	*824*
9	3				1		1		
538	547			31	139			1	
1585	1357	7	8	40	54	8		472	34
31411	28951	12	14	38	48	43	16	1250	782
10255	9519			1		1	5	127	8
119856	*117726*	*121*	*105*	*15*	*8*	*1030*	*739*	*11952*	*12869*
497	372								
119359	117354	121	105	15	8	1030	739	11952	12869
96711	**73704**	**894**	**579**	**2**	**1**	**52**	**120**	**4967**	**2643**
5172	4503	352	264					54	19
2745	2400	299	150	1	1	52	61	75	3
88794	66801	243	165	1			59	4838	2621
6	**6**							**1**	
6	6							1	

XII—PART II (A—

District or State		Total returning the mother-tongue		Using a language subsidiary to Pothwari					
				Subsidiary language Kashmiri		Subsidiary language Dogri		Subsidiary language Punjabi	
		M	F	M	F	M	F	M	F
1		*36*	*37*	*38*	*39*	*40*	*41*	*42*	*43*
JAMMU AND KASHMIR STATE	..	**19237**	**18435**			**2**		**6**	
Jammu Province	..	**19236**	**18431**			**2**		**6**	
(a) Total Districts	..	*19236*	*18431*			*2*		*6*	
Jammu	..								
Kathua	..								
Udhampur	..	1						1	
Reasi	..							5	
Mirpur	..	19235	18431			2		5	
(b) Total Jagirs	..								
Chenani Jagir	..								
Poonch Jagir	..								
Kashmir Province	..	**1**	**4**						
Baramulla	..		1						
Anantnag	..	1	3						
Muzaffarabad	..								
Frontier Districts	..								
Ladakh	..								
Astore	..								
Gilgit (Leased Area)	..								
Gilgit Agency	..								

BILINGUALISM)—CONTD.

(LAHNDA) Subsidiary language Hindustani M	F	Total returning the mother-tongue M	F	USING A LANGUAGE SUBSIDIARY TO LAHNDA (LAHNDA) Subsidiary language Kashmiri M	F	Subsidiary language Dogri M	F	Subsidiary language Punjabi M	F	Subsidiary language Hindustani M	F
44	*45*	*46*	*47*	*48*	*49*	*50*	*51*	*52*	*53*	*54*	*55*
45	**34**	**22931**	**22330**				**2**	**35**	**1**	**10**	**14**
44	**31**	**22931**	**22330**				**2**	**35**	**1**	**10**	**14**
44	*31*	*22931*	*22330*				*2*	*35*	*1*	*10*	*14*
			41				2				
44	31	22931	22289					35	1	10	14
1	**3**										
1	3										

XII—PART II(A—

District or State		Total returning the mother-tongue		Using a language subsidiary to Gojri					
				Subsidiary language Kashmiri		Subsidiary language Dogri		Subsidiary language Punjabi	
		M	F	M	F	M	F	M	F
1		*56*	*57*	*58*	*59*	*60*	*61*	*62*	*63*
JAMMU AND KASHMIR STATE	..	**150188**	**132780**	**2216**	**1144**	**3911**	**3114**	**186**	**107**
Jammu Province	..	**97822**	**89386**	**298**	**134**	**3909**	**3113**	**122**	**94**
(a) TOTAL DISTRICTS	..	*73455*	*65957*	*284*	*117*	*3867*	*3078*	*103*	*66*
Jammu	..	21162	18830	11	6	859	725	27	16
Kathua	..	4091	3573			407	348		
Udhampur	..	11789	11423	34	96	1804	1629	69	30
Reasi	..	33037	28769	239	15	797	375	7	1
Mirpur	..	3376	3362				1		19
(b) TOTAL JAGIRS	..	*24367*	*23429*	*14*	*17*	*42*	*35*	*19*	*28*
Chenani Jagir	..	243	239	3		42	35		
Poonch Jagir	..	24124	23190	11	17			19	28
Kashmir Province	..	**50165**	**42226**	**1918**	**1010**	**2**	**1**	**64**	**13**
Baramulla	..	18108	14651	738	520			7	
Anantnag	..	14526	12205	1175	490	2	1	22	
Muzaffarabad	..	17531	15370	5				35	13
Frontier Districts	..	**2201**	**1168**						
Ladakh	..								
Astore	..	14	8						
Gilgit (Leased Area)	..	416	355						
Gilgit Agency	..	1771	805						

BILINGUALISM)—CONTD.

(RAJASTHANI) Subsidiary language Hindustani		Total returning the mother-tougue		USING A LANGAUGE SUBSIDIARY TO BALTI (BALTI) Subsidiary language Kashmiri		Subsidiary language Dogri		Subsidiary language Punjabi		Subsidiary language Hindustani	
M	F	M	F	M	F	M	F	M	F	M	F
64	*65*	*66*	*67*	*68*	*69*	*70*	*71*	*72*	*73*	*74*	*75*
3845	**1682**	**67698**	**66225**	**17**	**3**	**8**	**5**	**5**	**1**	**2678**	**48**
3471	**1498**	**173**	**11**	**1**		**8**	**5**	**2**		**30**	
1453	*797*	*114*	*11*	*1*		*8*	*5*	*2*		*27*	
536	385	14	2	1				2		8	
649	188	21	1			8	5			19	
262	221	78	8								
6	3	1									
2018	*701*	*59*								*3*	
10	8	59								3	
2008	693										
260	**75**	**320**	**32**	**16**	**3**			**3**		**24**	**8**
46	1	32	32		3					7	8
15	7	209		16						17	
199	67	79						3			
114	**109**	**67205**	**66182**						**1**	**2624**	**40**
		66994	66169							2533	39
		59	13						1	9	
114	109	152								82	1

XII—PART II (A—

District or State	Total returning the mother-tongue		USING A LANGUAGE SUBSIDIARY TO LADAKHI					
			Subsidiary language Kashmiri		Subsidiary language Dogri		Subsidiary language Punjabi	
	M	F	M	F	M	F	M	F
1	76	77	78	79	80	81	82	83
JAMMU AND KASHMIR STATE ..	**20664**	**20994**	**1**	**6**				
Jammu Province ..								
(a) TOTAL DISTRICTS ..								
Jammu ..								
Kathua ..								
Udhampur ..								
Reasi ..								
Mirpur ..								
(b) TOTAL JAGIRS ..								
Chenani Jagir ..								
Poonch Jagir ..								
Kashmir Province ..	**29**	**193**		**4**				
Baramulla ..	3	1						
Anantnag ..	25	190		4				
Muzaffarabad ..	1	2						
Frontier Districts ..	**20635**	**20801**	**1**	**2**				
Ladakh ..	20634	20798	1	2				
Astore ..	1	2						
Gilgit (Leased Area) ..		1						
Gilgit Agency ..								

BILINGUALISM—CONTD.

(LADAKHI) Subsidiary language Hindustani		Total returning the mother-tongue		USING A LANGUAGE SUBSIDIARY TO SHINA (SHINA) Subsidiary language Kashmiri		Subsidiary language Dogri		Subsidiary language Punjabi		Subsidiary language Hindustani	
M	F	M	F	M	F	M	F	M	F	M	F
84	*85*	*86*	*87*	*88*	*89*	*90*	*91*	*92*	*93*	*94*	*95*
532	**32**	**40234**	**35754**	**332**	**93**			**237**	**22**	**3252**	**700**
		2								**2**	
		2								2	
										2	
15	**7**	**4023**	**3736**	**327**	**91**			**210**	**19**	**293**	**114**
1		4011	3734	326	91			210	19	289	112
14	7	10	2							3	2
		2		1						1	
517	**25**	**36209**	**32018**	**5**	**2**			**27**	**3**	**2957**	**586**
516	25	3162	2922	3						114	4
1		8496	7946					24		706	17
		9606	8360	2	2			3	3	2137	565
		14945	12790								

USING A LANGUAGE SUBSIDIARY TO KISHTWARI

District or State	Total returning the mother-tongue M	Total returning the mother-tongue F	Subsidiary language Kashmiri M	Subsidiary language Kashmiri F	Subsidiary language Dogri M	Subsidiary language Dogri F	Subsidiary language Punjabi M	Subsidiary language Punjabi F
1	96	97	98	99	100	101	102	103
JAMMU AND KASHMIR STATE ..	**5807**	**5363**	**6**	**7**	**97**	**5**	**413**	**10**
Jammu Province ..	**5772**	**5356**	**2**	**4**	**96**	**5**	**410**	**10**
(a) TOTAL DISTRICTS ..	*5772*	*5356*	*2*	*4*	*96*	*5*	*410*	*10*
Jammu ..	19	3			2		1	
Kathua ..								
Udhampur ..	5752	5353	2	4	93	5	409	10
Reasi ..								
Mirpur ..	1				1			
(b) TOTAL JAGIRS ..								
Chenani Jagir ..								
Poonch Jagir ..								
Kashmir Province ..	**32**	**7**	**4**	**3**	**1**		**3**	
Baramulla ..								
Anantnag ..	30	7	4	3	1		3	
Muzaffarabad ..	2							
Frontier Districts ..	**3**							
Ladakh ..	2							
Astore ..	1							
Gilgit (Leased Area) ..								
Gilgit Agency ..								

BILINGUALISM)—CONTD.

(KASHMIRI) Subsidiary language Hindustani M	(KASHMIRI) Subsidiary language Hindustani F	Total returning the mother-tongue M	Total returning the mother-tongue F	USING A LANGUAGE SUBSIDIARY TO BODHI (LADAKHI) Subsidiary language Kashmiri M	Subsidiary language Kashmiri F	Subsidiary language Dogri M	Subsidiary language Dogri F	Subsidiary language Punjabi M	Subsidiary language Punjabi M	Subsidiary language Hindustani M	Subsidiary language Hindustani F
104	*105*	*106*	*107*	*108*	*109*	*110*	*111*	*112*	*113*	*114*	*115*
821	**368**	**2413**	**2563**	**1**		**1**		**2**		**6**	
802	**207**	**135**	**164**			**1**		**2**			
802	*207*	*135*	*164*			*1*		*2*			
1											
801	207	135	164			1		2			
18	**161**	**8**		**1**						**5**	
		1									
16	161	6		1						5	
2		1									
1		**2270**	**2399**							**1**	
		2270	2399								
1										1	

XII—PART II (A—BILINGUALISM)—Concld.

District or State	Total returning the mother-tongue		Using a language subsidiary to Dardastani (other Kafir languages)							
			Subsidiary language Kashmiri		Subsidiary language Dogri		Subsidiary language Punjabi		Subsidiary language Hindustani	
	M	F	M	F	M	F	M	F	M	F
1	116	117	118	119	120	121	122	123	124	125
JAMMU AND KASHMIR STATE ..	**22**	**17**		**2**					**3**	
Jammu Province ..										
(a) Total Districts ..										
Jammu ..										
Udhampur ..										
Reasi ..										
Mirpur ..										
(b) Total Jagirs ..										
Chenani Jagir ..										
Poonch Jagir ..										
Kashmir Province ..	**22**	**17**		**2**					**3**	
Baramulla ..	16	8								
Anantnag ..	6	9		2					3	
Muzaffarabad ..										
Frontier Districts ..										
Ladakh ..										
Astore ..										
Gilgit (Leased Area) ..										
Gilgit Agency ..										

Note.—Bilingualism figures for Gilgit Agency are not available.

XII—PART II (B—POLYLINGUALISM)

District or State	Speaking three languages			Speaking four languages			Speaking five languages			Speaking six languages			Speaking seven languages		
	P	M	F	P	M	F	P	M	F	P	M	F	P	M	F
1	2	3	4	5	6	7	8	6	10	11	12	13	14	15	16
JAMMU & KASHMIR	**3125**	**2315**	**810**	**457**	**218**	**239**	**321**	**314**	**7**	**37**	**37**		**1**		**1**
Jammu Province ..	**1436**	**1031**	**405**	**133**	**101**	**32**	**6**	**1**	**5**	**4**	**4**				
(a) TOTAL DISTRICTS ..	*605*	*498*	*107*	*118*	*86*	*32*	*6*	*1*	*5*	*4*	*4*				
Jammu ..	**169**	141	28	**57**	57					**4**	4				
Kathua ..	**87**	76	11	**4**	4										
Udhampur ..	**140**	134	6	**45**	16	29	**6**	1	5						
Reasi ..	**131**	90	41												
Mirpur ..	**78**	57	21	**12**	9	3									
(b) TOTAL JAGIRS ..	*831*	*533*	*298*	*15*	*15*										
Chenani Jagir ..	**34**	22	12												
Poonch Jagir ..	**797**	511	286	**15**	15										
Kashmir Province ..	**1119**	**890**	**229**	**266**	**62**	**204**	**313**	**311**	**2**	**28**	**28**		**1**		**1**
Baramulla ..	**327**	251	76	**48**	34	14	**15**	15							
Anantnag ..	**420**	323	97	**46**	16	30	**4**	2	2	**18**	18				
Muzaffarabad ..	**372**	316	56	**172**	12	160	**294**	294		**10**	10		**1**		1
Frontier Districts ..	**570**	**394**	**176**	**58**	**55**	**3**	**2**	**2**		**5**	**5**				
Ladakh ..	**25**	21	4	**23**	23					**1**	1				
Astore ..	**53**	47	6	**2**	2					**4**	4				
Gilgit (Leased Area)	**492**	326	166	**33**	30	3	**2**	2							
Gilgit Agency ..															

NOTE.—No figures for Gilgit Agency are available.

APPENDIX

CLASSIFICATION OF DIALECTS

Language	Dialects	Speakers P	M	F	District
1	2	3	4	5	6
Balti		**134012**	**67787**	**66225**	
	Balti	**133923**	67698	66225	Ladakh
	Baltistani	**24**	24		Ladakh
	Khipumah	**3**	3		Gilgit Agency
	Kundpali	**45**	45		Gilgit Agency
	Malti	**17**	17		Gilgit Agency
Bhotia (Others)		**328**	**185**	**143**	
	Bhotia	**312**	173	139	Udhampur
	Khapli	**16**	12	4	Astore
Burushaski		**33132**	**17424**	**15708**	
	Brukshas	**1633**	1075	558	Gilgit (Leased Area)
	Bargasket	**244**	122	122	Ladakh
	Burshas	**37**	24	13	Gilgit (Leased Area)
	Broshki	**31123**	16147	14976	Gilgit Agency
	Hunzai	**95**	56	39	Gilgit (Leased Area)
Gujrati		**191**	**113**	**78**	
	Gujrati	**168**	95	73	Gilgit Agency
	Goanese	**12**	11	1	Anantnag
	Karnatki	**1**	1		Jammu
	Malabari	**5**	3	2	Baramulla
	Parsee	**5**	3	2	Jammu
Kashmiri		**1549460**	**837357**	**712103**	
	Banjwahi	**747**	386	361	Udhampur
	Kashmiri	**1512912**	818196	694716	Anantnag
	Kishtwari	**11170**	5807	5363	Udhampur
	Poguli	**5812**	3036	2776	Udhampur
	Rambani	**1202**	371	831	Udhampur
	Siraji	**17617**	9561	8056	Udhampur
Kohistani		**1160**	**638**	**522**	
	Bambagi	**590**	332	258	Jammu[1]
	Kaghani	**491**	272	219	Udhampur
	Kohistani	**79**	34	45	Baramulla
Ladakhi		**46953**	**23253**	**23700**	
	Bodhi	**4976**	2413	2563	Ladakh
	Changpa	**5**	3	2	Ladakh
	Dangpa	**20**	11	9	Ladakh
	Kiango	**285**	155	130	Ladakh
	Ladakhi	**41658**	20664	20994	Ladakh
	Lhassi	**9**	7	2	Ladakh
Lahnda		**82993**	**42194**	**40799**	
	Hazara	**7**	5	2	Astore
	Lahnda	**45261**	22931	22330	Mirpur
	Mirpuri	**46**	16	30	Jammu
	Pothweri	**37672**	19237	18435	Mirpur
	Punchi	**7**	5	2	Jammu and Anantnag

APPENDIX

CLASSIFICATION OF DIALECTS—CONTD.

Language	Dialects	Speakers F	M	F	District
1	2	3	4	5	6
Marathi	..	**17**	**7**	**10**	
	Koli ..	1	1		Kathua
	Marathi ..	16	6	10	Anantnag District including City
Oriya	..	**7**	**7**		
	Udesi ..	5	5		Jammu
	Udia ..	2	2		Jammu
Other Eranian Languages	..	**351**	**186**	**165**	
	Afgani ..	49	29	20	Anantnag
	Yagisthani ..	302	157	145	Gilgit (Leased Area)
Other Kafir Languages	..	**4291**	**2278**	**2013**	
	Dardistani ..	39	22	17	Baramulla
	Wakhi ..	4252	2256	1996	Gilgit Agency
Panjabi	..	**1075273**	**559439**	**515834**	
	Dogri ..	659995	349730	310265	Jammu
	Gurmukhi ..	194	35	159	Reasi
	Gojali ..	1	1		Gilgit (Leased Area)
	Kangri ..	68	48	20	Udhampur
	Khaski ..	23	16	7	Chenani
	Khokhri ..	1	1		Kathua
	Kandiali ..	22	5	17	Gilgit Agency
	Multani ..	7	5	2	Baramulla
	Panjabi ..	413754	208995	204759	Mirpur
	Powadhi ..	1208	603	605	Anantnag
Pashto	..	**4197**	**2554**	**1643**	
	Pashto ..	4121	2491	1630	Anantnag District including City
	Pathani ..	75	62	13	Jammu
	Peshawari ..	1	1		Jammu
Persian	..	**309**	**179**	**130**	
	Badakhshani ..	1	1		Anantnag
	Persian ..	308	178	130	Gilgit Agency
Rajasthani	..	**283741**	**150581**	**133160**	
	Gojari ..	282968	150188	132780	Reasi
	Labhani ..	771	392	379	Jammu
	Marwari ..	2	1	1	Jammu and Anantnag
Shina	..	**84604**	**44716**	**39888**	
	Astori ..	1		1	Baramulla
	Brukpa ..	6639	3402	3237	Ladakh
	Balshan ..	1		1	Gilgit (Leased Area)
	Chillasi ..	34	24	10	Anantnag
	Dassiali ..	08	60	48	Gilgit Agency

APPENDIX

CLASSIFICATION OF DIALECTS—Concld.

Language	Dialects	Speakers P	M	F	District
1	2	3	4	5	6
Shina—concld.					
	Domialies ..	**175**	99	76	Gilgit Agency
	Dareshk ..	**1**	1		Gilgit Agency
	Dakhani ..	**15**	11	4	Gilgit Agency
	Gilgitti .	**1043**	545	498	Ladakh
	Hanko ..	**1**	1		Gilgit (Leased Area)
	Hindko ..	**119**	60	59	Gilgit Agency
	Khibchi ..	**142**	90	52	Gilgit (Leased Area)
	Khiwali ..	**40**	24	16	Gilgit (Leased Area)
	Kaliwal ..	**80**	52	28	Gilgit (Leased Area)
	Khandia ..	**3**	2	1	Gilgit Agency
	Khaloja ..	**26**	12	14	Gilgit Agency
	Khulcha ..	**100**	50	50	Gilgit Agency
	Malakhi ..	**2**		2	Gilgit Agency
	Nagri ..	**42**	22	20	Gilgit (Leased Area)
	Punyali ..	**4**	1	3	Gilgit (Leased Area)
	Patri ..	**27**	15	12	Gilgit (Leased Area)
	Reshkori ..	**1**		1	Gilgit Agency
	Shina ..	**75988**	40234	35754	Gilgit Agency
	Saloni ..	**1**		1	Gilgit (Leased Area)
	Shikwar ..	**10**	10		Gilgit Agency
	Tokot ..	**1**	1		Gilgit Agency
Tamil ..	..	**44**	**30**	**14**	
	Banglori ..	**2**	2		Anantnag
	Dranali ..	**5**	5		Anantnag
	Daward ..	**2**	2		Anantnag
	Madrasi ..	**17**	9	8	Jammu
	Tamil ..	**16**	10	6	Anantnag
	Travedi ..	**1**	1		Anantnag
	Travancori	**1**	1		Anantnag
Turkish ..	..	**283**	**188**	**95**	
	Yarkandi ..	**283**	188	95	Gilgit (Leased Area)
Western Pahari ..	..	**531319**	**280165**	**251154**	
	Bhadrawahi ..	**22948**	11487	11459	Udhampur
	Bakerwali ..	**454**	256	198	Reasi
	Chambiali ..	**1572**	752	820	Kathua
	Gaddi ..	**6364**	3179	3185	Udhampur
	Padari ..	**5900**	3086	2814	Udhampur
	Pangwali ..	**4**		4	Udhampur
	Sarori ..	**1893**	1032	861	Udhampur
	Pahari ..	**492184**	260371	231813	Poonch Jagir

XII—(i) LANGUAGES

DISTRIBUTION OF THE POPULATION BY LANGUAGE ACCORDING TO LINGUISTIC SURVEY

(Languages returned as mother-tongue by less than 500 persons have been omitted)

Family, sub-family branch and sub-branch	Group	Language	Number per 10000 of the population 1941 M	1941 F	1931 M	1931 F	Tehsils where chiefly spoken
1	2	3	4	5	6	7	8
		A.—Languages of India					
	TOTAL ..		**429**	**476**			
Tibeto-Chinese family Tibeto-Burman sub-family Tibeto-Himalayan branch ..	Tibetan group	Bhotia of Baltistan or Balti ..	318	350			Kargil and Skardu
		Bhotia of Ladakh or Ladakhi ..	109	125			Ladakh and Kargil
		Bhotia of Tibet or Tibetan	2	1			
	TOTAL ..		**9482**	**9438**			
Indo-European family Aryan sub-family Eranian Branch ..	Eastern group	Pashto ..	12	9			
Dardic Branch ..	Khowar group ..	Khowar ..	4	3			
		Chitrali ..	15	17			
	Dard group ..	Shina ..	210	211			Kargil, Astore, Gilgit (Leased Area) and Gilgit Agency excepting Yasin Illaqa
		Kashmiri ..	3931	3764			Kishtwar, Ramban, Bhadrawah, Reasi, Haveli, Uttarmachipura, Baramulla, Sri Pratapsinghpura, Khas, Pulwama, Kulgam, Anantnag,, Uri and Karnah
		Kohistani ..	3	3			
	Kafir group ..	Other Kafir languages ..	11	11			
Indo-Aryan Branch Outer sub-branch ..	North-Western group	Lahanda or Western Panjabi ..	198	216			Kotli
Inner Sub-branch ..	Central group	Hindustani ..	445	442			Jammu, Bagh
		Rajastnani ..	707	704			Akhnoor, Kishtwar, Reasi, Rampur-Rajouri, Haveli Mendhar, Muzaffarabad, Uri and Chilas
		Panjabi (Dogri) ..	2627	2727			Jammu, Ranbirsinghpura Mirpur, Bhimbar, Uri,, Karnah, Samba, Akhnur, Kathua, Jasmergarh, Basohli, Udhampur, Kishtwar, Ramban, Ramnagar, Bhadrawah, Reasi and Chenani
	Pahari group	Naipali ..	4	3			
		Western Pahari ..	1315	1328			Rampur-Rajouri, Bagh Sadhnuti, Haveli, Mendhar, Muzaffarabad, Uri, and Karnah
	TOTAL ..	..	**82**	**83**			
Unclassed Languages ..		Burushaski ..	82	83			Hunza. Nagar and Yasin in Gilgit Agency

XII—(ii) DISTRIBUTION BY LANGUAGE OF THE POPULATION OF EACH DISTRICT

District	Number per 10,000 of the population speaking: Kashmiri as mother-tongue	Kashmiri as subsidiary to Dogri	Kashmiri as subsidiary to Panjabi	Dogri as mother-tongue	Dogri as subsidiary to Kashmiri	Dogri as subsidiary to Panjabi	Panjabi as mother-tongue	Panjabi as subsidiary to Kashmiri	Panjabi as subsidiary to Dogri	Hindustani as mother-tongue	Hindustani as subsidiary to Kashmiri	Hindustani as subsidiary to Dogri	Hindustani as subsidiary to Panjabi
1	2	3	4	5	6	7	8	9	10	11	12	13	14
Jammu	61	3		6494	3	24	1813	6	61	635	23	233	103
Kathua	131	2	1	8616	21	4	185	2	28	376	2	136	8
Udhampur	3135	8	2	3388	71	3	39	19	34	65	166	70	8
Reasi	972	1	1	3183	94	13	568	3	5	517	20	80	10
Mirpur	3			848			5784		4	540	1	40	113
Chenani Jagir	655	5		7282	36	6	70		2	655	16	53	24
Poonch Jagir	444			19			518	12	1	2285	163	7	49
Baramulla	8900	1	50	3			195	15		65	239		18
Anantnag	9400	4	24	28			112	7	1	37	674	6	22
Muzaffarabad	907		5	2			1817	26		134	50	1	46
Ladakh	60			11			12			1	9	11	3
Astore	78		1	7			133	1		3	52	2	40
Gilgit (Leased Area) ..	76						105			49	65		78
Gilgit Agency*	2						11			51			

*No information is available as regards subsidiary languages used.

XII—(iii) COMPARISON OF THE TRIBE AND LANGUAGE

Tribe	Language	Tribe		Tribal mother-tongue only		Tribal mother-tongue plus subsidiary language		Subsidiary language used
		Males	Females	Males	Females	Males	Females	
1	2	3	4	5	6	7	8	9
Balti ..		49742	49606					
	Balti ..			64990	66168	2708	57	Kashmiri, Dogri, Panjabi, Hindustani
Buddhist ..		20268	20428					
	Boddhi ..			2403	2563	10		Kashmiri, Dogri, Panjabi, Hindustani
Gujjar ..		202534	178923					
	Gojri ..			140030	126733	10158	6047	Kashmiri, Dogri, Panjabi, Hindustani
Kashmiri ..		803298	682132					
	Kashmiri ..			739945	677412	78251	17304	Dogri, Panjabi, Hindustani
Ladakhi ..		18360	17947					
	Ladakhi ..			20131	20956	533	38	Kashmiri, Hindustani
Shin ..		3076	2747					
	Shina ..			36413	34939	3821	815	Kashmiri, Panjabi, Hindustani

IMPERIAL TABLE XIII AND ITS SUBSIDIARIES

Community

NOTES

1. This table gives the population of the State by communities but as the communities of the State are recognised by religions rather than by tribes there is little change from 1931 when the corresponding table was for population by Religion—No. XVI. In 1931 the table showed the following religions :—Hindu with details of Brahmans, Aryas and Brahmos given separately, Sikh, Jain, Buddhist, Zoroastrian, Muslim, Christian and Tribal. On this occasion we give as communities Hindus, with Scheduled Castes shown separately, Muslims, Christians, with details of Indian Christians, Anglo-Indians and Others given separately, Sikhs, Jains, Parsees, Buddhists, Jews, Tribes and Others.

2. The figures for Arya Samajists were extracted by special request and since they are available they are given below :—

	Persons	Males	Females
State	87356	46657	40699
Jammu Province	85656	45674	39982
Kashmir Povince	1675	968	707
Frontier Districts (excluding Gilgit Agency)	25	15	10

The figures for Aryas for Gilgit Agency are not available. In any case they are negligible. Aryas, whatever their origin, have been included with Hindu—Others, columns 8 to 10 of the table.

3. (i) The following fourteen castes have been included in the figures given for Scheduled Castes :—Barwala (Barwar), Basith, Batawal, Chamar, Chuhra, Dhiyar, Dom, Gardi, Jolaha, Mang (Megh), Ratal, Saryara, Watal and Harijan. The individual strength of these castes is given separately in Table XIV. The first thirteen named are the same as those treated similarly in 1931. On this occasion we have added those describing themselves as Harijans with the approval of the Census Commissioner for India.

(ii) The table shows 39072 fewer persons under Scheduled Castes than in Table XIV. This is because that number, having joined the Arya Samaj, were treated as Hindus—Others. The total of persons of Scheduled Castes origin is however 152536 as shown in Table XIV.

4. To meet the special request of local representatives the figures for Shias were separately extracted. These are included with Muslims in the table. The figures given below do not include Gilgit Agency as the record for that area was not sorted separately for Shias. A large proportion of the Muslims of the Gilgit Agency belong to the Shia Sect.

	Persons	Males	Females
Jammu and Kashmir State ..	205999	107014	98985
Jammu Province ..	4595	2436	2159
Kashmir Province	59717	32336	27381
Frontier Districts (excluding Gilgit Agency)	141687	72242	69445

In 1931 the population of Shias was 279819 including Gilgit Agency. At this Census inclusive of Gilgit Agency it may be assumed they totalled 280000. This figure is necessarily approximate.

5. The entry under Tribes is misleading. It includes those only of the tribes known as Shins, Yashkuns and Sansis who, according to the record, have not embraced Islam or Hinduism. Those Shins and Yashkuns who are now Muslims have been included with Muslims in this table and the Sansis who have been admitted to Hinduism have been included with 'Hindus—Others'. The following table reconciles the seeming discrepancy between Tables XIII and XIV :—

Tribe		Shown in Table XIV			Converted to Islam			Converted to Hinduism			Those not converted (Total shown in Table XIII)		
		P	M	F	P	M	F	P	M	F	P	M	F
1		2	3	4	5	6	7	8	9	10	11	12	13
Shin	..	5823	3076	2747	5822	3075	2747				1	1	
Yashkun	..	21886	11569	10317	21885	11568	10317				1	1	
Sansis	..	1665	856	809				1616	829	787	49	27	22
Total	..	29374	14501	13873	27707	14643	13064	1616	829	787	51	29	22

The figures for Shins and Yashkuns in the Gilgit Agency were not extracted and cannot be shown here or in Table XIV.

6. The entry under 'Others' consists of 93 persons who showed no community at all in reply to the census questions on which the table is based and 2 atheists who gave no details by which their real community could be decided. Of these 95 persons 15 were males and 80 females; those describing themselves as atheists were both females living in Srinagar City.

7. The figures given below show at a glance by communities the population figures in 1931 and 1941 respectively, the percentage increase in the decade 1931-41 and the proportion each community bears to the total population. The smaller communities have been included with 'Others' here for the sake of convenience.

	1931	1941	Increase	Proportion
			Per cent.	Per cent.
Total ..	3646243	4021616	10.29	
Muslims	2817636	3101247	10.07	77.11
Hindus	736222	809165	9.90	20.12
Sikhs	50662	65903	30.08	1.64
Buddhists	38724	40696	5	1.01
Others	2999	4605	53.55	.11

The above figures are given in greater detail in Subsidiary (i).

8. **Subsidiary (i)**—

(a) The table gives the general distribution of the population by communities and localities. The communities are the same as those shown in the similar table in 1931 except that we have added 'Others'. The localities are the same—Natural Divisions.

(b) Since 'Others' have been shown on this occasion for the first time no entries can be made in columns 3-11.

(c) In the case of blanks in column 2 it should be understood the proportion is less than 1 in 10000 and in the case of blanks in columns 3-11 that the figures are not available from previous census reports.

(d) Variations all represent an increase except where a minus sign is given.

9. **Subsidiary (ii)**—

(a) The table is the same as the corresponding subsidiary in 1931 except that we have added 'Others' to the main communities to cover the whole population.

(b) Gilgit (Leased Area) and Astore are separate Census Divisions on this occasion; together they constituted the Gilgit District in 1931. As separate figures are not available for these two districts previous to 1941 we have given the figures for the old Gilgit District taken from the 1931 report for periods 1911 to 1931.

(c) The blanks under the Buddhist community should be taken to indicate either that no Buddhists live in the areas to which the columns refer or that the numbers are too small to show.

(d) In a few cases only are any figures available for 1901. As 'Others' appears for the first time no figures can be given for periods previous to 1941.

10. **Subsidiary (iii)**—

(a) This is similar to the corresponding subsidiary in 1931 except that on this occasion there is no column for the actual number of Christians in each district. The numbers are small but are given below by provinces for the benefit of those who require them :—

	Actual Number 1941	Actual Number 1931	Percentage variation.
Jammu and Kashmir State ..	3509	2263	55
Jammu Province	2788	1753	59
Kashmir Province	555	339	63.7
Frontier Districts	166	171	—2.9

(b) The standard form for this subsidiary provides two columns to show the variations for 1901-1911 and 1901-1941 respectively. As the information necessary to complete these two columns is not available by districts from previous census reports the two columns have been omitted. The figures for 1901 are however available for the whole State and by Provinces and are reproduced below :—

	Actual Number 1941	Actual Number 1901	Variation
Jammu and Kashmir State ..	3509	422	732 %
Jammu Province	2788	145	1823 %
Kashmir Province	555	244	127 %
Frontier Districts	166	33	403 %

(c) The variations shown in the table and in these notes are all increases unless a minus sign is given.

(d) The figures required for columns 3 and 4 are not complete ; where they are not available in the corresponding table for 1931 the spaces have been left blank.

11. A 1/50 random sample was extracted for Imperial Table XIII ; the results are given in tabular form following subsidiary (iii). In the table given below the results of the sample are compared with the actuals in the main table. It will be observed that the results of the Sample are fairly accurate in the case of the main communities but naturally are far from satisfactory in the case of small communities. The figures for Gilgit Agency are not included in the Sample. The total 3945090 is the total population of the State (4021616) less that for Gilgit Agency (76526).

Comparison between Imperial Table XIII and the results of a 1/50 Random Sample.

JAMMU AND KASHMIR STATE

(Excluding Gilgit Agency)

Community	Figure in Sample Results	Figure in Col. 2×50	Actual strength from Table XIII
1	2	3	4
All Communities	78901	3945050	3945090
Scheduled Castes	2328	116400	113464
Other Hindus	13875	693750	695627
Muslims	60444	3022200	3024820
Christians—			
Indian Christians	69	3450	3077
Anglo-Indians			7
Others	14	700	421
Sikhs	1338	66900	65882
Jains	23	1150	910
Parsees			29
Buddhists	809	40450	40696
Jews			11
Tribes			51
Others	1	50	95

NOTE.—P stands for Persons, M for males and F for Females.

XIII—COMMUNITY

District and State	Population			Hindus: Scheduled Castes			Hindus: Others			Muslims		
	P	M	F	P	M	F	P	M	F	P	M	F
1	2	3	4	5	6	7	8	9	10	11	12	13
JAMMU AND KASHMIR STATE ..	**4021616**	**2129872**	**1891744**	**113464**	**60772**	**52692**	**695701**	**369911**	**325790**	**3101247**	**1641701**	**1459546**
JAMMU PROVINCE ..	**1981433**	**1034410**	**947023**	**113422**	**60746**	**52676**	**609413**	**320999**	**288414**	**1215676**	**630318**	**585358**
(a) Total Districts ..	*1547809*	*814016*	*733793*	*110342*	*59110*	*51232*	*578775*	*305348*	*273427*	*830749*	*434759*	*395990*
Jammu (including city) ..	**431362**	233976	197386	**51120**	27725	23395	**197053**	106912	90141	**170789**	92578	73211
Kathua ..	**177672**	94134	83538	**18849**	10404	8445	**112974**	59044	53930	**45214**	24355	20859
Udhampur ..	**294217**	153608	140609	**21645**	11263	10382	**143175**	73916	69259	**128327**	67878	60449
Reasi ..	**257903**	135502	122401	**15720**	8163	7557	**65005**	34048	30957	**175539**	92412	83127
Mirpur ..	**386655**	196796	189859	**3008**	1555	1453	**60568**	31428	29140	**310880**	157536	153344
(b) Total Jagirs ..	*433624*	*220394*	*213230*	*3080*	*1636*	*1444*	*30638*	*15651*	*14987*	*384927*	*195559*	*189368*
Chenani Jagir ..	**11796**	6475	5321	**2670**	1378	1292	**6911**	3597	3314	**2205**	1491	714
Poonch Jagir ..	**421828**	213919	207909	**410**	258	152	**23727**	12054	11673	**382722**	194068	188654
KASHMIR PROVINCE ..	**1728705**	**934738**	**793967**	**42**	**26**	**16**	**85538**	**48362**	**37176**	**1615478**	**871499**	**743979**
Baramulla ..	**612428**	330050	282378	**7**	5	2	**12912**	7574	5338	**590936**	317983	272953
Anantnag (including Srinagar city) ..	**851606**	463571	388035	**27**	18	9	**66788**	37452	29336	**778684**	422619	356065
Muzaffarabad ..	**264671**	141117	123554	**8**	3	5	**5838**	3336	2502	**245858**	130897	114961
FRONTIER DISTRICTS ..	**311478**	**160724**	**150754**				**750**	**550**	**200**	**270093**	**139884**	**130209**
Ladakh ..	**195431**	98478	96953				**455**	361	94	**154492**	77925	76567
Astore ..	**17026**	8948	8078				**113**	72	41	**16878**	8852	8026
Gilgit (Leased Area) ..	**22495**	12471	10024				**108**	72	36	**22296**	12342	9954
Gilgit Agency ..	**76526**	40827	35699				**74**	45	29	**76427**	40765	35662

XIII—COMMUNITY—Contd.

District and State	Christians									Sikhs			Jains			Parsees		
	ndian Christians			Anglo-Indians			Others											
	P	M		P	M	F	P	M	F	P	M	F	P	M	F	P	M	F
1	*14*	*15*	*16*	*17*	*18*	*19*	*20*	*21*	*22*	*23*	*24*	*25*	*26*	*27*	*28*	*29*	*30*	*31*
JAMMU AND KASHMIR STATE ..	**3079**	**1675**	**1404**	**7**	**4**	**3**	**423**	**209**	**214**	**65903**	**34779**	**31124**	**910**	**490**	**420**	**29**	**17**	**12**
JAMMU PROVINCE ..	**2737**	**1505**	**1232**				**51**	**32**	**19**	**38566**	**20036**	**18530**	**901**	**482**	**419**	**23**	**14**	**9**
(a) Total Districts ..	*2737*	*1505*	*1232*				*48*	*30*	*18*	*23679*	*12501*	*11178*	*901*	*482*	*419*	*23*	*14*	*9*
Jammu (including city) ..	**2262**	1245	1017				**35**	20	15	**9151**	4980	4171	**895**	481	414	**23**	14	9
Kathua ..	**204**	103	101							**431**	228	203						
Udhampur ..	**89**	54	35				**9**	7	2	**445**	243	202	**6**	1	5			
Reasi ..	**96**	54	42				**2**	2		**1541**	823	718						
Mirpur ..	**86**	49	37				**2**	1	1	**12111**	6227	5884						
(b) Total Jagirs ..							*3*	*2*	*1*	*14887*	*7535*	*7352*						
Chenani Jagir ..										**10**	9	1						
Poonch Jagir ..							**3**	2	1	**14877**	7526	7351						
KASHMIR PROVINCE ..	**207**	**97**	**110**	**6**	**3**	**3**	**342**	**160**	**182**	**27034**	**14557**	**12477**	**9**	**8**	**1**	**6**	**3**	**3**
Baramulla ..	**48**	24	24				**64**	30	34	**8458**	4433	4025						
Anantnag (including Srinagar city) ..	**119**	56	63	**6**	3	3	**273**	130	143	**5654**	3260	2304	**9**	8	1	**6**	3	3
Muzaffarabad ..	**40**	17	23				**5**		5	**12922**	6864	6058						
FRONTIER DISTRICTS ..	**135**	**73**	**62**	**1**	**1**		**30**	**17**	**13**	**303**	**186**	**117**						
Ladakh ..	**127**	68	59				**11**	6	5	**182**	107	75						
Astore ..	**4**	3	1							**30**	20	10						
Gilgit (Leased Area) ..	**2**	2		**1**	1		**17**	9	8	**70**	44	26						
Gilgit Agency .	**2**		2				**2**	2		**21**	15	6						

XIII—COMMUNITY—Concld.

District and State	Buddhists			Jews			Tribes			Others		
	P	M	F	P	M	F	P	M	F	P	M	F
1	*32*	*33*	*34*	*35*	*36*	*37*	*38*	*39*	*40*	*41*	*42*	*43*
JAMMU AND KASHMIR STATE ..	**40696**	**20268**	**20428**	**11**	**2**	**9**	**51**	**29**	**22**	**95**	**15**	**80**
JAMMU PROVINCE ..	**522**	**247**	**275**				**29**	**16**	**13**	**93**	**15**	**78**
(a) Total Districts ..	*522*	*247*	*275*				*29*	*16*	*13*	*4*	*4*	
Jammu (including city) ..	2	2					29	16	13	3	3	
Kathua ..												
Udhampur ..	520	245	275							1	1	
Reasi ..												
Mirpur ..												
(b) Total Jagirs ..										*89*	*11*	*78*
Chenani Jagir ..												
Poonch Jagir ..										89	11	78
KASHMIR PROVINCE ..	**10**	**10**		**11**	**2**	**9**	**20**	**11**	**9**	**2**		**2**
Baramulla ..	1	1		2		2						
Anantnag (including Srinagar city) ..	9	9		9	2	7	20	11	9	2		2
Muzaffarabad ..												
FRONTIER DISTRICTS ..	**40164**	**20011**	**20153**				**2**	**2**				
Ladakh ..	40164	20011	20153									
Astore ..							1	1				
Gilgit (Leased Area) ..							1	1				
Gilgit Agency ..												

XIII—(I) GENERAL DISTRIBUTION OF POPULATION BY COMMUNITIES

Community	Community and locality	Proportion per 10000 of population in 1941	1931	1921	1911	1901	Variation per cent 1931-41	1921-31	1911-21	1901-11	1901-41
	1	2	3	4	5	6	7	8	9	10	11
Hindu	**State**	**2012**	**2019**	**2086**	**2186**	**2372**	**9**	**6.29**	**—1.1**	**—.2**	**17**
	I.—The Sub-montane and Semi-mountainous Tract ..	4627	4668	4761			13.3	7.7	1		
	II.—The Outer Hills ..	2965	3092	3305			4	4.6	—1		
	Jammu Province ..	3648	3720	3819	3921	4116	8.7	6.1			15
	III.—The Jhelum Valley ..	496	440	458	482	524	23.5	7.2	3.5	2.8	41
	IV.—The Indus Valley ..	24	58	44	58	98	—55.4	35.3	—19.2	—26.9	—195.2
Muslim	**State**	**7712**	**7727**	**7675**	**7594**	**7416**	**10**	**10.5**	**6.3**	**11.3**	**43.9**
	I.—The Sub-montane and Semi-mountainous Tract ..	5080	4406	5075	5119		14.2	11			
	II.—The Outer Hills ..	6871	6775	6661	6535		10	10.3	5.8		
	Jammu Province ..	6134	6100	6034	5966	5762	11.4	10.2	3.8	8.7	38.7
	III.—The Jhelum Valley ..	9345	9420	9413	9402	9364	9.3	11.6	8.8	12.4	49.1
	IV.—The Indus Valley ..	8673	8607	8584	8574	8566	8.7	5.9	3.2	16.9	39
Sikh	**State**	**164**	**138**	**119**	**100**	**89**	**30**	**28.2**	**25.8**	**22.2**	**155.2**
	I.—The Sub-montane and Semi-mountainous Tract ..	249	218	135	93		30	77.8	47.5		
	II.—The Outer Hills	157	129	130	112		31.8	7.9	20		
	Jammu Province ..	195	163	132	104	86	31.7	35.3	29.8	27	194.1
	III.—The Jhelum Valley ..	156	135	126	114	109	27.6	19.4	20.1	16.8	114
	IV.—The Indus Valley ..	9	6	4	5	3	59.5	37.2	13.1	56.4	288.5
Buddhist	**State**	**101**	**106**	**113**	**116**	**121**	**5**	**2.7**	**3.2**	**4.2**	**16.1**
	I.—The Sub-montane and Semi-mountainous Tract ..						—350	225			
	II.—The Outer Hills	4	4	4	5		4.4	13.6	—.3		
	Jammu Province ..	3	2	3	3	32	3	14.7	—2.2	—90.6	—825.5
	III.—The Jhelum Valley ..						100	250	—33.3	100	
	IV.—The Indus Valley ..	1289	1324	1364	1360	1332	5.1	2.6	3.3	19.3	32.9
Christian	**State**	**9**	**6**	**5**	**3**	**1**	**55**	**38.4**	**67.6**	**131**	**731.5**
	I.—The Sub-montane and Semi-mountainous Tract ..	32	22	18	10		58.2	34.9	85.4		
	II.—The Outer Hills ..	2	1				68.3	966.6	—48.3		
	Jammu Province ..	14	9	7	4	1	59	45.2	79.6	366.2	1823
	III.—The Jhelum Valley ..	3	2	2	2	2	63.7	—.6	56.4	—10.6	127.5
	IV.—The Indus Valley ..	5	5	3	3	1	—3	98.8	1.2	157.5	403
Jain	**State**	**2**	**1**	**2**	**1**	**1**	**52.4**	**13.2**	**53.3**	**—21.9**	**105.9**
	I.—The Sub-montane and Semi-mountainous Tract ..	11	8	8	5		53.8	11.1	54.1		
	II.—The Outer Hills ..						—500	500	—66.6		
	Jammu Province ..	5	3	3	2	3	52.5	11.9	53	—21.4	105.2
	III.—The Jhelum Valley ..						200	300		100	350
	IV.—The Indus Valley ..						—300			100	
Others	**State**										
	I.—The Sub-montane and Semi-mountainous Tract ..	1									
	II.—The Outer Hills ..	1									
	Jammu Province ..	1									
	III.—The Jhelum Valley ..										
	IV.—The Indus Valley ..										

XIII—(II) DISTRIBUTION OF THE MAIN COMMUNITIES BY DISTRICTS

XIII—(II) DISTRIBUTION OF THE MAIN

NUMBER

District and Natural Division	Hindu					Muslim				
	1941	1931	1921	1911	1901	1941	1931	1921	1911	1901
1	2	3	4	5	6	7	8	9	10	11
JAMMU AND KASHMIR STATE ..	**2012**	**2019**	**2016**	**2186**	**2372**	**7712**	**7727**	**7675**	**7594**	**7416**
I. The Sub-montane and Semi-mountainous Tract ..	**4627**	**4886**	**4497**	**4773**		**5080**	**4406**	**3074**	**5119**	
Jammu District ..	5753	5784	5728	6002		3960	3979	3901	3877	
Kathua District (Jasmergarh and Kathua Tehsils only) ..	6849	6901	6113	7032		3099	3032	2953	2928	
Mirpur District (Mirpur and Bhimbar Tehsils only) ..	2003	2056	2025	2162		7606	7958	7654	7720	
II. The Outer Hills ..	**2965**	**3177**	**3145**	**3348**		**6871**	**6775**	**6660**	**6535**	
Kathua District (Basohli Tehsil only)	8285	8368	8450	8489		1707	1631	1542	1509	
Mirpur District (Kotli Tehsil only)	755	763	753	824		9117	9123	9094	9125	
Udhampur District ..	5602	5692	6058	6062		4362	4277	3906	3912	
Reasi District ..	3130	3359	3298	3912		6806	6603	6420	6065	
Chenani Jagir ..	8122	8612				1870	1383	3999		
Poonch Jagir ..	572	657	590	658		9073	9047	9107	9051	
JAMMU PROVINCE ..	**3648**	**3720**	**3679**	**3921**	**4116**	**6134**	**6100**	**6033**	**5986**	
III. The Jhelum Valley ..	**496**	**442**	**458**	**482**	**524**	**9345**	**9420**	**9412**	**9402**	**9364**
Baramulla District ..	211	191	206	237		9649	9694	9685	9684	
Anantnag District ..	785	701	722	748		9143	9243	9226	9209	
Muzaffarabad District ..	222	189	202	241	248	9290	9350	9370	9369	9358
IV. Indus Valley ..	**24**	**58**	**44**	**58**	**98**	**8673**	**8607**	**8583**	**8574**	**8566**
Ladakh District ..	23	17	15	23		7904	7983	7933	8040	
Gilgit (Leased Area) ..	48 }	324	248	340		9910 }	9636	9717	9628	
Astore ..	67 }					9916 }				
Gilgit Agency ..	10	51	36	54		9987	9946	9960	9941	

COMMUNITIES BY DISTRICTS

PER 10000 OF THE POPULATION

Sikh					Buddhist					Others				
1941	1931	1921	1911	1901	1941	1931	1921	1911	1901	1941	1931	1921	1911	1901
12	13	14	15	16	17	18	19	20	21	22	23	24	25	26
164	**138**	**119**	**100**	**89**	**101**	**106**	**113**			**11**				
249	**218**	**135**	**93**							**44**				
212	182	146	97							75				
39	49	27	12							13				
388	341	160	117							3				
157	**129**	**130**	**112**		**4**	**4**	**4**	**5**		**3**				
2		3	1					2		6				
128	113	117	49											
15	11	15	6		18	17	20	20		3				
60	218	36	24							4				
8	5	301	288											
353	292	2								2				
195	**163**	**132**	**104**	**86**	**3**	**2**	**3**	**3**	**32**	**20**				
156	**135**	**126**	**114**	**109**				**116**	**121**	**3**				
138	111	106	99	1						2				
67	51	47	40							5				
488	460	426	390	393										
9	**6**	**5**	**5**	**3**	**1289**	**1324**	**1363**	**1360**	**1532**	**5**				
9	5	3	2		2055	1468	2030	1932		9				
34 }	26	24	24							8				
15 }										2				
3	1	3	4											

XIII—(III) CHRISTIANS—PERCENTAGE VARIATION

Natural Division and District	Percentage Variation		
	1931-1941	1921-1931	1911-1921
1	2	3	4
JAMMU AND KASHMIR STATE	**55**	**38.4**	**67.6**
I. Sub-montane and Semi-mountainous Tract	**58.2**	**34.9**	**85.4**
Jammu District	68.7	30.9	124.6
Kathua District (Jasmergarh and Kathua Tehsils only)	— 3.6	13	— 16.4
Mirpur District (Mirpur and Bhimbar Tehsils only)	8.6	1250	— 66.7
II. The Outer Hills	**68.3**	**866.6**	**— 93.3**
Kathua District (Basohli Tehsil only)	1025		
Mirpur District (Kotli Tehsil only)			
Udhampur District	206.2	1500	
Reasi District	206.2		—100
Chenani Jagir			
Poonch Jagir	— 96.1	533.3	—133.3
JAMMU PROVINCE	**59**	**45.2**	**79.3**
III. The Jhelum Valley	**63.7**	**— .5**	**56.4**
Baramulla District	83.6	84.8	— 15.4
Anantnag District	48.5	— 11.2	82.7
Muzaffarabad District	350	66.6	— 64.7
IV. The Indus Valley	**— 2.9**	**98.8**	**1.2**
Ladakh District	13.1	74.2	11.1
Astore District / Gilgit (Leased Area)	— 36.8	153.3	— 28.6
Gilgit Agency	— 63.6	+1000	

XIII—1/50 SAMPLE

TABLE XIII—

District or State	Total slips examined			Hindus — Scheduled Castes			Hindus — Others		
	P	M	F	P	M	F	P	M	F
1	*2*	*3*	*4*	*5*	*6*	*7*	*8*	*9*	*10*
JAMMU AND KASHMIR STATE ..	**78901**	**41773**	**37128**	**2328**	**1249**	**1079**	**12875**	**7354**	**6521**
JAMMU PROVINCE ..	**39638**	**20674**	**18964**	**2328**	**1249**	**1079**	**12149**	**6382**	**5767**
(a) TOTAL DISTRICTS ..	*30973*	*16275*	*14698*	*2275*	*1220*	*1055*	*11548*	*6075*	*5473*
Jammu ..	8648	4688	3960	1090	582	508	3902	2126	1776
Kathua ..	3558	1885	1673	335	190	145	2293	1190	1103
Udhampur ..	5878	3062	2816	464	251	213	2852	1459	1393
Reasi ..	5157	2707	2450	314	165	149	1321	683	638
Mirpur ..	7732	3933	3799	72	32	40	1180	617	563
(b) TOTAL JAGIRS ..	*8665*	*4399*	*4266*	*53*	*29*	*24*	*601*	*307*	*294*
Chenani Jagir ..	236	130	106	53	29	24	128	69	9
Poonch Jagir ..	8429	4269	4160				473	238	235
KASHMIR ROPVINCE ..	**34563**	**18701**	**15862**				**1712**	**965**	**747**
Baramulla ..	12244	6625	5619				246	146	100
Anantnag ..	17026	9258	7768				1345	749	596
Muzaffarabad ..	5293	2818	2475				121	70	51
FRONTIER DISTRICTS ..	**4700**	**2398**	**2302**				**14**	**7**	**7**
Ladakh ..	3911	1971	1940				12	6	6
Astore ..	340	178	162				2	1	1
Gilgit (Leased Area) ..	449	249	200						
Gilgit Agency									

1/50 SAMPLE

	Muslims			Christians									Sikhs			Jains		
				Indian Christians			Anglo-Indians			Others								
	P	M	F	P	M	F	P	M	F	P	M	F	P	M	F	P	M	F
	11	*12*	*13*	*14*	*15*	*16*	*17*	*18*	*19*	*20*	*21*	*22*	*23*	*24*	*25*	*26*	*27*	*28*
	60444	**31995**	**28449**	**69**	**39**	**30**				**14**	**7**	**7**	**1338**	**713**	**625**	**23**	**14**	**9**
	24264	**12565**	**11699**	**64**	**37**	**27**							**804**	**424**	**380**	**21**	**13**	**8**
	16556	*8647*	*7909*	*64*	*37*	*27*							*501*	*279*	*222*	*21*	*13*	*8*
	3389	1825	1564	**55**	33	22							**191**	109	82	**21**	13	9
	919	498	421	**4**	2	2							**7**	5	2			
	2544	1343	1201	**2**		2							**8**	5	3			
	3491	1842	1649	**2**	1	1							**29**	16	13			
	6213	3139	3074	**1**	1								**266**	144	122			
	7708	*3918*	*3790*										*303*	*145*	*158*			
	55	32	23															
	7653	3886	3767										**303**	145	158			
	32306	**17443**	**14863**	**1**		**1**				**13**	**6**	**7**	**528**	**285**	**243**	**2**	**1**	**1**
	11827	6382	5445							**2**	1	1	**169**	96	73			
	15567	8450	7117							**11**	5	6	**100**	52	48			
	4912	2611	2301	**1**		1							**259**	137	122	2	1	1
	3874	**1987**	**1887**	**4**	**2**	**2**				**1**	**1**		**6**	**4**	**2**			
	3088	1562	1526	**4**	2	2				**1**	1		**5**	3	2			
	338	177	161										**1**	1				
	448	248	200															

TABLE XIII—1/50 SAMPLE—CONCLD.

District or State		Parsees			Buddhists			Jews			Tribes			Others		
		P	M	F	P	M	F	P	M	F	P	M	F	P	M	F
1		29	30	31	32	33	34	35	36	37	38	39	40	41	42	43
JAMMU AND KASHMIR STATE					**809**	**401**	**408**							**1**	**1**	
JAMMU PROVINCE	..				**8**	**4**	**4**									
(a) TOTAL DISTRICTS	..				**8**	**4**	**4**									
Jammu	..															
Kathua	..															
Udhampur	..				8	4	4									
Reasi	..															
Mirpur	..															
(b) TOTAL JAGIRS	..															
Chenani Jagir	..															
Poonch Jagir	..															
KASHMIR PROVINCE	..													**1**	**1**	
Baramulla	..															
Anantnag	..													1	1	
Muzaffarabad	..															
FRONTIER DISTRICTS	..				**801**	**397**	**404**									
Ladakh	..				801	397	404									
Astore	..															
Gilgit (Leased Area)	..															
Gilgit Agency	..															

NOTE.—Sample was not available for Gilgit Agency.

P=Persons.
M=Males.
F=Females.

IMPERIAL TABLE XIV

Variation in Population of Selected Tribes, Scheduled Castes and Important Elements

NOTES

1. This table corresponds to Imperial Table XVIII of the 1931 report. It has been expanded beyond the scope for which provision was made in the standard form to include information of local interest. It is in three parts. Part I gives detail of Selected Tribes, Part II of Scheduled Castes and Part III of other Important Elements.

2. In column 1 of the table only those districts have been shown in which the particular tribes, Scheduled Castes or elements dealt with are found. It would serve no purpose to give the names of districts for which there are no entries.

3. The tribes, Scheduled Castes and important elements are given in alphabetical order.

4. (i) Figures are not available for the Gilgit Agency as the record was not sorted for this table.

(ii) The figures for Astore and Gilgit (Leased Area) Districts are given separately for 1941. As these two districts together previously constituted the old Gilgit District the figures given for 1931 are for the old Gilgit District ; they cannot be split up for Astore and Gilgit (Leased Area) separately. For this reason the variations cannot be shown separately for these two districts.

5. The only classes of the population treated as tribes in 1931 were the Pernas and Sansis, who were described as criminal tribes, and the Shins and Yashkuns who were described as primitive tribes. These four tribes have been selected for Part I of the table on this occasion but to call them 'Selected Tribes' is not a correct description. The fact is the distribution of the population of the State cannot be given satisfactorily on a tribal basis ; it can be shown by community (religion), caste and to some extent by race but before it can be shown by tribes an authoritative classification of the various 'tribes' constituting the whole population is necessary. It is reasonable to show the few Pernas and Sansis there may be as 'Tribes' but to classify Shins and Yashkuns as 'Primitive Tribes' without comment when all have embraced Islam would be misleading. The Shins and Yashkuns have only been shown on this occasion because they were so shown in 1931.

6. (i) There were 42 Pernas shown in 1931 in the whole State ; on this occasion there are none. These people earn their living as wandering minstrels and dancers and are said to have a very low standard of morals.

(ii) The Sansis are classified as a criminal tribe ; they are gipsies and are described as adepts in theft and house-breaking. In 1931 they numbered 134 and on this occasion 1665. The large proportionate increase, the whole of which and more is shown by the Jammu District must be attributed to an influx of these gipsies from the Punjab at a time just previous to the actual census.

(iii) The Shins and Yashkuns belong to the Astore and Gilgit Districts. Whatever their origin they have now all embraced Islam. The Shins are said to be of Hindu origin. The Yashkuns were described by the Political Agent, Gilgit in 1931 as being of Turanian origin but that intermarriage with people of Tartar and Aryan descent had obliterated most of their original characteristics.

7. A decrease is shown in the totals of both Shins and Yashkuns because there are no figures available for either for Gilgit Agency for reasons already given. For the areas for which figures are available there are increases of both and had the figures for Gilgit Agency been forthcoming there would certainly have been an increase of both in the totals. It will be seen that the decrease shown on the totals of each is less than the total for each shown for Gilgit Agency in 1931. Had figures for Gilgit Agency been made available the percentage increase for all districts for these two tribes would probably have been about the same as the percentage increase for the whole population.

8. The caste system is the result of the ancient Indian custom of classifying the population according to different social and working orders. The number of castes has been multiplied due to the increase through the ages of occupational and social differences. There are some who recognise the caste system as sound owing to the inevitableness of differences in occupation and social standing; others condemn the caste system on the grounds that it withholds from many privileges and opportunities which afford advantages which should be within the reach of all irrespective of birth and occupation. In Part II of our table we give figures for those castes which together are covered by the collective term 'Scheduled Castes'. These classes are variously known as 'Depressed Classes', 'Uutouchables', or 'Harijans'. They are the backward and lower class elements of the Hindu community. In recent years their lot has been improved by the activities of various social, religious and political societies, by legislation and by Government orders removing many of the disabilities under which they previously suffered. The total population of those included in the Scheduled Castes in 1941 was 152536 against 170928 in 1931. In 1941 they represented 18.8 per cent. of the total Hindu population against 23.2 per cent. in 1931. This decrease of 18392 is probably due partly to conversion to other religions, partly to the activities of Arya Smajists and partly to a reluctance on the part of some to show themselves as belonging to the Scheduled Castes. There is a distinct tendency for members of the Scheduled Castes to lose their old identity.

9. Blank spaces should be understood to mean that in 1941 or 1931, as the case may be, no members of this caste were recorded in the district against which the blank is shown.

10. The figures for Scheduled Castes given are for those only who described themselves as Hindus by religion. Sikhs, Muslims and others belonging to the same or equivalent castes have not been included.

'Harijan' has been added to the list of the thirteen Scheduled Castes for which figures were given in the 1931 report. This was done with the approval of the Census Commissioner for India because a number of members of the Scheduled Castes now describe themselves as Harijans. It will be noticed that 2815 did so in 1941.

11. Part III gives some of the information given in Imperial Table XVII—'Race, Tribe and Caste' in 1931. There is no provision for giving information regarding castes at this census in the standard tables. In view of the fact that our tables for tribes is of little interest or value it was decided to give the figures for the more important groups in addition to those for Scheduled Castes, under the heading 'Important Elements.' The figures given are of local interest. The 34 groups given were selected from :—

(i) Castes with numbers exceeding 10000 in 1931.

(ii) Those whose social status, political importance or special character are such as to justify inclusion.

12. It is not easy to adduce reasons for the decreases shown by some castes. The record was not sorted for all castes so it is not possible to compare a large decrease in one caste with a phenomenal increase in an allied caste with any certainty. Nor is it possible to give details to show the number of enumeration slips in which caste was not recorded at all. It is possible that legislation declaring certain castes to be agricultural and to be qualified to purchase agricultural land and others as non-agricultural, and precluded from such purchases in certain circumstances, has had some effect on the record. In spite of the fact having been stressed that the census record is not used, and cannot be under the Census Act, as evidence in connection with any subject other than the census, it is possible that some have not declared a caste which is not recognised as being one which includes agricultural classes.

13. (i) In 1931 the Brahman caste was shown under four heads—Kashmiri Pandits, Mohyals, Sikhs and others; on this occasion Kashmiri Pandits have been shown separately; the heading Brahmans includes Mohyals and others only; it does not include Sikh Brahmans. The 1931 figures given are for the same classes.

(ii) The caste shown as Hajjam (M) on this occasion was shown as Hajam in 1931 and then included Hindus and Sikhs. Hajams were also shown as a sub-caste of 'Kashmiri Muslims'. In the present table Hajjam (M) refers to Muslims only. The figures shown for 1931 include the Muslim Hajams shown in 1931 plus the sub-caste shown under Kashmiri Muslims on that occasion. Similar action has been taken with respect to the Hanjis (M), Syeds (M) and Sheikhs (M).

(iii) In the 1931 table for Jats figures are given separately for Hindus, Muslims and Sikhs. In the present table only the Hindu and Muslim elements have been given. The 1931 figures are for these two classes only.

(iv) Figures for Jhiwars were shown separately for Hindus, Muslims and Sikhs in 1931. The present table gives the figures for Hindu Jhiwars only both for 1931 and 1941.

(v) The total for Kashmiri Muslims is not shown in the table for 1931 ; the totals for sub-castes were then given separately. To arrive at the 1931 total given in the present table for Kashmiri Muslims we have taken the totals of all the sub-castes with the exception of Hajams, Hanjis, Syeds and Sheikhs; the latter have been shown separately.

(vi) In 1931 figures for Khatris were given separately for Hindus, Sikhs and Jains.. On this occasion they are given for Hindu Khatris only ; the 1931 figures are accordingly given for Hindus only. Similar action has been taken in the case of Kumiars (M), Lohars (M), Lohars (H), Mahajans (H), Tarkhans (M) and Telis (M).

(vii) Figures have been given for Buddhist Mangriks only on this occasion ; the Muslim element has been excluded.

(viii) Thakkars or Thakars have been included with Rajputs (H) as in 1931 but those describing themselves as 'Rattan Rajputs', have not been included as Rajputs (H).

(ix) 'Qureshis' have been included with 'Syeds'. As there is some doubt about the correct classification of those describing themselves as 'Qureshis' it may be stated that the number of those so included is 16564 consisting of 8593 males and 7971 females. Their inclusion with Syeds in this table does not of course in any way alter their actual status.

(x) The caste returns are believed, for various reasons, some of which have been mentioned in note 12 above, not to be correct but they are probably accurate enough in most cases for general purposes. The fall in the number of Gujjars can be partly balanced against the large increase in the closely connected group called Bakerwals. Similarly, the big fall in the numbers for Tarakhehas may be connected with the large increase in Tarkhans. The number of Syeds in Ladakh could not normally increase from 9 in 1931 to 2601 in 1941. There must be some factor to account for this abnormal preference for the Syed caste. Makmis who numbered 77347 in Ladakh in 1931 are not shown at all at this census in the Ladakh District. It is probable that the big increase in those describing themselves as Baltis is largely responsible for this.

There is a very heavy fall in the numbers of those describing themselves as Bafindas. This is particularly noticeable in the districts Poonch Jagir, Mirpur, Reasi and Kathua. The large increase in Rajputs (M) in the same districts may have a close connection. In any case minor caste distinctions are not important enough to call for more detailed inquiry and discussion.

XIV—VARIATION IN POPULATION OF SELECTED TRIBES, SCHEDULED CASTES AND IMPORTANT ELEMENTS.

XIV—PART I—SELECTED TRIBES

Tribes and locality	Persons			Males			Females		
	1941	1931	Variation	1941	1931	Variation	1941	1931	Variation
1	2	3	4	5	6	7	8	9	10
Pernas ..		**42**	**—42**		**5**	**—5**		**37**	**—37**
Jammu ..		6	— 6		5	—5		1	— 1
Kathua ..		36	—36					36	—36
Sansis ..	**1665**	**134**	**+ 1531**	**856**	**78**	**+ 778**	**809**	**56**	**+ 753**
Jammu ..	1620	41	+ 1579	829	17	+ 812	791	24	+ 767
Baramulla ..	25	58	—33	16	41	—25	9	17	— 8
Anantnag ..	20	35	—15	11	20	— 9	9	15	— 6
Shins ..	**5823**	**14139**	**— 8316**	**3076**	**7126**	**—4050**	**2747**	**7013**	**—4266**
Astore ..	2178			1137			1041		
Gilgit (Leased Area) ..	3645	4408 }	+ 1415	1939	2348 }	+ 728	1706	2060 }	+ 687
Gilgit Agency ..		9731	— 9731		4778	—4778		4953	—4953
Yashkuns ..	**21886**	**36160**	**—14274**	**11569**	**19091**	**—7522**	**10317**	**17069**	**—6752**
Ladakh ..	338		+ 338	143		+ 143	195		+ 195
Astore ..	10390			5340			5050		
Gilgit (Leased Areo) ..	11158	17352 }	+ 4196	6086	9360 }	+2066	5072	7992 }	+2130
Gilgit Agency ..		18808	—18808		9731	—9731		9077	—9077

XIV—PART II—SCHEDULED CASTES.

Scheduled castes and locality		Persons			Males			Females		
		1941	1931	Variation	1941	1931	Variation	1941	1931	Variation
1		2	3	4	5	6	7	8	9	10
Barwala	..	**5526**	**5682**	**− 156**	**2984**	**3011**	**− 27**	**2542**	**2671**	**− 129**
Jammu	..	4516	4473	+ 43	2443	2365	+ 78	2073	2108	− 35
Kathua	..	62	15	+ 47	37	10	+ 27	25	5	+ 20
Udhampur	..	243	335	− 92	133	171	− 38	110	164	− 54
Reasi	..	51	98	− 47	25	43	− 18	26	55	− 29
Mirpur	..	622	695	− 73	319	392	− 73	303	303	
Chenani Jagir	..	24	66	− 42	24	30	− 6		36	− 36
Muzaffarabad	..	8		+ 8	3		+ 3	5		+ 5
Basith	..	**1613**	**6213**	**− 4600**	**833**	**3071**	**− 2238**	**780**	**3142**	**−2362**
Jammu	..	207	225	− 18	104	109	− 5	103	116	− 13
Reasi	..	495	3171	− 2676	272	1537	− 1265	223	1634	−1411
Mirpur	..	911	2817	− 1906	457	1425	− 968	454	1392	− 938
Batawal	..	**7509**	**5645**	**+ 1864**	**4107**	**3045**	**+ 1062**	**3402**	**2600**	**+ 802**
Jammu	..	7234	5376	+ 1858	3928	2897	+ 1031	3306	2479	+ 827
Kathua	..	110	130	− 20	69	73	− 4	41	57	− 16
Udhampur	..	7	48	− 41	4	29	− 25	3	19	− 16
Reasi	..	158	91	+ 67	106	46	+ 60	52	45	+ 7
Chamar	..	**40439**	**41189**	**− 750**	**20953**	**21672**	**− 719**	**19486**	**19517**	**− 31**
Jammu	..	16725	15734	+ 991	8834	8488	+ 346	7891	7246	+ 645
Kathua	..	8438	7586	+ 852	4422	4084	+ 338	4016	3502	+ 514
Udhampur	..	6435	6226	+ 209	3180	3225	− 45	3255	3001	+ 254
Reasi	..	4954	5089	− 135	2558	2628	− 70	2396	2461	− 65
Mirpur	..	3507	6014	− 2507	1770	2955	− 1185	1737	3059	−1322
Poonch Jagir	..	50	185	− 135	10	98	− 88	40	87	− 47
Chenani Jagir	..	328	316	+ 12	177	170	+ 7	151	146	+ 5
Baramulla	..	1		+ 1	1		+ 1			
Anantnag	..	1	39	− 38	1	24	− 23		15	− 15
Chuhra	..	**577**	**1607**	**− 1030**	**328**	**846**	**− 518**	**249**	**761**	**− 512**
Jammu	..	41	225	− 184	28	123	− 95	13	102	− 8
Kathua	..	94	27	+ 67	42	16	+ 26	52	11	+ 41
Udhampur	..	66	3	+ 63		2	− 2	66	1	+ 65
Reasi	..	13	26	− 13	9	14	− 5	4	12	− 8
Mirpur	..		40	− 40		22	− 22		18	− 18
Poonch Jagir	..	355	1264	− 909	243	655	− 412	112	609	− 497
Chenani Jagir	..	2	3	− 1	2	2			1	− 1
Baramulla	..	6		+ 6	4		+ 4	2		+ 2
Anantnag	..		19	− 19		12	− 12		7	− 7
Dhiyar	..	**2742**	**3165**	**− 423**	**1229**	**1555**	**− 326**	**1513**	**1610**	**− 97**
Udhampur	..	391		+ 391				391		+ 391
Reasi	..	2351	3165	− 814	1229	1555	− 326	1122	1610	− 488
Dom	..	**14802**	**34329**	**−19527**	**8045**	**18400**	**−10355**	**6757**	**15929**	**−9172**
Jammu	..	3538	10715	− 7177	1933	5865	− 3932	1605	4850	−3245
Kathua	..	2065	8951	− 6886	1106	4886	− 3780	959	4065	−3106
Udhampur	..	5735	10350	− 4615	3201	5396	− 2195	2534	4954	−2420
Reasi	..	2329	3087	− 758	1225	1619	− 394	1104	1468	− 364
Mirpur	..	72	151	− 79	34	82	− 48	38	69	− 31
Poonch Jagir	..		46	− 46			− 28		18	− 18
Chenani Jagir	..	1063	1029	+ 34	546	524	+ 22	517	505	+ 12

XIV—PART II—SCHEDULED CASTES—Concld.

Scheduled castes and locality	Persons			Males			Females		
	1941	1931	Variation	1941	1931	Variation	1941	1931	Variation
1	2	3	4	5	6	7	8	9	10
Gardi ..	1118	173	+ 945	805	76	+ 729	313	97	+ 216
Jammu ..	398	105	+ 293	221	67	+ 154	177	38	+ 139
Kathua ..	642		+ 642	543		+ 543	99		+ 99
Reasi ..	48	9	+ 39	29	5	+ 24	19	4	+ 15
Mirpur ..	30	51	− 21	12		+ 12	18	51	− 33
Anantnag ..		8	− 8		4	− 4		4	− 4
Harijan ..	2815		+2815	1415		+ 1415	1400		+1400
Jammu ..	1665		+1665	881		+ 881	784		+ 784
Kathua ..	492		+ 492	262		+ 262	230		+ 230
Udhampur ..	475		+ 475	191		+ 191	284		+ 284
Reasi ..	63		+ 63	40		+ 40	23		+ 23
Mirpur ..	94		+ 94	25		+ 25	69		+ 69
Anantnag ..	26		+ 26	16		+ 16	10		+ 10
Jolaha ..	873	40	+ 833	869	20	+ 849	4	20	− 16
Jammu ..	7		+ 7	3		+ 3	4		+ 4
Udhampur ..	865		+ 865	865		+ 865			
Reasi ..	1	40	− 39	1	20	− 19		20	− 20
Megh ..	70577	70030	+ 547	37201	37062	+ 139	33376	32968	+ 408
Jammu ..	35502	28791	+6711	19052	15692	+ 3360	16450	13099	+3351
Kathua ..	7434	6153	+1281	4108	3295	+ 813	3326	2858	+ 468
Udhampur ..	19252	25609	−6357	9618	13053	− 3435	9634	12556	−2922
Reasi ..	5899	6073	− 174	3144	3240	− 96	2755	2833	− 78
Mirpur ..	703	1573	− 870	368	814	− 446	335	759	− 424
Poonch Jagir ..		32	− 32		28	− 28		4	− 4
Chenani Jagir ..	1784	1779	+ 5	908	929	− 21	876	850	+ 26
Anantnag ..	3	20	− 17	3	11	− 8		9	− 9
Ratal ..	648	488	+ 160	372	262	+ 110	276	226	+ 50
Jammu ..	34	7	+ 27	18		+ 18	16	7	+ 9
Kathua ..	188	92	+ 96	110	44	+ 66	78	48	+ 30
Udhampur ..	227	196	+ 31	147	115	+ 32	80	81	− 1
Reasi ..	199	193	+ 6	97	103	− 6	102	90	+ 12
Saryara ..	3265	2354	+ 911	1713	1243	+470	1552	1111	+ 441
Jammu ..	1398	1063	+ 335	679	548	+ 131	719	515	+ 204
Kathua ..	846	609	+ 237	486	345	+ 141	360	264	+ 96
Udhampur ..	685	282	+ 403	367	140	+ 227	318	142	+ 176
Reasi ..	336	390	− 54	181	206	− 25	155	184	− 29
Poonch Jagir ..		10	− 10		4	− 4		6	− 6
Watal ..	32	13	+ 19	30	10	+ 20	2	3	− 1
Udhampur ..	22		+ 22	22		+ 22			
Poonch Jagir ..	5		+ 5	5		+ 5			
Anantnag ..	5	13	− 8	3	10	− 7	2	3	− 1

XIV—PART III—IMPORTANT ELEMENTS

Important elements and locality	Persons			Males			Females		
	1941	1931	Variation	1941	1931	Variation	1941	1931	Variation
1	2	3	4	5	6	7	8	9	10
Arain (M) ..	**23366**	**22922**	**+ 444**	**12613**	**12727**	**− 114**	**10753**	**10195**	**+ 558**
Jammu ..	15995	14170	+ 1825	8772	8094	+ 678	7223	6076	+ 1147
Kathua ..	2258	2093	+ 165	1197	1168	+ 29	1061	925	+ 136
Udhampur ..	145	350	− 205	68	171	− 103	77	179	− 102
Reasi ..	234	350	− 116	110	166	− 56	124	184	− 60
Mirpur ..	4681	5776	− 1095	2432	3032	− 600	2249	2744	− 495
Poonch Jagir ..		117	− 117		72	− 72		45	− 45
Chenani Jagir ..	5	62	− 57	4	21	− 17	1	41	− 40
Baramulla ..	36		+ 36	18		+ 18	18		+ 18
Anantnag ..	10	2	+ 8	10	1	+ 9		1	− 1
Muzaffarabad ..		2	− 2		2	− 2			
Astore ..	2		+ 2	2		+ 2			
Bafinda (M) ..	**9826**	**33872**	**−24046**	**5139**	**17679**	**−12540**	**4687**	**16193**	**−11506**
Jammu ..	356	1059	− 703	196	572	− 376	160	487	− 327
Kathua ..	972	6301	− 5329	514	3487	− 2973	458	2814	− 2356
Udhampur ..	448	307	+ 141	245	168	+ 77	203	139	+ 64
Reasi ..	876	2516	− 1640	470	1316	− 846	406	1200	− 794
Mirpur ..	4695	9958	− 5263	2416	5179	− 2763	2279	4779	− 2500
Poonch Jagir ..	475	11570	−11095	237	5785	− 5548	238	5785	− 5547
Chenani Jagir ..	2	4	− 2	1		+ 1	1	4	− 3
Baramulla ..	101		+ 101	46		+ 46	55		+ 55
Anantnag ..	215		+ 215	112		+ 112	103		+ 103
Muzaffarabad ..	1686	2157	− 471	902	1172	− 270	784	985	− 201
Bakarwal (M) ..	**15299**	**5349**	**+ 9950**	**8353**	**2888**	**+ 5465**	**6946**	**2461**	**+ 4485**
Jammu ..	690	362	+ 328	391	216	+ 175	299	146	+ 153
Kathua ..	1044	109	+ 935	571	71	+ 500	473	38	+ 435
Udhampur ..	1379	918	+ 461	778	483	+ 295	601	435	+ 166
Reasi ..	10688	2368	+ 8320	5771	1280	+ 4491	4917	1088	+ 3829
Mirpur ..	344	29	+ 315	196	20	+ 176	148	9	+ 139
Poonch Jagir ..	282	12	+ 270	159	8	+ 151	123	4	+ 119
Chenani Jagir ..	84		+ 84	49		+ 49	35		+ 35
Baramulla ..	7	27	− 20	4	12	− 8	3	15	− 12
Anantnag ..	769	1523	− 754	423	797	− 374	346	726	− 380
Muzaffarabad ..	12	1	+ 11	11	1	+ 10	1		+ 1
Balti (M) ..	**99348**	**47326**	**+52022**	**49742**	**23274**	**+26468**	**49606**	**24052**	**+25554**
Jammu ..	1	24	− 23	1	19	− 18		5	− 5
Udhampur ..		53	− 53		53	− 53			
Reasi ..		144	− 144		144	− 144			
Poonch Jagir ..		7	− 7		5	− 5		2	− 2
Chenani Jagir ..	93	1	+ 92	93		+ 93		1	− 1
Baramulla ..	42	23	+ 19	22	14	+ 8	20	9	+ 11
Anantnag ..	301	274	+ 27	161	141	+ 20	140	133	+ 7
Muzaffarabad ..	4	1	+ 3	4	1	+ 3			
Ladakh ..	98810	46733	+52077	49387	22855	+26532	49423	23878	+25545
Astore ..	59			40			19		
Gilgit (Leased Area) ..	38	37 }	+ 60	34	27 }	+ 47	4	10 }	+ 13
Gilgit Agency ..		29	− 29		15	− 15		14	− 14
Brahman (H) ..	**198004**	**190441**	**+ 7563**	**103024**	**98183**	**+ 4841**	**94980**	**92258**	**+ 2722**
Jammu ..	63050	58411	+ 4639	33556	30941	+ 2615	29494	27470	+ 2024
Kathua ..	35330	35911	− 581	18150	16986	+ 1164	17180	18925	− 1745
Udhampur ..	35804	33039	+ 2765	18597	17425	+ 1172	17207	15614	+ 1593
Reasi ..	26939	26768	+ 171	13988	14153	− 165	12951	12615	+ 336
Mirpur ..	14271	13215	+ 1056	7326	6813	+ 513	6945	6402	+ 543
Poonch Jagir ..	19518	20385	− 867	9552	10345	− 793	9966	10040	− 74
Chenani Jagir ..	1335	1365	− 30	702	742	− 40	633	623	+ 10

XIV—PART III—IMPORTANT ELEMENTS—CONTD.

Important elements and locality	Persons 1941	Persons 1931	Persons Variation	Males 1941	Males 1931	Males Variation	Females 1941	Females 1931	Females Variation
1	2	3	4	5	6	7	8	9	10
Brahman (H)—concld.									
Baramulla ..	**52**	**48**	+ 4	34	26	+ 8	18	22	—
Anantnag ..	**665**	**157**	+ 508	474	100	+ 374	191	57	+ 134
Muzaffarabad ..	**922**	**1009**	— 87	540	549	— 9	382	460	— 78
Ladakh ..	**82**	**9**	+ 73	75	8	+ 67	7	1	+ 6
Astore ..	**33**	}	}	28	}	}	5	}	}
Gilgit (Leased Area) ..	**3**	**124**	— 88	2	95	— 65	1	29	— 23
Brukpa (M) ..	**12237**	**13104**	**— 867**	**6323**	**6691**	**— 368**	**5914**	**6413**	**— 499**
Ladakh ..	**12237**	**13102**	**— 865**	6323	6689	— 366	5914	6413	— 499
Gilgit (Leased Area) ..		**2**	— 2		2	— 2			
Dhund (M) ..	**17670**	**17523**	**+ 147**	**8926**	**8839**	**+ 87**	**8744**	**8684**	**+ 60**
Jammu ..	**8**	**5**	+ 3	8	3	+ 5		2	— 2
Udhampur ..	**175**		+ 175	58		+ 58	117		+ 117
Reasi ..		**43**	— 43		31	— 31		12	— 12
Mirpur ..	**11**	**1**	+ 10	7	1	+ 6	4		+ 4
Poonch Jagir ..	**13016**	**12105**	+ 911	6488	5980	+ 508	6528	6125	+ 403
Baramulla ..	**57**	**9**	+ 48	29	5	+ 24	28	4	+ 24
Anantnag ..	**2**		+ 2	2		+ 2			
Muzaffarabad ..	**4400**	**5360**	— 960	2333	2819	— 486	2067	2541	— 474
Astore ..	**1**		+ 1	1		+ 1			
Gujjar (M) ..	**381457**	**402781**	**—21324**	**202534**	**216958**	**—14424**	**178923**	**185823**	**— 6900**
Jammu ..	**68644**	**62439**	+ 6205	36324	33558	+ 2766	32320	28881	+ 3439
Kathua ..	**19473**	**17936**	+ 1537	10461	9463	+ 998	9012	8473	+ 539
Udhampur ..	**25194**	**24871**	+ 323	13331	13057	+ 274	11863	11814	+ 49
Reasi ..	**67200**	**71725**	— 4525	35590	38232	— 2642	31610	33493	— 1883
Mirpur ..	**28564**	**26414**	+ 2150	14255	14027	+ 228	14309	12387	+ 1922
Poonch Jagir .	**62862**	**76647**	—13785	33060	41031	— 7971	29802	35616	— 5814
Chenani Jagir ..	**494**	**578**	— 84	271	278	— 7	223	300	— 77
Baramulla ..	**32447**	**33982**	— 1535	17862	18048	— 186	14585	15934	— 1349
Anantnag ..	**28170**	**29742**	— 1572	15208	15605	— 397	12962	14137	— 1175
Muzaffarabad ..	**47589**	**55349**	— 7760	25713	31901	— 6188	21876	23448	— 1572
Astore ..	**47**	}	}	32	}	}	15	}	}
Gilgit (Leased Area) ..	**773**	**644**	+ 176	427	359	+ 100	346	285	+ 76
Gilgit Agency ..		**2454**	— 2454		1399	— 1399		1055	— 1055
Hajjam (M) ..	**38678**	**33379**	**+ 5299**	**20910**	**17949**	**+ 2961**	**17768**	**15430**	**+ 2338**
Jammu ..	**2183**	**2292**	— 109	1156	1257	— 101	1027	1035	— 8
Kathua ..	**301**	**242**	+ 59	164	140	+ 24	137	102	+ 35
Udhampur ..	**2009**	**1028**	+ 981	1111	528	+ 583	898	500	+ 398
Reasi ..	**3082**	**2542**	+ 540	1590	1242	+ 348	1492	1300	+ 192
Mirpur ..	**3636**	**3797**	— 161	1874	1988	— 114	1762	1809	— 47
Poonch Jagir ..	**3287**	**3557**	— 270	1722	1861	— 139	1565	1696	— 131
Chenani Jagir ..	**20**	**9**	+ 11	9	6	+ 3	11	3	+ 8
Baramulla ..	**10103**	**8501**	+ 1602	5436	4709	+ 727	4667	3792	+ 875
Anantnag ..	**11507**	**9503**	+ 2004	6468	5199	+ 1269	5039	4304	+ 735
Muzaffarabad ..	**2341**	**1711**	+ 630	1263	917	+ 346	1078	794	+ 284
Ladakh ..	**41**	**56**	— 15	24	31	— 7	17	25	— 8
Astore ..	**168**	}	}	93	}	}	75	}	}
Gilgit (Leased Area) ..		**141**	+ 27		71	+ 22		70	+ 5
Hanjis (M) ..	**7403**	**4124**	**+ 3279**	**4103**	**2341**	**+ 1762**	**3300**	**1783**	**+ 1517**
Jammu ..		**6**	— 6		5	— 5		1	— 1
Kathua ..		**9**	— 9		7	— 7		2	— 2

XIV—PART III—IMPORTANT ELEMENTS—Contd.

Important elements and locality		Persons 1941	Persons 1931	Persons Variation	Males 1941	Males 1931	Males Variation	Females 1941	Females 1931	Females Variation
1		2	3	4	5	6	7	8	9	10
Hanji (M)—(concld.)										
Udhampur	..		295	− 295		164	− 164		131	− 131
Mirpur	..		1	− 1					1	− 1
Baramulla	..	2231	1725	+ 506	1228	918	+ 310	1003	807	+ 196
Anantnag	..	5172	2088	+ 3084	2875	1247	+ 1628	2297	841	+ 1456
Jat (H)	..	**25170**	**23371**	**+ 1799**	**12760**	**12287**	**+ 473**	**12410**	**11084**	**+ 1326**
Jammu	..	7313	7014	+ 299	3930	3880	+ 50	3383	3134	+ 249
Kathua	..	1430	1549	− 119	836	929	− 93	594	620	− 26
Udhampur	..	163	152	+ 11	80	95	− 15	83	57	+ 26
Reasi	..	42	27	+ 15	29	24	+ 5	13	3	+ 10
Mirpur	..	16097	14460	+ 1637	7817	7256	+ 561	8280	7204	+ 1076
Poonch Jagir	..	1	64	− 63	1	38	− 37		26	− 26
Chenani Jagir	..	86	88	− 2	47	49	− 2	39	39	
Anantnag	..	30	4	+ 26	12	4	+ 8	18		+ 18
Muzaffarabad	..	3	12	− 9	3	11	− 8		1	− 1
Ladakh	..	5		+ 5	5		+ 5			
Gilgit (Leased Area)	..		1	− 1		1	− 1			
Jat (M)	..	**121696**	**120083**	**+ 1613**	**62692**	**62227**	**+ 465**	**59004**	**57856**	**+ 1148**
Jammu	..	10658	9258	+ 1400	5775	5228	+ 547	4883	4030	+ 853
Kathua	..	257	175	+ 82	125	101	+ 24	132	74	+ 58
Udhampur	..	46	100	− 54	21	66	− 45	25	34	− 9
Reasi	..	2802	2443	+ 359	1485	1272	+ 213	1317	1171	+ 146
Mirpur	..	103025	103096	− 71	52646	52805	− 159	50379	50291	+ 88
Poonch Jagir	..	4782	4808	− 26	2561	2631	− 70	2221	2177	+ 44
Chenani Jagir	..	4	32	− 28	4	32	− 28			
Anantnag	..	102	141	− 39	63	73	− 10	39	68	− 29
Muzaffarabad	..	10	4	+ 6	5	3	+ 2	5	1	+ 4
Astore	..	7	}	}	7	}	}		}	}
Gilgit (Leased Area)	..	3	26	− 16		16	− 9	3	10	− 7
Jhiwar (H)	..	**12099**	**10157**	**+ 1942**	**6364**	**5338**	**+ 1026**	**5735**	**4819**	**+ 916**
Jammu	..	7761	7043	+ 718	3993	3738	+ 255	3768	3305	+ 463
Kathua	..	2500	1941	+ 559	1291	1037	+ 254	1209	904	+ 305
Udhampur	..	269	330	− 61	168	194	− 26	101	136	− 35
Reasi	..	151	187	− 36	87	98	− 11	64	89	− 25
Mirpur	..	1022	483	+ 539	534	133	+ 401	488	350	+ 138
Poonch Jagir	..	107	79	+ 28	49	45	+ 4	58	34	+ 24
Chenani Jagir	..	60	31	+ 29	30	31	− 1	30		+ 30
Baramulla	..		6	− 6		5	− 5		1	− 1
Anantnag	..	218	12	+ 206	202	12	+ 190	16		+ 16
Muzaffarabad	..	1	7	− 6	1	7	− 6			
Ladakh	..	10		+ 10	9		+ 9	1		+ 1
Gilgit (Leased Area)	..		38	− 38		38	− 38			
Kashmiri Muslims (M)	..	**1270261**	**1242281**	**+27980**	**685547**	**671044**	**+14503**	**584714**	**571237**	**+13477**
Jammu	..	2596	5834	− 3238	1699	3449	− 1750	897	2385	− 1488
Kathua	..	2843	3185	− 342	1467	1676	− 209	1376	1509	− 133
Udhampur	..	58989	68554	− 9565	32223	36727	− 4504	26766	31827	− 5061
Reasi	..	21761	21346	+ 415	11720	11432	+ 288	10041	9914	+ 127
Mirpur	..	15163	16371	− 1208	7603	8717	− 1114	7560	7654	− 94
Poonch Jagir	..	27871	23352	+ 4519	13796	12145	+ 1651	14075	11207	+ 2868
Chenani Jagir	..	537	287	+ 250	386	207	+ 179	151	80	+ 71
Baramulla	..	476362	457626	+18736	256673	246316	+10357	219689	211310	+ 8379
Anantnag	..	633965	618657	+15308	343713	335655	+ 8058	290252	283002	+ 7250
Muzaffarabad	..	27319	24580	+ 2739	14648	13317	+ 1331	12671	11263	+ 1408
Ladakh	..	1596	1900	− 304	906	1058	− 152	690	842	− 152
Astore	..	799	}	}	425	}	}	374	}	}
Gilgit (Leased Area)	..	460	189	+ 1070	288	166	+ 547	172	23	+ 523
Gilgit Agency	..		400	− 400		179	− 179		221	− 221

XIV—PART III—IMPORTANT ELEMENTS—Contd.

Important elements and locality	Persons 1941	Persons 1931	Persons Variation	Males 1941	Males 1931	Males Variation	Females 1941	Females 1931	Females Variation
1	2	3	4	5	6	7	8	9	10
Kashmiri Pandits (H) ..	**76868**	**63088**	**+13780**	**42958**	**35060**	**+ 7898**	**33910**	**28028**	**+ 5882**
Jammu ..	1367	1008	+ 359	858	686	+ 172	509	322	+ 187
Kathua ..	37	6	+ 31	17	6	+ 11	20		+ 20
Udhampur ..	791	928	− 137	447	476	− 29	344	452	− 108
Reasi ..	112	65	+ 47	66	45	+ 21	46	20	+ 26
Mirpur ..	51	35	+ 16	30	31	+ 1	21	4	+ 17
Poonch Jagir ..	328	62	+ 266	169	37	+ 132	159	25	+ 134
Chenani Jagir ..	15	7	+ 8	7		+ 7	8	7	+ 1
Baramulla ..	11203	9441	+ 1762	6524	5515	+ 1009	4679	3926	+ 753
Anantnag ..	62039	50617	+11422	34247	27558	+ 6689	27792	23059	+ 4733
Muzaffarabad ..	697	668	+ 29	467	517	− 50	230	151	+ 79
Ladakh ..	166	162	+ 4	95	119	− 24	71	43	+ 28
Astore ..	35			17			18		
Gilgit (Leased Area) ..	27	81	− 19	14	62	− 31	13	19	+ 12
Gilgit Agency ..		8	− 8		8	− 8			
Khatris (H) ..	**25219**	**20556**	**+ 4663**	**13870**	**11254**	**+ 2616**	**11349**	**9302**	**+ 2047**
Jammu ..	9584	6812	+ 2772	5323	3626	+ 1697	4261	3186	+ 1075
Kathua ..	1769	1035	+ 734	955	570	+ 385	814	465	+ 349
Udhampur ..	2125	2039	+ 86	1137	1097	+ 40	988	942	+ 46
Reasi ..	2123	1923	+ 200	1145	1034	+ 111	978	889	+ 89
Mirpur ..	4047	3641	+ 406	2168	1998	+ 170	1879	1643	+ 236
Poonch Jagir ..	1535	1645	− 110	841	943	− 102	694	702	− 8
Chenani Jagir ..	129	198	− 69	68	110	− 42	61	88	− 27
Baramulla ..	925	811	+ 114	557	480	+ 77	368	331	+ 37
Anantnag ..	875	626	+ 249	520	383	+ 137	355	243	+ 112
Muzaffarabad ..	2031	1689	+ 342	1113	918	+ 195	918	771	+ 147
Ladakh ..	19	21	− 2	13	14	− 1	6	7	− 1
Astore ..	25			8			17		
Gilgit (Leased Area) ..	32	78	− 21	22	54	− 24	10	24	+ 3
Gilgit Agency ..		38	− 38		27	− 27		11	− 11
Kumiar (M) ..	**25457**	**12283**	**+13174**	**13449**	**6550**	**+ 6899**	**12008**	**5733**	**+ 6275**
Jammu ..	1113	1154	− 41	607	673	− 66	506	481	+ 25
Kathua ..	97	158	− 61	39	92	− 53	58	66	− 8
Udhampur ..	2496	904	+ 1592	1302	428	+ 874	1194	476	+ 718
Reasi ..	944	1075	− 131	452	549	− 97	492	526	− 34
Mirpur ..	3757	4493	− 736	1923	2411	− 488	1834	2082	− 248
Poonch Jagir ..	2909	3459	− 550	1521	1834	− 313	1388	1625	− 237
Chenani Jagir ..	108	39	+ 69	56	22	+ 34	52	17	+ 35
Baramulla ..	5059		+ 5059	2629		+ 2629	2430		+ 2430
Anantnag ..	6979		+ 6979	3863		+ 3863	3116		+ 3116
Muzaffarabad ..	1824	897	+ 927	972	489	+ 483	852	408	+ 444
Astore ..	171			85			86		
Gilgit (Leased Area) ..		104	+ 67		52	+ 33		52	+ 34
Lohar (H) ..	**12401**	**10788**	**+ 1613**	**6539**	**5756**	**+ 783**	**5862**	**5032**	**+ 830**
Jammu ..	3274	2837	+ 437	1813	1686	+ 127	1461	1151	+ 310
Kathua ..	2012	1587	+ 425	1079	870	+ 209	933	717	+ 216
Udhampur ..	3260	3029	+ 231	1644	1521	+ 123	1616	1508	+ 108
Reasi ..	2771	2770	+ 1	1399	1365	+ 34	1372	1405	− 33
Mirpur ..	417	291	+ 126	260	165	+ 95	157	126	+ 31
Poonch Jagir ..	110	77	+ 33	59	35	+ 24	51	42	+ 9
Chenani Jagir ..	184	168	+ 16	108	85	+ 23	76	83	− 7
Baramulla ..	367		+ 367	171		+ 171	196		+ 196
Anantnag ..	4	7	− 3	4	7	− 3			
Muzaffarabad ..		3	− 3		3	− 3			
Ladakh ..	2		+ 2	2		+ 2			
Astore ..									
Gilgit (Leased Area) ..		15	− 15		15	− 15			
Gilgit Agency ..		4	− 4		4	− 4			

XIV—PART III—IMPORTANT ELEMENTS—CONTD.

Important elements and locality		Persons			Males			Females		
		1941	1931	Variation	1941	1931	Variation	1941	1931	Variation
1		2	3	4	5	6	7	8	9	10
Lohar (M)	..	**28823**	**16131**	**+12692**	**15194**	**8487**	**+ 6707**	**13629**	**7644**	**+ 5985**
Jammu	..	1284	1295	— 11	703	737	— 34	581	558	+ 23
Kathua	..	38	64	— 26	22	36	— 14	16	28	— 12
Udhampur	..	1434	538	+ 896	644	268	+ 376	790	270	+ 520
Reasi	..	3608	2511	+ 1097	1863	1249	+ 614	1745	1262	+ 483
Mirpur	..	4209	4675	— 466	2172	2378	— 206	2037	2297	— 260
Poonch Jagir	..	5699	5066	+ 633	2940	2742	+ 198	2759	2324	+ 435
Chenani Jagir	..	15		+ 15	15		+ 15			
Baramulla	..	3440		+ 3440	1846		+ 1846	1594		+ 1594
Anantnag	..	6260	111	+ 6149	3448	55	+ 3393	2812	56	+ 2756
Muzaffarabad	..	2600	1717	+ 883	1393	947	+ 446	1207	770	+ 437
Ladakh	..	34	3	+ 31	23	3	+ 20	11		+ 11
Astore	..	142			86			56		
Gilgit (Leased Area)	..	60	94 }	+ 108	39	52	+ 73	21	42 }	+ 35
Gilgit Agency	..		57	— 57		20	— 20		37	— 37
Machi (M)	..	**248**	**115**	**+ 133**	**140**	**11**	**+ 129**	**108**	**104**	**+ 4**
Jammu	..	86	70	+ 16	48	11	+ 37	38	59	— 21
Mirpur	..	60	45	+ 15	32		+ 32	28	45	— 17
Baramulla	..	102		+ 102	60		+ 60	42		+ 42
Mahajan (H)	..	**23445**	**21009**	**+ 2436**	**12779**	**10973**	**+ 1806**	**10666**	**10036**	**+ 630**
Jammu	..	10499	8989	+ 1510	5911	4850	+ 1061	4588	4139	+ 449
Kathua	..	3385	2582	+ 803	1858	1351	+ 507	1527	1231	+ 296
Udhampur	..	4471	4214	+ 257	2286	2040	+ 246	2185	2174	+ 11
Reasi	..	1455	1203	+ 252	779	608	+ 171	676	595	+ 81
Mirpur	..	2809	3365	— 556	1483	1729	— 246	1326	1636	— 310
Poonch Jagir	..	352	292	+ 60	211	179	+ 32	141	113	+ 28
Chenani Jagir	..	264	204	+ 60	122	121	+ 1	142	83	+ 59
Baramulla	..	9	20	— 11	7	13	— 6	2	7	— 5
Anantnag	..	72	29	+ 43	49	20	+ 29	23	9	+ 14
Muzaffarabad	..	124	105	+ 19	69	57	+ 12	55	48	+ 7
Astore	..	5			4			1		
Gilgit (Leased Area)	..		5 }			5 }	— 1		}	+ 1
Gilgit Agency	..		1	— 1					1	— 1
Makmi (M)	..	**253**	**77347**	**—77094**	**253**	**38980**	**—38727**		**38367**	**—38367**
Udhampur	..	253		+ 253	253		+ 253			
Ladakh	..		77347	—77347		38980	—38980		38367	—38367
Mangrik (Buddhists)	..	**35104**	**34107**	**+ 997**	**17395**	**16943**	**+ 452**	**17709**	**17164**	**+ 545**
Udhampur	..		32	— 32		11	— 11		21	— 21
Ladakh	..	35104	34075	+ 1029	17395	16932	+ 463	17709	17143	+ 566
Moghal (M)	..	**42256**	**30148**	**+12108**	**21490**	**15770**	**+ 5720**	**20766**	**14378**	**+ 6388**
Jammu	..	1161	1238	— 77	651	738	— 87	510	500	+ 10
Kathua	..	197	72	+ 125	108	49	+ 59	89	23	+ 66
Udhampur	..	573	309	+ 264	292	135	+ 157	281	174	+ 107
Reasi	..	5149	3519	+ 1630	2652	1817	+ 835	2497	1702	+ 795
Mirpur	..	9628	6467	+ 3161	4624	3467	+ 1157	5004	3000	+ 2004
Poonch Jagir	..	16500	8496	+ 8004	8355	4261	+ 4094	8145	4235	+ 3910
Chenani Jagir	..	36	10	+ 26	29		+ 29	7	10	— 3
Baramulla	..	1109	312	+ 797	582	110	+ 472	527	202	+ 325
Anantnag	..	1337	157	+ 1180	712	121	+ 591	625	36	+ 589
Muzaffarabad	..	6192	9389	— 3197	3247	4964	— 1717	2945	4425	— 1480
Ladakh	..	51	35	+ 16	35	25	+ 10	16	10	+ 6
Astore	..	72			49			23		
Gilgit (Leased Area)	..	251	143 }	+ 180	154	82 }	+ 121	97	61 }	+ 59
Gilgit Agency	..			— 1		1	— 1			

XIV—PART III—IMPORTANT ELEMENTS—CONTD.

Important elements and locality	Persons			Males			Females		
	1941	1931	Variation	1941	1931	Variation	1941	1931	Variation
1	2	3	4	5	6	7	8	9	10
Pathan (M) ..	**22399**	**19288**	**+ 3111**	**11821**	**10554**	**+ 1267**	**10578**	**8734**	**+ 1844**
Jammu ..	1664	2083	− 419	919	1362	− 443	745	721	+ 24
Kathua ..	227	209	+ 18	149	104	+ 45	78	105	− 27
Udhampur ..	1203	982	+ 221	621	495	+ 126	582	487	+ 95
Reasi ..	1113	989	+ 124	539	535	+ 4	574	454	+ 120
Mirpur ..	1064	1239	− 175	506	726	− 220	558	513	+ 45
Poonch Jagir ..	5492	5218	+ 274	2918	2800	+ 118	2574	2418	+ 156
Chenani Jagir ..	37	70	− 33	26	49	− 23	11	21	− 10
Baramulla ..	3420	1316	+ 2104	1789	696	+ 1093	1631	620	+ 1011
Anantnag ..	3044	1046	+ 1998	1610	558	+ 1052	1434	488	+ 946
Muzaffarabad ..	4292	4924	− 632	2245	2554	− 309	2047	2370	− 323
Ladakh ..	81	4	+ 77	45	1	+ 44	36	3	+ 33
Astore ..	96	}	}	55	}	}	41	}	}
Gilgit (Leased Area) ..	666	501	+ 261	399	292	+ 162	267	209	+ 99
Gilgit Agency ..		707	− 707		382	− 382		325	− 325
Rajput (H) ..	**168582**	**159517**	**+ 9065**	**91040**	**87339**	**+ 3701**	**77542**	**72178**	**+ 5364**
Jammu ..	35781	30879	+ 4902	20689	18040	+ 2649	15092	12839	+ 2253
Kathua ..	36153	36167	− 14	19202	20581	− 1379	16951	15586	+ 1365
Udhampur ..	61488	58184	+ 3304	31771	30162	+ 1609	29717	28022	+ 1695
Reasi ..	20871	21216	− 345	10939	10630	+ 309	9932	10586	− 654
Mirpur ..	8414	7531	+ 883	4881	4468	+ 413	3533	3063	+ 470
Poonch Jagir ..	532	702	− 170	305	389	− 84	227	313	− 86
Chenani Jagir ..	3010	3004	+ 6	1548	1653	− 105	1462	1351	+ 111
Baramulla ..	166	98	+ 68	95	77	+ 18	71	21	+ 50
Anantnag ..	1862	1120	+ 742	1341	768	+ 573	521	352	+ 169
Muzaffarabad ..	145	116	+ 29	116	90	+ 26	29	26	+ 3
Ladakh ..	135	68	+ 67	134	68	+ 66	1		+ 1
Astore ..	5	}	}	5	}	}		}	}
Gilgit (Leased Area) ..	20	344	− 319	14	334	− 315	6	10	− 4
Gilgit Agency ..		88	− 88		79	− 79		9	− 9
Rajput (M) ..	**226404**	**196570**	**+29834**	**115979**	**102480**	**+13499**	**110425**	**94090**	**+16335**
Jammu ..	19379	16865	+ 2514	10470	9561	+ 909	8909	7304	+ 1605
Kathua ..	1691	470	+ 1221	937	299	+ 638	754	171	+ 583
Udhampur ..	3928	7521	− 3593	2035	3949	− 1914	1893	3572	− 1679
Reasi ..	20041	16886	+ 3155	10116	8511	+ 1605	9925	8375	+ 1550
Mirpur ..	68983	51012	+17971	34153	25805	+ 8348	34830	25207	+ 9623
Poonch Jagir ..	78152	61843	+16309	39979	31982	+ 7997	38173	29861	+ 8312
Chenani Jagir ..	163	90	+ 73	85	56	+ 29	78	34	+ 44
Baramulla ..	1608	2998	− 1390	896	1721	− 825	712	1277	− 565
Anantnag ..	2826	4710	− 1884	1840	2580	− 740	986	2130	− 1144
Muzaffarabad ..	29259	33961	− 4702	15227	17906	− 2679	14032	16055	− 2023
Ladakh ..	32	33	−1	14	10	+ 4	18	23	− 5
Astore ..	88	}	}	84	}	}	4	}	}
Gilgit (Leased Area) ..	254	121	+ 221	143	92	+ 135	111	29	+ 86
Gilgit Agency ..		60	− 60		8	− 8		52	− 52
Rigzong (Buddhists) ..	**985**	**1547**	**− 562**	**573**	**739**	**− 166**	**412**	**808**	**− 396**
Udhampur ..		15	− 15		8	− 8		7	− 7
Ladakh ..	985	1532	− 547	573	731	− 158	412	801	− 389
Sheikh (M) ..	**109781**	**103959**	**+ 5822**	**59253**	**55887**	**+ 3366**	**50528**	**48072**	**+ 2456**
Jammu ..	1201	2830	− 1629	681	1505	− 824	520	1325	− 805
Kathua ..	698	412	+ 286	356	214	+ 142	342	198	+ 144
Udhampur ..	10136	5968	+ 4168	5369	3091	+ 2278	4767	2877	+ 1890
Reasi ..	2926	3610	− 684	1519	1974	− 455	1407	1636	− 229
Mirpur ..	1917	2444	− 527	1025	1364	− 339	892	1080	− 188
Poonch Jagir ..	10529	11664	− 1135	5482	6096	− 614	5047	5568	− 521
Chenani Jagir ..	148	91	+ 57	100	59	+ 41	48	32	+ 16
Baramulla ..	28908	28289	+ 619	15598	15084	+ 514	13310	13205	+ 105
Anantnag ..	42612	37943	+ 4669	23356	20738	+ 2618	19256	17205	+ 2051
Muzaffarabad ..	10068	10228	− 160	5417	5479	− 62	4651	4749	− 98

XIV—PART III—IMPORTANT ELEMENTS—Contd.

Important elements and locality	Persons 1941	Persons 1931	Persons Variation	Males 1941	Males 1931	Males Variation	Females 1941	Females 1931	Females Variation
1	2	3	4	5	6	7	8	9	10
Sheikh (M)—concld.									
Ladakh ..	550	313	+ 237	300	192	+ 108	250	121	+ 129
Astore ..	48			28			20		
Gilgit (Leased Area) ..	40	108	− 20	22	62	− 12	18	46	− 8
Gilgit Agency ..		59	− 59		29	− 29		30	− 30
Sudhan (M) ..	**78412**	**68594**	**+ 9818**	**37226**	**33201**	**+ 4025**	**41186**	**35393**	**+5793**
Jammu ..	16	27	− 11	15	26	− 11	1	1	.
Kathua ..		5	− 5		5	− 5			
Udhampur ..	18		+ 18	10		+ 10	8		+ 8
Reasi ..	61	307	− 246	34	131	− 97	27	176	− 149
Mirpur ..	3480	2521	+ 959	1753	1402	+ 351	1727	1119	+ 608
Poonch Jagir ..	74210	65193	+ 9017	35085	31365	+ 3720	39125	33828	+5297
Baramulla ..	16		+ 16	10		+ 10	6		+ 6
Anantnag ..	8		+ 8	5		+ 5	3		+ 3
Muzaffarabad ..	603	541	+ 62	314	272	+ 42	289	269	+ 20
Syed (M) ..	**52293**	**52303**	**− 10**	**27395**	**27431**	**− 36**	**24898**	**24872**	**+ 26**
Jammu ..	2790	2773	+ 17	1485	1503	− 18	1305	1270	+ 35
Kathua ..	60	65	− 5	36	44	− 8	24	21	+ 3
Udhampur ..	910	459	+ 451	495	247	+ 248	415	212	+ 203
Reasi ..	3038	2774	+ 264	1591	1562	+ 29	1447	1212	+ 235
Mirpur ..	5209	5076	+ 133	2600	2655	− 55	2609	2421	+ 188
Poonch Jagir ..	11786	15054	− 3268	6153	7627	− 1474	5633	7427	−1794
Chenani Jagir ..	7	1	+ 6	7		+ 7		1	− 1
Baramulla ..	4792	5655	− 863	2481	3002	− 521	2311	2653	− 342
Anantnag ..	6930	5715	+ 1215	3548	3060	+ 488	3382	2655	+ 727
Muzaffarabad ..	13637	13281	+ 356	7123	6965	+ 158	6514	6316	+ 198
Ladakh ..	2601	9	+ 2592	1594	7	+ 1587	1007	2	+1005
Astore ..	43			25			18		
Gilgit (Leased Area) ..	490	450	+ 83	257	226	+ 56	233	224	+ 27
Gilgit Agency ..		991	− 991		533	− 533		458	− 458
Tarakhehas (M) ..	**3026**	**10155**	**− 7129**	**1539**	**5221**	**− 3682**	**1487**	**4934**	**−3447**
Udhampur ..	10		+ 10				10		+ 10
Ladakh ..	3016	10150	− 7134	1539	5216	− 3677	1477	4934	−3457
Gilgit (Leased Area) ..		5	− 5		5	− 5			
Tarkhan (M) ..	**35249**	**14405**	**+20844**	**18611**	**7616**	**+10995**	**16638**	**6789**	**+9849**
Jammu ..	2113	1950	+ 163	1127	1103	+ 24	986	847	+ 139
Kathua ..	35	67	− 32	15	40	− 25	20	27	− 7
Udhampur ..	615	41	+ 574	332	10	+ 322	283	31	+ 252
Reasi	2946	2052	+ 894	1500	1083	+ 423	1440	969	+ 471
Mirpur ..	6595	6340	+ 255	3402	3285	+ 117	3193	3055	+ 138
Poonch Jagir ..	3342	3455	− 113	1682	1817	− 135	1660	1638	+ 22
Chenani Jagir ..	3		+ 3	3		+ 3			
Baramulla ..	8564	1	+ 8563	4559		+ 4559	4005	1	+4004
Anantnag ..	9379	48	+ 9331	5087	13	+ 5074	4292	35	+4257
Muzaffarabad ..	1557	405	+ 1152	844	233	+ 611	713	172	+ 541
Astore ..	42			22			20		
Gilgit (Leased Area) ..	58	46	+ 54	32	32	+ 22	26	14	+ 32
Teli (M) ..	**28134**	**15834**	**+12300**	**15153**	**8221**	**+ 6932**	**12981**	**7613**	**+5368**
Jammu ..	7100	6551	+ 549	3803	3415	+ 358	3297	3106	+ 191
Kathua ..	2391	2747	− 356	1283	1559	− 276	1108	1188	− 80
Udhampur ..	538	511	+ 27	299	284	+ 15	239	227	+ 12
Reasi ..	958	966	− 8	508	403	+ 105	450	563	− 113

XIV—PART III—IMPORTANT ELEMENTS—Concld.

Important elements and locality		Persons			Males			Females	
	1941	1931	Variation	1941	1931	Variation	1941	1931	Variation
1	2	3	4	5	6	7	8	9	10
Teli (M)—concld									
Mirpur ..	**3514**	**3388**	− 474	1850	1968	− 118	1664	2020	− 356
Poonch Jagir ..	**759**	**735**	+ 24	391	377	+ 14	368	358	+ 10
Chenani Jagir ..	**50**	**16**	+ 34	26	8	+ 18	24	8	+ 16
Baramulla ..	**5066**		+ 5006	2763		+2763	2243		+2243
Anantnag ..	**7458**		+ 7458	4049		+4049	3409		+3409
Muzaffarabad ..	**328**	**270**	+ 58	167	147	+ 20	161	123	+ 38
Ladakh ..	**32**		+ 32	14		+ 14	18		+ 18
Gilgit Agency ..		**50**	− 50		30	− 30		20	− 20

M=Muslims H=Hindus

IMPERIAL TABLE XV

Europeans and Allied Races and Anglo-Indians by race and age

NOTES

1. The table is in exactly the same form as the corresponding Table XIX for 1931.

2. Badami Bagh Cantonment does not appear in the detail given under "Cities and Cantonments." This is due to the fact that the villages Sonawar and Bonimsar though lying within the administrative area of the Badami Bagh Cantonment were censused under arrangements made by the Census Officer for Khas Tehsil by arrangement with the Cantonment authorities. The elements dealt with in this table living within the area of the two villages named are included in the figures for Anantnag District.

3. All districts have been shown; blanks indicate that none of the elements shown in this table live in such districts.

4. Allied races include non-Asiatic races such as Australians, Canadians, Americans and South Africans, in fact all white races as distinct from Asiatic, Mongol, Negroid and Polynesian races.

5. Only those describing themselves as Anglo-Indians have been treated as such. The numbers are very small and suggest wrong descriptions in a number of cases. The number recorded as Europeans and Allied Races was 423 in 1941 against 321 in 1931; the number of Anglo-Indians 7 in 1941 against 123 in 1931. This fall of 116 in Anglo-Indians since 1931 accounts in full for the increase of 102 Europeans. The number of true Europeans and Allied races living in the State in 1941 is believed to have been less than in 1931.

6. The figures given against Jammu City and Cantonment are also included in the Jammu District and those against Srinagar City in the figures for Anantnag District.

NOTE.—P stands for Persons, M for Males and F for Females.

XV—EUROPEANS AND ALLIED RACES AND

A—EUROPEAN AND ALLIED

District or State	Total			(a) British subjects																
				All ages			0-13		14-16		17-23		24-33		34-43		44·53		54+	
	P	M	F	P	M	F	M	F	M	F	M	F	M	F	M	F	M	F	M	F
1	2	3	4	5	6	7	8	9	10	11	12	13	14	15	16	17	18	19	20	21
JAMMU AND KASHMIR STATE ..	**423**	**209**	**214**	**373**	**193**	**180**	**81**	**32**	**6**	**7**	**4**	**9**	**23**	**36**	**22**	**28**	**21**	**27**	**36**	**41**
JAMMU PROVINCE ..	**51**	**32**	**19**	**46**	**31**	**15**	**8**	**4**	**1**	**1**		**2**	**8**	**4**	**3**	**1**	**6**	**2**	**5**	**1**
(a) TOTAL DISTRICTS	*48*	*30*	*18*	*43*	*29*	*14*	*8*	*4*	*1*	*1*		*2*	*8*	*4*	*3*	*1*	*4*	*1*	*5*	*1*
Jammu ..	**35**	20	15	**30**	19	11	6	3	1	1		1	4	3	1	1	3	1	4	1
Kathua ..																				
Udhampur ..	**9**	7	2	**9**	7	2	2					1	4	1					1	
Reasi ..	**2**	2		**2**	2										1		1			
Mirpur ..	**2**	1	1	**2**	1	1		1							1					
(b) TOTAL JAGIRS ..	*3*	*2*	*1*	*3*	*2*	*1*											*2*	*1*		
Chenani Jagir ..																				
Poonch Jagir ..	**3**	2	1	**3**	2	1											2	1		
KASHMIR PROVINCE	**342**	**160**	**182**	**302**	**147**	**155**	**71**	**23**	**5**	**6**	**4**	**7**	**7**	**28**	**15**	**27**	**14**	**24**	**31**	**40**
Baramulla ..	**64**	30	34	**36**	25	11	6	2	4		3	1	4	3	3	2	2	1	3	2
Anantnag ..	**273**	130	143	**261**	122	139	65	21	1	6	1	6	3	21	12	25	12	22	28	38
Muzaffarabad ..	**5**		5	**5**		5								4				1		
FRONTIER DISTRICTS	**30**	**17**	**13**	**25**	**15**	**10**	**2**	**5**					**8**	**4**	**4**		**1**	**1**		
Ladakh ..	**11**	6	5	**7**	4	3	1	1					2	1			1	1		
Astore ..																				
Gilgit (Leased Area)	**17**	9	8	**16**	9	7	1	4					4	3	4					
Gilgit Agency ..	**2**	2		**2**	2								2							
CITIES AND CANTONMENTS																				
Jammu City ..	**5**	2	3	**5**	2	3							1	1		1		1	1	
Jammu Cantonment	**9**	5	4	**7**	5	2	2							2			1		2	
Srinagar City ..	**235**	118	117	**224**	110	114	62	21		5		4	3	18	12	21	11	17	22	28

ANGLO-INDIANS BY RACE AND AGE

RACES (INCLUDING ARMENIANS)																		B—ANGLO-INDIANS		
(b) Others																		All ages		
All ages			0-13		14-16		17-23		24-33		34-43		44-53		54+					
P	M	F	M	F	M	F	M	F	M	F	M	F	M	F	M	F		P	M	F
22	*23*	*24*	*25*	*26*	*27*	*28*	*29*	*30*	*31*	*32*	*33*	*34*	*35*	*36*	*37*	*38*		*39*	*40*	*41*
50	**16**	**34**	**2**	**4**	**1**		**1**	**3**	**4**	**8**	**3**	**9**	**4**	**4**	**1**	**6**		**7**	**4**	**3**
5	**1**	**4**	**1**					**1**						**1**		**2**				
5	*1*	*4*	*1*					*1*						*1*		*2*				
5	1	4	1					1						1		2				
40	**13**	**27**	**1**	**4**	**1**			**2**	**3**	**6**	**3**	**8**	**4**	**3**	**1**	**4**		**6**	**3**	**3**
28	5	23	1	4	1			2	3	5		7		2		3				
12	8	4								1	3	1	4	1	1	1		**6**	3	3
5	**2**	**3**					**1**		**1**	**2**		**1**						**1**	**1**	
4	2	2					1		1	1		1								
1		1								1								1	1	
2		2						1								1				
11	8	3								1	3	1		1	1			**6**	3	3

XV—EUROPEANS AND ALLIED RACES AND ANGLO-INDIANS BY RACE AND AGE—CONCLD.

B—ANGLO-INDIANS—concld.

District or State	0-3 M	0-3 F	4-6 M	4-6 F	7-13 M	7-13 F	14-16 M	14-16 F	17-19 M	17-19 F	20-29 M	20-29 F	30-39 M	30-39 F	40-49 M	40-49 F	50-59 M	50-59 F	60-69 M	60-69 F	70 + M	70 + F
1	42	43	44	45	46	47	48	49	50	51	52	53	54	55	56	57	58	59	60	61	62	63
JAMMU AND KASHMIR STATE ..					1			1					1		1			1	1	1		
JAMMU PROVINCE																						
(a) TOTAL DISTRICTS																						
Jammu ..																						
Kathua ..																						
Udhampur ..																						
Reasi ..																						
Mirpur ..																						
(b) TOTAL JAGIRS ..																						
Chenani Jagir ..																						
Poonch Jagir ..																						
KASHMIR PROVINCE					1			1							1			1	1	1		
Baramulla ..																						
Anantnag ..					1			1							1			1	1	1		
Muzaffarabad .																						
FRONTIER DISTRICTS													1									
Ladakh ..																						
Astore ..																						
Gilgit (Leased Area)													1									
Gilgit Agency ..																						
CITIES AND CANTONMENTS ..																						
Jammu City ..																						
Jammu Cantonment																						
Srinagar City ..					1			1							1			1	1	1		

P=Persons M=Males F=Females

IMPERIAL TABLE XVI

Summary of figures for Districts

NOTES

1. The table is in the same form as the corresponding Imperial Table XX in the 1931 report. There is a small change in the communities given. In 1931 figures were given separately for Hindus, Muslims, Sikhs, Christians, Buddhists and others ; on this occasion they are given for Hindus, Muslims, Indian Christians, Tribes and Others. The figures for those communities not included in this table are however given in Imperial Table XIII.

2. In the figures for Density fractions have been eliminated ; fractions of less than .5 have been ignored and those in excess treated as whole numbers.

3. The 'Tribes' for which figures have been given have been discussed in the notes to Table XIII.

4. The figures for 1931 are not available separately for districts Astore and Gilgit (Leased Area) as in 1931 these constituted the old Gilgit District. The 1931 figures given in columns 6 and 10 are the population and density figures respectively for the old Gilgit District.

5. The variations in every case show an increase.

NOTE.—P stands for Persons, M for Males and F for Females.

XVI—SUMMARY FIGURES FOR DISTRICTS

District or State	Area in square miles	Population 1941 P	Population 1941 M	Population 1941 F	Population 1931 P	Percentage of variation 1931-1941	Percentage of variation 1921-1931	Density 1941	Density 1931
1	2	3	4	5	6	7	8	9	10
JAMMU AND KASHMIR STATE	**84471**	**4021616**	**2129872**	**1891744**	**3646243**	10.29	**9. 8**	**48**	**43**
JAMMU PROVINCE ..	**12378**	**1981433**	**1034410**	**947023**	**1788441**	**10.79**	**9.03**	**160**	**144**
(a) Total Districts ..	*10656*	*1547809*	*814016*	*733793*	*1390132*	*11.34*	*8.78*	*145*	*130*
Jammu ..	1147	**431362**	233976	197386	**375240**	14.95	11.16	376	327
Kathua ..	1023	**177672**	94134	83538	**161232**	10.19	4.55	174	158
Udhampur ..	5070	**294217**	153608	140609	**273668**	7.50	11.58	58	54
Reasi ..	1789	**257903**	135502	122401	**235245**	9.63	5.18	144	131
Mirpur	1627	**386655**	196796	189859	**344747**	12.15	8.68	238	212
(b) Total Jagirs ..	*1722*	*433624*	*220394*	*213230*	*398309*	*8.86*	*9. 9*	*252*	*231*
Chenani Jagir ..	95	**11796**	6475	5321	**10925**	7.97	2.87	124	115
Poonch Jagir ..	1627	**421828**	213919	207909	**387384**	8.89	10.12	259	238
KASHMIR PROVINCE ..	**8539**	**1728705**	**934738**	**793967**	**1569218**	**10.16**	**11.52**	**202**	**184**
Baramulla ..	3317	**612428**	330050	282378	**559828**	9.39	11.47	185	169
Anantnag ..	2814	**851606**	463571	388035	**771943**	10.31	12. 1	303	274
Muzaffarabad ..	2408	**264671**	141117	123554	**237447**	11.46	9.87	110	99
FRONTIER DISTRICTS ..	**63554**	**311478**	**160724**	**150754**	**288584**	**7.93**	**5.64**	**5**	**5**
Ladakh ..	45762	**195431**	98478	96953	**192138**	1.71	4.72	4	4
Astore ..	1632	**17026**	8948	8078 }	**31902**	23.88	11.13	10 }	10
Gilgit (Leased Area) ..	1480	**22495**	12471	10024 }				15 }	
Gilgit Agency ..	14680	**76526**	40827	35699	**64544**	118.56	5.82	5	4

XVI—SUMMARY FIGURES FOR DISTRICTS—Concld.

District or State	Distribution by Communities									
	Hindus		Muslims		Indian Christians		Tribes		Others	
	M	F	M	F	M	F	M	F	M	F
1	11	12	13	14	15	16	17	18	19	20
JAMMU AND KASHMIR STATE	**430683**	**378482**	**1641701**	**1459546**	**1675**	**1404**	**29**	**22**	**55784**	**52290**
JAMMU PROVINCE ..	**381745**	**341090**	**630318**	**585358**	**1505**	**1232**	**16**	**13**	**20826**	**19330**
(a) Total Districts ..	*364458*	*324659*	*434759*	*395990*	*1505*	*1232*	*16*	*13*	*13278*	*11899*
Jammu ..	134637	113536	92578	78211	1245	1017	16	13	5500	4609
Kathua	69448	62375	24355	20859	103	101			228	203
Udhampur	85179	79641	67878	60449	54	35			497	484
Reasi ..	42211	38514	92412	83127	54	42			825	718
Mirpur ..	32983	30593	157536	153344	49	37			6228	5885
(b) Total Jagirs ..	*17287*	*16431*	*195559*	*189368*					*7548*	*7431*
Chenani Jagir ..	4975	4606	1491	714					9	1
Poonch Jagir ..	12312	11825	194068	188654					7539	7430
KASHMIR PROVINCE ..	**48388**	**37192**	**871499**	**743979**	**97**	**110**	**11**	**9**	**14743**	**12677**
Baramulla ..	7579	5340	317983	272953	24	24			4464	4061
Anantnag ..	37470	29345	422619	356065	56	63	11	9	3415	2553
Muzaffarabad ..	3339	2507	130897	114961	17	23			6864	6063
FRONTIER DISTRICTS ..	**550**	**200**	**139884**	**130209**	**73**	**62**	**2**		**20215**	**20283**
Ladakh ..	361	94	77925	76567	68	59			20124	20233
Astore ..	72	41	8852	8026	3	1	1		20	10
Gilgit (Leased Area) ..	72	36	12342	9954	2		1		54	34
Gilgit Agency ..	45	29	40765	35662		2			17	6

STATE TABLE I

Area and Population of Tehsils

NOTES

1. The table is in the same form as State Table I for 1931 except for the addition of columns 13 and 14.

2. (i) The areas of Tehsils are not authoritative; they have been adjusted to agree in total with the areas of the districts in which they are located. They are accurate enough for all practical purposes.

(ii) In 1931, the area 4 square miles of three villages, two located in the Jammu Tehsil and one in the Ramnagar Tehsil, belonging to the Poonch Jagir, was included in the area given for the Poonch Jagir. In the present table the areas of these villages have been included in the areas of the tehsils in which they are located *viz.*, 3 square miles with the Jammu Tehsil and 1 square mile with Ramnagar Tehsil. The population of these three villages has been shown accordingly as discussed in note 4 to Imperial Table I.

3. The details of the two cities of Jammu and Srinagar given separately at the end of the table have been included in the figures of the tehsils in which they are located, *viz.*, Jammu Tehsil and Khas Tehsil.

4. The names shown in brackets against tehsils Uttarmachipura, Sri Pratapsinghpura and Pulwama in the Kashmir Province are the local names by which these tehsils are frequently known.

5. The changes in the number of towns shown in each district have been discussed in note 7 to Imperial Table I.

6. All variations represent increases unless a minus sign has been given.

7. (i) The mothertongue shown in column 13 is that returned as mothertongue by the majority of the population of the area.

(ii) The number of those shown as speaking any particular mothertongue against Districts, (other than Gilgit Agency) Provinces and for the whole State will be found to agree with the figures given in Table XII Part II-A and not with those given in Part I of that table as the figures shown in the latter include dialects.

(iii) The details given in columns 13 and 14 for the Gilgit Agency and the illaqas of that district are those supplied by the Census Superintendent, North-West Frontier Province, who sorted the record.

8. (i) As the districts Astore and Gilgit (Leased Area) together constituted the old Gilgit District in 1931, they are joined together by a bracket for the purposes of columns 9, 10 and 11.

(ii) The illaqas Kuh and Ghizar of the Gilgit Agency were shown separately in 1931 but constitute one unit in 1941 according to the details supplied by the Census Superintendent, North-West Frontier Province.

9. The figures given in column 14 show clearly that Kashmiri and Dogri are the two languages in greatest use.

10. The figures given in column 12 indicate a high density in many tehsils which are entirely agricultural.

NOTE.—P stand for Persons, M for Males and F for Females.

STATE TABLE I—AREA AND POPULATION OF TEHSILS

Tehsil	Area in square miles	Number of Towns	Number of Villages	Occupied houses	Population 1941 P	Population 1941 M	Population 1941 F	Population 1931 P	Percentage variation 1931 to 1941	Percentage variation 1921 to 1931	Density (sq. mile) 1941	Prevailing mother-tongue Language	Prevailing mother-tongue P
1	2	3	4	5	6	7	8	9	10	11	12	13	14
JAMMU & KASHMIR STATE ..	**84471**	**39**	**8740**	**764424**	**4021616**	**2129872**	**1891744**	**3646243**	**10.29**	**9. 8**	**48**	Kashmiri	**1512912**
JAMMU PROVINCE ..	**12378**	**21**	**4533**	**400226**	**1981433**	**1034410**	**947023**	**1788441**	**10.79**	**9.03**	**160**	Dogri	**657143**
(a) TOTAL DISTRICTS	*10656*	*20*	*4004*	*319141*	*1547809*	*814016*	*733793*	*1390132*	*11.34*	*8.78*	*145*	Dogri	*647771*
Jammu District ..	**1147**	**5**	**1165**	**88263**	**431362**	**233976**	**197386**	**375240**	**14.95**	**11.16**	**376**	Dogri	**280108**
Jammu Tehsil (including Jammu city) ..	346	2	334	33223	**156556**	88970	67586	**132840**	17.85	10.8	452	Dogri	98552
Samba ..	327	1	319	16840	**89464**	47103	42361	**79181**	12.98	17.67	274	Dogri	73432
Sri Ranbirsinghpura	157	1	294	20005	**96521**	51400	45121	**82788**	16.58	7.82	615	Panjabi	47479
Akhnur ..	317	1	218	18195	**88821**	46503	42318	**80431**	10.43	9.27	280	Dogri	**61158**
Kathua District ..	**1023**	**3**	**563**	**37598**	**177672**	**94134**	**83538**	**161232**	**10.19**	**4.55**	**174**	Dogri	**153085**
Kathua ..	224	2	168	10132	**47378**	25954	21424	**43299**	9.42	6.01	212	Dogri	**42086**
Jasmergarh ..	185		257	12393	**59670**	31433	28237	**51957**	14.04	8.5	323	Dogri	**54391**
Basohli ..	614	1	138	15073	**70624**	36747	33877	**65976**	7.04	.75	115	Dogri	**56608**
Udhampur District ..	**5070**	**4**	**926**	**55947**	**294217**	**153608**	**140609**	**273668**	**7.50**	**11.58**	**58**	Dogri	**99682**
Udhampur ..	383	1	194	11045	**52937**	28065	24872	**48880**	8.29	7.03	138	Dogri	**44713**
Kishtwar ..	3021	1	156	9915	**60893**	32077	28816	**56496**	7.78	18.44	20	Kashmiri	**30878**
Ramban ..	588		130	13176	**75793**	39750	36043	**71043**	6.68	14.55	129	Kashmiri	**40945**
Ramnagar ..	525	1	137	13057	**60076**	30908	29168	**55666**	7.92	6.52	114	Dogri	**51294**
Bhadrawah ..	553	1	309	8754	**44518**	22808	21710	**41583**	7.05	10.55	81	Bhadrawahi	**21740**
Reasi District ..	**1789**	**3**	**648**	**48502**	**257903**	**135502**	**122401**	**235245**	9.63	**5.18**	**144**	Dogri	**82098**
Reasi ..	983	2	324	22251	**117059**	61858	55201	**106876**	9.52	5.90	119	Dogri	**49894**
Rampur Rajouri ..	806	1	324	26251	**140844**	73644	67200	**128369**	9.71	4.59	175	Pahari	**60295**
Mirpur District ..	**1627**	**5**	**702**	**88831**	**386655**	**196796**	**189859**	**344747**	**12.15**	**8.68**	**238**	Panjabi	**223427**
Kotli ..	574	1	224	24883	**111037**	56706	54331	**102787**	8.02	8.95	193	Chabhali	**43326**
Mirpur ..	355	1	288	28492	**113115**	56739	56376	**101102**	11.88	8.26	319	Panjabi	**104116**
Bhimbar ..	698	3	190	35456	**162503**	83351	79152	**140858**	15.36	8.79	233	Panjabi	**115057**
(b) TOTAL JAGIRS ..	*1722*	*1*	*529*	*81085*	*433624*	*220394*	*213230*	*398309*	*8.86*	*9. 9*	*252*	Pahari	*237582*
Chenani Jagir ..	**95**		**46**	**2562**	**11796**	**6475**	**5321**	**10925**	**7.97**	**2.87**	**124**	Dogri	**8590**
Chenani ..	95		46	2562	**11796**	6475	5321	**10925**	7.97	2.87	124	Dogri	**8590**
Poonch Jagir ..	**1627**	**1**	**483**	**78523**	**421828**	**213919**	**207909**	**387384**	**8.89**	**10.12**	**259**	Pahari	**236713**
Bagh ..	321		111	19507	**101091**	50859	50232	**93956**	7.59	12	315	Hindustani	**81309**
Sadhnuti ..	348		101	22564	**108300**	52046	56254	**100470**	7.79	12.76	311	Pahari	**105218**
Haveli ..	479	1	173	18085	**110733**	58477	52256	**101151**	9.47	5.85	231	Pahari	**49581**
Mendhar ..	479		98	18367	**101704**	52537	49167	**91807**	10.78	10.28	212	Pahari	**68313**

STATE TABLE I—AREA AND POPULATION OF TEHSILS—Concld.

Tehsil	Area in square miles	Number of		Occupied houses	Population				Percentage variation		Density (sq. mile) 1941	Prevailing mother-tongue	
		Towns	Villages		1941 P	1941 M	1941 F	1931 P	1931 to 1941	1921 to 1931		Language	P
1	2	3	4	5	6	7	8	9	10	11	12	13	14
KASHMIR PROVINCE	**8539**	**15**	**3518**	**298829**	**1728705**	**934738**	**793967**	**1569218**	**10.16**	**11.52**	**202**	Kashmiri	**1369534**
Baramulla District ..	**3317**	**4**	**1370**	**106573**	**612428**	**330050**	**282378**	**559828**	**9.39**	**11.47**	**185**	Kashmiri	**545032**
Uttarmachipura (Handwara) ..	2239	1	550	44614	**274942**	146180	128762	**247849**	10.93	11.98	123	Kashmiri	**224895**
Baramulla ..	590	2	353	29740	**162903**	88597	74306	**149009**	9.32	11.29	276	Kashmiri	**154503**
Sri Pratapsingh-pura (Badgam)..	488	1	467	32219	**174583**	95273	79310	**162970**	7.12	10.87	358	Kashmiri	**165634**
Anantnag District ..	**2814**	**9**	**1380**	**145473**	**851606**	**463571**	**388035**	**771943**	**10.31**	**12.1**	**303**	Kashmiri	**800487**
Khas Tehsil (including Srinagar city)	743	2	219	48109	**333881**	181554	152327	**282457**	18.26	16.62	449	Kashmiri	**315171**
Pulwama (Awantipura) ..	449	1	384	28240	**156526**	86464	70062	**149807**	4.48	11.04	349	Kashmiri	**147498**
Kulgam ..	588	1	452	29440	**157372**	83831	73541	**146147**	7.68	7	268	Kashmiri	**151542**
Anantnag ..	1034	5	325	39684	**203827**	111722	92105	**193532**	5.31	10.55	197	Kashmiri	**186276**
Muzaffarabad District	**2408**	**2**	**768**	**46783**	**264671**	**141117**	**123554**	**237447**	**11.46**	**9.87**	**110**	Pahari	**155595**
Muzaffarabad ..	546	1	423	22888	**125585**	66965	58620	**112798**	11.33	8.42	230	Pahari	**98250**
Uri ..	520	1	231	14078	**80223**	42770	37453	**71570**	12.09	10.72	154	Panjabi	**26[illegible]65**
Karnah ..	1342		114	9817	**58863**	31382	27481	**53079**	10.89	11.89	44	Pahari	**35925**
FRONTIER DISTRICTS	**63554**	**3**	**689**	**65369**	**311478**	**160724**	**150754**	**288584**	**7.93**	**5.64**	**5**	Balti	**133387**
Ladakh District ..	**45762**	**2**	**468**	**46255**	**195431**	**98478**	**96953**	**192138**	**1.71**	**4.72**	**4**	Balti	**133163**
Ladakh ..	29848	1	110	10591	**36307**	18360	17947	**34423**	5.47	4.14	1	Ladakhi	**32797**
Kargil ..	7392		163	9566	**52853**	26192	26661	**50238**	5.2	5.36	7	Balti	**32451**
Skardu ..	8522	1	195	26098	**106271**	53926	52345	**107477**	—1.12	4.60	12	Balti	**100176**
Astore District ..	**1632**		**39**	**2506**	**17026**	**8948**	**8078**				**10**	Shina	**16442**
Astore ..	1632		39	2506	**17026**	8948	8078	**31902**	**23.88**	**11.13**	10	Shina	**16442**
Gilgit Leased Area	**1480**	**1**	**45**	**3787**	**22495**	**12471**	**10024**				**15**	Shina	**17966**
Gilgit ..	1480	1	45	3787	**22495**	12471	10024				15	Shina	**17966**
Gilgit Agency ..	**14680**		**137**	**12821**	**76526**	**40827**	**35699**	**64544**	**18.56**	**5.82**	**5**	Broshki	**31131**
Chilas ..	2800		10	2799	**15364**	8401	6963	**13534**	13.52	3.03	5	Shina	**11373**
Nagar ..	1600		21	2879	**14874**	8309	6565	**13672**	8.79	—3.63	9	Broshki	**10792**
Hunza ..	3900		28	3000	**15341**	7999	7342	**13241**	15.85	9.27	4	Broshki	**11249**
Punial ..	1600		24	1218	**8164**	4270	3894	**6108**	33.66	11.21	5	Shina	**7402**
Ishkuman ..	1600		11	528	**4282**	2228	2054	**2986**	43.4	8.46	3	Wakhi	**1980**
Yasin ..	1200		24	1294	**9989**	5143	4846	**8083**	23.58	14.4	8	Broshki	**8723**
Kuh ..	480		19	1103	**8512**	4477	4035	**2808**	23	22.72	4	Chitrali	**5317**
Ghizar ..	1500							**4112**		4.02			
CITIES													
Jammu ..	2	1		9535	**50379**	2[illegible]817	20562	**38613**	30.47	22.11	25190	Hindustani	**18987**
Srinagar .	11	1		27053	**207787**	112460	95327	**173573**	19.71	22.46	18890	Kashmiri	**202185**

STATE TABLE II

Population of Districts and Tehsils by Communities and Literacy

NOTES

---

1. The form and detail of the table are the same as in the corresponding table in 1931 except that in 1931 the details given under Hindus were for Brahmans, Other Hindus and Depressed Classes whereas on this occasion the details under Hindus are given for 'Scheduled Castes', and 'Other Hindus.' The term 'Scheduled Castes' refers to the same elements of the population as those described as 'Depressed Classes' in 1931. Also, Buddhists have been omitted on this occasion and Tribes included. The details under 'Others' almost entirely relate to the Buddhists. The form adopted is in accordance with that prescribed by the Census Commissioner for India.

2. The heading 'Christians' includes Indian Christians, Anglo-Indian and Other Christians and the figures for literacy given thereunder are for all classes of Christians.

3. The population figures for all communities given for the whole State include the population of the Gilgit Agency but the figures for literacy do not. This is because the figures for literacy for the Gilgit Agency were not made available. The same remarks apply to the figures shown against 'Frontier Districts.'

4. The three districts Chenani Jagir, Astore and Gilgit (Leased Area) each consist of one tehsil only ; they are each shown twice, as districts and as tehsils, for the sake of uniformity.

5. Blanks throughout the table indicate that there are no figures to give.

STATE TABLE II—POPULATION OF DISTRICTS AND TEHSILS BY COMMUNITIES AND LITERACY

P=Persons L=Literate LE=Literate in English

District and Tehsil	Hindus								Jains			
	Scheduled Castes				Other Hindus							
	P		L		P		L		P		L	
	M	F	M	F	M	F	M	F	M	F	M	F
1	2	3	4	5	6	7	8	9	10	11	12	13
JAMMU AND KASHMIR STATE	**60772**	**52692**	**1827**	**209**	**369911**	**325790**	**84310**	**20531**	**490**	**420**	**272**	**178**
JAMMU PROVINCE ..	**60746**	**52676**	**1818**	**208**	**320999**	**288414**	**52192**	**13039**	**482**	**419**	**267**	**177**
(a) TOTAL DISTRICTS ..	*59110*	*51232*	*1802*	*208*	*305348*	*273427*	*48725*	*12257*	*482*	*419*	*267*	*177*
Jammu District ..	**27725**	**23395**	**1001**	**131**	**106912**	**90141**	**22559**	**6491**	**481**	**414**	**266**	**174**
Jammu Tehsil (including Jammu city) ..	9406	7927	403	88	44684	32077	15342	5390	478	413	265	174
Samba ..	4202	3492	82	8	22864	21921	2526	421			1	
Sri Rabirsinghpura ..	8133	6933	411	31	16603	14606	2496	490	3	1		
Akhnur ..	5984	5043	105	4	22761	21537	2195	199				
Kathua District ..	**10404**	**8445**	**123**	**3**	**59044**	**53930**	**6967**	**1052**				
Kathua ..	1213	1041	23		15286	12591	1954	320				
Jasmergarh ..	3545	2984	53	3	18973	17679	2068	179				
Basohli ..	5646	4420	47		24785	23660	2945	553				
Udhampur District ..	**11263**	**10382**	**461**	**51**	**73916**	**69259**	**8409**	**1623**	**1**	**5**	**1**	**3**
Udhampur ..	4102	3567	106	9	17702	16178	2698	813	1	2	1	1
Kishtwar ..	37	24	99	31	12909	11961	1324	210				
Ramban ..	857	809	7	1	10602	9780	724	89		3		2
Ramnagar ..	5668	5338	124	7	21118	20136	1892	217				
Bhadrawah ..	599	644	125	3	11585	11204	1771	294				
Reasi District ..	**8163**	**7557**	**108**	**9**	**34048**	**30957**	**4022**	**869**				
Reasi ..	7012	6501	81	6	20599	18389	2758	606				
Rampur Rajouri ..	1151	1056	27	3	13449	12568	1264	263				
Mirpur District ..	**1555**	**1453**	**109**	**14**	**31428**	**29140**	**6768**	**2222**				
Kotli ..	75	78	20	6	4249	3979	1378	485				
Mirpur ..	13	22			3501	2993	2123	1206				
Bhimbar ..	1467	1353	89	8	23678	22168	3267	531				

STATE TABLE II—POPULATION OF DISTRICTS AND TEHSILS BY COMMUNITIES AND LITERACY—Contd.

P=Persons L=Literate LE=Literate in English

District and Tehsil	Sikhs P M	Sikhs P F	Sikhs L M	Sikhs L F	Muslims P M	Muslims P F	Muslims L M	Muslims L F	Christians P M	Christians P F	Christians L M	Christians L F	Tribes P M	Tribes P F	Tribes M	Tribes F
1	14	15	16	17	18	19	20	21	22	23	24	25	26	27	28	29
JAMMU AND KASHMIR STATE	**34779**	**31124**	**13240**	**4525**	**1641701**	**1459546**	**101051**	**9641**	**1888**	**1621**	**367**	**289**	**29**	**22**	**2**	
JAMMU PROVINCE ..	**20036**	**18530**	**6678**	**2215**	**630318**	**585358**	**44305**	**5768**	**1537**	**1251**	**102**	**39**	**16**	**13**	**2**	
(a) Total Districts ..	*12501*	*11178*	*4162*	*1420*	*434759*	*395990*	*29849*	*4502*	*1535*	*1250*	*100*	*38*	*16*	*13*	*2*	
Jammu District ..	**4980**	**4171**	**1528**	**476**	**92578**	**78211**	**8713**	**2302**	**1265**	**1032**	**77**	**34**	**16**	**13**	**2**	
Jammu Tehsil (including Jammu city) ..	1816	1158	942	388	31903	24441	5064	1704	672	566	61	32				
Samba ..	996	970	104	12	18970	16913	743	68	71	65	1	1				
Sri Ranbirsinghpura ..	1790	1688	426	68	24401	21548	2000	358	448	327	13	1	14	13	2	
Akhnur ..	378	355	56	8	17304	15309	906	112	74	74	2		2			
Kathua District ..	**228**	**203**	**43**	**11**	**24355**	**20859**	**1291**	**139**	**103**	**101**	**2**					
Kathua ..	41	29	21	8	9343	7695	622	91	71	68	1					
Jasmergarh ..	177	170	15	1	8728	7394	352	11	10	10						
Basohli ..	10	4	7	2	6284	5770	317	37	22	23	1					
Udhampur District ..	**243**	**202**	**100**	**25**	**67878**	**60449**	**4060**	**450**	**61**	**37**	**13**	**2**				
Udhampur ..	93	73	49	15	6140	5038	393	105	27	14	9	2				
Kishtwar ..	57	66	13	5	18830	16490	1104	110								
Ramban ..	29	18	17	3	28248	25422	1490	51	13	14						
Ramnagar ..	26	6	6		4076	3676	163	12	20	9	3					
Bhadrawah ..	38	39	15	2	10584	9823	910	172	1		1					
Reasi District ..	**823**	**718**	**253**	**72**	**92412**	**83127**	**3466**	**251**	**56**	**42**	**3**					
Reasi ..	173	143	63	21	34018	30126	1181	108	56	42	3					
Rampur Rajouri ..	650	575	190	51	58394	53001	2285	143								
Mirpur District ..	**6227**	**5884**	**2238**	**836**	**157536**	**153344**	**12319**	**1360**	**50**	**38**	**5**	**2**				
Kotli ..	725	692	264	105	51657	49582	2798	151								
Mirpur ..	1161	1064	666	377	52064	52297	5501	376	50	38						
Bhimbar ..	4341	4128	1308	354	53815	51465	4020	833			5	2				

STATE TABLE II—POPULATION OF DISTRICTS AND TEHSILS BY COMMUNITIES AND LITERACY—CONTD.

P=Persons L=Literate LE=Literate in English

District and Tehsil	Others				Number Literate								Remarks
	P		L		Age 0-15		Age 15-20		Age 20+		LE		
	M	F	M	F	M	F	M	F	M	F	M	F	
1	30	31	32	33	34	35	36	37	38	39	40	41	42
JAMMU AND KASHMIR STATE	**20302**	**20529**	**1907**	**35**	**40374**	**12118**	**31442**	**6685**	**131160**	**16605**	**45254**	**2361**	
JAMMU PROVINCE ..	**276**	**362**	**7**	**2**	**21928**	**6748**	**15829**	**3952**	**67614**	**10748**	**17542**	**1013**	
(a) TOTAL DISTRICTS ..	*265*	*284*	*7*	*2*	*17954*	*5900*	*12690*	*3468*	*54270*	*9236*	*16211*	*974*	
Jammu District ..	**19**	**9**	**4**	**2**	**6508**	**2939**	**5192**	**1771**	**22450**	**4900**	**9416**	**799**	
Jammu Tehsil (including Jammu city) ..	11	4	4	2	4097	2423	3224	1394	14760	4021	7661	773	
Samba ..					750	137	592	109	2116	254	591	12	
Sri Ranbirsinghpura ..	8	5			1032	255	890	195	3423	499	852	11	
Akhbnur ..					629	124	486	73	2151	126	312	3	
Kathua District ..					**1806**	**388**	**1224**	**246**	**5396**	**571**	**988**	**25**	
Kathua ..					523	139	391	87	1707	193	445	19	
Jasmergarh ..					542	59	399	47	1547	88	163	3	
Basohli ..					741	190	434	112	2142	290	380	3	
Udhampur District ..	**246**	**275**	**3**		**2545**	**697**	**1769**	**379**	**8733**	**1078**	**1621**	**27**	
Udhampur ..					589	251	397	154	2270	540	545	18	
Kishtwar ..	244	275	3		508	130	389	53	1666	173	336	3	
Ramban ..	1				409	59	337	27	1462	58	175	4	
Ramnagar ..					473	66	260	58	1455	114	153	2	
Bhadrawah ..	1				566	191	386	87	1880	193	412		
Reasi District ..					**1416**	**367**	**1079**	**251**	**5357**	**583**	**548**	**10**	
Reasi ..					740	239	534	154	2812	358	358	2	
Rampur Rajouri ..					676	128	545	97	2545	225	190	8	
Mirpur District ..					**5679**	**1509**	**3426**	**821**	**12334**	**2104**	**3638**	**113**	
Kotli ..					1095	270	643	150	2722	327	357	4	
Mirpur ..					2393	636	1469	334	4528	989	2287	94	
Bhimbar ..					2191	603	1314	337	5084	788	994	15	

STATE TABLE II—POPULATION OF DISTRICTS AND TEHSILS BY COMMUNITIES AND LITERACY—CONTD.

P=Persons L=Literate LE=Literate in English

District and Tehsil	Hindus								Jains			
	Scheduled Castes				Other Hindus							
	P		L		P		L		P		L	
	M	F	M	F	M	F	M	F	M	F	M	F
1	*2*	*3*	*4*	*5*	*6*	*7*	*8*	*9*	*10*	*11*	*12*	*13*
(b) TOTAL JAGIRS ..	*1636*	*1444*	*16*		*15651*	*14987*	*3467*	*782*				
Chenani Jagir ..	**1378**	**1292**	**14**		**3597**	**3314**	**287**	**17**				
Chenani ..	1378	1292	14		3597	3314	287	17				
Poonch Jagir ..	**258**	**152**	**2**		**12054**	**11673**	**3180**	**765**				
Bagh ..	12	15			599	522	187	76				
Sadhnuti ..	190	94			6608	6908	1284	96				
Haveli ..	9	3	1		2871	2315	1303	548				
Mendhar ..	47	40	1		1976	1928	406	45				
KASHMIR PROVINCE ..	**26**	**16**	**9**	**1**	**48362**	**37176**	**31830**	**7439**	**8**	**1**	**5**	**1**
Baramulla District ..	**5**	**2**			**7574**	**5338**	**4690**	**529**				
Uttarmachipura (Handwara)	5	2			3240	2250	2016	230				
Baramulla ..					2943	2108	1844	247				
Sri Pratapsinghpura (Badgam) ..					1391	980	830	52				
Anantnag District ..	**18**	**9**	**9**	**1**	**37452**	**29336**	**25432**	**6220**	**8**	**1**	**5**	**1**
Khas Tehsil (including Srinagar city) ..	17	9	9	1	26169	20237	18774	5671	8	1	5	1
Pulwama (Awantipura) ..	1				2335	1951	1339	98				
Kulgam ..					3627	2823	2162	230				
Anantnag ..					5321	4325	3157	221				
Muzaffarabad District ..	**3**	**5**			**3336**	**2502**	**1708**	**690**				
Muzaffarabad ..					2213	1750	1156	562				
Uri ..					866	628	399	107				
Karnah ..	3	5			257	124	153	21				

STATE TABLE II—POPULATION OF DISTRICTS AND TEHSILS BY COMMUNITIES AND LITERACY—CONTD.

P=Persons L=Literate LE=Literate in English

District and Tehsil	Sikhs				Muslims				Christians				Tribes			
	P		L		P		L		P		L		P		L	
	M	F	M	F	M	F	M	F	M	F	M	F	M	F	M	F
1	*14*	*15*	*16*	*17*	*18*	*19*	*20*	*21*	*22*	*23*	*24*	*25*	*26*	*27*	*28*	*29*
(b) TOTAL JAGIRS ..	*7535*	*7352*	*2516*	*795*	*195559*	*189368*	*14456*	*1266*	*2*	*1*	*2*	*1*				
Chenani Jagir ..	**9**	**1**	**4**		**1491**	**714**	**64**	**2**								
Chenani ..	9	1	4		1491	714	64	2								
Poonch Jagir ..	**7526**	**7351**	**2512**	**795**	**194068**	**188654**	**14392**	**1264**	**2**	**1**	**2**	**1**				
Bagh ..	4036	4015	1374	505	46212	45680	5565	820								
Sadhnuti ..	2071	2230	494	95	43175	46950	3418	85								
Haveli ..	1302	1032	605	192	54293	48905	3490	268	2	1	2	1				
Mendhar ..	117	74	39	3	50388	47119	1919	91								
KASHMIR PROVINCE ..	**14557**	**12477**	**6464**	**2286**	**871499**	**743979**	**53035**	**3722**	**260**	**295**	**205**	**222**	**11**	**9**		
Baramulla District ..	**4433**	**4025**	**2109**	**828**	**317983**	**272953**	**15097**	**504**	**54**	**58**	**30**	**38**				
Uttarmachipura (Handwara)	1841	1632	847	393	141085	124869	8096	308	9	9	7	5				
Baramulla ..	1395	1235	689	218	84217	70918	4196	156	41	45	19	31				
Sri Pratapsinghpura (Badgam) ..	1197	1158	573	217	92681	77166	2805	40	4	4	4	2				
Anantnag District ..	**3260**	**2394**	**1471**	**349**	**422619**	**356065**	**30935**	**2836**	**189**	**209**	**162**	**168**	**11**	**9**		
Khas Tehsil (including Srinagar city) ..	1272	547	696	158	153878	131307	18115	2404	187	205	160	166	11	9		
Pulwama (Awantipura) ..	1232	1255	498	160	82896	66856	3482	103								
Kulgam .	155	128	37	3	80049	70588	3485	177		2						
Anantnag .	601	464	240	28	105796	87314	5853	152	2	2	2	2				
Muzaffarabad District ..	**6864**	**6058**	**2884**	**1109**	**130897**	**114961**	**7003**	**382**	**17**	**28**	**13**	**16**				
Muzaffarabad ..	4574	4236	2096	913	60161	52607	3340	265	17	27	13	15				
Uri ..	1982	1635	679	191	39922	35189	2223	108		1		1				
Karnah ...	308	187	109	5	30814	27165	1440	9								

STATE TABLE II—POPULATION OF DISTRICTS AND TEHSILS BY COMMUNITIES AND LITERACY—CONTD.

P=Persons L=Literate LE=Literate in English

District and Tehsil	Others				Number Literate								Remarks
	P		L		Age 0-15		Age 15-20		Age 20+		LE		
	M	F	M	F	M	F	M	F	M	F	M	F	
1	30	31	32	33	34	35	36	37	38	39	40	41	42
(b) TOTAL JAGIRS ..	11	78			3974	848	3139	484	13344	1512	1331	39	
Chenani Jagir ..					**44**	**5**	**47**	**3**	**278**	**11**	**23**		
Chenani ..					44	5	47	3	278	11	23		
Poonch Jagir ..	**11**	**78**			**3930**	**843**	**3092**	**481**	**13066**	**1501**	**1308**	**39**	
Bagh ..					1600	389	1079	221	4447	791	211	3	
Sadhnuti ..	2	72			1068	67	887	51	3241	158	218		
Haveli ..					948	343	779	187	3674	479	775	36	
Mendhar ..	9	6			314	44	347	22	1704	73	104		
KASHMIR PROVINCE ..	**15**	**14**	**8**	**11**	**17781**	**5286**	**14929**	**2682**	**58846**	**5714**	**27240**	**1315**	
Baramulla District ..	**1**	**2**		**2**	**3634**	**671**	**3757**	**391**	**14535**	**839**	**4010**	**94**	
Uttarmachipura (Handwara)					1893	328	1917	172	7154	436	1665	27	
Baramulla ..	1				1069	243	1168	156	4513	253	1679	54	
Sri Pratapsinghpura (Badgam) ..		2		2	672	100	672	63	2868	150	666	13	
Anantnag District ..	**14**	**12**	**8**	**9**	**11774**	**3933**	**9500**	**1933**	**36748**	**3718**	**21880**	**1200**	
Khas Tehsil (including Srinagar city) ..	12	12	7	9	8506	3459	6187	1663	23073	3288	18258	1172	
Pulwama (Awantipura) ..					903	128	908	81	3508	152	823	6	
Kulgam ..					895	195	919	97	3870	118	944	5	
Anantnag ..	2		1		1470	151	1486	92	6297	160	1855	17	
Muzaffarabad District ..					**2373**	**682**	**1672**	**358**	**7563**	**1157**	**1350**	**21**	
Muzaffarabad ..					1482	531	950	282	4173	942	875	16	
Uri ..					594	144	461	70	2246	193	366	4	
Karnah ..					297	7	261	6	1144	22	109	1	

STATE TABLE II—POPULATION OF DISTRICTS AND TEHSILS BY COMMUNITIES AND LITERACY—CONTD.

P=Persons L=Literate LE=Literate in English

District and Tehsil	Hindus: Scheduled Castes P M	P F	L M	L F	Hindus: Other Hindus P M	P F	L M	L F	Jains P M	P F	L M	L F
1	2	3	4	5	6	7	8	9	10	11	12	13
FRONTIER DISTRICTS ..					**550**	**200**	**288**	**53**				
Ladakh District ..					**361**	**94**	**199**	**24**				
Ladakh ..					201	16	100	5				
Kargil ..					61	36	37	8				
Skardu ..					99	42	62	11				
Astore District ..					**72**	**41**	**47**	**13**				
Astore ..					72	41	47	13				
Gilgit Leased Area ..					**72**	**36**	**42**	**16**				
Gilgit (Leased Area) ..					72	36	42	16				
Gilgit Agency ..					**45**	**29**						
Chilas ..					35	20						
Nagar ..												
Hunza ..												
Punial ..					2	2						
Ishkuman ..												
Yasin ..												
Kuh, Ghizar ..					8	7						
CITIES ..												
Jammu ..	566	429	175	68	17237	11332	10199	4721	412	372	2	
Srinagar ..	17	9	8	1	23870	19130	17474	5557	8	1	5	1

STATE TABLE II—POPULATION OF DISTRICTS AND TEHSILS BY COMMUNITIES AND LITERACY—CONTD.

P=Persons L=Literate LE=Literate in English

District and Thesil	Sikhs P M	Sikhs P F	Sikhs L M	Sikhs L F	Muslims P M	Muslims P F	Muslims L M	Muslims L F	Christians P M	Christians P F	Christians L M	Christians L F	Tribes P M	Tribes P F	Tribes L M	Tribes L F
1	14	15	16	17	18	19	20	21	22	23	24	25	26	27	28	29
FRONTIER DISTRICTS ..	**186**	**117**	**98**	**24**	**139884**	**130209**	**3711**	**151**	**91**	**75**	**60**	**28**	**2**			
Ladakh District ..	**107**	**75**	**52**	**12**	**77925**	**76567**	**2246**	**71**	**74**	**64**	**51**	**23**				
Ladakh ..	5	4	2	1	2100	1986	350	37	69	60	47	20				
Kargil ..	18	24	7	5	22084	22326	920	15	3	3	2	2				
Skardu ..	84	47	43	6	53741	52255	976	19	2	1	2	1				
Astore District ..	**20**	**10**	**16**	**4**	**8852**	**8026**	**476**	**17**	**3**	**1**			**1**			
Astore ..	20	10	16	4	8852	8026	476	17	3	1			1			
Gilgit Leased Area ..	**44**	**26**	**30**	**8**	**12342**	**9954**	**989**	**63**	**12**	**8**	**9**	**5**	**1**			
Gilgit (Leased Area) ..	44	26	30	8	12342	9954	989	63	12	8	9	5	1			
Gilgit Agency ..	**15**	**6**			**40765**	**35662**			**2**	**2**						
Chilas ..	9	1			8356	6942			1							
Nagar ..					8309	6565										
Hunza ..	1	1			7998	7341										
Punial ..	2	3			4266	3889										
Ishkuman ..					2228	2054										
Yasin ..					5143	4846										
Kuh } Ghizar } ..	3	1			4465	4025			1	2						
CITIES ..																
Jammu ..	1322	813	132	37	9751	6169	3914	1666	519	443	16	12				
Srinagar ..	943	469	554	149	87439	75531	15174	2323	171	175	152	142				

STATE TABLE II—POPULATION OF DISTRICTS AND TEHSILS BY COMMUNITIES AND LITERACY—CONCLD.

P=Persons L=Literate LE=Literate in English

District and Tehsil	OTHERS				NUMBER LITERATE								REMARKS
	P		L		Age 0-15		Age 15-20		Age 20+		LE		
	M	F	M	F	M	F	M	F	M	F	M	F	
1	30	31	32	33	34	35	36	37	38	39	40	41	42
FRONTIER DISTRICTS ..	**20011**	**20153**	**1892**	**22**	**665**	**84**	**684**	**51**	**4700**	**143**	**472**	**33**	
Ladakh District ..	**20011**	**20153**	**1892**	**22**	**399**	**44**	**441**	**25**	**3600**	**83**	**236**	**25**	
Ladakh ..	15985	15881	1869	22	120	31	180	14	2069	40	54	15	
Kargil ..	4026	4272	23		151	9	130	7	794	14	101	2	
Skardu ..					128	4	131	4	737	29	81	8	
Astore District ..					**85**	**10**	**67**	**6**	**387**	**18**	**71**	**1**	
Astore ..					85	10	67	6	387	18	71	1	
Gilgit Leased Area ..					**181**	**30**	**176**	**20**	**713**	**42**	**165**	**7**	
Gilgit (Leased Area) ..					181	30	176	20	713	42	165	7	
Gilgit Agency ..													
Chilas ..													
Nagar ..													
Hunza ..													
Punial ..													
Ishkuman ..													
Yasin ..													
Kuh ..													
Ghizar ..													
CITIES ..													
Jammu ..	10	4	4	2	3183	2188	2309	1234	9918	3580	6655	723	
Srinagar ..	12	12	7	9	7800	3390	5500	1624	20074	3168	17551	1131	